War and Revolution

Also by Norman E. Saul

Distant Friends: The United States and Russia, 1763–1867

Concord and Conflict: The United States and Russia, 1867–1914

War and Revolution
The United States and Russia, 1914–1921

Norman E. Saul

 University Press of Kansas

To Alyssa, Kevin, and Julia

Published by the University Press of Kansas (Lawrence,
Kansas 66049), which was organized by the Kansas Board
of Regents and is operated and funded by Emporia State
University, Fort Hays State University, Kansas State
University, Pittsburg State University, the University of
Kansas, and Wichita State University.

Library of Congress Cataloging-in-Publication Data
Saul, Norman E.
    War and revolution : the United States and Russia,
1914-1921 / Norman E. Saul.
        p. cm.
    Includes bibliographical references and index.
    ISBN 0-7006-1090-1 (alk. paper)
    1. United States—Relations—Russia.   2. Russia—
Relations—United States.   3. United States—Relations—
Soviet Union.   4. Soviet Union—Relations—United
States.   5. United States—Foreign relations—1931-
1921.   6. World War, 1914-1918.   7. Russia—
History—February Revolution, 1917.   8. Soviet Union—
History—Revolution, 1917-1921.   I. Title.
E183.8.R9 S384 2001
303.48'273047—dc21   00-012851

British Library Cataloguing in Publication Data is available.

Printed in the United States of America

10 9 8 7 6 5 4 3 2 1

The paper used in this publication meets the minimum requirements of the American National Standard for Perma-
nence of Paper for Printed Library Materials Z39.48-1984.

The luncheon table was set in a large, high-ceilinged room with red velvet hangings. A crackling fire blazed on the hearth, and in the center of the table a gleaming tree stepped from a mossy bed of crimson tulips. We pulled down the blinds and shut out war and revolution, while we laughed merrily over the Russian conception of mince pie, and wondered secretly, each in his own terms, what they were doing off there across the world at home.

—Bessie Beatty, describing Christmas Day 1917 at the Red Cross Mission in Petrograd in *The Red Heart of Russia*

Contents

Illustrations

Preface

The relations between the United States and Russia during World War I, the Russian revolutions of 1917, and the civil war and intervention that followed were a true "time of troubles." For Russia it corresponded in many ways to the period of its history in the early seventeenth century that is defined by that term and heralded the end of a dynasty, foreign invasion and intervention, civil war, economic decline and famine, and social and political unrest. The 1914–21 period is also similar to a more recent era of upheavals in Russian history in the 1990s that witnessed the collapse of a rigid centralized economic and political system and the empire that it maintained. Failure of leaders and institutions to adapt to and cope with the currents of the times was evident in all three cases.

By contrast, the United States remained on firm political and social foundations that had evolved over more than a century. Yet the emergence of the United States as a major political and economic power and its first participation on a large scale in a major European conflict had revolutionary consequences and resulting strains at home and abroad. Because of the destruction inflicted by war and revolution in Europe, the United States emerged as clearly the strongest economic and political power in the world. Some observers contended that it could have determined Russia's destiny, and in some ways it did. By entering the world conflict relatively late, in April 1917, after the overthrow of the tsar, the United States virtually forced a democratically oriented Russia to stay in the war and continue to face its severe economic and political consequences. In fact, most American leaders saw Russian participation as vital to their cause of winning the war.

Another focus is the theme developed in the first two volumes, *Distant Friends* (1991) and *Concord and Conflict* (1996), that of Americanization or mirror-imaging. This is a description and analysis of the ways that Americans and Russians saw themselves as having a common relationship that is distinguished from other European or Asian nations. Russians continued to look to America, in different ways, for ideas and models, while Americans expected Russians to follow an American path in developing resources and reforming institutions. The time span covered is from the beginning of World War I through the Russian civil war and intervention that followed until March 1921, which marked both the end of the Wilson administration and beginning of the New Economic Policy in Soviet Russia and a shift to more moderate policies in both domestic and foreign affairs.

An examination of the relations between the two powers throughout this period is not a simple one, because of the turmoil and varied means of communication. It is made more difficult by the uneven quantity and quality of the surviving source materials. Much was done "off the record" in private conversations in person and by telephone. The availability of typewriters, carbon paper, and cheap printing produced, on the other hand, mountains of documentation on the many people and events involved. Bureaucratic paperwork had clearly come of age. And at least some of the participants felt the need to record their activities and impressions in considerable detail in diaries, letters, and memoirs. The Russian Revolution and its aftermath definitely sold books in America at the time, and publishers and authors who rushed books to print reaped financial rewards, often at the expense of accuracy and subject to later misinterpretations.

The revolutionary upheavals naturally created gaps in the documentation, as papers were destroyed or lost in the process of moving and transition. The volume of material involved often led to periods of culling, sometimes by insensitive archivists in Washington and Moscow, especially in the case of military records. Whereas a few materials, such as some of the papers of the Petrograd consulate for 1918, have surfaced more recently in the former Soviet Union and have been transferred to the National Archives, others, such as the Odessa consulate post records, appear to have been lost. Some middle-level but key figures in the story, such as Maddin Summers, consul general in Moscow during 1917–18, General Lavr Kornilov, and Xenophon Kalamatiano, died prematurely, without leaving much of a personal record. And at the very top, disability and death prevented both Woodrow Wilson and Vladimir Lenin from giving a final reckoning, leaving historians to debate much of their contemporary writings and actions.

On the other hand, the very centrality of the events and early recognition of their significance caused a greater concern with obtaining and preserving records and soliciting memoirs and both private and official papers. Three examples can be singled out on the American side: the Hoover Institution Library and Archive at Stanford University, founded by Herbert Hoover specifically to preserve the records of war and revolution; the Columbia University oral history project that recorded the recollections of many Americans of this period; and the Bakhmeteff Archive, also at Columbia University, that was begun by the last ambassador of pre-Soviet Russia and houses important émigré Russian and American collections. Another very large collection of personal (and some official) papers is, of course, the Library of Congress Manuscripts Collection.

One of the problems of research on this general subject is that the documentation is quite scattered in other archives: state historical societies, libraries, and universities, the main ones being the State Historical Society of Wisconsin, the Missouri Historical Society in St. Louis, the New York Public Library, the Mudd Library at Princeton, the Sterling Library at Yale, and the Regenstein Library at the University of Chicago. The most important and revealing of these personal collections were those of Boris Bakhmeteff, Mark Bristol, David Francis, Samuel Harper, Robert Lansing, Breckinridge Long, Cyrus McCormick, Frank Polk, Edward House, Charles Russell, and William Allen White. These "personal" papers contain a surprising amount of governmental office material.

Official records of government and nongovernment agencies are, of course, vital for this study, and many on the American side are readily available on microfilm. Choices were made in some cases, for example, in relying more heavily on the Post Records (Record Group 84 in the National Archives) rather than the State Department case files (Record Group 59). The former are the files maintained at the diplomatic and consular posts and include much interpost communication and other incoming and outgoing traffic; they usually are arranged in chronological order, which provides a better sense of what is happening than the case files, which are cataloged by subject. The latter were reviewed, however, for any significant intraoffice or interdepartment communications and notations.

Archival documentation is weaker on the Russian side, partly because of the absence of formal relations after 1917 but also because of the inability to gain access to materials in the Archive of the Foreign Policy of the Russian Federation (AVPRF) that houses the diplomatic records from 1918 onward. Much but certainly not all of them are available in the Soviet documentary series that was begun in the Khrushchev era, and they have been thoroughly researched by other American and Russian scholars. Perhaps more important, however, was access to the papers of the Commissariat of People's Economy in the State Archives of the Russian Federation (GARF) and personal and party records in the Center for the Preservation of Documents.

Even more than in my previous researches, the assistance of library staff, archivists, and attendants has been crucial because of the volume and condition of the materials. By this time I have become accustomed to the different procedures and rules of these institutions (no two are the same) and even enjoy the variety. The preservation and maintenance of so much material is too often taken for granted and underappreciated.

This period of Russian-American relations has already been the subject of several investigations, and these have been of great value to my own work. They fall into two groups chronologically: one is from the period of the late 1950s and 1960s, when the easing of the cold war made access to Russian sources and scholarship easier and more objective study possible. The other is from the late 1980s and 1990s, when even more Russian archival access was possible, a substantial amount of American material was declassified, and the waning of the cold war inspired fresh perspectives. In the first category were the groundbreaking works of George F. Kennan, William Appleman Williams, Richard Ullman, and Betty Unterberger. This work owes much to them and to the important newer studies of David Foglesong, David McFadden, Christine White, William Allison, and others, more than is indicated by note references that concentrate on documentary materials. In contrast to most of the previous studies, mine provides a larger picture, linking the war itself with revolution and civil war and offering more of a sense of what was going on "in the trenches," among businessmen, reporters, and the various consular, diplomatic, and military staffs.

Any long-term research of this type depends heavily on funding from a variety of sources, making trips away from Mid-America possible for short and sometimes more extended periods: American Philosophical Society grants, IREX-Russian Academy of Sciences exchange, Kennan Institute for Advanced Russian Studies' short-term grants, and a Hoover Presidential Library Association fellowship. The University of Kansas has been very generous in its support: General Research Fund grants (summer stipends), sabbatical leave, Higuchi Research Award, Hall Center for the Humanities fellowship, Hall Center travel award, and Graduate School/International Programs international travel grant.

Acknowledgments for feedback and encouragement at conferences, in correspondence, and on-line are too numerous to list. Special mention, however, must be made of the unwavering support I received at all stages from Alexander Dallin, Basil Dmytryshyn, John Gaddis, W. Bruce Lincoln, and Walter LaFeber, and for the helpful advice of colleagues John Alexander, Anna Cienciala, Donald R. McCoy, John Clark, and Theodore Wilson. David Foglesong read and commented extensively on the manuscript, much to its improvement. My family—Mary Ann, Alyssa and Jim Lyon, Debbie and Kevin Saul, and Julia and Jim Mechler—did yeoman jobs as first readers of various parts of the manuscript and were patient and understanding through some difficult moments. The staffs of the Department of History, the Center for Russian and East European Studies, and the College of Liberal Arts and Sciences Word Processing Center handled the product in all its manifestations with their usual love and care.

Russian specialists on Russian-American relations have been invaluable in their advice and unsparing of their time in aiding my research. Foremost are my associate and friend Academician Nikolai Bolkhovitinov and his senior colleagues Academician Grigori Sevostianov, Aleksandr Chubarian, and Vladimir Lebedev. Members of the staff of the Center for North American Studies of the Institute of Universal History of the Russian Academy of Sciences, especially Vladimir Pozniakov and Ilya Gaiduk, have been expert guides for archival research in Moscow. It is hoped that conditions for Russian-American scholarly collaboration will continue to improve and expand.

Technical Notes

The Western, Gregorian calendar is used throughout, except when the Russian (Julian) date has significance. The few cases of doubt (as with a Russian writing to an American) are indicated. The official adoption of the Western calendar by the Soviet government in February 1918 fortunately eliminated this problem. Spelling of Russian names is somewhat arbitrary, following in general a modified Library of Congress format but straying from it for common usage (Trotsky instead of Trotskii). Russian first names with double vowels on the end are shortened to one (Grigori rather than Grigorii). The two Russian ambassadors of the same name are distinguished as Bakhmetev and Bakhmeteff, since the latter was the form used during his long permanent residence in the United States.

Readers are warned that the note references to manuscript collections may not coincide with current listings. My research was done over a period of several years, and some collections have been reprocessed, for example, the diplomatic and consular Post Records in their transfer to Archives II in College Park. Many documents exist in multiple copies, either in carbon or by contemporary or later machine reproduction, and can be found in several places. Only in cases of special relevance are originals and copies distinguished in citations.

Abbreviations Used in Notes

ACRER	Administrative Commission of Railway Experts to Russia
AE	American Embassy
ARC	American Red Cross
AVPR	Arkhiv Vneshnoi Politiki Rossii (Archive of the Foreign Policy of Russia)
BA	Bakhmeteff Archive, Columbia University
BFDC	Bureau of Foreign Trade, Department of Commerce
(c)	copy
CAB	Cabinet Office
CG	Consul General
CPI	Committee on Public Information
CU	Columbia University
d.	delo (box or package of documents)
DPR	Diplomatic Post Records
DSA	Divinity School Archives, Yale University (New Haven)
DSAR	*Documents of Soviet American Relations*
f.	file or folder; fond (collection)
FO	Foreign Office
FRUS	*Papers Relating to the Foreign Relations of the United States*
GARF	State Archive of the Russian Federation
GU	Georgetown University Libararies (Washington, D.C.)
HIA	Hoover Institution Archives (Stanford)
HPL	Hoover Presidential Library (West Branch, Iowa)
IH	International Harvester
LC	Library of Congress
M	Microcopy

MD   Manuscript Division (or Department)
MFA   Ministry of Foreign Affairs
MinnHS   Minnesota Historical Society
MoHS   Missouri Historical Society (St. Louis)
Mudd   Mudd Library Archives, Princeton University
NA   National Archives and Records Administration
NYPL   New York Public Library
(o)   original
op.   opis (inventory, part of collection)
o.s.   Old Style Russian calendar (thirteen days behind the Western
            calendar in the early twentieth century)
PRO   Public Record Office (London)
PWW   *Papers of Woodrow Wilson*
RG   Record Group
SHSW   State Historical Society of Wisconsin (Madison)
(t)   telegram
UC   University of Chicago, Regenstein Library Manuscript Collection
UCB   University of California-Bancroft Library
UIA   University of Illinois Archives
UOA   University of Oregon Archives
WCD   War College Division

1

War

The clash of arms that would ignite an unprecedented, bloody contest for political and military supremacy that started in August 1914 was a surprise to most people. But to others, and in hindsight, conditions were present that could act as the spark that would ignite the second most terrible, costly, and momentous war of the twentieth century. Even more, this "Great War" was, in fact, the forerunner and main cause of the Second World War, thus shaping much of world history of the twentieth century. All the participants would suffer momentous consequences in the political, economic, and social spheres, but none more than Russia. In the course of war and revolution, Russia would be transformed from a conservative hereditary monarchy into the first radical, visionary socialist state.

A simplified explanation for the war is that a developing national consciousness in European empires and states, as well as in America, had mutated into a rabid patriotism that restricted and limited compromise or negotiation. While most people primarily wanted to avoid a costly war, they were caught up in complex national and historical issues that they could not fully comprehend. The alliance system, born to protect and shield one set of countries from another, served war instead. By a unique set of circumstances, Russia had become allied, first with France in the 1890s, in a coalition against Germany and its client, Austria-Hungary, then with Britain, an unlikely partnership of Eastern conservatism with Western liberalism. Germany, the more natural ally by way of dynastic affiliation and economic rationality, became Russia's chief enemy and nemesis.

An almost hysterical overconfidence in victory on each side overshadowed saner perspectives that cautioned against too much reliance on the virtues of preventive war. This led to an underestimation of dangerous and volatile situations in the world, especially in the Balkans. Many, especially within the governments concerned, believed that war was not only a natural but also a desirable extension of diplomacy. Moreover, they felt prepared for such an outcome with confidence in a quick resolution by the huge investments in arms and munitions, and strategy and tactics, and were inclined to test their expectations of a glorious victory rather than pursue tiresome and mundane negotiations.[1]

Because of its militant nationalism in a complex, volatile region, its Orthodox religion, and its need for a protective "Big Brother," Serbia had allied itself with the Russian Empire to solidify and expand its base in the Balkans with the goal of additional aggrandizement. This aroused the concern of the neighboring but vulnerable multinational empire of Austria-Hungary, which had recently (in 1908) annexed a section of the Balkans, Bosnia-Herzegovina, that it had held under "temporary" occupation since the Congress of Berlin. It sought and received the willing support of a newer and stronger German Empire, which had expansionist designs in the area, symbolized by the project for a Berlin-Baghdad railway.[2] In part, the cause of conflict was the failure of the "European System" that had emerged from the Napoleonic peacemaking to adjust to shifts in power.

The assassination of the heir to the Austro-Hungarian crown by a Serbian nationalist in Sarajevo, the capital of a restless Slavic province that was annexed only in 1908, produced a series of ultimatums that naturally provoked resistance, a consequent failure of diplomatic solutions, and the advent of war. What made this Balkan tempest into a world war was the Franco-Russian alliance that obliged each partner to aid the other in the case of attack and made Russia an accomplice to French revanchist desires to get even with Germany (from the Franco-Prussian War of 1870-71) for the loss of Alsace-Lorraine. The arms race, and especially the escalating naval developments from battleships to dreadnoughts, from torpedo boats to submarines, added fuel to the sparks of national friction and diplomatic failures. Although actual war came as a surprise to most, few would try to avoid it. People would rather fight for realm and empire—or simply for personal advancement. Russia, rather than face insult and loss of prestige, thus backed Serbia in its conflict with Austria-Hungary by mobilizing on the western borders, including those with Germany. The latter's military plans could not allow for full Russian military preparations and declared war by launching

---

1. Few voices were raised about the possible consequences of failure. One, at least privately, was that of Andrew Dickson White, former diplomat and esteemed university president: "It bids fair to be one of the most terrible wars in history." Diary entry, 31 July 1914, reel 134, White Papers, Cornell.

2. A full-page article in the *New York Times* on the beginning of the war by Professor Albert Bushnell Hart was headlined "Austrian Fear of Serb Empire Is Real War Cause," *New York Times*, 2 August 1914 (V:1:1).

its main assault against France, under the assumption that France could be quickly disposed of (as in 1870) and the slower Russian military machine could then be dealt with—the German solution to a two-front war.

General mobilization and the first movements of armies across borders were met in most countries with enthusiasm and popular demonstrations, especially, to the surprise of some, in Russia. One of the largest peaceful crowds in Russian history assembled in front of the Kazan Cathedral on Nevsky Prospect, leading a *New York Times* reporter to observe, "Never within living memory have Russians lived through a day of such emotions."[3] At the outset this Russian popular support for the war may have been illusory, confined mostly to the capital, and at least partly stage-managed by local officials, as, on the contrary, opposition and rioting accompanied the calling up of reserves in a number of provincial cities.[4] And some rejoiced for other reasons, especially exiled revolutionaries who saw the war prophetically as an opportunity for their cause such as occurred during the Russo-Japanese War in 1905.[5]

Some thought that an alliance with Western democracies would make a difference. Ambassador Walter Page, Woodrow Wilson's trusted informant on European matters, thought Britain relished a war that could employ the hatred of Slavs against Teutons, and that Russia considered the time right to deal once and for all with Austria-Hungary while it was headed by an aged emperor, while the Slav portion of his empire was restless, and while Britain could be counted on to weaken Germany. He added, "Russia feels the need of a patriotic race cry at this stage of her growth and the need of a war to cause forgetfulness of the Russian-Japanese disaster."[6]

While Germany's plans were to throw the best of its fortress armaments—submarines and dreadnoughts—against Britain and a siege line artillery strategy against France, Russia loomed more and more as an unknown quantity, as perhaps a serious threat from the east. A backward military power recently suffering defeat to an upstart Japan, Russia clearly showed signs of new military resurgence in naval and field army advances, much of it sponsored by French

3. "Czar Orders Mobilization," *New York Times*, 1 August 1914 (3:2). For more on the initial support for war and subsequent efforts to sustain this "patriotic culture," see Hubertus F. Jahn, *Patriotic Culture in Russia During World War I* (Ithaca, N.Y.: Cornell University Press, 1995).

4. For this interpretation, see Josh Sanborn, "The Mobilization of 1914 and the Question of the Russian Nation: A Reexamination," *Slavic Review* 59, no. 2 (summer 2000): 267–89.

5. "Chance for Revolutionists," *New York Times*, 30 July 1914 (3:8).

6. Page to Wilson, 2 August 1914, in Burton J. Hendrick, ed., *The Life and Letters of Walter H. Page*, vol. 3 (Garden City, N.Y.: Doubleday, 1925), 129.

money. The Central Powers (Germany, Austria-Hungary, and the Ottoman Empire) did not have an easy solution to this dilemma, only the hope that in 1914 there was still time to salvage the von Schlieffen strategy of initial concentration of force in the west on the theory that Russia would be slow to mobilize. The rapid Russian advance in August of that year required the transfer of German units from the Western Front, thus crippling that plan and producing a military stalemate that would have dire consequences for all participants and for the rest of the century.

Although all participants in the "Great War" failed to envisage the war that was to come, Russia was probably the least prepared for it. With the help of French loans and the lessons of the Russo-Japanese War, the Russian armed forces did indeed modernize, especially the navy, with much new construction (necessitated by the destruction of a large part of the Baltic Fleet at Tsushima). Yet much of this was ephemeral, with the old officer class slow to adapt to modern tactics. Offensive planning dominated over defensive, little thought went into the use of reserves, and most new signs of modernity such as field telephones and radios were illusory. While failing to stock supplies for more than a brief conflict, the army relied on cavalry and bayonet charges to carry the day in battle.[7]

Russia in American Eyes

Evidence of a progressing, modernizing Russia was still apparent to most observers on the eve of the war but especially to those Americans who were particularly interested in finding a mirror image for continental conquest and industrial and agricultural development. And, indeed, they were in the forefront of promoting that modernization—with the success of American enterprises such as Singer and International Harvester, the electrification of Petrograd by Westinghouse, and the extraordinary gains in insurance sales by New York Life and Equitable. Granted, these American initiatives were largely symbolic and still small in comparison with native and other foreign ventures in major industries such as oil, steel, and machine tools. Nevertheless, most economic indices show Russia in the early twentieth century catching up with the rest of the world. This was remarkable, especially considering the setbacks from war and revolution in 1904–5, continuing revolutionary unrest, the cost of maintaining a virtual police state, and the drain through emigration of some of its most productive citizens.

---

7. For a full analysis, see Bruce W. Menning, *Bayonets Before Bullets: The Imperial Russian Army, 1861–1914* (Bloomington: Indiana University Press, 1992).

But with outside assistance Russia was also developing major resource bases for economic expansion in oil, coal, iron, copper, nickel, manganese, gold, platinum, and other essential metals of modern industry.

Credit for Russia's economic advances must be shared by foreign entrepreneurs and new Russian capitalists, such as Alexander Guchkov and Michael Tereshchenko, both of whom would play major roles in the Provisional Government in 1917. Symbolizing the rise of large-scale native industries was the organization of the Association of Industry and Trade in 1906.[8] Behind all this were the economic development policies of Sergei Witte, minister of finance from 1892 to 1903, that were carried forth by his successors. This is not to say that Russian industrialization was solid and sound. It had a number of weaknesses, as the war would soon demonstrate. The concentration was mainly in St. Petersburg, Moscow, Warsaw, and the Urals; St. Petersburg (as Petrograd) would be too close to the front, Warsaw behind it, and the Urals too far away for ideal support of an Eastern Front. Transportation was heavily dependent on long-distance railroads that would prove quite vulnerable under the stress of war.[9] Most important, as recent studies have demonstrated, Russia's new industrial elite was hampered by bureaucratic obstacles and little sense of community with merchants, professional groups, or the landed aristocracy.[10]

A variety of American businessmen, journalists, and diplomats were busy reporting the changing times in Russia before the war. They saw great opportunity in Russia's economic advance. The Singer Sewing Machine Company's factory at Podolsk, outside Moscow, employed 6,000 workers and produced an average of 10,000 machines per week in 1913. Sales and service income through hundreds of its shops throughout Russia was rising sharply before the war, from 13,725,000 rubles in 1904 to 91,900,000 in 1914 (one dollar equals two rubles).[11]

---

8. See, for example, Ruth AmEnde Roosa, *Russian Industrialists in an Era of Revolution: The Association of Industry and Trade, 1906–1917* (Armonk, N.Y.: M. E. Sharpe, 1997).

9. Neither then nor later was there anything like "the good roads movement" in the United States, Britain, and elsewhere.

10. See, as examples, Alfred J. Rieber, *Merchants and Entrepreneurs in Imperial Russia* (Chapel Hill: University of North Carolina Press, 1982); Thomas Owen, *The Corporation Under Russian Law: A Study in Tsarist Economic Policy* (New York: Cambridge University Press, 1991); Timothy McDaniel, *Autocracy, Capitalism, and Revolution in Russia* (Berkeley: University of California Press, 1988); and Leonid Shepelev, "Business Organization in the Russian Empire, 1906–14," *Russian Studies in History* 34, no. 1 (1995): 40–88.

11. "Historical notes," 1949, box 156, Singer Company Papers, SHSW; "Singer Protocol," 22 September 1915, AE Petrograd, DPR 290, RG 84, NA. The total company payroll in mid-1914 was over 30,000 employees, making it probably the largest private employer in Russia. Annual sales of machines had risen from 110,000 in 1900 to 678,986 (counting

Similar growth was recorded by International Harvester for both imported and Russian-made agricultural implements. John Grout, American consul in Odessa, reported that 500 automobiles were sold there in 1913, 75 of them from the United States. The majority were from Germany, but a Russian auto was also being assembled in Moscow with imported parts. Grout noted that motorcycles were becoming popular, that 100 mostly American tractors were sold in 1913, despite a poor harvest the previous year, and that there were new sales of American corn seeders and cultivators for Bessarabia, where the planting of corn was advancing rapidly. An American married to a Russian with family estates near Poltava, in Russia's Ukrainian breadbasket, describes the remarkable progress being made in rural Russia in the years just before the war. Modern steam-powered threshing machines improved the marketability of grain, and the local village took on an air of prosperity, with many new peasant homes.[12] Symbolizing the need to accommodate new forms of mobility, steam-powered rock crushers and road rollers and graders were being purchased by the local zemstva (land assemblies). Americans especially sought out these new Russian market possibilities.[13]

Obviously, the trade situation changed drastically in August 1914. The American embassy, in assessing the impact of the war on trade in December 1914, noted the following major items of import from the United States that were most affected: cotton, cottonseed oil, lathes and other machine tools, hardware, automobiles, agricultural implements, petroleum jelly, typewriters, and carbon paper (for which there is ample direct evidence in the archives).[14] Most of the cotton had come through Bremen and was recorded in official records as American exports to Germany and Russian imports from Germany. The same was true of machine tools, most of which were handled by the German firm of Scheuhardt and Schutte, while the Vera Company of Berlin distributed American shoes and boots throughout eastern Europe.[15] Exactly how much of the large officially re-

---

imports) in 1914. Fred V. Carstensen, *American Enterprise in Foreign Markets: Studies of Singer and International Harvester in Imperial Russia* (Chapel Hill: University of North Carolina Press, 1984), 56.

12. Julia Cantacuzene-Speransky, *Russian People: Revolutionary Recollections* (New York: Charles Scribner's Sons, 1920), 20–23.

13. Grout economic report, 22 March 1914, AE St. Petersburg, DPR 283, RG 84, NA. The consul general's records for 1914 indicate that he had received inquiries about selling baking machinery, electric motors, canning machines, water pumps, insulators, oil filters, knitting machines, sprayers, printing presses, match-making machines, grain dryers, meat cutters and grinders, veneer lathes, and automatic sprinklers. CG Moscow 1914, DPR 8, RG 84, NA.

14. Unsigned embassy report, 28 December 1914, AE Petrograd, DPR 284, RG 84, NA.

15. Ibid.

corded Russian trade with Germany before the war was actually American is difficult to calculate, but the American consul general in Moscow, John Snodgrass, estimated that after separating this out the United States would rank a close second to Germany as a source of Russian imports.

This conclusion is also borne out by a detailed study of Russian-American trade completed by the Russian Customs Bureau just before the war. In 1910, 36.8 percent of Russian imports of agricultural machinery were of American manufacture, but just over half of "complex" agricultural machinery (such as binders) came from America. From German sources, the report found that of the substantial German imports of implements from the United States in 1911, over 60 percent were reexported, mostly to Russia. Perhaps even more significant for American industry, 31.5 percent of the total exports of agricultural machinery in 1910 went to Russia (up from 25 percent in 1905). France was second (21 percent) and Germany a distant third (10 percent).[16]

The main explanation for so much American trade going through Germany is that American companies preferred to avoid the complex Russian tariffs and financial and credit arrangements. Instead, they left these matters in the hands of experienced German middlemen. Those that did deal directly frequently complained of Russian red tape and inconsistent practices. For example, Xenophon Kalamatiano, the J. I. Case Implement Company's representative in Odessa, complained that Russian customs treated imported threshing machines as separate from the steam engines that accompanied them, and that Russian officials were increasingly baffled by the large dimensions of American machinery and were inconsistent in the assessing of duties. The extent and growth of American exports to Russia provide ample additional evidence of a country modernizing on the eve of the war.[17]

Tracking American capital investments in Russia and their profits and losses is even more difficult, as many of them were part of the operations of multinational companies. This was especially true for mining enterprises, such as the Caucasus Copper Company, near the Turkish frontier, where a number of

16. The figures were given in German marks, for 1911: total German imports from the United States, 12 million; reexported, 7.8 million; of these to Russia, 5.7 million. "Review of the Conditions of Russian-American Trade for 1827–1910, Compiled by the Department of Customs Collections of Russia," in *Rossiia i SShA: torgovo-ekonomicheskie otnosheniia, 1900–1930: sbornik dokumentov*, chief editor G. N. Sevost'ianov (Moscow: Nauka, 1996), 39–47.

17. A number of other reports show a rising demand for sophisticated agricultural machinery from America. Kalamatiano to Curtis Guild, 9 April 1913, AE St. Petersburg, DPR 178, RG 84, NA; Snodgrass memorandum, "Agricultural Machines in Russia," 18 November 1914, CG Moscow, DPR 7, RG 84, NA.

American engineers were employed. The same was true of an even larger copper smelter at Kyshtim, near Ekaterinburg in the Urals, operated by a firm with headquarters in London but with Herbert Hoover as a major investor. One of the more successful "American" enterprises was that of Vacuum Oil Company of Rochester, New York, whose St. Petersburg refinery increased production substantially immediately before the war and, through its own retail operations in Moscow, Warsaw, Riga, Odessa, and Nizhni Novgorod, achieved remarkable profit gains, from 92 million rubles in 1910 to 338.4 million in 1913.[18]

In general, and in spite of Russian bureaucratic obstacles, American business in Russia was definitely on the rise, causing some public and official resentment about this rising foreign dependency.[19] This was especially true of New York Life Insurance Society, by far the largest insurer in Russia, which invested its income in local stocks so that by 1914 it was reported to be the largest single holder of Russian securities. Initially a strong competitor to New York Life in Russia, the Equitable Life Assurance Society had withdrawn from seeking new business by 1914, but it still had many outstanding policies.[20]

American companies quickly responded to pressure to support the war effort. According to company records, Singer invested over $20 million (about 44 million rubles) in Russian war bonds by 1917. The company also sustained considerable losses due to falling sales, more costly imports of parts, inflation, and a shift of part of its factory to the production of munitions. It still had an inventory on hand, just at Podolsk, of around $10 million.[21]

Impact of War

Americans in Russia, as less involved neutrals, were perhaps more surprised than others by the commencement of hostilities. A number of prominent members of the American community in Russia were away on vacation at the time, traveling either abroad or in the southern regions. Such was the case with

18. V. V. Lebedev, *Russko-Amerikanskie ekonomicheskie otnosheniia (1900–1917 gg.)* (Moscow: Mezhdu-otnosh., 1964), 141.

19. Charles Wilson to Guild, 5 March 1914, AE St. Petersburg, DPR 284, RG 84, NA.

20. Much information about the life insurance business in Russia is obscured by the many lawsuits regarding outstanding policy claims that the two American companies faced a number of years later. R. Carlyle Buley, *The Equitable Life Assurance Society of America, 1859–1964*, vol. 2 (New York: Equitable, 1967), 859–61, 952ff.

21. These figures were collected later especially for filing claims against the Soviet government. F. 1, box 157, Singer Papers, SHSW.

Frederick Corse, general manager of the main offices of New York Life. He was a longtime resident of St. Petersburg, dean of the expanding American colony in that city, and an important adviser to the embassy.[22]

The American diplomatic headquarters, located in a poorly furnished two-bedroom "palace" that was considered a "laughing stock among Russians and diplomats alike,"[23] even lacked an ambassador. Several months had passed since Curtis Guild had withdrawn from the post. Charles Crane, Russophile and prominent Democratic campaign contributor, declined to be his replacement in May 1914.[24] The Wilson administration, taking its time in filling the post, in July finally appointed businessman George Marye from San Francisco, who was in no hurry to reach Petrograd. He arrived in late October to find the small staff swamped with work and immediately pressed Washington for additional personnel.[25] In the interim between Guild and Marye, Charles Wilson served competently as chargé d'affaires, though he drew the fire of some visiting countrymen for not paying enough attention to their needs.[26]

22. Corse, who was a Phi Beta Kappa graduate of the University of Vermont and earned an M.A. at Columbia, had been in Russia since 1898, working first for Singer, and since 1903 with New York Life. "Memorandum Concerning *Frederick Merritt Corse*," 14 September 1927, General Biographical File, RG 3, New York Life Insurance Archives. For Ambassador Marye's impression:

> He is a man of keen intelligence, with good powers of observation; he speaks Russian well and can mix pleasantly with men so that he has the ability and the opportunity to get pretty accurate knowledge of the feelings and thought of the Russian People. I look upon him as my best source of information about Russia and things Russian, about present and prospective conditions in the country, social, economic and political.

George Thomas Marye, *Nearing the End in Imperial Russia* (London: Selwyn and Blount, 1929), 132–33.

23. Charles Wilson to Bryan, 2 January 1914, AE Petrograd, DPR 281, RG 84, NA. Bryan considered a proposed alternative, the Obolensky palace, too large and too expensive. Bryan to C. Wilson, 7 July 1914, ibid.

The American facilities in Petrograd were the subject of repeated complaints. Ambassador David Francis, soon after his arrival in May 1916, observed that his colleagues' "elegantly founded, well located embassies put me to shame," and that his abode was "inconvenient, ill-adapted, almost absolutely unequipped." Francis to Lansing, 30 May 1916, AE Russia, DPR 296, RG 84, NA.

24. Crane cited inability to arrange business affairs. Crane to Wilson, 14 May 1914, box 1, Crane Papers, BA, CU.

25. Marye to State Department, 28 October 1914, DPR 281, RG 84, NA.

26. For example, Hoffman Nickerson of the New York Zoological Society, who had come to Russia to seek help in preserving the walrus, complained of Wilson's lack of cooperation. To William Phillips (State Department), 13 July 1914, AE Petrograd, DPR 287, RG 84, NA.

The first and most immediate task of the American embassy and consular staffs was accounting for Americans marooned in Russia by the war, especially since quite a number were near the rapidly forming military fronts. A quick survey listed 57 Americans (apparently not including children) in St. Petersburg and around 50 more in Moscow.[27] Others were scattered about the country but especially in the border regions of Poland and the Caucasus. Chargé d'affaires Charles Wilson estimated that he needed at least $5,000 to $6,000 to provide emergency transportation for about 200 Americans who wanted to leave by way of Sweden.[28]

The most complicated situation was in Poland, where a number of American Jews had come as usual to visit relatives during the summer. Many of them, mostly women, were there illegally, having obtained false German or Russian papers to enter Russia. The consul in Warsaw, Hernando de Soto, tried to sort through the confusion that was exacerbated by the panic caused by a forced evacuation of the Jewish population from front areas and the resulting crunch of refugees pouring into Warsaw.[29] Many of the "American" Jews found at least temporary shelter in the Warsaw ghetto along with many others, often twenty to a room.[30]

The Warsaw consul also described a wave of brutality and persecution caused by Russian and Polish distrust of the loyalty of the Jewish population. Poles had resented the recent influx of Jews into their cities as a result of anti-Semitic "cleansing" policies in Russia proper.[31] The Jewish population of Warsaw, for example, had grown from 210,000 in 1897 to 337,000 in 1914, or almost 40 percent of the population.[32] As usual in Russian history, when things do not go well (as they certainly did not in Poland in 1914 and 1915), Jews became scapegoats caught in a Catch-22, with the Russian government no longer allowing them to emigrate because of transport priorities and their liability to military service.

27. North Winship (Petrograd) to Charles Wilson, 8 August 1914, DPR 285, RG 84, NA.

28. Wilson to American Embassy, London, 19 August 1914, DPR 285, RG 84, NA.

29. De Soto to C. Wilson, 12 September 1914, AE Petrograd, DPR 281; and to Marye, 25 November 1914, DPR 284, RG 84, NA.

30. De Soto to Bryan, 10 June 1915, AE Petrograd, DPR 293, RG 84, NA.

31. Ibid. Ironically, De Soto noted, the Poles considered these *Russian* Jews agents of Russification. Roman Rosen, former ambassador to the United States, was one who lamented this outburst of violence: "It is a page in our history of which every patriot who has at heart the honour of his country must be deeply ashamed." Rosen, *Forty Years of Diplomacy*, vol. 2 (London: Allen and Unwin, 1922), 191.

32. Stephen D. Corrsin, "Warsaw: Poles and Jews in a Conquered City," in *The City in Late Imperial Russia*, ed. Michael F. Hamm (Bloomington: Indiana University Press, 1986), 130.

Although Russia refused to recognize temporary passports issued to the American "Hebrew women," they did accept consular registration certificates, thus allowing them to return home.[33]

But a number of Americans caught in Russia by the war were reluctant to accept assistance in leaving. Many wanted to stay to help their families during a time of crisis, while others decided to wait it out for one reason or another. For example, Consul General Snodgrass in Moscow was annoyed that Charles Johnson, an African American with the Lewis Douglas Theatrical Company, accepted a small sum of money (ten rubles) from him for leaving—but then stayed.[34] The same was true of the stranded Phillips sisters, who, after performing at the famed Aquarium nightclub in Moscow, were scheduled to go on to Dresden but obviously now could not go there directly.[35] After causing considerable extra work for the consular staffs, most of those stranded by the war eventually left Russia by the only convenient route through Scandinavia.

Another special concern was the employees of the Caucasus Copper Company at Alexandrovsk near the Armenian-Turkish frontier, not only because of being located near the border but also because of anticipated bloody reprisals there against the Armenian population, if and when the Ottoman Empire entered the war. When that happened at the end of October, H. Willoughby Smith, consul in Batum, rushed to the scene and helped arrange the evacuation of thirty Americans and a number of British employees to Petrograd.[36]

Another problem, also in the south of Russia, attracted early American attention—the Mennonites. Their situation was compounded by the fact that they were German-speaking and also opposed military service. Americans were interested in their fate because many of their brethren (and relatives) had emigrated to the United States, they had been good customers for American agricultural equipment, and they resisted any direct participation in the war effort. Frederick Corse, after passing through a colony in the spring of 1915, noted that the Mennonites were being denied loans and forced to liquidate property and were not planting fields, despite the fact that "the land is in a high state of cultivation and most modern agricultural machinery has been introduced."[37] The next spring an 1873

33. Lansing to Marye, 15 May 1915, AE Petrograd, DPR 289, RG 84, NA.

34. Snodgrass to Wilson, 31 October 1914, AE Petrograd, DPR 282, RG 84, NA.

35. Phillips sisters (Moscow) to Wilson, 29 August 1914, AE Petrograd, DPR 282, RG 84, NA.

36. Smith (Batum) to Wilson, 13 August 1914, AE Petrograd, DPR 281; Smith (Tiflis) to Marye, 24 November and 14 December 1914, DPR 283, RG 84, NA. A mining engineer, Robeson T. White, was reported as wounded but recovering.

37. Corse to Marye, 21 April 1915, AE Petrograd, DPR 294, RG 84, NA.

immigrant to the United States, Peter Jansen, complained that his kinsmen, who were among the most productive elements of the Russian populations, were being dispossessed and reduced to poverty.[38]

The advent of war naturally had a significant impact on economic relations. American exports to Russia that passed through Germany or other major European countries were suddenly cut off. Passage by rail through Scandinavia was quite restricted, mainly limited to passengers, while other access points, through the Arctic and White Sea to Archangel or across the Pacific to Vladivostok, required considerable reorientation and greater expense. The latter route would, of course, give the United States an apparent advantage over European traders, one that was rapidly reduced, however, by the deteriorating condition of the mostly single-tracked Trans-Siberian Railroad.

American business operations in Russia fared quite differently from the war's effects. This was especially true of the American "flagship" companies, International Harvester and Singer. Harvester was initially left relatively undisturbed by the war, except for import difficulties, and was actually in a position to gain from the reduced foreign competition. Sales and production thus increased in 1915. Perhaps because of this boost, or because the continuation of hostilities dimmed future prospects, the company offered to sell its Lubertsy plant to the Russian government in early 1916.[39]

Singer, on the other hand, took quite a beating at the beginning of the war. Although recognized officially as mainly American (actually Americans and British held all the stock in the Russian branch), Singer was considered, in public eyes, as German. This, in part, was because of the unfortunate spelling of the Russian affiliate's name, "Kompaniia Zinger,"which appeared on every machine made in Russia and on its "headquarters" on Nevsky Prospect (no. 28) in the capital, but also because a number of administrators were indeed (or had been) of German origin, due to the initial opening up of the Russian market to Singer machines by its Hamburg office.[40] Singer had also aroused popular resentment

38. Jansen (Beatrice, Nebraska) to Francis, 28 March 1916, AE Russia, DPR 304, RG 84, NA.

39. Bakhmetev to Sazonov, 26 February 1916, f. 133, op. 470, d. 53, AVPR.

40. Walter F. Dixon (director of Russian Singer) to Marye, 9 June 1915, DPR 291, RG 84, NA. Ironically, the distinctive building on Nevsky no longer housed Singer offices. It suffered some superficial vandalism, such as having the *American* eagle torn off.

Dixon also explained that Albert Flohr, a target of Russian charges, was an invalid who had not been involved in the company since 1905 and held only 3 shares of stock (out of 50,000). Although Dixon was thoroughly American, Ottar Myslik was in charge of sales and Heinrich Bertling was the chief financial officer, both formally Russian subjects. Ibid.

from its monopoly on service in the countryside and its collection tactics (down payments with extended payment schedules with interest).

Russian patriotically inspired anger against Germany thus found easy targets in the many sales and repair shops scattered across the country, a large number of which were ransacked and vandalized at the beginning of hostilities. Local authorities usually stepped in to prevent further violence but then sequestered many of these facilities, essentially putting them out of business for a time. A zemstvo commission, supported by the central government, also leveled charges against Singer for harboring German spies and placed the Podolsk factory briefly under its superintendency.[41] In an effort to placate officials and repair the company's public image, the Singer management cooperated fully in diverting much of the plant's operations to munition (artillery shells) production but "suffered extremely serious financial losses" in the process.[42]

Singer admitted to having labor problems that went back to before 1905 and blamed disgruntled employees for some of the negative publicity. Nonetheless, facing threats to future operations and with the war continuing through 1915, the president of the company, Douglas Alexander, rushed to Petrograd in October 1915 to negotiate directly with Russian foreign minister Sergei Sazonov, accompanied by the American ambassador. Marye quoted Sazonov as saying:

> You tell me you only had a hundred and forty Germans in your employment out of between thirty-four and thirty-five thousand employees. That may be, but those Germans all held the most responsible and prominent positions in your service and were allowed to create, and did create, the popular impression that you were a German company.

Sazonov went on to charge Singer officials in the Warsaw area with "the most criminal and dangerous kind of spying."[43] Although Alexander felt that his persistent efforts bore fruit with the Russian administration, around 700 shops remained closed at the end of 1915, no doubt a popular measure in the countryside that would curtail or seriously hamper collection of payments on machines

---

41. A translation of the twenty-eight-page zemstvo report, dated 8 August 1915, is in the Singer Papers, box 155, SHSW, and in DPR 290, RG 84, NA. The company's detailed defense revealed information about the operations of the factory. At the beginning of the war, 5,047 (897 women) were employed, earning an average of 505 rubles per year. Conscription removed 1,297, with the effective workforce reduced to 4,662 by August 1915.

42. Dixon to Francis, 24 November 1916, AE Russia, DPR 300, RG 84, NA.

43. Marye to Lansing, 28 October 1915, AE Petrograd, DPR 291, RG 84, NA.

already sold.[44] The Russian government restricted its own direct actions against Singer, however, due to its reliance on heavy-duty sewing machines for making uniforms.

Singer was not the only foreign company to be targeted by a population frustrated by a war that was increasingly going poorly for Russia. In a series of riots in Moscow at the end of May and in early June 1915, a number of businesses were looted in what Consul General John Snodgrass termed a "pogrom." National Cash Register, for example, lost 330 machines in an attack by over 2,000 Muscovites on its warehouse, sustaining a total loss of $185,250. Even the private homes of some foreign businessmen, no matter what nationality, were targets of vandals, though apparently no loss of life resulted.[45]

Some American businesses were simply caught with goods on hand that could not be shipped, because of outlets being closed or government edicts. The latter were especially annoying because of their fickleness and inconsistency. Theodore Bassett of New York could no longer export scrap rubber out of Odessa or even through Vladivostok. Sheepskins could not be sent out, but horse manes could. Chesborough Manufacturing Company of New Jersey, the major supplier of Vaseline to Russia, discovered that Russian authorities refused to allow the return of empty tins.[46] And Russia, in many ways desperately needing trade, insisted that the American government guarantee that any items imported would not be reexported to enemy countries, which that government could not do.[47] Then, as the war lengthened, there was concern that even though Russia might have a surplus of a particular commodity, such as casings for sausage, its allies might have a shortage. All of this created more confusion and frustration for consuls and businessmen in both Russia and the United States.

A number of Russians and Americans, however, saw a great opportunity for commercial expansion created by the war and the suppression of trade with Germany. Although many rushed to be on the ground floor, most expectations would be frustrated by Russian policies or American apathy. For example, increasing American demand for Russian flax and linen brought several traders to Russia who subsequently lost their investments when the Russian government without warning prohibited their export. Snodgrass frequently complained of

---

44. Alexander to Marye, 15 November 1915, AE Petrograd, DPR 291, RG 84, NA.

45. Snodgrass report, 26 May 1915, CG Moscow, DPR 5; and Snodgrass to Marye, 1 October 1915, and A. Krilachevsky (attorney for Americans) to Marye, 30 October 1915, AE Petrograd, DPR 291, RG 84, NA.

46. A. B. Richardson (Chesborough Russian branch) to Marye, 12 August 1915, AE Petrograd, DPR 292, RG 84, NA.

47. Wilson to F. Blumenthal Co. of New York, 31 August 1915, ibid.

the lack of enthusiasm in Washington to his pleas on behalf of commercial opportunities: "I am hoping that in the future the eyes of those in authority at home may be so thoroughly opened that they will accept the suggestions of the men in the field, rather than those of the men who sit in the seats provided for those who are presumed to understand conditions abroad."[48] For a variety of reasons, expansion of trade between the United States and Russia was a lost dream.

Journalist Arthur Ruhl also observed the American frustration in exploring opportunities in Russia:

> It was interesting to watch the change come over Americans—see them arrive full of steam and the notion of getting a lot done in a hurry, and gradually lose their energy and optimism until they either went home defeated or got a sort of second wind, and understood that the game in Russia was a new one and called for an amount of patience, leisure, politeness, and apparently aimless palavering which they never dreamed of at home.[49]

Perhaps the most successfully exported Russian commodity was, in fact, sausage casings (sheep's entrails), thanks to the large demand in immigrant sections of American cities and the success of the Petrograd firm of Kamensky Brothers, which handled much of the business.[50] Casings had normally been imported into the United States from Germany but were probably of Russian (Caucasus and Central Asia) origin. Other items sometimes allowed export licenses were vetch, mustard, and beet seeds, furs, licorice root, and goatskins, none of which could be considered of great importance. Henry Baker, newly appointed American commercial attaché for Russia, summed up the situation: "The policy as regards granting permits has been so changing and uncertain that American firms which purchase such goods here, run the risk of serious loss and embarrassment."[51]

Petrograd professor of political economy and trade proponent Ivan Ozerov thought that a major problem was structural, the lack of a special Russian-American bank.[52] The war inspired a vision of brighter future prospects for

48. Snodgrass to Harper, 29 May 1915, f. 12, box 2, Harper Papers, UC.

49. Arthur Ruhl, *White Nights and Other Russian Impressions* (New York: Charles Scribner's Sons, 1917), 50.

50. Kamensky Bros to Wilson, 26 April 1915, and Wilson to Kamensky Bros, 23 June 1915, AE Petrograd, DPR 292 (15), RG 84, NA. A leading American importer was the Oppenheimer Casing Company of Chicago.

51. To State Department, 29 May 1916, AE Russia, DPR 302, RG 84, NA.

52. Ozerov to Snodgrass, 5 November 1914, CG Moscow, DPR 4, RG 84, NA.

American business and reinvigorated the dormant Russian-American Chamber of Commerce in Moscow under a new director, Alexander Behr.[53] It also sparked the creation of an American counterpart in New York—the American-Russian Chamber of Commerce—under the leadership of Charles Boynton and E. Chapell Porter, who quickly made clear their frustration with Russian restrictions. Porter was experienced in the promotion of American trade as New York agent of the Bureau of Foreign and Domestic Commerce.[54] Behr came to America in September 1915 to coordinate and publicize these efforts but incurred the opposition of J. P. Morgan (Guaranty Trust), which aspired to a major portion of future Russian trade and investment.[55] Nonetheless, a closer relationship was forged between the Russian and American branches.

Another problem, however, was a rival trade organization promoted actively by Ivan Narodny, a quasi socialist exiled in America for several years who was also convinced of a great future for Russian-American trade. Denounced by the Russian embassy and New York consulate, Narodny struck back by pointing out that a particularly valuable asset of Russia's, quite marketable in the West, was the wealth of art, gold, silver, and so on held by the church, crown, and nobility.[56] These were resources that the future Soviet government would not hesitate to use for its own benefit and survival.

One more Russian-American trade organization entered the fray. Alexander Postnikov and Xenophon Kalamatiano set up the International Manufacturers Sales Company of America in 1915 in Chicago and published the short-lived *Russian-American Journal of Commerce.* Unlike the other two organizations, this one was led by knowledgeable and experienced businessmen of Russian background who were resident in America with good connections in both countries.[57] Going one step further, Kalamatiano returned to Russia in 1916 to establish an

53. Snodgrass, who, along with Ivan Ozerov, had first organized the chamber, considered its "takeover" by Behr unfortunate because of his checkered career as a cotton trader and as an agent for Fidelity Deposit Company of Baltimore. To Marye (confidential), 18 August 1915, AE Petrograd, DPR 291, RG 84, NA.

54. "Move to Win Trade of Russian Empire," *New York Times,* 24 September 1915 (14:1).

55. At least this was the impression of David Francis. Francis to House, 13 April 1916, box 56, Francis Papers, MoHS. Complicating the picture was an escalating rivalry between Morgan and Frank Vanderlip's New York City Bank, which had already established a branch in Russia.

56. "Russia Aims Blow at Ivan Narodny," *New York Times,* 7 May 1915 (10:2); Narodny, "Russia's Fabulous Untouched Wealth," *New York Times,* 12 May 1915 (10:7–8).

57. Postnikov to Harper, 7 November 1915, f. 17, box 2, Harper Papers, UC; L. N. Burns (Case & Co.) to Francis, 18 March 1916, box A, Francis Papers, MoHS; Adee (State Dept.) to Dearing, 7 April 1916, AE Russia, DPR 301, RG 84, NA.

office in Moscow and gained the support of American commercial attaché Henry Baker.[58]

With the possibility opened for a great postwar commercial expansion, due to the expectation that Germany would not regain its former dominant position, Washington pushed for a renewed commercial expansion in Russia and a new treaty to assist it. Even more cognizant of this opportunity was Great Britain, which considered the United States its chief rival. Britain had the disadvantage of being forced to concentrate its economic efforts on the war but the advantages of having a commercial treaty in place and Russia as an important ally. As the war continued and popular hostility toward Germany grew, a new agreement seemed even more urgent for the United States. Marye sought and received an audience with Nicholas II within a week of his arrival and was pleased with the long, friendly conversation that emphasized past cooperation and future trade prospects.[59] The appointment of Henry Baker as commercial attaché was another sign that Washington was finally taking trade prospects more seriously. And Baker was pleased to discover that in early 1916 National City Bank seemed about to seal a $260 million loan to Russia in cooperation with its main rival, Guaranty Trust.[60]

The primary American diplomatic goal in 1915 and 1916 was thus a new treaty of commerce to replace the one abrogated by the United States in 1911 over a dispute that involved Russian discriminatory screening in issuing visas to American Jews ("the passport question"). This commercial treaty, which dated to 1832, needed revision and clarification and, in any event, remained more or less in effect even after the abrogation. Marye pursued a new foundation for trade but to no avail. From the time of his appointment in the spring of 1916, Ambassador David Francis's number one priority was also to sign a new accord.[61] Although welcoming such overtures, Foreign Minister Sazonov put off any negotiation until the end of the war.[62]

Temporary and short-term adjustments were the only alternative strategy. Prodded by American pressure, in mid-1916 Finance Minister Petr Bark finally

58. Postnikov to Baker, 3 April 1916, copy in box 46, Francis Papers, MoHS.
59. Marye, *Nearing the End in Imperial Russia*, 40.
60. Baker to Pratt, 12 February 1916, box 435, BFDC, RG 151, NA.
61. Francis to Lansing, 18 April 1916 (o), f. 187, box 6, Polk Papers, Yale-Sterling.
62. Wilson to Bryan, 11 September 1914, AE Petrograd, DPR 284; and David Francis to Lansing, 11 December 1916, AE Russia, DPR 305, RG 84, NA. Francis thought that one reason for the lukewarm Russian response was that Finance Minister Bark and Foreign Minister Sazonov were under British influence. Francis to Polk, 3 May 1916, f. 187, box 6, Polk Papers, Yale-Sterling.

Nicholas II

produced a long list of prohibited items and a short list of those allowed for export that featured corn, butter, eggs, timber, and furs, the latter having only a relatively small market in the United States.[63] Major strategic items, such as copper, manganese, and oil products, might have been handled by American shippers, except that they faced transportation obstacles through the closure of the Baltic and Black Seas and Russian sensitivity about their reaching enemy hands through neutral carriers.

The commencement of hostilities and the accompanying export restrictions also brought to an end, or severely curtailed, a number of American-Russian endeavors in the agricultural sphere. With both scientific and economic motives

63. List, dated 15 July 1916, AE Russia, DPR 302, RG 84, NA.

in mind, two Americans were separately trying to develop herds of karakul sheep, native to the region of Bokhara in Central Asia, in America. C. C. Young (Karl Jung), originally from a German colony in Bessarabia, had become a successful Chicago eye surgeon before getting involved with agricultural ventures. Several prewar shipments had failed to produce a sustainable herd on his Belen, Texas, ranch, so he returned to Russia in fear that war disruptions might wipe out his larger herd in Bessarabia.[64] Similarly, Robert Nabours, a zoologist at Kansas State Agricultural College, had a small herd stranded in 1914 at Samara that was destined as an addition to one he had helped establish near Cottonwood Falls, Kansas.[65]

Certainly one of the greatest economic effects from the war on both Russia and the United States was the cessation of Russian grain exports that normally left Russia through the Baltic and Black Seas for European markets. The loss of income from grain sales naturally had dire economic consequences for all who were directly involved, while the United States reaped the benefit of a sharply increased demand for its farm products abroad, essentially filling the gap in the needs of Russia's allies.

But in other respects neutrality raised complications for the United States. The war caused disruption in the operations of New York Life Insurance and personal embarrassment to its chief director in Russia. Many of the company's 35,000 policies written in Russia had been sold in Russian Poland, most of which fell under German occupation by 1916, and the administration of these policies was transferred to the Berlin office. In order to coordinate with German representatives and transfer case files, Corse and his wife went to Stockholm in early February 1916. At Torneo, the Russian customs point, both were subjected to a thorough strip search, causing embarrassment to all concerned, since Corse was "said to be the most prominent and respected man in the American colony in Petrograd."[66] Sharp protests to the Russian foreign ministry brought only a declaration of the right to interfere with anyone doing business with Germany.[67]

64. Young to Francis, 1 July and 13 August 1916, AE Russia, DPR 307, RG 84, NA.

65. Nabours to Snodgrass, 12 January and 8 March 1915, CG Moscow, DPR 3, RG 84, NA.

66. Fred Harris Baring (Stockholm) to Sazonov, 25 April 1916 (c), and Corse to Marye, 11 February 1916, AE Petrograd, DPR 297, RG 84, NA. A rival, with whom apparently Corse did not get along, was Harry Fessenden Meserve, director of the Petrograd branch of the National City Bank of New York.

67. Marye to Sazonov, 12 February 1916, and Sazonov to Marye, 16 March 1916 (o.s.), AE Petrograd, DPR 297, RG 84, NA. The ministry seemed insensitive to the claim that the company was the largest holder of Russian securities in the country.

More successful was the evacuation through Russia in 1916 of over eighty Standard Oil employees who had been working in the Ploesti oil field in Romania.[68]

The war produced yet one more aggravation for foreign diplomats and businesses—a crunch for office space in Petrograd, especially with a booming military bureaucracy and the fact that the city soon became a major reserve and supply center for the Northern Front. Use of the more spacious Austro-Hungarian embassy, now under temporary American care, alleviated the cramped conditions in the American building, and some members of the enlarged staff worked out of apartments or from leased offices in the Singer building.[69] Harry Fessenden Meserve was relieved that the threatened takeover of the main branch of National City Bank in Petrograd for military purposes was abandoned.[70] Finding space for more staff was not an easy task, given the housing shortage, meager resources from Washington, and pressure from other diplomatic missions as well.

War Matériel

The Russian government was slow to realize that it would need additional military supplies to sustain the large army that was being mobilized. At first, under the influence of Lord Kitchener, Britain was willing to share its production facilities with Russia, but by the time Russia made its needs clear in the summer of 1915, Britain's requirements for its expeditionary forces had outstripped production. The recourse was mainly to the United States and Japan. Unfortunately for Russia, by late 1915 Britain, with the ascendancy of the strategy of concentrating on the "western front" of Chief of Staff William Robertson, insisted on coordination and approval of all Allied munitions orders.[71]

Auxiliary supplies could still be negotiated directly, but a serious problem at the beginning was failing to take advantage of American agents in Russia for large government orders, for which American consular agents were partly to blame. Thus a large order from the Ministry of War for 800 badly needed trucks from the White Motor Company was delayed and then canceled.[72] The main

68. Standard Oil to Francis, 7 November 1916, AE Petrograd, DPR 299, RG 84, NA.
69. The German embassy, also technically in American custody, was not available, since it had been completely ransacked and virtually destroyed at the beginning of the war.
70. Meserve to Francis, 16 November 1916, AE Russia, DPR 297, RG 84, NA.
71. For an excellent, detailed account, see Keith Neilson, *Strategy and Supply: The Anglo-Russian Alliance, 1914–17* (London: Allen and Unwin, 1984).
72. Upon first inquiry in August, White promised delivery within sixty days through Archangel and Vladivostok, but Sidney Friede, the White agent who was on vacation in

obstacle was that Russian bureaucratic procedures prevented swift placement of orders, and there was a natural tendency for Russians to believe that deliveries would take so long that the war would be over before they arrived. One supplier complained in October that "people in Russia have so delayed things as to lose all chance of obtaining any large number of trucks out of immediate stock." He noted that 750 Kelly-Springfield trucks could have been delivered in fifteen days, but with France buying 600 finished trucks and ordering 1,100 more, very few, if any, would be available for Russia. Russia could have had all of them. "Is it not possible to bring before our friends there the idea that matters are now moving in this country with great speed?"[73]

As another example of faulty Russian business practice, Rice and Hutchins, a major American shoe company, signed a contract in August 1914 to deliver 1 million pairs of knee-high boots for $5 million. But just as the first delivery was about to be made, the Russian police arrested the company's agents in Russia on charges of spying because they had previously been attached to the Berlin office. Russia rescinded the agreement and held the Americans for six weeks, incurring a lengthy lawsuit and bad publicity. Consul General Snodgrass was especially upset: "This is the most shameful and unspeakable offence against citizens of a friendly country I have experienced during my six years in Russia."[74] Russians had a way of literally shooting themselves in the foot (unprotected by American boots!).

Russian officials instead preferred to deal directly in the United States, but that took time. The first provisional purchasing commission, consisting of military and commercial agents already in the country, formed in New York in September to place orders for the most immediate and pressing need—medicines, bandages, dressings, and chloroform, a sad reflection on the initial costs of the war to Russia and its lack of basic preparedness.[75] Russia was quick to react, however, to fill one other military need—barbed wire—that would signal the type of fighting to come. Having no production capability of its own, Russia ordered 8,000 tons to be shipped through the Panama Canal to Vladivostok.[76] That route would consume valuable

August, insisted on negotiating the order for the sake of commissions. Snodgrass to White (t), 19 August 1914, and White to Snodgrass (t), 20 August 1914; Friede to Snodgrass, 21 August 1914; Snodgrass to Beliaev (Ministry of War), 26 August 1914; Snodgrass to Friede, 8 October 1914, CG Moscow, DPR 8, RG 84, NA.

73. R. B. Bedford, president Railway Export Corp., to Snodgrass, 15 October 1914, CG Moscow, DPR 8, RG 84, NA.

74. Snodgrass to Wilson, 7 September 1914 (t), CG Moscow, DPR 3, RG 84, NA.

75. Bakhmetev to Sazonov, 25 September 1914 (t), f. 133, op. 470, d. 48, AVPR.

76. Sherman Miles (U.S. military attaché) to WCD, 26 October 1914, f. 8806-3, box 359, RG 165, NA.

time but was cheaper than paying high insurance for a North Atlantic passage to Archangel. Other initial items of purchase included Overland touring cars, Garfield trucks, and a number of locomotives and other railroad equipment.

Details of many of the Russian purchases in the United States are obscured by secrecy, confusion, delays, and the inability of American companies to fulfill or keep up with orders.[77] Russia at the beginning also lacked the technical advisers required to draw up the specifics in contracts, which was crucial for Russia because of the much greater variance in equipment—caliber of shells, wider axles for railroad equipment—than was the case with its Western allies. For several months after the beginning of the war, Russian military authorities thought that their own production of rifles would meet their needs. The American military attaché finally received his first inquiry about ordering rifles from the United States in November 1914.[78]

Russian officials were slow to take advantage of opportunities for a number of other reasons. Financing had to be arranged, mainly through Guaranty Trust and J. P. Morgan to avoid reliance on Jewish banks.[79] It also required backing by British credits and awkward coordination through other Russian purchasing agents in Britain and France and with Allied buyers in the United States.[80] Britain and France dominated most of the market and restricted Russian purchases by denying credit in order to meet their objectives of maintaining a high priority on supplies for the Western Front. Nor was Russia trustful of a number of opportunistic yet well-intentioned gestures coming from American sources. Even the aging Wharton Barker, who had been the agent for Russian warship purchases during the Russo-Turkish War of 1877–78, offered his assistance directly to Nicholas II (by registered mail).[81]

Preferring direct negotiations, little could really be done by Russia to initiate substantial contracts until a "properly authorized" purchasing commission under Major General A. V. Saposhnikov arrived in late November 1914, followed by other technical personnel.[82] Matters improved some with the hiring in April

77. It must be admitted, however, that Russian archives on this subject have not been thoroughly mined.

78. Sherman Miles to WCD, 12 November 1914, box 359 (8806), RG 165, NA.

79. Agents of the Ministry of Commerce opened lines of credit of $7 million with Guaranty and $5 million with Morgan. Bakhmetev to Sazonov, 14 November 1914, f. 133, op. 470, d. 105 (1914), AVPR.

80. See Neilson, *Strategy and Supply*, especially 172–78.

81. Barker to Nicholas II, 21 September 1914 (c), box 12, Barker Papers, MD, LC. He concluded, "Permit me to say again that I am at your command in any way within my power and that I am sure no other American now living has had the intimate relations with Russians that I have had."

82. Bakhmetev to Sazonov, 25 November 1914, f. 133, op. 470, d. 48 (1914), AVPR.

1915 of a prominent New York law firm, Coudert Brothers, to oversee all legal matters regarding doing business in America.[83] By that time most key American industries had extensive back orders for all kinds of munitions from Britain and France. Saposhnikov advised Ambassador George Bakhmetev that Dupont, despite a threefold expansion in production of gunpowder, would only take orders for deliveries in 1916. His aide, Colonel Zhukovskii, nevertheless signed a contract for 5 million pounds, at 97½¢ per pound, in March 1915, with the hope that delivery might begin by November.[84]

Other Russian initiatives met with mixed success. To alleviate the access route problem, Russia decided to build a railroad almost 1,000 miles long from Petrograd north to the Kola Peninsula, where a new port could be kept open through the winter. The Lackawanna Steel Company made most of the rails, reportedly its largest order ever, and increased its blast furnaces in operation from two to six, while the Maryland Steel Company of Baltimore furnished another 100,000 tons of rails.[85]

Russian efforts to initiate such agreements independently were often sabotaged by British refusal to extend credit. Currency exchanges were another problem. An offer of a $25 million contract for 50,000 badly needed freight cars to the Pullman Company of Chicago fell through because of Russian insistence on paying in rubles and the condition that most of the cars be assembled in shops built in Russia.[86] Charles Flint's negotiations for field artillery shells also collapsed because of Russian insistence on using Russian securities for payment.[87] Flint did arrange, however, for the purchase of an undisclosed number of "tractor tanks, well adapted for snow," from a Chicago firm for $5,600 each, but delivery could not be made before April 1917 and then was preempted by American military needs.[88] And the successful completion of several especially large and expensive aircraft for the

83. Bakhmetev to Sazonov (t), 23 April 1915, f. 133, op. 470, d. 60 (1915). This did not come cheap, with a retainer of $1,250 per month plus commissions.

84. Bakhmetev to MFA for Zhukovskii, 31 March 1915, f. 133, op. 470, d. 139, AVPR. There are indications that out of desperation this order to Dupont was enlarged with a substantial bonus offered for early completion. "$60,000,000 Russian Order," *New York Times*, 8 July 1915 (9:3).

85. "Russia Places Rail Order," *New York Times*, 16 July 1915 (15:2); and "Russia Buys Steel Rails Here," *New York Times*, 8 August 1915 (14:2); *New York Times*, 3 July 1915 (3:1).

86. "Refused 25,000,000 Order," *New York Times*, 2 July 1915 (3:1).

87. C. M. Carter to Hayley Eames (Flint and Company), 17 March 1916, box 2, Flint Papers, NYPL.

88. W. N. Smith (Monarch Tractor Co.) to B. N. Sverdlov, 27 November 1916, ibid. Such involvement with Russian war business contributed to the bankruptcy of Flint and Company in 1917.

Russian navy at the Curtiss plant in Toronto was probably not a wise investment of Russian military resources.[89]

Russian orders, along with those of the other Allies, promoted a substantial increase in American capacity for producing munitions and other military needs, thus helping prepare the United States for the military and financial burdens that lay ahead. But, in the process, the Russian treasury was drained, and faith in an American supply miracle faded.

Another problem was coordination. For security purposes, all Russian communications with Petrograd were at first handled through the embassy in Washington, though the purchasing commission was headquartered in New York and worked mainly out of the office of the Russian consul general. The size of the commission, by 1916 over eighty officers, few of whom knew any English, was also a problem.[90] And it took some time for the Russians to learn the ropes, such as negotiation with Canadian firms, which could subcontract orders to American companies. This was a way around compromising American neutrality while at the same time circumventing suspicion and distrust from certain areas of American labor about producing munitions for autocratic, antirevolutionary Russia.

Finally, in July and August 1916, Boris Bakhmeteff, an engineering professor with experience in the United States, led another commission sent by the Ministry of Commerce and Industry to achieve greater coordination. Although he did improve on the social sophistication required in dealing with American companies, it was too late to have much effect on supplies for 1917.[91] While noting the difficulty of obtaining reliable data, the American military attaché in Russia believed in June 1915 that Russia had placed orders for 1 million rifles with Remington and another for 25,000 machine guns and 5 million shrapnel shells, few of which could reach Russia before 1917.[92]

89. "Flying Destroyers Ordered by Russia," *New York Times*, 10 July 1915 (2:4). These were delivered to Archangel lashed to the deck of the *Czaritza*. *New York Times*, 15 November 1915 (3:6).

90. Already in June 1915, Bakhmetev expressed "his disgust" with the operations of the purchasing commission for failing to consult with Russian consul Sergei Korff and for getting so little done. To Sazonov, 17 June 1915, f. 133, op. 470, d. 60 (1915), AVPR.

91. Bakhmeteff oral history, CU; Loyall Osborne (vice president of Westinghouse Electric) to Bakhmeteff, 20 July 1916, box 20, Bakhmeteff Papers, BA, CU, inviting Bakhmeteff for a weekend in the country.

92. Bakhmetev to Sazonov, 12 May 1916, f. 133, op. 470, d. 54, AVPR. Sherman Miles to WCD, 4 June 1915, f. 8806-23, box 359, RG 165, NA.

Russians ignored other possibilities of assistance. General M. M. Macomb, chief of the War College Division in Washington, thought it was strange that he had never met the Russian military attaché who resided permanently in New York. Macomb to Riggs, 12 September 1916, f. 9241-27, box 422, RG 165, NA.

Even if sorely needed munitions and other supplies could be produced in America for Russia, they could not be delivered to the war zones in a timely fashion. Russia possessed little shipping of its own and was forced to rely on whatever could be spared by its allies. Chartering vessels for Archangel and Murmansk encountered high costs and insurance fees, while using the alternative route of the Panama Canal and across the Pacific to Vladivostok required at least two and a half months in transit. The latter was at least open throughout the year, and some of the first cargoes of American arms—heavy field guns—went by that route.[93] Russia expended much time and effort in trying to overcome such obstacles and in combating security breaches and moral lapses, such as were alleged in an investigation of Colonel Vladimir Nekrasov and his purchase in late 1916 of field artillery shells.[94]

The combination of Russian bungling and delays, financial complications, the overtaxing of American capacity to produce, Allied priority on supplying the Western Front, and scarcity of shipping meant that any relief from America for significant Russian shortages would be little and late. Russian expectations of American help would be disappointed, adding to the decline in morale. Dmitri Protopopov, a patriotic liberal, wrote his friend Samuel Harper, the founder of Russian studies at the University of Chicago: "We are astonished that America is so slow in making ammunition for us. What is the reason? Might it be German influence? Or what is it?"[95] And on a visit to the front at the end of 1915, Naval Attaché Newton McCully found officers wanting to know when they would receive rifles ordered from America and complaining about how rich America was becoming because of the war. Then and later, McCully thought a British conspiracy was keeping American business out of Russia.[96]

Nevertheless, the United States supplied Russia with an increasing quantity of munitions, railroad equipment, medicines, and other vital needs. As in the case of Singer, crucial additional materials and equipment shipped from America allowed the company to supply sewing machines and spare parts to army outfitters and to increase the production of munitions at the Podolsk factory.[97] Other

93. "American Guns for Russia," *New York Times*, 3 January 1915 (2:4).

94. Russian Artillery Commission in North America file, MD, NYPL. The sordid—and complicated—details involved an alleged Austrian plot (Baroness Seidlitz), Sidney Reilly's exposé, and the transportation of women across state lines for immoral purposes by Nekrasov.

95. Protopopov to Harper, 12 August 1915, box 2, f. 15, Harper Papers, UC.

96. McCully to CNO, 20 December 1915 and 11 January 1916, box 710, WA-6, RG 45, NA.

97. Dixon to Francis, 24 November 1916, AE Russia, DPR 300, RG 84, NA.

opportunities were missed because of misguided Russian policies. For example, the Walkover Shoe Company closed its Russian operations in 1916 because of a price limit of nineteen rubles for the sale of any pair of shoes, regardless of quality.[98]

American Attitude Toward Russia

George Bakhmetev, the Russian ambassador to the United States since 1910, had several advantages over his American counterparts in Petrograd. First, he occupied a stately mansion, the largest embassy-residence in Washington. It had been built a few years before for Mrs. George Pullman and was located not far from the White House on Sixteenth Street. Second, his wife, the former Mary Beale, was prominent in Washington social circles and entertained frequently there and at their Newport, Rhode Island, summer home. Her father served as minister to Austria in the 1870s, and her brother, Truxtun Beale, was a well-known diplomat in Greece and the Middle East. Both she and her brother were connoisseurs and collectors of classical and Renaissance art.[99] She was also renowned for her interest in birds and for her "wild garden" beside the embassy.

With several years of service in Washington behind him, Bakhmetev was also fortunate to have an experienced staff that was both familiar with America and well placed in Russian political society. It included Aleksandr Shcherbatskoi, Konstantin Nabokov (uncle of the author), Iosef Loris-Melikov, Konstantin Medzhikovskii, and Baron Renard Ungern-Shternberg.[100] Unfortunately for the Russian mission, some of these would soon be transferred to other, "more important," posts. First Loris-Melikov was called home. When Nabokov was moved to London in late 1915, Petrograd granted Bakhmetev his request that Loris-Melikov be sent back to Washington, but within months he was "promoted" to ambassador to Siam instead.[101]

Bakhmetev seemed genuinely surprised by the outpouring of support for the Entente and hostility toward Germany in America at the beginning of the war. He reported from his summer residence in Newport that almost all of the

98. Francis to Phillips (c), 13 July 1916, Francis Papers, box 30, MoHS.

99. Jerome Landfield, "'Operation Kaleidoscope': A Melange of Personal Recollections," typescript memoir, UCB.

100. For a description, picture, and interview with Mrs. Bakhmetev, see "Russian Women's Part in the War," *New York Times*, 11 April 1915 (V:11).

101. Bakhmetev to Sazonov, 13 November 1915, f. 133, op. 470, d. 60 (1915), AVPR.

George Bakhmetev and Mary (Mamie) Beale Bakhmetev, in front of Russian Embassy, Sixteenth Street, Washington, D.C., 1917, courtesy of the Prints and Photographs Division, Library of Congress

press, including that formerly opposed to Russia, was against Germany and that 8,000 people appeared outside Saint Nicholas Cathedral in New York to celebrate the initial Russian victories.[102] A crowd even gathered at a casino near Bakhmetev's summer home to serenade him with the Russian national hymn.[103] He tempered this report of pro-Russian sentiment with a warning that influential Jewish banking circles were pro-German, citing Jacob Schiff in particular as being a close friend of the German ambassador, and that Jewish Russian-language newspapers continued their anti-Russian stance.[104]

Bakhmetev was also amazed, however, that Oscar Straus, a widely recognized leader of the American Jewish community and former ambassador to the Otto-

102. Bakhmetev to Sazonov (t), 3 and 10 August 1914, f. 133, op. 470, d. 48 (1914), AVPR.

103. Bakhmetev to Sazonov, 28 August 1914, f. 133, op. 470, d. 49 (1914), AVPR.

104. To Sazonov (t), 19 September 1914, ibid.

man Empire, asked for a meeting with him to explain that he was not anti-Russian and that he actually hated Germany. Straus predicted that Jews in America would cease all agitation against Russia and support loans to that country. Straus went on to argue that Jews should have the same rights (future autonomy) as Poles, only to have the ambassador point out that the status of Jews was different, never having had a state or been independent in that region.[105] Bakhmetev's rebuff of such overtures and fixation on a continuing Jewish menace to Russia would only aggravate the persisting Russian difficulties in America.

America's view of Russia's war, at least on the East Coast, was somewhat the same as the attitude toward Japan at the beginning of the Russo-Japanese War in 1904—sympathy for the underdog, a generally regarded weaker country being taken advantage of and attacked by a superior military force; a peaceful, pacifist "Tolstoyan Russia" confronting a Napoleonic demon. Publicity given to Russia's quick signing of a treaty with the United States, as part of William Jennings Bryan's peace program begun before the war, reinforced this image of a reluctant participant trapped in a war not of its own making.[106]

Two other aspects of Russia's early military program caught the fancy of broad segments of the American public. First and foremost was Russia's declaration of prohibition. Although the American temperance movement had fascinated a number of Russians and inspired their own quiet campaign before the war, little was known about this response in the United States. Suddenly, and to the great surprise of everyone, a large country known for its alcoholism and social and political ostentation had landed a socially progressive knockout punch that antisaloon leagues in the United States had been anticipating for many years, but with little countrywide success. A huge country had suddenly become "as dry as a Maine town."[107]

Chicago Daily News correspondent John Foster Bass credited Mikhail Chelishev, a self-made millionaire, with having laid the foundation for the imperial decision with successful experiments in limiting alcohol sales as mayor of Samara

---

105. Bakhmetev to Sazonov, 12 December 1914, f. 133, op. 470, d. 105 (1914), AVPR.

106. Actually the Russian government had been slow to join other countries in the rather meaningless declarations of peaceful intentions put forward by the secretary of state. Now it benefited from favorable publicity, especially since Germany and Austria-Hungary had refused to sign. "Russia and America Sign Peace Treaty," *New York Times*, 2 October 1914 (5:4–5).

107. "Russia in War Time," Sherman Miles report to WCD, 21 October 1914, f. 8806-2, box 359, RG 165, NA.

and by an emotional interview with Nicholas II.[108] Isabel Hapgood, a well-known traveler to Russia and a prolific translator of Russian literature, followed this up by explaining that the real force behind the Russian temperance movement was Mikhail Alekseev, who had visited the United States in 1886 and was impressed by the energetic American movement there. He subsequently wrote widely on the subject, including a book, *Concerning Drunkenness*, published in several editions. Hapgood recounted being very impressed with Alekseev's devotion to the cause, apparent from a conversation with him at Tolstoy's residence in Moscow in 1890. Although Alekseev died in Siberia before the war, he had won many converts, including Chelishev (and apparently Hapgood).[109]

Glowing reports of the positive impact of prohibition on family life and moral character—with increased personal savings and improved worker productivity, family life, and fighting capability—filled the pages of the American press, bolstered by firsthand reports such as one by Tiffany's longtime buyer in Russia, Henry W. Hiller:

> The marvelous change has swept over Russia like a cyclone with the noise left out. On payday the wives who came, so underfed, so badly clothed, to wheedle from their husbands part of their earnings to buy food for the children usually came too late. Now the men come to their work cheerful and sober, and their work has improved incredibly. And the women have ceased coming after their husbands' pay and the children are looking well, as if they had three meals a day. This is the outward and visible sign of the change, a change from a people starving, hopeless, inefficient, slaves to drink, to a people well-nourished, industrious, regenerated.[110]

Even George Kennan, a noted severe critic of both Hapgood's translations and the Russian autocracy, joined the chorus in praise of Russia's surprising reform in an article in *Outlook*.[111]

Little attention was paid by the American public to the reality of the situation. Since alcohol production was a state monopoly, there was no opposition to face

---

108. "How Prohibition Came to Russia," reprinted in *New York Times*, 19 November 1914 (4:2–3).

109. Isabel Hapgood, "America's Share in New Russian Reforms," *New York Times*, 21 February 1915 (V:15, entire page).

110. [Henry W. Hiller,] "Sees Russia Regenerated," *New York Times*, 27 December 1914 (IV:4:7), though mistakenly citing the author as "Miller."

111. George Kennan, "Prohibition in Russia," *Outlook* 108 (16 December 1914): 875–78, 887–88.

from distilling interests, and military advisers had favored the measure in order to avoid the drunken chaos that had ensued during mobilization at the beginning of the Russo-Japanese War. An edict of the tsar was all that was needed, with no legislative debate or action required or allowed. While a number of reporters rushed to the scene to write what they thought Americans wanted to read about the positive aspects of Russian prohibition, a few saner heads remarked on yet another disparity between upper and lower classes, between officers and soldiers, in the ability to obtain alcoholic beverages, and the increased availability of moonshining and bootlegging (shades of speakeasy America). The irony of a country entering a major war while at the same time abolishing its largest single source of revenue (about 25 percent of total) was also noted. There can be no question, however, that Russia, unwittingly, had given the American temperance movement a big shot in the arm.

American fascination was similar in another "progressive arena"—women's rights. Although the civilized West claimed the leadership in the fight for women's suffrage, few of its leaders had considered full social and political equality to extend to women being drafted or willingly volunteering for combat. Already in 1914, stories circulated in the American press about Russian women serving in combat roles out of patriotism, desire to share the sacrifices with their male kinfolk, or other reasons.[112] One explanation was that traditionally Russian women had served as auxiliaries or as nurses with units on the front line. Thus it was relatively easy for them to take up arms, especially in critical defensive situations.[113]

The number of Russian women combatants was still surprisingly large, with as many as 350 serving by as early as February 1915. They included Colonel Kokovtseva, who commanded the 6th Ural Cossack Regiment, Mariia Isaakova, Aleksandra Lagareva, Liubov Ugliskaia, and Anna Krasilnikova.[114] Most were from the upper and middle classes and, even though frequently detected, fought dressed as men. Although the interest in Russian prohibition waned as enforcement slackened and results diminished, the American obsession with the role of Russian women in combat would culminate with much publicity given the 1917 formation of official female combat units of battalion size. Probably the greatest Russian military hero of the war, in American eyes, was one of the commanders, Colonel Maria Bochkareva, who began fighting alongside her husband in 1915.

112. "Girls Don Uniforms, Fight as Soldiers," *New York Times*, 3 November 1914 (3:7).
113. "Women, Too, Are at war," *Kansas City Star*, 21 February 1915 (9a:1-2).
114. Ibid. For a more complete accounting, see Laurie Stoff, "Russian Women in Combat: Female Soldiers of the First World War" (M.A. thesis, University of Kansas, 1995), 14–32; for a picture of Kokovtseva, see *New York Times*, 6 June 1915.

The great bulk of Russia's fighting forces were, of course, men. And most of them were taken from villages in the countryside, where the great majority of the population lived. The draft, however, especially decimated the ranks of the factory workers because they could be reached more quickly at the start of the war and little thought was given to defer certain workmen. This caused a severe shortage of skilled labor in most industries and reduced production in many of them. The wife of American mining engineer Norman Stines noted that the replacement of men by women was causing serious problems at the large copper mines and smelter near Ekaterinburg in the Urals. She attributed part of the slowdown to the women not needing to work as hard as the men did, because they did not need money to spend on vodka.[115] Perhaps, however, this displacement of men by women in the workforce was less in Russia than among other participants because women already by necessity occupied many low-paying jobs.

Publicity

Russia started the war with a surprisingly good image in America, buoyed especially by anticipation of a great advance in direct trade by both sides. Bakhmetev hoped to keep it that way but feared German propaganda success and Jewish and Russian émigré-socialist opposition. He tried to deal with the latter by subsidizing various Russian-language newspapers in competition with the antigovernment socialist and mainly Jewish émigré press in New York that was led by *Novaia Vremia* (New Times) and *Russkoe Slovo* (Russian Word). He was constantly hampered, however, by a shortage of funds and consequent defection of writers and editors. After *Russkii Emigrant* (Russian Emigrant) failed, the embassy financed an Orthodox Church paper, *Russkaia Zemlia* (Russian Land).[116] This probably reached only an already pro-Russian audience, but, in the face of an aroused patriotism and prevailing American sentiment toward the Allied cause, the formerly sharp critics of Russia remained comparatively subdued.

Bakhmetev relied at first on the staff of the New York consulate for his publicity efforts. Then Sergei Syromiatnikov, a freelance Americanophile, arrived in late 1915. A journalist, editor of the newspaper *Rossiia*, and onetime philosopher,[117] Syromiatnikov had spent three years in China, had visited the United

---

115. To Folks, 2 June 1915, Stines Papers, HIA.
116. Bakhmetev to Sazonov (t), 3 September 1915, f. 133, op. 470, d. 60 (1915), AVPR. He stressed the need for at least $20,000 per year to keep the church newspaper in operation.
117. His one known book was *Opyty Russkoi mysli* (St. Petersburg: Suvorin, 1901).

States a couple of times before, and hoped to get in on the ground floor of Russian-American commercial expansion.[118] He was fluent in English and an old friend of Russian-American Zenaida Ragozin, who had recently worked with him on *Rossiia;* through her, he knew Elizabeth Reynolds, a devoted student of Russian language, literature, and society who was by this time prominent in New York social circles. With their help he developed a number of influential contacts and for almost a year, into early 1916, served as Russia's chief (but secret) publicity agent in New York.[119]

In addition to assisting Bakhmetev with the Russian press initiatives, Syromiatnikov wrote articles for English-language newspapers defending Russia's policies and positions.[120] The Russian ambassador considered Syromiatnikov too independent, unpredictable, and ambitious for his limited budget, and especially opposed his plan to establish a press bureau to plant news directly in American newspapers.[121] Bakhmetev thought one of Syromiatnikov's articles in the *New York Tribune* had gone too far in accusing the U.S. government of being pro-German while representing himself as the independent voice of Russian public opinion, and he asked for his recall.[122] Bakhmetev wanted to replace him with an American, Jerome Landfield, who knew Russia and Russian, was married to a Russian noblewoman, and was an experienced lecturer (University of California–Berkeley). But Landfield wanted $10,000 plus a secretary and expenses, more than Bakhmetev thought he could afford. He also feared opposition from Petrograd to hiring an American.[123] From this experience, Bakhmetev seemed to have concluded that having a publicity agent was worse than having none.

Despite the ambassador's repeated appeals to Petrograd for additional modest funds, the Russian press bureau in mid-1916 consisted of only a woman

118. One of his first articles was "American Chance for Russian Trade," *New York Times,* 15 March 1915, in Hapgood Scrapbook 1915, box 15, Hapgood-Reynolds Papers, MD, LC.

119. Bakhmetev to Sazonov, 13 May, 10 June 1915, and 2 January 1916, f. 133, 470, d. 60 (1915), AVPR. Syromiatnikov consistently denied being a Russian agent and worked under a front, "Russian Translation Service," at 280 Broadway. To Reynolds, 4 December 1915, box 12, clipping of interview with *Rochester Herald,* 28 August 1915, Syromiatnikov file, box 15, Reynolds-Hapgood Papers, MD, LC.

120. For example, "Russia's Big, Slow-Beating Heart," *New York Times,* 23 May 1915 (III: 2:7–8).

121. Bakhmetev to Sazonov, 10 June 1915, f. 133, op. 470, d. 60 (1915), AVPR.

122. Bakhmetev to Sazonov, 25 November 1915, ibid. Stanley Washburn thought Syromiatnikov had been "an absolute failure." To Harper, 24 January 1916, box 3, f. 2, Harper Papers, UC.

123. Bakhmetev to Sazonov, 15 November and 15 December 1915, f. 133, op. 470, d. 60 (1915), AVPR.

named De Bogori and her secretary in a small New York office. Their work consisted of sending translations of articles from Russian newspapers to specialized commercial-industrial publications with a limited audience. De Bogori herself recommended that Syromiatnikov be brought back to broaden the scope of the publicity, an idea that was opposed by the ambassador.[124]

Lacking adequate financial resources, Bakhmetev did not hesitate to employ the good offices of American Russophiles such as Charles Crane, Curtis Guild (until his sudden death in early 1915), Xenophon Kalamatiano, Elizabeth Reynolds, Isabel Hapgood, Samuel Harper, and Stanley Washburn. Washburn was especially valuable because of his recent tour of the Russian front, his speaking ability, his political connections (his father was a senator), and his independent wealth (from a Minnesota flour-milling empire). Loris-Melikov accompanied him to Minneapolis and was quite impressed with his social position, dedication, and ability.[125] In a detailed report on this trip, however, Loris-Melikov stressed the fickleness of American opinion. He observed that before the war Americans had believed all the bad impressions of Russia under the influence of George Kennan and various Jewish causes, but now their views had reversed. He strongly recommended an increased publicity effort to keep it that way but wisely cautioned that care should be taken in targeting audiences: "What works in Chicago may not in California."[126] Loris-Melikov also warned that Russia sometimes defeated its purpose by blaming Jews, which only alienated American audiences.

Both Harper and Washburn spoke to President Wilson individually about Russian matters. But Charles Crane was the most important conduit for such contacts because of his more direct access to the president and to Colonel Edward House, Wilson's chief political adviser, and indirectly through his son, Richard, who was Lansing's private secretary. Crane was practically a second Russian ambassador because of his intimate and sympathetic knowledge of Russia and his high-level contacts in both Russia and the United States.[127] Curtis Guild, the former American ambassador, was another Russia advocate, literally work-

124. Bakhmetev to Bark, 14 November 1916, and to Miliukov, 7 April 1917, f. 133, op. 470, d. 53 (1916), AVPR.

125. Loris-Melikov to Bakhmetev, in Bakhmetev to Sazonov, 30 March 1916, f. 138, op. 473, d. 170 (1916–17), AVPR.

126. Ibid.

127. For example, he wrote from Petrograd to Charles W. Eliot, president of Harvard, on 15 December 1914 that he was now "seeing Russia at its best" and compared it to the time of Napoleon's invasion and the great reform era of Alexander II. Box 1, Crane Papers, BA, CU.

ing himself to death on Russian causes. He was bitter that John D. Rockefeller's foundation had given a million dollars for Belgium but not a cent for relief in Poland. He asked Harper to approach the philanthropist about this, since Rockefeller had given essential support to Harper's father for the founding of the University of Chicago.[128]

An important vehicle for the "truth about Russia" was *Harper's Weekly*, an influential pictorial journal with wide distribution that was owned by Crane and edited by another Russophile and experienced newspaperman, Norman Hapgood, who was assisted in gathering news about Russia by Elizabeth Reynolds, his future wife.[129] Hapgood (no relation to Isabel Hapgood) was also a prominent and valued supporter of Wilsonian internationalism (as editor of *Collier's*) and a close friend of Supreme Court Justice Louis Brandeis. Thus the management of Russian news became intertwined with the promotion of the Wilsonian political agenda.[130]

Reynolds was first converted to Russian culture by her godmother, Zenaida Ragozin; had spent a couple of summers with her in Russia; and then earned a master's degree at the Sorbonne in "oriental languages," studying under a leading Western Slavicist, Paul Boyer. She was probably the author of several anonymous letters, such as one signed "American" in the *New York Times* that argued for increased attention to Russia, and she wrote the lead article on Russia for the last issue of *Harper's* in 1916.[131] Other support for the Russian cause also came unsolicited. For example, Philadelphian Wharton Barker campaigned through letters to the editor of several "provincial" newspapers.[132] Ambassador

---

128. Guild to John Conner (former consul in Russia), 7 December 1914, in Conner to Harper, 9 December 1914, f. 6, box 2, Harper Papers, UC. Guild also complained that his millionaire predecessor, George Meyer, was supporting Germany.

Bakhmetev remarked on the death of Guild in April 1915: "The loss of this courageous champion of our cause is very lamentable, and I am sure that his poor widow would be deeply touched if she received from Petrograd some expressions of sympathy." To Sazonov, 7 April 1915, f. 133, op. 470, d. 60, AVPR.

129. Crane bought controlling interest in *Harper's* in June 1913, and even with a circulation of around 25,000 it ran an estimated loss of $4,000 per month until it merged with the *Independent* in May 1916. E. W. Scripps to Crane, 31 December 1913, and Hapgood to Crane, 1 September 1914, reel 2, Crane Papers, BA, CU; *Harper's Weekly*, 6 May 1916.

130. Hapgood to Francis, 15 March 1916, box A, Francis Papers, MoHS. Hapgood, like Crane and Harper, was, along with his better-known socialist brother, Powers, originally from Chicago.

131. "Russia and America," *New York Times*, 21 September 1915 (10:7). The author obviously knew both Russian and French in making the case that Russian was easy to learn. Reynolds, "America Realizes Russia," *Harper's Weekly*, 6 May 1916, 483.

132. For example, "The Forces Behind Russia's Great Offensive," in *Detroit Free Press*, 27 January 1916; *Syracuse Herald*, 28 January 1916; and *Philadelphia North American*, 30 January 1916, box 12 and scrapbooks in box 27, Wharton Papers, MD, LC.

Bakhmetev also had an inside track to the *Washington Post* through his wife, whose sister was married to the publisher, John McLean.

Although many Russophiles such as Harper and Crane had not hidden their distaste for the imperial regime and their support for its liberal opponents such as Paul Miliukov, a leader of the Constitutional Democratic Party, they were quick to jump on the bandwagon in support of Russia's war, while at the same time keeping a distance from Bakhmetev and other "imperial" representatives. Some found the situation ironic, as Frederick Corse wrote to Harper: "I'm wondering how long it is to be fashionable here to be reactionary. Until the tide turns play the cards carefully. I don't want you to be out of favor here when the time comes to reconstruct Europe."[133] They took solace in the belief that the war would be a catalyst for progressive reforms in Russia.

The New York offices of the American-Russian Commercial Company were also used as a channel of favorable publicity, especially since its chief executive, Charles Boynton, was a member of the New York Stock Exchange, was married to a Russian, and was a friend and former associate of Melville Stone, head of the Associated Press. A number of other public events, such as charity bazaars sponsored by Elizabeth Reynolds, provided free and helpful publicity as well as material aid. Other offers of assistance had to be refused for lack of money or for other reasons. C. C. Young, of karakul sheep fame, offered to send 5,000 copies of his *Abused Russia* on behalf of the Russian embassy to various American political leaders for $3,750, but he was turned down after the ambassador looked at this short, contentious book that was mainly a defense of Russia's Jewish policies.[134]

Another book, by Richard Washburn Child, would probably have pleased the ambassador more for its overt support of the imperial regime. Child, in fact, went to Russia expressly to give authenticity to a book that would correct the generally negative picture of Russia in the United States. "To have a faithful picture of the Czar appear in the United States would help in creating greater friendly interest between the United States and Russia."[135] While many Americans were genuinely pro-Russian, others were primarily interested in courting future favors.

In prosecuting the war and dealing with allies, Russians at home had little time left for courting the United States, and that was devoted primarily to fostering the hopes for commercial expansion. The Society for Promoting Mutual

133. Corse (Petrograd) to Harper, 3 November 1914, box 2, f. 4, Harper Papers, UC.
134. Bakhmetev to Sazonov, 3 July 1915, f. 133, op. 470, d. 60, AVPR.
135. Richard Washburn Child, *Potential Russia* (New York: Dutton, 1916), 73.

Friendly Relations Between Russia and America emerged in Petrograd in March 1915.[136] Baron Roman Rosen, former ambassador to the United States and a member of the Russian State Council (the upper house of the legislature) organized the Russian-American Society, which foresaw the need to prepare for changed circumstances after the war. It called for closer cooperation between the two countries, echoing a nineteenth-century refrain of commonality of interests:

> There are no two countries whose natural conditions are in such a degree similar as Russia and the United States of America with their vast territories and the variety of their national elements. Both countries could profitably learn from each other. In the United States we can observe the newest methods of agriculture, the highly developed organization of transport, the unification of various and sometimes antagonistic national elements and the development of a true harmony between different social groups. For all these reasons the study of the various sides of America and its social life is a question of vital importance for Russians.[137]

Rosen's laudable cause had limited results among Russians because of his German name, his pronounced antiexpansionist views, and his advocacy of separate peace overtures to Germany.[138]

During the war, another member of the State Council, University of Moscow economist Ivan Ozerov, continued to publicize an Americanized business future for Russia in his many writings.[139] He was also active in the Moscow-based Russian-American Chamber of Commerce, headed by Nikolai Guchkov, a prominent cotton textile manufacturer and brother of a leader of the opposition Octobrist Party in the Third and Fourth Dumas.

Relief

Combined with the modest but effective Russian publicity campaign in the United States was a genuine and somewhat spontaneous movement to mitigate the

136. Snodgress report, 16 March 1915, CG Moscow, DPR 5, RG 84, NA.

137. As quoted in Henry Baker, Commercial Attaché report, 17 May 1915, Bureau of Foreign and Domestic Commerce, f. 1, box 435, RG 151, NA.

138. See his memoirs, *Forty Years of Diplomacy.*

139. Norman E. Saul, *Concord and Conflict: The United States and Russia, 1867–1914* (Lawrence: University Press of Kansas, 1996), 547, 560. See Ozerov's *Problemes economiques et financiers de la Russie modern* (Lausanne: Payot, 1916).

horrors of war on the Russian side. Similar to their sympathy for victims of the German "rape" of Belgium, many Americans responded to the need to alleviate the suffering in Russia caused by a very large refugee problem and the inadequacy of medical facilities to handle an overwhelming number of battle casualties. In small amounts, Americans contributed indirectly to Russian relief through religious organizations, especially Orthodox Church organizations, and fund-raising events.

The Russian embassy, and especially the ambassador's American wife, received many such individual bequests and either sent the funds directly or purchased supplies, such as bandages, for shipment to the large Russian relief organization sponsored by Empress Dowager Maria Fedorovna (mother of Nicholas II), the Russian Red Cross, or similar agencies.[140] Other contributions went directly to Americans in Russia. For example, Harold McCormick, younger brother of International Harvester president Cyrus McCormick Jr., sent over 3,000 rubles to Julia Cantacuzene-Speransky, a granddaughter of President Grant who was married to a Russian regimental commander.[141]

A series of concerts and other benefits were held in New York and other American cities to obtain funds for Russian relief. One benefit sponsored by Ruth Erford in early January 1915 raised $3,770 for this cause.[142] Elizabeth Reynolds organized another at Carnegie Hall in mid-March that featured Russian-American entrepreneur C. C. Young as speaker.[143] A New York "bazaar" at the 71st Regimental Armory sponsored by the Russian-American War Relief Society and assisted by the Russian embassy and consulate netted 50,000 rubles ($25,000) in mid-April.[144] And a benefit performance by the famous ballerina Anna Pavlova for the American Red Cross added another $3,000. More help came through the YMCA, which received substantial contributions from the Cranes and McCormicks (and John D. Rockefeller), who had a particular interest in the Russian cause.[145]

---

140. For example, at the end of October, 10,000 bandages were sent. Bakhmetev to Sazonov, 30 October 1914, f. 133, op. 470, d. 105 (1914), AVPR.

141. Cantacuzene-Speransky to Harold McCormick, 25 May 1916, f. 1916, box 29, 1F (Harold McCormick Papers), International Harvester Papers, SHSW. Julia was also much involved with Russian Red Cross work. 22 December 1915, f. 1915, ibid.

142. Bakhmetev to Sazonov, 7 January 1915, f. 133, op. 470, d. 105 (1914), AVPR. Unfortunately, very little has been done, either in Russia or abroad, on the apparently very large and impressive Russian relief efforts during World War I.

143. Reynolds to Harper, 13 March 1915, f. 10, box 2, Harper Papers, UC.

144. Bakhmetev to Sturmer, 19 September 1915, f. 133, op. 470, d. 62 (1915), AVPR.

145. C. Howard Hopkins, *John R. Mott, 1865–1955: A Biography* (Grand Rapids, Mich.: William Eerdmans, 1979), 449–73.

One problem encountered in 1915 concerned the funds collected by the Russian Orthodox Church in New York that were forwarded to the local American Red Cross for use in Russia. After Jacob Schiff, Red Cross treasurer for the city, objected, an arrangement was made to transfer these amounts to the Russian embassy for dispatch to Russian relief agencies.[146] From that point Mary Bakhmetev served as the coordinator for raising funds for Russian relief agencies. In no case were these amounts really large, especially considering what was being spent on armaments, but cumulatively they represented a significant part of total American world relief. The contributions received wide publicity and were important as symbols of genuine sympathy, duly reported as such to Petrograd and widely exposed in the presses of both countries.

An even larger bazaar was held at the 71st Regimental Armory on Lexington Avenue in December 1916, sponsored by the Russian-American Relief Association, headed by Mary Bakhmetev and Maria (Dmitrenko) Boynton. The invitation made clear that "the proceeds from the sale of your donations to this Bazaar, will go to the sick and wounded in Russia, regardless of race or creed and such funds will be forwarded to Russia through the Imperial Russian Embassy in Washington." Frank Vanderlip served as treasurer, and checks and money orders could be sent directly to National City Bank on Wall Street.[147]

A separate important source of assistance was the American Jewish community, once the serious plight of Jewish refugees in Poland, and then in Russia proper, became widely known. The American consul in Warsaw, Hernando de Soto, reported in June 1915 that over 50,000 Jews had sought refuge in the city and were living in conditions "beyond description."[148] Their situation had been aggravated by summary orders to evacuate the military zone issued by local authorities and by Russian reluctance to relocate so many Jews in Russian provinces.[149] This aid was usually funneled through a Russian Jewish relief society, headed by Baron David Gintsburg, or through the Central Polish Relief Committee. The worst of conditions were believed because of wide knowledge—from

146. Mary Bakhmetev to Mabel Boardman, 23 and 24 August 1915; Boardman to M. Bakhmetev, 27 August 1915; B. Bakhmetev to Boardman, 22 November 1915, f. 958, box 69, RG 200 (American Red Cross Papers), NA.

147. General invitation, n.d. (November 1916), reel 2, Crane Papers, BA, CU.

148. To Bryan, 10 June 1915, AE Petrograd, DPR 293, RG 84, NA.

149. For a description of "great suffering and most appalling distress," see De Soto (Warsaw) to Bryan, 10 June 1915, AE Petrograd, DPR 293, RG 84, NA.

This must have registered, since Samuel Harper received a similar answer to his inquiry to the State Department about the Jewish situation. Alvey Adee (State) to Harper, 23 July 1915, f. 14, box 2, Harper Papers, UC.

immigrants or published accounts—of the harsh life for Jews in prewar Russian Poland.[150]

In some respects the Jewish refugee problem damaged American relations with Russia, as when Judah Magnes, an American Jewish investigator, was denied admission to Russia.[151] Francis attempted to mend such gaps by coordinating the efforts of American and Russian Jewish organizations. After conferring with Russian Jewish leader Mark Varshavskii, he noted, "I learned a great deal about Russia that I did not know before."[152] But it also facilitated new contacts between American Jewish organizations and their official Russian counterparts, which previously had been deemed tainted by their pro-government bias. In general, however, aid from foreign Jewish sources and the movement of large numbers of Jewish refugees into central Russia, due to the German advances in Poland, exacerbated anti-Semitism.

American Protestant missionary activity also faced new restrictions after the war began. In the years just before the war, following a few years of relative freedom after 1905, Russia's stricter treatment of such activities had discouraged many religious groups from funding missionary work in Russia. Baptists and Seventh-Day Adventists were especially targeted, probably because of their focus on the German population on the Volga. The Reverend George Simons, who arrived in 1907 to establish Methodist churches in the Baltic region and St. Petersburg, fared better and was enthusiastic about new possibilities, but the Methodist Board of Foreign Missions in America denied his repeated requests for more funding. His close connections with the American colony and its relief activities helped raise the Methodist profile.[153] The American-inspired religious institution that gained most by the war, however, was the Young Men's Christian Association that already had a flourishing base of operations in the "Mayak" (lighthouse) organization in Petrograd.

150. For example, Kurt Aram, "Warsaw and Its Incredible Conditions of Life," *New York Times*, 12 July 1914 (VI:9:1–5).

151. Magnes (Stockholm) to Francis, 15 August 1916, AE Russia, DPR 300, RG 84, NA. Magnes proclaimed, "Who would not be happy to suffer personal indignity, if thereby he might bring bread to the hungry, clothing to the naked, comfort and encouragement to the widow, the orphans, the old, and the sick?"

152. Francis to Felix Warburg, 15 July 1916, AE Russia, DPR 301, RG 84, NA. The ambassador conferred several times with Sazonov about Jewish and Polish relief, the last time just before the latter's breakdown and resignation. Francis to Lansing, 25 July 1916, ibid. For an analysis of progressive Russian Jews who tried to work within the system to ameliorate conditions, see Christoph Gassenschmidt, *Jewish Liberal Politics in Tsarist Russia, 1900–1914: The Modernization of Russian Jewry* (New York: New York University Press, 1995).

153. See David S. Foglesong, "Redeeming Russia? American Missionaries and Tsarist Russia, 1886–1917," *Religion, State and Society* 25, no. 4 (1997): 356–59.

Other Americans simply volunteered for "Samaritan" service in Russia. One such "missionary" "doing all the good he could" was Thomas Whittemore, a noted Byzantinist who was also an acquaintance of Syromiatnikov.[154] Knowing the terrain and its institutions, he became an important conduit and inspiration for a variety of Russian relief efforts. By 1916 he was serving as "director in Russia" for Refugees in Russia of the International Reconstruction League, which was sponsored by Crane, Charles Eliot, and others, with Elizabeth Reynolds as secretary.[155]

Another special volunteer was Dr. Eugene Hurd, a tall, handsome surgeon from Seattle, who offered his services to the Russian army at the beginning of the war and soon found himself directing a large field hospital on the Southwestern Front that served an army corps of 40,000 men and operating on as many as ninety patients a day.[156] In a plea for outside news from the embassy, Hurd wrote that he was "at the front all the time and under fire when ever there is a fire, and that was all winter, trying to save a few poor wounded soldiers from bleeding to death, with three surgeons, three nurses, and sixty one soldiers under me working some days twenty three out of twenty four hours."[157]

Perhaps the most effective and self-sacrificing of America's unsung heroes of the Russian war was Dr. Archibald C. Harte, who was affiliated with the YMCA and had already logged many years of experience in international relief work. He set an example of service that inspired many others, but even he complained that his work was hampered by extreme shortages of supplies by 1917.[158] The most significant medical relief for Russia, however, came through the auspices of the American Red Cross, which sent a unit of eight surgeons and twenty-four nurses and a considerable quantity of medical supplies in September 1915, in charge of Dr. Philip Newton and a nurse, Lucy Minnigrod.[159] After languishing in Petrograd for a month, the unit was finally put to good use in a military hos-

---

154. Francis to Baron Nolde (MFA), 19 December 1916, AE Russia, DPR 297, RG 84, NA.

155. Elizabeth Reynolds to Norman Hapgood, 16 October 1916, box 16, Hapgood-Reynolds Papers, MD, LC.

156. Francis to Newton Baker, 16 May 1916, and to Hamilton Cook, 9 October 1916, box 56, Francis Papers, MoHS. Francis described Hurd as a large man, 250 pounds and six feet two inches. For details and pictures, see Florence MacLeod Harper, *Runaway Russia* (New York: Century, 1918), 79–161.

157. Hurd (Grodno) to Wilson, 23 May 1915, AE Petrograd, DPR 295, RG 84, NA.

158. John R. Mott to Harper, 1 February 1917, box 3, f. 11, Harper Papers, UC.

159. Mabel Boardman (ARC) to Mary Bakhmetev, 27 August 1915; and, expressing Russia's "profound appreciation of this noble work of charity and humanity, which has added another strong link to the traditional bonds of friendship that so happily unite our two countries," Bakhmetev to Boardman, 22 November 1915, box 69, RG 200 (American Red Cross Papers), NA.

Dr. Eugene Hurd and his surgical unit's priest. From
Donald Thompson in Russia

pital in Kiev.[160] One problem that was never solved was effecting close coopera‑
tion with the Russian Red Cross, because instead of being an independent
charity organization, its field operations were directly subordinated to military
commands.[161] The American unit was withdrawn after a few months, ostensibly
because of lack of funds, but Newton returned in 1916 with sixteen ambulances
to head the Princess Tatiana Ambulance Corps.[162]

160. The unit was ordered withdrawn in July 1916, ostensibly because its services were
needed elsewhere but actually because of complaints about terrible working conditions. Lan‑
sing to Marye, 22 July 1916, AE Petrograd, DPR 294, RG 84, NA.
161. D. L. Hough (U.S. naval attaché and secretary of Russian Committee of ARC) to
ARC, 4 November 1916, box 67, RG 200, NA.
162. Francis to Phillips, 13 July 1916 (c), Francis Papers, box 30, MoHS.

Another important relief service came from the American colony in the capital. Under the leadership of the Corses, two adjoining apartments were secured and modified into a small hospital, where up to twenty patients could be cared for, all expenses covered by contributions from the American residents.[163] Friction within the community led to one faction separating to sponsor an orphanage for forty refugee children; its backers were Mr. and Mrs. Harry Fessenden Meserve (of National City Bank), Lee Hagood, Mrs. David Hough, and "Lady" Mercedes and L. McAllister Smith (of Guaranty Trust).[164] Both factions received the blessings and additional financial support of the American embassy.

Prisoners of War

By far the largest American relief effort in Russia involved aid not to Russians but to German and Austro-Hungarian prisoners of war and civilians marooned in Russia by the war. Already in 1915 a large number of prisoners were concentrated around Kiev and scattered in camps east of Moscow, mainly along the Trans-Siberian Railroad.[165] By virtue of the neutral status of the United States and provisions of the Geneva Convention, Americans assumed the role of inspecting the camps and providing medical and other relief for the inmates, mostly paid for by their native countries. At first the American embassy responded to its new role by mobilizing American residents Reginald Lehrs and Alessandro Carasso, who both spoke German, while calling for new personnel from Washington.[166]

Because of the growing number and more remote locations of the camps, inspection and relief turned out to be major operations, and the United States was slow in realizing the magnitude of its task. Over a year passed before a makeshift American Red Cross detachment of ten doctors and forty nurses was organized from units in Germany at the behest of the German Red Cross. Armed with German medical supplies and money, it reached Petrograd via Stockholm

163. This was obviously a drop in the bucket, as the military attaché estimated that at least 40,000 beds were needed. Miles to WCD, 30 November 1914, box 359 (8806), RG 165, NA.

164. "Semi-annual Statement of the American Refuge for Refugee Women and Children from the War Zone, 1 June–1 December 1916" (Petrograd: Unicat, 1917), list of officers and committees. The prime mover, according to one source, was Mercedes Smith. Ragozin to Reynolds, 10 February 1916, Box 9, Hapgood-Reynolds Papers, MD, LC.

165. For a thorough examination of the treatment of prisoners of war in all countries during World War I, see Richard B. Speed III, *Prisoners, Diplomats, and the Great War: A Study in the Diplomacy of Captivity* (New York: Greenwood Press, 1990).

166. Wilson to Bryan, 30 September 1914, AE Petrograd, DPR 281, RG 84, NA.

on 1 October 1915 and immediately encountered obstructions.[167] Organizing this outfit in Germany with German-speaking (and largely German-named) Americans was probably unwise, since the Russian government was immediately suspicious of it. Another problem was that the Russians first understood that the American Red Cross was paying the expenses of the operation but then learned that Germany financed it. And Russia refused to commit funds for their own prisoners of war in Germany.[168]

The Americans eventually received necessary permits and farmed out over the area east of Moscow during the winter of 1915–16, the Moscow consul general's office becoming the most important administrative center. The actual hands-on distribution of relief, especially in Siberia, was delegated largely to affiliated organizations such as the American Red Cross and the YMCA. Donald Lowrie of the latter sensed a real challenge and responsibility when he was assigned to the prison camps in and around Tomsk in western Siberia. In preparation he requested extra underwear and several magazine subscriptions from home.[169]

By 1916 this "diplomatic" oversight staff was designated the "Second Division" of the embassy and headquartered appropriately in the former Austrian embassy in Petrograd, adding one more link to the difficulty of coordination.[170] The head of the division by the end of March 1916 was Edward T. Devine, a Columbia University professor of social welfare and expert on philanthropy. He served directly under First Counselor Fred Dearing and the ambassador and coordinated the fieldwork of the division through Assistant Foreign Minister Vladimir Artsimovich, who had spent several years as consul in San Francisco and was married to an American. The division's rather sudden establishment and rapid growth added a major problem to American diplomatic and consular operations in Russia and created an even more intensive scramble for space, telephones, typewriters, secretaries, and interpreters. Under such circumstances the mix of reliefers and diplomatic staffs was not very congenial. Consular officials, especially Consul General Snodgrass in Moscow, also had added advisory and support responsibilities in their areas.[171]

167. Cary A. Snoddy, report of American Red Cross Russian Relief Detachment (Prisoners of War), 20–22 September 1915, box 607, RG 200, NA.
168. Charles Wilson to Lansing, 23 November 1915, and ARC notes of 27 November, ibid.
169. Lowrie to Father, 3 August 1916, f. 1916, box 1, Lowrie Papers, UIA.
170. The German embassy was also under nominal American supervision, but it had been thoroughly looted and vandalized at the beginning of the war and was considered unfit for use without expensive repairs.
171. "Memoranda on the Present State of the Second Division, 1917," DPR 457, RG 84, NA.

When Devine arrived in March 1916, he found that up to that month Germany had supplied over 10.5 million rubles in funding and Austria 2.5 million, but the combined monthly relief support from those sources was rising to 1,650,000 rubles. In addition, each week the Swedish Red Cross was shipping in twenty-four to twenty-six carloads of supplies for prisoners of war, adding one more burden to Russia's strained rail distribution system and to the demands on American reliefers.[172] An additional problem for all involved was that Germany furnished at least 75 percent of funds and supplies, but around 75 percent of the prisoners were from the Austro-Hungarian army. Tacked on as a footnote was responsibility for Ottoman Turkish prisoners, but, under the circumstances of most relief coming from Germany, they were left to the cursory observation of the American consul in Tiflis.

The Second Division was fortunate to have regular and expert assistance from the War Prisoners' Aid section of the YMCA, headed by Archie Harte. With more materials and guidance from an influx of specially recruited and trained "Y" secretaries, the prisoners themselves established steam baths, delousing stations, tailor and shoe shops, schools and libraries, and even medical and dental clinics. Nathaniel Davis, a YMCA recruit, described bringing into Russia a compound material for making 40,000 sets of false teeth.[173] The American Red Cross and YMCA field personnel were especially busy during and after the 1916 Brusilov summer offensive and the resulting capture and large defection of Austro-Hungarian soldiers.[174]

In accomplishing their complex mission, the Americans regularly submitted prisoner complaints of poor treatment and harsh conditions to the Russian government, earning them a reputation of being overzealous and a formal request (later withdrawn) that they be recalled. A frustrated State Department counted on the new ambassador in 1916, David Francis, to calm matters: "It seems utterly hopeless to try to do anything in Russia, and I am counting the hours until you can get there and straighten out this very bad and complicated mess."[175] Devine was accused of being pro-German, giving the ambassador one more tense situation to settle with Foreign Minister Sazonov. Thinking the division could use more expertise on Russian affairs, Francis recommended that Samuel Harper, who was visiting Russia in 1916, be appointed as a special

172. Devine to Bicknell, 29 March 1916, box 607, RG 200, NA.

173. Nathaniel P. Davis, *Few Dull Moments: A Foreign Service Career* (Philadelphia: Dunlap, 1967), 33.

174. For a description, see Ruhl, *White Nights*, 135–59.

175. Phillips to Francis, 23 March 1916, box A, Francis Papers, MoHS.

assistant.[176] The outcome, however, was Devine's recall by the State Department over Francis's objections, while Harper returned to his teaching duties in Chicago.[177] Devine's replacement, Philip Lydig, also proved unsatisfactory because of his demand for ambassadorial rank and his business (Flint and Company) connections.[178] Basil Miles, an experienced diplomat, sent initially to backstop Francis, finally took over the Second Division. Despite these problems, Francis agreed with Devine that the Russians are

> a kind hearted people and are far from being cruel; and if prison camps are neglected in Russia, it is either want of system or inability properly to provide for them, and not the result of malice or retaliation. The Germans, on the other hand, have design in everything and if the Russian prisoners are maltreated there, I fear it is intentional and inspired by a spirit of reprisal.[179]

Contrarily, German efficiency and discipline in the Russian camps made up to some extent for Russian neglect and American inexperience.

The jurisdiction of the Second Division was limited to European Russia and western Siberia, mainly to the Volga and Urals regions, where the bulk of the prisoners were located. Another American Red Cross unit, based in China—with substantial assistance from the YMCA—undertook the task of overseeing camps, many of them former Russian army cantonments from the Russo-Japanese War, in eastern and central Siberia, where conditions were especially bad. Relief was even slower in getting started there, although initial inspection by Roger Burr revealed intense suffering from the cold and inadequate clothing during the winter of 1914-15.[180] Coordination with local officials was even more difficult in eastern Siberia because of distances of travel and communications, a tradition of harsh treatment of Siberian prisoners, the climate, and the more open funding of the operation by Germany, to the extent of furnishing a num-

176. Francis to Polk and Phillips, 20 June 1916, box 29, ibid. Francis noted that the POW work was greater than all other business of the embassy combined, and "We are doing all in our power to avoid friction with the Russian authorities while discharging the trust we have assumed in representing the German and Austrian interests." To Phillips, 13 July 1916, ibid.

177. Francis to Lansing, 18 July 1916, box 30, ibid.

178. Francis to Polk, 6 November 1916, f. 189, box 6, Polk Papers, Yale-Sterling.

179. Francis to Lansing (personal and confidential), 16 May 1916, box 56, Francis Papers, MoHS.

180. Burr report, 30 January 1915 (Tientsin, China), f. ARC Papers Siberia, box 607, RG 200, NA.

ber of nurses, who entered Siberia literally under the cloaks of the American Red Cross.

Regular inspection of camps commenced only in February 1916 and revealed that many of the initial shipments of 1915 had been kept by the Russians. Still, distribution of clothing and medical supplies proceeded apace with YMCA, Swedish, and Danish assistance, and a conference superintended by Consul Caldwell in Vladivostok in July 1916 improved coordination.[181] By the spring of 1917 the clothing situation had improved considerably with substantial shipments of Chinese and Japanese cloth, along with sewing machines for camp workshops.[182]

These extensive but little-known American operations in Russia were of great delicacy and difficulty. There was natural resentment by Russians at having to cooperate in admitting and transporting aid and relief throughout the country, while their own military units and civilian populations were in desperate need. Moreover, most of the American personnel recruited for this mission were necessarily German-speaking, thus leading to initial suspicions of their being spies. This largely dissipated as the "field delegates," as the Russians preferred to call them, won the trust of most local authorities while earnestly performing their tasks.[183]

Even in the best of times, travel by foreigners in Russia, especially to prisons and labor camps, was difficult or impossible (after George Kennan's 1880s exposé), and now inspection teams were traversing remote areas, bothering local officials, and drawing up detailed maps and reports on what they saw. In typical American fashion (or Russian or German, for that matter), reams of paper were consumed to prove to everyone that Americans were doing their job, to show that Russia was abiding by the international rules, and to account for German funds used in the process. A saving grace for Russia, however, was the fact that the United States was performing the same role in Germany, Austria,

181. Memorandum of conference, 18 July 1916, ibid. Willy Wadsted, Danish vice-consul in Omsk, is especially singled out for praise, but accounts had still not been settled in 1926. Detailed reports on other aspects of Siberian prisoner relief, especially those of Roger Amos Burr, are in ibid. Distribution in 1916 included 140,000 complete sets of winter clothing ordered by Germany from China to be delivered to approximately 100,000 prisoners in eastern Siberia and 200,000 in central Siberia. Burr report, 10 April 1917, ibid.

182. Burr report to ARC, 10 April 1917, box 607, ARC Papers Siberia, RG 200, NA.

183. Chiefs of field posts included Griffin Barry, Kazan; George Bakeman, Penza; Tom Devine, Ufa; Read Lewis, Voronezh; Lere Cathcart and A. B. Rudd, Moscow; W. H. Mallou and Graham Taylor, Orenburg; W. W. Pettit, Saratov; and R. J. Scovell, Samara. Edward Devine to Dearing, 19 July 1916, AE Petrograd, DPR 293, RG 84, NA. The records of the division compose approximately twenty volumes in RG 84.

and the Ottoman Empire for Russian prisoners of war, though Russia could afford little relief support for them.[184]

The American prisoner relief in Russia also played a key role in sorting out from the "Austrian" prisoners those of Slavic descent, mainly Czechs, Slovaks, and Serbs, who were willing to fight for Russia or their own nation on the Allied side. The overall mission was indeed a large one. By mid-1916 the United States was superintending the care of over 1.2 million prisoners and 150,000 civilians and dispersing $1 million monthly in relief sent by Germany and Austria.[185] That most of this came through European Red Cross and neutral diplomatic channels and had to be strictly accounted for caused additional headaches for both Red Cross and State Department officers in Washington.[186]

Although a detailed study is yet to be done on this rather unique American war contribution, its conclusion would probably be that on the whole it was a surprising success, that many prisoner lives were saved by providing more food, heat, and medicine—and especially attention—than would otherwise have been the case. The fact that the United States performed this task probably brought about more than the usual amount of cooperation from Russian and German authorities. The American administrators were also wise in soliciting and obtaining additional neutral assistance from such respected organizations as the International Red Cross, the YMCA, and the Society of Friends. And, also surprising, since this administration could not be easily or quickly replaced, it remained in service through much of 1917, months after the United States had entered the war, and until the Swedish Red Cross could assume most of the burdens. Unfortunately, many of the prisoners would suffer from the increasing scarcity of food and medicine resulting from the breakdown of transportation, the departure of American supervision, and the chaos and turmoil of revolution and civil war.[187]

184. Among the many prisoners held by Germany, the death rate was higher among Russians than among British, French, or Americans, primarily because of this little aid from Russia but also because they were in poorer condition upon capture. More of them also died in the unsettled circumstances after the Armistice and while the Russian civil war delayed repatriation. Speed, *Prisoners, Diplomats, and the Great War*, 73-74, 170-74.

185. Francis to Daniel Taylor, 31 July 1916, Francis Papers, MoHS. In March 1916, Naval Attaché McCully estimated the prisoners as 750,000 "Austrian" and 250,000 German. McCully to Oliver (CNO), box 710, WA-6, RG 45, NA.

186. See ARC (Washington) to Devine, 6 May 1916, box 607, RG 200, NA.

187. The best estimate is that of close to 2 million prisoners in Russia, as many as 400,000 to 600,000 perished. Speed, *Prisoners, Diplomats, and the Great War*, 108-9. But this was a very confused period, and this figure may not take into account all of the Czechs, Slovaks, and Serbs who were no longer prisoners and Germans and others who fought with White armies and became "Russian refugees."

Newspapermen

A number of other Americans entered Russia to cover the scene, and, judging from the results, news from the Russian front sold newspapers and journals in the United States. Nearly every issue of an American newspaper or journal on contemporary affairs carried something about Russia. While some older veterans, such as George Kennan, were called upon for their views at home, most journalists went to Russia to gather firsthand reports and advance their careers.[188] They included both those on assignment and freelancers; few had difficulty getting into print. In fact, almost any American who wanted to write on Russia could find an audience, even if just a letter to an editor.

John Bass of the *Chicago Daily News* and Stanley Washburn capitalized on being first on the scene, and their reports were picked up by a number of other newspapers. Washburn, who had covered the Russo-Japanese War and 1905 revolution together with Bass, was already widely known as a war correspondent. Employed by Lord Northcliffe for the *Times* of London, he benefited from the prestige of that paper, a practically unlimited expense account, and being the representative from an ally. He also wrote articles for American journals.[189] Possessing a good knowledge of Russian, he was the first American reporter to interview both Nicholas II and Foreign Minister Sazonov and to reach, along with Bass, the front lines in October to witness the Russian advance into Austrian Galicia and the retreat in Poland.[190]

Clearly, Washburn cultivated connections in the government such as Prince Ivan Kudachev, who represented the Foreign Ministry at Staff Headquarters. Washburn was genuinely dedicated to presenting Russia in a more favorable light than had been the recent Western custom. As he wrote privately, "Russia both in what she represents and in what she is doing continues to be a great

188. Kennan wrote a series of at least thirty articles for *Outlook* and produced new editions of *A Russian Comedy of Errors* and *Tent Life in Siberia*, but his main work during the war years was on the life of E. L. Harriman.

189. Washburn recalled leaving the United States on 14 August. At first Lord Northcliffe wanted him to pose as an American reporter in Germany, but that seemed too much like spying, so Russia was the alternative assignment. Another reason for employing an American was that many British correspondents were enlisting in the army. Washburn, oral history, pp. 81–86, CU; Stanley Washburn, *On the Russian Front in World War I: Memoirs of an American War Correspondent* (New York: Robert Speller, 1982), 26.

190. Sazonov decided to designate Washburn an official guest of the government rather than a war correspondent. Washburn's initial foray produced the pro-Russian *Field Notes from the Russian Front* (London: Andrew Melrose, 1915), enhanced by many poignant pictures taken by British photographer George Mewes.

Stanley Washburn (left front) getting unstuck on the Russian Front. From his Field Notes from the Russian Front

mystery in the West and at this time when any news from here is read by everyone there is an incredible opportunity to interpret to the Western World what Russia really represents in this war and in her new spirit."[191] After a brief visit to London in February 1915 to meet his wife and confer with Northcliffe, Washburn returned to cover more of the Eastern Front around Warsaw at the end of March.[192] After time out to rest in America and a monthlong tour of the Western Front, Washburn went back to Russia once more to cover the 1916 Brusilov offensive.[193]

By the spring of 1915 a number of others had joined the fray to pester the overworked American diplomatic staff and Russian ministers with their requests for travel permits and information. They included Walter Whiffen,

191. Washburn to Kudachev, 11? March 1915, box 1 (Correspondence, 1912–23), Washburn Papers, MD, LC.

192. Washburn, *On the Russian Front*, 80–85. The reports to London inspired a second volume, dedicated to his wife, *The Russian Campaign: April to August, 1915* (New York: Charles Scribner's Sons, 1916), followed by *Victory in Defeat: The Agony of Warsaw and the Russian Retreat* (Garden City, N.Y.: Doubleday, Page, 1916). *On the Russian Front* is a later compilation and abridgment of the three contemporary volumes.

193. Washburn, *On the Russian Front*, 163–83; Stanley Washburn, *The Russian Advance* (Garden City, N.Y.: Doubleday, Page, 1917).

D. B. Macgowan, and Charles Stephenson Smith of the Associated Press,[194] Walter Austin of the *Boston Transcript*, veteran Russianist Montgomery Schuyler for the *New York Times*, Lucien Kortland of *Leslie's Weekly*, William Sims of United Press,[195] Robert R. McCormick and Donald Thompson of the *Chicago Tribune*, and Arthur Ruhl of *Collier's*. Isaac Don Levine replaced Bass in reporting for the *Chicago Daily News*, while John Reed and Canadian artist Boardman Robinson were under contract with *Metropolitan Magazine*. Covering the Russian front was not without danger, as both Bass and Whiffen were wounded during visits to the battle zone.[196] Many would go on to distinguished careers, at least partly based on Russian experiences. Typically, a journalist would secure letters of introduction from the State Department and from other political leaders and businessmen to the American ambassador, who would then write more letters to various Russian ministries.[197]

In spite of bureaucratic logjams and delays, and a few arrests and deportations, American journalists generally gave Russia a good grade in pursuing its military goals and coping with domestic disruptions. Their positive views of the Russian scene may have been tempered by a desire to ingratiate themselves with Russian authorities for possible future benefit or simply to provide their editors with what they and the public wanted to read. But more often it came from a sincere sympathy for the Russian cause, especially the liberal side of that cause. Continuing upbeat reports on the Russian military scenes, despite obvious setbacks, may have had a detrimental result, as Northcliffe of the *Times* wrote to Washburn:

> There is a point in connexion with your cables that I think I ought to mention, and that is, that their extremely optimistic tone has the effect here of seeming to entirely minimize Russia's task. . . . I remember you wrote to me that the Germans would never take Lemberg, but by the time your letter reached me, the Germans were comfortably settled in that city. That does not matter in private letters, but anything that appears in The Times

194. Whiffen was favored with a letter of introduction from Marye to Sazonov, 20 June 1915, AE Petrograd, DPR 295, RG 84, NA.

195. Crane cabled Francis directly: "Sims articles united press sympathetic and widely read should be encouraged return Russia given wider field." 8 August 1916, AE Russia, DPR 308, RG 84, NA.

196. Robert W. Desmond, *Windows on the World: World News Reporting, 1900–1920* (Iowa City: University of Iowa Press, 1980), 322, 355–59.

197. See, for example, Marye to Sazonov, 20 June 1915, for Whipple, and William Phillips (State Department) to Francis, 17 October 1916, for Austen, AE Petrograd, DPR 295, RG 84, NA.

calculated to give the English and French the idea that they need not do any work—that the Russians will do it all—is, I think, undesirable.[198]

Among those whose tours were curtailed for entering battle areas without permission or for being too critical were Bass, Reed, and Robinson.[199] Most were content to report behind the scenes from Petrograd and Moscow in lieu of obtaining official permits.

Reports from Russia were not the end of the journalists' contribution. Impressed by the uniqueness of their experiences, they continued to write about them, gave lectures, and talked to anyone who would listen. Sonya Lieven of *Metropolitan Magazine* wrote Harper that Reed and Robinson "have had the most interesting experiences in Russia and are constantly hanging around our office." She advised him to come in and meet them sometime.[200] As in the past, many journalists, like Reed, were bitten by the Russian bug.

Another dimension of the reporting on the Eastern Front was the cooperation between American and British journalists. Noted British reporter Harold Williams (of the *Manchester Guardian*), who happened to be in Warsaw when the war began, was highly respected by Americans and passed on influential contacts.[201] Many of his articles were picked up by the *Christian Science Monitor* and other papers. Clearly the dean of Western journalists in Russia, he added one more bent toward the liberal side through his marriage to Ariadna Tyrkova, who was an important writer on Russia in her own right and a prominent activist with Miliukov in the Constitutional Democratic Party. Another friend of Russian progressives, Bernard Pares, who might be termed one of the "grandfathers" (along with George Kennan) of Western Russian studies and was the founder of its first real center in Liverpool, also rushed to cover the Russian scene, but he wrote little that was immediately publishable and managed to alienate past associates, such as Williams and Harper.[202]

198. Northcliffe to Washburn, 22 September 1915, Washburn Papers, MinnHS.

199. Reed complained bitterly that the American embassy refused to help him and that he was released only because of action by the British embassy. Reed to Marye (draft), 19 July 1915, Reed Papers, Harvard-Houghton.

200. Lieven to Harper, 12 January 1916, f. 2, box 3, Harper Papers, UC.

201. He was at least partly responsible for Harper coming back to Russia in 1915. "You wouldn't know Russia. Everyone is cheerful and full of life. . . . rights and lefts have been thrown into a kind of cauldron and I haven't the faintest idea what is to become of it." Williams to Harper, 10 November 1914, box 2, f. 5, Harper Papers, UC.

202. Pares allegedly was having an affair in Russia that did not set well with friends of the family that included two small children. For one of his reports, see clipping "From the Russian Front: Professor Pares in London," *London Daily Chronicle*, 7 August 1915, in box 2,

Most of the American press reports from Russia provide excellent firsthand historical material on the Russian war scene, especially since Americans in general had better access to sources and places and a more neutral perspective. One special additional contribution was that of Donald C. Thompson, a diminutive photographer from Kansas, whose images have been reproduced in many pictorial surveys of the war and revolution. His full-length motion picture documentary of 1915, *With the Russians at the Front*, sponsored by the *Chicago Tribune*, premiered later that year to sellout houses.[203] Another promoter of the "illustrated" approach was Gilbert Grosvenor and his *National Geographic Magazine*, which featured Russia during these years more than any other country, except the United States. All this attention to Russia at war even brought George Kennan back to the fore with a new edition of *Tent Life in Siberia* and a collection of his articles and speeches, *A Russian Comedy of Errors*. Significantly, his much more negative *Siberia and the Exile System* exposé was not reissued during this period.[204]

Other Americans came on personal missions but wrote articles to pay expenses. Isabel Hapgood managed to annoy the embassy staff so much in 1916 in getting access to library resources that she was dismissed as "a crank," while Samuel Harper at the same time was welcomed as a valued special adviser.[205] Some just wanted an excuse for being there. By the summer of 1916, the number of Americans, including journalists, businessmen, diplomatic and attaché staffs, and amateur observers in the Russian capital, had swelled to over 200 (from only about 50 in 1914).[206] Russia was reaching a point of overexposure, to add to its other problems. And, not surprisingly, as the tide turned against the Russian government, economically and militarily, news coverage became sharply more critical.

One result of increased publicity about Russia in the United States was a sharp escalation of interest in Russian literature, language, music, and folk art, facilitated

---

f. 15, Harper Papers, UC. But most of his diary impressions of the war were published in book form: *Day by Day with the Russian Army* (London: Constable and Company, 1915).

203. A print is in the Museum of Modern Art in New York. David Mould, "Donald Thompson: Photographer at War," *Kansas History: A Journal of the Central Plains* 5, no. 3 (autumn 1982): 157–58. For a description of Thompson filming a battle scene, see Robert R. McCormick, *With the Russian Army* (New York: Macmillan, 1915), 94–96, which also includes a number of excellent still photographs.

204. Kennan to George F. Kennan, 12 November 1916, box 10, Kennan Papers, MD, NYPL, enclosing copies for his twelve-year-old namesake.

205. Hapgood was apparently just demonstrating her usual impatience. "Ask the ambassador, P-L-E-A-S-E!!! to furnish me with an up-to-date, latest model Bessemer steel Burglar's Jimmy, to crack the Imperial Treasury!" To Johnston, 21 November 1916, AE Russia, DPR 297, RG 84, NA.

206. Harper (Petrograd) to his mother, 7 May 1916, box 3, f. 5, Harper Papers, UC.

"Refugees" in Russia by artist Boardman Robinson. From Reed, The War in Eastern Europe

by the background established in previous decades. Some of Russia's most famous performers—for example, Pavlova, Nijinsky, Chaliapin, Nazimova—were already well known from their widely acclaimed public appearances in the United States. In fact, Anna Pavlova and Nazimova were in America when the war began and remained. Pavlova even organized, and invested $75,000 in, her own "opera" company in Boston and toured the country.[207] Nijinsky, at first detained in Austria and then employed by the New York Opera Company, encountered difficulties and bad publicity for failing to respond to a general order for draft-age men to return to Russia.[208] The Ballet Russe de Monte Carlo, under direction of Sergei Diaghilev, also found enthusiastic audiences in the United States during the war years.

The Crane Circle

Russian studies also expanded due to the publicity about Russia and their promotion by Charles R. Crane. In fact, much of the American expertise that emerged

207. "Pavlowa Revealed as an Impresario," *New York Times,* 27 October 1915 (11:1).
208. Bakhmetev recommended that Nijinsky be granted an extended leave. To Sturmer, 7 October 1916, f. 133, op. 470, d. 53, AVPR.

during the war owed its existence, directly or indirectly, to Crane's encouragement and financing. Most of his enterprises were somewhat spontaneous, with
his verbal instructions implemented by a trusted secretary and financial manager, Roger Williams, while Crane spent much of his time as one of America's
most visible world travelers. By 1914 the "Crane circle" of beneficiaries included
such diverse people as Isabel Hapgood, Samuel Harper, Elizabeth Reynolds,
Stanley Washburn, Norman Hapgood, Jerome Landfield, Charles Boynton, John
Dyneley Prince (Columbia), Louis Brandeis, John R. Mott (YMCA), Charles
Eliot (Harvard), and Robert Kerner (University of Missouri).

By 1890 Crane had moved east to become the director of an affiliated enter-
prise, the Crane Valve Company of Bridgeport, Connecticut. His interest in
Russia began soon afterward through a business partnership with Westinghouse
Air Brake, which won a lucrative contract to supply equipment for the Trans-
Siberian Railroad, and Crane went to Russia to oversee this operation. He soon
passed the management to his brother-in-law, William E. Smith, but never lost
his fascination with Russian culture and society. In 1900 he introduced William
Rainey Harper, founding president of the University of Chicago, to Russia and
to Leo Tolstoy, thus establishing what would become a permanent Chicago
connection with Russian studies, especially through the career of Harper's son,
Samuel. By 1916 his niece, Helen Smith, would be managing a special exhibi-
tion of Russian folk art on Michigan Avenue.[209]

During the war years, the circle widened significantly to include by exten-
sion or on the fringes Frederick Corse of New York Life, Ambassador Francis,
Ray Stannard Baker, Raymond Robins, Walter Lippmann, Arthur Ruhl, William
Allen White (Emporia Gazette), Frederick Dickson (Christian Science Monitor),
Christabel Pankhurst, Columbia professor Richard Gottheil, and a number
of Russians and other Slavs of varied social backgrounds and political views:
Miliukov, Syromiatnikov, Ragozin, Rostovstsev, Bakhmetev, Postnikov, Rosen,
Breshko-Breshkovskaia, Archbishop Nicholas, and especially the Masaryk
family (a daughter married Jan Masaryk, the son of the founder of Czechoslovakia and future foreign minister).[210] Although the members of the Crane
circle were quite diverse in personality, ambition, talent, and ability, they agreed

209. Helen Smith to Harper, 4 November 1916, f. 6, box 3, Harper Papers, UC.
210. This group was far from cohesive but instead fraught with jealousy and competition. Harper and Syromiatnikov, for example, could not stand each other. Syromiatnikov to
Crane (c), 1 April 1915, f. 4, box 3, Harper Papers, UC. This letter, mainly a note of thanks
for hospitality of a weekend at Crane's Woods Hole home, makes clear that Crane preferred
dealing individually with his "agents." It is interesting that Crane forwarded to Harper a
copy, containing the Russian's charges against him.

Charles R. Crane, courtesy of the Prints and Photographs
Division, Library of Congress

fully that Americans should prepare themselves for the future by acquiring
a knowledge of, and appreciation for, Russian culture and society. It was
also probably not a coincidence that Bridgeport became a center for Russian
immigrants.

An unflattering characteristic of Crane and most of his associates, however,
was that they tended to be anti-Jewish, simply because some of the most influential American Jews were vocally anti-Russian. Crane wrote to his daughter in
early 1916: "A little bunch of them, self-constituted, but not at all representative, have for a long time controlled the bridge between Russia and America and
so the 98,000,000 Christians here have had no relations with the 170,000,000
Christians over there—although there are the strongest bases for both political

and social sympathy." Professor Gottheil (Semitic languages) at Columbia was an exception, "the finest Jew I know."[211]

One of Crane's best-known accomplishments was the establishment of a chair of Russian studies at the University of Chicago. Having inspired William Rainey Harper's interest in Russia, Crane paid for most of his son's educational expenses, including several extended trips to Russia before the war. In 1914 Crane agreed to a four-year contract extension for Samuel Harper's professorship, on an annual basis: $2,000 in salary, $500 for public lecturers, $1,000 for books, and $500 for library maintenance.[212] Fred Corse in Petrograd was delighted to act as book buyer for Harper: "A man who is going to be Assistant Professor of Slavonic and Russian and all those queer things should be amply stocked with Hiroglyphics [sic]."[213]

Crane also backed Syromiatnikov's project of a Russian studies center at Columbia University, where John Dynelly Prince had laid the groundwork with courses in Slavic languages and culture.[214] Young Elizabeth Reynolds (B.A. Bryn Mawr, M.A. Sorbonne) was hired to teach Russian language, history, and society as an experiment during the summer of 1915.[215] There she met middle-aged, divorced Norman Hapgood, who was also lecturing at Columbia, beginning a whirlwind May-September romance that took the many others interested in Reynolds by surprise. Hapgood had recently developed a curiosity about Russian affairs through his role as a freelance theater critic and a consequent fascination with the work of Constantine Stanislavsky, whom he planned to bring to New York in 1915.[216]

---

211. Crane to JCB, 5 April 1916, box 1, Crane Papers, BA, CU. One problem in assessing Crane's role is that he wrote very little himself, preferring lunch and dinner meetings—and the telephone.

212. Henry Pratt Judson (president, University of Chicago) to Crane, 14 November 1914, reel 2, Crane Papers, BA, CU.

213. Corse to Harper, 5 March 1915, f. 9, box 2, Harper Papers, UC.

214. Prince was a noted philologist with training primarily in Czech and Slovak. He was well known to President Wilson, since he had been the leader of the New Jersey Senate when Wilson was governor and served as acting governor during his absences. With enrollments of forty in the winter term of 1915, the university constituted a separate Department of Slavonic Languages for the first time. Prince to Harper, 10 May 1915, f. 12, box 2, Harper Papers, UC.

215. Ibid. Her appointment at Columbia received much publicity in New York, not only for the expansion of an exotic curriculum but especially because it was being done by a twenty-one-year-old female socialite. A full page was devoted to it—with a large picture—in the New York Herald, "Young American Girl Becomes Head of New Russian Department of Columbia University," 11 July 1915, and printed course announcement for summer session 1915, box 3 (scrapbooks), Elizabeth Reynolds Hapgood Papers, Billy Rose Theater Collection, NYPL.

216. Hapgood was divorced and had a daughter older than Elizabeth. Her family and close friends were clearly shocked by the marriage in December 1916, after which the couple immediately left for Europe. By all accounts, the marriage was a very successful one, though she outlived him by thirty-five years.

Largely because of the general attention given to Russia in the press, enrollments increased in any university where an instructor of competence in Russian language and culture existed. This was certainly true of several universities: Chicago (Harper), Harvard (Wiener and Coolidge), Michigan (Clarence Meader), Columbia (Prince and Reynolds), UC-Berkeley (Alfred Noyes and Alexander Kaun), Western Reserve (Samuel Cross), and Missouri (Robert Kerner). Quite a few other neophytes also sought assistance from Harper and others for self-teaching or tutorial instruction. Success depended on sustained desire, natural ability, and circumstances. William Chapin Huntington of Chicago, for example, managed to become quite fluent in the language on his own prior to accepting an appointment as commercial attaché in Russia in 1916.

To augment the availability of reading material about Russia, Alfred Knopf published Kaun's translation of Alexander Kornilov's *Modern History of Russia* in early 1916.[217] And many articles and letters by "experts" found their way into print. The only "expert" more prolific than Samuel Harper was that old warhorse of Russian studies, the "independent" George Kennan.[218] A number of these, especially Harper and Landfield, found themselves besieged and overtaxed as lecturers but usually drew large audiences wherever they appeared. As a result, the Russian message was getting across in the United States as never before.

One of Crane's pet projects was the New York Russian Orthodox Saint Nicholas Cathedral and its choir and balalaika orchestra. Crane supported and encouraged these for publicity and benefit purposes, but his main goal was to expose Americans to a greater variety of Slavic religious and musical culture. Although such largesse was relatively small in comparison with that of the great philanthropists of the period, such as Rockefeller and Carnegie, it was targeted largely on Russian matters, and even Crane's substantial contributions to the YMCA were understood to be for expansion of work in Russia and in the Near East, another of his interests.[219] Above all, Crane's goal was to correct the bad impressions of Russia fostered by political exiles and hostile American Jews.

It is difficult to track Crane's influence on America's Russian policy because most of what he did took place in personal meetings or through his son (Lansing's personal secretary). Crane and Harper may have been decisive in Wilson's sum-

217. Knopf to Harper, 9 February 1916, f. 11, box 3, Harper Papers, UC.

218. Harper wrote primarily for the *Christian Science Monitor*, while Kennan was under contract to *Outlook*; both publications circulated nationally and had high reputations. Given the looseness of syndication and copyright at this time, many of these articles were reproduced or quoted extensively in local newspapers.

219. Hopkins, *John R. Mott*, 464; Mott to Crane, 3 August 1916, reel 2, Crane Papers, BA, CU.

mary recall of Marye and choice of David Francis as his replacement. He recounted one private meeting with the president in March 1916: "I had some talk with the President about Russia, our problems and our opportunities there now, and my own strong hope that *now* was the time and Ambassador Francis the man to put our relations with Russia on a better basis than they have been for half a century."[220] He also gained Wilson's approval to assure that the new ambassador was properly prepared to steer a pro-Russian path through his own counsel and the tutorial work of Harper, who accompanied Francis to Russia in April 1916 at Crane's expense.[221]

Crane's support for expanding the American awareness of Russian culture did have limitations. A major project to publish a multivolume series of Slavic classics failed for lack of an adequate subvention from Crane. At least part of the problem was caused by squabbling among the project's main proponents, John Prince, Isidore Singer, and Isabel Hapgood. The latter blamed Singer for disorganization ("changes of views, plans, methods"), his rivalry with Prince (which only a woman could mediate), repeated pestering of Crane's secretary, and of being of Austrian background.[222]

With the foundations prepared, if not set, for a new, closer Russian-American relationship, Crane himself planned to go to Russia in early 1917. He—and Americans and Russians generally—would soon be overtaken by events. At least the expectation had been raised that both Russia and the United States were moving toward a radically different relationship. No one could tell exactly what the future would hold.

---

220. Crane to JCB (daughter), 19 March 1916, box 1, Crane Papers, BA, CU. Ironically, some Russians believed that Marye was removed because he was too pro-Russian, while Francis was viewed at first as pro-German because he came from St. Louis. Francis to Hamilton Cook, 9 October 1916, box 56, Francis Papers, MoHS.

221. Ibid.; Roger Williams to Harper, 18 March 1916, f. 4, box 3, Harper Papers, UC. Crane believed Harper was the jewel in his Russian crown:

> Not only is Samuel very well informed about Russia, but he has a unique position in that he is trusted by all of the various groups there—by the Government, by the Revolutionists, and by the Jews. . . . Everyone else I have known who has tried to study Russia has been taken up by one or another of these groups and been alien to the others. In Samuel's case President Harper and I were careful to have him understand that he must not have this limitation.

To JCB, 19 March 1916, box 1, Crane Papers, BA, CU.

222. Hapgood to Harper, 13 July and 1 August 1915, f. 14, box 2, Harper Papers, UC. Singer predicted that the Bohemian (Czech) and Polish sections could be sustained by sales, but that the Russian section would need a subsidy. Singer to Harper, 1 July 1915, f. 14, box 2, ibid.

2

Revolution

Many interested observers, both inside and outside Russia, predicted that the war would bring major political and social changes to that country. Very few, however, could forecast the degree and range of the impact of events of the February–March Revolution of 1917, the ease by which the imperial government fell, terminating a 300-year-old dynasty, or their long-term effects. Not only would Russia itself go through one of the most extreme transformations of any state in history, but the end of the Russian autocracy would signal the demise of most of the old, established order in Europe and provide a precedent for the republicanizing (Americanizing?) or socialization of Europe and much of the rest of the world. That neither Russia nor many other areas were really prepared for the rapidity and degree of change would shape much of the history of the twentieth century; the costs and victims would be great and numerous.

Americans were much better prepared than most other nations to welcome the first Russian Revolution. The French were accustomed to the ideological compromises and mutual trust that formed the Franco-Russian alliance—of a republic and a monarchy—that set the stage for the war. The British expected a moderate constitutional arrangement on their model to emerge for Russia that would preserve the Romanov dynasty; after all, Empress Alexandra was the granddaughter of Queen Victoria. But this unpopular European import, some would argue, did more than anyone else to shorten her husband's reign, aided by British impatience with the prosecution of the war by the Russians.

American Diplomats and Military Observers

During the first year of war, the public American accounts of Russia's performance were overwhelmingly positive despite shocking early major setbacks. Typical was a lengthy article from the Russian army headquarters by Robert

59

McCormick in June 1915, which was headlined in the *New York Times* "Found Czar's Army Highly Efficient" and emphasized such attributes as a model kitchen and skill with bayonets.[1] This article illustrates the pro-Ally, pro-Russian bias in the American press from the beginning. Another reason for this positive depiction of the Russian war was that the government channeled foreign observers to the Southwestern Front, where morale was higher and limited military successes had been achieved.

Behind the scenes, in more private communications, Americans observed signs of serious problems. The astute American military attaché Sherman Miles reported as early as January 1915, after visiting the front, about the careless waste of equipment, especially the practice of leaving rifles loaded in trenches at all times.[2] After a second trip in May, he was not surprised to find "the great majority of rifles dirty and rusty" and two regiments training behind the lines without any.[3] Marches were slow walks, officers lived carefree lives with plenty of wine and vodka, despite prohibition, and he often heard the comment *nichevo* (it doesn't matter).[4] By the end of the year, Russian officers at headquarters were asking Miles's colleague, Naval Attaché Newton McCully, when the rifles from America would arrive.[5] McCully himself wondered about this and concluded the British were delaying shipments.[6]

Nearing the end of his Russian assignment in September 1915, Lieutenant Miles noted: "If Petrograd is to be taken as a criterion, the Germans have come very near their purpose of shattering the morale of the Empire. The city is in the first stages of panic."[7] And he was one of the first to foresee the consequences of the assumption of the role of commander in chief by the tsar on 1 September 1915 from the popular Grand Duke Nikolai Nikolaevich. "It may lead to most serious internal troubles in Russia. . . . The danger is that the Court Party will

1. *New York Times*, 23 June 1915 (3:2–4).

2. Miles to WCD, 25 January 1915, f. 8806-20, box 359, RG 165, NA.

3. Miles to WCD, 21 May 1915, ibid. John Bass reported essentially the same thing but blamed it on the German spies. "Ammunition Famine Laid to German Spies," *New York Times*, 21 June 1915 (2:7).

4. 30 May 1915, f. 8806-24, box 359, RG 165, NA.

5. McCully to DNO (Director of Naval Operations), 20 December 1915, box 770, WA-6, RG 45, NA. McCully, who had observed the Russo-Japanese War from the Russian side and made a number of useful connections, was clearly one of the best American observers of the Russian wartime scene. For a thorough analysis of his importance, see Charles J. Weeks Jr., *An American Naval Diplomat in Revolutionary Russia: The Life and Times of Vice Admiral Newton A. McCully* (Annapolis, Md.: Naval Institute Press, 1992).

6. To Oliver, 1 May 1916, box 710, WA-6, RG 45, NA.

7. Miles to WCD, 4 September 1915, f. 8806-27, box 359, RG 165, NA.

command through the mouth of the Emperor."[8] But by the end of the year he saw some improvement and thought the tsar had actually been a stabilizing influence.[9]

Those who traveled around Russia during the war—and many Americans did—found the transportation system to be breaking down rapidly. Already by October 1915, Miles reported, "The great discouraging factor is the gross incompetency of the railroad service"; he noted that it took six and a half days to travel from Moscow 600 miles directly west to the front near Minsk.[10] From afar, Samuel Cross, a professor of Slavic literature who had spent the winter of 1913-14 in Russia, put the problem in perspective: "Our poor Russians seem to be having a hard time of it. Maybe fifty years from now they will have learned to four-track the Trans-Siberian, and then not be hard up for munitions."[11]

The extent of and reasons for the Russian munitions shortage in 1915 and 1916 have been much debated. Besides transport difficulties and American failure to deliver orders, the complexities of manufacture of modern weaponry on a large scale played a significant role. Actual productive capacity was not so much a problem as organization of production, the shortage of skilled labor, and quality control. The Russian army wasted large amounts of ammunition in the field, while the government diverted substantial stocks for a Baltic naval offensive that never occurred and continued to count on huge quantities of imports. By November 1916, of foreign orders of over 40 million artillery shells, only 7 million had arrived.[12]

In January 1916, on an inspection trip north of Petrograd, Miles was surprised to discover that war supplies were already being landed at Kola, although the new railroad line was far from complete and storage facilities were practically nonexistent.[13] This project of building a railroad through difficult terrain almost 1,000 miles north from Petrograd to the new port of Murmansk consumed much valuable labor and material during the war, but the railroad would not be fully operative until the mid-1920s. Meanwhile, Commercial Attaché Henry Baker

8. 7 September 1915, ibid.
9. 14 December 1915, ibid.
10. Miles to WCD, 19 October 1915, f. 6494-6, box 359, RG 165, NA.
11. To Leo Wiener, 21 August 1915, corresp. 1884-1935, Wiener Papers, Harvard University Archives.
12. For a more detailed discussion, see Norman Stone, *The Eastern Front, 1914-1917* (New York: Charles Scribner's Sons, 1975), 144-64.
13. "The Railroad from Petrograd to Kola, Russia," 3 January 1916, f. 6494-3, RG 165.

discovered yet another growing problem—a severe shortage of horses caused by increased military needs and the large number of battlefield losses.[14]

By August 1915, after nine months on the job, Ambassador George Marye felt an atmosphere of doom descending: "Russia is a land, it seems to me, which lends itself to depression of spirits."[15] He added, "There is a strange and strong propensity here to criticize in an unfriendly and fault-finding spirit everything that is done, or left undone by the Government or by anyone connected with the Government." And after sitting through a session of the Duma in October, Marye observed: "Of men of a high order of intelligence there is an abundance; of safe and clear-sighted leaders there is an entire absence. . . . That should not surprise; the people of Russia have never had any experience in the organization and administration of a liberal government."[16]

Despite such astute observations, Marye's reputation for not being strictly neutral, for being pro-Russian and anti-German, may have caused his summary recall by a cable from Lansing on 24 January 1916.[17] Marye promptly complied, causing another embarrassing gap in high-level American diplomatic representation. Neither seemed to be aware that cable traffic was routinely intercepted and decoded by Russian intelligence.[18]

David Francis

President Wilson hoped to fill the Petrograd vacancy with an old personal friend, Brand Whitlock. However, Whitlock declined because of insufficient personal resources and his current involvement with Belgian relief.[19] It is not exactly clear how the president settled on David Francis, a businessman (banker-stockbroker-publisher) from St. Louis, but Wilson gave two speeches in that city on 3 February and no doubt would have met Francis, whose newspaper (the *Republic*)

14. Baker to BFDC, 22 July 1915, box 435, RG 151, NA. By 1917, even though horses were decreasing in numbers, a Studebaker agent in Russia, H. W. Russell, reported that a large Russian order ($2,225,000) for harnesses and saddles was vetoed by the purchasing commission in London. Francis to Lansing, 25 January 1917, AE Russia, DPR 313, RG 84, NA.

15. Quoting his diary, Marye, *Nearing the End*, 206.

16. Ibid., 252.

17. Colonel House had complained to Lansing about Marye and advised his recall when convenient; House diary extract, 15 December 1915, *PWW* 35:358.

18. Lansing to Marye, 24 January, and Marye to Lansing, 25 January, in f. 133 (special dossier USA), op. 470, d. 120, AVPR.

19. Lansing to Whitlock (t), 1 February 1916, and Whitlock to Lansing, 5 February 1916, *PWW* 36:86, 135–36.

Ambassador David R. Francis, inscribed in his hand to Cyrus McCormick, courtesy of the Francis Papers, Missouri Historical Society

was the only one there that printed a full text of the addresses.[20] Clearly, he was an important political figure in the Midwest.

The eventual new occupant of the humble American headquarters in Russia, to no one's surprise, lacked diplomatic credentials. He did, however, have important prerequisites—personal resources to support his appointment and considerable

20. The president spoke at a breakfast meeting of the Business Men's League of St. Louis and then before a crowd of 12,000 at the Coliseum. *PWW* 36:110-21.

Wilson made the offer to Francis by 17 February, apparently without consulting House (who was in France) or Lansing, but he did receive Crane's approval. Crane to Wilson, 17 February, and Wilson to Crane, 21 February 1916, ibid., 191-92, 201-2. The original of the latter is in Crane Papers, reel 2, BA, CU.

administrative and Democratic political experience as mayor of the city, governor of the state, and secretary of the interior in the second Cleveland administration. He could also claim to have some international expertise as commissioner of the St. Louis World's Fair of 1904. Although older than most (sixty-five), he typified American diplomatic appointees, who, thrown into a complex new situation, usually rose to the occasion. Perhaps his contemporary in Stockholm had Francis in mind when he observed, "Throughout Europe certain men are, as it were, born to diplomacy. . . . In America, however, diplomats, like Topsy, just grow."[21]

Gaining both respect and ridicule in over two tumultuous years in Russia, Francis worked hard at his post while never really succeeding in avoiding the reputation as the bumbling midwestern politician at Tsar Nicholas's court. One of the first things he did after arriving in Russia was to order from Henry Ford himself an auto delivered through Archangel to facilitate his regular forays to the golf course. Renowned for his fondness for long evenings of poker and bridge—and whiskey—and hearty breakfasts of bacon and eggs prepared by his African-American valet, Francis was a strong adherent to the motto of a later fellow Missouri politician: "The buck stops here." Whether all the crucial decisions he made were the correct ones remains debatable. He often listened to advice, but, given the times, found much of it conflicting.[22]

Although knowing virtually nothing about Russia before his appointment, Francis responded quickly to the urgings from the State Department and from Charles Crane to become as informed as possible in a short time. Samuel Harper became his close but unofficial adviser before his departure and accompanied him to Russia. He also consulted Columbia University instructor Elizabeth Reynolds, Professor Richard Gottheil, Norman Hapgood, and others in New York and Washington. Crane may have had the most influence in steering him away from Jewish influence, after Francis was feted by leading anti-Russian Jews in New York, and by arranging a meeting for him with the influential Colonel House.[23] Francis claimed that at a luncheon with twelve leading American Jews

---

21. Ira Nelson Morris, *From an American Legation* (New York: Knopf, 1923), 3.

22. One of the best of many descriptions of Francis in Russia is by his French colleague, Joseph Noulens, who found as much humor as folly in the American's antics—such as Francis's habit of chewing tobacco during diplomatic conferences and displaying his uncanny accuracy in hitting the spittoon several feet away. Noulens, *Mon ambassade en Russie soviétique, 1917-1919* (Paris: Librairie Plon, 1933), 2:243-44.

23. This was done, typically, by telephone. Diary of Colonel House, 2 April 1916, *PWW* 36:401-2.

Crane complained to his daughter, "This week has been full of problems relating to the departure of Ambassador Francis and keeping him level on the Jewish questions." Crane to JCB, 5 April 1916, box 1, Crane Papers, BA, CU.

at the Lotus Club, when they asked what they could do to help him, he responded, "By not talking so much."[24] Francis had two more attributes for his job—a skill in summing up and a proclivity to leave a record.

Further insight into Francis's tutelage on Russia appears in a letter to Norman Hapgood on trade:

> If this war had been deferred ten years, or even five, Germany's interests would so completely have dominated Russia that no other country would have been able to break in. . . . the foreign commerce of Russia will have to pay tribute to England in the future, as it has paid to Germany in the past. . . . If our Jewish friends, who number about 2% of the population of our country, insist upon interfering to the extent of preventing the growth of direct trade between the United States and Russia, there will grow up in our country an anti-Semitic sentiment in large proportions.[25]

Francis betrayed his (or Crane's) anti-Jewish bias, since Russian trade was not really a concern of many Jews.

From the first landfall of his ship, the *Oskar II*, at Kirkwall, Scotland, Francis thanked Crane for all his advice and especially for the guidance of Harper:

> Mr. Harper and I have talked a great deal about Russia and shall have many other conversations on the same subject. His presence on this steamer is, of course, attributable to you, as is his visit to Russia at a season other than that which he had planned. His familiarity with the Russian language, and his knowledge of Russian politics will be valuable to me, and his companionship agreeable.[26]

He also had the foresight to bring along a stenographer with a typewriter and dictated 150 letters from the ship. His valet, Philip Jordan, was an educated former Pullman porter, whose letters to Mrs. Francis are another valuable source of information on the embassy and Russia.

Francis carried considerable business baggage with him to Russia. As a member of the board of directors of New York Life and having a son who was a regional manager, he was naturally partial to that company's considerable opera-

24. Francis to Wilson, 6 April 1916, and to House, 13 April 1916, box 56, Francis Papers, MoHS.
25. To Hapgood, 25 April 1916, ibid.
26. To Crane, 19 April 1916, ibid.

tions in Russia. Thanks to Harper he quickly came under the influence of its manager in Russia, Frederick Corse, an old friend of Harper's.[27] Francis also understood from conversations in New York that J. P. Morgan's Guaranty Trust was lukewarm to a direct loan to Russia because of its involvement in handling British accounts in the United States. Francis believed that Morgan was undermining joint efforts in that direction initiated by its chief rival and occasional financial partner, National City Bank. Francis invested $50,000 of his own money in a Russian loan proposed by National City Bank and actively supported Samuel McRoberts, the bank's agent and vice president, during a visit to Petrograd. He was then rebuked by the State Department for transmitting private business correspondence in government code.[28] Also with his own money, Francis dabbled in the Russian stock market, proposed investing in the bricketting of peat found near Moscow to a business friend, and tried unsuccessfully to revive an old irrigation project of Charles Flint's.[29]

Besides Harper, personal secretary Arthur Dailey, and Jordan, Francis was accompanied on the *Oskar II* by Captain Hayden Eames, a St. Louis business associate who hoped to ride Francis's coattails to lucrative military contracts on behalf of Flint and Company, and by Edward C. Riley of New York Life.[30] On the ship he also became acquainted with Mrs. Matilda de Cram (Kramm), a Russian woman married to a Baltic German still in the United States. Her long and frequent visits with Francis at the embassy would later do much to damage his reputation.

The American Embassy

Arriving in Petrograd at the end of April, after a short sojourn in Sweden, Francis found a troublesome situation at the embassy. The state of the embassy building was a problem. After making the requisite calls on the other ambassadors, Francis

27. Francis to David Kingsley (president of New York Life), 13 April 1916, box 56, Francis Papers, MoHS. Kingsley had hosted a dinner for Francis in New York.

28. Francis to Lansing, 16 May 1915, box 56, Francis Papers, MoHS; Francis to Perry Francis, 15 September 1916, ibid. Francis explained that he felt compelled to support the loan because not doing so might be misconstrued as opposition to it.

29. Francis to David Jr., 25 July 1916, explaining his request for more funds from home, box 30, Francis Papers, MoHS.

30. Eames was the brother of a renowned opera singer, Emma Eames, while Riley had assisted Corse for a number of years and was expected to be his eventual replacement. Francis to Perry F., 13 July 1916, box 30, Francis Papers, MoHS; Francis to Polk, 25 April 1916, f. 187, box 6, Polk Papers, Yale-Sterling; Eames to C. M. Carter, 14 March 1916, box 2, Flint Papers, NYPL; Thomas Buckner to ?, 1 October 1909, Agency Committee Correspondence, Board of Directors, RG 01, New York Life Archives.

cabled Washington: "Just completed visits to my colleagues whose elegantly founded, well located embassies put me to shame. Am[erican] embassy inconvenient ill adapted almost absolutely unequipped."[31] But as bad as the building was, the status of its employees was worse.

Fred Dearing, the counselor (and interim chargé d'affaires) and also from Missouri, was exhausted, in poor health, and nearly deaf, while the first secretary, John C. White, had to be transferred for having insulted a provincial official and having a brother-in-law on the German general staff. Next in rank, Frederic Sterling, left for ninety days to attend to family affairs at home. William Cresson temporarily filled in as first secretary but proved intolerable to nearly everyone and was sent off to be consul in Tiflis.[32]

Although Francis commendably decided to set up an apartment at the embassy for himself and his valet, he put a further strain on the already congested space by assigning an adjoining office to Devine of the Second Division and agreeing to share his stenographer with him.[33] This only gave Devine a greater tendency to behave like an ambassador and blurred his jurisdiction (prisoners of war) with Francis's. Unfortunately for Francis, another able member of the staff, Military Attaché Sherman Miles, was recalled and replaced by one lacking any Russian experience. Second Lieutenant E. Francis Riggs, from a prominent Washington banking family, arrived in February 1916 to find his low rank an embarrassment. Since there was little likelihood of getting permission to visit the front, he decided to spend the winter away from the embassy studying Russian in Moscow.[34] Finally, to disturb staff continuity even more, Washington decided that John Snodgrass, longtime consul general in Moscow, should be relieved by Maddin Summers, who was married to a Muscovite noblewoman (Gorianova) he had met in Spain. One staff member commented succinctly, "The Embassy does not arouse admiration for its efficiency."[35]

The State Department finally responded to the pleas of Dearing and Francis for additional help. Within a few months after Francis's arrival, Sheldon Whitehouse and Norman Armour, who were from prominent eastern business fami-

---

31. Francis to Lansing, 30 May 1916, AE Russia, DPR 296, RG 84, NA.

32. Francis to Phillips, 26 June 1916, box 29, Francis Papers, MoHS.

33. Francis to Lansing (private and confidential), 16 May 1916, box 56, Francis Papers, MoHS.

34. Riggs to family, 26 February and 17 October 1916, box 124, Riggs Family Papers, MD, LC; and to WCD, 10 and 31 October 1916, f. 9241-33-34, box 422, RG 165, NA. His later superior, General William Judson, described Yale graduate Riggs as socially popular, very English, and somewhat spoiled. Judson to wife, 10 August 1917, Judson Papers, Newberry Library.

35. J. C. Breckinridge to Oliver, 5 June 1916, f. 5, box 710, (WA-6), RG 45, NA.

lies and had Ivy League educations and diplomatic experience, joined the staff. Armour literally left his yacht at sea to serve the Petrograd embassy and, to his credit, stuck it out through the turmoils to come. Whitehouse's sister was married to a member of a prominent Anglo-Russian family, Baron Constantine Ramsay, which gave him social connections in the Russian capital. Although Wilsonian and internationalist in outlook, this well-heeled, eastern presence in the American embassy oriented it toward the aristocratic elements in the Russian capital.

North Winship, the new vice-consul for Petrograd, added more youth to an American cast that exuded energy and poise and maintained a very active social and cultural calendar. The arrival of (Marine) Colonel John C. Breckinridge, son of a former ambassador to Russia, to assist Naval Attaché Newton McCully was probably more of an embarrassment than an aid, since he frequently showed up at formal events out of uniform; fortunately, his stay would be brief. Thus Francis was hampered during his first six months in Russia by a shifting and inexperienced (with Russia) diplomatic staff, sometimes giving the impression of an old hen trying to control a brood of unruly chicks.

Francis had one more complaint, namely, a severe shortage of women to serve at—and decorate—embassy functions and to chat with. In fact, there was only one, Dorothy Dearing, to assist him in receiving over a hundred guests on the Fourth of July, 1916, and she was soon pregnant and returned home.[36] Partially making up for the abundance of young men at social occasions were American women married to Russians—such as Baroness Frances Ramsay (Whitehouse's sister), Countess Julia Cantacuzene-Speransky (née Grant), Princess Beloselskaia (née Whitman), and the wife of General Grigori Nostitz, an aide to Nicholas II.[37] They, along with a number of longtime residents such as the Corses, Messerves, and Smiths, added even more age and conservatism to the American appearance in Russia.

Of greater value to Francis were the appointments later in 1916 of William Chapin Huntington as commercial attaché, Joshua Butler Wright, a career foreign service officer, as counselor, and Livingston Phelps as first secretary. From Chicago, Huntington had already mastered Russian in a few weeks with the help of Harper and immediately departed for an eight-week, 6,000-mile tour of the

36. Francis to Jane, 5 July 1916, box 30, Francis Papers, MoHS.
37. Francis, *Russia from the American Embassy: April 1916–November 1918* (New York: Charles Scribner's Sons, 1921), 66; Francis to Phillips, 3 May 1916, describing hosting his first dinner at the embassy, f. 187, box 6, Polk Papers, Yale-Sterling. Countess Nostitz was the former Anne (Madelaine) Bouton, a dazzling circus performer who had charmed the Russian military attaché in Paris into marriage.

country, returning quite enthusiastic about business prospects: "Country is marvellous . . . in *present, definite, solid, realizable* opportunities for the best sort of business." But then he added that the difficulties were as staggering as the possibilities.[38]

Since Wright and Phelps were accompanied by their wives, the shortage of women at the embassy was temporarily alleviated.[39] After Wright's arrival in November, systematic office procedures were adopted, based on a thirty-two-page draft by Dearing, and a considerable burden was lifted from the ambassador's own duties.[40] The new counselor was appalled at the amount of work facing him and noted in his diary after the first week, "Still trying to get acquainted with my job—which grows more colossal in dimensions as I study it." His initial impression of Francis was of a kindly man with a "great sense of natural business and common sense—but very little conception of the social amenities as regards the diplomatic service. Ergo, I will have to coach him."[41]

Finally, at the end of October 1916, Basil Miles replaced the aloof Devine as head of the Second Division in charge of supervising German and Austrian prisoners of war. He brought valuable experience of a previous assignment in Russia during a volatile time, 1904–5. Through the persistence of State Department counselor Frank Polk, Miles was induced to leave a position with the Chamber of Commerce of the United States to accept another Russian assignment.[42] He proceeded to reorganize the Second Division at a conference of its personnel in Moscow in early January 1917, stressing pecuniary responsibility and coordination of work with consular offices in the various districts.[43]

In early 1917 two more secretaries, William Franklin Sands and James G. Bailey, were added. By that time, however, the staff member with the most expe-

38. Huntington to Harper, 19 October 1916, f. 6, box 3, Harper Papers, UC.

39. Frank Polk in the State Department was sorry to part with Wright, who headed the Latin American Division. Polk to Francis, 13 October 1916, reel 2, Francis Papers, MoHS. For a good description of the new operations, see Francis to Dorothy Dearing, 20 February 1917, reel 2, Francis Papers, MoHS.

E. C. Pratt, director of the Bureau of Foreign and Domestic Commerce, first offered the attaché position to Harper, who was already committed to assist Francis, but Harper felt obligated to return to the university and recommended Huntington. Pratt to Harper, 7 March 1916, f. 4, box 3, Harper Papers, UC.

40. Dearing to Francis, 7 October 1916, AE Petrograd, DPR 288, RG 84, NA; Francis to Jane Francis (wife), 12 December 1916, Francis Papers, MoHS.

41. Diary, 23 November 1916, box 2, Joshua Butler Wright Papers, Princeton-Mudd.

42. Polk to Francis, 22 September 1916, Francis Papers, MoHS; Huntington to Harper, 19 October 1916, f. 6, box 3, Harper Papers, UC.

43. Minutes of Conference of 11–18 January 1917, Francis Papers, MoHS.

War Prisoner Relief Division conference, Moscow, 11 January 1917. Seated behind table from left to right: North Winship, Petrograd consul; William F. Sands, assistant director, Second Division; Ambassador Francis; Basil Miles, director of Second Division; Consul General Maddin Summers; D. B. Macgowan, vice-consul Moscow; and embassy secretary Norman Armour is seated far right, courtesy of the Francis Papers, Missouri Historical Society

rience, McCully, was being recalled (though Francis managed to delay it a few months).[44] At least fifty people made up the American diplomatic mission in Petrograd: twenty-eight in the "first division" (regular staff) and twenty-two in the Second Division, making it the largest in Russia, though both Britain and France naturally had more substantial military missions. Finally having a sufficient workforce for the demands, Francis now faced another problem—coordination and communication. His staff members were scattered over the city, between the consulate in the Singer building on Nevsky Prospect, the embassy a block off Liteiny and not far from the Tauride Palace where the Duma met, and the Austrian embassy located near a Putilov arms factory to the west of Liteiny.

44. Francis to Josephus Daniels, 17 January 1917, ibid.

To add further complications, the Russian ministries were also scattered about the city but with the Foreign Ministry conveniently situated on the Winter Palace Square. Negotiation with the Swedish firm of Erickson to install an intercom telephone system fell through because of the expense and the time required to install it. Additional messenger boys were hired instead.[45] And Francis's plan for a direct cable to the United States through Iceland and Newfoundland also never materialized because the State Department insisted that it had to be entirely a private affair and no one anticipated that it could pay for itself.[46]

Meanwhile, Francis kept busy, playing golf when weather permitted and hosting small dinner parties on a regular basis. During the summer, Harper continued orienting Francis and Huntington, enjoying ragtime music at the Corses', writing articles, guiding visiting YMCA chief John Mott around Petrograd, and sympathizing with Russian liberals about the political and military situation. In September he returned to his university post in Chicago.[47] Harper took pride in his tutoring of the ambassador: "He is very energetic, very clear on most of the points, and has shown a kindly friendly attitude toward Russia, which is realized and appreciated."[48]

One thing that united such different personalities as Harper, Francis, McCully, and most other Americans was their resentment of British dominance to the extent that rumors circulated that Americans were pro-German.[49] One reason for this was the seriousness with which the reorganized Second Division pursued the task of improving conditions for German prisoners of war. Another may have been the sharp contrast between the casual Francis and the stuffy and proper British ambassador, George Buchanan.

45. Francis to Dearing, 23 August 1916, AE Russia, DPR 308, RG 84, NA.

46. Francis to Lansing, 9 August 1916; Newton Carlton (president, Western Union) to Francis, 21 September 1916; and Lansing to Francis, 22 December 1916, AE Russia, DPR 308, RG 84, NA.

47. Harper to his mother, 7 and 22 May, 10 June, and 6 July 1916, f. 6, box 3, Harper Papers, UC. Mott wrote, "What do I not owe to you for your rare service of interpretation in the largest use of that term!" To Harper, 27 July 1916, ibid.

48. To Crane, 21 June 1916, ibid. Privately, Harper apparently had serious reservations about Francis as ambassador. J. R. Mott, whom Harper regularly saw in Petrograd, later wrote him: "With you I share the sense of sorrow and mortification in the fact that we are not better represented in our Embassy in Petrograd. In some way a change must be brought about. I am taking this matter up with Crane." Mott to Harper, 27 March 1917, f. 12, box 3, Harper Papers, UC.

49. Francis to Perry (son), 1 May, and to Polk, 3 May 1916, box 56, Francis Papers, MoHS.

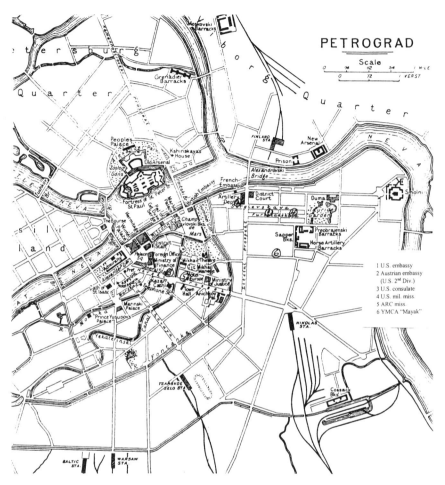

Petrograd, showing locations of American offices. Adapted from Knox, With the Russian Army

Policy Problems

At the beginning of his mission, Francis tried once more to open negotiations for a new commercial treaty, but Foreign Minister Sazonov again turned a deaf ear. As the ambassador informed Secretary of Treasury William McAdoo, Sazonov "told me very emphatically in our first interview that Russia would negotiate no commercial treaty with any neutral country until her commercial relations with her Allies should be established and defined."[50] When he again broached the subject to Sazonov's inexperienced successor later in 1916, he was surprised to hear that this was the province of the minister of finance. After this error was corrected, the Sazonov line remained in force.

The ambassador was disappointed that no change appeared imminent in Russia's policy of special restrictions on native and foreign Jews alike, a corollary to any commercial agreement. Russia was concerned especially about the previous record of Jews emigrating to the United States, becoming naturalized citizens, and then returning to Russia with full rights to do business like any other American citizen. The United States naturally and firmly opposed any discrimination based on religion or ethnic background. What brought the problem to a head before the war and caused the abrogation of the commercial treaty was that Russian consular agents in the United States began screening out and denying visas to applicants who admitted being of the Jewish religion.

Harper had led Francis to believe that the war might produce a promise of liberalization to appease friends abroad, but the government turned more conservative in 1916, dooming hopes for the time being. "The prejudice against the Jews here is very deep rooted and is not confined to Government officials nor to the Nobility nor even to the upper commercial circles. The peasants fear the Jews in spite of the law prohibiting Jews from owning land in Russia other than under severe restrictions. The Army also dislikes the Jews."[51]

Under these circumstances, nothing much could be done to improve relations between the two countries until the political stance of one or both of them changed. In fact, communication problems and war needs aggravated the situation. The business of the embassy was conducted in spurts, usually behind schedule, and often in the dark, because of the irregularity of mail, a situation that worsened considerably during the winter of 1916-17. At the end of February 1917, Francis was expecting the delivery of a backlog of twenty-seven pouches—

50. Francis to McAdoo, 25 February 1917, reel 3, Francis Papers, MoHS.

51. Ibid. See also Francis to Lansing, 25 July 1916, AE Petrograd, DPR 306, RG 84, NA, for a similar appraisal of the war's effect on Russian Jews.

and eight cases of whiskey—that had piled up at Stockholm over several weeks. Communication in the other direction was no better, with a private letter written 28 December from Japan arriving in Petrograd on 20 February.[52]

Munitions Contracts

One of the most sensitive and complicated issues that caused friction between Russia, the United States, and Britain in the last year of Nicholas II's reign was the fulfillment of contracts for war supplies for Russia by American companies. The careless and haphazard preparation of them resulted in additional costs and delays, combined with the fact that Americans accepted far more orders than they could fill. By 1916 it was clear to most observers that General Sapozhnikov, chief of the Russian Supply Mission in New York, was far from adequate to the task. He was characterized by the departing Russian assistant naval attaché in the summer of 1916 as having "done a great deal toward lowering Russian prestige in the United States by his entire lack of *savoir faire*, his outrageous nepotism, and his friendships with some of the shadiest characters among the munitions crowd."[53]

Despite vociferous complaints about Russian violation of joint agreements and about their making contracts independently, the British opposed the replacement of Sapozhnikov because he at least had some experience with the American business scene and knowledge of the technical specifics of equipment. The process thus proceeded in a disorderly fashion throughout 1916, with Russians generally resentful of British financial controls and the British trying to figure out what the Russians were doing and what their needs really were. Finance Minister Petr Bark blamed his dependence on British funding for the confusion and delays.[54] The situation was certainly not helped by squabbles in all countries among and between banks and ministries about the extension of credit and shipments of gold.[55]

Mounting war needs and increasing orders placed in the United States in 1916 produced a severe credit crunch at the end of the year that threatened crucial shipments to both Britain and Russia and disruptions in the American

52. Francis to Dorothy Dearing, 20 February 1917, reel 3, Francis Papers, MoHS.
53. Dmitri Fedotoff White, *Survival Through War and Revolution in Russia* (Philadelphia: University of Pennsylvania Press, 1939), 56.
54. As confided to Francis, Francis to Lansing, 12 November 1916, AE Russia, DPR 305, RG 84, NA.
55. Neilson, *Strategy and Supply*, 188–92.

economy. Simply stated, the very large but unfulfilled orders for Russia were blocking loans for more British contracts. Two particular Russian contracts worth over $110 million, one with Bethlehem Steel for 4 million three-inch howitzer shells and one with Westinghouse for 1 million rifles, were felt to be clogging the works.[56] Although production for both of these orders was far behind schedule, British efforts to cancel them in early 1917 failed owing to Russian obstruction and American willingness to reduce the required advances and extend credit on more favorable terms. This meant the postponement of delivery deadlines beyond July 1917.[57]

Many Russians began to feel that the only solution was American entry into the war and large-scale direct American loans, but in the heat of the presidential campaign and heightening conflict with Germany, few in Washington paid much attention to these affairs, while the Petrograd embassy reported the end result—Russians wondering where American munitions were.

Government Changes

As if Francis did not have enough problems to confront within the American community and in communications with Washington, the Russian government went through some dramatic changes. Sergei Sazonov, who had been minister of foreign affairs since 1910 and had essentially steered Russia into and through its wartime alliances and secret treaties, was forced to resign (on formal grounds of ill health) on 10 July 1916. He was replaced by Boris Sturmer (or Stuermer), the reactionary chairman of the Council of Ministers (since the previous December) and minister of interior. At the time, Francis thought it was simply because Sazonov was too liberal, but on reflection he added that it was probably the minister's pro-British tendencies and thorough commitment to the alliance.[58] This interpretation agrees with Sazonov's own version, which blamed the reputedly pro-German Rasputin clique at court and Sturmer's political ambitions for his removal.[59]

56. Ibid., 213-17.
57. Francis to Lansing, 25 January 1917, AE Russia, DPR 313, RG 84, NA.
58. Francis to Lansing, 25 July 1916, box 30, Francis Papers, MoHS; Francis to Lansing, 31 October 1916, AE Petrograd, DPR 306, RG 84, NA. Just before the resignation, however, Francis had remarked about how tired and broken down Sazonov seemed. To Lansing, 16 June 1916, box 29, Francis Papers, MoHS.
59. Sergei Sazonov, *Fateful Years, 1909–1916: The Reminiscences of Sergei Sazonov* (London: Jonathan Cape, 1928), 306-7.

Stability was further disrupted by the dismissals of the incompetent Sturmer a few months later and of Vladimir Artsimovich, America's chief friend and contact in the ministry.[60] A new "liberal" head of the Council of Ministers, Aleksandr Trepov, lasted only a month (mid-November to mid-December) before being replaced by the reactionary Nikolai Golitsyn. In this last shake-up of the old regime, Nikolai Pokrovskii, a budget expert, won the distinction of serving as the last imperial foreign minister. These changes posed problems for all diplomats, especially since Nicholas II was more and more isolated from them.

One element of continuity was Petr Bark, who had been generally friendly to American economic overtures and who retained his position as minister of finance but seemed to have less voice in governmental affairs. Perhaps betraying his own gullibility and naïveté, Francis was positively impressed by both Sturmer (who spent over an hour in conversation with him at the embassy) and Pokrovskii.[61] Or perhaps he was only putting the best possible face on an increasingly depressing political scene.

These government changes, the failure of the 1916 summer offensive on the Southwestern Front to produce any real results, and the worsening economic situation produced a decided drop in public morale by the fall of 1916. Critical voices were mounting in the shops, fields, factories, and garrison units, and even within the officer corps and civil bureaucracy. Blame tended to focus on the nefarious but uncertain influence of Grigori Rasputin and Empress Alexandra, who were credited with exercising more influence and were reputedly pro-German.

As was the custom, Francis attended the opening session of the Duma on 14 November 1916, along with the rest of the diplomatic corps, but he withdrew at Sturmer's request after the initial formalities in a fruitless effort to avoid encouraging Duma members from taking the opportunity to display their outrage with the ministerial changes. He returned on 2 December to listen to mounting cries of German influence and sympathy in the government from the opposition

60. Artsimovich to Francis, 17 August 1916, AE Petrograd, DPR 296, RG 84, NA, warning him that he may be accused of a state crime and cannot be seen.

Assistant Minister Artsimovich had served for several years as Russian consul general in San Francisco in the 1890s. For his skill in mending a difficult situation there, see Terence Emmons, *Alleged Sex and Threatened Violence: Doctor Russel, Bishop Vladimir, and the Russians in San Francisco, 1887–1892* (Stanford, Calif.: Stanford University Press, 1997).

61. Francis to Lansing, 23 July 1916, and Francis to Bark, 17 December 1916, AE Petrograd, DPR 306, RG 84, NA. Bark seemed to go out of his way to court American friendship, writing to Francis in English: "I should be, of course, extremely pleased to keep up frequent intercourse with you, both because of my real sympathy to you personally and the deep esteem I entertain for your Excellency as the worthy representative of the great American country here." 21 December 1916, ibid.

Rasputin and friends. Photo by Donald Thompson from his Blood Stained Russia

Progressive Bloc. To his son, the ambassador confided: "My opinion, however, is that whatever may be the outcome of this controversy, the danger of a separate peace being made by Russia is greatly diminished, if not entirely removed. These meetings of the Duma have given expression in a public way to rumors which have been circulated secretly for the past two months."[62]

The murder of Rasputin, itself at least partly motivated by the erratic course of government, shook the Petrograd court and society at the end of the year. Although Rasputin had been the subject of gossip for years, the end of his "reign" seemed to lift a veil of secrecy from around the imperial family and brought everything out into the open, including especially more charges of German sympathies at the highest levels.[63] Extensive public exposure and the demise of this

62. Francis to Perry, 5 December 1916, Francis Papers, MoHS. The entire letter is published in *Dollars and Diplomacy: Ambassador David Rowland Francis and the Fall of Tsarism, 1916–17*, ed. Jamie H. Cockfield (Durham, N. C.: Duke University Press, 1981), 63–65.

63. Public discussion seemed to break into a frenzy in the first week of January 1917 (Western calendar). J. Butler Wright diary entries, 1–4 January, box 2, Wright Papers, Princeton-Mudd. Nicholas II brought attention upon himself by making a dramatic appearance in the capital. Francis to Polk, 4 January 1917, f. 190, box 6, Polk Papers, Yale-Sterling.

Journalist Dosch-Fleurot, who accompanied Francis to the famous November Duma session, credits Miliukov's reference to "dark forces at work in Russia" as setting off the chain

particular nefarious influence did not improve matters, however, but only forced the family into even deeper isolation and depression.

Still, Nicholas II displayed a brave diplomatic front publicly for one more time at the annual New Year's Day reception, 14 January 1917. Perhaps because of his growing estrangement from British ambassador George Buchanan and being forced to listen to another lecture from him, he paid particular attention to the Americans attending, drawing "his old friend" Newton McCully aside for a long conversation, ironically about Mexico and the fall of Porfirio Díaz.[64] Another eyewitness, Butler Wright, noted that the emperor spent more time with the American mission than any other, but he seemed very nervous, and his "hands fidgeted continually."[65]

Buchanan's negative views of the government of Nicholas II were no secret. He and the tsar had already had a heated exchange about giving in to demands of Duma progressives on more representative government in order to head off revolution during a special audience at Tsarskoe Selo on 12 January.[66] The ambassador's impolitic cable of 16 January advising the Foreign Office of growing opposition to Nicholas II was promptly intercepted and decoded: "Here the general feeling is that if Emperor does not yield something will occur in some next weeks, either in form of palace revolution or in form of assassination."[67] Whether this intelligence was passed on to Nicholas II is unknown; if so, it would have only added to his state of depression.

---

of events. *Through War to Revolution: Being the Experiences of a Newspaper Correspondent in War and Revolution, 1914–1920*, 2d ed. (London: John Lane, the Bodley Head, 1931), 107.

64. Weeks, *An American Naval Diplomat in Revolutionary Russia*, 106. Nicholas II, despite his self-chosen role as commander in chief of the largest army ever assembled up to that time, much preferred ships and naval affairs, which probably accounts for his close relationship with McCully.

Norman Armour, who apparently overheard the "conversation" between Buchanan and Nicholas II, thought the British ambassador was quite indiscreet. Armour reminiscences, f. 4, box 2, Armour Papers, Princeton-Mudd.

65. Diary, 14 January 1917, box 2, Wright Papers, Princeton-Mudd.

66. Buchanan recalled in some detail the meeting on 12 January, "my last audience," but nothing about the 14 January reception. Buchanan, *My Mission to Russia and Other Diplomatic Memories*, vol. 2 (Boston: Little, Brown, 1923), 43–50. This led one historian, George Katkov, to conclude that the British ambassador was part of a cabal to remove the tsar. *Russia 1917: The February Revolution* (London: Collins, 1967), 309–10.

67. Translated from Russian translation, Buchanan to Balfour, 16 January 1917, f. 138, op. 467, d. 651/673, AVPR. Intercepts of cables of the Japanese ambassador reporting on his conversations with Buchanan in January and February are also revealing. After his speech to the tsar of 14 January advising major changes in his government, Nicholas II said one word, "Merci." Marumo to Ichiri Motono, 16 January 1917, ibid.

Despite the ministerial and other upheavals in Russia during the winter of 1916-17, little changed in the personnel of its servants abroad. Key veteran diplomats retained their portfolios: in Britain (Aleksandr Benkendorf), France (Aleksandr Izvolskii), Italy (Mikhail Giers), and, of course, the United States. This probably gave a deceptive picture of stability to the waning months of the Russian imperial government in distant capitals, but, at least in the case of George Bakhmetev, there is more than a hint of distrust and disillusionment with Petrograd creeping into the diplomatic correspondence.

Washington

Although references to Russia within official circles in Washington are sparse for 1916, owing primarily to preoccupations with a national election and deteriorating relations with Germany, the Russian shift to a decidedly conservative direction at the end of the year elicited concern from the president. An important British agent in America, Sir William Wiseman, telegraphed the Foreign Office on 16 January: "President and advisors are particularly anxious about the Russian situation, fearing that power has gone back into the hands of the reactionaries." He added, "President says that Russia stands in the way of complete sympathy between United States and Allies."[68] Wiseman blamed French ambassador Jean Jules Jusserand for indiscretion in drawing the president's attention to this development and at the same time betraying the British goal to control American perceptions of European politics.[69]

The little attention paid to Russia in Washington frustrated Bakhmetev, who continued to press for closer commercial relations, blaming Jewish financial interests for his lack of success. Like Francis in Petrograd, the Russian ambassador was increasingly isolated from the State Department and the other Allied missions, though he took some solace in seeing American public opinion shift against Germany in 1916.[70] His worries mounted, however, about incidents of sabotage in both the United States and Canada at munitions production and storage facilities for supplies destined for Russia, especially a $17 million loss at a Canadian factory.[71]

68. Sir William Wiseman to Foreign Office, 16 January 1917, in *PWW* 40:503-4.
69. Ibid.
70. Bakhmetev to Sturmer, 31 July 1916, f. 133, op. 470, d. 54, AVPR.
71. Bakhmetev to Pokrovskii, 14 January and 3 February 1917, f. 133, op. 470, d. 61, AVPR; and secret telegram, 14 January, f. 134 (war file), op. 473, d. 189, AVPR.

Bakhmetev was also on the receiving end of many complaints about trade restrictions and transportation and communication problems encountered by Americans wanting to conduct private business with Russia. Shipping priorities remained confused and inconsistent and became more and more critical with German resumption of unlimited submarine warfare. Nevertheless, some items were coming through Scandinavia during the 1916–17 winter: sheep's casings for American sausage, several shipments of Remington typewriters for Russia (totaling around 7,000), as well as some agricultural equipment and a number of Central Asian rugs for B. Altman of New York.[72] The British probably were less interested in these items, since they made their own typewriters and had plenty of sheep.

Bakhmetev had at least some good news to report to Petrograd—the American breaking off of relations with Germany on 3 February.[73] Suspense was definitely in the air in both Washington and Petrograd by this time. The counselor for the State Department, Frank Polk, summed it up best in a letter to Francis:

> We are having stirring times here, but still do not know quite where we are "at." We are neither flesh, fish, nor fowl. We would be in a better position, to my mind, if the break would actually come. A break seems inevitable and the sooner we get at it, the better. No one hates the thought of war more than I do, but the time seems to have come to go to bat, to put it crudely, and we would count more if we were actually at it.[74]

Stormy Petrel

Anyone who was reading at least some of the American dispatches from Petrograd in early 1917 would know that a storm was on the horizon. Once more Newton McCully led the way. His forty-two-page report, dated 6 March 1917, just before the beginning of the February-March Revolution but probably accumulated over several weeks, signaled the onset of a tumultuous Russian revolutionary year.

---

72. Konstantin Modzykhovskii (Russian Commercial Attaché) to Robert Hudson (Department of Commerce), 9 and 29 December 1916; to Ferdinand Mohrenschildt, 30 November 1916; and to Bakhmetev, 9 and 13 February 1917, f. 170, op. 512/2, d. 132–33, AVPR.

73. Bakhmetev to Pokrovskii, 8 February 1917, f. 133, op. 470, d. 61, AVPR.

74. Polk to Francis, 12 February 1917, Francis Papers, MoHS.

The anarchist elements are of little strength but unite with any disorderly movement, seeking to take advantage of it for their own purposes. . . . In the principal towns, particularly Moscow and Petrograd, reside the Revolutionary and other elements of disorder, and it is here that any organized movement is likely to commence.

He saw the Russian government losing control not only over the local political scene but also over its foreign policy, which he ascribed to the British involvement in a budding conspiracy.

In political matters recently British influence has become very strong, and occupies itself almost as much with the internal politics of Russia, as with the financial and commercial conditions, where it is in supreme control. In Petrograd, the British ambassador acting in cooperation with the Progressive "block" of the Duma, is hardly less powerful than the Emperor himself.[75]

The main problem, McCully advised, was a 600 percent inflation in the price of wood for fuel since 1914, posing special hardships during an extraordinarily severe winter. He estimated the following price increases in essential goods between October 1916 and February 1917: fuel 90 percent, potatoes 120 percent, cabbage 125 percent, milk 72 percent, and flour 41 percent. Only black bread was available, but it was increasingly scarce because of the price of fuel to bake it and the consequent wrecking of a number of bakeries by disgruntled crowds. The underlying problem was distribution: "Great as are the difficulties in administration, labor and supply, those of transportation are now by far the greatest."

On the peasantry, McCully observed, "In its heart this body would follow any party which promised peace. Economically it is in the best condition of any of the population—it has sufficient food until the next harvest, plenty of firewood grows near at hand, and now for the first time in years has plenty of money." But it could purchase nothing and resented the demands of cities for its grain and had a bitter dislike of bureaucracy. He concluded by noting the rapid rise of fatalism in the capital:

---

75. To Captain James H. Oliver (Chief of Naval Operations), 6 March 1917, f. 6497-12, RG 165, NA. Oliver was an Annapolis classmate of McCully's, and the reports read like private letters.

Moral restraint and self control have diminished. One of the most striking evidences of this is the increasing vogue of spiritualism. . . . Combined
with the general disturbance of moral ideas, uncertain means of existence,
and loss of the sense of responsibility due to war conditions, the problem of preserving internal order becomes more and more difficult. An
organized movement of any kind against the Government would find
support from many elements in Russia. Flesh and blood is the cheapest
thing in Russia.[76]

One factor that gave McCully an especially keen and critical sense of the situation was his knowledge of the conditions in the Russian Baltic Fleet, where the
lid would blow off during the February-March Revolution. An old friend of
McCully's, Admiral Robert Viren, the commandant of the main training base
of the fleet at Kronstadt, about twenty miles out in the Gulf of Finland from
Petrograd, would literally be torn apart by sailors in the most savage outburst of
the February-March Revolution.[77]

As early as November, Francis complained about the growing difficulty of
acquiring food for his staff. He had to ration sugar and exhaust the reserve stock
of the Austrian embassy during the winter. He observed, "The securing of food
. . . is becoming a very serious problem throughout Russia and especially in
Petrograd where there are said to be at present one million refugees from war
territories and other outlying sections."[78]

Upon arriving on 18 January to assist with prisoner-of-war work, James
Lawrence Houghteling recorded in his diary that there was much talk of the
Rasputin affair, of a coming revolution, and about expectations of America entering the war.[79] In Moscow on 17 February he noted that bread lines had grown
considerably longer and slower in a week but that the crowds were still good-
natured. "A decent government need fear nothing from the people, but this fi-

76. Ibid.
77. For details on the revolution in the fleet, called by one observer "October in February," see Norman E. Saul, *Sailors in Revolt: The Russian Baltic Fleet in 1917* (Lawrence: Regents Press of Kansas, 1978).
78. To Lansing, 12 November 1916, AE Russia, DPR 306, RG 84, NA. Butler Wright
observed on 1 February 1917 that diplomats can get bread and butter at special prices, "but
what do people do?" Diary, box 2, Wright Papers, Princeton-Mudd.
79. James L. Houghteling, *A Diary of the Russian Revolution* (New York: Dodd, Mead,
1918), 7-16. The perception that Rasputin had undermined loyalty to the imperial family
was widespread. Another eyewitness, a National City Bank employee, placed special emphasis on this. Leighton Rogers, "An Account of the March Revolution 1917" (typed copy),
p. 1, HIA.

asco of a system is constantly in danger of a revolution."[80] He reported the lines were even longer on 3 March; the next day he noted, "People are beginning to rebel and to cry out there is plenty for the rich and powerful, but only bread-cards and scarcity for the poor."[81] But Houghteling still seemed unaware of an imploding revolution when he shared a box with several other Americans to see Tchaikovsky's *Queen of Spades* at the Bolshoi Theater on 9 March.[82]

From Petrograd, Consul North Winship noted an especially severe shortage of black bread on 4 March. "All other prime necessities within the means of the working classes had already gradually disappeared as the winter advanced: meat, sugar, white flour, buckwheat, potatoes." Fish, fowl, milk, cheese, and butter could still be found but were far too expensive for the average citizen.[83] *Leslie's Weekly* correspondent-photographer Donald Thompson wrote to his wife on 6 March that black bread was not only scarce but also of much reduced quality. He observed a bread line from his hotel window when he went to bed. The same people were standing in it the next morning.[84]

The kaleidoscope of events that began with massive street demonstrations in Petrograd on 8 March,[85] International Women's Day, and an unusually warm day during a severe winter still caught most observers and participants by surprise. Demonstrations initially featured cries of "Give us bread,"[86] but they continued for several days, gaining momentum through isolated incidents, as is often the case in revolutionary situations. Another American observer, Leighton Rogers, described a scene on 11 March at a fancy pastry shop on Nevsky Prospect near the Europe (Evropeiskii) Hotel. Angry workers broke the window, and then a couple of them were killed in a confrontation with police.[87] This only added fuel to the fire.

Most Americans in Petrograd during the March days of disruption were constrained by official positions, duties to perform, obligations to families, or simple

80. Ibid., 33–34.
81. Ibid., 50–52.
82. Ibid., 54–55.
83. Winship report, 20 March 1917, U.S. Consulate Petrograd, box 3, RG 84, NA.
84. Thompson, *Donald Thompson in Russia* (New York: Century, 1918), 34.
85. This was 23 February by the Old Style Julian calendar still officially in effect in Russia, hence the more popular reference to the events as the "February Revolution."
The best general studies of the February Revolution are Tsuyoshi Hasegawa, *The February Revolution: Petrograd 1917* (Seattle: University of Washington Press, 1981); Marc Ferro, *The Russian Revolution of February 1917* (Englewood Cliffs, N.J.: Prentice-Hall, 1972); E. N. Burdzhalov, *Russia's Second Revolution: The February 1917 Uprising in Petrograd*, ed. and trans. Donald J. Raleigh (Bloomington: Indiana University Press, 1987); and Katkov, *Russia 1917*.
86. Diary, 8 March 1917, box 2, Wright Papers, Princeton-Mudd.
87. "An Account of the March Revolution 1917," p. 6, HIA.

*Funeral procession of "Fallen Heroes," Nevsky Prospect, Petrograd,
April 1917 (probably by Donald Thompson) courtesy of the Francis
Papers, Missouri Historical Society*

rules of safety to stay off the streets and to observe from windows or at a safe
distance. Not so with journalists such as Florence Harper and Donald Thompson, who resided at the Astoria Hotel, a focus of mob attacks, and who were on
the streets looking for and finding action. In Thompson's firsthand accounts in
pen and on film (mostly taken by a camera hidden under his coat), the revolutionary scenes come through as confused, violent, and unpredictable. He was
indeed lucky to have survived with no more than getting bloodied (from other
victims), bruised, and briefly arrested.[88]

88. See his letters to his wife, 8–19 March 1917, in Thompson, *Donald Thompson in
Russia*, 41–108.

The joining of the demonstrations by most garrison units, extreme violence in some of those units and in the Baltic Fleet, and hopes of saving his family and Russia's military capability caused the tsar to abdicate on 13 March, not only for himself but also for his one son, Grand Duke Alexis, then thirteen, and in favor of his brother. Although it was widely rumored that the tsarevich was sickly, few knew the nature of his blood disease, hemophilia. The fact that the "miracle worker," Rasputin, was no longer around and that Alexis also happened to have the measles, considered a particularly dangerous disease for him, may have contributed to the decision of Nicholas II to abdicate.

A New Government

Many liberal members of the Progressive Bloc in the Fourth Duma, such as Paul Miliukov, had anticipated the likelihood of a transitional constitutional monarchy under a regency for Alexis. However, they were now faced with an unpredictable alternative, the tsar's younger brother, Grand Duke Michael, who was next in line of succession. Leaders of the bloc, while forming a provisional government to replace the reactionary imperial regime, convinced Michael not to accept the crown until it might be offered to him after the adoption of a new constitution limiting autocratic power. They may have exaggerated concerns for his safety, but the grand duke signed such a proclamation on 16 March, and it was made public the following day.

The leaders of the hastily assembled new government were severely handicapped in three important ways. First, since they were committed to Western-style representative democracy, they lacked a clear mandate to act through an electorally confirmed process. This they believed could be achieved only through a popularly elected "constituent assembly" that would draw up a new constitution. Second, and in the meantime, they were forced to share the "mandate" of the street crowds and military garrisons of Petrograd and Moscow, with equally hastily improvised bodies, styled "soviets," that is, councils of workers and soldiers on the pattern of the 1905 Revolution (before there was a Duma). These organizations were havens for the ideas and actions of Russia's long-established and most radical and revolutionary political groups: the agrarian Socialist Revolutionary Party, the Marxist Social Democrats divided into the commonly designated Bolsheviks and Mensheviks (after positions taken at a 1903 party congress), anarchists, and other splinter groups.

Third, and perhaps most important, the new Provisional Government was forced by circumstances to continue an increasingly unpopular war and to bear the brunt of the conditions that the war was creating. Clearly inclined toward liberal and democratic goals and institutions, it could hardly abandon an alliance with Britain, France, Italy, Serbia (its longtime little Slavic brother), and soon the United States. Russian liberals also considered the German and Austro-Hungarian regimes as repugnant as the Romanov. The war suddenly became much more ideological: a battle between republics and empires, between parliamentary democracy and autocracy. Many hoped and expected that a resurgent Russian military, buoyed by the revolutionary spirit, would turn the tide and bring the war quickly to a close in 1917 and that the Western Allies would then come to Russia's aid with massive economic and moral assistance.

Unfortunately, Russia's military capability had been severely weakened by three years of fighting. It had suffered demoralizing defeats and serious disruptions of the chain of command in crucial units, especially in and around Petrograd, by the organization of Soviet-sponsored unit committees that could veto command orders. The latter were authorized on 14 March by the infamous Order Number One of the Petrograd Soviet because of concerns about the possibility of an officer-led counterrevolution. The order provided for limiting officer authority by empowering rank-and-file soldiers and sailors to elect commanders and approve their orders in the Petrograd Military District. The Provisional Government, too hastily, in retrospect, approved and extended it to the whole country. The result, as Consul North Winship observed, was that "many regiments [are] now commanded by reserve lieutenants."[89]

American Reaction

Americans in Russia were better prepared than most other foreigners to accept the new regime. The March changes were greeted with general approval if not elation, reminding many Americans of their own revolutionary origins. Some, however, felt regret and sorrow for Nicholas II and the imperial family, who, after all, had been unusually friendly toward Americans. Although thinned in ranks by the harsh winter that had driven off many reporters and curiosity seekers (even the Corses returned home for a rare visit), Americans through marriage or diplomatic and consular positions were situated as few others to appraise and record the events.[90] Now the dispersal of Americans around the capital and

---

89. Winship report, 27 March 1917, U.S. Consulate Petrograd, box 3, RG 84, NA.
90. Counselor J. Butler Wright was in the habit of recording a few weather details in his diary, for example, 1 January: very, very cold; 4 January: cold!; 9 January: so cold, canceled

throughout the country was an advantage. Many Americans—just to get to work—moved through the crowds on the streets.[91]

Most of the remaining American diplomatic staff were imbued with the traits of the eastern U.S. establishment. Armour, Whitehouse, McCully, Riggs, Basil Miles, and Wright all had upper-middle-class backgrounds and Ivy League educations. Armour had a law degree from Harvard and had toured Europe extensively. The senior member of the group, Miles (B.A., University of Pennsylvania) was invariably described as sophisticated, skilled in languages, diligent, and calm and collected, which fits his upbringing in a prominent Philadephia educator's family. These traits are apparent in a fourteen-page report he filed as an eyewitness to events.

On his way down Nevsky on Saturday, 9 March, Miles stopped by the Anichkov Bridge over the Fontanka Canal as a small cavalry unit charged into a crowd. To his surprise, good humor prevailed on both sides, and there was no violence. He walked the length of Sadovaia, another major street that was filled with people, and described seeing a short "battle" between rioters and loyal troops as like watching a baseball game. After several days of moving around the city, Miles summed up his impressions through the prism of his American liberalism:

> The vicious and highly centralized police system which for ten years I have considered to be like a cancer in the whole Russian system of Government, had been wiped out. . . . [I was surprised by] the amazing good-nature and self restraint of the soldiers and populace; the immediate order which emerged from what looked like chaos; the almost fabulous rapidity with which the revolution took place; and the totally unexpected facility with which it was effected. There seemed to be no one in Russia who favored the Czar or the rule of his family. A hopelessly inefficient government and ruler had crumbled through being rotten to the core.[92]

Consul Winship probably had the best working view, from the third floor of the Singer Building on Nevsky Prospect, and was in the eye of the storm, as the

---

opera engagement; 30 January: −22 degrees below zero, bluish mist in air, horses covered with ice; 3 February: −28, depressingly cold; 8 February: bitterly cold; 18 February: very cold. Diary, 1917, box 2, Wright Papers, Princeton-Mudd.

91. The two military attachés were strategically placed: McCully near the Winter Palace and Riggs, along with Armour, in an apartment that overlooked Liteiny, where much of the action occurred. William Sands report, 30 March 1917, AE Russia, DPR 325, RG 84, NA; Houghteling, *Diary of the Russian Revolution*, 65-69.

92. Miles report, 12 April 1917, AE Russia, DPR 325, RG 84, NA.

building, associated with its "German" name, was the subject of several attacks on 11 and 12 March. "During these two days the fighting around the Consulate was severe, and on several occasions it seemed as if nothing could save the Singer Building from total demolition." It was especially vulnerable because police had set up a machine gun on the roof, finally cleared by revolutionary forces on the twelfth. "No damage was done in the Consulate, but other offices and the building itself were considerably injured." Winship successfully prevented the American eagle on the front from being torn off as it was in August 1914.[93] Other American personnel had a scare on 13 March when a detachment of soldiers demanded the right to search the Austrian embassy but were persuaded to withdraw.[94]

Thomas Whittemore, who was busy at the time installing a ventilation system in the American home for refugee children, composed a sad epitaph for the old regime, in pondering the indefinite course of Russia:

> The future is clear that the dynasty has come to an end. Not a ray of poetry falls across Russian Imperialism to light it on its way to dusty death. Are there no young Royalists, like the French and the Scots, one asks beautifully to die. Yes, but there is nothing to die for. The Emperor is a foolish ghost and the Empress is a despised German intrigante.[95]

Another American who viewed the events from the street level was Frank Golder, who was spending the winter searching Russian archives for material about America and Russian-American relations. He sensed the revolution as "like a rotten tree just fell over. . . . It was lots of fun." And when released prisoners joined the crowds, "What a gathering of freaks and patriots."[96]

Throughout most of these tumultuous days, the American ambassador stayed in the embassy receiving reports from staff members on what they saw and heard and trying to inform Washington, but few cables were getting through. After things calmed down somewhat, on 15 March, he ventured out with his secretary for a midnight walk and was soon stopped by a patrol. Identifying himself as the ambassador, he was allowed to pass on. That day he sent a somewhat confused and contradictory report to Washington:

---

93. Winship report, 20 March 1917, U.S. Consulate Petrograd, USSR file, box 3, RG 84, NA. These records remained behind in Russia and were returned to the United States only in the 1980s.

94. Franklin Sands report, 30 March 1917, AE Russia, DPR 325, RG 84, NA.

95. To Crane, 2 April 1917, reel 2, Crane Papers, BA, CU.

96. Golder to "Friends," 20 March 1917, f. 1, box 11 (Correspondence, 1917–1926), Golder Papers, HIA.

This is undoubtedly a revolution, but it is the best managed revolution that has ever taken place for its magnitude. The Duma is assuming control and is exercising its authority in Petrograd with rare good judgment. . . .

A great many acts of violence have been perpetrated in Petrograd, and some almost within sight—certainly within hearing distance—of this embassy, which appears to have been in the center of the revolutionary movement. The first regiment that mutinied was in barracks not two blocks from this embassy; the arsenal, which was immediately captured by this regiment and the people, is within a block and a half of this embassy. There are passing in front of the embassy now stray soldiers in uniform, some with guns, and some without.[97]

One factor that provoked and sustained a special American interest in the Russian Revolution was the interconnection of the new Provisional Government leadership with Americans. Paul Miliukov, a leader of the Constitutional Democratic Party and its chief spokesman in the Duma, was the new foreign minister and actual head of the government. He had a number of ties with the United States, having lectured widely there and formed close associations with Harper and Crane.[98] Moreover, his brother Aleksei had been the architect for the Singer factory at Podolsk. Similarly, Alexander Guchkov, the new minister of war, was well known to American business circles from his wartime economic role and through his brother Nikolai, who had been a leading organizer of the Russian-American Chamber of Commerce in Moscow.[99] The Guchkovs spoke excellent English and were frequently mentioned as either guests or hosts of Americans in that city.

Even Prince Georgi Lvov, the nominal head of the Provisional Government as chairman of the Council of Ministers and minister of interior, had an American connection: Consul General Maddin Summers's mother-in-law was his first cousin.[100] Others with American connections were Finance Minister Nikolai Nekrasov and Vladimir Nabokov, whose brother Konstantin served at the Russian embassy in Washington during the war. The new assistant minister of

---

97. Francis to Lansing, 15 March 1917, in Cockfield, *Dollars and Diplomacy*, 91.

98. Besides Crane's sponsorship of Miliukov's lectures and visits to the United States, he accompanied him on a tour of the Balkans in October 1912 and saw the beginning of the First Balkan War. Paul Miliukov, *Political Memoirs, 1905–1917*, ed. Arthur P. Mendel, trans. Carl Goldberg (Ann Arbor: University of Michigan Press, 1967), 247–50.

99. Saul, *Concord and Conflict*, 547. Houghteling dined at the Guchkovs' in Moscow on 4 March. Houghteling, *Diary of the Russian Revolution*, 52.

100. Summers to Francis, 15 March 1917, Francis Papers, MoHS.

commerce, Boris Bakhmeteff, had just returned from heading a purchasing commission in America and would soon be on his way back.

Farther to the left of the Russian political spectrum, a number of leading representatives attracted American attention, thanks especially to George Kennan. Peter Kropotkin, the "anarchist prince," had lectured in America, while "little grandmother" Catherine Breshko-Breshkovskaia was worshiped by millions during her publicity and fund-raising tours. Another elder statesman of Russian socialism, Nikolai Chaikovskii, had lived among Americans in the heartland while trying to make a Russian-style commune work in Kansas. These, like Kennan, were practically "over the hill" and would play relatively minor roles after their return to Russia. Younger radicals—such as Leon Trotsky and Nikolai Bukharin—also came back with an American experience and would have a definite impact on the revolution, but their stays in the United States were relatively short and virtually unnoticed.

In the United States

The February–March Revolution came as more of a surprise to Americans at home because they were engrossed with other matters—Mexico, the Far East, the election and second inauguration of President Wilson, but mainly the breaking off of relations with Germany and the approach of war. They were also ingrained with the habit of thinking of Russia as backward, autocratic, imperial, and unchanging, with a lot of lost souls wandering the globe preaching revolution and looking for handouts. For that picture suddenly to alter required some adjustment.

The first news came, oddly, on the ides of March and through German channels, but it still created a sensation. George Kennan first learned of the event through telephone calls to his Central Park West apartment in New York. He rushed down to the corner to pick up a special edition of the *Globe* and soon found a *New York Times* reporter at his door and his phone ringing every twenty minutes day and night.[101] In a letter written to Colonel House about the need for a publicity bureau if the United States entered the war, Arthur Bullard added, "Today's news from Russia may have vast significance."[102]

Information, however, was sketchy and confused because the revolution had disrupted the already strained channels of communication between Russia and

101. 1916-17 diary, 15 and 19 March 1917, box 14, Kennan Papers, MD, LC.
102. Bullard to House, 15 March 1917, box 9, Bullard Papers, Princeton-Mudd.

the United States. The State Department was still in the dark on 17 March, when Third Secretary Breckinridge Long recorded in his diary: "Russia is overthrowing the government—papers full, A.P. cables get through, but no word from Francis."[103] But the proclamation by Grand Duke Michael on 17 March asking the Russian people to obey the new Provisional Government arrived promptly by cable and was generally interpreted as signaling the end of the Romanov dynasty. Some, such as Harper, remained dubious that Russia could shed the monarchy so easily.[104] Others saw the revolution as a definite turning point not only for Russia but also for the world, leaving Austria and Germany "as the last exponents of absolutism and divine right."[105] For the many critics of the old regime and sympathizers with Russian liberal and radical causes, celebrations were now in order.

Kennan's appearance naturally highlighted a mass meeting sponsored by the Friends of Russian Freedom at Carnegie Hall on 23 March. There were speeches by him, Herbert Parsons, Lillian Wald, Mayor Mitchell, and Rabbi Stephen Wise. Nikolai Sokolov's Russian orchestra played Tchaikovsky's Fourth Symphony, lantern slides of the new Russian leaders were shown, and the rafters rang with the singing of the "Marseillaise." Kennan thought the speeches were too long and disorganized, but "it was on the whole a very enthusiastic and successful meeting."[106] Similar meetings were held on subsequent nights, with one on 28 March setting up a political exile relief fund to assist the return of revolutionaries in the United States. The Russian consul general in New York was besieged with requests for permissions, and, in response to Bakhmetev's query, the Provisional Government agreed to advance sums for travel expenses for Russia's wayward exiles to return home.[107]

Inveterate traveler Charles Crane came back from the inauguration in Washington and packed his bags for yet another trip to Russia to see what was going on firsthand, but first he took time to pledge $150,000 for YMCA work in Russia. He advised both the president and the State Department on Russian affairs, especially on the sending of a special mission.[108] Joining him for the journey

103. Diaries, 1917, box 1, Long Papers, MD, LC. Long went several months with hardly a mention of Russia in his diary.
104. Harper to Crane, March ?, 1917, reel 2, Crane Papers, BA, CU. "The extreme radical element, the students and some of the workmen, may be talking republic, but the monarchical idea is, as you know, strong throughout the peasantry, who are now the army."
105. Samuel Cross (Cleveland) to Leo Wiener, 18 March 1917, Wiener Papers, Harvard University Archives.
106. Diary, 23 March 1917, box 14, Kennan Papers, MD, LC.
107. Bakhmetev to Miliukov, 22 and 26 March 1917, f. 133, op. 470, d. 61, AVPR.
108. J. R. Mott to Roger Williams, 22 March 1917, reel 2, Crane Papers, BA, CU; and to Harper, 27 March 1917, f. 12, box 3, Harper Papers, UC.

George Kennan, courtesy of the Prints and Photographs
Division, Library of Congress

was muckraking journalist Lincoln Steffens, who appears to have been inspired
by Robert LaFollette to go help write a new Russian constitution. In steerage on
their Norwegian ship—at least as far as Halifax—was a man whose name would
soon be a household word: Leon Trotsky.[109]

109. *The Autobiography of Lincoln Steffens* (New York: Harcourt, Brace, 1931), 744-45;
"LaFollette Sends Envoy," *New York Times*, 21 April 1917 (1:4).
    Trotsky, his wife, and two sons were taken off the ship at Halifax by British authorities.
He was held at Amherst, a camp for German prisoners of war, for a month, on the grounds
that he represented a threat to the new Russian government, despite the fact that his visa had
been granted by the Russian consul general in New York. The future Bolshevik leader certainly had nothing good to say about his illegal arrest, search, and detention by the British.
Trotsky, *My Life* (New York: Grosset and Dunlap, 1960), 278-85.
    Samuel Harper, who had been to New York to see Crane off, observed Trotsky "address-

Many Americans quickly connected the revolution with America entering the war. Andrew Dickson White, whose first direct contact with Russia dated back to the Crimean War, recorded in his diary on 31 March: "The Revolution in Russia has seemed to awaken every sort of warlike hope. Americans are talking now not merely of defense but of sending troops to Europe."[110] Old and new warrior and ex-president Theodore Roosevelt pronounced, "I rejoice from my soul that Russia, the hereditary friend of our country, has ranged itself on the side of orderly liberty, of enlightened freedom, and for the full performance of duty by free nations throughout the world."[111] He probably also thought, "and will now sacrifice even more to win the war."

From the Midwest, Indiana governor James P. Goodrich echoed, "Freed from the autocracy that has misruled them for many generations, Russia with all of its marvelous resources will make rapid strides toward the development of the nation in every way and I sincerely wish them success in everything they do in that direction."[112] Samuel Gompers, on behalf of American labor, was more succinct in a cable to Soviet leader Nikolai Chkheidze: "We rejoice with Russia's workers in their newly achieved liberty."[113] Others on the American "Left" were equally enthusiastic. Rose Strunsky simply wrote, "What a glorious world it has suddenly become."[114] Clearly, Americans basked in the bright light of what they thought was a new Russian era.

Recognition

Despite communication problems, the United States was the first state to formally recognize the new Provisional Government, sanction the abdication of the tsar, and welcome the entrance of Russia upon a new era. Technically this was in response to Miliukov's 17 March announcement to the diplomatic community of the formation of a new government.[115] The credit for this probably goes to Ambassador Francis himself, who claimed that upon his own initiative and without consulting other members of his staff, he drafted a cable recommend-

---

ing the crowd from the pier as we stood there." Harper to Richard Crane, 12 April 1917, part II, box 1, Richard Crane Papers, GU.

110. Diaries, 1912-1918, reel 134, White Papers, Cornell.
111. Undated photostat, f. business correspondence 1917, box 3, Flint Papers, NYPL.
112. Goodrich to Flint, 2 April 1917, ibid.
113. Quoted in Gompers to Flint, 4 April 1917, ibid.
114. To Harper, n.d., f. 12, box 3, Harper Papers, UC.
115. Miliukov to Francis, 17 March 1917, AE Russia, DPR 325, RG 84, NA.

immediate recognition. He personally secured permission from Miliukov to send it directly from the Ministry of Foreign Affairs on 18 March.[116] He explained his action to his son as based on his impression that the new government was striving to maintain law and order and to remain in the war:

> Such a government merits the support of all good citizens and is entitled to the recognition of all foreign governments that favor law and order and especially of that government represented in Russia by myself.
>
> As the result of this reasoning I cabled to the Department the evening of Sunday March 18th asking for authority to recognize the provisional government and based this request on the following facts. The government to which I came accredited has ceased to exist and has no probability of a restoration in the immediate future; the government which succeeds the Imperial system is the practical realization of the principle which my government has advocated and is advocating and of which the United States of America has been the champion for 140 years, and that is a government by the consent of the governed; both the high officials [Lvov and Miliukov] with whom I have conferred assured me that it is the firm determination of the provisional government to vigorously prosecute the war.[117]

The Francis cable reached responsive people in Washington. In fact, Robert Lansing had already sought additional information on Russian affairs from Samuel Harper through his secretary Richard Crane on 16 March; on the seventeenth, Colonel House advised the president to recognize the new government "as soon as England and France do so."[118] Wilson, after conferring with Charles Crane, decided instead to take the initiative, and Lansing formally replied to Francis on 20 March, instructing him to secure an appointment as soon as possible with Miliukov to relay the American decision: "At your interview state that the Government of the United States recognizes the new Government of Russia, and that you, as the ambassador of the United States, will continue intercourse with Russia through the medium of the newly established regime."[119] Francis formally pre-

---

116. One source credits Chapin Huntington with giving the ambassador strong support.
117. To Perry, 19 March 1917, reel 3, Francis Papers, MoHS.
In a follow-up cable on 20 March, Francis hinted at another motive, that U.S. recognition come before it would appear as influenced by Jewish opinion. To Lansing, 20 March 1917, f. 138, op. 467, d. 651/673, AVPR.
118. *PWW* 41:422–23. See Richard Crane to Harper, 15 March 1917, and Harper to Crane, 15 March 1917, f. 12, box 3, Harper Papers, UC. The date in *PWW* of Harper's telegram is 16 March, perhaps the date of receipt of a night transmission.
119. Lansing to Francis, 20 March 1917, AE Russia, DPR 325, RG 84, NA.

Paul Miliukov, Russian foreign minister. From World's Work, *April 1917*

sented his credentials to the new Russian government on 22 March. Thus the United States became the first country to recognize the new Provisional Government of Russia. Two days later, Britain, France, and Italy followed suit.

New American Relief for Russia

A variety of American assistance for field hospitals and for refugees from the battle zones had entered Russia before 1917, but most of it went through Russian administrative auspices, mainly the Russian Red Cross and the Russian YMCA "Mayak" organization. By far the largest direct American administration of relief had been for German and Austrian prisoners of war, and that was resented by many Russians who were aware of it. In fact, this extensive program, in which the American YMCA had a large role, relieved the Russian agencies of some of this burden—of providing medical supplies, improving sanitation, and so on—and at the same time reducing international condemnation of the bad conditions of Russian prisoner-of-war internments.

Direct operation of YMCA relief facilities in Russia encountered obstacles and frustration before the revolution, except for some limited activity allowed in Central Asia, at least in part because of the concentration of this relief on Russia's enemies. Even the new government was reluctant to allow the YMCA to open facilities to serve the Russian army.[120] Finally, special permission was granted for the first YMCA "hut" in Petrograd during the first week of April with two large rooms, one as a tea room and the other as a library and reading and writing room. Classes were organized in Russian language for regular soldiers and in English for officers, with direction in the hands of a Russian committee, supervised by a "Y" secretary. Credit for developing this new opportunity should go to Archibald ("Archie") Harte, who by this time had considerable Russian as well as international experience.

Harte also planned for other such operations, especially in Moscow, where two more had already started, but warned his colleagues there to be careful to keep prisoner-of-war funds separate from funds for service to Russian soldiers. He also cautioned that the work should start slowly: "Do not attempt to start twenty Y.M.C.A.'S, or even ten, but do intensive work with the two you have started until you have a real Army Y.M.C.A." He continued, "I do want us, because we have learned to love these Russian soldiers, to do for them a service that will be called a good work now, and that will grow better through the years."[121] The new funding was coming from Crane and other subscribers who were inspired by the great political and social change in Russia.

America Goes to War

It is unlikely that a direct cause-and-effect connection can be made between the Russian Revolution and American entry into war. The latter would no doubt have occurred regardless of what happened in Russia, but it certainly made the

120. Jerome Davis, "Relationship of the Young Men's Christian Association to the Russian Government from January 1917 to March 1918," f. YMCA Inter. Com., box 5, Anderson Papers, UIA.
121. Harte to Jerome Davis, 2 April 1917, copy in f. War Prisoner's Aid, box 5, Paul Anderson Papers, UIA.

President Woodrow Wilson and his cabinet, summer 1917, who frequently discussed policies regarding Russia. Front row, from left to right: Secretary of Commerce William Redfield, Secretary of State Robert Lansing, Secretary of Agriculture David Houston, President Wilson, Secretary of Treasury William McAdoo, Postmaster General Albert Burleson; back row: Secretary of Navy Josephus Daniels, Secretary of Labor Charles Wilson, Secretary of War Newton Baker, Attorney General Thomas W. Gregory, Secretary of Interior Franklin K. Lane, courtesy of the Prints and Photographs Division, Library of Congress

declaration of war more enthusiastic and wholehearted. The most crucial factor in the decision was the German submarine sinking of three American merchant vessels. Secretary of the Navy Josephus Daniels recorded his impressions of the debate at a special cabinet meeting with the president on the afternoon of Tuesday, 20 March, the same day that the United States recognized the Provisional Government. The discussion was decidedly pro-war, with Wilson speaking of "the glorious act of Russia, which, in a way, had changed things, but he could not give that as a reason for war."[122] Breckinridge Long, who was not present, sensed the change in atmosphere, that the United States was "practically in a state of war."[123]

Probably the most complete record of the 20 March meeting was kept by the secretary of state, who noted that Wilson, in his opening remarks, reviewed the situations in the belligerent countries, "particularly in Russia where the revolution against autocracy had been successful."[124] As the cabinet members spoke in favor of the central question of calling a special session of Congress to hear a war message, Lansing stressed the new Russian situation:

> I said that the revolution in Russia, which appeared to be successful, had removed the one objection to the [sic] affirming that the European war was a war between Democracy and Absolutism; that the only hope of a permanent peace between all nations depended upon the establishment of democratic institutions throughout the world; that no League of Peace would be of value if a powerful autocracy was a member, and that no League of Peace would be necessary if all nations were democratic; and that in going into the war at this time we could do more to advance the cause of Democracy than if we failed to show sympathy with the democratic powers in their struggle against the autocratic government of Germany.
>
> I said that the present time seemed to me especially propitious for action by us because it would have a great moral influence in Russia, because it would encourage the democratic movement in Germany, because it would put new spirit in the Allies already flushed with recent military successes, and because it would put an end to the charges of vacillation and hesitation, which were becoming general, and bring the people solidly behind the President.[125]

At the time Wilson was dubious about Lansing's suggestion that he stress these points in his message to Congress, but in the middle of his speech on 2 April, Wilson declared:

> Does not every American feel that assurance has been added to our hope for the future peace of the world by the wonderful and heartening things

122. Robert V. Daniels, *Red October: The Bolshevik Revolution of 1917* (Boston: Beacon, 1984), 117.
123. Diary, 20 March, box 1, Long Papers, MD, LC.
124. Lansing memorandum, 20 March, *PWW* 41:438.
125. Ibid., 440.

that have been happening within the last few weeks in Russia? Russia was known by those who knew it best to have been always in fact democratic at heart, in all the vital habits of her thought, in all the intimate relationships of her people that spoke their natural instinct, their habitual attitude towards life. The autocracy that crowned the summit of her political structure, long as it had stood and terrible as was the reality of its power, was not in fact Russian in origin, character, or purpose; and now it has been shaken off and the great, generous Russian people have been added in all their naive majesty and might to the forces that are fighting for freedom in the world, for justice, and for peace. Here is a fit partner for a League of Honour.[126]

The sentiments expressed by the president are quite remarkable given his lack of expertise on Russia. His interpretation of a latent but naturally democratic Russia was quite unexpected. And no one else in the government in Washington had any better knowledge. True, the president received some information through Samuel Harper's long telegram, elicited by Richard Crane, on 16 March.[127] But the real source of this passage was probably Charles Crane, whom Wilson trusted and considered an expert on Russia. Crane and his wife lunched at the White House on 23 March. The next day, when the Wilsons visited the Navy Department, Secretary Daniels was surprised to find the president full of detailed information about Russia.[128] And on 25 March Crane lunched with

126. Ibid., 524. The president wrote the address on his own typewriter and refused to have it read by any cabinet member, though he did read it himself shortly before delivery to House, who thought that he had inspired at least some of it: "It would be interesting to know how much of his address the President thinks I suggested. He does not indicate, in any way, that he is conscious that I had any part in it. I think it is quite possible that he forgets from what source he receives ideas and suggestions." House diary, ibid., 529.

127. Harper to R. Crane, 16 March 1917, encl. in Lansing to Wilson (personal and private), 16 March, *PWW* 41:415-17. Harper stressed the roles of the Duma and zemstvo local government organizations.

128. Diary of Josephus Daniels, 24 March 1917, ibid., 466. Part of the conversation dealt with Miliukov's difficulty in learning English, which could only have come directly from Crane or indirectly from Harper.

Crane was quite busy in Washington. He called on Louis Brandeis on the evening of 22 March, spreading his Russian democracy message:

Crane thinks the Russian Cabinet is the ablest body of men in the world & that Russia will teach the world democracy. Says their local self government, and cooperative system, with which 15,000,000 people are connected, is greatest essay in practical democracy the world knows today—& Crane is generally as happy as a clam over the outlook.

Louis Brandeis to Alfred Brandeis, 23 March 1917, *Letters of Louis D. Brandeis*, vol. 4, ed. Melvin I. Urofsky and David W. Levy (Albany: State University of New York Press, 1975), 276-77.

Colonel House, who the same day wrote the president, "If it is convenient to you I will come down on Tuesday [28 March] for there are some things I would like to talk over with you."[129] Crane's parting shot, on that day, stressed "that the men in the provisional government of Russia are the best group running any one of the great powers."[130]

Reinforcement came from Harper, Crane's trusted lieutenant, who was summoned to Washington at the end of March to confer with the State Department, in addition to giving a lecture at the National Geographic Society. The *Washington Post*, in covering his arrival, referred to Harper as "America's foremost authority" on Russia.[131] He spoke with Lansing and, through Richard Crane, met Breckinridge Long for the first time on 31 March.[132] Harper's views on Russia also may have influenced the president directly during an interview on Sunday morning, 1 April; at least Harper thought they did, as he wrote upon his return to Chicago that the paragraph in Wilson's war speech was "the message to Russia which I hoped could be secured."[133]

In any event, the Russian Revolution added another cause to the American reasons for entering the war. Saving Russia for democracy was apparently a concern in cabinet discussions before Wilson made his war speech. Franklin Lane, secretary of interior, wrote his brother on 1 April:

> The meetings of the Cabinet lately have been nothing less than councils of war. . . .
>
> The first thing is to let Russia and France have money. And the second thing, to see that Russia has munitions, of which they are short—depending largely, too largely, upon Japan. I shouldn't be surprised if we would

129. House to Wilson, 25 March, and House Diary entry, 25 March, *PWW* 41:466, 468.

130. To Wilson, *PWW* 41:493; and reel 1, Crane Papers, BA, CU. Crane shared the president's dislike and fear of Japan: "With Russia and China directed by their peoples we shall not have to concern ourselves so much about the military autocracies of Germany and Japan." Ibid.

131. "Harper Will Tell of the New Russia," *Washington Post*, 27 March 1917, clipping in f. 12, box 3, Harper Papers, UC.

132. Diary, 31 March, box 1, Long Papers, MD, LC.

133. Harper to R. Crane, 4 April 1917, f. 13, box 3, Harper Papers, UC; see also to Washburn, 6 April, f. 14, ibid.

Washburn, who might have had the ear of the president, was recuperating from exhaustion in Minnesota. Similarly, Norman Hapgood, close to the White House on Russian matters, was honeymooning—with Elizabeth Reynolds—and reporting the war from London.

operate the Russian railroads. . . . The lovable, kindly Russians are not to be conquered,—and it makes me rejoice that we are to be with them.[134]

In fact, Assistant Secretary of the Navy Franklin Roosevelt had already consulted with Bakhmetev about warships that would be needed to secure greater use of the Arctic supply route to Murmansk and Archangel.[135] And the ambassador found it surprisingly easy to arrange a series of short loans with Riggs National Bank to cover debts, based on the assumption that a large government loan would soon be available.[136]

While the Russian Revolution made it easier for Washington to mobilize its forces for war, the country was far from united in support. From the beginning of the great European conflict, a strong pacifist trend existed in the United States, though it lacked cohesion. It consisted of such disparate groups as conservative religious sects, radical socialists, suffragettes, and some active politicians such as William Jennings Bryan. Several of these groups had ties to, or interests in, Russia: for example, Mennonites, Tolstoyans, and socialists.

Some of these pacifists hoped the Russian Revolution could keep America out of war by forcing Russia to leave it. Celebrations of the revolution and anti-war meetings sometimes merged, and it was difficult to separate them. George Kennan agreed to preside over a meeting of the Humanitarian Cult in New York on 27 March on the condition that it not be pacifist in tone. Despite reassurances, to his chagrin the speeches turned out to be quite antiwar in focus.[137] Differing interpretations of the Russian Revolution exacerbated the fissures in American society, embittering feelings and adding another dynamic to the Russian-American equation.

Exit Bakhmetev, Enter Bakhmeteff

Because of the revolution, it became Russia's turn to experience instability and gaps in diplomatic representation abroad. Once it became clear that there was little likelihood that the monarchy in some form would be retained in Russia,

---

134. Franklin Lane to George Lane, 1 April 1917, in *The Letters of Franklin K. Lane: Personal and Political*, ed. Anne Wintermute Lane and Louise Herrick Wall (Boston: Houghton Mifflin, 1922), 243.
135. Bakhmetev to Miliukov, 31 March 1917, f. 133, op. 470, d. 61, AVPR.
136. Bakhmetev to Miliukov, 5 and 7 April 1917, ibid.
137. 1916-17 diary, 27 March, box 14, Kennan Papers, MD, LC.

George Bakhmetev, on 17 April, cabled Miliukov his resignation as ambassador, delegating Konstantin Onu, the first counselor, as chargé d'affaires.[138] It was generally expected that Bakhmetev's predecessor, Roman Rosen, would return to the post, and he himself anticipated it, perhaps too much.[139] Although identified with pro-American and liberal causes and a critic of the Romanov war record, Rosen was considered too tainted by service to the old regime and by being an outspoken advocate of peace to serve as an ambassador in a wartime alliance.[140] His age—seventy—was another drawback.

The new Russian ambassador, Boris Bakhmeteff, was an unrelated namesake of his predecessor.[141] A professor of engineering at Petrograd Polytechnic Institute, he served as a technical adviser to various purchasing commissions and as assistant minister of commerce in the new government. He was no stranger to Americans in Russia, due to his associations with selling a patent to General Electric and with the Russian-American Chamber of Commerce, but he was without any diplomatic experience.[142] Appointed by Miliukov in early May, Bakhmeteff would not reach Washington for another month, via the Pacific route, to take up his duties. In the meantime, America was preoccupied with getting ready for war and its new role as a major ally in the Entente.

138. Bakhmetev to Miliukov, 17 April 1917, f. 133, op. 470, d. 61, AVPR.

139. Roger Williams to Harper, 5 April 1917, relaying the contents of a cable from Rosen to Crane, f. 13, box 3, Harper Papers, UC.

140. Rosen, *Forty Years of Diplomacy,* 2:235. As a member of the tsar-appointed State Council, he served as a representive, along with Miliukov, in a Duma/State Council delegation to the Allies in April–May 1916. He was quite vocal in pressing for peace negotiations and in disagreement with Miliukov. He could claim later to be one of the few who saw where staying in the war would lead Russia.

141. To separate the two, and to conform to Bakhmeteff's own usage throughout his life, the Anglicized spelling "Bakhmeteff" is used for the second ambassador by that name.

142. Bakhmeteff oral history, pp. 249–50, CU.

3

Alliance

The February–March Revolution occurred just three weeks before America's entry into the war to save the world for democracy. Even before the revolution, the United States was moving irrevocably toward war, but Woodrow Wilson was among the first to realize that the Russian Revolution made a formal declaration much easier and removed at once much of the leftist opposition to the Russian autocracy and to American entry on the side of democratic ideals. The considerable anti-Imperial Russian and often, as a corollary, pro-German, elements could now identify with a crusade to save Russia for democracy—and possibly for more revolution—even if that meant an end to Imperial Germany.

Throughout its relatively short history, the United States strove to maintain a policy of avoiding "entangling alliances." This is not to say, of course, that this country was not involved in major world conflicts. In fact, its own war for independence produced a Russian intervention in the form of the Declaration of Armed Neutrality of 1780. The greatest preceding world conflict, the Napoleonic Wars, also very much involved the two countries, though not in direct alliance or conflict. America's War of 1812 began almost simultaneously with the historic Napoleonic invasion of Russia. In fact, in almost all the other nineteenth-century conflicts both countries were interested parties, especially during the Crimean War in the 1850s, which occurred during a high point of American Anglophobia. Partly out of gratitude for America's friendly neutrality and partly out of self-interest, Russia sided with the Union during the Civil War, but in the relatively recent Russo-Japanese War American sympathies, at least at the beginning, were with Japan.

The initial American euphoria about the Russian Revolution continued through April but under a cloud of growing concern about the future, in consideration of the deterioration of economic conditions and an ensuing political turmoil in a free Russia. The latter was accompanied by reports of German intrigue and radical troublemaking. While many American Russophiles could revel in the prospects of a United States of Russia, the suppressed energies of Russia's political life suddenly came to the fore in ways that Americans failed to predict or immediately comprehend. A new Russia had definitely materialized, but was it what Americans expected, a Russia in their own image? Americans, it turned out, had different ideas regarding what the Russian future should or would be. The American model was immediately challenged by a new, futuristic ideal of a revolutionary society—from the backwardness of autocracy to a great new socialist world.

Four days after his historic war message to Congress and on the day of the formal American declaration of war, Woodrow Wilson approved the sending of special instructions to his envoy in Russia:

> You may say to Doctor Miliukoff that the United States in thus arraying itself against the greatest enemy of and menace to democracy in the world does so with a feeling of confidence in the ultimate triumph of those principles of liberty and justice which it has maintained for nearly a century and a half and in devotion to which by all civilized nations lies the hope of universal peace.
>
> You may also say that the Government and people of the United States rejoice that the great Russian people have joined the powerful democracies which are struggling against autocracy and wish to express to the Russian Nation their sincere gratification that thus a new bond of friendship is added to those which have so long united the peoples of the two countries. It is the earnest hope and expectation of this Government that a Russia inspired by these great ideals will realize more than ever the duty which it owes to humanity and the necessity of preserving internal harmony in order that by a united and patriotic nation it may overcome the autocratic power which by force and intrigue menaces the democracy which the Russian people have proclaimed.[1]

This message, received in Petrograd at 9:30 P.M. on 7 April, created an immediate sensation at the embassy and in the new government. It not only signaled a new relationship between the United States and Russia, one of military and political alliance, but also indicated genuine concern about Russia's future participation in the war.[2] The United States placed its full weight on Russia's "duty"

---

1. Lansing to Francis, 6 April 1917, *FRUS 1918: Russia* 1:20–21; Wilson to Lansing, 6 April 1917, *PWW* 41:552.
2. Diary, 7 April 1917, box 2, Wright Papers, Princeton-Mudd.

to stay the course and uphold the cause of democracy everywhere, motivated especially by information about the wave of radical violence in military units in the Petrograd area in the wake of the revolution.

Missions to Russia

News from Russia throughout the winter of 1916-17 had portrayed a country on the verge of economic collapse. As American participation in the war drew near in late March, considerations of what to do about the Russian situation could hardly be avoided. America's new Western allies were also hard-pressed. They were willing to pass the buck of bolstering Russia to Washington as long as they still received the bulk of American support and the United States did not take over their economic stakes in Russia. After all, the United States was a next-door neighbor to Russia, across the Pacific, and with its enormous economic resources should be able to keep Russia in the war.

What could America do? One thing was clear: the Russian transportation system was extremely fragile and threatening the flow of essential supplies to cities and to the front, so a technical commission, made up primarily of railroad experts, could be sent to investigate needs and render advice. It also might prepare the way for more direct American involvement in overseeing and operating vital communications, particularly the Trans-Siberian Railroad, a key artery for the infusion of American products into Russia.

Second, the preceding would require funding, special long-term loans to pay for large quantities of railroad equipment and war matériel. In anticipation of this, the Russian embassy suddenly found borrowing small amounts relatively easy. The first such loans were used to finance the return of a large number of political exiles in the United States, a program supported and assisted by the Society of Friends of Russian Freedom.[3] So, ironically, the United States indirectly financed the return of many individuals, such as Leon Trotsky and Nikolai Bukharin, who would devote their energies to overthrowing the Provisional Government.[4]

3. Paul Kennaday to Kennan, 30 April 1917, box 4, Kennan Papers, MD, LC.
4. Trotsky and Bukharin had worked together in New York during the winter of 1916-17 on the editorial staff of *Novyi Mir*, along with Mosei Volodarskii and Grigorii Chudnovskii, who would also play important roles in the Bolshevik seizure of power. Trotsky and his family left on the Atlantic route at the end of March, while Bukharin departed about a week later via the Pacific. Trotsky, *My Life*, 273-76; Stephen F. Cohen, *Bukharin and the Bolshevik Revolution: A Political Biography, 1888-1938* (New York: Vintage, 1973), 43-44.

Finally, the United States would also send a "political" commission to display the new American ally's support for "democratic" Russia, to stabilize and strengthen the "Americanophile" Miliukov-Guchkov-Lvov government, and to build up military morale. The idea for this floated around Washington in early April, one of its chief promoters being, ironically, Oscar Straus, certainly no Russophile. Straus first proposed his plan to Lansing, House, and Andrew White, before calling George Kennan on 9 April. At lunch the next day, he tried to convince Kennan to head such a mission without success. Nor would Kennan even consent to be one of its members.[5] Quite clearly Straus had in mind being included himself, or at least assuring a strong Jewish presence on the commission.

The idea of a special, highly visible commission also was urged independently by America's new Western allies, who were concerned about more indications that Russia might leave the war. Colonel House reported to the president on 10 April that the heads of the French Information Bureau (Stephane Joseph Vincent Lauzanne and Marcel Knecht) urged him to suggest this special mission:

> They think it important that Russia be told authoritatively that if they are to have the good will and financial support of this country, they must compose their internal differences and not make a separate peace at this time. These men thought that a prominent Jew, a business man, a labor leader and an educator should compose the commission.[6]

He also suggested a few names beginning with Straus, Willard Straight, Samuel Gompers, and Benjamin Wheeler, and also stressed that it would be an opportunity to include a leading Republican, citing a speech delivered the previous night by Elihu Root calling on all Republicans to support the president's war policies.[7] It is, of course, quite possible that Straus was behind this French initiative, too, since he was seeing Lauzanne socially and discussing political matters with him at the time.[8]

Engrossed in other business, Washington moved slowly to compose the commission. Perhaps this was only in the nature of American foreign policy: if the situation is confused and murky, wait for it to clear. But the idea of a small,

5. Kennan diary, 9 and 10 April 1917, box 14, Kennan Papers, MD, LC.
6. House to Wilson, 10 April 1917, *PWW* 42:30.
7. Ibid.
8. Oscar Straus, *Under Four Administrations from Cleveland to Taft: Recollections of Oscar S. Straus* (Boston: Houghton Mifflin, 1922), 390–91. Unfortunately, Straus writes nothing about the commission itself.

representative delegation for Russia had clearly emerged. On 12 April, Lansing suggested John R. Mott, as a religious leader (YMCA executive secretary) known in Russia, with Cyrus McCormick and financier Samuel Bertron to represent business interests. He thought it was not wise to send a Jew and vetoed Straight. He assumed Charles Crane, who was already on his way to Russia, would be included.[9] After a week, Wilson followed Lansing's advice and decided on Root, Mott, Crane, McCormick, and Bertron and asked Lansing to consult with Root about heading the commission. Still intending to have a Jewish representative, he named Eugene Meyer Jr. of New York; for a railroad specialist, he chose John F. Stevens of the New York Central.[10] All were from either New York or Chicago.

Root was already an elder statesman with a stellar career in international law behind him. He had considerable political experience as secretary of state under Theodore Roosevelt and subsequently as a senator from New York. He was known as an excellent public speaker, a prerequisite for the job. His appointment to head the commission was backed by members of Wilson's inner circle, particularly Secretary McAdoo, but was not unopposed, since some voices supported Roosevelt, an old warrior much better known in Russia.[11] As soon as rumors circulated of his appointment, Rabbi Stephen Wise wrote Wilson:

> Whatever be Mr. Root's repute as a lawyer, he stands out before the American people as the most eminent and powerful representative of those theories of government and political life to which you as the leader of the American democracy are opposed. It would seem to me that much of the great service which you have rendered the Russian people by your heartening reference in the Message of April 2nd would be lost if Mr. Root should be singled out as the chief representative of the American government and American opinion in the matter of co-operating with the Russian people as one of our Allies in the battle for the security of democratic peoples.[12]

9. Lansing to Wilson, 12 April 1917, *PWW* 42:45. Crane later claimed to have urged the selection of Mott. Extract of letter of Crane's, dated 27 June 1917, f. 243, box 13, Mott Papers, DSA.

10. Wilson to Lansing, 19 April 1917, *PWW* 42:95.

11. McAdoo to Wilson, 17 April 1917, *PWW* 42:80.

12. Wise to Wilson, *PWW* 42:124. Years later, Stanley Washburn was of the opinion that Wilson sent Root to Russia to discredit him. Washburn to Thomas Lamont (n.d.) in answer to Lamont to Washburn, 26 March 1946, Root file, box 3, Washburn Papers, MinnHS.

In any event, the president had already come to a decision, and Root consented the night before (at a dinner party for British foreign secretary Arthur Balfour) he received Wise's critique.[13]

According to Florence Harriman, prominent Washington socialite and political arranger, the designation of Root was very unpopular in the capital. She was asked to intercede directly with House and Root to obtain his withdrawal and replacement by Roosevelt. "It would pacify the Colonel and give him the sense of active service abroad; and the Russians . . . would dote on the honor of having our foremost citizen representing America amongst them."[14] With Roosevelt as head, it certainly would have been a different mission. John Hays Hammond was another Washington insider who urged Roosevelt's selection. According to him, when House suggested this to the president, he blew up. "It was not that he failed to recognize the force of my argument; it was because of the pettiness he [Wilson] often showed in treatment of those who had previously offended him. The Root Commission was a failure."[15]

On the other end of the political spectrum and in consideration of the looming role of socialist groups in the new Russia, the choice of a pro-war, not-so-radical socialist was not so easy. After first considering William English Walling, who had been to Russia several years before, the president selected Charles Edward Russell, journalist and twice a candidate for governor of New York on the Socialist Party ticket.[16] Russell was an outspoken critic of the majority of his party's leadership that opposed the war. To represent American labor, after Gompers was rejected for his antisocialist stance, was the elderly James Duncan, vice president of the American Federation of Labor.

Military representatives had, of course, to be included—Army Chief of Staff Hugh Scott and Vice Admiral James Glennon—making a total of nine members. General Scott was an appointment of convenience, since he was considered too old-fashioned to retain his post in a wartime administration. Glennon, like Scott, knew nothing of Russia but was much respected for his knowledge of ordinance and as commandant of the Washington Navy Yard. At least he was handy and not out to sea.[17] The railroad expert was dropped from the political commission in favor of sending a separate "technical commission" to be headed

13. Thomas W. Brahany Diary, 24 April 1917, *PWW* 42:126.

14. Harriman, diary, 6 May 1917, in *From Pinafores to Politics* (New York: Henry Holt, 1923), 224.

15. John Hays Hammond, *The Autobiography of John Hays Hammond* (New York: Farrar and Rinehart, 1935), 667.

16. William B. Wilson to Wilson, 30 April 1917, *PWW* 42:165-66.

17. Weeks, *An American Naval Diplomat in Revolutionary Russia*, 114-15.

by Stevens. Samuel Harper, discouraging his own full membership on the commission in order to retain a "free hand" and to complete unfinished business at home, agreed to be an unofficial interpreter and guide in Petrograd.[18]

After much discussion no Jew was included, partly because of disagreement among various factions about who should be chosen. Columbia University professor Gottheil thought, for example, that Meyer would be perceived as representing German-Jewish money interests. He also claimed that Crane had advised Jews to lie low on the Russian situation.[19] Samuel Harper agreed and wondered why the New York Jews did not "form societies of Friends of German Freedom and let Russia alone."[20] Others of various denominations scrambled to be chosen, including a son of Leo Tolstoy, who wanted to go as an interpreter.[21] Final arrangements were left to Breckinridge Long, who had many other chores to perform in a meagerly staffed State Department that was now facing a whole range of international problems.[22]

The "Root mission" to Russia, though rather elderly, was distinguished, thoroughly Anglo-Saxon Christian, and conservative, but it included one definite "expert" on Russia (Crane) and two people who could claim prior knowledge (McCormick and Mott). All three of these had fairly extensive contacts with Harper. One other advantage, whether planned or not, was that several members—Crane, Bertron, Mott, and McCormick—were known to Ambassador Francis.[23] None of the mission members, however, had a real understanding of the Russian economic and military situation in May 1917. Nor were they allowed much opportunity to become better informed on the journey, since Crane was already in Russia, and Harper hoped to speed his own arrival on the Russian scene by going separately via the Atlantic route.

18. Harper to Roger Williams, 6 May 1917 (confidential), f. 3, box 4, Harper Papers, UC. Harper apparently also believed that he would be better prepared to assist in Russia if he kept his distance and remained able to speak independently. "I like to stay here [Chicago] where I have time to reflect over each bit of news, and then give my conclusions with careful thought behind them. This is how I managed to date to avoid any real mistake." To Gottheil, 6 May 1917, ibid.

19. Gottheil to Harper, 3 May 1917, f. 3, box 4, Harper Papers, UC. He also thought Root was "a plutocrat, the worst possible choice."

20. Harper to Gottheil, 6 May 1917, f. 3, box 4, Harper Papers, UC.

21. Leo Tolstoy Jr., to Root, 1 May 1917, box 136, Root Papers, MD, LC; and Root to Wilson, 3 May 1917, *PWW* 42:216.

22. Long diary, 10–13 May 1917, box 1, Long Papers, MD, LC.

23. Francis to Willoughby Smith (consul in Tiflis), 14 May 1917 (personal and confidential), reel 3, Francis Papers, MoHS. McCormick's calling card read "Envoy Extraordinary of the United States of America on Special Mission." Envelope of miscellany, 9C, McCormick Papers, SHSW.

George Kennan counseled those who urged his inclusion that he could not go because of age and health, but he was not sanguine about the mission.[24] To a friend he warned about Crane's optimism reflected in published cables: "I don't share his optimistic views & nobody could who had ever made a study of Russian psychology & Russian history." "The country [meaning Russia]," Kennan wrote, "is full of idealists, pacifists, socialists & half-baked reformers, who all think that the nation can be saved & made prosperous & happy only though the adoption of their visionary & impracticable schemes."[25] Kennan was not alone in passing from initial euphoria about the revolution to wary watchfulness, even disillusionment.

Harper on Russia

Before leaving, Harper consulted individually with McCormick, Mott, and Root and recommended reading material, while Stanley Washburn briefed Bertron.[26] None of the members were provided with more than vague instructions about advancing American cooperation with the Provisional Government, promoting democracy, and encouraging military efforts. Theoretically, Crane, on the ground in Russia ahead of the commission, would be in a position to guide the members on arrival, but it was early May by the time the commission was fully constituted and over a month had passed since the idea was first broached.

In contrast to Kennan, Harper put up a brave front of optimism and encouragement but felt handicapped owing to a series of negative reports coming from Russia. To Walling he wrote, "It is discouraging to find America so pessimistic over the Russian situation. But I believe one explanation is that Russia is trying an experiment in real democracy, and many of our good Americans are afraid of real democracy."[27] By this he apparently had in mind the American tendency to be alarmed about unruly street demonstrations. And to the editor of the *Christian Science Monitor* he complained that they say in Washington, "Oh yes, Harper is an optimist on the Russian situation, just as though I had smallpox or something." But then, lamenting the delay in extending credit to Russia, he betrayed another kind of pessimism: "We are

24. Draft letter to Oscar Straus, 27 May 1917, box 8, Kennan Papers, MD, LC.
25. To Fairchild, 16 May 1917, ibid.
26. Washburn to Root, 5 May 1917, apologizing for inability to see Root, box 136, Root Papers, MD, LC.
27. 10 May 1917, f. 4, box 4, Harper Papers, UC.

Moscow's Okhotnaia Riad (Hunter's Row), a major street (during Soviet days Prospect Marx), with Metropole Hotel on right and the Maly Theatre on left. At the end of the street is Lubianka Square, site of the imperial and later Soviet police headquarters, and also where the American consul general's office was located, courtesy of the National Archives

skeptical about Russia. I wonder if we are not contributing to whatever instability there is over there, by our attitude?"[28]

He thought the problem was that the press was finding difficulty getting real information, so the publication of rumors filled the gaps.[29] A cable from his old friend Kalamatiano bolstered his optimism: "It does not try to paint things too brightly. But it shows clearly that eventually everything will turn out all right. . . . What they needed was our confidence. There was every ground for extending to them moral and material support."[30] On Harper's optimistic side, there was an exaggerated belief that just showing the American flag could achieve miracles.

28. Harper to Frederick Dixon, 12 May 1917, f. 5, box 4, Harper Papers, UC. Harper also objected to a *Chicago Tribune* editorial. "Sam Harper Gets Peevish Again," clipping from *Tribune*, 16 May 1917, f. 6, ibid.
29. To Arthur Bullard, 21 May 1917, f. 6, ibid.
30. To Postnikov, 22 May 1917, f. 7, box 4, Harper Papers, UC.

The Root Mission Departs

Further delays ensued in processing aides and staff and by deciding to send the commission the long way—across America leisurely by train, then by ship to Vladivostok, and by the Trans-Siberian Railroad to Petrograd. Chief among the list of "assistants" to the mission were Colonel T. Bentley Mott, who had served as military attaché in Russia during the Russo-Japanese War; Scott's personal aide-de-camp, Colonel R. E. L. Michie; Colonel William V. Judson, also a veteran observer of the Russo-Japanese War; Lieutenant Alva Bernhard as aide to Glennon; and Navy Surgeon Lieutenant Commander Holton Curl as tour physician. At least ten more went as clerks, orderlies, and valets.[31]

According to Bentley Mott, half the congressional secretaries in Washington wanted to join the expedition. Although serving officially as aide to Scott, Mott was chosen by Root to act as his personal troubleshooter. When the delays in Washington seemed unreasonable, he instructed Mott, "I wish you would go over to the State Department and see if you can get this expedition started. Nobody seems to be doing anything about it and if we are going every day is precious."[32] In the meantime Root did some homework, meeting with George Kennan on the first of May for an hour and a half and with Russian publicists Arkady Sack and Boris Shatsky.[33]

The decision to take the longer Pacific passage was based on its greater safety and a belief that arrival in Petrograd after crossing much of the country would impress their hosts. To the regret of most members, a vintage Spanish-American War cruiser, the *Buffalo*, virtually a tramp steamer, was assigned to carry them through the middle lap. Finally, on 15 May a train carrying the Root party of thirty departed Washington with Harper again available for consultation as far as Chicago.[34] Following the Northern Pacific route to Seattle, the commission sailed on 20 May. After a stormy, rough voyage, on 3 June the *Buffalo* dropped anchor in Vladivostok harbor.

Greeting the commission were Attaché E. Francis Riggs, Frank Golder, who was in Russia to survey archives and now on embassy interpreting assignment, Eugene Prince as another interpreter, "Major" Stanley Washburn, and a few

31. "Personnel of Special Diplomatic Mission of the United States of America," box 192, Root Papers, MD, LC.
32. T. Bentley Mott, *Twenty Years as Military Attaché* (New York: Oxford University Press, 1937), 193.
33. Kennan diary, 1 May 1917, box 14, Kennan Papers, MD, LC; Sack to Harper, 5 May 1917, f. 3, box 4, Harper Papers, UC.
34. Cyrus McCormick traveled separately on a brief visit to the family summer home in Pasadena before joining the group in Seattle.

members of the railroad commission that had managed to arrive first.[35] Russell was impressed by the political and economic chaos that greeted them, noting especially the supplies from the United States piled all around in streets, docks, and along railroad tracks in general disorder. Because of the political uncertainty (due to a hostile demonstration arranged by some returned Russian exiles from America who arrived ahead of them), the mission's sojourn in the city was as brief as possible, with Washburn whisking them off to a secluded train.[36]

During the ocean journey Root reluctantly agreed to pressure from McCormick to hold daily discussion sessions, and Bentley Mott organized exercise routines.[37] While Scott was seasick and thus confined to his cabin most of the time (fully clothed and comatose, according to Russell),[38] the others read, talked, and recorded their thoughts in diaries, the most complete, that survives at least, being Russell's. The rail excursion across Siberia was leisurely and pleasant; at Harbin in Manchuria, they transferred to the nine-car imperial blue train (Nicholas II's favorite) and traveled in luxury the rest of the way to Petrograd, a land trip of over 5,000 miles. Riggs reported, "There is a good red wine (Crimean) aboard which Admiral Glennon and I are putting out a [sic] sight at a rapid rate."[39] At least they learned something about former imperial taste and the deteriorating condition of the country's railroads, and McCormick had an opportunity to confer with Harvester agents along the way for more bad news.[40] At Ekaterinburg, Basil Miles and Sheldon Whitehouse of the embassy met the mission and escorted it the remainder of the way through Vologda to Petrograd, bypassing Moscow.

35. Golder, reflecting on the trip across Russia, wrote, "Things are in a terrible mess and I am sure the Russian people would somehow work out their salvation if the war were only out of the way." He found Vladivostok surprisingly bountiful, however, and stocked up on supplies to take back to Petrograd. To Henrietta Eliot, 31 May 1917, box 12, Golder Papers, HIA.

In addition to Russian speakers Prince, Golder, and Washburn, the American missions would use the services of Harper and Alexander Gumberg. Prince, Golder, and Gumberg were Russian-born but resident in the United States for several years. Russell to Gumberg, thanking him for his services, 9 July 1917, f. 3, box 1, Gumberg Papers, SHSW; and Francis to Stevens, 17 May 1917, reel 3, Francis Papers, MoHS, explaining that Golder was not just an interpreter but a professor of history at Washington State College in Pullman.

36. Russell Notebooks, 3 June 1917, box 25, Russell Papers, MD, LC.

37. Hopkins, *John R. Mott*, 480–81.

38. Russell diary, 23 May 1917, box 25, Russell Papers, MD, LC.

39. Riggs to Jane Riggs, 9 June 1917, box 124, Riggs Family Papers, MD, LC. Judson reported that the dining car was where Nicholas II signed his abdication. To Mrs. Judson, 5 June 1917, Judson Papers (one file), Newberry Library.

40. "Memorandum of Interviews," Special Diplomatic Mission of USA to Russia, box 113, McCormick Papers 2C, SHSW. McCormick compared the trip on the Trans-Siberian to an ocean voyage, where

The Russian Embassy

The reduced staff of the Russian embassy in Washington handled the changed situation and increased activity as best it could. They were obviously hampered after mid-April in not having an ambassador. Upon Bakhmetev's sudden resignation, Onou served as chargé d'affaires without an experienced first secretary and did what he could to arrange the Russian receptions of the Root and Stevens delegations. The main problem was in keeping up with the revolutionary times in Russia, not easy for professionals accustomed to dealing with a traditional, unchanging bureaucratic structure.

One task, public information, was pursued with new energy and skill, thanks to the arrival in March of Boris Shatsky, actually sent in February before the revolution. Hampered by conflicting and irregular communications from Russia, the New York office of the Russian Information Bureau nevertheless underwent a major improvement over what had existed before. Harper naturally considered its new goal of advancing the development of Russian departments in universities farsighted and supported the Russian plan to open a second office in Chicago.[41]

Bakhmetev had already assigned an energetic assistant, Arkady Sack (Zak), to assist Shatsky.[42] Ironically, these agents of the former tsarist government found their chief task to be explaining and defending the revolution, but they did so fairly effectively. Because of the changed situation in Russia and the indefinite status of Bakhmetev, Shatsky and Sack faced a problem in recruiting prominent Americans to serve as honorary advisers and to give the publicity effort more clout. Cyrus McCormick, for one, urged caution while soliciting the advice of others.[43] Fortunately for the continuity of Russian public information in the

---

day after day passes with the same flat plains and low, sloping hills, the same vast distances, the same groups of low, wooden buildings huddled together like a flock of sheep preparing to withstand a coming storm; the same kind of stations, the same crowds of people, the same endless groups of soldiers—this experience makes the journey seem much more than ten days.

He also quoted Root as observing, "At last we have reached the country described in the hymn 'Where congregations ne'er break up / And Sabbaths have no end.'" "Vladivostok, June 3, to Petrograd, June 13," undated memorandum, enclosed in McCormick to Legge, 26 June 1917, 2C, box 113, McCormick Papers, SHSW.

41. Harper to Clarence Meader (University of Michigan), 5 April 1917, f. 13, box 3, Harper Papers, UC.

42. Bakhmetev to Miliukov, 16 and 21 March 1917 (nos. 91 and 104), f. 133, op. 470, d. 61; Harper to Sack, 4 April 1917, f. 13, box 3, Harper Papers, UC.

43. Memorandum on Russian Information Bureau, 10 May 1017, box 115, 2C, McCormick Papers, SHSW.

United States, Shatsky was not included in the Root mission as Onou had urged and Harper had strongly opposed.[44] He continued to direct his attention to correcting what he characterized as one-sided, incomplete, and negative reports sent from Russia by American correspondents.[45]

Still, the new Russian government was considerably hampered by its low-level presence and visibility in Washington and was omitted from important Allied conferences. Constantine Nabokov, Russian chargé in London, lamented "the pitiful state of our present representation in America" in a report to Foreign Minister Miliukov:

> I deem it my duty not to conceal from you that the absence at the present moment of an energetic chief at the head of the embassy, one acquainted with the situation, capable of directing the press, and informed of the political and financial relationship between Russia, America, and England, impressed the Americans themselves as a misfortune that should be remedied as soon as possible.[46]

A new ambassador was soon on his way.

Russian Émigrés

Another serious and more complicated problem for the Russian diplomats and consular agent in America was handling the requests of Russian émigré exiles to return home. Many were Jewish socialists or anarchists living in New York City on the Lower East Side, who did not have the means to pay for passage. They had been among tsarist Russia's most vocal opponents but were unhappy with their existence in America and anxious to seize an opportunity to participate in a real revolution. The Provisional Government, under pressure from the Petrograd Soviet, agreed to welcome any such "victims" of tsarist oppression and to authorize funds to cover travel expenses. Following these instructions, Onou borrowed $150,000 from National City Bank at 6 percent interest at the end of April.

---

44. Onou to Miliukov, 1 May 1917 (no. 213), f. 133, op. 470, d. 61, AVPR; Harper to Richard Crane, 6 May 1917, f. 4, box 4, Harper Papers, UC. To Harper Shatsky was "a boot-licker," "a Jew," and simply "second rate."
45. Onou to Tereshchenko, 21 May 1917 (no. 279), f. 133, op. 47, d. 61, AVPR.
46. Nabokov to Miliukov, 2 May 1917, in *The Russian Provisional Government 1917: Documents*, ed. Robert Browder and Alexander Kerensky (Stanford, Calif.: Stanford University Press, 1961) 2:1053–54.

Within two weeks it had been expended, and he requested another $300,000.[47] The bulk of the processing of these applications naturally fell to the consul general's office in New York, creating additional coordination problems.

After Samuel Harper expressed concern about the character of some of these expatriates, Onou assured him that Petrograd was being consulted.[48] The Russian consular offices in Chicago, Pittsburgh, and San Francisco also faced complex problems in deciding who legitimately should be allowed passports and funds to leave the United States. Guidelines from Petrograd proved to be vague and contradictory, at first lenient (in the immediate postrevolutionary euphoria), then tighter (when Miliukov sensed the dangers of easy access by all kinds of radicals), looser again in June (under Kerensky and Soviet pressure), and more difficult finally in August.[49] By that time even American officials were suspicious of possible draft-dodging and law-evading motives in leaving the country and concerned about the negative influences on the Russian situation of so many returning radical exiles.

The stream continued through September, however, occupying much of the time and resources of Consul General Mikhail Ustinov and Vice-Consul Evgenyi Omelchenko in New York.[50] Complications grew as some of the émigrés were alleged to be criminals fleeing persecution, who were now coming from such cities as Pittsburgh and Cleveland with vague evidence of Russian origins, while others were desirable specialists and physicians who demanded $300 each for passages.[51] Grigori Chirkov, the consul in Pittsburgh, complained that after so long with little to do, he was now swamped with paperwork and expenses as his district included all of Pennsylvania, New Jersey, Maryland, and Virginia.[52] The main problems for all of them were the conflicting directives from Petrograd and resulting protests within the immigrant communities.

---

47. Onou to Miliukov, 2 and 13 May 1917 (nos. 213 and 254), f. 133, op. 470, d. 61, AVPR. Some returning exiles also received funds from local American charitable organizations with funds earmarked for Russian refugee relief.

48. Harper to Onou, 1 May 1917, and Onou to Harper, 3 May 1917, f. 3, box 4, Harper Papers, UC.

49. Onou to Miliukov, 27 April 1917, f. 133, op. 470, d. 61, AVPR.

50. Bakhmeteff to Ustinov, 30 July and 17 August 1917, f. 170, op. 512/5, d. 34/31, AVPR.

51. Ustinov to Bakhmeteff, 10 August 1917, f. 170, op. 512/5, d. 34/35; Bakhmeteff to Tereshchenko, f. 170, op. 512/5, d. 34/36, AVPR. A list compiled in December included 100 dentists, 50 doctors, 50 pharmacists, 50 engineers, 30 nurses, and 60 other medical specialists. Bakhmeteff to Tereshchenko, f. 133, op. 470, d. 61, AVPR.

52. Series of letters from Chirkov to Omel'chenko for August and September in f. 170, op. 512/5, d. 34/41, AVPR.

Supplies for Russia

Although the embassy suddenly found easy credit in the United States due to the expectation of major loans from the new ally, the American government was again in no hurry to bolster Russia. Miliukov in Petrograd kept promising publicly that loans were coming. Finally, with pressure from Root and McCormick, who wanted to ensure a good landing in Russia,[53] the United States Treasury extended a credit line of $100 million to Russia on 16 May, too late to give Miliukov some additional credence. Immediately, a contract for 1 million rifles was under negotiation with Remington.[54] The publicity given to this advance also helped speed cargoes of goods waiting in American ports. Onou reported on 23 May that in New York alone 100,000 tons of rails (for the new Petrograd-Murmansk line), 30,000 tons of agricultural machines, and 70,000 tons of munitions were released to Grace Line ships destined for Arctic ports.[55]

Shippers and suppliers were counting on using the new port of Murmansk on the Kola Peninsula that was open year-round, thanks to the Gulf Stream, and the services of the new 900-mile railroad connecting it with Petrograd. James Wood Colt traveled over the line in June, however, and found it still far from satisfactory. "[Murmansk] has great possibilities but it is just commenced and everything is in confusion." There were no warehouses, and hay and flour were piled outside, exposed to the weather.[56]

New money and the facilitating of orders demanded much time and energy of embassy and consular personnel. Many previous contracts had to be renegotiated because of the rapid depreciation of the ruble, which by mid-May was down to twenty-six to the dollar (prewar two rubles = one dollar).[57] And fulfilling them was further delayed by the highest priority being placed on meeting America's

53. "Its [Russia's] pressing need is financial assistance. Could not this, to some extent be extended without awaiting for arrival of commission? If no financial aid is extended before Commission arrives there will be a long period of uncertainty and discouragement in Russia. There is double danger in delay." McCormick telegram copy to Wilson, 12 May 1917, box 114, 2C, McCormick Papers, SHSW.

54. Three separate dispatches, dated 16 May (265, 267, 268), f. 170, op. 512/5, d. 34/41, AVPR. Harper credits Cyrus McCormick with influencing the announcement, and he may have been behind McCormick. Harper to Roger Williams, 17 May, f. 6, box 4, Harper Papers, UC.

55. To Tereshchenko, 23 May (285), f. 133, op. 470, d. 61, AVPR.

56. Diary, 25 June 1917, f. 4, box 1, James Wood Colt Papers, Manuscript Division, University of Rochester, Rush-Rhees Library.

57. Onu to Miliukov, 11 May 1917, ibid.

greatly expanded military requirements and, of course, the increased reliance of the major Western Allies on supplies from the United States. Russian bureaucratic methods certainly did not help the situation. By 1 September 1917, the embassy employed 1,248 people for supply work alone.[58]

American Charity

The "democratic" revolution in Russia and American entry into the war inspired an increase in other assistance, most of it flowing from a variety of new and old charitable organizations in the United States to agencies in Russia, especially to the Russian Red Cross. Both the American Red Cross and the YMCA planned for a much greater presence in Russia, but this expansion also took time to organize and to arrange transportation, and it also was limited by pressure for much more service on the Western Front.

Dr. (Colonel) Eugene Hurd, after a short leave home, returned in April to his field hospital behind the front lines in Ukraine. Although technically under the administration of the Russian Red Cross, Hurd made certain that the hospital had the best American Red Cross supplies. Medical needs slackened in 1917, at least until July, though the revolution intruded in the form of soldiers' committees, confusion, and reduced discipline.[59] Hurd's operations, reported to have reached 6,500 patients by July, fared better than most thanks to his ability to build up a thriving medical community with log infirmaries and ample food supplies that included the raising of 2,000 pigs, several cows for fresh milk and meat, chickens, geese, and even turkeys for an anticipated Thanksgiving dinner.[60]

The hospital sponsored by the American colony in the capital (officially Petrograd City Lazaret No. 137) also reduced its operations in 1917 because many of its patients joined the revolutionary activities or simply deserted and went home, and with combat practically ceased, at least in the Petrograd region, few new ones appeared. One notable new enterprise, however, was the American

58. Bakhmeteff to Lansing, 7 January 1921, f. State Department (4), box 21, Bakhmeteff Papers, BA, CU. Bakhmeteff was justifying the need for continued operations after 1917.

59. For an extended, detailed description of the scene—with pictures—by a visiting reporter, see Harper, *Runaway Russia*, 79–161.

60. Donald Thompson reported having his best meals there since leaving Topeka, Kansas. To his wife, 7 June 1917, in *Donald Thompson in Russia*, 242–43; Mott to his wife, Leila, 9 July 1917, f. 1838, Mott Papers, DSA.

Ambulance in Russia, formed by Dr. Philip Newton with assistance from American agencies, especially the Red Cross, but it retained a vague independence under its own executive committee.[61]

The "corps" consisted of 24 six-cylinder Studebaker ambulances, 3 transport trucks, 2 passenger cars, 1 gasoline tank truck, 1 motor repair shop, and 1 small field hospital. Designed to serve a Russian infantry division in the field, the corps was manned by Newton and about seventy-five Russian personnel.[62] It was not fully assembled until mid-July, however, and when Newton was assigned to a new Red Cross commission, he left for Washington to straighten matters out.[63] Its subsequent deployment is unknown.

Postrevolutionary Russia

In some ways the end of the Romanov dynasty changed very little in Russia in regard to official policy. Despite the formation of a new cabinet, considerable continuity existed in the staffs of the new ministries. Shortages, lines, and price and wage inflation continued, abated slightly by the arrival of warmer weather and a slackening of demand for fuel. Few in government seemed to know how to deal with the conditions that had provoked the revolution in the first place. At least the immediate imperial family, under protective custody, could no longer be the chief target of rumors and complaints.

The euphoria and general harmony that greeted the transition to a new, supposedly democratic Russia was short-lived, as news of the more violent events in certain quarters, especially within naval units at Kronstadt and Helsingfors, circulated in the rest of the country in late March. McCully, who was acquainted with many of the officer victims, was especially dismayed by the failure of the Provisional Government to regain full control of the Baltic Fleet and to punish those guilty of murder and torture of officers. Even worse, in American eyes, was that sailors and soldiers in the Petrograd region were devoting most of their

---

61. The committee was chaired by Hamilton Fish Jr. and included Nicholas Murray Butler, Robert McCormick, former ambassadors to Russia George Meyer and John Riddle, Alton Parker, Philip Lydig, Theodore Roosevelt Jr., and Willard Straight. Letterhead, Newton to Francis, 24 August 1917, reel 3, Francis Papers, MoHS.

62. Newton to Francis for Surgeon General, 21 May 1917, AE Russia, DPR 320, RG 84, NA.

63. Francis to Tereshchenko, 10 July 1917, seeking release of equipment from Customs, and Newton to Francis, 23 August 1917, ibid.

time to political matters in various committee and soviet meetings, with military capability virtually disappearing.[64]

Maintaining an excellent record of objective reporting of the Russian scene, Lieutenant Riggs observed from the Russian military headquarters on 11 April that "the city of Petrograd is quiet but the Provisional Government is anything but firmly in the saddle."[65] Americans, now naturally more interested in Russia's fighting capability, were especially concerned about the rapidly disintegrating transportation system and the dim outlook for any immediate improvement.

Worried about reports from Russia, Lansing cabled Francis to do his best to bolster the Provisional Government, to use the carrot-and-stick approach: "If new government can maintain order and successfully prosecute the war, it is impossible to overestimate the enthusiastic friendship that will be engendered in this country, opening up tremendous possibilities for Russian development after the war."[66] By most accounts, Francis was handling the new demands of his position successfully. He seemed to have developed a knack for sailing through the Russian political storms and keeping his staff of bright young eastern men in line while at the same time giving them some slack. Judson, who was not one of them, described Francis as "a typical old Southern politician with plenty of money, and much homely wisdom. He is getting along well with the Russians."[67]

His friends and advisers, the Corses, returned to their business in Russia as quickly as possible but by the safer Siberian route. On the long train journey they dined regularly with Walter and Pauline Crosley. Captain Crosley was on his way to relieve McCully as naval attaché. Signs of a different Russia were quickly apparent in the difficulty they had getting porters to handle baggage and in the surly attitude of train attendants. They felt constantly threatened by roving bands of drunken soldiers who took over the corridors and toilets and had to be bribed to allow passage.[68]

Arriving in Petrograd on 6 May, Corse was quite shocked to find totally new circumstances:

64. McCully report, 20 May 1917, AE Russia, DPR 325, RG 84, NA; "Personal Accounts of Persons Taking Part in the Revolution," Office of Naval Intelligence report, 24 April 1917, f. 6497-15, RG 165, NA.
65. Riggs to Jane Riggs (his aunt), 11 April 1917, box 124, Riggs Family Papers, MD, LC.
66. Lansing to Francis, 21 April 1917, f. 138, op. 467, d. 651/673, AVPR. This was another intercepted cable with awkward phrasing due to retranslation of Russian translation.
67. To his wife, 12 July 1917, Judson Papers, Newberry Library.
68. Pauline S. Crosley, *Intimate Letters from Petrograd* (New York: Dutton, 1920), 1-12.

Ambassador Francis, J. Butler Wright, and valet-chauffeur Philip Jordan in the Ford, Petrograd, 2 June 1917, courtesy of the Francis Papers, Missouri Historical Society

Immediately the old regime was thrown down and the new order of things established here, the laborers, who possessed a complete organization, came forward with insistent and excessive demands, and the labor organizations caught up all office employees and clerks not only in Petrograd, but the movement seems to have spread throughout Russia. Notwithstanding that some of the strongest and best known men in Russia were placed at the head of the Government, the real power has remained with the so-called Council of Laborers and Soldiers. Up to the present all matters of Government, and the direction of the army has been in the hands of this Council and the Ministers have so far been obliged to take orders from them.[69]

He felt forced to submit to demands for substantial salary increases for the fifty-three office employees of New York Life, along with a reduction of the workday to six hours, and faced additional costs of three months extra wages and a scheme of insurance. Moreover, three-quarters of the staff were "hysterical young women upon whom we have no personal hold," who had replaced the men conscripted for the army.[70]

69. Corse to Walker Buckner (2nd Vice President, New York Life Insurance Company), 31 May 1917, copy in f. Dept. of Commerce, box 115, 2C, McCormick Papers, SHSW.
70. Ibid.

A onetime critic of the ambassador, Corse now admitted, "The Governor, under present democratic conditions finds himself very much at home. His counsel is widely sought and I must say he has surprised us all by the apparent grasp which he has on the movement and influence which he has achieved in Government spheres. We pronounce him the right man in the right place."[71]

Among Francis's accomplishments was a close friendship with Minister of Foreign Affairs Tereshchenko, with whom he conferred on a daily basis either directly or by telephone and was thus kept confidentially informed.[72] He was, however, restricted in another way after the United States entered the war, and that was by the necessity of conferring with his diplomatic colleagues from the other Allied embassies on all important matters, and this meant bowing to the overdignified British dean of the colony, George Buchanan.[73]

Another problem Americans faced was the dual power structure of Provisional Government and Soviet assemblies as a result of the revolution. Corse advised Harper to "keep in mind that the Council of Laborers and Soldiers Deputies are in the ascendant and that most extreme socialistic ideas are struggling for supremacy." He thought that the government was caught in the middle with a return to the former administration no alternative.[74] "A Government such as the present, working by moral suasion, cannot, of course, do anything dramatic. Perhaps after all there is wisdom in adopting that plan as the old system of pouring lead into disorderly mobs, although temporarily effective, left behind it unforgettable hatreds."[75]

But Americans still had ample opportunity for digressions. The Russian opera and ballet continued to dazzle American visitors with regular performances, but now the royal box was usually occupied by sailors and soldiers, and the orchestra was frequently required to play the "Marseillaise" before performances. The better restaurants were still open, though with fewer selections and deteriorating service. The embassy was able to obtain a reserve of food supplies for the

---

71. Corse to Harper, 12 June 1917, f. 8, box 4, Harper Papers, UC.
72. Francis, *Russia from the American Embassy*, 118-19.
73. Francis to son Perry, 25 September 1917, reel 4, Francis Papers, MoHS, regarding a rumor that the Provisional Government would move the capital to Moscow and whether the embassy would follow.
74. Corse to Harper, 12 June 1917, 1-8, box 4, Harper Papers, UC.
75. Ibid. Corse obviously did not realize Harper was on his way to Petrograd. About the same time, Kalamatiano wrote Harper, "When will you be in Russia again? Stirring times we are having." 21 June 1917, f. 8, box 4, Harper Papers, UC.

usual, perhaps increased, dinner parties, with corn bread and biscuits made by Philip Jordan (Francis's valet-cook) especially appreciated by the American colony.[76]

Nevertheless, a cloud of depression hung over the land. Frank Golder, who was in the middle of things as an interpreter for the Stevens mission, by mid-June was sounding a somber note: "The situation here is most pitiful and heartbreaking; for so many years the people have been kept in bondage and fear and as soon as that was removed they have gone to pieces. They (a great many at least) have no conception of liberty. . . . No one knows whether we have an army or a mob."[77]

The role of the American diplomats and consuls became especially onerous in trying to decipher the course of events, but also with the arrival of more Americans on the scene under YMCA and Red Cross auspices, and especially the return of many political exiles who would do their best to negate the official objectives of stabilizing the Provisional Government through their radical and revolutionary activities. A. C. Harte, returning from leave to his YMCA post in early June, wrote that he had traveled with around 500 of them, who were constantly complaining about America, speaking bitterly about their lives there, and looking forward to making a new Russia.[78]

Consul General Summers reported from Moscow that class interests were uppermost, that there was no desire to continue the war, that taxes were not being paid, and that no one even paid tram fares any more. The largest department store, the British-owned Muir and Mirrieless, had closed. At the International Harvester plant outside the city, "The workers threaten to run the plant themselves and the Manager is practically a figurehead. The same state of affairs exists at the factory of the Singer Sewing Machine Company. The plant is threatened with serious losses and may have to close down."[79]

The revolution had also let loose a torrent of grievances in the country as a whole against foreigners and those with economic or administrative authority. An American wife of a Baltic German nobleman wrote to Francis from Yalta that their house had been searched and ransacked by twenty-five armed sailors from Sevastopol, who had pointed revolvers at their heads.

76. Jordan to Mrs. Francis, 19 September 1917, reel 4, Francis Papers, MoHS.
77. To "K," 18 June 1917, f. 1, box 11 (Correspondence 1917–1926), Golder Papers, HIA.
78. Harte to Francis, 5 June 1917, AE Russia, DPR 325, RG 84, NA.
79. Summers to Francis, 5 June 1917, ibid.

The fact of having a Baltic Province name and being the wife of a man who had a Court position is of course enough to rouse suspicions at the present time. Added to that the fact that we speak English at home has seemed dangerous in the eyes of people who can not distinguish between that language and any other foreign tongue.[80]

She was seriously considering leaving Russia.

The Root Mission Arrives

Arriving in Petrograd on the afternoon of 13 June, the delegation headed by Elihu Root was met at the station by Ambassador Francis, Butler Wright, the military attachés, and several government ministers, including the new Russian foreign minister, Mikhail Tereshchenko, and then escorted grandly to the Winter Palace, where Root and Scott occupied what was represented as the private apartment of Catherine the Great. To their discomfort, the rest of the party was lodged at the other end of the palace, "five blocks" from the dining room.[81]

Although the members of the mission had plenty of time to adjust to a change in environment and their new roles on the monthlong journey, they seemed dazed, confused, and off balance from the beginning. Russell sensed "a new and tremendous power unleashed and what do we know of it?"[82] Scott thought, probably from a briefing by Riggs, that "the Russian army is almost dissolved, officers disappeared, millions of deserters."[83] They and the others probably did not have much spare time to read many of the fifteen lengthy reports furnished by the American consul in the city.[84] All could observe with their own eyes what

80. Anne Huene to Francis, 29 April 1917, AE Russia, DPR 315, RG 84, NA.
81. Notebooks, 13 June 1917, box 25, Russell Papers, MD, LC; Scott diary, 13 June, box 71, Scott Papers, MD, LC. Judson claimed the apartment was that of the mistress of Alexander III—possibly both. To Mrs. Judson, 24 June 1917, Judson Papers, Newberry Library.
82. Notebooks, 13 June 1917, box 25, Russell Papers, MD, LC. McCormick observed, "We find everything in a good deal of confusion here." To Legge, 26 June 1917, box 113, 2C, McCormick Papers, SHSW.
83. Diary, 13 June, box 71, Scott Papers, MD, LC. Washburn, probably unfairly, characterized Scott as "a man who knew very little about war, and he spent most of his time asleep." Washburn oral history, p. 112, CU.
84. North Winship to Stanley Washburn, 16 June 1917, Petrograd Consulate, DPR 3, RG 84, NA. One immediate impact of the mission was on the workload of the already overtaxed embassy staff. Wright noted, "The embassy work waits." Diary, 14 June 1917, box 2, Wright Papers, Princeton-Mudd.

"Billy" Judson noted simply: "The people stand in line for hours to buy bread, milk, and some other articles and the shops are out of nearly everything else. . . . There is plenty of food in Russia but they can't haul it to town."[85]

The next day after arrival, by dressing formally for a government reception, Russell thought they got off to a bad start: "I don't know why we cling to these fol-de-rols, nor why we refuse to see the plain sign that all this has passed away in Russia. The red flag floats from one end of the country to the other, and nothing but the red flag."[86] Indeed, the Russia they found was quite different from the one to which they were sent.

A New Provisional Government

Paul Miliukov, friend of America, liberal politician, and occasional professor of history, accepted the portfolio of minister of foreign affairs in the first cabinet that replaced the government of Nicholas II. Although Georgi Lvov, a leader of the central zemstvo (local government) organization, was designated chairman of the new council of ministers (cabinet), Miliukov, a long-acknowledged leader of the Constitutional Democratic (Kadet) Party,[87] was considered the real head of the government that was constituted mostly from the Progressive (opposition) Bloc of the Fourth Duma.

In one of his first acts as minister, Miliukov assured the Allies that Russia would uphold all its treaty arrangements, thus committing the country to continue the war and to receiving the spoils stipulated in various secret treaties, the main one being the annexation and control of the Straits of the Bosporus and the Dardanelles including the city of Constantinople, a long-cherished Russian expansionist goal. Dispensing with much of the stuffy formality of the imperial ministry, Miliukov retained most of its personnel, and in appearances, at least as far as foreign policy was concerned, very little change occurred as a result of the revolution.

The first and fundamental problem that Miliukov faced was that the Provisional Government was thrust into a position of sharing actual power with that of the Petrograd Soviet of Workers and Soldiers Deputies that had spontaneously risen during the chaos of the February Revolution on the precedent of the strike

85. Judson letter to his wife, 14 June 1917, Judson Papers, Newberry Library.
86. Notebooks, 14 June 1917, box 25, Russell Papers, MD, LC.
87. Those affiliated with the party that was most responsible for the formation of the first government were generally referred to as Kadets, after the pronunciation in Russian of its initials—"ka, de."

"council" created during a similar situation in the 1905 Revolution. The social-ist leadership of that body favored an early end to the war negotiated on the basis of "no annexations, no indemnities," quite different from the policy Miliukov proclaimed. This was one of a number of conflicts between the rather weak and inexperienced liberal establishment and the social populism generated in the street and voiced by the Soviet, the so-called dual power of the February–October 1917 period.

Miliukov was also handicapped by having insisted, much longer than was politically wise, on retaining the monarchy in the form of a regency to provide continuity with the old regime and to ward off expected counterrevolutionary efforts to restore the monarchy.[88] The fact that the latter failed to materialize pushed power to the left. Through his arrogant manner (political naïveté?) and inability or refusal to compromise sufficiently, he lost the support of some of the fellow Kadets in the cabinet who were drawn toward the idea of closer coopera-tion with the Soviet, a view argued by Alexander Kerensky, the one "token" Soviet representative in the cabinet (and also a former leader of the Progressive Bloc), in the interests of stabilizing government and society.

The result of this standoff and a division both within the forces of the Febru-ary Revolution and within the cabinet was the "April crisis" of 1917 and popular demonstrations, coinciding with May Day and during the following week, call-ing for the resignation of "Miliukov Dardanelskii" and "Down with the War."[89] After much angry debate in the cabinet, Miliukov resigned on 15 May, the day the Root mission sailed. His successor was Mikhail Tereshchenko, a tall and handsome but young and inexperienced Ukrainian millionaire (beet sugar) and, more important, a close friend of Kerensky's. His fluency in English facilitated contact with the American embassy. In the shake-up Guchkov also retired from the government as minister of war, to be replaced by the upwardly mobile Kerensky.

Petrograd consul North Winship summed up the situation on the eve of the Miliukov crisis:

> The power which the Temporary Government now administers is fictitious
> to a certain extent. . . . If this power is not handled with the greatest versa-

88. For this section, see Melissa Kirschke Stockdale, *Paul Miliukov and the Quest for a Liberal Russia, 1880–1918* (Ithaca, N. Y.: Cornell University Press, 1996), 250-57.

89. Ibid., 256. Miliukov himself, relying on the memoirs of the French ambassador, saw the turning point as a concert-meeting on 2 May at which he and Kerensky were the chief speakers. After Miliukov's successful patriotic appeal, the meeting was interrupted by an outburst by a Siberian exile against the war, followed by a hysterical, extremist speech by Kerensky that swayed the crowd. Miliukov, *Political Memoirs*, 446-47.

tility and tact it will pass to the leaders of the Council of Workers' and Soldiers' Deputies who openly prefer and personify the expectations of the majority of the lower classes.

Prophetically, he added:

If the Council ... openly assumed authority it could, after street fighting, control Petrograd, but all the provinces would not support it. Secession and civil war would follow, in all probability, degenerating into anarchy in many localities.[90]

Winship returned to the subject a week later:

The Consulate cannot forbear to mention here what it considers the gravest menace to Russia at the present time, namely the narrow partisanship, the bigotry and fanaticism of the socialists and the socialist press. They are Jesuitized in their casuistry, and supersensitivity to any criticism or opposition. ... The socialists wield enormous power, infinitely more than any other party or parties in Petrograd today, but have been, up to the present, unwilling to accept any responsibility for that power.[91]

And when Guchkov also resigned: "Gootchkoff not being versed in military and naval affairs was not sufficiently firm during the first days that the Temporary Govt. was in power, and the army and navy, where too much liberty cannot be given, got beyond his control."[92]

The new Provisional Government was a coalition of socialists and nonsocialists but definitely more aligned with the political temperament of the current leaders of the Soviets, who, however, were being challenged by the more radical voices of newly returned political exiles such as Lenin, Martov, and Trotsky. Embassy staff members were immediately aware of Lenin's arrival on the Russian scene on 21 April because of rumors that he had urged an attack on the embassy in protest of American arrests of radicals such as Alexander Berkman and Emma

90. Winship reports, 8 May 1917, U.S. Consul Petrograd, box 3, RG 84, NA.
91. Report to Lansing, 15 May 1917, ibid.
92. Ibid., 22 May. Actually, Guchkov had more military experience—going back to the Boer War—than political acumen. To his son in Secretary of State Lansing's office, Crane expressed even more pessimism: "At present ... there is a food crisis, a railroad crisis, a financial crisis, a ministerial crisis, a military crisis, and an industrial crisis. Money is losing its value and there is a buyer's panic. ... There is little continuous responsible government." To Richard Crane, 5 June 1917, part II, box 1, Richard Crane Papers, GU.

Goldman.[93] And at least one of them noticed immediately the impact of Lenin's arrival in creating a sharp division in the Petrograd Soviet over support for the Provisional Government.[94]

The departures of key makers of the February Revolution, Miliukov and Guchkov, was not so much a change as the rise of Kerensky and the great boost to the antiwar political forces, centered in many urban local soviets. The Bolsheviks, a term derived from their having a majority on a few key votes at the second congress of the Russian Social Democratic Workers Party that met abroad in 1903, were for years a relatively insignificant political faction. Vladimir Lenin (Ulianov) was soon the recognized leader of this elite group of Marxist revolutionaries, most of whom remained in foreign exile. After the beginning of the war, they were in the forefront of the Zimmerwald movement, organized in Switzerland to continue an international campaign to convert the war into revolution. The Bolsheviks, in contrast to the other social democratic faction, the Mensheviks, most of whom supported the Russian war effort, were able to take advantage of the growing disillusionment during the summer of 1917.

Mission Impossible

The Root mission, chosen to represent American diversity, was now mostly to the right of the Russian political spectrum, with some (Root and Scott at least) more in tune with the former imperial regime, a middle phalanx of pragmatic though antisocialist capitalists, and pro-war socialists. The middle ground, occupied by Charles Crane, had been thoroughly undermined by the dethronement of Miliukov.[95] Russell found him in Petrograd depressed and bewildered: "From

---

93. Francis to Lansing, 24 April 1917, f. 9, box 1, Lansing Papers, Princeton-Mudd. At Francis's urging Miliukov sent forty militia to defend the embassy. Wright commented succinctly, "Strain of it all!!" Diary, 24 April 1917, box 2, Wright Papers, Princeton-Mudd.

94. Winship report, 23 April 1917, U.S. Consul Petrograd, box 3, DPR, RG 84, NA. Perhaps influenced by Winship, Francis also credited Lenin with the new divisiveness and expressed a common view that German money was behind him. "I am inclined to the opinion that Lenin is in the pay of the German Government and this Government thinks so too." To son David, 8 May 1917, reel 3, Francis Papers, MoHS.

95. Crane wrote dejectedly from Moscow on 5 June:

> The men directing the revolution did a thorough job. Apparently a very different type is required for reconstruction. At any rate the revolutionists have lost control of the country and now there are no leaders. . . . Aside from the war, the world's greatest problem is here and peace may be forced in order to set Russia on a permanent new basis.

To Francis, 5 June 1917, AE Russia, DPR 310, RG 84, NA.

the beginning of the revolution Mr. Crane's hopes were centered upon Milliukoff [sic] and when that scholar was ejected Crane suffered a deep and genuine disappointment. He cannot see how a Russian government can be a success without Milliukoff, and the outlook to him is without a hope."[96]

Crane sought solace and probably found more depression in the company of old Russian friends. To his protégé, Elizabeth Hapgood, he wrote that "it seems entirely natural to be here and my place near the samovar seems as natural as tho' I had never left it."[97] Crane's pessimism spread among members of the mission, but they varied considerably in their opinions about what, if anything, America could do about Russia.

Hoping to find better prospects, Crane led John Mott, with Harper as interpreter, to Moscow to attend a special Orthodox Church Council and to find consolation in an apparent revival of religious spirit and amusement in the prominence given Father Alexander, a priest in Native American attire from San Francisco, who represented the Orthodox Church in Alaska.[98] The tall, distinguished, and athletic-appearing Mott made quite an impression on the assemblage, according to both Crane and Russian sources.[99] They also visited the philosopher-prince Evgenyi Trubetskoi and Princess Bobrinskaia and attended an Old Believer service. While they correctly sensed a budding religious renaissance in the country, the political mood was going in another direction.

In Petrograd, after the formal round of meetings and receptions, and Root's speech before what was left of the State Council, the mission held its own first conference to discuss the situation. By then Russell had come to the conclusion that the only way out for Russia was an end to the war through revision of treaties to eliminate imperialist goals and, by promising a peace with no loss of ter-

96. Notebooks, 17 June 1917, box 25, Russell Papers, MD, LC. Fred Corse, not realizing Harper was soon to arrive in Petrograd, wrote him on 12 June that Crane was "very much depressed and rather pessimistic" after Miliukov's resignation. In f. 8, box 4, Harper Papers, UC.

What role Crane played in the last days of Miliukov's political career is not clear from available sources, but they must have seen each other frequently.

97. Crane to Elizaveta, 23 May 1917, f. 1916-29, box 10, Hapgood-Reynolds Papers, MD, LC.

98. Notebooks, 20 June 1917, box 25, Russell Papers, MD, LC; Mott to his wife, Leila, 25 June 1917, f. 1838, box 107, Mott Papers, DSA.

99. Translation of an article from *Birshevnaya Gazeta* of 22 August, reel 4, Francis Papers, MoHS. For Mott's own account, including high praise from Metropolitan Platon, see Hopkins, *John R. Mott*, 491-92. He describes meeting "Reverend V. V. Aleksandrov" from California but does not mention his dress. Mott's addresses reminded Crane of St. Paul. "Extract from Private Letter of Mr. Charles R. Crane, 27 June 1917, f. 243, box 13, Mott Papers, DSA.

ritory, provoke revolution in Germany. For Russia and its "fifty-seven varieties" of political programs, the solution was a gigantic American propaganda effort, and Russell asked Root to demand $5 million immediately for that purpose. When Root agreed to ask for only a $100,000 emergency authorization, Russell said we could use it, but that $100 million would be worth keeping Russia in the war.[100] Root thus made his first formal report to Washington a request for money for a publicity and morale campaign, with the YMCA (Mott) assigned a special role.[101]

Upon return from the Moscow Church Council, Crane drafted a message to President Wilson recalling that the United States entered the Spanish-American War to free Cuba but then took responsibility for the Philippines. "The present war is vastly greater and we may come out of it with vastly greater responsibilities for the future of Russia"[102]—a clear call for some kind of active American intervention. Without Miliukov, Crane wanted to place his trust in the Russian church but still saw difficulties:

> The enthusiasm of the revolution is being followed by dismay over the magnitude of the new problems and the difficulties of firmly establishing a new state on the wreckage. The one unified element in the empire is the church but that went through more changes in the month of May than it had gone through in two hundred years before.[103]

He found Moscow more congenial than the "socialistic, materialistic carnival at Petrograd" and spent more time there visiting with Nikolai Guchkov, the former mayor, and Evgeniia Lineva, a collector of folk songs whose chorus Crane had sponsored in New York and at the fair Chicago in the 1890s.[104]

The economic members of the delegation, McCormick and Bertron, lunched on 16 June with Andrei Shingarev, minister of finance, and were clearly unimpressed: "We found him a most intelligent and interesting man, but as he has only held the position of minister of finance about two weeks he knows very little about the subject, and his profession as a physician at Moscow did not help to qualify him for this position." At another session a couple of days later,

100. Notebooks, 18 and 19 June 1917, box 25, Russell Papers, MD, LC.
101. Root cable to Lansing, 17 June 1917, box 136, Root Papers, MD, LC.
102. Crane to Wilson, 21 June 1917, reel 1, Crane Papers, BA, CU. This letter may not have been sent or delivered, since it does not appear in the published papers of the president.
103. Ibid.
104. Crane to daughter Josephine, 25 July 1917, reel 1, Crane Papers, BA, CU.

Special Diplomatic Mission from U.S. to Russia (the Root mission) in the Winter Palace, Petrograd, 9 July 1917. Front row, from left to right: Samuel R. Bertron, Charles R. Crane, James Duncan, General Winfield Scott, Elihu Root, Ambassador Francis, Rear Admiral John Glennon, John R. Mott, Cyrus McCormick Jr., Charles E. Russell; back row: behind Francis, Colonel William V. Judson; third from right, Lt. Alva Bernhard, courtesy of the Francis collection, Missouri Historical Society

Shingarev described to them "a distressing condition of affairs financially."[105] McCormick's conclusion probably summed up that of the mission as a whole: "The officers of the new government are trying their best to get things in shape, and I believe with plenty of time they will be able to do this. The difficult question is whether they can pull themselves together in time for the necessities of the war."[106]

On a tour of local factories on 19 June, Scott was impressed by the large number of the 30,000 workers of the Putilov Works who were absent, by a boisterous

105. Undated memorandum, enclosed in McCormick to Legge, 26 June 1917, box 113, 2C, McCormick Papers, SHSW.
106. McCormick to Legge, 26 June 1917, ibid.

meeting in one shop, and by the many airplanes in another factory that were in an advanced state of construction, although none were ready to fly.[107]

Everywhere the mission went, the theme of "We are in this together" was repeated. The message was clear that to save Russia for democracy, victory over the enemy was required. Root gave the last of fifteen formal speeches on the afternoon of 21 June before the Russian-American Chamber of Commerce in Petrograd.[108] He indicated his own limited definition of the mission's role:

> The Mission has no function to discharge in respect to industrial or commercial life. That was intentionally excluded from the scope of its duty. We came to Russia to bring assurances of the spiritual brotherhood of the two great democracies, and we came, moreover, to learn how we could best do our part as allies of the Russian democracy by material as well as spiritual aid, in the great fight for the freedom of both our nations.

He emphasized that the United States sought no commercial advantage, but then added:

> Yet, when the war is over and the world is by victory made safe for democracy, then, of course, as between brothers who have fought together, mutual knowledge and confidence and friendship will lead to all those relations of industrial and commercial life which make up the peaceful activities of the civilized world.[109]

In other words, the United States did in fact have an economic agenda. According to Russell, Root slipped from the prepared text and actually said that the role of Americans was "to teach these people democracy," and he hoped that this did not get out to the press.[110]

That evening the mission and Ambassador Francis dined at the home of oil magnate Emanuel Nobel, "the Rockefeller of Russia," who, like his American counterpart, was a major donor to the activities of the Russian "Mayak" YMCA.

107. Scott diary, 19 June, box 71, Scott Papers, MD, LC.

108. Speakers included three former ministers—Pokrovskii, Vyshnegradskii, and Stepanov. "Order of Addresses," 21 June 1917, box 192, Root Papers, MD, LC.

109. Elihu Root, *The United States and the War: The Mission to Russia Political Addresses*, ed. Robert Bacon and James Brown Scott (Cambridge, Mass.: Harvard University Press, 1918), 105-6.

110. Notebooks, 21 June 1917, box 25, Russell Papers, MD, LC.

Appropriately, John Mott delivered the key address in praise of YMCA wartime activities.[111]

Russell was clearly as disenchanted with the mission as with the Russia that surrounded it. He commented on a mission conference on 20 June: "All sorts of objections. Objections are the thing we do best. It seems like that the sum total will be a bunch of negatives. At a time like this!"[112] When most of the mission, including Crane and Mott, who had just returned, left for Moscow on 22 June, he and Judson remained behind. "It seems that Col. Judson has as little taste as I for sightseeing at a time when hell is poppin and the fate of the world is teetering, so he too cut out the kremlin."[113] Instead, Russell spent the time investigating the Soviet organizations and the Russian Left in general, conversing with Georgi Plekhanov, Maxim Gorky, and other veterans of the revolutionary movement. Others, such as Maria Spiridonova, a leader of the radical wing of the Socialist Revolutionaries, he found elusive as they were off speaking somewhere every day and night.

After attending a few sessions of the Petrograd Soviet, Russell was invited to speak at one. His appearance was delayed, however, by the need to translate his text into Russian, then by advice to revise it and tone down its pro-war emphasis. He finally said what he wanted to about the war on the night of 25 June with the right and center rising and responding enthusiastically while "the extreme left, headed by the stage figure of Lenine, sat still and did not applaud."[114] Obviously, Russell was getting around in quarters left untouched by other members of the commission.

On 27 June, Russell ran into Trotsky, "and I had a cordial, rather josting [sic] talk with him." "Trotsky is the regular thing in the dreamy, hot headed utopian Jew: bushy haired, sanguine, highly-strung, excitable, and a gifted talker."[115] Russell also wanted to make his own special impact in celebrating the Fourth of July at the city circus with a gala occasion open to the public; he obtained the support of Ambassador Francis for this, but Root opposed it as "undignified." He probably had an image of Trotsky and all sorts of other "quasi-Americans" crashing the party. The commission settled instead for a quiet reception at the

111. "Address at a Dinner Given by Mr. Emanuel Nobel, Petrograd, June 21, 1917," f. 2293 (Addresses), box 140, Mott Papers, DSA.
112. Ibid., 20 June.
113. Ibid., 22 June. Actually Judson wanted to spend the time being briefed by the much larger British and French military missions. To Mrs. Judson, 24 June 1917, Judson Papers, Newberry Library.
114. Notebooks, 25 June 1917, box 25, Russell Papers, MD, LC.
115. Ibid., 27 June 1917.

Foreign Ministry.[116] As if to ward off one possible interpretation of that historic date, Root gave a pointedly pro-British speech.[117] Perhaps it was here that the commission had the opportunity of imbibing well-aged bourbon that had been purchased in 1878 for hosting former president Ulysses Grant.[118] Francis then presided over a larger crowd of more than 300 at the embassy and reported that all went well except for one fistfight over the continuation of the war.[119]

At and in between receptions and appearances in the capital before various groups, the mission members were bombarded by requests for audiences by various parties having axes to grind. Most persistent to the point of being a nuisance was Roman Rosen, onetime ambassador to the United States. Some felt obliged to listen to him politely, but he did not succeed in getting an opportunity to address the mission as a whole, no doubt because of his arguing for a negotiated peace, a matter that did not fit with the mission's agenda.[120] He may, in fact, have had the best answer for Russia's 1917 dilemma.

At times members went their separate ways, with Root and Scott accompanying Tereshchenko for a visit to the army headquarters at Mogilev to meet General Aleksei Brusilov, hero of the Russian offensive of 1916. The military members, with their respective attachés, covered the most ground, with Scott reaching the far Romanian front (and writing most of his final report about it) and Glennon having an adventurous time in Baltic and Black Sea naval bases, where rank-and-file sailors held the upper hand. He reached Sevastopol just as yet another demonstration of sailor power deposed the Black Sea Fleet commander, Admiral Alexander Kolchak. Glennon, accompanied by McCully, Crosley, and Bernhard, was met officially by three officers, a sailor, and a worker, who, according

116. Ibid., 26 and 29 June and 4 July 1917. In connection with the reception, Russell noted that British ambassador George Buchanan "struck me as a dull, cold, formal man and I could well understand, looking him over, why he is so unpopular here," and "I see that sinister old figure, Baron Rosen, hovering around the Commission more than is good for it." Ibid., 4 July. Understandably, Wright found Russell "a most interesting and queer soul." Diary, 28 July 1917, box 2, Wright Papers, Princeton-Mudd.

117. "Address at a Luncheon Given by the Minister of Foreign Affairs Petrograd, July 4, 1917," in Root, *The United States and the War*, 132–35. Root characterized the Revolutionary War as a "civil war between two groups of the people of Great Britain," perhaps too apt given what was approaching in Russia.

118. According to Norman Armour's reminiscences, f. 4, box 2, Armour Papers, Princeton-Mudd.

119. Francis to Lansing, 5 July 1917, AE Russia, DPR 330, RG 84, NA.

120. His program is best presented in a seventeen-page letter to Harper, in which he lamented his failure with the mission, the foolishness of Miliukov, and the inexperience of Tereshchenko. To Harper, 29 July 1917, f. 9, box 4, Harper Papers, UC. Rosen also belabors his point in an "I told you so" vein in his memoirs. *Forty Years of Diplomacy*, 2:283–87.

Elihu Root and Russian Foreign Minister Tereshchenko on his left, July 1917, courtesy of the Francis Papers, Missouri Historical Society

to Pauline Crosley, was dirty and unshaven, then were forced to lunch under the gaze of hungry sailors.[121] Glennon's valiant attempts at patriotic speeches were, however, politely received and credited by his Russian guide and interpreter as having prevented a full-fledged mutiny of the fleet.[122]

The Kerensky Offensive

While the American mission was in Petrograd, the Russian army launched an offensive on the Galician front on 1 July against the Austro-Hungarian forces, which also had little enthusiasm left for fighting. This June (old calendar), or

121. Weeks, *An American Naval Diplomat in Revolutionary Russia*, 116–17; Crosley, *Intimate Letters from Petrograd*, 66–67. The most complete and graphic account of the Black Sea Fleet visit is in Fedotoff White, *Survival Through War and Revolution*, 145–57.

122. Fedotoff White, *Survival Through War and Revolution*, 154.

"Kerensky," offensive resulted at first in significant gains after hopes that Russia would contribute to Allied victory in 1917. After more than two weeks and the deployment of German reinforcements to that area, the Russians were thrown back in disorder and with over 200,000 casualties, and thus further demoralized by failure, a major cause of which was Bolshevik and other antiwar agitation throughout the army.[123]

It has been claimed that this last Russian offensive on the Eastern Front was inspired by the presence of the American mission or intended to demonstrate to it real Russian military capability. General Scott, who toured behind the front during the offensive, reported, "The most they expected was a successful local battle, which would prove to Russia and to America that the army would and could fight. . . . It was hard to believe that the whole thing was not a maneuver to which I had been invited and whose elaborate arrangements for my entertainment had been made beforehand."[124]

The presence of the mission may indeed have played a role,[125] but this campaign mainly carried out a plan that was already in place but delayed in execution by the February–March Revolution. In fact, the Root mission arrived after the offensive had been approved by both the Provisional Government and the moderate Soviet leadership and may actually have counseled against it.[126] According to Washburn, General Brusilov wanted him to have Root ask Kerensky personally not to launch an offensive, but Root refused for fear of being accused of meddling in Russian affairs.[127] The result was certainly not a good omen for the mission's goal of keeping Russia in the war, as the British photographer John Memes reported total chaos and demoralization during the retreat.[128]

123. See the detailed examinations by Allan K. Wildman, *The End of the Russian Imperial Army*, vol. 2, *The Road to Soviet Power and Peace* (Princeton, N. J.: Princeton University Press, 1987); and Louise Erwin Heenan, *Russian Democracy's Fatal Blunder: The Summer Offensive of 1917* (New York: Praeger, 1987).

From Kerensky's own memoirs, a major reason for launching the offensive may have been the false sense of loyalty and support he perceived during a May tour of military units at the front. *Russia and History's Turning Point* (New York: Duell, Sloan and Pearce, 1965), 268–88.

124. Report to Secretary of War, 25 July 1917, box 71, Scott Papers, MD, LC.

125. A few days before the offensive began, McCormick wrote in a private letter that "our Commission is helping them as far as possible to prepare for another advance on the Austrian and Roumanian fronts." To Legge, 26 June 1917, box 113, 2C, McCormick Papers, SHSW. And Scott reported, "It was impossible for the members of the Mission to escape the belief that our presence was a factor in the determination to order an attack at that particular time." Report to the Secretary of War, 25 July 1917, box 71, Scott Papers, MD, LC.

126. Heenan, 56, citing T. Bentley Mott.

127. Washburn oral history, p. 118, CU.

128. Thompson, *Donald Thompson in Russia*, 345.

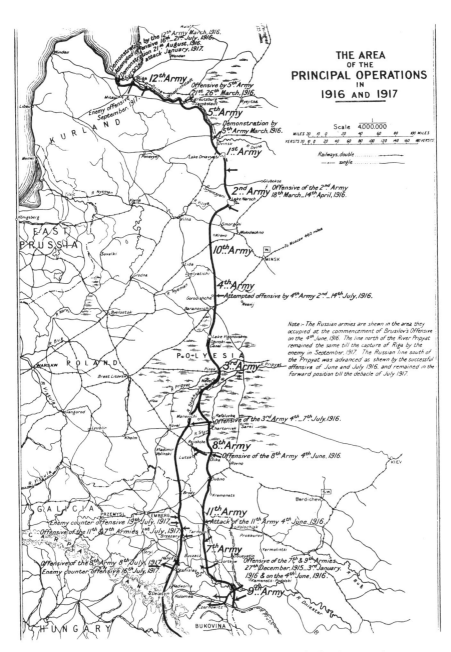

Russian Front and the Kerensky offensive. From Knox, With the Russian Army

The Russian radical press charged the American representatives with having economic motives and advancing the interests of American imperialism at Russia's expense, and their well-publicized dinners with Nobel and Baron David Gintsburg (the Jacob Schiff of Russia) provided some grounds. Root was also personally vulnerable for his involvement in the Platt amendment of 1901 and the heavy-handed American policy in Cuba. There is at least some truth to this also in regard to the business interests of Cyrus McCormick. He took advantage of the mission to confer with a number of representatives of International Harvester in Russia and gathered information about special business opportunities that could be exploited due to Russia's economic depression for the specific goal of postwar expansion of the company's operations.[129]

After just less than a month on the ground, and with the news of a victorious Russian offensive ringing in their ears, members of the Root mission had a farewell lunch with Tereshchenko, then departed Petrograd on 9 July for the long trip back the way they came, leaving behind Crane, John Mott, and Judson, the latter to be senior military attaché. UP correspondent Shepherd tried to cheer up Russell at the station by saying the mission had accomplished much, but he then added that "the people were dead sick of the war, they could see nothing in this war that interested them, and soon or late they would pull out."[130] But if the mission had one real goal, it was to keep Russia in the war. The first day on the train, Russell noted, "we were a silent crew" and slept most of the time.[131] Russia had actually been relatively restrained and on good behavior during the mission's sojourn; a little more than a week after its departure, the streets of Petrograd would again be the scene of chaos and revolt.

Harper and Crane in Russia

Samuel Harper, delayed by lecture commitments and in transit, finally arrived on 24 June. He then spent most of the remainder of the mission's stay in Russia with Mott and Crane but tried to remain upbeat, unlike Crane, about the chaotic situation in Russia in both his private and official correspondence. To Richard Crane, he wrote that his optimism was not shaken but then acknowledged

129. Clyde Scott Stilwell, "With Harvester Men in Russia," *Harvester Age*, November 1917, 1–5.

130. Notebooks, 9 July 1917, box 25, Russell Papers, MD, LC.

131. Ibid., 10 July. Perhaps it was symbolic that the return trip was held up a day at Viatka because of a bridge that had burned in front. The train was parked next to a garbage dump, and the mission endured an avalanche of odors and flies. Ibid., 11 and 12 July.

the main difficulty: "Russia has a problem such as no other nation has ever had to face. She must at one and the same time consolidate the revolution and wage a war."[132] He also remarked that John Mott "had been better able to seize the human side of the great revolution than the other men of the commission."[133] A factor that gave Harper encouragement was that he, almost alone among Americans in Russia, knew Kerensky and some other members of the new government from previous contacts and for a while at least had some confidence in them.[134]

Admitting to his mother on 9 July that "the 'hang-over' of the old regime has been worse than I expected," Harper was pleased that no one wanted to return to it. "But the demoralization of the old police system was enormous. So every thing has gone slowly, especially in the matter of reorganization." He thought that the Kerensky offensive would severely damage Lenin's influence and that Russia would again play a key military role in the war.[135]

Harper was especially dismayed by the critical reporting of Russia during the summer of 1917 and picked a fight with Associated Press correspondent Robert Crozier Long for depicting a blundering, lost Russia that led to charges of slander by Long: "Harper has neither the experience of journalism nor the knowledge of Russian affairs necessary for authoritative criticism."[136] An extended exchange culminated in Harper's apology, apparently just to get Long off his back.[137] Although Mott left on 23 July, Harper stayed on with Crane and departed when he did in September. By that time his optimism was cured.

The behavior of Crane is something of a mystery. By going home with the Root mission, he would have given it more clout in Washington, owing to his personal connections with the president. In Russia he spent most of his time

132. Harper to Crane, 8 July 1917, f. 8, box 4, Harper Papers, UC.
133. Harper to Henry Pratt Judson (president, University of Chicago), 8 July 1917, ibid.
134. Harper to Paul Harper (brother), 12 August 1917, f. 10, box 4, Harper Papers, UC.
135. To Mother, 9 July 1917, f. 9, box 4, Harper Papers, UC.
136. Long to Francis, 22 July 1917, AE Russia, DPR 315, RG 84, NA. For Long's sharp criticism of the Provisional Government and emphasis on the "independence" of the Kronstadt naval base, see his *Russian Revolution Aspects* (New York: Dutton, 1919).
137. Long to Harper, 2 July 1917, and Harper to Long, 7 July 1917, f. 9, box 4, Harper Papers, UC. For a compendium of Long's sharp critiques, see *Russian Revolutionary Aspects*. He typically begins one chapter:

The decay of the Revolution into disorder and anarchy began very much sooner after the deposition of the Tsar than foreigners usually believe. It began almost immediately; and it was only the brave front kept up at Petrograd and the emphatic announcements that Russia's Army would continue to fight that had the effect of blinding observers in Ally Countries. (32)

with church affairs and sharing his pessimism with various visiting Americans. The few messages that reached the president through Francis and Crane's son Richard were short, confused, and empty of substantive advice.[138] Both he and Harper were in transit during the critical month of October.

In the meantime, the rest of the Root mission traveled slowly across Siberia giving patriotic speeches at various stops, usually to chilly receptions, and reached Vladivostok on 21 July, where Russell observed that the great piles of supplies had remained untouched since their arrival. There were just more of them, since several ships were unloading.[139] The mission reboarded the waiting *Buffalo*, and most members reached Washington by 7 August, after a welcome-home party at the Chicago Club arranged by McCormick on the sixth.[140] Over three months after their departure, the members were ready to present voluminous—and largely unread—reports on what they had seen and done.

Bentley Mott summed up the mission with mild praise for Root:

> As the seas of floating ice off Kamchatka changed to the endless plains of Siberia, as the tiresome visits in Moscow succeeded the midnight seances with the Cabinet in Petrograd, and when finally the dreary journey empty-handed back to Washington in seething heat terminated this thankless task, it was evident that the commissioners had not only yielded to the influence of Mr. Root's wisdom but had fallen under the charm of his nature.[141]

That may not have been the best outcome.

The July Crisis

While the Root mission was on its way home, another major change in the Russian political climate occurred, comparable to the resignations of Miliukov and Guchkov. A growing reaction to the Kerensky failure to carry out a success-

138. Cables for Richard Crane, dated 6 and 21 July, in Richard Crane to Tumulty, 11 and 27 June 1917, *PWW* 43:149–50, 298–99. Actually, these were sent to his son, probably with the expectation that they would be forwarded to the president, but without precise instructions.

139. Notebooks, 14 and 21 July 1917, box 25, Russell Papers, MD, LC.

140. McCormick telegram to Junia Williams (personal secretary), 6 August 1917, f. Special Diplomatic Mission to Russia, 9C, box 113, McCormick Papers, SHSW.

141. Mott, *Twenty Years as Military Attaché*, 195.

ful offensive produced a series of street demonstrations, inspired by the radical party leadership in the soviets—Bolsheviks, anarchists, and a new antiwar split in Kerensky's own Socialist Revolutionary Party who styled themselves "Left Socialist Revolutionaries" and gained strength especially among sailors and soldiers in the capital region.

The demonstrations became a crisis in mid-July, when many of these followers came into the streets of Petrograd with weapons. The arrival of a sizable contingent of sailors from the Kronstadt naval base was especially threatening. It appeared that the Provisional Government might be toppled as a larger but unarmed crowd had overthrown the tsarist government in February. But the radical leadership, including Lenin himself, hesitated to press the issue, and Kerensky was able to summon enough loyal units to put down the demonstrators and disarm them.

The results of this affair were considerable not only for Russia but also for the alliance and American interests. It polarized the society, especially in and around Petrograd, into pro-war and antiwar and the Provisional Government against the growth of radical parties in the soviets. The government was able, however, to arrest a number of important leaders such as Trotsky and force others like Lenin to go into hiding. In a major publicity campaign the pro-war side then charged them with being German agents, based on evidence of communications intercepted by British intelligence in Stockholm. These were alleged to prove that the Bolsheviks especially had received substantial sums of German money to finance their radical propaganda and activities.

The charges and evidence were accepted almost universally by the Allies as valid, giving the Bolsheviks a particularly unsavory reputation in their eyes, especially since it was widely circulated in the Western press as well. And this would, of course, affect the strain in relations after the Bolsheviks took power in October. Most contemporary and later historians of the Russian revolution have accepted the charges to various degrees, some explaining that the acceptance of German money did not necessarily make the Bolsheviks German agents. A recent study, however, has shown the evidence of the intercepted communications to be very weak, and they would not have stood up to close examination in a court of law.[142] For their part the embittered Bolsheviks treated the whole business cynically as typical bourgeois dirty tricks.

---

142. See Semion Lyandres, *The Bolsheviks' "German Gold" Revisited: An Inquiry into the 1917 Accusations*, Carl Beck Papers in Russian and East European Studies, (Pittsburgh: Pittsburgh University Press, 1995).

The Railroad Mission

One reason for some of the difficulties of the Root mission was that it had been upstaged by the "technical" mission led by John F. Stevens. The separation of this Advisory Commission of Railway Experts to Russia from the political one seemed to make sense at the time, but in retrospect it probably was a mistake. Stevens, a trained engineer and businessman, could claim credit for building the Denver and Rio Grande and had won fame as one of the chief engineers for the Panama Canal.[143] Similar to Root, now retired to a consulting role, Stevens was considered an elder statesman of American railroading, but he had not been much involved in politics.

The president entrusted Daniel Willard of the Department of Commerce with organizing this "delegation," and with the help of Stanley Washburn he did so effectively and efficiently.[144] Besides Stevens, the mission consisted of other appropriate experts: William Lafayette Darling (consulting engineer), Henry Miller (Chicago, operations), George Gibbs (New York, rolling stock and repair shops), and John E. Greiner (Baltimore, bridges) with Stevens's son Eugene, Frederick Mason, Edward Shannon, Leslie Fellows, Stanley Washburn, and Clinton Decker as aides, and a woman, Mrs. John Bass, to handle publicity. Against his doctor's advice, Washburn left a sanatorium where he was recovering from shell shock and exhaustion to serve as guide and probably claimed undue credit for organizing the mission.[145]

It also sailed across the Pacific but from Vancouver to Yokohama in commodious first-class quarters on the *Empress of Asia* and reached Vladivostok on 31 May ahead of the Root mission, the members well rested and ready to go to work. Portents were not good when returning revolutionary exiles raised red flags over the ship from Japan to Vladivostok.[146] Planning initially to take their time and gather information on the Trans-Siberian, "so they can see all of the railroad by daylight," they raced the Root mission to Petrograd instead.[147] The railroad men had already practically stolen the show in Petrograd

143. Biograpical data, Stevens Papers, MD, LC.
144. Wilson to Lansing, 5 May 1917, *PWW* 42:222.
145. Washburn oral history, pp. 100–104, CU.
146. Darling diary, 29 May 1917, HIA, with the added comment that most of them were Jewish and included several women.
147. Clinton Decker to Gertie (fiancée), 2 June 1917, box 1, Decker Papers, Princeton-Mudd. The credit for this change of plan was given to Aleksandr Mitinskii, the official Russian guide for the mission. Many of Decker's letters were published in a private edition, edited by his son; see Clinton J. Decker, ed., *Mission to Russia, An American Journal: Letters by Clinton A. Decker* (New York: n.p., 1994).

John F. Stevens. From World's Work, *July 1917*

before the Root mission arrived. Under the firm authority of Stevens, it set to work learning the ropes and knots of the Russian transportation system, not an easy task. Darling probably reflected the group's first impression: "Russia is certainly going thro an adjustment period; it seems to be license rather than freedom."[148]

Stevens believed that his mission was at least the equal of Root's, much to Root's consternation and disapproval.[149] When Root suggested the idea of sending

148. Darling diary, 14 June 1917, HIA.
149. "The one and only thing I asked assurance of from President Wilson . . . was that this Commission should not be interfered with in any transportation matters in Russia, either by any other commission or member of any other commission, which assurance President Wilson granted very quickly and emphatically." Stevens to Root, 1 July 1917, box 136, Root Papers, MD, LC.

existing American railroad equipment to Russia, he was quickly refuted and told to mind his own business.[150] The dissension between the two was eased, unfortunately for the goal of immediate American technical assistance to Russia, by Stevens becoming seriously ill in Petrograd with erysipelas and having to spend much valuable time in the hospital while the other members could do little but gather information without him. As in the case of the Root mission, Stevens was handicapped in having his delegation of experts labeled a "commission," and by devoting too much attention to data collection and time-consuming conferences and less to problem solving.

The railroad men suffered an additional obstacle in being considered as representing commercial interests by Russian authorities, who remained suspicious of American motives regarding the railroads. Proposing in some informal conversations that the United States simply take over the operation of the Trans-Siberian may have contributed to Russian caution. The transport ministry even rejected a proposal by Miller, who was supported by British experts, that the road be organized in 150-mile sections instead of 75 because the locomotives were in bad shape and could not handle the longer distances.[151]

Hugh Moran, the YMCA secretary in Irkutsk who had been working on relief to prisoners of war, outlined such a plan to Francis as early as mid-April for the line from Vladivostok to Chita or Irkutsk and recommended that one-way traffic be established for the existing one-track line westward through Manchuria and eastward on the Amur River line through Khabarovsk. He also warned against sending more of the heavy American engines that were breaking down the track and bridges of the road.[152] Whether this proposal was brought to the attention of the Stevens commission is not known, but it would probably have been dismissed for its author's lack of professional expertise.[153]

Only on 29 June did the American railroad advisers really get down to business with a meeting—without Stevens but with Francis present—at the ministry with Nekrasov and other officials. They enthusiastically seconded a request for 40,000 new freight cars and 2,000 locomotives to be ordered in the United States.

150. Stevens, Miller, Gibbs, Darling, and Greiner to Root, 21 June 1917, box 136, Root Papers, MD, LC.

151. Darling diary, 19 and 22 June 1917, Darling Papers, HIA.

152. Moran to Francis, 13 April 1917, reel 4, Francis Papers, MoHS.

153. Moran admitted his lack of expertise but claimed to be a habitual car counter, and he had been watching trains going in and out of Irkutsk for over a year, as well as riding on a number. Ibid.

They also discussed the delivery of new American coal chutes, water stations, turn tables, and repair facilities.[154]

The commission again took time off, however, to join the Root mission and most of the American colony for a special Orthodox service in English on 1 July at the Kazan Cathedral, conducted by Father Vladimir Aleksandrov of the Cathedral of the Holy Trinity in San Francisco, and to celebrate the Fourth at the embassy.[155] Then they matched the Root mission's wanderings with a week's tour of Moscow and Ukraine.[156] Back in Petrograd, comfortably housed at the Hotel Europe, they endured some frightening experiences during the July crisis and considered going home.[157]

Also unfortunately for their mission, Minister of Communications Nekrasov was more interested in the volatile politics of the Kerensky regime than in railroads and then switched positions at the end of July—to minister of finance—in midstream.[158] When James Colt recommended to the mission improvements on the Murmansk line, Nekrasov objected: "We promised to take up the question with Mr. Nekrasof at once and we did so but Mr. Nekrasof did not worry over it; Mr Stevens told Colt that he could do nothing until invited by Mr. Nekrasof."[159]

The Stevens mission finally developed a comprehensive plan for a major overhaul of the Russian railroads, including new coaling stations (although coal was increasingly scarce), longer traffic divisions, larger engines, and heavier tracks—a complete modernization of 140,000 miles of Russian track. After delays caused by slow Russian consideration and political interruptions with changes in ministerial personnel, the commission met at the ministry on 26 July, six weeks after its arrival, to discuss in detail the American recommendations.[160]

154. Minutes of meeting of 29 June 1917, ACRER, f. 1, box 1, RG 43 (Records of International Conferences, Commissions and Expositions), NA; Stevens to Nekrasov, 3 and 5 July 1917, f. 4, ibid.

155. Darling diary, 18 June and 1 July 1917, HIA; Hopkins, *John R. Mott*, 506–7; Francis to wife, 30 June–1 July 1917, reel 4, Francis Papers, MoHS.

156. On the return trip from Ukraine, an awkward scene occurred when interpreter Frank Golder attempted to allow Miliukov to join them, but the Russian guides refused, and Golder left with him. Decker to Gertie, 14 July 1917, box 1, Decker Papers, Princeton-Mudd.

157. Darling diary, 17 and 24 July 1917, HIA.

158. For a description of the internal politics of the Provisional Government at this time, see *V. D. Nabokov and the Russian Provisional Government, 1917*, ed. Virgil D. Medlin and Steven L. Parsons (New Haven, Conn.: Yale University Press, 1976), 100–101.

159. Diary, 23 June 1917, Darling Papers, HIA.

160. Minutes of meeting of 26 July 1917, f. 1, box 1, ACRER, RG 43, NA. In the formation of a new cabinet on 25 July, Nekrasov moved to finance and Petr Iurenev replaced him in communications. Iurenev resigned at the end of August.

Only after this did Stevens decide to concentrate on short-term priorities, such as longer work sections and a special request for twelve mobile railroad workshops, each manned by fourteen men, to be attached to Russian repair stations.[161] He admitted that it would be several months before quantities of new equipment and technical personnel could arrive.[162] But in August Stevens was ill again, this time with dysentery, while some other members wasted two weeks going to Murmansk and back.[163]

More information on Russian transportation problems was reaching Washington from other sources. John Caldwell, consul in Vladivostok, reported in June that 13,000 large American cars, delivered the previous year, had allowed some improvement in traffic on the Trans-Siberian, but those cars departing in September did not start returning until February, and then most went straight to repair shops, "many nuts and small parts having been removed and air brake hoses cut off."[164] Still, by June 1917 the number of cars being dispatched from Vladivostok per day rose to around 100 from an average of 20 during the winter. During a good week in June, 22,000 tons of supplies of various kinds were forwarded by rail, but that same week 30,000 tons arrived by ship, and Caldwell estimated the total backlog of goods stored in Vladivostok and vicinity at 600,000 tons.[165]

Having finally perceived the enormity of the transportation problem, Stevens recommended and proceeded to follow a policy of concentrating on the Trans-Siberian Railroad, starting from Vladivostok, as the most important supply line into Russia. This, of course, meant that little attention would be paid to the chaotic situation of the railroads in Russia proper, at least until—or if—those in Siberia could be put into decent operating condition. It also entailed submitting a new plan to the Ministry of Communications and then discussing it at another meeting on 10 August.[166] By this time the British ambassador considered that the only practical solution was for the Allies, but mainly the United States, to take over completely the Russian railroads.[167]

---

161. Stevens to Commission, 27 July 1917, ibid.; Stevens to Francis and Francis to Lansing, 14 August 1917, AE Russia, DPR 303, RG 84, NA.

162. To K. N. Vanifant'ev, 7 August 1917, f. 4, box 1, ACRER, RG 43, NA.

163. Darling diary, 7–20 August 1917, HIA.

164. Caldwell to Lansing, 19 June 1917, AE Russia, DPR 329, RG 84, NA.

165. Ibid. Estimating the volume of this confused mess of supplies was not easy. About the same time, a member of the Stevens mission gave a figure of 700,000 tons. Darling diary, 31 May 1917, HIA.

166. Stevens to Minister P. P. Iurenev, 10 August 1917, and minutes of 10 August meeting, f. 1, box 1, ACRER, RG 43, NA.

167. Enclosed report from Buchanan, 6 August 1917, in Polk to Tumulty, 7 August 1917, *PWW* 43:387.

The mission then made another trip to Vladivostok and back to resurvey the needs, returning to Petrograd on 14 October,[168] three weeks before the Bolshevik seizure of power, to discover that the ministry had still not responded to the commission's plan submitted in July.[169] Most members of the mission then decided to go home and traveled again to Vladivostok, arriving in Vancouver on 12 November. So much for any substantial American technical assistance to Russia's Provisional Government. Meanwhile, the state of deterioration of railroads was relayed to Washington by Judson:

> General railroad situation growing more critical and exciting alarm of Russians and allies. Stevens and his Commission have all they can do on Trans-Siberian. They have been away from Petrograd and out of touch with general situation and people interested here for a month. The magnitude and difficulties of the problem demand immediate presence here of biggest railroad men available in United States with small but competent staff of four or five, but no commission, to act as constant advisers to Minister of Communications.[170]

Stevens's recommendation, however, was for a large technical advisory staff under his direction that was, in fact, formed and sent to Siberia the following year.

American Coverage of Russia in Revolution

After the February Revolution and American entry into the alliance against the Central Powers, what was happening in Russia again sold newspapers. A horde of journalists and pseudojournalists descended on the country like a tourist ship unloading at an island resort, adding more complications for the embassy and consulates, for beleaguered Russian officials, and for the confused American readers. They ranged widely in perspective but generally were more critical of the conditions they found, in contrast to those covering the initial months of the war. The avalanche of dispatches and articles, usually by courier to Stockholm to access reliable cables, had some positive features; they were unsupervised and free of censorship, to some, such as Harper's, regret. They covered the spectrum

168. Darling noted that this should have been done two months earlier. Diary, 22 August 1917, HIA.
169. Stevens to Francis, 18 October 1917, AE Russia, DPR 303, RG 84, NA.
170. Judson cable to War Department, 29 September 1917, f. 6494-16, RG 165, NA.

from fronts to city to countryside. And some at least strove for objectivity and fairness.

The reporters represented almost all principal publications but tended to possess particular political agendas regarding the Russian scene, such as Lincoln Steffens, Edward Ross (American Institute for Social Service and *Century Magazine* and *Atlantic Monthly*), Albert Rhys Williams and Bessie Beatty (*San Francisco Chronicle*), and, of course, latecomers John Reed (*Metropolitan*) and Louise Bryant. Others such as Long (AP), Arthur Ruhl (*Collier's*), Mrs. Walter Farwell (*Chicago Tribune*), Arthur Judson Brown (Presbyterian Board of Foreign Missions), William G. Shepherd (UP), Maynard O. Williams (*Christian Herald*), Arthur Bullard (*New Republic*), Samuel Harper (*Christian Science Monitor*), Frederick McCormick (freelance), Arno Walter Dosch-Fleurot (*New York World*), and photographer Donald Thompson and Florence MacLeod Harper (*Leslie's Weekly*) tried to be more positive and comprehensive.

Thompson and Harper were lucky to have reached Petrograd just before the revolution, while Dosch-Fleurot fortunately delayed his recall by the *World* because nothing was happening in Russia.[171] Among the first to arrive after it were Steffens and Shepherd, traveling with Crane. Both were caught up in the excitement of the revolution and stayed together at the same hotel, Steffens benefiting from Shepherd's prior experience in Russia. Unfortunately, most of Shepherd's reports were without a byline, and, unlike many, he did not write a book about his experiences. Steffens's autobiography captures some of the atmosphere of the period:

> [The Provisional Government's] little leaders had their own history to make, and we had to hear and report it if we could. History? How can you get history in the making, on the spot, as it happens? There were several histories all going on together, unconnected, often contradictory narratives that met and crossed, and—they were all "history." We heard aplenty of them; we must have missed many more. Nobody could, nobody will, ever hear them all. History is impossible.[172]

There is indeed something of the blind men and the elephant about American reporting on Russia in revolution. But more than most, Steffens saw the revolution through a dreamlike mist. Other American reporters, arriving just after the

---

171. Dosch-Fleurot, *Through War to Revolution*, 113. Despite his name, the author was thoroughly American, from Oregon. He also acknowledged a debt that novice American correspondents in Russia owed to veteran journalists Ludovic Naudeau of France and Guy Baringer of Britain, and all looked up to Harold Williams of the *Manchester Guardian*. Ibid., 103.

172. Steffens, *Autobiography*, 749.

February Revolution, took a misleadingly favorable view of the Provisional Government and its leaders.[173]

Some of these "reporters" were not really journalists but scholars who wanted to study the changes to earn money to pay their way. As a leading authority, Harper would naturally want to observe the new scene, especially since his friend Miliukov was in the middle of it. Edward Ross, a pioneering sociologist at the University of Wisconsin, was a newcomer to Russian studies who saw important sociological implications in the revolution but needed to secure advances for the expenses of the trip by contracting to write articles for *Mercury*.[174]

Another problem was getting to Russia because of its isolation and the crush for steamer space. After consulting with Harper, Boris Shatsky of the Russian embassy, and others, Ross decided to go the longer but safer Siberian route.[175] In contrast to most, however, Ross undertook the difficult task of seeing the Russian countryside—as far as Central Asia—instead of concentrating on the centers of revolutionary activity.

All Americans covering the scene, whether diplomats, journalists, businessmen and other residents, or just tourists, were frustrated by communications problems. Most simply did not rely on the irregular mail or undependable telegraph but instead gathered materials, made notes, or kept diaries to be taken out with them. Some opportunities existed for people leaving the country to take things out, but given the time involved in travel, this resulted in delays. A better option was to prevail on someone to send a cable from Stockholm or London. They also found being virtually cut off from family and friends for the duration of their stay painful and oppressive.[176]

The Women's Battalions

Despite the frustration about a Russia that would not stand still for a reporter's snapshot, certain new developments especially caught the attention of Americans. This was the case with the recruitment of women's battalions to be de-

173. See, for example, Arthur Judson Brown, *Russia in Transformation* (New York: Fleming Revell, 1917).

174. Nathaniel Pratt (American Institute of Social Service) to Ross, 12 May 1917, reel 10, Ross Papers, SHSW.

175. Harper to Ross, 7 May, Shatsky to Ross, 28 May, and Bullard to Ross, 2 June 1917, ibid.

176. Excellent examples are the letters describing the chaos in the countryside by Emma Cochrane Ponafidine, *Russia–My Home: An Intimate Record of Personal Experiences Before, During and After the Bolshevist Revolution* (Indianapolis: Bobbs-Merrill, 1931).

ployed in combat. Russia was carrying the fight for women's equality farther than most advocates of women's rights in the West intended, and journalists believed, correctly, that it would be of interest to readers at home.

Moreover, the government of Alexander Kerensky, whose misguided belief was that these special units would shame the regular army to fight harder, was quick to provide easy access and wide publicity to them. American reporters and general observers thus focused much attention on the spectacle of women in uniform in training or marching through the streets of Petrograd. Donald Thompson, photographer-reporter for *Leslie's Illustrated,* captured them in a series of revealing, if somewhat pathetic, pictures and featured Colonel Mariia Bochkareva, the leading advocate of female combatants and one of the commanders, in the frontispiece to his book.[177]

The Provisional Government seemed particularly anxious to expose this experiment to visiting Americans, inviting a Red Cross mission to a special assembly of women soldiers.[178] And Bessie Beatty devoted a whole chapter to the recruitment and training of 5,000 women during the summer of 1917, which she dubbed "the most amazing single phenomenon of the war."[179] The elaborate ceremony marking the dispatch to the front of one battalion on 21 August inspired both Raymond Robins of the Red Cross and William Darling of the railroad mission to compose detailed descriptions.[180]

Interestingly, Florence Harper, Thompson's partner, took a much more critical view of the female soldiers. While stating her bias that the battlefield was not the place for women, she admitted that many were patriotic and made good soldiers. To her, however, the whole thing was a failure.

> The only man who expressed admiration for the Women's Battalion was a private of the Death Battalion that rescued them from a dangerous position at the front. He said the women were splendid, but at the same time he added, "When the soldiers saw them, they laughed, and a great many men who were willing to fight refused to fight, because they said fighting

177. Donald C. Thompson, *Blood Stained Russia* (New York: Leslie-Judge, 1918), 96–115. Charles Russell, who was impressed that no fun was made of these women soldiers in public, provides a good description of Bochkareva and her second in command. *Unchained Russia* (New York: D. Appleton, 1918), 211–16.

178. Orrin Sage Wightman, *The Diary of an American Physician in the Russian Revolution, 1917* (Brooklyn, N.Y.: Brooklyn Daily Eagle, 1928), 48–49, 58–64, also with excellent pictures.

179. Bessie Beatty, *The Red Heart of Russia* (New York: Century, 1919), 90–114.

180. Robins to Bessie, 23 August 1917, f. August, box 12, Robins Papers, SHSW; Darling diary, 21 August, Darling Papers, HIA.

Drilling women soldiers. From Thompson, Blood Stained Russia

had become woman's work and therefore there was no need for them."
... He had splendid stories to tell of their bravery, but said they did more
harm than good.[181]

On the Street

Donald Thompson, with both still and motion picture cameras, was in the thick
of things until his departure in August. To him we are indebted for many revealing photographs, usually uncredited, of Russia in revolution. Unfortunately, a
print of his full-length feature documentary on the revolution, *The German Curse
in Russia*, first shown in New York in December 1917, appears not to have
survived, though fragments are included in a number of later educational films
on the Russian Revolution.[182] One dramatic scene of a crowd scattering at the
intersection of Nevsky Prospect and Sadovaia, usually depicted as during the

181. Harper, *Runaway Russia*, 168. Although on assignment for *Leslie's Weekly*, Florence
Harper was a British citizen.
182. For an analysis, see David Mould, "Donald Thompson: Photographer at War," *Kansas
History: A Journal of the Central Plains* 5, no. 3 (autumn 1982): 154–68.

July crisis (see, for example, *Russia: Czar to Lenin*), was really a panic that ensued during a demonstration on 3 May.[183]

By September more American journalists arrived who were particularly attracted
to the rise of the extreme left of the political spectrum; they included Albert Rhys
Williams, John Reed, and Louise Bryant, who were quickly caught up in an
enthusiasm for what they saw as a more positive outcome for the Russian Revolution and the world. To his former companion in Mexico and Russia, Reed
wrote, "For color and terror and grandeur this makes Mexico look pale."[184]

While Americans found certain aspects of Russia in war and revolution intriguing, Russians often turned to Americans for guidance and support in advancing prospects for new opportunities. Journalists and other Americans were
besieged by Russians for information on American institutions. Educational
reform was one area. Xenophon Kalamatiano, still seeking business opportunities in Moscow, found himself in June serving as an officer for a parent-teacher
organization, the All-Russian Union of Parents for the Reorganization of Russian Preparatory Schools.[185]

A book could be written about the various attempts to transplant to or graft
on American institutions during this period.[186] All Russian political groups
succumbed to some extent to *amerikanizm*, idealizing things American and believing they could be the salvation of their new Russia. The difficulty of finding
a good fit frustrated both Russians and Americans, and no anti-immunity vac-
cine was available. Americans, too, harbored the view that they might have the
answers for Russia's problems, and political leaders, ranging from Miliukov and
Kerensky to Trotsky and Lenin, bathed in the attention they garnered from the
American traveling salesmen, though they rarely understood it.

More Missions

The sending and hosting of various missions was not the ideal way to wage a
successful war or revolution but probably was inevitable under the circumstances.

---

183. In a letter to his wife on that day, he describes scrambling up on to a balcony to get
the shot. *Donald Thompson in Russia*, 167.
184. Reed to Boardman Robinson, 17 September 1917, f. 137-38, Reed Papers, Harvard-
Houghton.
185. Kalamatiano to Harper, 21 June 1917, f. 8, box 4, Harper Papers, UC.
186. For some good beginnings, see Hans Rogger, "America in the Russian Mind—or
Russian Discoveries of America," *Pacific Historical Review* 47, no. 1 (February 1978): 27-51;
and Robert V. Allen, *Russia Looks at America: The View to 1917* (Washington, D.C.: Library
of Congress, 1988).

Any mission sent had to be reciprocated, so to no one's surprise, one of the Provisional Government's early diplomatic endeavors was to form and send a mission to the United States in exchange for the Root mission. It was, however, far from a distinguished or very well known crowd of forty that made the trip across Siberia and the Pacific to the United States. Most were liberal friends and associates of Miliukov who probably could have made better use of their time by staying home.[187]

The mission that departed Petrograd on 17 May was headed not by an elder statesman of Russian liberalism but by a young engineering professor and recent assistant minister of commerce and industry, ambassador-designate Boris Bakhmeteff, who would never be able to return to his homeland. The new ambassador at least was familiar with the American scene, having spent a year in the United States as a graduate student and having just returned from heading a purchasing commission, and he was a friend of Tereshchenko.[188] He also took with him as secretary-attaché an English-speaking history student, Michael Karpovich, who would make his own, valuable contribution to the preservation of a true sense of the Russian past as a Harvard professor and founder of the Russian Research Center.

The reason for the large size of this mission was apparently that it was initially formed by Miliukov, and after his resignation, rather than dismiss and replace members, the new administration simply added more personnel. And, as if this were not enough, Lincoln Steffens tagged along to carry a personal message from Kerensky to President Wilson and attempt to be Bakhmeteff's guide and adviser.[189] During the long Siberia-Pacific trip, according to Steffens, excellent cuisine was served, thanks to the influence of one of the mission's members, railroad authority (and Menshevik) Georgi Lomonosov.[190] Further delays ensued at Vladivostok and in Japan in finding passage for so many on the same ship.[191]

Breckinridge Long was again the State Department officer assigned to mission duty. Upon receiving information about the Russian mission, he complained

---

187. After attending a farewell reception for the delegation on 13 May, the day before Miliukov's resignation, Butler Wright commented, "not very much impressed." Diary, 13 May 1917, box 2, Wright Papers, Princeton-Mudd.

188. Houghteling diary, 20 April 1917, AE Russia, DPR 325, RG 84, NA. Houghteling quoted him before his appointment: "Bakhmeteff says it will be necessary to put a live wire in place of George Bakhmetev in Washington."

189. Steffens, *Autobiography*, 764.

190. Ibid., 766–67.

191. Steffens (Tsuruga, Japan) to Crane (May ?, 1917), reel 2, Crane Papers, BA, CU.

in his diary: "Awful news. They bring *wives*—lady stenographers, etc., etc. Awful fate—40 persons 10 ladies." The Russian mission was also the opposite of the Root mission in being unprepared for the more formal American receptions. Perhaps already prejudiced against time-consuming missions, Long, after meeting this one in Chicago on 18 June, expressed his disappointment: "Not much impressed with them. . . . Long talk with Bakhmeteff. He will talk too much. All energy—little dignity. No style. They had to buy *silk hats* in Chicago so as to arrive in Washington properly attired."[192]

By this time Washington was under siege by various Allied delegations, but Long managed to combine the Russians with the Belgians for a trip to Mount Vernon on the presidential yacht, the *Mayflower*. He admitted, however, that Bakhmeteff made good speeches in separate appearances in the House of Representatives and the Senate.[193] A number of the delegates managed to prolong their stays in the United States in supply work—for example, Lomonosov to tackle railroad orders and the Soviet representative assigned to study Russian immigrant settlements.[194]

Ambassador Bakhmeteff

Boris Bakhmeteff finally assumed the post of ambassador on 23 June, over two months after George Bakhmetev's resignation. He was greeted with a gift of another loan of $100 million from the American government, followed by an additional credit of $75 million on 13 July, earmarked for exchange into Finnish marks to pay for allowances and supplies for the radicalized Baltic Fleet, at least some of which would end up in the coffers of the Bolsheviks and Left Socialist Revolutionaries, who were popular among the sailors.[195] The first loan was committed to badly needed supplies as follows: $55,338,000 for 500 locomo-

192. Diary, 2 and 18 June, box 1, Long Papers, MD, LC.
193. Long diary, 23, 24, and 26 June, box 1, Long Papers, MD, LC.
194. Bakhmeteff to Tereshchenko, 7 and 18 October 1917, f. 133, op. 470, d. 61, AVPR.
195. Bakhmeteff to Tereshchenko, 16 and 23 June and 13 July 1917, f. 133, op. 470, d. 61, AVPR. Tereshchenko to Francis, 8 August 1917, AE Russia, DPR 301, RG 84, NA. Root and Francis appealed for a special grant for Finnmarks on 8 July. Cable to Lansing, reel 5, Francis Papers, MoHS.

The newspapers of the Bolshevik and Left SR parties in Helsingfors (Helsinki) regularly reported sizable donations from naval units in Finnmarks, which unlike the ruble remained stable and not depreciated. Finland, formally a grand duchy of the Russian empire in the process of moving toward full independence, provided a relatively safe haven for Russian radical activists such as Lenin after the July crisis. See Saul, *Sailors in Revolt*, 103ff.

*Ambassador Boris Bakhmeteff, courtesy of the Prints and
Photographs Division, Library of Congress*

tives and 10,000 boxcars; $25 million for Remington rifles; $15.6 million for 3 million pairs of boots; and $12,665,000 for agricultural machinery.[196]

Bakhmeteff's was not the only Russian mission to the United States; apparently many Russians were happy to escape to America in an official capacity, and quite a few managed to do so. A mining engineering delegation headed by Vasily Soldatenkov followed the main mission. The Ministry of War sent its own, thankfully smaller, delegation, headed by General Aleksei Potapov (a Boer War veteran!), on 12 May, just before Guchkov's resignation.[197] Of course, the

---

196. Tereshchenko to Francis, 8 August 1917, AE Russia, DPR 301, RG 84, NA.

197. Guchkov to Francis, 12 May 1917, and Riggs memorandum for Francis, 9 May, AE Russia, DPR 330, RG 84, NA.

navy, too, had to have its own mission and designated the deposed Black Sea commander, Alexander Kolchak, to head it, thus saving him from any further humiliation in the Russia of 1917. Apparently, the idea of Admiral Kolchak heading this mission was hatched by Admiral Glennon of the Root mission, who thought the American navy might be able to use his advice if and when an attack on the Dardanelles was planned; at least that was Kolchak's impression.[198] He and six other officers traveled the easier path through Scandinavia and London to Halifax but did not arrive until early September in Montreal, where they were met by old acquaintances Newton McCully and Alva Bernhard. They spent several weeks in New York and Washington and at the Naval War College in Newport, technically in an advisory role. Kolchak concluded his tour in October with a visit to the U.S. Atlantic fleet and an interview with President Wilson.[199]

Assistance to the Provisional Government

The various Russian delegations and the new ambassador constantly appealed for more American attention and funding for Russia, but most of their input was too little and too late.[200] When a frustrated Bakhmeteff turned to Colonel House for help, he was advised not to bother the president, but House made a case on his behalf, even suggesting the sending of troops to Russia via the Pacific.[201] Petrograd did not improve the situation by Tereshchenko sending a long rhetorical message addressed to "the Government of the United States."[202] Unfortunately, no Russian in the United States was even close to the stature of

198. Charles J. Weeks Jr. and Joseph O. Baylen, "Admiral Kolchak's Mission to the United States, 10 September–9 November 1917," *Military Affairs* 40, no. 2 (April 1976): 64–65; Fedotoff White, *Survival Through War and Revolution*, 155–56.

199. Weeks, *An American Naval Diplomat in Revolutionary Russia*, 123–28. Evidence for Kolchak's visit with the president seems to be only from his own testimony at his trial after capture by the Bolsheviks in 1919. Breckinridge Long was relieved that the Navy Department took care of all the arrangements. Long diary, 31 August 1917, box 1, Long Papers, MD, LC.

200. Appeals were too often cloaked in rhetoric, such as "The Provisional Government is endeavoring to establish a full understanding and a close cooperation with the Government of this country whose immense resources and unlimited energy contribute most effectively to the achievement of our cause." Bakhmeteff to Wilson, 15 July 1917, f. 133, op. 470, d. 61, AVPR.

201. House to Wilson, 23 July 1917, *PWW* 43:248–49.

202. Lansing to Wilson, 15 August 1917, enclosing Tereshchenko's note of 3 August, *PWW* 43:473–75. This was meant apparently to reassure Washington after the July crisis.

the heads of other Allied missions and their special envoys—Sir Cecil Spring Rice, Sir William Wiseman, Jules Jusserand, and Marshall Joseph Joffree. Although that may not have made any difference in relations with the American government, it did affect respect from the other Allies.

The persistent calls of David Francis and John Stevens for American aid may also have struck some chords in Washington, but most of the diplomatic and consular pleas were probably lost on an overworked, undermanned, and frustrated State Department. Breckinridge Long wrote privately to Francis about a failure to respond to one of his requests:

> I fear you do not appreciate the real conditions in the Department. Everything is delayed. Telegrams come in here so thick and fast, and requests are so many, that it is quite impossible to attend to any of them on time and to some of them at all. As it is, we work practically all the time. For instance: last night I worked until half past one—and that is not the exception. . . .
>
> All the Embassies and Legations complain that we are not giving them sufficient attention. To make matters worse, the draft has taken a great many men from the Department and, because of the draft, we are not able to fill up our ranks. Every body wants to put on a uniform and no body wants to pound the typewriter.[203]

Long blamed part of the problem on delays in transmission of cables from Petrograd, with some arriving as much as ten days after they were written, the main hangup apparently being between Petrograd and Stockholm.[204] The situation was even worse on the Russian end, with Francis complaining of not receiving any mail communications from the United States for a five-week period that included the visit of the Root mission.[205]

Finally, at the end of July, Bakhmeteff responded to a request from McAdoo to be more specific about his requests by designating $145 million out of $154 million for 30,000 freight cars ($53 million) and 1,500 locomotives ($88 million) and improvements to the Trans-Siberian road ($5 million). Washington bureaucrats, however, were still trying to integrate and coordinate the Russian needs with those of the other Allies.[206] Like his colleague in Petrograd, Bakhmeteff

203. Long to Francis, 14 September 1917, reel 4, Francis Papers, MoHS.
204. Ibid.
205. Francis to Jane Francis, 16 July 1917, reel 4, Francis Papers, MoHS.
206. Bakhmeteff to Tereshchenko, 27 and 30 July 1917, f. 133, op. 470, d. 61, AVPR.

complained of disorder, indecision, and inexperience in the government he was dealing with.[207]

Hard-pressed American officials enduring the scorching heat of Washington in August expressed exasperation with Russia's repeated requests for more money. Josephus Daniels noted the 7 August cabinet meeting:

> Furnishing engines & men to Russia. Depended upon money. Very difficult to get statement of exact & most pressing needs. Rus Am "Please let us have $165 mill dollars. If this is not done it will cause misunderstanding." No particulars. Must have detailed list & secure treasury loan before can determine what can be advanced.[208]

Obviously some Russian affairs were simply getting lost in the shuffle, but the real reason for the late and inadequate American assistance to Russia was simply a matter of priority. Creating a large American army and bolstering with supplies the French and British armies on the Western Front clearly came first. Not only that, but these priorities became almost an obsession of the administration in the summer of 1917. Part of this, of course, was due to the influence of Britain and France, whose military strategy had been and continued to be that the war would be won or lost on Flanders fields, on the Western Front, but it also represented the conviction of influential members of the administration.

American Impressions of Russia as Ally

Reports from Russia painted a dismal picture of disintegrating military and economic conditions. The problem of shipping goods on the long, hazardous routes to Russia loomed large, while war mobilization at home encountered numerous obstacles. No wonder Secretary of War Newton Baker took a very dim view of American aid to Russia and argued consistently against it. Influenced by many pessimistic reports, he insisted that Russia would leave the war sooner or later, and thus any aid would be a waste. A large American army in Europe—to replace the Russians—would be a prime necessity for a successful military outcome on the Western Front. Baker was backed in this belief by the army's acting chief of staff, General Tasker Bliss, and by his permanent replacement, General Peyton

207. Bakhmeteff to Tereshchenko, 9 August 1917, ibid.
208. Diary, 7 August 1917, in *PWW* 43:389.

March.[209] At least in this area—military aid to Russia—there was remarkable American consistency.

Much of the pessimism about Russia's military capability was shaped by events of early summer: the failure of the June Kerensky offensive and massive antiwar demonstrations in the streets of Petrograd that followed in mid-July, both well covered by the American press. William Howard Taft, one of two presidents (the other being John Quincy Adams) to have seen Russia before taking the office, wrote from his summer home in Canada:

> The debacle in Russia is very discouraging. It would seem as if the Empire had fallen apart nearly. The dictatorship may help, but if meantime the Germans move in and take all the equipment of the Russians, I don't know what will happen. They will be able to secure food and all sorts of supplies. It will throw on us a greater burden than ever.[210]

The early American solution for Russian collapse was thus to make a greater effort in western Europe, especially since the situation there was little better militarily.

The Root Mission Returns

Perhaps the members of the long-awaited but now nearly forgotten Root mission could exercise some leverage in Washington. They did indeed try, but the Washington they left in May was not the same one they came back to in August. The rift between the War Department and the president on one hand and the State Department on the other had widened, and everyone was concerned more with saving the Western Front for the Allies than Russia for democracy.

At a two-hour-long reception for Root and other members of the mission, including Stanley Washburn, on 8 August, President Wilson listened to their appeals for assistance for the Russian transportation system but claimed not to have understood their repeated requests for funding of a public information campaign.[211] He graciously received the detailed reports written by each mem-

---

209. Baker was especially annoyed by General Hugh Scott's report that called for a major American investment in Russia. Frederick Palmer, *Newton D. Baker: America at War*, vol. 1 (New York: Dodd, Mead, 1931), 143.

210. To Mabel Boardman, 27 July 1917, f. 1917, box 8, Boardman Papers, MD, LC.

211. Scott to Judson, 14 August 1917, box 29, Scott Papers, MD, LC; Washburn oral history, p. 118, CU. Washburn claims that at a subsequent meeting the following week, the president stated that he had turned over Russian affairs to Creel. Ibid., 121.

ber on the return trip and probably only scanned them before forwarding them to the State Department for file. If he had read them carefully, he probably would have found Mott's the most succinct and perceptive:

> It appeared that the Provisional Government, established in Petrograd upon the downfall of the autocracy in the revolution of March, 1917, had not succeeded in fact to the centralized power of the old bureaucratic government, but that extraordinary decentralization had followed the revolution. . . . The Central Government had for the time being no power to require action or to prevent action.[212]

Secretary Lansing, however, gained the impression that the commission members were misguidedly optimistic about the Kerensky government, since it was overthrown "not long after their return."

> Thus their recommendations predicated on the success of the Provisional Government could not be adopted, or, if they had been, would have been useless. Yet the Root Mission was composed of very able men who were doubtless as capable of judging the situation and giving advice as any this Government could have sent out.[213]

Like Taft and many others, Lansing was on vacation when the Root mission returned.

Back in his office in the War Department, Bentley Mott informed Judson in Petrograd that Scott was doing his best to get aid to Russia, but he thought that communications with Russia were a serious obstacle: "The only medium for news to Russia seems to be the State Department and as far as I can find out this is very unsatisfactory."[214] Mott reflected the drift in Washington during the summer of 1917–that the war was being fought by the War Department, not the State Department.

Still, President Wilson listened to repeated appeals, especially from McCormick and Bertron, and agreed in late August to another $100 million in credit for Russia, to include the sending of 2,000 more locomotives and 40,000 cars,

212. Mott report, M 367 (Records of the Department of State Relating to World War I and Its Termination, 1914–1929), RG 59, NA, which contains all the mission reports.

213. "Memorandum on the Russian Situation," 7 December 1917, f. The Conduct of American Foreign Affairs, box 7, Lansing Papers, Princeton-Mudd.

214. Mott to Judson, 15 September 1917, Judson Papers, Newberry Library.

and additional funding for a propaganda campaign in Russia to be launched by the Committee on Public Information.[215] None of the new railroad equipment, however, could be obtained and shipped to Vladivostok before 1918, and the new order for locomotives could not be filled until February 1919.[216]

Some of the initial purchases of American locomotives and freight cars that began arriving in 1917 were shipped as parts by Baldwin and American Locomotive Works to be assembled in Russia. At first the parts were forwarded to Harbin to be put together, but this proved unsatisfactory because of the additional strain on the railroad and the low rate of production there. By October, assembly had been shifted back to Vladivostok, where a rate of only twelve cars per day could be reached by mid-October, though the Stevens mission optimistically planned on 120 per day. A new locomotive assembly facility was expected to open near the dock in late November.[217]

The uncertainty of transportation held up earlier orders, to await, as Hugh Scott put it, "a clearing up of the railway situation, and definite reports from the Stevens commission as to what can be expected."[218] Even he, a strong advocate for aid to Russia, believed in the wisdom of avoiding risk by making decisions only when the supplies were available: "If Russia by that time is wobbling, we of course could not send them, but keep them for ourselves; if she is steadfast, they would do more good on her front than on the French one."[219] Russia was already wobbling.

In all these orders for railroad equipment, no mention can be found of any requests for passenger cars to transport troops across Siberia. No need for them was anticipated because the Russian army, excepting officers, was accustomed to traveling in boxcars.[220] This would certainly not be the case for any American troops that might be sent.

---

215. Bertron to Francis, 27 August 1917, AE Russia, DPR 329, RG 84, NA. Bertron claimed that he had spent an hour and a half with the president alone, but the only written correspondence between them during this period has nothing to do with Russia. *PWW* 44:309, 335-37, 359. Harper credited his influence on McCormick for the timeliness of the loan. Harper to Williams, 17 May 1917, reel 2, Crane Papers, BA, CU.

216. Lansing to Francis, 5 October and 8 November 1917, AE Russia, DPR 303, RG 84, NA.

217. Decker to Gertie, 16 October 1917, in *Mission to Russia, An American Journal*, 144-45.

218. Scott to Root, 7 September 1917, box 71, Scott Papers, MD, LC.

219. Report to Secretary of War, 25 July 1917, box 71, Scott Papers, MD, LC.

220. For a description of the movement of a division by train, see Malcolm C. Grow, *Surgeon Grow, an American in the Russian Fighting* (New York: F. A. Stokes, 1918), 219-21.

American Propaganda Campaign

One of the Root mission's strongest recommendations for action in Russia was an extensive publicity campaign to counter the German efforts, to explain why the United States had entered the war, and to glorify the virtues of democratic institutions. It was advocated by the most influential members of the mission—Russell, McCormick, Bertron, and Mott—and by Root himself and also had the firm backing of Francis, Harper, and most of the American colony. What they wanted was a considerable fund, Root requesting $5 million to compete with the $1 million per month he claimed the Germans were spending, and more personnel to launch an effective campaign to produce and circulate political literature in Russian and to influence the Russian press.[221]

Francis suggested that Harper direct the work under the embassy's supervision.[222] More controversy ensued when Russell proposed himself as head but was strongly opposed by Duncan, who argued that his "only object is socialistic propaganda."[223] Finally, Francis drafted his friend Corse to head the work on a part-time basis and asked the State Department for $250,000 to fund it over a six-month period.[224] Perhaps because of the confusion and contradictory recommendations, Washington again delayed and temporized but eventually forwarded some very modest sums.

The Wilson administration agreed on the importance of such a publicity effort but wanted it coordinated and centralized under a new agency, the Committee on Public Information (CPI), headed by journalist George Creel, but that took time to get organized. From the beginning the State Department resented and opposed its independent authority, especially in regard to work abroad. Formed officially on 14 April, the committee was not fully operational until a month later, but its primary mission was the manipulating and censoring of the American press. Plans for Russia remained bogged down in Washington red tape until Arthur Bullard, another liberal journalist and friend of House, Crane, and Russell, was designated to head the Russian campaign.[225] After completing an assignment for Creel, he was finally ready to begin work in mid-June and attempted without success to obtain State Department credentials.[226]

---

221. Root to Lansing for McAdoo, and Root to Lansing (two separate cables), 2 July 1917, reel 4, Francis Papers, MoHS.
222. Francis to Lansing, 5 July 1917, AE Russia, DPR 299, RG 84, NA.
223. Francis to Lansing (decoded cable), 7 July 1917, reel 4, Francis Papers, MoHS.
224. Francis to Summers, 5 August 1917, reel 5, Francis Papers, MoHS.
225. Creel to Wilson, 10 May 1917, vol. 3, Creel Papers, MD, LC.
226. Bullard to Lansing, 13 June 1917, *PWW* 42:508–9; to House, 3 June 1917, box 9 (House correspondence), Bullard Papers, Princeton-Mudd; Edgar Sisson, *One Hundred Red*

Impatient with Washington's bureaucratic slowness, Bullard went on to Russia with the blessings of Creel and Colonel House, under the guise of a journalist, to scout the territory. Arriving at the end of July, he was baffled over how to proceed, given the publicity operations already under way. To House, he finally communicated in August that he had been reluctant to report because of the complexities of the situation but described transport woes, much talk of a separate peace, and a hostile impression of perceived American pressure: "The Americans treat us like mercenaries—they offer to pay us to fight." He thought that the Bolsheviks had been discredited as German agents and were on the wane, and he was in no hurry to take over the publicity work.[227]

Bullard recruited Malcolm Davis, a YMCA secretary who knew Russian, for translating CPI materials into Russian; he thought about using university professors in Moscow but was dismayed by the formidable task of trying to persuade Russians to continue the war. In a letter to Wright in October, he wrote, "'To keep Russia in war'—I find a great many of my friends here feel that this is our sole interest in Russia. . . . The psychological crisis is as acute as the political crisis and equally dangerous." He thought the departure of British subjects especially demoralizing. "More than one Russian friend has used the comparison of rats leaving a sinking ship. . . . With the best will in the world there is very little we can do to help Russia in the immediate crisis." He suggested long-term projects such as a model school, special American exhibits on education and agriculture, and Rhodes scholarships for Russia.[228] But there was little time left for that. By the end of October Bullard sensed the need for more immediate action because of the increasing deluge of anti-American articles produced by radical Jews from New York's East Side. He thought that Wright was trying to develop the publicity work, "but he is the busiest man in the Embassy."[229]

Bullard's main problem was that he still did not have a budget to implement much of anything. The Root mission had followed up its initial appeal, awkwardly entitled "Plans for American Cooperation to Preserve and Strengthen the Morale of the Civil Population and Army of Russia," for a major allocation of $5 million for a publicity campaign in Russia with a more detailed request on 15 August. It was broken down as follows: news service ($285,500), pamphlets and leaflets ($250,000 to 500,000), film service ($255,000), special

Days: A Personal Chronicle of the Bolshevik Revolution (New Haven, Conn.: Yale University Press, 1931), 75–76.

227. Bullard to House, 22 August 1917, box 9, Bullard Papers, Princeton-Mudd.

228. Bullard to Wright, 11 October 1917, DPR 299, Russia 1917, RG 84, NA.

229. Bullard to Creel, 1 November 1917, f. CPI, Russian Division, box 6, Bullard Papers, Princeton-Mudd.

advertising ($211,000), the hiring of 500 Russians to lecture ($405,000), sub-sidies for a soldiers' newspaper and for other Russian agencies ($250,000), contingency fund ($250,000), and expenses for 700 YMCA secretaries and 200 "huts" ($3,305,000).

The president passed this to Creel, who recommended cutting everything except news service ($500,000), film service ($300,000), and the soldiers' newspaper ($10,000). His objection to the large YMCA request was not that this would put the government in the position of sponsoring a religious organization but that it would take too long to implement.[230] For his part, Root was quite disappointed with the delays and the fact that any new shipments from America would be "pretty slow." He accurately, though, referred to his commission as "wandering amateur diplomatists."[231]

Mott, Root, and McCormick again conferred with the president at the White House on 30 August and presented a new, more general plan for a $2.2 million "educational campaign" in Russia and $2 million more to raise the morale of the Russian army, to which was added $1 million each for the British and French armies. Most of this latter total of $4 million seemed earmarked for the YMCA but apparently was not specifically designated. This, too, was referred to Creel for comment but with no apparent action taken.[232] Mott and McCormick per-sisted, with the latter calling on the president on 19 September and again in early October.[233] After another meeting with Mott on 26 September, Wilson, tightfisted as usual, approved a more modest funding but instructed Creel not to withdraw "a whole million" from the Treasury at once but to withdraw "por-tions of it from time to time."[234]

Although it finally earmarked $1 million for publicity in Russia, Washing-ton had moved slowly. Referring to "our conjectures" concerning lack of funding, Butler Wright instructed Summers in October, citing a new State Department instruction, "to hold in abeyance any further propaganda plans pending the receipt of forthcoming instructions regarding the completion by

230. Creel to Wilson, with enclosure, 20 August 1917, PWW 43:526-30.

231. Root to Francis, 29 August 1917, reel 4, Francis Papers, MoHS. Whether he was amateur or professional probably made no difference, but the president's personal dislike of Root did.

232. Mott to Wilson, 30 August 1917, and Wilson to Creel, 4 September 1917, PWW 44:92, 142.

233. McCormick to Tumulty, 29 September 1917, f. Woodrow Wilson, box 116, 2C, McCormick Papers, SHSW.

234. Wilson to Creel, 27 September 1917, and Mott's notes of conversation, PWW 44:270-71.

the Committee on Public Information in Washington of a comprehensive plan for propaganda."[235] Corse also expressed his disappointment:

> For reasons best known to themselves, our Washington friends have not given the support for publicity work in Russia which we had reason to expect from the diplomatic commission. As a result I have been unable to organize such a bureau as I had in mind when agreeing to take over the work which I am supposed to do in this connection.[236]

At least the State Department was able, belatedly, to send some forty-nine copies of a special film produced by the D. W. Griffith Company with Guy Crowell Smith.[237]

By the time the Creel Committee work could be amply funded and organized and staff dispatched to Russia, the Bolshevik revolution had occurred. The same story was again repeated for Russia—too little and too late, although the question remains open as to whether a barrage of American words could have made any difference in Russia by the middle of 1917. The committee ran the risk of arousing even more the Russian sensitivity to outside manipulation.

In the meantime, a modest publicity campaign was mounted with funds and personnel that could be spared from the diplomatic and consular offices and from the American colony. The head of this program in the capital was Frederick Corse, using the offices of New York Life and the informed advice of Harper and Mott. Francis praised Corse's initiative and advised against sending a new person to direct the campaign, but was disappointed that his request for $250,000 for expenses was not answered by the State Department.[238]

In Moscow, Consul General Summers instituted an even more ambitious operation with the assistance of his Russian wife and the expanded personnel of a new office, now centrally located on (later notorious) Lubianka Square, declared by some to be "the handsomest Consulate in Europe"—with electric multigraph machines mounted on the billiard tables.[239] Volunteers from

235. Wright to Summers, 9 October 1917, AE Russia, DPR 299, RG 84, NA.

236. Corse to Summers, 18 October 1917, ibid.

237. This was probably *Hearts of the World*, starring Lillian Gish as a French peasant girl enduring a brutal German occupation. Michael T. Isenberg, *War on Film: The American Cinema and World War I, 1914–1941* (Rutherford, N.J.: Fairleigh Dickinson University Press, 1981), 201. Its reception in Russia is unknown.

238. Cables to Lansing, 10 and 26 July and 11 August 1917, AE Russia, DPR 299, RG 84, NA.

239. Summers to Francis, 17 August 1917, reel 4, Francis Papers, MoHS.

International Harvester and Singer helped distribute 8,000 copies of one pamphlet.[240] Summers did see one possible drawback to what he considered a remarkable success: "I am afraid that all of this publicity will bring about, after the war, the greatest wave of immigration ever known to the human race."[241]

By mid-October the campaign broadened to include many films shipped over by both Creel and the State Department. Butler Wright, perhaps prompted by Bullard's interest in a long-term effort, wanted less emphasis in the films on battles and troop training and more on present and future problems such as hygiene, sanitary construction, agriculture, and rail transport, "and particularly the rights, privileges, and responsibilities of citizenship, the methods and machinery of elections, and the disposition of the public domain," because "in the mind of the ignorant soldier and the illiterate peasant (of which, God knows, there are an appalling number), law and order have been done away with in the temporary enjoyment of 'freedom.'"[242] He suggested a film showing a Russian married to an American who goes to the United States and views the work ethic in large factories, fire drills and calisthenics, and a traffic cop at Fifth Avenue and Forty-second Street, "in fact, anything to show the moral effect of law, order, system, individual responsibility."[243] Americans could not shed themselves of the idea of "Americanizing" Russia.

In practice, both of the Petrograd and Moscow centers were essentially information bureaus whose goal was to plant pro-American and pro-war news items in the Russian press. They ran into problems when they attempted to coordinate their work with the French and British, and, according to Summers, lost a couple of valuable weeks in August.[244] A shortage of resources was the key limiting factor. Francis continued to complain that he "had cabled the Department so often on this subject without receiving satisfactory replies that yesterday I sent through the Department a cable to Root, Mott, McCormick, and Bertron."[245] The Red Cross, YMCA, and some journalists assisted in promoting the American cause of democracy and victory through war and service.

240. Summers to Francis, 12 July 1917, AE Russia, DPR 299, RG 84, NA.
241. Summers to Wright, 24 July 1917, ibid.
242. Wright to Philip Patchen (State Department), 17 October 1917, AE Russia, DPR 329, RG 84, NA.
243. Ibid.
244. To Francis, 17 August 1917, reel 4, Francis Papers, MoHS.
245. To Summers, 12 August 1917, ibid.

Red Cross and YMCA Missions

More promising in the short term was the arrival of a new, high-powered Red Cross mission during the second week of August, inspired by "Colonel" William Boyce Thompson and headed officially by Colonel Frank Billings, a noted Chicago physician. The mission included Raymond Robins, a veteran of Hull House and a Republican Party activist, and twenty-five other men of varied distinction and experience. It had been organized virtually single-handedly by Thompson, a Montana copper magnate transplanted to Wall Street, who was convinced of the importance of supporting Russia and maintaining the Eastern Front.[246] Following the precedent of the Stevens delegation, the Red Cross commission traveled first-class on the *Empress of Asia* across the Pacific but did not come empty-handed. It arrived in Petrograd on 7 August well furnished with medical supplies and equipment, and Thompson proceeded immediately to subscribe for 500,000 rubles of a Russian liberty bond campaign and to contribute $20,000 more for Corse's Petrograd publicity work.[247]

The Red Cross commissioners set out immediately to catch up on Russian affairs. Francis held a dinner for them with embassy personnel on 9 August and the next day had a smaller luncheon for Billings, Thompson, Kerensky, and Tereshchenko, while Robins lunched with Crane.[248] Samuel Harper was again recruited to help them get situated and now found his time divided three ways between advising Francis on a regular basis, assisting with the Petrograd propaganda effort, and serving the new Red Cross mission.[249] The mission had a vague political agenda based on the belief that a democratic Russia could only be saved by military victory, and the maintenance of the Eastern Front was an important part of that goal. This program was sustained for several months by Thompson's money and Robins's enthusiasm. Like other such endeavors, it was at least partly damaged by insensitivity. The members arrived in resplendent uniforms (purchased by Thompson), were furnished with the finest luxury auto-

---

246. Neil V. Salzman, *Reform and Revolution: The Life and Times of Raymond Robins* (Kent, Ohio: Kent State University Press, 1991), 176–78. Thompson's $250,000 donation helped persuade the American Red Cross leadership in Washington to go along with the project. Francis to Summers, 12 August 1917, reel 4, Francis Papers, UC.

247. Francis to Summers, 12 August 1917, reel 4, Francis Papers, UC. Later in October, Thompson opened an account for $1 million at National City Bank to be used for the good of the cause.

248. Francis and Thompson to Lansing, 10 August 1917, AE Russia, DPR, RG 84, NA; Salzman, *Reform and Revolution*, 184.

249. Harper to brother Paul, 12 August 1917, f. 10, box 4, Harper Papers, UC.

mobiles (Arrow-Pierce and Rolls-Royce), were lodged in the most expensive quarters available, and spent much time at the ballet and opera, where they usually sat in the imperial box.[250]

The Red Cross members were not certain what else to do in Russia, since emergency military medical needs were waning. After dining with the Petr Kropotkins on 15 August, Robins thought he had found "the way for our Mission to serve Russia in the most supreme fashion in the organization and distribution of the food and clothing resources throughout the empire."[251] But then he was disappointed that "the Colonels" (Thompson and Billings) vetoed the plan: "The Commission has chosen the 'safety first' program! Personal security, a bit of charitable relief, and then home as fast as we can go. . . . The big door was closed by us after conference this morning. I was in a minority when it came to the real adventure."[252]

Despite Robins's opinion about a missed opportunity, the mission had already encountered serious obstacles in obtaining supplies. Shipping was scarce and backlogged on the Atlantic, and Pacific freighters had been diverted to the Atlantic. A solution was to try to purchase food and clothing in the Far East, mainly China, for shipment to Russia, but it was soon discovered that stocks of clothing were low there, rice exports were restricted, and flour was virtually unavailable.[253] In any event, the Trans-Siberian route was nearly impossible.

From the beginning, Raymond Robins was the most active of the Red Cross men, making numerous speeches, attending meetings, seeking out leaders, and especially conferring regularly with Ekaterina Breshko-Breshkovskaia at her suite in the Winter Palace.[254] "She is now a stage piece a bit of wonderful human scenery and with great influence as such to help Kerensky whom she adores and supports to the last limit of her power. . . . The old grandmother fears famine and cold and the return of the autocracy."[255] In September, Billings and some other members of the mission returned to America, apparently with the object of obtaining more support for operations in Russia, but they found the association too busy with national fund drives and with little interest in Russia.[256]

250. Robins at least professed to be embarrassed by this. To his wife, 24 September 1917, typed extracts, box 13, Robins Papers, SHSW.

251. Robins to wife, 16 August 1917, f. August, box 12, Robins Papers, SHSW.

252. To wife, 17 August 1917, ibid.

253. John Finch (Peking) to Thompson, 20 August 1917, f. Mission to Russia: Food and Clothing Supplies, box 187, ARC Papers, HIA.

254. To wife, 21 September 1917, box 13, Robins Papers, SHSW.

255. To wife, 15 August 1917, box 12, ibid.

256. Billings to Harper, 16 November 1917, f. 13, box 4, Harper Papers, UC.

Meanwhile, Robins, backed especially by Allen Wardwell and Thomas Thacher, weathered the storm of an attempted coup by General Lvar Kornilov in early September and gave full support to Kerensky. Later that month, after attending the Democratic State Conference, an assemblage of representatives of the various socialist parties in Petrograd, he was clearly impressed by Bolshevik leadership: "The most skillful and dangerous leader of the extreme left was Trotsky. He together with Karmeneff [Lev Kamenev] marshalled the Bolchivicki [sic]–Immediate Peace–Social revolutionary groups with judgment and precision."[257]

While Robins familiarized himself with the rising left wing of the political scene, others of the mission seemed not to know exactly how to spend their time and acted as tourists. Dr. Orrin Wightman, after consulting with Maddin Summers, traveled south to Romania, the chief objective being to take motion pictures of the collapse of fighting on that front. There is no indication from his own record that he accomplished anything medical during his time in Russia.[258] But Wightman saw a great need for supplies and ambulances for the Red Cross units in Romania and returned to Moscow on 25 October to arrange for them.[259] In fact, a major problem facing the Red Cross was that with very limited fighting by the Russian army, there was less need for its services but more for the basic supplies it could furnish.

After touring and sitting for a couple of months in Russia, Thompson became alarmed by the danger of an imminent fall of the last allied government of Russia and in early October transferred $1 million of his own money to Russia to prop it up through an expanded publicity campaign, coordinated with Creel and his Committee on Public Information.[260] Why he believed this action would have any effect or why he waited so long to take it remains unclear, but he was obviously frustrated by Washington's failure to respond to a number of requests for funds and believed that Russia was being lost by the input of German money.[261] The channel of distribution was Breshko-Breshkovskaia and David Soskice, Kerensky's private secretary, and their Committee on Civic Education in Free Russia, a sort of Kerensky slush fund. In any event, it was symbolic of American policy toward the pre-Bolshevik Russia—too little and too late.

257. To wife, 7 October 1917, f. September–October 1917, box 13, Robins Papers, SHSW.

258. See his *Diary of an American Physician.*

259. Robert Barr to Colonel Thompson, 25 October 1917, f. Mission to Russia, box 187, American Red Cross Papers, HIA.

260. Creel personally went to New York on 13 October to arrange the transfer of money. Creel to Wilson, 12 October 1917, vol. 3, Creel Papers, MD, LC.

261. Salzman, *Reform and Revolution,* 188–93.

Thompson supporting publicity campaign, in the Winter Palace (August 1917). Seated, from left to right: William Boyce Thompson, Lazarov, Ekaterina Breshko-Breshkovskaya; standing: Nikolai Chaikovskii, Frederick Corse, Viktor Soskice (Kerensky's secretary), and Raymond Robins, courtesy of the State Historical Society of Wisconsin

Under the leadership of John R. Mott, the American YMCA planned a major expansion in Russia through the transfer of personnel from German and Austrian prisoner-of-war work to serving the Russian military in the field and in the cities. The goal was to offer programs, facilities, and services to soldiers to improve their morale and their will to fight. The process was slow, however, because of the time needed for the transfer of the prisoner work to Swedish commissions and continuing obstructions of the Provisional Government. It may also have been the case that American "Y" workers were reluctant to leave the highly successful operations they had established. In Tomsk, Donald Lowrie wound up his work at the end of July, proudly reporting on what had been accomplished: dental and medical clinics, libraries of several thousand volumes, various classes in mechanics and languages, athletic clubs, orchestras and choirs, vegetable gardens, even bookkeeping courses for disabled prisoners. Clothing and shoes were in short supply, since the Russians had stopped supplying any, but surplus vegetables and medical supplies were shared with local Russian hospitals in exchange for other items.[262]

Although several approaches were made to the central government about serving military units, including one by Mott directly to Kerensky in July, little progress was made. In the meantime, by dealing with local authorities, such as the Moscow Soviet, YMCA activities expanded in the major cities. Finally, on 20 October 1917 the Provisional Government granted the "Y" general operational permission throughout the country, including the frontline units. The resolution provided for free transportation, exemption of supplies from customs duties, enlistment of soldiers and officers as workers, and free use of buildings.[263]

Mott planned to send in 200 secretaries during the winter and raise $2 to $3 million at home to support them.[264] In the meantime, after several weeks of preparation, the first YMCA "hut" opened in Odessa on 6 October with much fanfare, many speeches, a large, receptive crowd of soldiers, and the showing of American motion pictures.[265] A veteran "Y" man and Harvard graduate, Lowrie was in charge and proud that attendance soared from 508 the first night to a capacity house of 1,800 within a week.[266]

The YMCA had an excellent foundation for an increased presence in Russia. Besides Mott's special interest in Russia, backed by Crane and Harper, several able people with considerable Russian experience were available. They included Franklin Gaylord, a founder and adviser of the Russian "Mayak" (Lighthouse) organization since 1909; Archie Harte, who had already won much respect for his work during the war with prisoner relief; Hugh Moran, whose activities were mainly confined to Siberia; Jerome Davis, in charge of YMCA service to prisoners of war; as well as Lowrie, Paul Anderson, and several others.[267]

The "Y" added another dimension to its activities. In May, two experienced YWCA workers, Elizabeth Boies and Clarissa Spencer, arrived in Petrograd; after three months of preparation, they opened a school for young girls just off Nevsky Prospect that featured a tea room, a gymnasium, and classes in languages, with

262. Lowrie to Mott, 30 July 1917, f. 1917, box 1, Lowrie Papers, UIA.
263. Davis, "Relationship of the YMCA to the Russian Government," f. YMCA, Anderson Papers, UIA.
264. Mott to Harper, 5 October 1917, f. 12, box 4, Harper Papers, UC.
265. Wightman, who gave a speech, described the scene. *Diary of an American Physician*, 160–66. Lowrie described Odessa as quite different from other Russian cities—prosperous, bustling sidewalk cafes, cosmopolitan, with well-dressed women. To Folks, 16 September 1917, box 1, Lowrie Papers, UIA.
266. Lowrie to Folks, 14 October 1917, f. 1917, ibid.
267. Hopkins, *John R. Mott*, 494ff.

English being the most popular. Providing tea (with sugar!) and sandwiches guaranteed that the facility was quickly filled to capacity. The Americans were assisted in obtaining the rooms and necessary permissions by Russian women leaders, especially Anna Miliukova (Paul's wife), Ekaterina Vasilshchikova, and Madam Orzhevskaia, widow of a former tsarist head of political police in the 1880s.[268]

The "Y" personnel also had the advantage over the Red Cross people in having their own base of operations already established in Mayak, being less nationally oriented and at least making a show of having no political agenda, and exuding an aura of self-sacrifice. Then, too, the "Y" was reaping the rewards of its considerable success in serving troops behind the Western Front in France. Somehow the "Y" recruits were better prepared, trained, and motivated for service in Russia, and by November they were arriving in considerable numbers. They would come closest to a real American success story in revolutionary Russia.

But as more "Y" and Red Cross personnel began filing into Russia, other Americans prepared to leave, either frustrated and worn out, aware of the approach of a grim winter, or under the impression their service would be more valuable elsewhere. Major losses to Francis were the transfer of Petrograd consul North Winship to Milan and the departure of Samuel Harper, who had become the ambassador's chief interpreter and adviser.[269]

The very considerable American relief operations on behalf of prisoners of war naturally should have come to a conclusion with the ending of American neutrality, but it took some time to transfer the work to remaining neutrals, chiefly Scandinavian. Summers was left with the big job of straightening out a mess of paperwork and a considerable confusion in financial accounting.

> The complete chaos which I found in the office on my arrival, the absence of books showing certain disbursements, especially clothing, and the general disorderly state of accounts and correspondence since 1914, all had to be remedied. This, to a great extent, has been done, yet two years work, in a confused state, cannot be straightened out save with great patience.[270]

---

268. Boies to Miss Cratty, extracts of 24 June, 29 August, and 1 October 1917, f. Elizabeth Boies letters, box 3, Lowrie Papers, UIA; "Out of Russia with Uncle Sam," *War Work Bulletin*, no. 33 (14 June 1918): 1, based on a talk by Spencer.

269. Francis to Jane, 9 August 1917, and Jordan to Mrs. Francis, 19 September 1917, reel 5, Francis Papers, MoHS.

270. Summers to Francis, 23 July 1917, reel 9, Francis Papers, MoHS.

He suspected that large amounts of German money had been misappropriated and feared future investigations. The collapse of the Central Powers in November 1918 relieved the United States of any charges of malfeasance in prisoner-of-war relief.

The Kornilov Affair

What Russia did not need in August and September 1917 was another major crisis. After the armed demonstrations of mid-July against his government in the wake of the unsuccessful offensive, Kerensky appointed one of Russia's few war heroes, General Lavr Kornilov, as commander in chief of the army, with the hope that his reputation might yet restore a crumbling military system. Kornilov's task was certainly not an easy one, with discipline and morale in a state of free fall. Backed by most of the high officer corps, he believed that the maintenance of order and fighting capability of the armed forces demanded extreme measures, including the restoration of the death penalty for severe infractions such as desertion, but this required action by the Provisional Government. He conferred with Kerensky twice on this subject and seemed to have his agreement, but nothing was done.[271] The problem became more acute by the ease with which the Germans, resuming the offensive, captured Riga in mid-August.

Kornilov moved a number of Russia's best, most loyal divisions to the vicinity of Petrograd, ostensibly to deal with any continuing German advance. About the same time, an important assembly of Russian political leaders and businessmen was scheduled in Moscow for 25–28 August. Kornilov and Kerensky both

---

271. Raymond Robins describes one of these visits on 23 August:

Today we were at the Winter Palace when Korniloff came in to see Karensky [*sic*]. His escort dashed up to the inner entrance and formed a hollow square and out of the automobile jumped this swarthy Tartar in the gorgeous Cossack general's uniform. [With] [s]trong face and military air he passed into Karensky's suite and I felt the tingling that sometimes comes to me in the presence of men that shall interest me profoundly. I had a curious feeling that here was the man—the Dictator of tomorrow. I saw Karensky at the meeting and it seemed as if the one was passing and the other coming into his day of power. It is all quite childish but I felt it a strange certainty. Well we shall see what we do see. Korniloff was surrounded by his special Cossack guard. Each man carried a rifle a pistol a sabre and a dagger. They were barbaric and it was as if you looked upon a painting of some scene of the far gone yesterdays. I am wondering what was said between these two men who hold the fate of Russia for this hour? These are great days, Sweetheart Mine!!

To his wife, 23 August 1917, f. August 1917, box 12, Robins Papers, SHSW.

appeared at this "Moscow State Conference," but the former, with his pleas for more authority to restore law and order, was clearly in the ascendant. The general received ovations wherever he appeared and the direct encouragement of a number of influential moderates and conservatives in private meetings. The outcome of the conference was still ambiguous, with Kerensky believing he had received a vote of confidence. During the meeting in Moscow, Samuel Harper described to Mott a mood of optimism he detected regarding the Kerensky government. He thought it had turned a corner and was gaining the upper hand vis-à-vis the challenge from the radical left, but he was dismayed by the absence of strong support from the United States.

From this point the decisions and events in Russia remain confused, especially regarding the circumstances by which Kornilov and Kerensky understood or misunderstood each other's intentions. The general, however, definitely believed that the crux of the problem was to separate the Provisional Government from the influence of the Soviet and was prepared to use force to accomplish this. In early September he moved two loyal divisions toward Petrograd, an action that was interpreted by Kerensky as a bid to overthrow the Provisional Government and establish a military dictatorship. Kerensky then turned to the Soviet leadership for support and allowed the rearming of Red Guards, who had been disarmed following the July crisis, in order to defend the city and his government.[272]

The role of the Allied representatives in this impasse remains something of a mystery and has received relatively little investigation. Obviously, there was unanimity of concern with Russia's military disintegration but little consensus about what to do about it. Indications are that the influential British military representatives, General Charles Barter, liaison officer at Stavka, and General Alfred Knox, military attaché, backed by the War Office in London, actively supported Kornilov's insistence on establishing martial law. Barter even accompanied him to the Moscow State Conference.[273]

As tensions mounted in Petrograd and confusion reigned, the Allied diplomats, meeting regularly, urged compromise but basically sided with Kerensky. This was especially true of British ambassador George Buchanan, who was miffed by the independence of the military advisers and their lack of communication

272. For more details consult W. Bruce Lincoln, *Passage Through Armageddon: The Russians in War and Revolution, 1914–1918* (New York: Oxford University Press, 1986), 414–24; and George Katkov, *Russia 1917, The Kornilov Affair: Kerensky and the Break-Up of the Russian Army* (London: Longman, 1980).

273. Norman E. Saul, "British Involvement in the Kornilov Affair," *Rocky Mountain Social Science Journal* 10, no. 1 (January 1973): 43–50.

with him. David Francis was even more supportive of the Provisional Government in the several diplomatic conferences held during these days, owing perhaps to his close working relationship with Tereshchenko. For both Buchanan and Francis, the likelihood of civil war was a worse prospect than seeing the Russian army continue to decline.

William Judson, now with the rank of brigadier general, and Captain Crosley were certainly aware of the seriousness of the situation. In a prophetic memorandum to Francis, Judson advised that Kerensky be urged to compromise:

> The conditions are such that if the Army Chiefs lose in the present conflict with the Temporary Government anarchy will result with the utmost certainty. Russia will remain at war indeed, but not with the common enemy. The Kaiser will have won and Russia will have lost everything, including the peace that so many cherish.[274]

Kerensky, however, took his own counsel, appealed to the Petrograd Soviet for support, and challenged Kornilov. Poor planning and communication resulted in the disintegration of Kornilov's march on the city and his removal from command. The head of the Provisional Government won the day but at the expense of further erosion of his reputation and a capitulation to demands of the Soviet to release those arrested after the July crisis, such as Trotsky.

While sympathetic to the aims of Kornilov and quite critical of Kerensky, for basic philosophical reasons most American diplomats were not prepared to see Russia move in the direction of a military dictatorship or a restoration of the monarchy (rumored at the time). They had little contact with Kornilov and his headquarters, nor did they attend the Moscow conference.[275] Moreover, they lacked any instructions in the matter from Washington, perhaps an impossibility considering communication difficulties. Discounting American support, the British military mission apparently made no effort to coordinate policy with their American colleagues.

Everyone involved in or witnessing the events, except the radical left, agreed that the outcome offered dismal prospects for Russia's continued participation in the war and for much stability or support for the Kerensky government. Many believed that it had been dealt what Kerensky would later refer to as "the stab in

274. Judson memorandum, 10 September 1917, in *Russia in War and Revolution*, 74.

275. Butler Wright probably reflected the opinion of most of the embassy staff in his emphatic opposition to Kornilov. Diary, 13 September 1917, box 2, Wright Papers, Princeton-Mudd.

the back," but they saw no alternative to staying with the government, still committed to the war, to remaining aboard a sinking ship. American dispatches from Russia now more frequently warned of increasing chaos, anarchy, and the Bolshevik menace. Judson, noting rumors of the capital moving to Moscow, expressed the consensus view: "The situation here is most discouraging in every respect."[276]

Back in Washington, Hugh Scott expressed his concern to Judson: "It looks as if Russia is on the toboggan slide unless that army braces up right away."[277] Kept informed by Scott on a regular basis, General John J. Pershing, from his base in France, corrected on 1 October an earlier impression and saw the implications of the collapse of Russia:

> My optimism at that time [letter of 17 July] regarding the quick recovery of the Russian people and their establishment of a stable government has not been realized. The Russian situation today is probably the most serious obstacle to our success. Unless they can pull themselves together and make some sort of showing, there is nothing to prevent a large number of German divisions from coming to the western front. I still hope the Russians may realize their own precarious condition.[278]

276. To his wife, 19 and 24 September 1917, Judson Papers, Newberry Library.
277. Scott to Judson, 12 September 1917, box 71, Scott Papers, MD, LC.
278. Pershing to Scott, 1 October 1917, f. Sch–Sco, box 181, Pershing Papers, MD, LC; original to Scott, box 30, Scott Papers, MD, LC.

4

Soviet Power

By October 1917 Americans in Russia and at home had little good left to say about the Kerensky-led Provisional Government, though most realized that the deteriorating military and economic situation of Russia was not of its making and largely beyond its control. Nevertheless, Kerensky and his dwindling number of able associates and supporters, shared at least some of the responsibility. The sorry outcome of the Kornilov affair especially dashed hopes of some sort of miracle that would bring Russia fully back into the war. And because major victories eluded the Allies in 1917, the likelihood of the war continuing for at least another year increased concern about maintaining an active Eastern Front and focused more attention on Russia.

The withering away of the authority of the Provisional Government by the end of September 1917 left an enormous vacuum to be filled. Under the circumstances, much of the residue of power was falling naturally into the hands of leaders of local governments. This had already occurred in far-flung places such as Vladivostok and Archangel, in Ukraine, and in Finland, near the Russian capital. Pauline Crosley observed on 14 October, "Anarchy in general throughout Russia is on the increase, more and more cities and towns becoming involved."[1] At home George Kennan was equally discouraged: "I am not even sure that there will be a new Russia in the near future."[2]

In the key cities of Petrograd and Moscow, both in new soviet institutions and in the traditional dumas or city councils, one particular party had emerged as the clear alternative—the Bolshevik wing of the Russian Social Democratic Labor Party—commanding a majority or near majority. The party that had declined so precipitously between July and October was the Socialist Revolutionary Party, Kerensky's political base, which had also split into left and right wings,

1. Crosley, *Intimate Letters from Petrograd*, 188.
2. To Ely, 10 October 1917, box 15, Kennan Papers, MD, LC.

with only the latter supporting the war. What made the situation worse in the capital was the threat of German occupation, which was creating a near panic of evacuation of people and objects and consideration of moving the government to Moscow. Summing up the situation in a "better late than never" dispatch on 7 November, the American consul general noted, "I cannot but draw the Department's attention to a growing revulsion against the Government and its disintegrating policy."[3]

Underlying the transformation of the Russian empire toward a more radical socialist leadership and into breakaway national or local governments was the continuation of the war and economic decline. The first was being solved by the disintegration of a large portion of the military force by desertion of millions of fighting men, by destruction of the chain of command by unit committees and a consequent defection of officers, as in the case of the Baltic Fleet, or by a deliberate effort to cleanse the military of disloyal elements, initiated by Minister of War Verkhovskii. For want of materials the economy was gradually losing steam and shutting down. With military action and factory production drastically decreased, one might expect one vital area, transportation, to improve. Such does not seem to have been the case, as a frustrated, demoralized management was close to giving up and as masses of workers and soldiers took control of stations, cars, and whole trains.

American Business in Russia

The belief in 1914-15 in a golden opportunity for expansion of the American economic presence in Russia—to replace German—and revived after the overthrow of the tsar rapidly dissipated in 1917. Few could be found who had any faith in making money in Russia for the foreseeable future because of rampant inflation, little law and order to safeguard property, and a stalled transportation system. Even those companies with a well-established base could no longer hold out.

In September the Singer plant at Podolsk was still working on a government contract to supply 500 magnetos for military aircraft, with another order for 5,000 pending. Deliveries were slow, however, owing to the need to import ball bearings and wiring from abroad, which could be done only with hard currency, and bureaucratic obstacles prevented this.[4] The plant still had enough parts to

3. Summers to Lansing, 7 November 1917, AE Russia, DPR 326, RG 84, NA.
4. Thomas September report, f. 3, box 157, Singer Papers, SHSW.

assemble sewing machines through the end of the year, but it could not produce many stands for them, "on account of the lack of pig iron, and, although we have been promised supplies, the Government Departments regulating the supply of metals are so thoroughly disorganized that we cannot rely on any promises."[5]

This somewhat optimistic picture of operations belied the considerable losses the company sustained during the war and especially in 1917 and the increasing problem of workers usurping management control. In early October the company finally pulled the plug and made plans to shut down the plant. While noting that a number of problems at the beginning of the war had been eased, the company president stated that "conditions since the revolution . . . have become so extraordinary that it is no longer possible to carry on commercial business in Russia."[6] Actually, it would continue reduced operation through the civil war and until its formal takeover by the Soviet government in 1924.

A similar story was repeated at the International Harvester factory in Lubertsy. The company actually expected production to expand during 1917, thanks to a high priority placed by both the pre-March Imperial Government and the Provisional Government on expanding the availability of modern agricultural machinery. Since the Russian plant produced mainly war material and a simple Russian reaper (*lobogreika*), the Provisional Government reserved portions of the new American credits to purchase priority agricultural equipment in the United States, chiefly harvesters, tractors, twine, and hay balers (to supply forage to army horses more efficiently).[7] But shipping problems, bureaucratic snafus, and exchange difficulties caused most of this business to collapse by October. For several months the company had successfully followed the carrot-and-stick approach, increasing wages and improving conditions but refusing to allow workers any role in management, but by September Lubertsy production was slowed almost to a standstill by strikes and worker efforts to remove a number of experienced but mostly foreign foremen.[8]

The Bary boiler works in Moscow, which had been making military mines since the beginning of the war, closed at the end of July because costs of production had risen so sharply in 1917, and efforts to obtain revisions of the

5. Ibid.

6. Douglas Alexander (New York) to Robert Lansing, 3 October 1917, AE Russia, DPR 319, RG 84, NA.

7. Sandomirsky report to McCormick, 7 July 1917, and McCormick to Sandomirsky, 11 July 1917, box 113, 2C, McCormick Papers, SHSW.

8. A. A. Halvoran to H. F. Perkins (Chicago), 10 September 1917, box ?, McCormick Papers, SHSW.

government contract to take this into account had failed. It could still produce income from a large inventory (2 million rubles) of materials. Zenaida Bary, the Russian-born owner after her husband's death in 1913, and her manager son, Vladimir, both considered American citizens, simply went into semiretirement.[9]

While for the time being Americans with Russian connections were inclined to "seeing it through," others made a hasty retreat if possible. America's "Russian banker," H. Fessenden Meserve, was soon on his way home, while Ray Knickerbocker, a metallurgist with the Kyshtim Copper Company in the Urals, found the Trans-Siberian escape route temporarily cut.[10] Norman Stines, an engineer working in Sistert, also in the Urals near Ekaterinburg, was hired to assist the American military mission in September in the acquisition of strategic metals and arranged the purchase of 21,000 ounces of highly sought platinum from the Russian government. He also helped other Americans in Russia on business arrange passports and transportation.[11]

Although actual American private business in Russia already was at a virtual standstill before the Bolshevik revolution, major investments in plant, equipment, and training of workmen were still at stake. While Singer, International Harvester, and other companies had been anticipating expansion in May and June 1917, they were now looking for an opportunity to bail out of Russia entirely. Alexander Behr, a leading proponent of increased Russian-American business who led a life of unseemly luxury in Moscow, apparently benefited from the economic chaos by acting as a commission broker in the buying and selling of enterprises and goods.[12] Others hesitated after expected seizures of private enterprises failed to occur. In a conversation with Edward Ross on 9 December, Trotsky stated that American businesses would be allowed to continue operations under the new regime, but with their profits controlled.[13]

9. Summers to Lansing, 12 July 1917, and article "The Patriot Bary," *Kommersant*, 7 July 1917, AE Russia, DPR 331, RG 84, NA. The Bary family is credited—by DeWitt Poole—with providing considerable monetary support for the White armies of Alekseev, Deniken, and Kolchak. Notes of interview with W. A. Bary in New York, 3 March 1951, f. 10, box 7, Poole Papers, SHSW.

10. Knickerbocker to Tredwell, 8 December 1917, and Tredwell to Knickerbocker, 21 December 1917, Petrograd Consulate, box 1, DPR, RG 84, NA.

11. Hazel Stines to Folks, 3 October 1917, Stines Papers, HIA. The platinum eventually reached New York, where it was seized by the government and later, in 1921, became the focus of a lawsuit involving American engineer Charles Janin and M. D. Rothschild of the American Diamond Committee, in which Stines claimed ownership. Stines affadavit, 11 February 1921, f. G–H, box 5, Janin Papers, Huntington Library.

12. Huntington report to Pratt, 9 June 1917, copy in f. 1378, box 7, IH Papers, SHSW.

13. Ross journals, vol. 4, 1, reel 29, Ross Papers, SHSW.

Military Situation

Captain Francis Parker, relieved by Judson from his post as assistant military attaché in Russia, returned to Washington at the end of September. In his report he bemoaned the lack of American appreciation of the importance of maintaining the Russian front. The weakness of the Provisional Government, he concluded, had led to mutiny at the front, the only solution for which was a strong military leader. The United States had failed to realize the importance of this and did not back Kornilov, as it should have. He believed, however, that it was not too late to keep Russia in the war.[14] In a lecture prepared soon afterward, Parker emphasized the deleterious effects of the overthrow of the tsar on government authority and warned that Americans must disabuse themselves of the idea of a democratic Russia. "The average Russian has had no training whatever in self-government."[15]

Judson himself advised Scott on 1 October, "Things happen so quickly here that it is as though years and not months have passed since your Mission left." This must have been discouraging to members such as Scott who were making recommendations based on what they observed in June and July, and it probably hampered their ability to exercise leverage in Washington. Judson emphasized:

Discipline in the Army has been growing rapidly worse. Although some of the symptoms improve, the disease apparently increases. There is complete lack of confidence now between officers and men and the life of the officer is a very uncertain proposition, many having been murdered and many having committed suicide. . . .

We learn that the Army is very poorly supplied with winter clothing and with food. They have lost great quantities of ammunition and they offer but little resistance, relatively, to determined German movements.

The railroads seem to be getting worse rather than better. The other day the greatest locomotive works in Russia, largely engaged now in repair work, was closed down on account of strikes, and the deterioration among the cars and locomotives will probably occur more rapidly than will be offset by arrivals from America.

The food situation grows more acute in the cities.[16]

14. Parker report to War Department, 29 September 1917, box 1, Parker Papers, MD, LC.
15. "Russian lecture," undated, ibid.
16. Judson to Scott, 1 October 1917, box 30, Scott Papers, MD, LC.

Such descriptions, relayed also to Pershing, could not be very encouraging for those making plans for another year of war.

The American expeditionary force commander was especially alarmed at the news from Russia.

> 1. . . . I consider the Russian situation as very serious, but perhaps not yet hopeless. The important thing is, first, to prevent them from making a separate peace and, second, to encourage and possibly hold together as many troops as we can. . . . The situation there would justify the expenditure of any amount of money, if there still remains hope of its being spent to any good purpose.
>
> 2. With the collapse of Russia and a separate peace, practically the whole of the German and Austrian forces now on the Eastern front would be released for service on the Western front. . . . The relative strength on the Western front in that event would enable the Central Powers to assume the offensive, which, if begun in the early spring or sooner, would seriously reduce the chances of allied success. While it is not probable that Germany will be able to bring to the Western front all of these forces, yet it is imperative that we realize the full extent of the danger and hasten our preparations accordingly.[17]

The implications of the Russian military collapse to Pershing were to speed up the concentration of American troops and supplies on the Western Front by mobilizing "two million tons" of shipping.[18] Complementing the Anglo-French strategy and the thinking of Secretary of War Baker, Pershing's plan made a major American presence in France more crucial and immediate. But it also called for an active role in making use of what could be resurrected in Russia (avoiding any diversion of military units there, it went without saying).[19]

Bolshevik Seizure of Power

Having virtually given up on Kerensky and his government, Americans inside Russia or closely observing it should not have been surprised by their fall. Some expected it sooner, some later. A few believed, as did Kerensky himself, that he would regain control in a week or so. Colonel Thompson's last-ditch effort in

17. Memorandum for General Scott, undated but probably late October, ibid.
18. Ibid.
19. Ibid.

squandering $1 million of his own money to bolster Kerensky even met with sharp criticism.[20] Thompson, however, considered this only a stopgap and cabled the State Department that at least $3 million per month was needed. Responding to similar pleas from Bullard, George Creel recruited banker Robert Hutchins Jr. to go to Petrograd to lay out a broader plan for a propaganda campaign. Creel's assistant, Edgar Sisson, was quickly dispatched with $1 million to jump-start it, with the president's blessings.[21] Neither would reach their destination before the Bolsheviks took power.

In the meantime, the Russian Ministry of Finance had already spent $50 million of a special American credit to purchase and disperse Finnmarks that were needed to pay expenses of Russian operations in Finland,[22] a good portion of which probably ended up in Bolshevik hands. Most of the embassy staff, led by Francis, persisted in the belief that German money financed Bolshevik activism. Although exaggerated, this, too, was true to some extent but by a similar indirect path through Finland.[23]

Francis spent the last day of the Provisional Government, 6 November, visiting various officials, as if saying farewell. Tereshchenko fully expected and wanted

20. Francis thought the money did more harm than good, especially due to Thompson's misguided effort to cloak the transfer of funds by buying works of art and imperial hunting dogs. Francis to Lansing or Polk (personal and confidential), 26 October 1917, reel 8, Francis Papers, MoHS. One of the two copies in the Francis Papers is stamped "Secretary of State 27 November 1917" and "Assistant Secretary 28 November 1917." This appears to be the original signed—"Dictated not read by DRF"—in Francis's hand. And Francis indicated that it was being carried out of Russia by an American Red Cross mission to Romania that was leaving Petrograd for home the next day, so a month in passage would be about right. It is possible that in 1919, when Francis was preparing his memoirs, he took some papers from files in the State Department.

21. Creel to Wilson, 22 and 24 October 1917, and Wilson to Thompson, 24 October 1917, and to Sisson, 24 October 1917, *PWW* 44:424, 434-35.

22. Francis to Lansing, 27 October 1917, AE Russia, DPR 331, RG 84, NA. As a semi-autonomous grand duchy of the Russian empire, Finland was practically a neutral country with its own currency and freedom from conscription into the Russian army. Yet Helsinki was the main base of the highly radicalized Baltic Fleet. Because the ruble inflated so much in 1917, Finnish banks would no longer accept rubles, so the sailors and their mess funds had to be paid in Finnmarks, purchased with dollars or pounds. See Saul, *Sailors in Revolt*, 155-56, 242.

23. The anti-imperial Finnish Social Democratic Party, probably supported by German money, was a major source of funding for Bolshevik activities in the fleet, and most of the allegations that Bolshevik leaders in Petrograd received German funding involved conduits through Finland. Saul, *Sailors in Revolt*, 101-4; Michael Futrell, *Northern Underground: Episodes of Russian Revolutionary Transport and Communications Through Scandinavia and Finland, 1863-1917* (London: Faber and Faber, 1963), 172-91.

a Bolshevik takeover. "I hope so, . . . if you can suppress it," Francis responded. The foreign minister doubted that possibility but still wanted the suspense ended. In the same report, Francis recorded that at 10:30 the next morning, Sheldon Whitehouse burst into the embassy to report that his automobile, with American flags posted on the front, had been requisitioned at his residence to carry Kerensky "to the front."[24] Whitehouse, accompanied by his brother-in-law (Baron Ramsay), pursued the car to Kerensky's headquarters and after confronting him was told that the emergency was created by the disabling of a fleet of cars in the palace square during the night. Actually, the "minister-president," as mentally and physically exhausted as his government, rode in a second car borrowed from a friend.[25]

The remaining ministers in the Winter Palace awaited arrest—or a worse fate— through a confused, halfhearted defense conducted by a women's battalion and military cadets and a delayed and equally bungled assault orchestrated by the Military Revolutionary Committee of the Petrograd Soviet.[26] Late at night—with the ministers finally under arrest and the Provisional Government overthrown— the Second All-Russian Congress of Soviets, meeting at Smolny Institute, at the behest of its Bolshevik leadership elected a radical executive committee and declared itself the new government. Lenin and, more obviously, Trotsky were the stage managers of this "revolution" and spearheaded the Council of Peoples' Commissars that replaced the old cabinet.

The event, heralded in many later grandiose holiday celebrations, and immortalized especially by Sergei Eisenstein in his film *October, or Ten Days That Shook the World* on its tenth anniversary, was actually much smaller, briefer, and less dramatic than the revolution that overthrew the tsar. The power that was seized had suffered considerable attrition from the Provisional Government. Not many people noticed much immediate difference in the transition to what was expected to be just another *provisional* government. What did gain public attention and wide support was the vow by the new Soviet leadership to take Russia out of the war, which, in fact, was ending anyway as far as that country was concerned.

24. Francis to Lansing (personal and confidential), 20 November 1917, vol. 32, Lansing Papers, MD, LC; and in reel 7, Francis Papers, MoHS; see also Diary, 7 November 1917, box 2, Wright Papers, Princeton-Mudd.
25. Richard Abraham, *Alexander Kerensky: The First Love of the Revolution* (New York: Columbia University Press, 1987), 317.
26. During the siege but before the attack, John Reed and Louise Bryant wandered into the palace, their coats were taken, and they were treated like tourists.

Women's battalion after surrender at the Winter Palace, 27 October 1917, courtesy of the State Historical Society of Wisconsin

American Participants in the Bolshevik Revolution

What drama there was on the side of the victors—and, indeed, the sessions of the Soviet congress and the appearance of the cruiser *Aurora* in the Neva River not far from the Winter Palace provided some really stirring moments—was perhaps recorded best by Americans who were enthusiastic about the expectation of a drastic shift in government, economy, and society worldwide, part of the particularly American idealism of the times: John Reed, Louise Bryant, Bessie Beatty, and Albert Rhys Williams. Williams and Beatty had been in Russia since soon after the February–March Revolution. They quickly brought Reed and Bryant, who arrived during the Kornilov affair, up to date on the rise of the radical wing of the revolution.

In a discussion of the comparative merits of Trotsky and Lenin, Williams related to Reed an incident he had observed at the First All-Russian Congress of Soviets in early June. Irakly Tsereteli, a leader of the Mensheviks who supported the war and at that time was minister of communications, was speaking in defense of the Provisional Government. A fine orator, he made the point that there was no political party prepared to take over and accept the responsibility for government, then paused for effect. From the Bolshevik section came a growl and a single word in a low voice from Lenin: "Yest'," meaning, "There is."[27] In November the Bolshevik leader lived up to his word.[28]

The "American" Bolsheviks

The Bolshevik revolution had a definite but immeasurable American imprint upon it, similar in some ways to that of the February–March Revolution, with the Miliukov and Guchkov connections with Crane, Harper, and others. Many of the returning exiles and active socialists from America in 1917 gravitated quickly into the Bolshevik camp and especially to the support of the most radical Bolsheviks—Lenin, Trotsky, Aleksandra Kollontai, and Nikolai Bukharin (three of whom had come to Russia in 1917 from America). This gave the radical wing of the party a decided boost vis-à-vis the more moderate faction led by Lev Kamenev.

Among those who were well educated but mostly had led a worker's or mechanic's life in the United States were Grigori Chudnovskii, one of the directors of the capture of the Winter Palace; Vladimir Volodarskii (Moisei Goldstein), an excellent orator and organizer; Samuel Voskov; Mikhail Yanishev; Boris "Daddy" Reinstein from Buffalo (who assisted Trotsky with foreign propaganda); Grigori Petrovsky (member of the Military Revolutionary Committee, then peoples' commissar of the interior); and Iakov (Jake) Peters.[29] The latter, a Latvian who had only passed through the United States on his return to Russia from England, served as a member of the Military Revolutionary Committee in November but would be best known as "Bloody Peters," the chief assistant to Felix Dzherzhinsky in the organization and direction of the infamous Cheka, a predecessor to the even more infamous NKVD and KGB.

27. Albert Rhys Williams, *Journey into Revolution: Petrograd, 1917–1918*, ed. Lucita Williams (Chicago: Quadrangle Books, 1969), 31.

28. Among the best secondary accounts of the Bolshevik rise to power are Daniels, *Red October*; S. P. Melgunov, *The Bolshevik Seizure of Power* (Santa Barbara, Calif.: ABC-Clio, 1972); Richard Pipes, *A Concise History of the Russian Revolution* (New York: Random House Vintage, 1996); and Alexander Rabinowitch, *The Bolsheviks Come to Power: The Revolution of 1917 in Petrograd* (New York: Norton, 1976).

29. Albert Rhys Williams is the best source on American radicals in Russia. See also Georges Haupt and Jean-Jacques Marie, *Makers of the Russian Revolution: Biographies of Bolshevik Leaders* (Ithaca, N.Y.: Cornell University Press, 1974).

Besides these ardent Bolsheviks from America, some adhered to other Russian radical parties. Eccentric Bill Shatov remained loyal to his anarchist roots in the IWW (Wobblies) but was a strong supporter of Lenin and would perform important service directing rail traffic in and out of Petrograd in 1918.[30] Another anarchist, Samuel Agursky, was also a member of the Military Revolutionary Committee and soon joined the Bolsheviks.[31]

These Russian-American radical socialists, few of whom would survive the years of terror and civil war to follow, provided an important link to the rising Soviet leadership for left-leaning journalists Reed, Williams, Bryant, and Beatty and predisposed them to the Bolshevik side. Their open association with the political groups most ardently opposed to the Provisional Government and the war effort naturally alienated them from most of the "official" Americans of the embassy, consulates, businesses, and aristocracy. But they also infused the Bolshevik cause with a sense of international solidarity. Reflecting on speeches delivered by Reed and himself to a mass meeting of 10,000 factory workers on 21 October, essentially extending greetings from American socialists, Williams commented, "It was always surprising to see how important our few words to them seemed."[32] Convinced that the tide of "the masses" was with the radical left, Reed pressed for action. "The French would have torn things to pieces long ago. The Russians talk violently, but they do nothing particular about it all except to hoist tea and say, 'The situation is very grave.'" He added, "Kerensky is dying very fast."[33]

Other important contacts with the Russian Left were Alexander Gumberg, who came with the Stevens mission but stayed on as interpreter for Reed and Williams, as well as for Raymond Robins and Edgar Sisson, and Gregory Yarros, an Associated Press representative. These Russian-Americans were in an important strategic position, since they knew well both Russian and English.

The drama of 7–8 November, captured so memorably by Reed, could not but add further conviction and enthusiasm to the Russian-Americans and their jour-

---

30. Bruce Lockhart describes Shatov as squat, heavy-set, wearing overalls over his clothes, with two large revolvers tucked into his belt. "The general effect was a cross between a gunman and the rotund gentleman who furnishes the advertisement for Michelin tyres." Robert H. Bruce Lockhart, *Memoirs of a British Agent* (London: Putnam, 1932), 245.

31. For a lengthy discussion of their contributions, see Williams, *Journey into Revolution*, 43-63. Reed also mentions several in passing without fully identifying them. Petrovsky, for example, he credits with bringing the Obukhov workers into the revolution—and also made a seat for him at the key session of the Second All-Russian Congress of Soviets. John Reed, *Ten Days That Shook the World* (New York: Vintage, 1960), 124.

32. Williams, *Journey into Revolution*, 95.

33. To Boardman Robinson, 29 October 1917, f. 137-38, Reed Papers, Harvard-Houghton.

nalistic cohorts. After so much frustration in the city slums of America, their ideals were being realized in faraway Russia. Nothing probably galvanized their attention more than the Decree on Peace approved overwhelmingly by the Second All-Russian Congress of Soviets and signed by Lenin, though they might have been disappointed by the omission of the United States in its appeal to "the class-conscious workers of the three most advanced nations of mankind and the largest states participating in the present war, namely, Great Britain, France and Germany."[34]

The Russian-Americans facilitated the involvement of journalists in the revolutionary events. Albert Rhys Williams relates the story of going to the "front" to the south of Petrograd on 10 November. He, Reed, and Gumberg were standing outside of Smolny waiting for something to happen, when Vladimir Antonov-Ovseenko, who had been in direct command of the seizure of the Winter Palace, and Pavel Dybenko, a leading Bolshevik sailor, came out to get into a car to go take charge of the motley assembly of units preparing to defend the revolution from an anticipated attack by army units loyal to Kerensky.

Gumberg hopped in and motioned for Reed and Williams to follow. After delays resulting from the need to procure food—paid for by Gumberg—for Dybenko, who had just arrived from Helsinki, a mechanical breakdown, and the requisitioning of a passing auto with Italian flags on it, they reached Pulkovo Heights, about fifteen miles south of the city. Antonov-Ovseenko discovered immediately that the Red Guards and other units were short of ammunition; he decided to write an order for some to be sent but had to borrow paper and pencil from the Americans. Thus the first order of the embryonic Red Army was written on American paper with an American pencil.[35] As it turned out, the counterattack against the revolution fizzled out, and little force was needed.

Some stability gradually returned, as the new Council of Peoples' Commissars, chaired by Lenin, assumed control over the old ministries. Trotsky, designated commissar for foreign affairs, is reported to have walked into the old ministry and said, "We will now issue a few revolutionary proclamations and close up shop," meaning that with the approach of world revolution, no foreign relations would be needed. He did thoughtfully take time to inform the diplomatic mis-

---

34. For the text of the declaration, see Harold J. Goldberg, ed., *Documents of Soviet-American Relations*, vol. 1, *Intervention, Famine Relief, International Affairs, 1917–1933* (Gulf Breeze, Fla.: Academic International Press, 1993), 8–9.

35. Williams, *Journey into Revolution*, 138–42. For a different version that has Gumberg going alone and left stranded and having to walk back, see Louise Bryant, *Six Red Months: An Observer's Account of Russia Before and After the Proletarian Dictatorship* (New York: George H. Doran, 1918), 151–53.

sions of the official change in government.[36] But in actuality, Trotsky confronted a recalcitrant staff that refused to obey orders. He then detailed a scholarly but radical assistant (and his nephew), Professor Ivan Zalkind, who quickly brought the place under control by waving a pistol around and threatening arrests, thus obtaining the cooperation needed to extract copies of secret treaties from the archives for publication.[37]

Trotsky rarely appeared at the ministry subsequently, and he conducted the negotiations for peace at Brest-Litovsk out of the Smolny Soviet and party head-quarters. Besides Zalkind, who was friendly with Reed and Bryant but disdain-ful of all "bourgeois" diplomats, Russian-American Boris Reinstein headed the section on foreign propaganda in the ministry and supplied Reed and Williams with offices in return for their assistance.[38]

The Official Americans

Aside from these enthusiasts, the November revolution was largely unrecorded and unphotographed (most of it occurring at night), in contrast to the Febru-ary Revolution. Jack Reed and Rhys Williams were too involved in the action and too busy keeping up with events to do much more than take sketchy notes and collect documents. The American embassy and consular personnel and businessmen stayed out of range, and some time passed before they could fig-ure out what was happening, as communications and transportation were seri-ously disrupted.

Still, American officials could not avoid seeing some things and receiving information from the streets. The Crosleys watched the flashes of the field guns in the Peter and Paul Fortress from their apartment windows, and Raymond Robins had a ringside seat on a bank of the Neva to watch the cruiser *Aurora* and other ships arrive to menace the Winter Palace with their guns—and thought, "The story is much too great to try to write." From such sources, Ambassador Francis wrote a surprisingly accurate résumé of the situation on 8 November for Summers in Moscow.[39]

36. Trotsky to Francis, 7 November 1917, AE Russia, DPR 326, RG 84, NA.
37. Richard K. Debo, *Revolution and Survival: The Foreign Policy of Soviet Russia, 1917–1918* (Liverpool: Liverpool University Press, 1979), 19–20; Bryant, *Six Red Months*, 200–201.
38. Bryant, *Six Red Months*, 201–3; Williams, *Journey into Revolution*, 168–69.
39. Pauline Crosley letter of 7 November 1917, *Intimate Letters from Pettrograd*, 201; Robins to wife, 16 November 1917, f. Nov/Dec 1917, box 13, Robins Papers, SHSW; Francis to

What "the revolution" amounted to was armed Red Guards from factories, Kronstadt sailors, and some Russian and Latvian army units, about 30,000 total, under the loose direction of the Petrograd Soviet and its Military Revolutionary Committee, staging a rather chaotic and uncoordinated attack on the Winter Palace, arresting the remaining ministers of the Provisional Government, and escorting them to the Peter and Paul Fortress prison. Other detachments occupied the telephone and telegraph offices and a few other key points. The Second All-Congress of Soviets, with a Bolshevik majority, then announced the formation of a new government of people's commissars and issued decrees on peace and land that declared the new leadership's intention to end the war and to transfer remaining privately held land (about one-third of the total) to the peasant village communes. Both were already in progress.

In a letter to his wife, written five days after the main events, David Francis revealed his perplexity: "We have no government here since last Thursday; the ministers of the provisional government . . . were arrested by Bolsheviks and sent to St. Peter and Paul prison; . . . All of the government offices are closed as the employees therein have refused to work under Bolshevik ministers." The ambassador went on to describe how he organized an armed guard for the embassy from "Junkers," some of the same military students who had tried to defend the Winter Palace.[40]

That same afternoon, 12 November, Assistant Military Attaché Francis Riggs made the first "unofficial" contact with the new government. He was sent by General Judson to seek reassurances about the safety of Americans in Petrograd. "I had a very interesting and historic interview with Trotzky [sic]. He said the foreigners had nothing to fear from his people."[41] This was a breakthrough of a kind, beginning a series of informal contacts between the American military attaché's office and the Soviet government. This willingness to communicate was probably based on the belief that the revolution in Russia must simply run its course and that this was only a passing phase.[42]

Summers, 8 November 1917, reel 10, Francis Papers, MoHS. Robins was confused, however, when he wrote, "I was on the Neva bank and watched the shells from the cruiser break upon the Palace." The *Aurora* fired only very loud blank shells, but some minor damage was inflicted by smaller field guns from the Peter and Paul Fortress. Butler Wright was also under the wrong impression. Diary, 8 November 1917, box 2, Wright Papers, Princeton-Mudd.

40. To Jane, 12 November 1917, Francis Papers, MoHS. The letter was sent privately with Stewart Elliott, an agent of W. R. Grace & Co., who apparently carried a number of letters from others.

41. Riggs to Aunt Jane, 12 November 1917, box 124, Riggs Family Papers, MD, LC.

42. For example, Huntington's talk with old SR leader Nicholas Chaikovsky, cited in Edward Thomas to Harper, 13 November 1917, f. 13, box 4, Harper Papers, UC.

It appeared to Francis and others that the government was being shut down as much as being taken over. Many expected the Bolsheviks to fade away in failure and/or Kerensky to return with enough military force to suppress them. Ten days after the fall of the Provisional Government, rumor and confusion still reigned. Philip Jordan, the ambassador's African-American companion, wrote no doubt with some exaggeration,

The streets are full of thieves and cut throats, and they have started to rob and kill. The machine guns and cannons are busy every minute in the day and night. Thousands are being killed, Why we are alive I cannot tell. . . . All the prisons and jails have been fired, and the murderers and robbers are doing a land office business. . . . There are some horrible sights to be seen. Petrograd is shot all to pieces, but it is not near as bad as Moscow.[43]

This could not be very reassuring to the ambassador's family in St. Louis. Jordan also reported that a train, the last one, would take Americans out that night, just before the Bolsheviks planned to burn the city. But Francis still managed to host a "tea" for 250 Americans on the Thanksgiving holiday that turned into a kind of wake for pre-Bolshevik Russia.[44]

The confusion, anarchy, and chaos that seemed unending after the seizure of the Winter Palace and the flight of Kerensky were good reasons for no consideration of recognizing the new government, as had been done so quickly and with little hesitation in March. The other factors, of course, were its opposition to the war and promotion of world revolution, both anathema to the interests of the United States. Instead, Ambassador Francis prepared a small arsenal to defend the embassy against assault. William Judson, the military attaché, thought that this was a mistake and could lead to a serious confrontation, and instead wanted to seek adequate protection from the new authorities.[45]

Few Americans in Russia were totally detached from the events around them. In fact, discussions were hot and heavy around teas, such as the regular ones hosted by Pauline Crosley, and dinners at General Judson's apartment. Harry Brown, a Red Cross worker and former newspaperman, even circulated a daily newsletter containing the latest rumors.[46] The journalists, Raymond Robins, and

43. To Mrs. Francis, 18 November 1917, reel 5, Francis Papers, MoHS.
44. Jordan to Annie Pulliam and Francis family, 30 November 1917, Francis Papers, MoHS.
45. Judson, memorandum for ambassador, 19 November 1917, Francis Papers, MoHS.
46. Beatty, *The Red Heart of Russia*, 326–27.

others were able to reach Bolshevik sources regularly but on an informal basis. And even the ambassador got out a few times for his customary drive around the city in his Ford.

In Moscow a new YMCA/YWCA contingent arrived from a long trip across Siberia just after some of the worst violence occurred. Helen Ogden likened the frequent popping of guns to the Fourth of July. After being holed up for several days in a "Y" apartment,

> we sallied forth to see the town and the destruction. It is some mess!! Trolley wires down, thousands of windows smashed, the Hotel Metropole absolutely riddled, some of the Inner City gates very much battered, streets torn up for barricades, some buildings. . . . Altogether it was some revolution. But I wouldn't have missed it for a farm. It is thrilling to have been right in it.[47]

Many Americans were perplexed about what to do next, but most went on with their jobs and learned to stay inside when there was shooting. Almost all attested to good treatment, when "Amerikanets" was announced to the new "street" authorities.

Robins summed up the atmosphere two weeks after the seizure of power:

> It is now Fourteen Days since the Bolshevick Commune took control of the Government of this city and in so far as there is any, the government of Russia. The outlook is extremely uncertain but I have still hope for the people and the land of the Slavs. We have in Lenin a practical dictatorship of the extreme socialist type and it is marching toward a genuine control of the masses of the people. The rifles and the peasants are behind his leadership at this moment.
>
> It is a tremendous drama! Each day we face a new contingency and the interest of the play is breathless, and the element of danger adds to its power and absorption.[48]

Arthur Bullard was more succinct in registering his account of the situation in Moscow: "The Bolsheviki are in complete control and appear to be prepared to hold on by means of terrorizing everybody. These poor people do not seem to

---

47. Ogden to Family, 17 November 1917, f. Ogden Correspondence, box 3, Lowrie Papers, UIA.
48. To his wife, 20 November 1917, f. Nov/Dec 1917, box 13, Robins Papers, SHSW.

American Red Cross mission to Russia after Bolshevik revolution: William Boyce Thompson in middle seated with Raymond Robins on his left, courtesy of the State Historical Society of Wisconsin

know any other means of governing."[49] Americans clearly had wide-ranging views of Soviet power, but almost all were caught up in the excitement.

Finally, Judson, believing the new government was indeed the de facto authority over Russia, went to see Trotsky on 1 December to seek resolution of some misunderstood protests and an explanation of the peace negotiations that were announced to begin the following day.[50] After the additional urging of Naval Attaché Captain Crosley,[51] Francis agreed to this contact though he opposed

49. Bullard to Robins, 22 November 1917, f. November–December, Robins Papers, SHSW.

50. This may have been prompted by a handwritten note from Trotsky indicating the desire for a general, not a separate, peace. Trotsky to Judson?, 13/26 November 1917, f. 2070-12, roll 3 (M1443), RG 165, NA.

51. "Without recognizing the present 'government' here, I believe the representatives of the Allies can, with propriety, negotiate with the actual existing power that does exist, whether or not the Allies approve of it." Crosley, "Memorandum for the Ambassador," 23 November 1917, reel 9, Francis Papers, MoHS.

Judson doing it himself, which he feared could be interpreted as a step toward recognition, even though Judson made clear to Trotsky that the visit was personal and not official. Trotsky explained to Judson that all peace negotiations would be conducted openly and that the Allies were welcome to join in them at any time.[52]

Washington Befuddled

Understandably, the news that trickled into Washington from Russia was confused and contradictory. President Wilson was handicapped by having few close advisers on hand whom he trusted. House had left for London on a special mission, and Crane was still wandering around the trenches in France and delivering Russian tea to General Pershing.[53] Arthur Bullard was already in Russia, and Edgar Sisson was on his way. The president did not trust the State Department, and the department had its own reasons for doubting information it received from both the American embassy in Petrograd and the Russian embassy in Washington, which no longer represented a government in Russia. Samuel Harper was back at his teaching job in Chicago and busy writing articles for the *Christian Science Monitor* and lecturing in the area.[54] He apparently did not communicate with Washington for over a month, his input also limited by Crane's absence.

Stanley Washburn was off on his own mission to educate the American public about the importance of Russia, always giving the optimistic view, with the assistance and financing of the Russian embassy. In fact, both he and Bakhmeteff were scheduled to speak on behalf of the Chamber of Commerce in Memphis on 8 November, when they received the news of the revolution in Russia. The ambassador shortened his address to take a waiting overnight train back to Washington.[55] Washburn immediately advised redoubling the publicity effort, with the proviso "as long as there is a single division on the Russian Front which remains loyal to the Provisional Government and to the cause of the Allies."[56]

52. Francis to Lansing, 2 December 1917, reel 5, Francis Papers, MoHS.

53. House telegram to Wilson, expressing dismay, 9 November 1917, *PWW* 44:545; Crane to Richard Crane, 23 October 1917, reel 1, and Pershing to Crane, 14 November 1917, reel 2, Crane Papers, BA, CU.

54. Frederick Dixon to Harper, 19 and 27 November 1917, f. 13, box 4, Harper Papers, UC.

55. Bakhmeteff oral history, p. 342, CU.

56. Washburn to Bakhmeteff, 9 November 1917, Bakhmeteff Papers, BA, CU. He asked for a modest $5,000 to cover expenses for the next month.

Under the circumstances, President Wilson tried to assume an optimistic view, hoping that the worst of the news was not accurate. To a Florida congressman who suggested some action be taken, he wrote in metaphor: "I have not lost faith in the Russian outcome by any means. Russia, like France in a past century, will no doubt have to go through deep waters but she will come out upon firm land on the other side, and her great people, for they are a great people, will in my opinion take their proper place in the world."[57]

The president apparently first saw an official message direct from Petrograd only on 23 or 24 November, over two weeks after the flight of Kerensky. Not surprisingly, it was written by Judson and cabled on 14 November to the War College. After delays in transit and decoding, Secretary Baker forwarded it to the White House. It could not have been very encouraging reading, starting with "Shock of present crisis on top of past experiences may put Russia into anarchy and out of war" and, after some garbled and confused suggestions about an American peace offer, concluding, "Any Russian Government formed in the near future must have peace program but will remain at war if Germany does not meet fair terms unless complete anarchy prevents."[58] This was an awkward but fairly accurate representation of the confused state of affairs for several months.

The next communication was from Francis, containing a translation of Trotsky's speech of 21 November outlining peace proposals and taking the ideological stance that Wilson's foreign policy was controlled by Wall Street.[59] Received on 27 November, it was discussed but apparently not taken seriously at a cabinet meeting that day. The president noted that to answer "would imply recognition" and that "Lenine and Trotsky sounded like opera bouffe, talking of armistice with Germany when a child would know Germany would control & Dominate & destroy any chance for the democracy they desire."[60]

Prompted by a cable from House in Paris, Lansing followed this up with a clear six-page declaration of American policy toward the new Soviet regime that began:

> This Government has found it impossible to recognize Lenine, Trotsky and their associates as the *de facto* government of Russia since there is inadequate evidence that they are the real agents of the sovereignty of the Rus-

57. WW to Frank Clark, 13 November 1917, *PWW* 45:39. The contents of Clark's letter to Wilson are not known.
58. Judson to War College, 14 November 1917, enclosed in Baker to WW, 23 November 1917, *PWW* 45:104.
59. Francis to Lansing, 24 November 1917, *PWW* 45:119–20.
60. Diary of Josephus Daniels, 27 November 1917, *PWW* 45:147.

sian people. When the Bolshevik faction under the leadership of Lenine seized by force the public offices at Petrograd and Moscow arresting or expelling the provisional ministers and military commanders who had obtained authority through legal succession from the revolutionary body which had come into power on the abdication of the Czar, they set up in those two cities arbitrary and irresponsible authority based solely on physical control over the residents.[61]

Although this was a good statement of present and future American policy, the president at this time wanted to keep options open and would not approve its release.[62]

Railroad Assistance and Public Information

Events in Petrograd spurred movement on two major long-delayed projects, railroad assistance and the publicity campaign. Samuel Felton of the Office of Director General of Railways of the War Department asked George Emerson, general manager of the Great Northern Railroad, to direct a corps of railroad professionals recruited from northern railroads, where they presumably were more accustomed to cold weather.[63] Felton informed Francis on 17 November that "we are just sending about 350 men for Russia" from San Francisco for the railway service. After enumerating numbers and ranks, he added, "I hope they will not be too late to help save the day."[64]

The contingent included around seventy-five Baldwin Locomotive workers to help assemble engines being sent. They reached Vladivostok when it was in the throes of revolutionary turmoil in mid-December and were forced to endure frustrating delays aboard ship in Nagasaki harbor and then on Japanese soil. By March they even switched from studying Russian to Japanese.[65] About 100 finally moved to Harbin at the end of March. Nor could much be done to speed

61. House to Lansing, 2 December 1917, and untitled draft, 4 December 1917, box 2, Lansing Papers, Princeton-Mudd.

62. The secretary of state added a note in his own hand to this document: "I drafted this as a public statement but after conferring with the President did not use it. RL." Ibid.

63. Joe Michael Feist, "A Wisconsin Man in the Russian Railway Service Corps: Letters of Fayette W. Keeler, 1918–1919," *Wisconsin Magazine of History* 62, no. 3 (1979): 217–18.

64. Felton to Francis, 17 November 1917, reel 5, Francis Papers, MoHS.

65. Letters of Fayette Keeler, 31 January and 4 and 30 March 1918, "A Wisconsin Man," 221–23.

Committee on Public Information Press Bureau in Singer Building, Petrograd. From left to right: Arthur Bullard, William Adams Brown Jr., Graham Taylor Jr., and Malcolm Davis, courtesy of the Special Collections, Princeton University Libraries

the shipments of locomotives and freight cars because of the backlog of orders in factories and the special adjustments to equipment that were required to fit the wider gauge of the Russian tracks. Shipments to Vladivostok of an order of 500 locomotives and 10,000 cars began in November, with expected completion by February 1918, but further delays occurred.[66]

Arthur Bullard was slowly and unsurely taking charge of the American publicity campaign in Russia in cooperation with Consul General Summers in Moscow. On 6 November, Frederick Corse turned over his somewhat amateurish operation in Petrograd to Bullard, who was reluctant to expand further before the expected arrival of the new director or without precise instructions (and funds) from Washington.[67] Sisson finally arrived on 24 November, and soon came a message from Creel, awkwardly through Lansing and Francis:

66. Lansing to Francis, 8 November 1917, AE Russia, DPR 333, RG 84, NA.
67. Bullard to Wright, 6 November 1917, AE Russia, DPR 329, RG 84, NA. Chapin Huntington confided to Corse's friend Harper, "Corse was not the man for the publicity:

Dive ahead full speed regardless of expense. Coordinate all American agencies in Petrograd and Moscow and start [just now!] aggressive campaign. Use press, billboards, placards and every possible medium to answer lies against America. Make plain our high motives and absolute devotion to democratic ideals. . . . Engage speakers and halls. Urge Red Cross and YMCA to fullest effort.[68]

Sisson moved the center of the campaign to Petrograd, where better and cheaper supplies of paper were available from Finland. Russia was at last coming to the forefront of an American propaganda effort. As Bullard commented to House, "Our government, rather late in the day, has decided to back up the publicity work here."[69]

After Lansing's draft of a statement of nonrecognition died in the White House, the State Department adopted a more unequivocal attitude. William Phillips counseled resistance to French demands for a clear statement of opposition to the Soviet government for breaking the "covenant" signed in September 1914 not to seek a separate peace. He argued in favor of keeping doors open. The United States, after all, was not a signatory to that agreement.[70] The secretary of state reflected openly the consternation in the department in a 7 December "Memorandum on the Russian Situation":

There are a number of people who are telling us about Russia and advising us as to what the outcome will be and what we ought to do. . . . The conclusions and opinions are almost as many as the advisers, and their advice as to our policy is about as harmonious. I have yet to find one, who, pinned down to the application of his theory, is able to furnish a plan that is practical except one who frankly asserts that the best thing to do is to let things alone as far as it is possible to do so.

With this latter policy I am in entire accord. The Russian situation is to me an unanswered and unanswerable riddle. None of our observers, and some are well trained, has been able to find a way out or to advise a course of action leading to satisfactory results. . . .

Too slow to react and lacking bold initiative," but he did not acknowledge that Corse had major business obligations on his hands. Huntington to Harper, 7 December 1917, f. 15, box 4, Harper Papers, UC.

68. Lansing to Francis, Creel for Sisson, 8 December 1917, AE Russia, DPR 329, RG 84, NA.

69. Bullard to House, 12 December 1917, box 6, Bullard Papers, Princeton-Mudd.

70. Phillips to Lansing, 3 December 1917, vol. 33, Lansing Papers, MD, LC.

I confess that I do not feel warranted in hazarding even a guess as to what the outcome will be. This makes the adopting of an active policy most difficult.[71]

The de Cram Affair

The reputations of the Petrograd embassy, of David Francis personally, and of the State Department itself were soiled by accusations leveled at Francis that he had harbored a German agent, "Matilda de Cram," in the embassy and that they were jointly responsible for the disappearance of sensitive documents. The association of the elderly Francis with the middle-aged, attractive wife of a Baltic German Russian subject (Kramm) was not new and had been conducted openly, with de Cram tutoring Francis in French (and a little Russian). They had first met on the ship coming to Russia, and she proceeded to visit him regularly at the embassy, where he lived alone (with valet-cook Philip Jordan). Nor was it news that her husband was reported to be in custody in San Francisco, charged with illicit ordering of war supplies for Germany, in other words, being a German agent.

The new charges, however, were a serious attack on Francis's administration of American affairs in Russia. Two cables sent in late November by Lansing hinted that Francis should resign.[72] Lansing's source remains unknown but was probably a returning American such as Basil Miles, who reached Washington just a few days before the cables were sent. Hurt and angry, Francis stated specifically that de Cram "has never had access to any papers here, and in my judgment never desired to have."[73] He did not, however, deny that she had regular access to the embassy. In fact, William Judson later confirmed that she spent nearly every evening with him.[74]

To Breckinridge Long, his Missouri political colleague in the State Department, Francis wrote even more bitterly, "If this is an insinuation that I am in-

71. "Memorandum on the Russian Situation," 7 December 1917, f. 2 (Confidential Memoranda), box 7, Lansing Papers, Princeton-Mudd.

72. Lansing to Francis, 14 and 30 November 1917, box 2, Lansing Papers, Princeton-Mudd. The secretary of state apparently thought Francis was not taking the matter seriously enough and in the second cable assured him that his sources were reliable. "Under circumstances consider it will be safer for your reputation and for safety of Government not to take any chances and hope you will act immediately."

73. Francis to Lansing, 4 December 1917, Francis Papers, MoHS.

74. William Judson report to secretary of war, 18 June 1919, in Salzman, *Russia in War and Revolution*, 268–70. The reason for this late recitation of details was to recommend members of the Red Cross mission for distinguished service medals.

tentionally or otherwise giving away or permitting to be extracted from myself information injurious to my country it is an insult which I cannot permit to pass unnoticed."[75] He went on to cite his record of forty years of loyal public service and indicated that he would immediately request a leave of absence to defend himself were it not such an inconvenient time.

President Wilson apparently first learned about this embarrassing problem a couple of weeks later from reading a message sent by Sisson to Creel by means of Petrograd consul Roger Tredwell to Lansing.[76] It contained the following condemnation:

> *Have been* reluctantly convinced that no fruitful work can be done here by any division of our Government as long as Francis remains in charge of *Embassy.* Not only does he impress every one as a sick man absolutely unfitted to the strain physical and mental of his great post but also he has allowed himself to become subject of public gossip and of investigation by the secret police of the Allied nations because of open association with a woman suspected perhaps without sufficient evidence, of espionage.[77]

Actually, the alleged "affair" had been the source of much gossip, division, and mistrust in the American colony for some time. Bullard, arriving in August 1917, was interviewed in mid-October by a British agent about the de Cram–Francis connection; he knew only rumor but set out to discover more about it in conversations with Butler Wright and Raymond Robins. Both separately revealed their suspicions and embarrassment. Wright felt duty bound not to report the affair to Washington, to Bullard's chagrin, while Robins indicated that reports of a German agent in the embassy forced him and Thompson to act independently with Thompson's money without informing Francis, which naturally upset the ambassador. Not trusting the embassy for communications, they used Judson's War College code for cabling home.[78]

Judson was reportedly the only member of the American staff to approach Francis directly about this sordid business. In doing so, he caused Francis to

75. Francis to Long (strictly confidential), 4 December 1917, Francis Papers, MoHS.
76. Wilson to Lansing, 8 December 1917, *PWW* 45:243.
77. Tredwell to Lansing, 5 December 1917 (recd. 6th), *PWW* 45:217.
78. Bullard to Creel, 17 November and 20 December 1917, box 6, Bullard Papers, Princeton-Mudd. Bullard noted (17 November), "There has been a regrettable amount of jealousy and factionalism among the crowd over here who ought to have worked together." He also informed House of the details of the de Cram affair with a strong suggestion that Francis be recalled and Wright designated chargé, "which would be a vast improvement on Francis." To House, 12 December 1917, ibid.

think that Judson was responsible for informing Washington, thus incurring a personal enmity that, along with his desire to establish regular communications with the Soviet government, contributed to Francis's request for his recall at the end of December, when he was most needed on the scene. It also exacerbated the tension between Robins and Francis and damaged the reputation of the Red Cross mission (for having acted independent of the embassy) and the operations of the Committee on Public Information.[79] Bullard charged Francis and Lansing with screening dispatches sent by Sisson through the embassy in code relating to the affair.[80]

Although firm evidence is lacking that de Cram was actually a German spy (she had two sons by a previous marriage in the Russian armed forces), Francis was certainly at fault in permitting his connections with her to foment gossip and seriously hamper the conduct of American relations with Russia at such a critical time. Attaché Huntington saw Francis as increasingly tired, despondent, and in ill health, and believed that he really wanted to return to America and take part in the peacemaking.[81]

The matter apparently never surfaced publicly in Russia, discretion no doubt being the better part of valor. But it was alluded to by Herman Bernstein in a New York newspaper in December, eliciting a direct denial from both Francis and de Cram.[82] Why all this information from reliable sources—Sisson, Tredwell, Judson, Huntington, Robins, Bernstein—did not result in the immediate recall of Francis is not clear, especially considering that Allied representatives were informed (provoking a degree of mistrust) and the probable knowledge (and possible use) by Bolshevik leaders. Perhaps the answer is simply that a sudden

79. Judson report, 18 June 1919, in Salzman, *Russia in War and Revolution*, 269-70.

80. Bullard to Creel, 20 December 1917, box 6, Bullard Papers, Princeton-Mudd. Bullard claimed that the only American in Russia who did not support the recall of Francis was New York Life's Frederick Corse and went on to note pointedly that Francis had a financial stake in that company. Ibid. Bullard also highly recommended W. C. Huntington as an aide to House at the peace conference. "He is unusually well trained, his German is fluent, his Russian better than that of any American I know." To House, 14 December 1917, box 6, Bullard Papers, Princeton-Mudd.

81. Huntington to Harper, 7 December 1917, f. 15, box 4, Harper Papers, UC. This part of Huntington's letter was written in Russian.

82. De Cram to Bernstein, 5 January 1918, and Francis to Bernstein, 8 January 1918, copies enclosed in Francis to House, 8 January 1918, f. 1441, box 45, House Papers, Yale-Sterling. Francis was calling House's attention to the fact that Bernstein arrived in Russia during the summer with an introduction from House, and was asking advice on getting de Cram back to America. Interestingly, this correspondence does not appear in the Francis Papers, and House did not reply until July, but did refer to it as "absurd gossip" and indicated he had discussed the matter with Bernstein. House to Francis, 1 July 1918, ibid.

departure at this time would be subject to misinterpretation, or perhaps it was dismissed, as in Arthur Bullard's words: "I thought that it was mere gossip. The old boy doesn't look up to that sort of pastime."[83] For certain, it damaged the American ability to carry out effective policies in Russia at a crucial time. But having a novice replacement or no ambassador at all, as in the case of the British after Buchanan's departure, might have been worse.

Soviet Contacts

In various ways and to different extents, Americans in Russia adjusted and accommodated to the new reality of the radical socialist leadership. Some sought out officials of the new regime for journalistic reasons or simply out of curiosity. Others did so by way of carrying out their missions. A few were convinced that there was no alternative to a government dominated by the Bolsheviks in the near future. Most, however, believed that their authority was weak and transitory and sought to either ignore or escape it—or saw no harm in having some communication with it. Sisson, who arrived on 25 November to take charge of Bullard's publicity campaign, adhered at first to the latter view and supported Judson and Robins.

Some expressed sympathy with Soviet actions, such as the release of secret treaties. Commercial Attaché W. Chapin Huntington thought that foreign diplomats were "making fools of themselves" by not dealing with Trotsky: "The Bolsheviki have gotten where they are by demagogy, but they stay, and they are untouched because they touch a deep yearning. We hate their violence but something inside us says that it is good for the world that these damned treaties are to be aired."[84] He believed the United States should drop its hostility and send aid. "Let us feed Petrograd; let us feed Finland; let us play the game big and bold."[85] On a more practical matter, Huntington secretly secured approval by Soviet officials of the purchase of 1,440 pounds (40 *pud*) of Siberian platinum at $103 an ounce (for a total of close to $2.5 million!) for American munitions production and arranged a special car and armed guard for its transportation through Siberia.[86]

83. To Creel (personal and private), 20 December 1917, box 6, Bullard Papers, Princeton-Mudd.

84. Huntington to Harper, 27 November 1917, f. 14, box 4, Harper Papers, UC.

85. Ibid.

86. Huntington to Lansing, 4 December 1917, AE Russia, DPR 323, RG 84, NA. The War College Division continued to be concerned about acquiring platinum from Russia, which produced around 95 percent of the world's supply. "Russian Source of Platinum," 2 August 1918, f. 10276-66, box 551, RG 165, NA.

Such official and unofficial contacts served the purposes of both sides in terms of mission and finances.

The YMCA continued to expand its operations, with secretaries throughout the country reporting a thriving business. In Odessa, the indefatigable Donald Lowrie supervised the large "Y" house from a German-colony hospital, where he spent ten weeks recovering from typhoid fever. With the help of two American subordinates, Russian assistant Krachmalnikov, who had spent five years studying at Harvard and Columbia, and volunteers from the Soldiers Christian Circle, the Odessa "Y" averaged 1,700 patrons, mostly soldiers, each night.

> Our building is admirably suited to our purpose, and from the very opening night has been crowded with soldiers. We have a great writing-room, where all materials are free, a large library and reading-room, numerous evening classes (we have already graduated two classes in reading and writing), a tea-room, moving pictures, music, both real and canned, and many other wholesome means for filling the soldier's free time.[87]

Local authorities, who changed frequently, were universally supportive. The main problem was that there were so many more loose soldiers, and most of them were armed.[88]

Matters were even more chaotic in Kiev, where Edward Heald lamented the failure of the Kornilov affair and the breakdown of military discipline. He thought the only hope was for Japan to send in an army of 200,000, certainly not the first time that a large Allied force intervening in Russia was mentioned.[89] In Moscow the YMCA expanded its activities under the direction of Jerome Davis, Graham Taylor Jr., and Read Lewis, with the full support of local Soviet authorities.

In December a YWCA house for Russian girls opened in Moscow under the supervision of Elizabeth Dickerson, Clara Taylor, Marcia Dunham, and Helen Ogden, with the assistance of the experienced Elizabeth Boies. They had diffi-

---

Because of transportation delays and security precautions, this consignment of platinum would not reach the United States before the end of the war, and then it would be auctioned off at considerable loss, though $20,000 worth was carried out by Norman Stines in March. Hazel Stines to Folks, n.d. [c. March 1918], Stines Papers, HIA. Substantial but undetermined amounts of Russian platinum reached both sides of the war in 1918 through third parties.

87. Lowrie to Folks, 24 December 1917, f. 1917, box 1, Lowrie Papers, UIA.

88. Ibid.

89. Heald report of 2 December 1917, in Heald to Crawford Wheeler (Moscow), 5 December 1917, AE Russia, DPR 327, RG 84, NA.

culty finding quarters because Moscow was so crowded with noble and middle-class refugees from Petrograd, until Magarita Morozova, wife of a well-known textile magnate, came to their rescue to loan her backyard salon that was normally used by the Moscow Theosophical Society. It contained a hall that would seat 250 that was quickly converted into a reading room, tearoom, gymnasium, and four classrooms, where French, Russian, and English were taught.[90]

In contrast to the one in Petrograd that served mostly a non-Russian clientele (Latvians, Lithuanians, Poles, and Armenians), the Moscow "YW" attracted young Russian shop girls (cashiers, clerks, messengers), who especially enjoyed the gym classes, although protective screen had to be put up to cover the icons on one wall and the large windows on the other before basketball could be played.[91] Local Soviet officials were quite willing to provide special rations for this "working-class" facility.[92]

According to the letters of Helen Ogden, this was a happy, relatively carefree time in Moscow; the Russian girls were "most appreciative and lovable," while the American women took time out to enjoy the opera and the Moscow Art Theatre and apparently found the streets safer than in Petrograd, since they chose to walk home afterward. They staged parties for the American community on Thursday evenings, the one on Valentine's Day being especially festive, with the making of valentines, dancing and singing, and serving tea, fruit jelly, and home-made cookies.[93] All of this helped relieve the tension. YMCA worker William Duncan managed to attend both a Thanksgiving dinner for thirty in Moscow and a lavish Christmas party given by National City Bank for the Amerian community in Petrograd.[94]

The Kalpashnikov Case

The relative calm that existed between Bolshevik leaders and Americans in Petrograd was broken on 21 December with the arrest of Colonel Andrei Kalpash-

90. Helen Odgen to Family, 10 December 1917, f. Ogden Correspondence, box 3, Lowrie Papers, UIA; "The Russian Angle of the Blue Triangle," YWCA *War Work Bulletin*, no. 54 (3 January 1919): 2. Donald Lowrie later married Helen Ogden.

91. Extracts from Elizabeth Boies letter, "A Glorified Gymnasium," YWCA *War Work Bulletin*, no. 19 (15 February 1918), in box 3, Lowrie Papers, UIA.

92. Boies to "Miss Cratty," 15–28 January 1918, f. Elizabeth Boies letters, box 3, Lowrie Papers, UIA.

93. Helen Ogden to Family, 24 February 1918, f. Ogden Corres., box 3, Lowrie Papers, UIA.

94. Letter copies, 29 November and 27 December 1917, Duncan Papers, HIA.

nikov and by a violent public attack by Trotsky on American embassy officials, whom he charged with conspiring to deliver ambulances and other supplies to anti-Bolshevik military units in the area of Rostov-on-Don. The Ford ambulances had just arrived from America, where they had been ordered by Kalpashnikov for the American Red Cross unit in Romania. The director of that unit, Colonel H. W. Anderson, concerned about the collapsing Romanian front, where remnants of the Romanian army were caught between Austro-Hungarian forces and bolshevized Russian units, had asked the embassy on 5 December to relay an order to Kalpashnikov to dispatch the ambulances instead to Rostov, quite some distance from Romania and then the center of army units under Don Cossack General Aleksei Kaledin that were preparing to resist the Bolsheviks.

The embassy, for unknown reasons, failed to forward the communication, and Kalpashnikov continued to plan to send the ambulances to Jassy, the temporary Romanian capital. By 16 December the embassy received another message canceling the dispatch of materials to Rostov, because of the likelihood of Romania making a separate peace.[95] Francis then, probably without much thought, forwarded copies of these messages to Robins and Kalpashnikov. At about the same time, 17 December, Roger Perkins arrived from Jassy to assist with the arrangements and quickly got into a heated argument with Robins about including some of the ambulances in the shipment to an area that Robins considered in a state of military disintegration.[96]

Sisson, who may not be wholly reliable, accused Robins of providing Trotsky with the documentation, in part because of past friction between the two American Red Cross units, to keep the ambulances in Petrograd, and perhaps to court favors from Trotsky.[97] Actually, Robins was acting on the authority of Francis, who wanted to make clear the genuine innocence of the embassy in the affair. Complicating the scenario, Trotsky may have borne a personal grudge against Kalpashnikov for assisting in the British interrogation of him at Halifax, on his way to Russia. In any event, Trotsky devoted a considerable portion of a speech on 21 December to denouncing American complicity in aiding forces hostile to the Soviet government and accused Francis of being not an ambassador but a foreign adventurer.[98] The documents were pub-

---

95. Such was the view of the American minister in Jassy. Vopicka to Francis, 10 December 1917, AE Russia, DPR 330, RG 84, NA.

96. Perkins to Anderson, 17 December 1917, AE Russia, DPR 325, RG 84, NA. For an excellent and fuller treatment, see Kennan, *Russia Leaves the War*, 191–218.

97. Sisson, *One Hundred Red Days*, 148–55.

98. According to journalist Dosch-Fleurot, Trotsky was looking for a good excuse to attack "American business imperialism." *Through War to Revolution*, 187–88.

lished the next day and given considerable press attention in Russia and at home.[99]

Surprisingly, Francis treated the episode diplomatically and authorized Robins to try to smooth things over with the "appropriate persons." "I take it for granted that Mr. Trotsky will make every effort to remedy the false and harmful impression concerning the Embassy and the American Red Cross Mission which his speech of last evening was intended to make upon the Russian people."[100] Kalpashnikov, however, remained under arrest under harsh conditions for several weeks, the ambulances were not allowed to leave Petrograd, relations of Americans with the Soviet leadership were strained further, and Robins was rebuked for exceeding his authority in direct contacts with Soviet officials.

A Near Modus Vivendi

Even Francis, who at first treated the new regime with distrust and revulsion, felt that some accommodation was advisable. First of all, the Soviet efforts to get out of the war were proving difficult, and the temporary breaking off of the negotiations for peace at Brest-Litovsk at the end of December eroded the common Allied belief that the Bolsheviks were nothing more than German wolves in radical sheep's clothing and revived hopes of Russia actually staying in the war. After a second meeting with Trotsky, Riggs wrote, "Personally I am impressed, I frankly admit with Trotsky. I have had two interviews with him on business—he is a type of brilliant Jewish fanatic who knows what he wants. Personally I don't think him a German agent as many do—although he might have *taken German* money for his own uses."[101] Trotsky also assured Edward Ross on 9 December that the new government would not nationalize industries and businesses but only control their profits, and contrary to general Western expectation, the Soviet government seemed to be maintaining that policy at the end of the year, two months after coming to power. This revived

---

Although he did not mention it directly, Trotsky may also have known about direct contacts of American officials with Kaledin in the south of Russia, owing to the porous nature of American communications.

99. Judson diary, 21 and 22 December 1917, in Salzman, *Russia in War and Revolution,* 185–86. When finally released several months later, Kalpashnikov claimed that his copies of the letters were still safely hidden.

100. Francis to Robins, 22 December 1917, AE Russia, DPR 327, RG 84, NA.

101. Riggs to Aunt Janie, 1 January 1918, box 124, Riggs Family Papers, MD, LC; emphasis in original.

Vladimir Lenin and Leon Trotsky, unknown artist. From William Hard, Raymond Robins' Own Story

some American expectations for doing a profitable business with Russia in the future.[102]

In fact, workers were taking over factories, either through their own power or because the previous management had left. An effort to seize control of the International Harvester plant at Lubertsy was met with a firm refusal by the American management, and it continued to function, though on a reduced scale because of the shortage of coal and imported parts. S. G. McAlister thought that "the disastrous results of such control in other factories is causing our people to hesitate before such a move." In his view, with continued cooperation of Soviet agencies, the plant had a decent chance of achieving its goal of producing 24,000 machines in 1918.[103]

From his Moscow vantage point, Consul General Maddin Summers saw positive elements in the Soviet leadership: "The Maximalist leaders are not stupid. 'Trotsky' (Bronstein), who seems to exceed 'Lenin' in qualities of leader-

102. Ross journals, vol. 4, p. 1, reel 29, Ross Papers, SHSW.
103. McAllister to H. F. Perkins, 7 February 1918, box 1365, IH Papers, SHSW. According to McAllister, the greatest problem was in industries producing war materials where the owners had already made considerable profits and could not continue to do so with the war ending and under current worker demands.

ship, has displayed an intellect as acute as his will is daring."[104] And Francis reported that members of the former Provisional Government, and even monarchists such as Grand Duke Paul, were supporting the Bolsheviks, as well as pointing out certain signals from Trotsky of a desire to maintain normal trade relations with the United States.[105]

General Judson also continued to press for informal relations with the Bolsheviks. On 26 December he and his chief assistant, Lieutenant Colonel Monroe Kerth, wrote a clear, strong recommendation for this position to Francis that began, "The Bolshevicks [sic] are in control of Great Russia," but then noted that the embassy had no direct communication with them.

> As a result all American aid to the Russian people is at a standstill while the German emissaries are everywhere, working day and night in the interests of the enemy. The terrible responsibility for this deplorable condition, fraught with untold dangers not only to the Russian Democracy but to the Democracies of the world, rests primarily upon the Ambassador and the Chief of the Military Mission.[106]

Their specific recommendations began with "1: In view of the fact that the Bolshevick [sic] Government is the most important and extensive in Russia today, enter into helpful, sympathetic and friendly relations with it." Four more points stressed the need to extend assistance, concluding with "5: Act on the theory that Russia is entitled to sympathy not condemnation. She is passing through a dreadful experience in many ways unequalled in history. Under similar conditions no other nation might be expected to act otherwise."[107] The alternative, they warned, was that Russia would become a German colony.

Even Summers, normally a hard-liner in regard to Bolsheviks, reported getting along well with local Soviet authorities and argued for more contacts in the interests of protecting Americans and their property.[108] His colleague, Petrograd consul Roger Tredwell, also felt duty bound to maintain contact at the highest

104. Summers to Lansing, 15 December 1917, AE Russia, DPR 326, RG 84, NA.

105. Francis to Lansing, 14 December 1917, ibid.

106. Judson and Kerth to Francis, 26 December 1917, confidential ("Copy for Col. Raymond Robins"), f. Nov/Dec 1917, box 13, Robins Papers, SHSW.

107. Ibid.

108. Summers to Wright, 17 December 1917, AE Russia, DPR 327, RG 84, NA. Wright responded that contacts were valuable in gathering information. "I have read attentively and with great interest your various political reports and it is only out of all of this welter of conflicting reports, rumors, instructions, etc., that we can at least hope to arrive at a sane appraisal of the situation." Wright to Summers, 28 December 1917, ibid.

level and detailed his assistant, Henry Emery, to attend meetings of the Council of Peoples' Economy and the Commissariat of Trade and Industry under the direction of the eminent Marxist economist Iurii Larin.

The dean of American residents, Frederick Corse, had a different view: "Judson and Robins and Sisson are playing the Bolsheviks, hobnobbing with them a good deal to the Gov's [Francis's] disgust, and I think against the wishes of the President." And then he revealed another bias with regard to Trotsky: "This Jew is now playing with the idea of putting up a guillotin [sic] in the Winter Palace square. What have the Russians come to, to put up with a Jew who holds the lash over them and threatens them with the guillotin? These people have no spine, no bones, they are mere mush."[109] The "Jewish plot" theory of the Russian Revolution would have a long history.

Even before Judson's appeal and despite the personal attack on him in relation to Kalpashnikov's arrest, Francis was preparing a more flexible approach. He reported to the State Department on 24 December:

I am willing to swallow pride, sacrifice dignity, and . . . do all necessary to prevent Russia from becoming an ally of Germany. Possibly by establishing relations with Soviet Government allied representation could influence peace terms and in that way preserve Russian neutrality, thereby preventing war munitions stored in Russia being acquired by Germany.[110]

And after another conversation, Francis wrote Washington, "Robins believes Red Cross work is impossible without permission of Smolny and that sudden cessation of such visits will embitter the Bolshevik Government. I have therefore given my consent to Robins' visits to Smolny being continued."[111]

Finally, on 4 January 1918, Francis wrote the American consul in Helsingfors:

I have thought until recently that Lenin and Trotsky were German Agents and working wholly in the interest of that country. I am not satisfied now that some of their lieutenants have not been using German money and are possibly still doing so, but the position assumed by Lenin and Trotsky

109. Corse to Harper, 20 December 1917, f. 15, box 4, Harper Papers, UC.
110. AE Russia, DPR 327, RG 84, NA.
111. Francis to Lansing, 27 December 1917, AE Russia, DPR 327, RG 84, NA. On the same day, Francis evinced surprising eloquence to his colleague in London: "To analyze is difficult, to prophesy absolutely impossible, and so all we can do is to deal with the situation as it develops from day to day—which it does with the most extraordinary rapidity and unexpected turns." To Walter Hines Page, 27 December, ibid.

themselves and by Pokrovsky the Moscow Professor who is one of their peace commissioners, leads me to believe that they are sincere in their advocacy of a Democratic peace.[112]

The ambassador considered the Soviet recognition of the independence of Finland in December another factor in their favor.[113]

Boyce Thompson departed Russia on 28 November, after switching his support from Kerensky to Lenin and endorsing Robins's request that the Red Cross mission maintain regular contact with the Soviet government, for the sake especially of the security and continued distribution of a substantial quantity of relief material on hand, but also in the belief that the Soviet government might decide—or be forced—to continue in the war. Directly from Trotsky, Robins secured permission and an armed guard for a trainload of supplies to pass through Russian territory to Romania in late November. Robins was also convinced that the only practical possibility of preventing German influence from dominating Russia was to counter German propaganda and promise aid to the Bolsheviks that the Germans could not provide.

Bullard praised Robins for his efforts in this direction, while noting his past opposition to President Wilson as a Bull Moose and then Republican Party campaigner:

> But whether or not he has been on the right side before, he has been and is on the right side here. Of all the officials of our Government, whose trail I have encountered here, he has been the most important, the most intelligent, the most single minded in his patriotism and the most sympathetic to democracy—in short the best American. In these qualities he has been not only pre-eminent, but—unfortunately—almost unique.[114]

Jack Reed assisted Robins in securing a list of Russian needs from a number of peoples' commissars, who had taken over the old ministries. From the Commissariat of Transportation he learned that money for purchasing locomotives and spare parts would be greatly appreciated, but "*technicians, mechanics and railroad organizers are not wanted.*"[115] If more experts were needed, men would

---

112. Francis to Thornwell Haynes, 4 January 1918, reel 5, Francis Papers, MoHS.
113. Ibid.
114. Bullard to Creel, 9 December 1917 (confidential), f. CPI, box 6, Bullard Papers, Princeton-Mudd.
115. Reed memorandum, "Skeleton Report," for Robins, 6 January 1918, f. January 1918, box 13, Robins Papers, SHSW; emphasis in original.

be sent to America and Europe to study. In agriculture he discovered a plan for the very gradual introduction of tractors and complicated harvesters and planters. "Of all departments, however, that of Public Welfare is of the first importance. Before anything else the Russian people have got to have food, especially canned stuff, shoes, clothes and cloth, and enormous amounts of milk for the babies— *immediately.*"[116]

In short, the new government seemed to be counting on considerable American aid coming from sympathetic sources but without conditions or capitalist interference.

While cooperating with Robins in communications with the Soviet government, Reed made clear that his motives were quite different: a democratic peace without annexations or indemnities and an international socialist revolution. The Allies were "still a little Alsace-Lorrainish," referring to the French demand for the return of that territory from Germany. To Robins he confessed, "I am working for international democracy *from below*—the only way I believe it can come. There are conflicts, as you know, between our two ways of thinking. But I don't think you judge me right when you call my method a 'straitjacket' formula."[117]

Reed thanked Robins for his sympathetic understanding:

> I appreciate very much all you have done for me, and am most grateful for anything you can of your own free will say to signify that I am not corrupted by anybody's money—neither the Germans' nor the Americans'— that I am working for things I believe in, and am willing to sacrifice for, and that I have not knowingly violated my agreement with the State Department.

He even asked Robins to get "a statement from the Stuffed Shirt [Francis] to the effect that I am *not* the dangerous dynamiter and German spy that he has described me in official dispatches."[118]

Unfortunately, but perhaps unavoidably, there was a certain amount of duplicity in American policy toward Russia. At the same time that Francis pursued a more moderate approach toward Bolsheviks, Maddin Summers learned directly from General Brusilov in his Moscow hospital room about what he claimed

116. Ibid. Although studies of 1917 events are numerous through the Bolshevik revolution, examinations of the first few months of Soviet governance are rare and cursory.

117. Reed to Robins, 11 January 1918, ibid. The full text of the letter is in Williams, *Journey into Revolution*, 219–20.

118. Ibid.

was the formation of a sizable army in the south of Russia under General Mikhail Alekseev, commander in chief in the early Provisional Government, and Kaledin.[119] Apparently without informing Francis, he dispatched his assistant, DeWitt Poole, on a fact-finding mission to Rostov and to confer with them at their nearby military headquarters in Novocherkassk. On the crucial question of whether he was forming a government, Alekseev replied, "For the confidential information of your government, yes—I had hoped to gather what remained of the former provisional government, but this proved quite impossible." He admitted to complications regarding its composition but stressed that the first priority was to provide assistance to Kaledin's army.[120] Even Robins, while courting Trotsky, was reported to be still channeling funds to Kerensky's friend, Breshko-Breshkovskaia.[121]

Washington Responds

Deciding how to deal with the new situation in Russia caused much discussion and frustration in Allied capitals, none more than in Washington at the end of the year. There was also some embarrassment about a short-term editor of a small Lower East Side New York Russian-language newspaper now being in charge of the foreign affairs of a major ally. This was well beyond anything in even the "democratic" American republic's diplomatic experience.[122] In general, indecision reigned.

Also sensitive was the status of the Russian embassy that represented the previous Provisional Government. Although it remained formally recognized, a low profile was deemed in order. On the request of Basil Miles, the aggressive publicity campaign in progress by the embassy was curtailed, much to the chagrin of its featured lecturer, Stanley Washburn, who wound up a monthlong tour (twenty-nine appearances) on the West Coast in Portland and Spokane in early December.[123] The State Department was not certain how to proceed. William

119. Summers to Lansing, 6 December 1917, *PWW* 45:228–29.
120. Poole (Rostov) to Francis (t), 30 December 1917, AE Russia, DPR 327, RG 84, NA. It is not clear from Poole's report that he also saw Miliukov, who was in Rostov at the time attempting to establish a military-civil coalition government. Stockdale, *Paul Miliukov,* 263–65.
121. Summers to Lansing, 12 December 1917, AE Russia, DPR 326, RG 84, NA.
122. Trotsky was a topic of discussion at a cabinet meeting on 27 November. Diary of Josephus Daniels, 27 November 1917, *PWW* 45:147.
123. Washburn to Bakhmeteff, 17, 21, and 27 November 1917, Bakhmeteff Papers, BA, CU. Although Washburn argued for a second tour, he was ordered to report to army duty and ship out to France on 10 December. 17 November, ibid.

Phillips counseled against a request from the French government for a public declaration against recognizing the de facto government in Russia but thought that some statement regarding support of a democratic Russia was in order.[124] The situation was complicated by information brought first through Allied channels of the anti-Bolshevik army organizing in the south of Russia.

Philadelphia newspaperman Lincoln Colcord, for one, urged the president to take a more active role vis-à-vis the Bolsheviks and send a new special mission to investigate and assist. He believed the real danger was not so much Russia leaving the war, which was inevitable, but allowing Germany to take it over: "But if America and the Allies, in the meanwhile, refuse to recognize her government, and continue to revile it, thus fixing permanently in the hearts of the Russian People the belief that we are animated by predatory war motives, anything might happen."[125] The president professed to have given this a "great deal" of thought, but he did not know who could be sent.[126] Colcord returned to the subject, arguing that "Lenine and Trotsky, under the pressure of responsibility, will suffer a change of heart," that they would have to face the fact that Russia was not ready for the program they had in mind.[127]

At the same time that increased contact, if not outright recognition, was being urged on the president, Lansing believed that the best hope for keeping Russia in the war was to aid the Kaledin-Alekseev forces in the south; he advised against any overtures to the Bolsheviks that might endanger this option, one that might lead to a military dictatorship. He seemed to rely on Stanley Washburn's views (at a private luncheon on 9 December) regarding the superior leadership qualities of these officers.[128]

At a cabinet meeting on 11 December, the president admitted his frustration and puzzlement about Russia, and that "he hated to do nothing."[129] Following up his exposure to Russia on the Root mission, Samuel Bertron recommended stronger action and delivered a memorandum from Ambassador Bakhmeteff that emphasized the urgency of American aid to railroad transportation and sending basic goods of necessity, but he also cautioned against "pouring a stream of material assistance into a sea of chaos."[130] The dilemma was that anything the

124. Phillips to Lansing, 3 December 1917, Phillips Papers, Yale-Sterling.

125. To Wilson, 3 December 1917, *PWW* 45:193.

126. Wilson to Colcord, 6 December 1917, *PWW* 45:222. After seeing the president's reply, William C. Bullitt thought that Colcord himself was the ideal candidate for a one-man mission. Bullitt to Wilson, 7 December 1917, *PWW* 45:235.

127. Colcord to Wilson, 8 December 1917, *PWW* 45:251.

128. Lansing to Wilson, 10 December 1917, *PWW* 45:263–64.

129. Daniels diary, 11 December 1917, *PWW* 45:271.

130. Enclosure in Tumulty to Wilson, 14 December 1917, *PWW* 45:293.

United States might do in Russia could further destabilize the situation by fo-
menting civil war. The tendency again was to wait and see the results: of the
Bullard/Sisson propaganda effort; of the gathering of military forces in the south;
and of the negotiations for peace at Brest-Litovsk.

In the meantime, the British cabinet committed a large amount of money (10
million pounds for the Kaledin army and 10 million for Russian units that supported the Romanian army) by mid-December in the hopes of maintaining a
semblance of the Eastern Front and also to protect British interests in Persia.[131]
Where these funds were actually coming from and how much actually reached
their destination remain unclear, since the operation was quite secret and involved
obscure British agents and a shady Polish-Russian banker named Iaroshinskii.[132]
Significantly, Americans were not directly informed of this substantial British
"intervention" at the time. Another plan to use Russian soldiers still in France,
with Admiral Alexander Kolchak as commander, came from none other than
Winston Churchill.[133]

For a change, Washington should not have wanted for expertise on Russia at
the end of 1917. Charles Crane had finally returned home and resumed his
informal contacts with the president. He still seemed to be at a loss for advice,
however. To his daughter, he wrote:

> I feel that this year I have discovered two entirely new countries—Russia in
> revolution and America in evolution—and they are both overwhelming. I
> believe the object lesson will be sufficiently convincing to the world for a
> long time of the futility of revolution as a mode of progressing and the
> fearful disaster that may overtake a state and all of its citizens if it does not
> progress in orderly fashion.[134]

He probably supported assistance to the anti-Bolshevik commanders in the south,
since his old friend Miliukov was doing so. In 1917 he had supported Kornilov,
who was now also in the south.

Colonel Edward House, who had returned from his special mission to Europe,
conferred with the president on 17 December and had dinner with the Cranes

131. "Organisation of Military Forces in South Russia on the Persian Frontier," secret
memorandum reviewing War Cabinet decisions, prepared by Director of Military Intelligence
for General Staff, 21 December 1917, FO 371/3018, PRO.

132. Richard H. Ullman, Anglo-Soviet Relations, 1917–1921, vol. 1, Intervention and the
War (Princeton, N.J.: Princeton University Press, 1961), 52 and n. 33.

133. "A Loyal Russian Force," War Cabinet memorandum of Churchill, 10 December
1917, CAB 24/35, PRO.

134. To Josephine, 17 December 1917, reel 1, Crane Papers, BA, CU.

(Charles, Richard, and spouses) at his daughter's on 23 December.[135] The effect of House's return, however, was temporarily to divert attention from Russia to the Western Front priority, and most of their discussion centered on that. Nonetheless, the indefinite Russian situation regarding Brest-Litovsk influenced the president's decision to draft a more definite statement of war aims, though House suggested that he rest up over the holidays before drafting it.

Meanwhile, Isabel Hapgood lent some humor to the situation by referring to "Nikolai Lenin" as Nicholas III and Ekaterina Breshko-Breshkovskaia as Catherine III.[136] The American Historical Association, at its annual after-Christmas meeting in Philadelphia, featured a session on the Russian Revolution with papers by Samuel Harper, Frank Golder, and Alexander Petrunkevich (Yale), but they confined their historical analyses to the almost forgotten February–March Revolution.[137] By the end of the year, Harper had joined a mixed bag of American "experts" on Russia—Crane, McCormick, Bertron, Thompson, Norman Hapgood, Oscar Straus, Frank Vanderlip, John Dewey, Senator William Borah, and former president William Howard Taft—in forming the American League to Act and Cooperate with Russia. Its program and objectives, however, remained vague.

Adding to the confusion, Thompson came back to Washington at the end of December after spending a couple of weeks in Britain, where he conferred with British leaders, including lunch and a long interview with Prime Minister Lloyd George. With the help of Thomas Lamont, a business associate and a director of Morgan Guaranty Trust, he influenced the British decision for a more flexible approach toward the Bolsheviks, beginning with the withdrawal of the aristocratic Sir George Buchanan as ambassador and the appointment of Robert H. Bruce Lockhart as a "special commissioner" to Russia.[138]

In Washington, Thompson and Lamont spoke with Creel, Polk, McAdoo, Daniels, Lansing, and Brandeis but failed to see Wilson, as Creel requested on 31 December and despite the claim that "Colonel Thompson has more firsthand information than anyone yet reporting."[139] In a long memorandum for the president, Thompson warned once more about the successes of German

135. Wilson to House, 16 December, and House diary, 30 December 1917, PWW 45:313, 398-99.

136. To Samuel Harper, 18 December 1917, f. 15, box 4, Harper Papers, UC.

137. Program, in ibid.

138. Salzman, Russia in War and Revolution, 214-15. Wright thought this was unfortunate timing because it lowered Allied prestige at a critical time. Diary, 3 January 1918, box 2, Wright Papers, Princeton-Mudd.

139. Salzman, Reform and Revolution, 418 n. 36; Creel to Wilson, 31 December 1917, PWW 45:407, and in vol. 1, Creel Papers, MD, LC.

propaganda and urged an increased American effort in that direction. Beyond that, he had only vague ideas of what should be done.[140]

Former Root mission member Charles Edward Russell seconded Thompson's publicity plans, not that they would have any effect upon the Bolsheviks, but because the latter were "certain to fail," and the United States should be in position to influence the policies of the next government.[141] To Cyrus McCormick it seemed that nothing was being done, and he bemoaned the "dreadful situation of apathy."[142]

The Russian situation, however, and especially the break in peace negotiations at Brest-Litovsk at the end of December, certainly played a role in the president's famous message to Congress of 8 January 1918, formulating fourteen points for peace. Sisson claimed credit for inspiring the speech through a cable sent to Creel on 3 January emphasizing the importance of taking advantage in the interim at Brest-Litovsk of circulating a clear, official statement. He based this on a response from Creel of 10 January congratulating him "on great work—Go the limit."[143]

William Bullitt in the State Department's Division of Foreign Intelligence might also claim an influence, since he drafted a long memorandum on the same day (3 January) that concluded as follows:

> At the present moment, both the Bolsheviks and the German socialists are bitterly disillusioned in regard to the sincerity and the war aims of the German Government. A unique opportunity, therefore, exists for the President by a specific statement of the liberal war aims of the United States (and the Allies), to unite Russia against the German Government and to produce revolt against the Government within Germany. And in Austria-Hungary the effect of such a message would not be slight.
>
> To-day the iron is hot![144]

He also went over Lansing's head in advising House, "I do feel sure that Trotsky is the sort of man we need in power in Russia and I think that we should do

---

140. Thompson, "Memorandum on the Present Situation in Russia," 3 January 1918, *PWW* 45:442–47.

141. Russell to McCormick, 24 December 1917, f. Department of Commerce, box 115, McC, McCormick Papers, SHSW.

142. To Mott, 26 December 1917, f. 983 (McCormick), box 53, Mott Papers, DSA.

143. Sisson, *One Hundred Red Days*, 206. Creel independently also credited Sisson's request for a statement from the president. Handwritten note on his copy of Creel to Wilson, 31 December 1917, vol. 1, Creel Papers, MD, LC.

144. Memorandum written for William Phillips, in Bullitt to Polk, 3 January 1918, f. 089, box 3, Polk Papers, Yale-Sterling.

everything possible to strengthen his hands."[145] It is not easy to believe that these words came from Lansing's department and on the eve of an important American policy speech. Additional input came from Commercial Attaché W. Chapin Huntington, in a report forwarded by Crane with a note that Huntington was the best aide the ambassador had. "He takes a more sympathetic and intelligent interest in really Russian affairs and the Russian people than anyone else in Petrograd."[146]

Although the president, with guidance from House, had decided earlier on making a war aims statement, Bullitt and Sisson, Bullard, and perhaps Huntington, Francis, and others helped give the document a sharper Russian focus.[147] Clearly Wilson was being besieged by reports on Russia for several days just before delivering the address. But House drove in the last nail in the final hours:

> As to Russia, I urged him to be at his best. I read him a sentence that I had prepared regarding Russia. . . . I told the President that it did not make any difference how much we resented Russia's action, the part of wisdom was to segregate her, as far as we were able, from Germany, and that it could only be done by the broadest and friendliest expressions of sympathy and a promise of more substantial help. . . . What he wrote about Russia is I think, in some respects, the most eloquent part of his message.[148]

After the first five points covering generalities, such as open diplomacy and freedom of the seas, the first country specifically mentioned, in point six, was Russia, with the longest text of any of the points and, it might be argued, the most careful language. Wilson called for

> the evacuation of all Russian territory and such a settlement of all questions affecting Russia as will secure the best and freest cooperation of the other nations of the world in obtaining for her an unhampered and unembarrassed opportunity for the independent determination of her own poli-

145. Bullitt to House, 7 January 1918, f. 677, box 21, House Papers, Yale-Sterling.

146. Crane to Tumulty, 3 January 1918, reel 1, Crane Papers, BA, CU. The text of this report could not be found.

147. From Petrograd, Bullard noted that everyone, especially Francis, was claiming credit for some of the content of Wilson's statement: "The Governor has at least ten times told me the exact hour on which he filed his despatch urging the President to such action and accordingly to his theory, W.W. at once locked himself in with his typewriter and went to it. The Governor modestly hints that the President lifted some of his very phrases." To Summers, 24 January 1918, box 6, Bullard Papers, Princeton-Mudd.

148. Diary of Colonel House, 9 January 1918, *PWW* 45:553.

tical development and national policy and assure her of a sincere welcome into the society of free nations under institutions of her own choosing; and, more than a welcome, assistance also of every kind that she may need and may herself desire. The treatment accorded Russia by her sister nations in the months to come will be the acid test of their good will, of their comprehension of her needs as distinguished from their own interests, and of their intelligent and unselfish sympathy.

Textbook analyses often inadequately summarize this point, omitting the open-ended promise of assistance. Nor do they note the emphasis on the negotiations at Brest-Litovsk in the introductory paragraphs of the message, which included such statements as "The Russian representatives presented not only a perfectly definite statement of the principles upon which they would be willing to conclude peace, but also an equally definite programme of the concrete application of those principles" and "The Russian representatives were sincere and in earnest." Special mention of "autonomous development" of peoples of the Austro-Hungarian and the Ottoman empires, while avoiding that distinction for Russia, except for Poland (point thirteen), was left deliberately vague and could also be interpreted as favoring any Russian government.

Wilson's Fourteen Points address was promptly transmitted to Petrograd, where it was quickly translated and circulated by Bullard and Sisson, with the help of Huntington. On 11 January it was delivered personally by Sisson, Gumberg, and Robins to Lenin, who had just returned from a brief rest in Finland. The Bolshevik leader seemed pleased with the text and with its special delivery. According to Sisson, Lenin remarked in English, "It is a great step ahead toward the peace of the world," and made certain that the address was promptly telegraphed to Trotsky at Brest-Litovsk.[149]

Arthur Bullard thought that the declaration, in combination with the emphatic dissolution of the Constituent Assembly by the Bolsheviks, had considerably strengthened their position in Russia and may also have contributed to a stiffening of their negotiations at Brest Litovsk: "As far as the aims of the war and ideals of peace the U.S. finds itself more nearly in accord with Trotsky than with Milyukov and his hot air talk about Constantinople. . . . In these matters Mr. Wilson seems to be more in accord with Trotsky than with the Foreign Ministers of some of our other allies."[150]

---

149. Sisson, *One Hundred Red Days*, 208–9. Creel's Russian agents printed 100,000 poster copies of the Russian text and over a million handbills. Ibid., 210.

150. To Summers, 24 January 1918, box 6, Bullard Papers, Princeton-Mudd.

New signals from Russia caused other modifications of American opinion. After Thompson handed Theodore Roosevelt a lengthy letter from Robins, the former president admitted that this was "far and away the most illuminating and instructive statement of the situation that I have seen" and promised to "govern my conduct and my utterances hereafter absolutely by it, . . . because in my not unnatural indignation at much of the conduct of the Bolsheviki I have used expressions which I shall hereafter avoid."[151] That caution would soon again be abandoned.

President Wilson remained open to suggestions about relations with the new Russian government through January. After reading a proposal relayed from Copenhagen on 15 January that at least one of the Allied governments formally establish relations with it, he thought it "worth considering." "Here is the ever-recurring question. How shall we deal with the Bolsheviki?"[152] But he also personally distrusted Robins's increased meddling in affairs: "It is very annoying to have this man Robins, in whom I have no confidence whatever, acting as political adviser in Russia and sending his advice to private individuals." He wondered if Robins should not be reminded of his proper functions and their limitations.[153]

The Diamandi Affair

Much of Russia was obviously in a state of disarray and confusion after the Bolshevik seizure of power, none more so than the southwest border region, where Romania still remained in the war—barely. The Romanian government and much of what remained of its army had taken refuge in the formally Russian territory of Bessarabia. The Russian military units in that area were especially demoralized by Bolshevik agitation, and in late December the commanders asked the Romanians for assistance in disarming the mutinous units. They did so and arrested several radical agitators in the process. Trotsky vehemently protested to the Romanian minister, Constantine Diamandi, in Petrograd on 1 January 1918 and demanded that he report forthwith on punishments being administered to those responsible.[154]

151. TR to Robins, 14 January 1918, f. January 1918, box 13, Robins Papers, SHSW. Robins had also sent a letter of 18 September with "Some Observations on the Present Condition of Russia" with Harper. Copy with Robins to Margaret, 20 September 1917, f. September–October 1917, box 13, Robins Papers, SHSW.
152. Wilson to Lansing, 20 January 1918, *PWW* 46:45.
153. Wilson to Lansing, 4 February 1918, *PWW* 46:232.
154. Kennan, *Russia Leaves the War*, 330–32.

When more news of disarming and arrests followed, the Soviet police moved on the evening of 13 January (Russian New Year's Eve) to arrest Diamandi and four members of his staff and held them as hostages in the Peter and Paul Fortress. This clear violation of diplomatic immunity naturally aroused the indignation of the other Allied representatives, especially French ambassador Joseph Noulens, who requested that Francis, now the dean of the diplomatic colony after the departure of Buchanan, call a meeting of ambassadors and ministers. In the meeting at noon the next day, they decided to carry an appeal directly to Smolny, to Lenin, to whom a formal written statement would be presented by Francis with an oral explanation of the protest of diplomatic immunity delivered by Noulens.[155]

After some hasty communications by telephone, Lenin sent Francis a handwritten note agreeing to meet with representatives of the diplomatic missions at 4:00 in the afternoon.[156] Rather than agree on a few representative delegates, all decided to go. The result was an impromptu New Year's Day reception in Lenin's office in the Smolny Institute. After listening (in French) to Francis's interpreter, Livingston Phelps, and eighteen other diplomats take up the cause of diplomatic immunity and protection of mission property and receiving their formal note of protest, Lenin complained about the awkward situation of the Russian army in the southwest, where a pro-Bolshevik division was being starved to death by the Romanians. He promised, however, to take up the Diamandi matter with the Council of Peoples' Commissars that same evening.[157]

The Romanians were released the following day, after some additional behind-the-scenes maneuvering by Robins, which may have involved a face-saving announcement that Francis would protest to Romania for the actions in Bessarabia (which Francis later denied).[158] This first encounter of Francis and the other diplomats with the head of the Soviet government came off surprisingly well, with Lenin generally described as affable, attentive, and responsive. The harsh-

155. Noulens, *Mon ambassade en Russie soviétique*, 1:186–88.

156. The original in English is in reel 5, Francis Papers, MoHS. It reads: "Sir; Being unable to connect with you by telephone at 2 o'clock as agreed, I am writing in order to inform you that I shall be pleased to receive you at my office, Room 81, Smolny Institute at 4 o'clock p.m. to day. Respectfully, Lenine."

157. Noulens, *Mon ambassade en Russie soviétique*, 1:186–90. For Francis's sketchier version, see *Russia from the American Embassy*, 216–20. Stalin apparently was also present but typically quiet, remaining in the background.

158. Francis, *Russia from the American Embassy*, 220–21.

est words were reserved for Trotsky's assistant, Ivan Zalkind, "whose intervention was always the reverse of conciliatory."[159]

Probably prompted by Robins and fearing increasing chaos and conflict that would further endanger Bolshevik-Allied relations and the chances of Russia staying in the war, Judson appealed to Francis for authorization to lead a peace-keeping mission to Ukraine and Romania. Intending first to secure Trotsky's approval and accompanied by a special Soviet commissar, a railroad official, an economic expert, and other members of the American military mission, he hoped to avert civil war and maintain "the possibility of harmonious action along the Russian front if war shall be renewed."[160] Francis, knowing Judson had already been recalled, ignored the offer.[161]

Between Peace and War

Another sign of more hostile Allied-Bolshevik relations came on 18 January 1918, when the long-awaited Constituent Assembly finally met. As most observers expected, its composition, reflecting elections held throughout the country in November, resulted in a Socialist Revolutionary (SR) majority (with the Bolsheviks and Left SRs holding a sizable minority), and it was forcibly disbanded by armed sailors after a futile daylong session. With Kerensky and a number of other SR leaders discredited, it is not clear who might have emerged as its chief spokesman or how it might have drafted a workable alternative constitution, assuming that decisions would have required a two-thirds vote. Some concerned Americans, such as the manager of the International Harvester factory outside Moscow, thought that an SR government would be no improvement over a Bolshevik one.[162] This action and the narrow avoidance of more serious violence against Bolshevik opponents dashed many hopes that the Bolsheviks might bend to the democratic will of the people.

159. "Mr. Phelps Statement of Visit of Diplomatic Corps to Smolny Institute," 14 January 1918, Francis Papers, MoHS. Salzman, *Russia in War and Revolution*, 239. Zalkind had a reputation for being crude and brutal.

160. Judson to Francis, 15 January 1918, copy in box 13, Robins Papers, SHSW. Full text in Salzman, *Russia in War and Revolution*, 220–21.

161. Judson diary, 16 January 1918, in Salzman, *Russia in War and Revolution*, 224. The head of the mission was scheduled to leave in a week, after the arrival of his replacement, Lieutenant Colonel Ruggles.

162. S. G. McAllister to H. F. Perkins, 7 February 1918, box 1365, IH Papers, SHSW.

Judson's departure on 21 January, or rather the lack of any attempt to post-
pone it on the part of Francis, was symptomatic of important changes occurring
in the American missions in Russia in early 1918 that would seriously influence
the course of Soviet-American relations. Colonel Kerth, also recalled, left with
him. In a separate report to Judson, he clarified his support of a policy of aid
and recognition, regardless of a separate peace: "America must remain active in
Russia until the general peace for we must fight the exploitation of Russia by the
Central Powers to the bitter end and we must guard carefully against doing anthing
we ought not to do or leaving undone anything that we might do to accomplish
our purpose."[163]

Assuming Judson's position was Colonel James A. Ruggles, who was originally assigned in October as the replacement for Colonel Kerth as an assistant
to Judson.[164] Ruggles, having finally arrived at the end of January, had no knowledge of Russia nor of any foreign languages; he also lacked diplomatic experience and had no chance to be briefed by Judson. He was now, unexpectedly,
head of the American military mission in Russia at a crucial time and a chief
adviser to the dean of the diplomatic corps (which a number of observers were
now often referring to as "the corpse"). Fortunately, he still had Riggs as an
aide, but an important high-level American contact with Trotsky had been lost
by Judson's removal.

The Bolsheviks did not help matters. While seeking recognition of the Soviet
government by foreign powers, especially the United States, they made life difficult for resident diplomats by freezing bank accounts and allowing unruly anarchists to threaten an attack on the American embassy in a misguided effort to
free Alexander Berkman and Emma Goldman from jail. Nor could they really
escape, except for short intervals, their ideological blinders. For all his faults
and problems, Francis had the ability to sum up the situation succinctly. To
Ambassador Ira Morris in Stockholm, he described an ideological and class
conflict:

> The bolsheviks here are attempting to create a world-wise [*sic?*] social revo-
> lution and do not hesitate to preach violence in order to promote it. It begins
> to look as if it might become a problem for the bourgeoisie (in which you

163. Kerth to Judson, 22 January 1918, f. 2070-12, roll 3 (M 1443), RG 165, NA.

164. War Department to State Department, 25 October 1917, f. 10282-3, box 551, RG
165, NA. A "Captain Miller," who had some knowledge of the area, was dispatched to assist
Ruggles but then recalled for being publicly drunk at the Grand Hotel in Tokyo. Morris
(Tokyo) to Lansing, 29 January 1918, f. 10281-21, ibid.

and I and all men of education who wear white collars are classed) to make the world safe for society.[165]

The ambassador's trust in his military advisers was certainly not improved at this critical time by a memorandum prepared for him by Riggs on 9 February. According to the memo, reliable sources had reported that Matilda de Cram, referred to as "mistress of the American ambassador," had met and entertained Wilhelm von Mirbach and other members of the German delegation in Petrograd. After conducting his own investigation, Francis flatly denied all the charges.[166]

Almost everyone in the diplomatic corps and in its auxiliaries such as the Red Cross and the Creel mission was tired, frustrated, and ill-tempered from contending with the Russian circumstances—and each other. Arthur Bullard may have summed up the situation best:

It was not only that the various embassies were often at loggerheads. No one of the ambassadors was of strong enough character to dominate and control his own flock. Grouped about each embassy, there were military missions, secret services, publicity agents, commercial attachés, all busily engaged in trying to serve their country, but with no one to co-ordinate their actions. They were continually getting in each other's way.[167]

Still, some managed to relieve the tension with humor, as in Norman Armour's ironic description of the Petrograd scene:

The Ambassador now being Dean of the Corpse, the question of protocol is continually coming to the front in the many Ambassadorial dinners that are being given. The Judge [Butler Wright] and I have to continually decide the important question as to whether Lenin or Trotzky [sic] should sit on the Ambassador's right.[168]

The most that Ruggles seemed to accomplish was to quarrel with Francis, who was increasingly isolated—from Washington, the Soviet government, and

165. Francis to Morris, 31 January 1918, reel 9, Francis Papers, MoHS.

166. Francis to Riggs, 26 February 1918, reel 10, ibid.

167. *The Russian Pendulum: Autocracy–Democracy–Bolshivism* [sic] (New York: Macmillan, 1919), 111.

168. To Whitehouse (Stockholm), 18 January 1918, f. 52, box 2, Armour Papers, Princeton-Mudd.

his own staff. Sisson was going his own well-funded way, transforming his mission to inform Russia about the United States into a private intelligence-gathering agency. Malcolm Davis, who worked for Sisson, remembered his work as a combination of propaganda and spying.[169]

During the meeting of Sisson and Robins with Lenin on 11 January, the Bolshevik leader made a rhetorical reference to people thinking he was a German agent. Sisson then set out to prove just that—and collected quite a number of documents on the subject that would cause a major sensation when finally published in America, though most would later be proved to be forgeries. The main source was a former Russian newspaper editor, Evgeny Semenov, but the author of the forgeries was his former assistant, Antoni Ossendowsky.[170] In his acquisition Sisson was assisted by Davis, Bullard, and Berlitz teacher George Akerman and members of the military mission Bukovsky and Eugene Prince, as an adjunct to their intelligence mission.[171] As veterans of Russian affairs, Davis and Corse helped convince Sisson that the documents were authentic, while Bullard claimed to have doubts from the beginning.

Sisson caused other mischief by trying to take charge of American affairs in Russia. Having broken with Robins over the policy of seeking an understanding with the Soviet leaders, he proceeded to undermine Robins's credibility. Sisson was also especially annoyed by John Reed's speaking for America at the Third Congress of Soviets that met as the legitimate government of Russia just after the closing of the Constituent Assembly. The fact that Reed was soon to leave with credentials as the new *Soviet* consul general to the United States (later rescinded) and with much Soviet-generated revolutionary literature irritated Sisson greatly, so he helped arrange through Washington Reed's detention for several weeks in the Norwegian port of Christiana and the seizure of his papers when he finally reached New York.[172]

After Judson's departure, and unable to trust Ruggles, Francis became more and more reliant on Sisson for information and advice. On 5 February Francis received from Semenov, whose newspaper had been closed by the Bolsheviks, a copy of a letter purporting to be from Adolf Ioffe, Trotsky's assistant at Brest-Litovsk, written from there on 13 January and directing the arrest of the Romanian mission in compliance with German wishes. This was supposedly part of

169. Davis oral history, p. 43, CU.

170. For proof that the documents were fake, see George F. Kennan, "The Sisson Documents," *Journal of Modern History* 28, no. 2 (June 1956): 130–54.

171. Sisson, *One Hundred Red Days*, 340–73.

172. Robert A. Rosenstone, *Romantic Revolutionary: A Biography of John Reed* (New York: Knopf, 1982), 315–16.

a German plan to force Romania to make peace and to close down the entire Eastern Front. Francis asked Sisson to verify this. He promptly did so with the help of the British chief of intelligence, who vouched for Semenov, thus adding more fuel to the Bolshevik-German conspiracy theory.

Francis carelessly sent a coded cable to Washington with this information only, to his consternation, to have it intercepted. Trotsky almost immediately cited the ambassador's charges and denied them to Robins. Francis summed up the confused situation in Petrograd in an unsent cable to Lansing:

> Robins says Trotsky told him if I did not know that what I wired you about himself is untrue I am badly mistaken. Cannot imagine how he got such information as all was sent in special code . . . Robins Sisson disagreeing and each when asked how Trotsky got information insuates [sic] the other responsible. . . . Robins thinks all documents forged Sisson disagrees. These men who for two months were unitedly working contrary to my policy are now very confidential with me. Robins sees Trotsky daily. Sisson visits Smolny often but doubt his seeing Lenin or Trotsky.[173]

Quite a few more documents surfaced that professed to reveal a strong German influence upon Bolshevik leaders. Some even came into Sisson's hands through Robins, while most Sisson acquired easily on the street, since it was widely known that he had plenty of money for such purchases. By mid-February a clear rift was apparent between Sisson and the Red Cross men, Robins, Wardwell, and Thacher, with the former convinced that the Bolsheviks were paid German agents and that he had documents to prove it, while the latter believed that German money might have been involved before their coming to power, but that the Soviet authorities were now independent performers who might yet resume the war rather than sign a dictated peace.

Robins's position was strengthened by the arrival at the beginning of February of Robert H. Bruce Lockhart, an experienced British diplomat (former consul general in Russia) with a special commission to communicate with Soviet leaders. They quickly developed a close relationship that would endure for the remainder of Robins's stay in Russia. Lockhart came equipped with a letter of introduction from Maxim Litvinov, a special Soviet emissary to Britain, and quickly established regular, almost daily contact with Georgi Chicherin, who was now in charge of the Commissariat of Foreign Affairs during Trotsky's

---

173. Francis to Lansing, 18 February 1918, reel 10, Francis Papers, MoHS. At the top of this document in Francis's hand is "not sent but framed by me. DRF."

absence at Brest-Litovsk.[174] The British diplomatic-military staff was thus similarly split as the American between recognizers and nonrecognizers, with Chargé Francis Lindley, like Francis, caught in the middle. But with special instructions from the Foreign Office in London, Lockhart had much more authority than Robins.

While Sisson detached himself and quite a bit of money from the propaganda campaign and made plans to hurry home to publish his incriminating materials against the Bolsheviks, Robins vowed to stay and maintain contacts with the Soviet leadership with the lukewarm backing of Red Cross officials in Washington. This action seemed warranted by Trotsky's walking out and breaking off of the Brest-Litovsk negotiations in a huff on 11 February. He then pronounced his policy of neither peace nor war, that is, that Russia would stop fighting but would not sign a peace on terms demanded by Germany. The German army simply resumed its advance on Petrograd.

Robins's position as an intermediary was precarious, however, owing to hostile feedback reaching Washington. Henry Davison, director of the American Red Cross, prompted by the president, almost reeled him in in February but delayed after listening to General Judson's praise of his conduct.[175] Clearly, Robins was not an easy man for American officialdom to deal with.

Clarifying Russia

For the folks at home, the situation in Russia obviously needed some explanation, and many "experts" were on hand to try. The two extreme positions were represented by Thompson and Washburn. Thompson paid for his own inept articles advocating recognition of the Soviets but was generally dismissed as a crackpot. Washburn thought that he had been muzzled by his position in the State Department and in reaction volunteered for duty in France. He consistently advocated substantial armed intervention on the scale of 250,000

---

174. Lockhart, *Memoirs of a British Agent*, 220–29. Lockhart described Robins as follows:

Robins, who was a philanthropist and a humanitarian rather than a politician, was a wonderful orator. His conversation, like Mr. Churchill's, was always a monologue, but it was never dull, and his gift of allegory was as remarkable as it was original. With his black hair and his aquiline features, he had a most striking appearance. He was an Indian chief with a Bible for his tomahawk.

And he describes how Robins was a worshiper of "great men" such as Teddy Roosevelt and Vladimir Lenin. Ibid., 222.

175. Davison to Wilson, 21 February 1918, *PWW* 46:408–9.

troops.[176] Although John Reed was still cooling his heels in Norway, Louise Bryant and Bessie Beatty tentatively took up the pro-Bolshevik cause, but few paid much attention to their cries in the dark. The positions of major armed intervention and of immediate recognition tended to cancel each other out by their extremism and hostile positions.

For the time being in early 1918, most of the ground was left to the middle, those who opposed both recognition and major armed intervention but who urged understanding and the coupling of relief and assistance with any modest intervention that might be needed to keep ports secure and open. Charles Crane led the list but typically remained out of the limelight, while supporting and encouraging his followers such as Samuel Harper and Norman Hapgood. A number of others had developed a special interest in Russia, for example, leading journalists such as Walter Lippmann and William Allen White, who also pleaded the cause of understanding and patience.

Harper, who would later be a strong advocate of nonrecognition, best represented the moderate position. While noting that the Bolsheviks are "clever manipulators," he admired the work of both Trotsky and Lenin. He wrote to Richard Crane:

Of course Trotsky is not working for the same kind of democracy for which we are fighting. But up to a certain point he takes a line that fits in with ours, and to that point he represents not pure Bolshevism, but the principles of the first revolution, which the Bolsheviki have monopolized. To that point he will use us, just as we are using him, and it is a question of wits. But it is a difficult game for us to play, for these Bolsheviki are indeed mighty clever, and they are not handicapped by scruples.[177]

White, as publisher and editor of the *Emporia (Kansas) Gazette*, was already renowned as a Middle American voice of homespun but progressive views. He was riding the height of his fame from covering the arrival of the first American troops in France with his cousin Henry Allen in syndicated columns and in a widely circulated book, *The Martial Adventures of Henry and Me*. On the way back from Europe, he happened to be on the same ship as Harper, and they spent most of the crossing talking about Russia. His interest sparked, White devoted considerable attention to the kaleidoscoping events in Russia. He saw a progressivist silver lining in the Bolshevik revolution: "Today in Russia, all

176. Washburn oral history, p. 101, CU.
177. To Richard Crane, 22 February 1918, box 5, Harper Papers, UC.

uninformed, all blind, all mad and tremendously stupid, stands a new man in the world—the worker. This will be his century. . . . For the first time since history dawned he is having an international say."[178]

Privately, White wrote a friend in the administration, "I have faith in Russia. I believe that the Russian revolution is the greatest net gain of this war so far. And the best thing in the President's peace terms, it seems to me, is his consideration of Russia and the Russian views and rights in the matter."[179] He also resumed contact with Harper and offered to arrange a speaking tour for him through the Great Plains in February. Urged by Crane to explain Russia and in need of money, Harper was happy to accept.[180] Originally planned to include an area from Texas to Iowa, the tour was ultimately limited to Colorado and Kansas, concentrating on college and university campuses—Colorado College, University of Denver, University of Colorado, Kansas State Agricultural College, University of Kansas, and, of course, Kansas Normal College (Emporia State University) in White's home town in late February.

At the University of Kansas the chancellor canceled classes and declared Harper's lecture a university convocation, with all students and faculty required to attend. According to the local press that covered the event in detail, Harper stressed understanding and patience for Russia, arguing that it should be considered "an experimental laboratory" and that the Allies owed it a debt for not leaving the war a year earlier. He was optimistic that Russia might yet be saved from extremism. No mention of either intervention or recognition can be found.[181]

Harper thought that his audiences in the Midwest were more patient and open-minded in regard to Russia than those he had found in the East: "I was much encouraged by the calm determination and intelligent patriotism of those two States. . . . They look on the East as too emotional, given to panics. The idea that sound interpretation is as important as efficient administration seems to prevail out there."[182]

Harper was naturally busiest speaking in the Chicago area, and he welcomed the return of Edward Ross of the University of Wisconsin in February to share

---

178. Editorial, "The Bolsheviks," *Emporia Gazette*, 22 January 1918.

179. White to Victor Murdock, 14 January 1918, series B, vol. 32, pt. 1, White Papers, MD, LC.

180. White to Harper, 14 January 1918, ibid.; Harper to White, 6, 10, and 14 February 1918, series C, box 45, ibid.

181. *Lawrence Journal-World*, 26 and 27 February; *Lawrence Gazette*, 27 and 28 February; and *University Daily Kansas*, 27 February 1918.

182. Harper to Crane, 2 March 1918, box 5, Harper Papers, UC.

some of the burden. Privately, Harper believed that relief should continue, especially milk for children; that exchanges of students, workers, and peasants be organized; that the integrity of the empire be maintained; and that the Bolsheviks were likely to remain in power for some time. He was especially concerned about the quality of the American personnel in Russia and believed that a new ambassador was needed. "Men of unquestioned democratic sympathies, men of wide vision and men of action are required at this most critical post."[183]

Avoiding the extremes of recognition or major intervention was also the credo of respected members of the business and intellectual communities in early 1918. One lead was taken by Cyrus McCormick, who approached other Root mission members—Mott, Crane, Bertron, and Root—to call a meeting in early February to discuss the Russian situation.[184] He prepared a draft agenda that began as follows:

> Granting that we despise the Bolshevik movement and would much prefer to have nothing to do with them, is it not a fact that they have gained such an ascendency that the diplomatic thing would be to give them some attention and by a sort of quasi recognition in negotiating with them get them to act along more reasonable lines than they will if we hold aloof?[185]

He questioned whether Bakhmeteff, Francis, Corse, or Sisson, who "has mixed things up pretty well in Petrograd," could be of any use in a more moderate and sophisticated publicity effort in Russia, and suggested that pressure might be applied to Creel and Lansing to have both Sisson and Francis recalled. He also recommended consideration of another special mission to Russia and mentioned Myron Herrick or William G. Sharp, current ambassador to France, to head it.[186]

With any sign of significant intervention seeming to be in the distance, Washington was shocked by the news in late February that the War Council in Paris had authorized Japan to send troops to Siberia. This decision was due at least in part to the urging of Robert Cecil in the Foreign Office and the influence of George Buchanan and General Alfred Knox, recently returned

183. "Notes by Professor Harper," 7 February 1918, f. 20, box 4, Harper Papers, UC.

184. Copies of letters to Mott, Root, and Bertron, 2 February 1918, f. Department of Commerce, box 115, 2C, McCormick Papers, SHSW. Russell was omitted because he was on a speaking tour.

185. Draft, "prepared by CHM," copies to Bertron, Crane, Mott, Root, 8 February 1918, ibid.

186. Ibid.

from Russia. Cecil only regretted that the decision had not been made a month or six weeks earlier. "My own opinion, for what it is worth, is that if it [intervention] were carried through with vigour and decision the Russians would not object to it."[187] But the American alarm about the Japanese in Siberia would prevent this.

Breckinridge Long reported in his diary on 25 February: "This is blue Monday in the Allies camp. It is 'reported' the War Council in Paris 'unanimously' decided to send Japan to Russia and into Siberia."[188] That evening Colonel House dined with President and Mrs. Wilson and recorded:

> We discussed, at great length, the question of Japanese intervention in Siberia, but came to no conclusion. There are arguments both for and against it. My thought was that unless Japan went in under a promise to withdraw, or at least be subject to the disposition of the peace conference, the Entente in backing her would place themselves in exactly the same position as the Germans now occupied toward Western Russia, to which there is such vociferous objection among the Western Powers.[189]

The State Department was still sharply divided over the issue of a Japanese presence in Siberia, with Basil Miles recommending the prompt dispatch of American troops in China as far as Irkutsk to make it appear a joint effort and also with the goal of rescuing Francis, but Long opposed.[190] William Bullitt advocated a strong public protest against any Japanese move into Russia in a lengthy memorandum of 2 March 1918.[191] The matter was discussed at a cabinet meeting that day, with the president emphatically saying no to the idea of joining the Japanese "for the very practical reason," according to Franklin Lane,

> that we had no ships. We had difficulty in providing for our men in France and for our Allies. . . . How hopeless it would be to carry everything seven or eight thousand miles—not only men and munitions, but food!—for Japan

187. Cecil, "Memorandum on Russia," 23 February 1918, CAB 24/43, PRO.
188. Long diary, 25 February 1918, box 1, Long Papers, MD, LC.
189. House diary, 25 February 1918, *PWW* 46:445.
190. Long Diary, 28 February 1918, box 1, Long Papers, MD, LC.
191. The memorandum, prepared for Counselor Frank Polk, circulated through House and Auchincloss to the president, but he probably did not see it before the cabinet meeting. *PWW* 46:510-13.

has none to spare, and none we could eat. Her men feed on rice and smoked fish, and she raises nothing we would want. . . . So there is the end of talking of an American force in Siberia![192]

Concern was also expressed about avoiding being the focus of a strong Russian reaction. Long, however, gained the impression from Polk that "Prest decides to make no opposition to Jap going into Siberia but because of advisability of U.S. keeping diplomatic independence we will not join in request."[193]

After listening to appeals of Root, Bertron, Bakhmeteff, and even Bessie Beatty the next day, and having discussed the matter with the president "backward and forward during the last week,"[194] House sensed even more the danger of "the proposed Japanese intervention in Siberia." Perplexed about why Britain and France would support such an idea, House concluded, "The French have come to hate the Russians and do not care what ill fate befalls them and for reasons which are obvious. The English that are in power have such an intense hatred for Germany that they have lost their perspective."[195]

Economic Relations

Adding to the confusion of the limbo of nonrecognition and nonintervention were questions of economic relations. This was made more imperative by dire scarcity of many essential items in Russia, a crash program to equip a new Red Army, evidence of German attempts to purchase Russian products, and the existence of large quantities of "Allied" material in the ports of Murmansk, Archangel, and Vladivostok with very little protection.

Already in January reports circulated of large amounts of goods being purchased by Nuys-Banken and other Swedish and German agents, presumably for shipment to Germany. They included sleigh loads of frozen hogs, bales of cotton, 100,000 *pud* (one *pud* = 36 pounds) of railway oil, 200,000 *pud* of rubber,

192. Lane Memorandum, 2 March, *PWW* 46:515. Josephus Daniels's version is as follows: "Why not join Japan & go into Russia? B & W [Burleson and W. B. Wilson] said if Japan went in she would never come out & we ought to join No said WW. 'We have not ships to send soldiers and besides if we invade Russia will not Germany say we are doing exactly what she is doing. We will lose our moral position.'" Daniels diary, 1 March 1918, ibid., 508.
193. Long diary, 2 March 1918, box 1, Long Papers, MD, LC.
194. House diary, 3 March 1918, *PWW* 46:519.
195. House to Wilson, 3 March 1918, *PWW* 46:518-19.

and 10 million cowhides.[196] Major Henry Emery of the American military mission, attached to the Petrograd consulate, and R. R. Stevens of National City Bank verified these reports, so Tredwell cabled Washington: "Stevens convinced agents of Germany here are buying this stuff and exporting it."[197] This prompted Washington, to Tredwell's relief, to authorize $1 million in mid-February through National City Bank for the purchase of such commodities, just to prevent them from falling into German hands.[198]

On another front the Soviet leadership was concerned about acquiring important shipments of a wide range of items in ports or in transit. On 29 January (evidently Old Style calendar), Iwri Larin invited American and British consular representatives to a conference on 15 February (new calendar) at the offices of the old ministry of commerce and industry to discuss a number of issues. From the British he wanted assurances that no general or partial embargo would be imposed, that goods on ships at Murmansk would be unloaded, and that a basis for acquiring strategic raw materials, especially rubber, would be arranged.[199]

Larin queried Emery about a report that indicated several shiploads of locomotives and cars destined for Vladivostok had been detained in Japanese ports and demanded a statement of how many of these much-needed items ordered by the previous government would be delivered in 1918. He asserted the Soviet position that none of these shipments were to be paid for out of the loans secured by the Provisional Government but only by gold upon delivery. Other contracts would be renegotiated on the same basis. When asked for a guarantee that none of these goods would be sold to Germany, Larin was evasive but noted the critical needs in Russia itself and said he would refer the matter to the Council of Peoples' Commissars.[200] He also stated that he was sending a special expedition to Archangel to bring supplies there to the interior for the use of the Soviet government.

After seeing Emery's report, Consul General Summers in Moscow was quite upset by what he believed was a serious breach of authority and a wrongheaded policy.

I do not believe, unless there is a radical change in Russia's policy, that we should send a dollar's worth of goods here. Not only does this policy en-

---

196. Tredwell memorandum, 24 January 1918, box 2, Petrograd Consulate 1918, RG 84, NA.
197. Tredwell to Francis, 27 January 1918, ibid.
198. Tredwell to Lansing, 20 February 1918, ibid.
199. Emery report of 15 February, in Tredwell to Francis, 16 February 1918, ibid.
200. Ibid.

courage them to stop work and depend on others to provide for their needs, but the articles sent here are in danger either of falling into the hands of the enemy, or of being wantonly destroyed by the proletariat.[201]

Ironically, while the British, with at least some American blessing, were promising aid to anti-Bolshevik forces in the south, both British and Americans were holding open the door for the continuation of commerce in Soviet territory.

Exodus

During the first few weeks of 1918, a year thankfully shortened for Russians by the formal adoption of the Western calendar on 1 February, conditions in Petrograd deteriorated rapidly. The streets had not been cleaned of snow, and the freezing and thawing of an unusually mild winter left many of them virtually impassable. Food, fuel, and electricity were increasingly in short supply, but worst of all were the breakdown in law and order and the constant threat of robbery and violence from refugees, unemployed workers, or wandering ex-soldiers and sailors.[202]

Previously, such episodes were mostly confined to the streets, but now apartments, offices, and hospitals were no longer safe. Even the American embassy was threatened, and on 13 January the Italian embassy was invaded and relieved of its alcoholic beverages, prompting some Americans to drink more than usual while supplies were available.[203] Symbolizing the new extremism was the vile murder on 20 January of two leading liberals and Kadet politicians, Andrei Shingarev and Fedor Kokoshkin, both former ministers in the Provisional Government, in their Petrograd hospital beds by vigilante (and probably drunken) sailors.[204] Many current or former opponents or those who held positions in previous governments chose to leave for the countryside or other, hopefully safer, cities.

201. Summers to Tredwell, 25 February 1918, ibid.

202. For the heightened sense of difficulty and danger, see the letters of Pauline Crosley, *Intimate Letters from Petrograd*, 247–76.

203. Armour to Whitehouse, 18 January 1918, f. 52, box 2, Armour Papers, Princeton-Mudd.

204. For an account of its impact on Kadet policy vis-à-vis Bolsheviks and support for the Kaledin forces in the south, see William G. Rosenberg, *Liberals in the Russian Revolution: The Constitutional Democratic Party, 1917–1921* (Princeton, N.J.: Princeton University Press, 1974), 286–91.

By mid-February, with the German army again advancing, and with the realization that there was really nothing to stop it, panic ensued, beginning with 11 February (the breakoff of negotiations) and continuing through the remainder of the month.[205] Lenin's difficult but successful effort on 23 February to gain approval by the Soviet executive committee of new, more stringent German terms failed to stem the tide. They still had to be ratified by the Fourth Congress of Soviets that was to meet in the comparative security of Moscow. This change of venue was another reason for people to abandon Petrograd.

Ambassador Francis advised American residents to prepare to leave on 22 February. Several Americans, including the Corses, the Stines, the Emerys, and the Crosleys, sought to exit the country through Finland.[206] Francis thought it was a quicker and safer route for women, but they were detained, and endured a number of scares, in Finland, where a state of civil war existed between the left and right wings of the Finnish independence movement, before finally reaching safety in Sweden a month later. A larger detachment of twenty-five or more, mostly YMCA/YWCA and National City Bank employees, left Petrograd on 24 February for Vologda; after a brief stop they proceeded on to Vereshchagino, a minor station on the Trans-Siberian, where they waited a week for instructions.[207]

At a conference of Allied representatives on 20 February, the decision had been made to abandon Petrograd, but, as dean of the diplomatic colony, Francis did not want to be the first to leave. Upon the urging of Robins, however, he decided to remove himself and the rest of his immediate staff to the east, still uncertain on 25 February whether his destination would be Siberia or Murmansk, but in preparation cabled Lansing insisting on the immediate occupation of Vladivostok, Murmansk, and Archangel in order to provide safe exit. His main concerns were the advance of the German army toward Petrograd and the expectation of collapse of the Soviet government, with resulting anarchy throughout the country. He believed Russia was about to become a German ally or prov-

---

205. Pauline Crosley wrote on 20 February, "All of our previous surcharged atmosphere has been a mere nothing as compared with the last ten days." *Intimate Letters from Petrograd*, 273.

206. Crosley complained that Francis sent him out because "he didn't need a sailor in Siberia." Crosley (Christiania, Norway) to DNI, 12 April 1918, f. 9799, C-10-F, RG 38, NA.

207. Francis to Perry (son), 25 February 1918, reel 10, Francis Papers, MoHS. For a detailed account of this evacuation train that finally reached Vladivostok on 20 May, see Paul Anderson to mother, 5 April 1918, f. YMCA (Russian Work), box 5, Anderson Papers, UIA.

ince, with the likelihood of civil war.[208] On the afternoon of 26 February, Consul Tredwell ordered a train that could carry 150 people with a dining car and three luggage cars attached, not an easy task considering the confusion and rush to abandon Petrograd.[209]

The object was to remain in Russia if possible but not to go to Moscow, which might be viewed as a step closer to recognition, especially since many in the government were simultaneously moving to Moscow and because congestion was greatest on that route. After additional time to conduct inventories, pack and seal archives, and turn over custody to the Norwegian ministry, a second train with Francis, Tredwell, and others aboard—and Robins's Red Cross car attached—was ready to depart on 26 February, "after unspeakable confusion in getting the Chinese and Japanese staffs settled with their mountains of baggage."[210]

But permission to leave was held up by authorities who feared that news of the American desertion of the city would only aggravate the general panic. Robins made a quick trip to Smolny to obtain Lenin's personal permission.[211] Finally, in the early morning hours of 27 February, the American embassy literally and formally left the Russian capital, accompanied by the Japanese and Chinese missions, which were going in that direction anyway, and arrived in Vologda at 3:00 A.M. the next day.[212] Wright recorded, "It is a most extraordinary proceeding—5 diplomatic missions headed out into Siberia, in winter, with no news and not the slightest idea where we are going."[213]

208. Ibid.; Francis to Lansing, 24 February 1918, f. Siberia 1918, box 186, Long Papers, MD, LC.

209. Tredwell to Chicherin, n.d., AE Russia, DPR 325, RG 84, NA. A French observer thought the Americans "have shown more panic than anyone else over this business. Louis D. Robien, 26 February 1918, in *The Diary of a Diplomat in Russia, 1917–1918*, trans. Camilla Sykes (London: Michael Joseph, 1969), 235.

210. Wright diary, 26 February 1918, box 2, Wright Papers, Princeton-Mudd.

211. Salzman, *Reform and Revolution*, 243.

212. Francis diary, 26 and 28 February 1918, reel 11, Francis Papers, MoHS; "Report on Evacuation of Petrograd by Consulate," 31 March 1918, box 1, Petrograd Consulate, RG 84, NA. Tredwell lists 60 Americans, 40 Japanese, and 35 Chinese on the first train. The second all-American contingent included several marines guarding crates of confidential archives.

213. Wright diary, 27 February 1918, box 2, Wright Papers, Princeton-Mudd.

5

Vologda

For five months in 1918, the provincial town of
Vologda, with a population of around 40,000, would be the diplomatic capital
of Russia, at least as far as the United States was concerned.[1] Its main advantages were direct rail and telegraph links with Petrograd and Moscow and to
Archangel to the north and less regularly with Siberian points to the east. Although this destination was chosen at short notice and without much forethought,
it was also fairly safe from German attack. Francis recounted a conversation with
Allied representatives, after he assured them that he was not leaving Russia:

> "Where are you going?" one of them asked.
> "I am going to Vologda," I said.
> "What do you know about Vologda?"
> "Not a thing except that it is the junction of the Trans-Siberian Railway
> and the Moscow-Archangel Railway and that it is 350 miles farther away
> from the Germans."
> "Well, if it is unsafe there, what are you going to do?"
> "I am going east to Viatka, which is 600 miles east, and if it is unsafe
> there, I am going to Perm. If it is unsafe at Perm, I am going to Irkutsk,
> and if it is still unsafe, I am going to Chita, and if necessary from there I
> am going to Vladivostok, where I will be protected by an American man-
> of-war, the *Brooklyn*, under Admiral Knight."[2]

1. This is the figure given by Consul Roger Tredwell in his report on the move, 31 March
1918, box 1, Petrograd Consulate, RG 84, NA, but the population may have been somewhat
in flux in 1918, since Ambassador Francis claimed 65,000. Francis to family, 15 April 1918,
reel 9, Francis Papers, MoHS.
2. Francis, *Russia from the American Embassy*, 234-35. At home, Herbert Hoover, from
his office as director of the United States Food Administration, correctly guessed the situation and advised Francis, facetiously:

A few days after arrival at Vologda, it appeared that the German advance had halted and, at the same time, that the Soviet government might resist the peace terms, which were due to be ratified at a Soviet congress in Moscow, scheduled for 12 March. After some initial confusion and difficulty in finding food—"Never was an Embassy in such a plight"[3]—Francis decided to send the first detachment of Americans under the charge of James Bailey on toward Siberia on a train carrying the Japanese and Chinese missions. He also instructed Chapin Huntington to go along as far as Irkutsk to investigate and report on conditions there.[4] Then, on 5 March, apparently with the motive of finding out what was going on in the Far East, he dispatched Butler Wright, who had really been running the day-to-day affairs of the embassy, to Vladivostok and on to Washington.[5]

At the same time, consular offices were retained in both Petrograd and Moscow, and Vologda, after a week of indecision, became a sort of summer residence of the ambassador. He and his immediate staff found quarters in a former merchant's house, currently being used as a commercial club, while others took rooms in the Hotel Ermitage. Meanwhile, a secretary of Finnish origin, Karen Sante, and Russian clerk Raisa Loviagin kept the embassy and consulate, respectively, on a semioperational basis in Petrograd.[6] In the absence of Huntington, "Livy" Phelps (on courier duty), Wright, and Whitehouse (previously detached to Stockholm), Francis was left with few able assistants at Vologda.[7] Remaining

---

By this time you will be scurrying all over Russia trying to find a place to sleep. There is a very good house that I lived in for some time at Kyshtim—a station on the trans-Siberian line outside of Ekaterinburg—that was in fact a country palace built by a former owner of a property that I operated there for some time. You will find some very good pictures in it and the place is very decent to live in! But to be serious, I am anxious for your safety in this melee.

Hoover to Francis, 8 March 1918, f. Francis, pre-Commerce, HPL.

3. Wright diary, 4 March 1918, box 2, Wright Papers, Princeton-Mudd.

4. Francis to Huntington, 3 March 1918, reel 9, Francis Papers, MoHS.

5. Wright diary, 5-6 March 1918, box 2, Wright Papers, Princeton-Mudd. French military adviser Jacques Sadoul, who was on a visit to Vologda, connects Wright's departure with Francis's concern with Japanese intervention. Letter of 7 March 1918 to Albert Thomas, in *Notes sur la révolution bolchevique octobre 1917–janvier 1919* (Paris: François Maspero, 1971), 254-55.

6. Sante, who is described by Francis as "twenty four, crosseyed but very bright and efficient," did yeoman service during difficult times. Francis to wife, 23 June 1918, reel 10, Francis Papers, MoHS.

7. One factor in these departures was Francis's concern for family affairs. Phelps was accompanying his wife out of the country as far as Norway, and Francis felt sorry for Wright, who had parted from his pregnant wife the previous December. Those who took the early road through Finland were also with wives. Francis to family, 15 April 1918, reel 9, Francis Papers, MoHS.

behind in Petrograd were four YMCA secretaries, six Creel men (including Sisson and Bullard), twelve National City Bank employees, and some Red Cross personnel.[8] Sisson, however, departed for the United States through Finland on 4 March with the documents he had collected, while Thomas Thacher of the Red Cross headed for Murmansk to be in position to carry the Robins story home.

One of the first things that Robins did at Vologda was to wire Lenin of their arrival and inquire about the status of the peace negotiation. Lenin quickly responded, "Peace not signed. Situation without change."[9] Robins made plans at once to return to Petrograd on 3 March, accompanied by Consul Roger Tredwell, followed two days later by Ruggles and Riggs, who were instructed by Francis to consult with Soviet authorities about military preparations.[10] The relocation of the embassy to Vologda and the subsequent transfer of the Soviet government to Moscow naturally gave Maddin Summers and the consul general's office more responsibility and authority but also blurred the lines between the ambassador, the consul general, and Robins's quasi-official diplomatic role.

Intervention?

While the American embassy was in the chaos of movement, Washington was immobile, more perplexed than ever about what to do. Vologda was even less known there, as remote as Timbuktu. It was as if an important embassy in Washington had taken off into the Rocky Mountains for a prolonged, indefinite winter expedition, virtually out of touch. At the same time there came from Paris the shock of a more concrete proposal for a major Japanese military foray into Siberia. After conferring with Lansing, Breckinridge Long noted, "Sect'y doubtful as to course to pursue, Will take up with Pres't. [Lansing] fears resentment in Siberia and Russ. at intervention army, if such to be so, wants Jap. to have blame. Says it most complicated problem he has ever had. Biggest problem & most complicated."[11]

Long himself advised holding the Japanese off in order to consult with the Chinese and local Russian authorities; he also opposed Basil Miles's suggestion

8. Tredwell to Lansing, 28 February 1918, box 186, Long Papers, MD, LC. Bullard thought "they seemed inclined to leave much sooner than was necessary." Russian CPI Report May 1918, box 6, Bullard Papers, Princeton-Mudd.

9. Robins to Lenin, 28 February 1918, 2:45 p.m., and Lenin to Robins, 28 February, 3:10 p.m., reel 9, Francis Papers, MoHS.

10. Francis to Ruggles, 5 March 1918, reel 8, Francis Papers, MoHS.

11. Diary, 26 February 1918, box 1, Long Papers, MD, LC.

that a marine regiment stationed at Tsienstin be sent in to rescue Francis. Using American forces in the area, however, continued to be a major topic of discussion in the State Department through March, encouraged by the arrival of the USS *Brooklyn* at Vladivostok on the first of that month.[12] The issue of whether Japanese units should go into Russia remained high on the agenda of cabinet meetings. Josephus Daniels reported that on 8 March the president was grim, determined, and definitely opposed—"it might throw Russia into protecting arms of Germany"—and he resented British pressure on him to support it.[13]

The Brest-Litovsk Peace

In the meantime, still vulnerably located in Petrograd, the Soviet government debated the acceptance of new, more onerous peace terms. Upon return to Petrograd on 5 March, Robins and Gumberg went directly to Smolny for a long conversation with Trotsky. A disagreement was immediately apparent between Trotsky and Lenin, with the former opposed to ratifying the dictated peace and the latter arguing that it was the only way out of a precarious situation. Trotsky counted on the unwillingness of Germany to renew an offensive in the East with so much of its manpower already shifted to the West and also on support from German workers, while Lenin gave highest priority to saving "his" Russian revolution and discounted the possibility of any near-term German revolution.[14]

Trotsky apparently thought he might gain the balance over Lenin if he could get assurances of assistance from the Allies in the event of rejecting the terms. He and Robins worked out a simple question—"Can the Soviet government rely on the support of the United States of North America, Great Britain, and France in its struggle against Germany?"—to forward to Washington. Trotsky also wanted to know details of any such support. Robins also met with Lenin to plea for time to allow a response that could be considered and immediately relayed the Trotsky proposal to Vologda, using a military code that was considered more secure than the diplomatic ones.

Robins assumed that the proposal would be sent at once to Washington, but Ruggles and Riggs had left that day (5 March) for Petrograd, carrying with them the codebooks.[15] Their return was prompted by the arrival at Vologda of Cap-

---

12. Long diary entries, ibid.; Logbook 1918, USS *Brooklyn*, RG 24, NA.
13. Daniels, *Red October*, 288.
14. For a detailed examination of the background of the treaty, see John W. Wheeler-Bennett, *Brest-Litovsk: The Forgotten Peace, March 1918* (London: Macmillan, 1963).
15. Salzman, *Reform and Revolution*, 243–46.

tain Jacques Sadoul, French military attaché. He had also interviewed Trotsky and brought from him a plea for American assistance directly to Francis that even included the use of American officers to assist a Soviet defense of its territory.[16] Francis dispatched Ruggles and Riggs, with Eugene Prince as interpreter, back with Sadoul to Petrograd, where they met separately with Trotsky and with General Mikhail Bonch-Bruevich, the Soviet army chief of staff. Their discussions included a possible Japanese intervention in the Far East, the Soviet request to Robins, and the need for professional officers to guide a new army of 1 million, to be composed mainly of workers.[17] Ruggles immediately returned to Vologda to inform Francis, leaving Riggs to conduct further negotiations with Bonch-Bruevich and Georgi Chicherin, Trotsky's new assistant in the Commissariat of Foreign Relations.[18] Riggs had another interview on 11 March with Trotsky, who "repeated his statement of the other day that a new army on a non-political basis with a strong discipline must be formed."[19]

Although Robins returned to Vologda to stress the urgency of the message upon the ambassador, Trotsky's first communication through him was not sent to Washington for seventeen days, the cause of the delay remaining unclear.[20] In the meantime, the government hastily moved to Moscow on 11–12 March, where the Fourth All-Russian Congress of Soviets would consider ratification of the treaty. That meeting was postponed two days, according to Robins, to allow more time for a response to the request for assistance from the United States.[21] It finally convened on the fourteenth with the usual preliminaries, which were highlighted by Yakov Sverdlov's reading of a message from President Wilson.[22] Then the debate on ratification ensued, with strong speeches on both sides. Late

16. Sadoul to Thomas, 7 March 1918, *Notes sur la révolution*, 254–55; Riggs memorandum, 5 March 1918, box 41, Riggs Papers, BA, CU.

17. Two Riggs memorandums of 8 March 1918, ibid.

18. Two Riggs memorandums of 10 March 1918, ibid.

19. Riggs memorandum, 11 March 1918, ibid.; Riggs to Family, 13 March 1918, box 124, Riggs Family Papers, MD, LC.

20. Salzman, *Reform and Revolution*, 245.

21. George F. Kennan, discounting the likelihood of a response making any difference to Lenin, attributes the confusion of the move to the postponement. *Russia Leaves the War*, 513–16. Indeed, several important Bolsheviks, including Trotsky, Lunacharsky, and Shlapnikov, did not leave Petrograd before 12 March. Sadoul to Thomas, 13 March 1918, *Notes sur la révolution*, 261–62.

22. Summers to Lansing, 15 March 1918, in Goldberg, *Documents of Soviet-American Relations*, 1:43. According to Norman Hapgood, the message was prompted by William Boyce Thompson asking him to call House, who in turn rang up the White House. Hapgood, *The Changing Years: Reminiscences of Norman Hapgood* (New York: Farrar and Rinehart, 1930), 249.

in the evening, again according to Robins, Lenin appeared on the platform and asked Robins, seated nearby, if he had received a response to Trotsky's inquiry; learning that there was none, he then addressed the congress, strongly advocating ratification of the treaty, which followed by a two-thirds majority in the early morning of 15 March.[23] Russia's participation in the Great War had at last come to a formal conclusion.

To the end of his life, Robins believed that a golden opportunity had been lost to keep Russia in the war and to avoid intervention and the hostile environment that it would create. And this position, echoed in the writings of historian William Appleman Williams, became part of the great debate over early Soviet-American relations. Robins, however, must assume part of the blame for relying so much on Ruggles and not following up by repeating the message.[24] And, strangely, Robins kept this important matter mostly to himself and ignored other possible channels. Bullard, for example, was unaware of it and, writing on 14 March, fully expected the congress to "rubberstamp Lenin's decision to accept this peace."[25] Above all, Robins did not seem to realize that Trotsky was using him to gain more political leverage at the congress. Both Trotsky and Lockhart, who were clearly as opposed to ratification as Robins, did not even appear in Moscow until 17 March, after the vote.[26]

Under the treaty an enormous amount of valuable territory was separated from what had been the Russian Empire: Ukraine including Crimea (in recognition of a separate German agreement with a Ukrainian government), the Russian part of Poland, the Baltic States (described as Estonia and Livonia), and a large section of western Russia—a total of 780,000 square kilometers, 56 million population, three-fourths of iron ore production, and 90 percent of coal resources.

---

23. Lenin's speech, which lasted one hour and twenty minutes, emphasized a historical analogy with the Peace of Tilsit, dictated by Napoleon to Alexander I in 1807. For the text, see Wheeler-Bennett, *Brest-Litovsk*, 409–26.

One card that the United States held but apparently did not play in this high-stakes poker game was its support for the integrity of the Russian Empire—except for Poland, while Germany was actively dismantling it in Ukraine, Finland, and the Baltic region. Probably the most distasteful aspect of the treaty to the Soviet leaders was their recognition of an independent but German-dominated Ukraine.

24. He and Francis did send other messages to Washington during these days, but they all assumed the prior arrival of the "lost" Trotsky appeal. Salzman, *Reform and Revolution*, 246–48.

25. To Creel, box 6, Bullard Papers, Princeton-Mudd.

26. For a vivid description of their departure from Petrograd on the sixteenth, see Lockhart, *Memoirs of a British Agent*, 244–45. During the long delay in handling luggage and arranging the train, American socialist Bill Shatov, in charge of the station, regaled the party with East Side stories and added humor to the spectacle.

Any Russian armed forces remaining in this territory, especially Ukraine and Finland (already recognized as independent), were to be withdrawn immediately and the whole Russian army and navy demobilized.[27]

Although the treaty proper specified that neither side would pay any indemnities for war costs, a supplementary agreement obliged each to reimburse the other for the costs of maintaining prisoners of war. This actually entailed a very large indemnity payment for Russia, considering the larger number and higher cost of its prisoners in Germany. While all prisoners were to be repatriated immediately, most of the Russian prisoners remained in the Central Powers as laborers until the war ended (though Russia would not be liable for the costs for this period), and transportation difficulties and political chaos slowed the return of German and Austrian prisoners from Siberia.[28] Russia also agreed to silence any pro-Allied propaganda on its territory. Neither side had much faith in such onerous terms actually being carried out; in fact, voices were raised in Germany as well as Russia for that very reason: that it was not in Germany's long-term best interests to strip Russia of its dignity as a great power.[29]

In Petrograd, confusion reigned in the wake of the peace and all the diplomatic departures. A German occupation was still widely believed to be possible, with only a few observers such as Arthur Bullard discounting it, and the government announced its definite intentions of abandoning the city for Moscow.[30] Consul Tredwell reported that up to 20,000 former POWs were roaming the streets of Petrograd. He was prepared to leave at a moment's notice and planned to send a cryptic message, "Scooting," in that event.[31] "The situation here becomes most interesting. Stevens, Taylor, and I feel like the last of the Mohicans and have no idea what may happen at any minute."[32]

Washington Responds

What difference did the Robins-Ruggles communication fiasco in Russia make? Probably none. Francis learned from several other sources of Trotsky's interest in American assistance and, according to Thomas, was prepared to offer the Stevens technical railroad mission, which had arrived in the Far East and was

27. Wheeler-Bennett, *Brest-Litovsk*, 269–75.
28. Ibid., 273.
29. Debo, *Revolution and Survival*, 157–61.
30. Tredwell (Petrograd) to Wright (Vologda), 6 March 1918, reel 9, Francis Papers, MoHS.
31. Tredwell to Francis, 14 March 1918, box 2, Petrograd Consulate, RG 84, NA.
32. Ibid., 16 March 1918.

awaiting instructions and shipments of food to the Bolsheviks.[33] Washington, as well as the other Allied capitals, was well-informed about the approaching Soviet congress and its main business—consideration of the peace terms negotiated at Brest-Litovsk. There was nothing to prevent the United States, with or without its allies or a message from Francis, from attempting to head it off by a promise of substantial aid to the Soviet government, but nothing of this kind was considered. The president, in fact, upon the urging of House and after consultation with Polk,[34] did send a message to the Fourth All-Russian Congress of Soviets on 11 March:

> May I not take advantage of the meeting of the Congress of the Soviet to express the sincere sympathy which the people of the United States feel for the Russian people at this moment when the German power has been thrust in to interrupt and turn back the whole struggle for freedom and substitute the wishes of Germany for the purposes of the People of Russia.

The next phrase was crucial: "Although the Government of the United States is unhappily not now in a position to render the direct and effective aid it would wish to render, . . ."[35] There was Trotsky's answer. And the presidential message was promptly dispatched by Polk to Summers in Moscow and delivered the next day (12 March) personally (by Robins!) to Lenin.[36]

Washington was obviously viewing the Brest-Litovsk treaty as a fait accompli instead of thinking of possibilities of direct intervention. The disarray among the country's representatives in Russia may have been a factor. The State Department had granted permission for a departure of the embassy from Petrograd some weeks before but was surprised by the suddenness of the event. Reacting to concerns of safety from both Francis and Summers, Third Assistant Secretary Breckinridge Long, who was more and more becoming the chief department officer responsibile for Russian matters, recommended for the first time serious consideration of the dispatch of American troops to Siberia, namely, the 15th Marine Infantry Regiment stationed in China, but then withdrew this suggestion: "After writing this it seems that circumstances and known facts do not *now* warrant the proposed action."[37]

33. Sadoul to Thomas, 8 March 1918, *Notes sur la révolution*, 254–55.
34. House to Wilson, 10 March, and Polk diary, 11 March 1918, *PWW* 46:597.
35. Ibid., 598.
36. The speed of this particular transmission may have caused Lenin to expect a similar result from his message through Robins.
37. Long to Lansing, 1 March 1918, box 186, Long Papers, MD, LC.

Nevertheless, after learning of the withdrawal of the American embassy in the direction of Siberia, Long drafted a much larger project for intervention, based on the apparent inevitability of a Japanese presence in eastern Siberia and on developing an American political center in western Siberia, headed by the American ambassador and backed by a substantial Japanese military expedition. "He [Francis] would be the first on the ground and would become the head of the whole undertaking. His diplomatic and economic staffs could be later augmented by appropriate specialists."[38] He also proposed sending a special mission to Japan to coordinate this action.

The goals of this operation, however, were not to maintain a second front but to establish a stronger American presence in Asia, and especially Siberia, that would compete economically with Germany in Russia proper and indirectly drain that country of its gold supply. The president responded that the plan "interested me very much, but in view of what seems to me the necessary limitations of our action over there I do not think that it would be practicable to carry out your suggestion. I mean that we have not the instrumentalities through which to act alone, and cooperation where alone it is possible cuts in many directions."[39] He was also very sensitive to negative Russian reaction to a Japanese invasion and received support for this position from men he trusted.[40] Thus, even before the ratification of Brest-Litovsk and a major shift in the military situation on the Western Front, President Wilson was still disinclined to make a substantial commitment to intervention in Siberia, especially since it would involve close cooperation with Japan.

On 4 March, Basil Miles in the State Department circulated a different proposal to buy Soviet support of the war with assistance, exactly what Trotsky and Robins were simultaneously seeking. He concluded, "I do not believe I am wrong in saying that we can do more to relieve Russia at present than it is possible for Germany and her Allies to do; but in the absence of any relief from America, Russia will turn to Germany for what she can get parceled out to her."[41] This "second option" would remain on the table until well after intervention had become a reality.

---

38. Memorandum attached to Long to Wilson, 4 March 1918, f. Woodrow Wilson (Jan.-March 1918), box 41, ibid.

39. Wilson to Long, 14 March 1918, ibid.

40. Wilson to Mott, 11 March 1918, f. 1762, box 100, Mott Papers, DSA.

41. Memorandum, 4 March 1918, box 117, 2C, McCormick Papers, SHSW. This copy has "Basil Miles" at the top. Informed references to the lenient Russian treatment of Austrian prisoners of war and to credit societies would seem to authenticate that source, though it could conceivably be a file copy of a document McCormick sent to Miles.

Independently, British military planners in March were working out a project for a major investment of Allied resources in Siberian intervention. Their goal was to reopen the Eastern Front, in the light of Russia's separate peace with Germany, with a force of up to 600,000 men, mostly Japanese and American. The main object would be to prevent the diversion of more German divisions to the West and thus make victory there more likely in the spring of 1918. Completed for review by 2 April, the plan apparently did not consider the logistical problems of moving that many troops through Siberia along a practically paralyzed Trans-Siberian Railroad, and the planners did not even include or inform the United States, which would bear the primary responsibility for sending and supplying these units.[42]

A sense prevailed in both the United States and Russia in February and most of March that particular events did not matter, that the general drift was certain: Russia was disintegrating, and Germany would soon be defeated with the arrival of substantial American armed forces in Europe. With the war over, aid and possibly military intervention could be sent in quantity to a nation that probably would have sorted itself out by then anyway. Harper and Mott fully agreed with Chapin Huntington's report from Petrograd.

> The Bolsheviki are slipping. It was inevitable. The Germans seemed to treat them and their emissaries as inferiors, and to have made such selfish conditions that the negotiations were broken off for a week. I think the Germans are very afraid of the social revolution, and fear they may become infected by bolshevism. They are in a worse quandry [sic] than we.[43]

The German March Offensive

In any event, plans for intervention in Russia in 1918 were drastically affected by the launching of a major Ludendorff-inspired offensive on the Western Front on 21 March. This was made feasible by the shifting of over 1 million men from the Eastern Front since November at the rate of ten divisions per month. Although the attack was expected by the Allies, it came through a weak sector on the right flank where the British had recently taken over responsibility from

42. Some historians have emphasized Allied betrayal of Russia by failing to implement this plan. See Victor M. Fic, *The Collapse of American Policy in Russia and Siberia, 1918: Wilson's Decision Not to Intervene (March–October, 1918)* (Boulder, Colo.: East European Monographs, 1995), 120–23.

43. Quoted in Harper to Mott, 7 February 1918, f. 21, box 4, Harper Papers, UC.

the French. Its goal was to destroy British forces to the extent of forcing a surrender before American presence could be much of a factor—and it nearly succeeded.

Within two weeks the German offensive had driven a salient south of Arras more than thirty miles deep. Insufficient reserves forced a halt in the attack by the end of April after having inflicted 300,000 casualties, mainly on the British, but at considerable cost to German strength as well. Delays in the signing of the peace in the East contributed to the German inability to shift more troops westward in time to sustain the attack.[44] A major result as far as future Allied policy in Russia was to reconfirm the Western Front imperative and the concentration of shipping, supply, and troop movements on the Atlantic and to the Western Front.[45] For the United States it meant that troops would move east on trains and ships, not west, and plans for a major military commitment to Russia would not be feasible for the remainder of the war.

Other factors certainly were important in shaping the American intervention in Russia that eventually did come. One was the generally accepted view of various shades of American opinion that, excepting Poland and Finland, the integrity of Russia should be maintained. The fear was that a partitioning of the empire would result in the various parts coming under foreign, especially German, political and economic influence or a large volatile and unstable region. And Woodrow Wilson was certainly not alone in being especially leery of the prospect of a Japanese protectorate over the Russian Far East and possibly the whole of Siberia or of a British stranglehold over the Caucasus oil fields. Another American tendency was to be suspect of any leaders of the former monarchy or of the "failed" first revolution, which would include all admirals and generals and "ineffective" politicians such as Miliukov and Kerensky.

In the midst of the confusion surrounding the peace negotiations and moves to Vologda and Moscow, an Allied armed presence in Russia began. For some time both Soviet and Allied leaders had been concerned about the vulnerability of the large depot of supplies in and around the port of Murmansk to German or pro-German Finnish forces advancing from the southwest. By agreement with the local soviet and with the approval and support of Trotsky, a detachment of 130 Royal Marines landed on 6 March from HMS *Glory*. Although almost unnoticed in the chaos of the time, it set a precedent for a greater military pres-

---

44. Raymond Robins would later claim credit for saving the Allies on the Western Front by delaying the Bolshevik signing of the peace and a consequent shift of German troops through his holding out the possibility of American assistance.

45. V. H. Rothwell, *British War Aims and Peace Diplomacy, 1914–1918* (Oxford: Clarendon Press, 1971), 186-87.

ence in that area to follow and for the first Japanese landing of substantial forces in Vladivostok a month later.

The British initiative at Murmansk was also unique in being by invitation and in cooperation with both local and central Soviet authorities. This led many Americans, both in Russia and in the United States, in particular President Wilson, to believe in intervention by invitation, thus contributing to delays in the timing and limiting the spheres of any commitments of armed forces on Russian territory. In fact, Francis believed from information from Robins that Trotsky had agreed to an American supervisory role at Vladivostok and a "virtual control of the Siberian railway."[46]

Enemy Prisoners of War

One of the Allies' main concerns about the impact of the revolution in Russia was the status of German and Austro-Hungarian prisoners of war, especially with Russia leaving the war. With the Russian army disintegrating and local authority tenuous, released prisoners might arm themselves, take control of local areas, and serve as agents of Germany or the Bolsheviks. Disruptions in communications and the general state of confusion led to wild rumors of the danger posed by the many thousand prisoners, especially in Siberia, where they were virtually trapped by the collapse of transportation. In fact, some of the first skirmishes of the civil war were over jurisdiction of the Trans-Siberian and other railroads.

One reason for Francis's sending of Butler Wright across Siberia and Chapin Huntington to Irkutsk was to report on conditions. In Moscow, Robins and Lockhart were also alarmed by rumors of large-scale arming of former prisoners, and they sent assistants William Webster of the Red Cross and Will Hicks, a British captain, to Irkutsk to investigate. Webster was familiar with prisoners in Siberia from his relief work there in 1916. Arriving at Irkutsk on 29 March, they consulted with local leaders and found evidence of only a few hundred armed Hungarians, who were sympathetic to the revolution and acting to bolster Bolshevik control in the region.[47]

---

46. Francis to Lansing (cable), 9 March 1918, reel 8, Francis Papers, MoHS. Francis explained to Summers his realism with a Missouri homily: "You probably know my estimate of the bolshevik regime but I realize that the only power in Russia which can offer any resistance whatever to the German advance is the Soviet Government. When my house is on fire I don't ask the quality of the water used to extinguish the flame." To Summers, 9 March 1918, ibid.

47. Kennan, *The Decision to Intervene,* 75–79; Lockhart, *Memoirs of a British Agent,* 251–52; Ullman, *Anglo-Soviet Relations,* 1:157–58.

In fact, the great majority of the released prisoners in Siberia were from the Austro-Hungarian army and wanted most of all to go home. Despite this and the Webster-Hicks findings being verified by other observers, reports persisted that a large number of prisoners were armed either by themselves or by the Bolsheviks and had the potential of seizing Siberia. Some of these exaggerations emanated from the Japanese, who saw this as a convenient excuse for intervention. Certainly, large numbers of released prisoners in 1918 added even more confusion to the Siberian economic and political chaos.

Communications

The new situation in Russia further complicated the flow of information because of the scattering of personnel in several locations, a sustained state of confusion, and the general breakdown in reliability of rail and telegraphic services. Much depended on courier service and direct conversations by wire or in person (thus much is lost to the historian). Because of the danger in carrying codebooks around the country, other methods were often employed. Initially, Consul Tredwell resorted to a baseballeze slang over open telegraph lines that he thought only an American would comprehend, for example: "Slid into home plate for four runs while many were leaving bleachers inform umpire bulls and frogs intend to make circle of bases on a long outfield hit and that a member of home team is supposed to have dropped the bag of peanuts report on next game will follow Culver."[48] And the first indication of an approaching landing of troops at Murmansk was recorded as follows: "The Captain of the British team at Murmansk has requested his manager to see that he had at least 6,000 fans to watch the game on his field up there."[49]

The American diplomatic corps generally adapted well to the new situation and took it in stride, except for bemoaning the long gaps in regular mail. Assistant Military Attaché Riggs observed from Moscow on 13 April that he had received no mail since 20 January.[50] In Washington, the State Department and other agencies, in frustration, simply attempted little communication, thus add-

48. Tredwell (Petrograd; Culver was his little-known middle name) to Robert Imbrie (Vologda), 5 March 1918, box 1, Petrograd Consulate, RG 84, NA. At least some of this can be translated: home plate = Petrograd; umpire = Francis; bulls and frogs = British and French. Some other code names were too transparent, such as referring to Robins as "Red Breast." Malcolm Davis also admitted to resorting to this "code." Davis oral history, p. 48, CU.
49. Lee (Vologda) to Tredwell (Petrograd), 4 March 1918, ibid.
50. Riggs to Family, 13 April 1918, box 124, Riggs Papers, MD, LC.

American embassy and staff, Vologda, July 1918. Francis center with Norman Armour on his immediate right and Philip Jordan holding the flag, courtesy of the Francis Papers, Missouri Historical Society

ing more difficulties for Americans trying to do their jobs in Russia. Colonel House responded to a February inquiry of Francis only in July with the excuse that he thought his homecoming was imminent.[51]

Although the ambassador and a small staff remained resident at Vologda, Moscow became the main focus of American contacts with each other and the Soviet authorities, now relocating in Moscow in early March. Robins naturally moved most of his Red Cross unit to Moscow with the goal of continuing his liaison activities, but even the Committee on Public Information, after Sisson's departure, found Moscow the only practical center for its operation simply because many newspapers were moving there and the printing service it relied on was also the main press of the Soviet government and had moved to Moscow

51. House to Francis, 1 July 1918, f. 1441 Francis, box 45, House Papers, Yale-Sterling.

with it.[52] Bullard, who had the best channel of communications with the out-side, published regular bulletins but did not share any of them with Francis until mid-April.[53]

In the absence of instructions from Washington, Francis, through Robins, supported Trotsky's plan to build a new army, "because I hope and expect that such army after being organized will be more under the influence of the Allies than under Trotsky who is amenable to flattery, vain, loves to be conspicuous, plays to the galleries and is I understand now dressing like a gentleman."[54] This apparently accounts for his surprising lack of concern in March and April about the Bolshevik evacuation of critical military supplies from Petrograd and Arch-angel. Francis remained convinced that the Bolsheviks had accepted German money but doubted that "they were staying bought."[55]

It probably also did not seem ironic at the time that both the American and Soviet governments relied on the same press for their printing needs, and, there-fore, that profits from American dollar business helped subsidize Soviet propa-ganda. Both Bullard and Robins, however, retained bases in Petrograd, because of unfinished business and supplies still stored there. Still, including the well-staffed consul general's office, there were probably about as many Americans in Moscow on official business during the spring and summer of 1918 as there had been in Petrograd in 1917. Even the Vologda staff spent many days in Petrograd or Moscow attending to business, and Francis himself spent four days in each city in May and June.

Increasing difficulty of communication contributed to an important policy shift by Francis. At the end of April, Soviet authorities declared a ban on telegraphic communications in code. Francis was just recovering from being incapacitated by illness for ten days.[56] Although the Soviet action was probably directed pri-

52. Bullard to Creel, 5 and 14 March, box 6, and to House, 7 March 1918, box 9, Bullard Papers, Princeton-Mudd. Despite repeated requests to Washington, cables from there were still being sent to Petrograd as late as May. Taylor (Petrograd) to Bullard, 1 May 1918, box 6, ibid.

53. Francis to Summers, 12 April 1918, reel 8, Francis Papers, MoHS.

54. Francis to Summers, 27 March 1918, ibid. Francis's trust in Robins at this time was probably due, at least in part, to his disgust with Sisson, who, he had learned, was strongly urging his recall. Francis to Lansing (personal and confidential), 20 March 1918, ibid.

55. Francis to Lansing, cipher telegram, 26 March 1918, ibid.

56. This illness seems not to have been related to his later prostate problems, but per-haps more to the change in location and his running out of whiskey that earlier may have had a purification effect. Francis himself thought it was food poisoning. Francis to Lansing, 2 May 1918, reel 9, ibid. Summers tried to supply the ambassador with whiskey, but the only store that sold it in Moscow had been plundered by "anarchists." Summers to Francis, 23 April 1918, ibid.

marily against the French, Francis suddenly went into action, urging, in a cable sent 2 May, immediate intervention, and he continued to insist on it for the remainder of his tenure.[57] But even then, the next day he sounded out Robins about the Soviet government not opposing such intervention and admitted that he could "understand the difficulty of the position of Lenin and Trotsky and their colleagues," especially if it was coupled with military and railway assistance missions.[58]

More and more, the only certain and safe means of communication was in person or by hand-carried message, but this required enduring the deteriorating and randomly scheduled trains. The Allied operatives shared couriers, so that the "Ace of Spies," Sidney Reilly, for one, carried American dispatches between Petrograd, Moscow, and Vologda.[59] Harrison Smith, a correspondent for *Century* and *New Republic*, after sharing a compartment for four with sixteen people from Petrograd to Samara, told Helen Ogden that he was preparing a new phrase book for foreigners in Russia. Instead of a phonetical rendition of "Excuse me, is this seat engaged?" he would substitute, "Pardon me, Madame, if I sleep on your shoulder," "Sir! Your baby is eating my leg!" and "Kindly remove your foot from my lap."[60]

Another improvised solution was direct-line telegraphic conversations, especially employed by Robins in communicating with Vologda. This usually involved the bribing of agents at the telegraph office, and on one occasion on 9 April Robins suffered the embarrassment of having his automobile stolen by "anarchists" while he was inside, "at the apparatus."[61] He received an immediate handwritten apology from Foreign Commissar Chicherin, followed by raids by the Cheka to recover it that signaled the beginning of serious test of strength of the Soviet government against a growing opposition from former Left Socialist Revolutionary and anarchist supporters.[62]

---

57. Another influence may have been a conversation with Chapin Huntington, who left Irkutsk for Vologda on 29 April. From his experience in Siberia, Huntington shifted firmly toward viewing intervention as inevitable and being welcomed by Siberians. Report of 28 April 1918, f. 5, box 5, Harper Papers, UC. Although this document was not signed by Huntington, it is obviously his from internal evidence. This was also the conclusion of George F. Kennan, who wrote on it, "probably from Chapin Huntington (GFK)." Ibid.
58. Francis to Robins, 3 May 1918, reel 9, Francis Papers, MoHS.
59. Imbrie note, 28 July 1918, box 4, Petrograd Consulate, RG 84, NA.
60. Helen Ogden (Samara) to family, 7 April 1918, f. Ogden March–April 1918, box 3, Lowrie Papers, UIA.
61. Salzman, *Reform and Revolution*, 260.
62. Robins described this as "a battle of three hours in 26 different quarters of the city." To Margaret, 14 April 1918, f. April 1918, box 14, Robins Papers, SHSW.

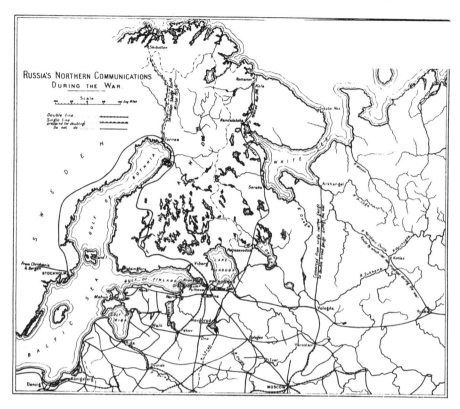

Northern Russia. Adapted from Knox, With the Russian Army

Stress and Strain

The frustrations with communications and living conditions and the increased isolation from both inside and outside added considerably to the trials and tribulations of Americans in Russia. There was also a sense of helplessness. One of the first things observed after arriving in Vologda was the passage through the station of trainloads of munitions from Archangel headed south toward Moscow, the result of Larin's previously announced effort to move supplies from there to the interior. Tredwell at first thought they were mainly of British origin, but Consul Felix Cole in Archangel clarified and confirmed the shipment of 210,000 American Remington and Westinghouse rifles and 16 million cartridges, a substantial arsenal for the embryonic Red Army.[63]

63. Tredwell (Vologda) to Summers, 9 March 1918, and Cole to Tredwell, 11 March 1918, box 2, Petrograd Consulate 1918, RG 84, NA.

Despite the scarcity of basic needs and threats to life and property, a number of nonofficial Americans remained, placing further strain on consular personnel. In requesting additional passport forms for the consular office in Moscow, Frank Lee commented, "The natives seem to have drifted into Moscow from all over the world, each with an expired passport."[64] From Petrograd Robert Imbrie responded:

> I note that you in Moscow are blessed with 50 Americans and, while this Consulate is cursed with about 20, I am prepared to back these 20 against your 50 when it comes to making demands, getting into trouble and generally making nuisances of themselves. If you care to accept this challenge, please notify and I shall be on hand with my gang.[65]

Most unsettling was being surrounded by indefiniteness and inconsistency on all sides—from the Soviet and anti-Soviet Russians, within the Allied missions, and by confused or nonexistent instructions from their respective departments. Bullard observed, "The situation is so complicated that it is dizzying. The explanation is, I think, that no one is all honest nor all dishonest. Some of the council of the Peoples' Commissaires [sic] are 90% crooked and some are nearly as much honest. It is impossible for such a team to play a consistent game."[66] Especially awkward were the division and rivalry in Moscow between Robins (Red Cross), Bullard (Committee on Public Information), and Summers (consul general). While Summers had staff, offices, and experience with the Moscow surroundings, Bullard had ample funds and better communications with Washington, and Robins had the ear of Soviet leaders and support of British and French counterparts—Lockhart and Sadoul. Unlike them, however, Robins lacked clear diplomatic authority. All of them faced unusual difficulties, for example, in even finding the Soviet Commissariat of Foreign Affairs, which moved three times during its first month in Moscow.[67]

Most of the dirty, tedious work of taking care of American business fell to Summers and his overworked staff, which included the capable assistant Poole and new recruits from the Moscow business community, John Lehrs Jr. and Xenephon Kalamatiano.[68] They took on the particularly difficult cases that in-

64. Lee to Imbrie, 10 July 1918, box 4, ibid.
65. To Frank Lee, 23 July 1918, box 4, ibid.
66. To House, 7 March 1918, box 9, Bullard Papers, Princeton-Mudd.
67. Robins to Francis, 1 April 1918, reel 8, Francis Papers, MoHS.
68. Francis observed to Consul Tredwell, "Poor Summers appears overwhelmed and is reaching in every direction for help." 31 March 1918, box 1, Petrograd consulate, RG 84, NA.

volved extensive involvement with Soviet officials. For example, Lehrs and Poole interceded in regard to charges levied against members of the wealthy Bary family. The Cheka raided and searched the Bary house on 14 April and arrested Vladimir Bary for directly financing anti-Bolshevik movements in the south. Lehrs and Poole were able to ameliorate his condition and eventually secure his release from the clutches of the Cheka into the custody of the consulate.[69] Another complicated matter was the responsibility for continued purchasing of Russian strategic goods, the cost of which had now greatly exceeded in commitments the $1 million authorized in February.[70]

In personality and views, Summers differed sharply from Robins. In addition, Summers felt uncomfortable and even threatened by his wife's connections with the old Russian nobility and repeatedly asked Washington for reassignment in April. He was especially annoyed by Robins's interference in his efforts to arrange the exit of a number of Serbian refugees who had found their way to Russia through Romania.[71] Still, Summers relied on Robins to solve certain difficulties, such as an anarchist seizure of the building housing the military missions. He complained to Francis, "I think Robbins [sic] is handling the situation. I phoned him about it and he did not seem to relish my referring to the matter. Frankly speaking I am getting rather sick of this dual situation and am anxious to put an end to it."[72]

Francis, however, obviously wanted Summers to stay as a check on Robins and for the valuable service he performed; he also wanted to use Robins for "unofficial relations," "notwithstanding Summers expressed humiliation thereat."[73] Meanwhile, one of the best American minds in Russia, a person who seemed to get along with everybody—Commercial Attaché Chapin Huntington—was stuck and apparently forgotten in Irkutsk with nothing to do but study the local flora and fauna with his assistant, Edward Thomas.[74] He would finally be retrieved at the end of April, but Thomas stayed behind.

Unfortunately for Summers, the last straw came at the end of April, when the local press published reports that Robins was now or was soon to be head of

69. Lehrs to Summers, "Memorandum re Woldemar Bary's Case," 17 April 1918, reel 9, Francis Papers, MoHS. Years later Bary admitted that he had furnished "large scale financial aid" to Alekseev and Denikin. Interview of Bary by DeWitt Clinton Poole at Century Club in New York, 3 March 1951, f. 10, box 7, Poole Papers, BA, CU.

70. Summers to Francis, 30 April 1918, ibid.

71. Summers to Francis, 23 April 1918, ibid.

72. Summers to Francis, 3 April 1918, ibid.

73. Francis to Lansing, 2 May 1918, ibid.

74. Huntington to Harper, 15 April 1918, box 5, Harper Papers, UC.

the American mission, displacing both Summers and Francis.[75] Although Robins denied having anything to do with this and thought it was due to erroneous reports in the press about a resignation or recall of Francis,[76] Summers suspected otherwise and even more deeply resented Robins's interference in diplomatic and consular affairs. Francis attempted to heal the wound by issuing a statement deploring the "false rumors" and questioning their source and object. He added, "Colonel Robins and I are friends and understand each other thoroughly; we have the same object in view which is to make the world safe for Democracy, and we agree that such a desirable end cannot be accomplished without the defeat of Germany."[77]

Summers was not satisfied and complained to Francis on 30 April:

> With all the Consulates closed in Russia and with the immense work imposed upon the office of furnishing the Department with information regarding the situation, you can imagine that we are almost exhausted. Night and day we are endeavouring to do all we can, but personally I am getting very tired. I do not have the time to do all I wish and this aggravates me. . . .
>
> I cannot understand how a Red Cross officer can so leave his work as to engage in matters which do not belong to his position.[78]

The next day Summers was shocked to have his view verified by a notice in the papers that a dispute over taxes being paid by the Singer Company in Irkutsk had been referred "to the American Representative in Moscow, Colonel Robins."[79] On Friday, 3 May, at the end of a particularly trying week, Summers died suddenly of a cerebral hemorhage that all agreed had been precipitated by the intense strain of his situation—the first major American casualty of the Russian Revolution.

75. Robins admitted the problem but did not take it very seriously:

All kinds of tales are floating around. I am a German Agent, I have been corrupted by Trotzki and Lenin, I am under the malign influence of a Russian Princess, I am selling Russia to Wall Street, I have immense concession in the Urals, I have turned traitor to the allied cause for control of the Siberian railway, I have secured a monopoly upon the platinum of Russia, I was an anarchist in America, etc., etc.

Robins to Margaret, 14 April 1918, f. April 1918, box 14, Robins Papers, SHSW.
76. Robins to Francis, 26 April 1918, reel 9, Francis Papers, MoHS.
77. Francis statement, 28 April 1918, ibid.
78. Summers to Francis, 30 April 1918, ibid.
79. To Francis, 1 May 1918, reel 9, ibid.

Soviet-American Hiatus

During and after the period of transition of the center of Soviet power from Petrograd to Moscow in March and the signing of the peace, Robins was the main American contact with the Soviet leadership. He continued to believe that by cultivating closer relations the peace with Germany might be modified or at least German influence limited. Soviet leaders still seemed willing to consider the option of accepting substantial American aid in return. They were quite aware that immediate assistance was a possibility from cargoes already in Russian ports, material and advisers in transit, and the services provided by the American Red Cross and YMCA, whereas Germany could afford little and was more likely to take what it could.[80]

Having established themselves in the comparative safety of Moscow and cognizant of the shift of substantial German forces to the West, the Bolshevik leaders had much less reason to fear a German advance. Moreover, they were fully aware of a substantial opposition to the peace and resulting prospects of an increasing German presence, especially from their erstwhile allies, the Left Socialist Revolutionaries. Thus, the almost daily contacts of Robins with the commissar for foreign affairs, Georgi Chicherin, and others were sustained by mutual interest.

With Trotsky busy building a new army, foreign relations fell on the shoulders of Chicherin, who was not even a Bolshevik but a trained civil servant who had worked eight years in the tsarist foreign ministry. He had, however, sympathized with the revolutionary movement, associating especially with the Mensheviks, and had conducted antiwar propaganda in Britain. For this he spent most of 1917 in a British jail. He is invariably described as cultured, Western-oriented, mild-mannered, and indecisive, quite a contrast to Trotsky and Zalkind, but he also was quite aware that many Bolsheviks could not fully trust him.[81] Huntington described him as "a man in middle life, thin and ill looking, dressed in baggy suit of rough material of a green shade, large apparently all-steel watch chain, with red hair and brown eyes to match it. To me he has the furtive abnormal expression of most of those men who have worked all their lives by conspiracy rather than in the open."[82]

80. Although the war was essentially over, many patients remained in hospitals wounded and shell-shocked, and the Russian Red Cross and other agencies were in a state of almost complete collapse, financially and politically, even to the point of abandoning hospitals full of wounded. Memorandum of Russian Red Cross conference of 2 April 1918, box 67, ARC, RG 200, NA.

81. Debo, *Revolution and Survival*, 87–90.

82. Huntington to Francis, 17 May 1918, AE Russia, DPR 314, RG 84, NA. For a similar description, see Lockhart, *Memoirs of a British Agent*, 221.

Flanking and assisting Chicherin in the commissariat were two other mis-
fits of the revolution. Karl Radek was an "Austrian Jew," born in Galicia as
Sobelsohn and nurtured in the German social democratic movement; he had
veered left during the war into the international Zimmerwald movement in
Switzerland, where he caught the attention of Lenin and was recruited into the
Bolshevik fold. He first set foot in Russia after the seizure of power in November and was immediately drafted for the negotiating team at Brest-Litovsk for
his fluency in German. Always a left-wing troublemaker, he acquired immediate notoriety by passing out revolutionary fliers to German soldiers at Brest-
Litovsk and stood out among ranking Bolsheviks as clean-shaven, wearing thick
glasses, and always with a huge cigar or pipe in his mouth. Arrogant, self-
assured, radical, he yet seemed more at home intruding himself socially among
the foreign diplomats.[83]

Radek was counterbalanced by Lev Karakhan, a friendly, always smiling but
devious Armenian, nominally in charge of the "Asian desk" but who was left
with much of the day-to-day contact with the diplomatic community, such as it
was. Acting as "gofer" for the commissariat was an even stranger Voznesensky,
who spent much time going back and forth between Moscow and Vologda. These
contrasting personalities presented additional obstacles for doing any business
with the Soviet government.

While moving more toward favoring active intervention in April, at least for
the military occupation of the three ports, Francis hoped it could be achieved
through an invitation from the Soviet government and coupled with guarantees
of American aid, and Robins might be the key link to realizing such a plan. He
was disappointed, however, at receiving no response from Washington to his
repeated requests for special shipments of foodstuffs through Murmansk or
Archangel. He was finally informed that tonnage was unavailable, but that the
State Department feared in any event that the supplies would fall into the hands
of the Germans.[84]

Ambassador Francis, though ill and confined to his bed for a number of days
in April, was no longer as isolated, since several Allied missions—French, Italian, Belgian, and Serbian—unsuccessful in exiting through Finland, returned to

---

83. This description is from several sources, but see Bruce Lockhart, *Memoirs of a British
Agent*, 254–55, who adds, "Almost every day he would turn up in my rooms, an English cap
stuck jauntily on his head, his pipe puffing fiercely, a bundle of books under his arm, and
a huge revolver strapped to his side. He looked like a cross between a professor and a bandit." Ibid., 255. See also, Warren Lerner, *Karl Radek: The Last Internationalist* (Stanford,
Calif.: Stanford University Press, 1970).

84. Francis to Poole, 29 May 1918, reel 9, Francis Papers, MoHS.

join him at Vologda, making the town truly the diplomatic capital, but in a temporary state except for the Americans, since most of the other missions had tight quarters aboard trains at the station.[85] Even a diplomatic pouch finally came through from Stockholm. To brighten the springtime, Francis gave teas on Saturday afternoons for the motley assembly that included a couple of unhappy wives and the Siamese minister, whom he delighted in teaching how to play poker.[86] Francis even had time to send some provisions to, and correspond with, Matilda de Cram in Petrograd.[87]

In these respects Francis seemed to fit perfectly with the tragicomic opera aspects of Soviet-Allied relations in 1918. Bruce Lockhart, who was guest for a few days in May, recalled:

> He did not seem to have any decided views about Russia. Knowledge of Russian politics he had none. The only political entry in my diary for that evening is the laconic note: "Old Francis doesn't know a Left Social Revolutionary from a potato." . . .
>
> As soon as dinner was over, Francis began to fidget like a child who wishes to return to its toys. His rattle, however, was a deck of cards, and without loss of time they were produced. The old gentleman was no child at poker. We played late, and . . . he took my money.[88]

Other Americans, besides Francis, were also more optimistic in April about Soviet cooperation. Tredwell resumed his consular chores in the Singer Building in Petrograd and found life relatively tranquil there and at his dacha at Strelna.

---

85. During a dinner given him by the mayor of the city in the second week of March, Francis formally "designated Vologda as the diplomatic capital of Russia." Francis to son Perry, 15 March 1918, reel 8, Francis Papers, MoHS. In June 1998, Vologda businessman Aleksandr Bykov and local historian Leonid Panov launched a gala opening of a museum and a scholarly conference in the restored "American embassy." See their publication, *Diplomaticheskaia stolitsaia Rossii* (Vologda: Ardvisura, 1998).

86. Francis to family, 15 April 1918, reel 9, Francis Papers, MoHS.

87. Francis to Cram, 18 April 1918, ibid. Although the ambassador continued to be indiscreet in these communications, for example, "I miss you greatly and often wish you were in Vologda," and in sending Philip Jordan with supplies, he was also upset that Mrs. Cram continued to expect the use of the embassy carriage and coachman in Petrograd. Francis to Cram, 22 March 1918, ibid.

Francis was not without female company in Vologda, as his small staff included women secretary-clerks by the names of Kennedy, Woodward, and Knox. He was also quite impressed by a young Russian who entertained (piano and voice) at his tea parties. Francis to Miles, 8 April 1918, reel 9, ibid.

88. Lockhart, *Memoirs of a British Agent*, 282–83.

The manager of the International Harvester plant sought out Robins's assistance in obtaining six carloads of imported materials in Vladivostok that were needed to maintain the production schedules of harvesting machines. Looking to the future, he asked Robins to emphasize the importance of the continuation of such imports on Soviet officials for agriculture.[89] Another knowledgeable intermediary was Methodist "superintendent" George Simons, who offered his services as courier and voiced his approval of the food parcels that the American Red Cross was doling out to Americans in Petrograd: "How we do appreciate this timely help and 'praise God from whom all blessings flow!'"[90]

By the end of April, Bullard was looking forward to continued expansion of the publicity campaign, which clearly violated the terms of the Brest-Litovsk treaty, with more reliance on regular news releases to the countryside as well as to the cities and the distribution of films in Moscow, Petrograd, and other towns. He made up for the departures of American staff by hiring more Russians. Even the "Y" people who had been shunted off to the Far East made plans to return to Petrograd.[91]

The rift between Summers and Robins was a source of constant tension in the American community, but they also managed to cooperate on some issues, such as the exodus of a number of Serbian refugees through the north.[92] Until mid-April Francis tolerated Robins as a valuable conduit for achieving Soviet agreement to limited Allied intervention and to mollify objections to the Japanese landing at Vladivostok.[93] Even that was likely to end, since Francis, annoyed especially by Robins's proclivity to pronounce American policy, such as firm opposition to Japanese intervention. Francis was upset that Robins not only cooperated closely with Lockhart in gaining more contacts with the Soviet government but also seemed to have convinced Riggs and Stevens (of National City Bank) of the correctness of this course.[94]

One truly "official" American, Felix Cole, consistently opposed intervention in northern Russia. From his perspective as consul in Archangel, he believed that Russians simply did not want to fight anymore. The idea that a small Allied force would rally a Russian army for the cause either of continuing the war or of overthrowing the Bolsheviks, he thought, was absurd. He considered the ques-

89. S. G. McAllister to Robins, two letters of 4 April 1918, f. April 1918, box 14, Robins Papers, SHSW.
90. Simons to Francis, 12 April 1918, reel 9, Francis Papers, MoHS.
91. Paul Anderson to mother, 5 April 1918, f. YMCA, box 5, Anderson Papers, UIA.
92. Summers to Francis, 23 April 1918, reel 9, Francis Papers, MoHS.
93. Francis to Summers, 14 April 1918, ibid.
94. Francis to Summers (personal and confidential), 19 April 1918, reel 9, Francis Papers, MoHS.

tion of the Bolsheviks being German agents to be totally irrelevant, since intervention would throw them into the hands of Germany regardless. Unfortunately, he was somewhat late in putting all this into a coherent argument, which he sent to Francis on 1 June. After some delay it was sent on by pouch, arriving Washington in mid-July, well after intervention was under way.[95]

British Intervention in Murmansk

From almost the beginning of the war, a British naval squadron defended the northern supply route to Archangel and Murmansk from possible German attack. In November 1917 the small squadron, commanded by Rear Admiral Thomas Kemp, withdrew as usual to the Kola Peninsula near Murmansk for the winter. In early March, with the German army continuing an almost unhindered advance toward Petrograd and poised to land in Finland, the British became alarmed about the security of the enormous amount of supplies that might fall into German hands.[96]

On 6 March, with the approval of the local soviet, 130 British marines landed and took up residence in Murmansk, though Kemp was warned by Thomas Thacher, who had just arrived there from Petrograd, that this might upset the work of Lockhart to keep Bolshevik Russia in the war.[97] In fact, the Soviet government, while raising questions, preferred to ignore the operation as long as it remained small and posed no direct threat. Chicherin and Trotsky, too, had little interest in seeing such supplies in German hands, at least not without some bargaining for payment. Both the Allies and the Soviet authorities were also concerned about the fate of the main part of the Russian Baltic Fleet marooned by ice in Helsinki harbor, especially because a British submarine squadron was stationed with it.

Japanese Intervention in Siberia

On 5 April 1918, about 400 Japanese marines debarked from ships in the harbor into the city of Vladivostok. The announced purpose was to protect Japanese people and property after an incident the previous day that involved the

95. For details on the Cole story, see Allison, "Our Man in Archangel," in *American Diplomats in Russia: Case Studies in Orphan Diplomacy, 1916–1919* (Westport, Conn.: Praeger, 1997), 127–38.
96. Ullman, *Anglo-Soviet Relations*, 1:118–19.
97. Ibid.; Thacher report, 6 April 1918, box 609, WA-6, RG 45, NA.

robbery of a Japanese shop and the killing of the tradesman and wounding of two employees. This was the beginning of a Japanese armed intervention in the Russian Far East that would eventually involve a much larger force and last for several years. It provoked much negative reaction in both Russia and the United States and quite a bit of opposition within Japan as well.

The Japanese landing, however, came as a surprise to no one, since it had been discussed openly in Allied capitals, including Japan's. The background cause was the instability and unrest in the region created by the Russian Revolution and the collapse of the Russian imperial chain of command. Even before the Bolshevik seizure of power in Petrograd, the veteran American consul, John Caldwell, reported that anarchists were numerous and active and that there was much fear of the Japanese taking over the area. He recommended visits of American warships as a calming effect.[98] Subsequently, the cruiser *Brooklyn*, flagship of the American Pacific Squadron, called at the Russian port from 23 November to 11 December 1917, attended by the usual reciprocal shore and sea visits and entertainments.[99]

Vladivostok was especially vulnerable to unrest because of disruptions created by the increased harbor and rail traffic and consequent piling up of supplies as attractive loot, and many of the returning radical émigrés who came across the Pacific from America decided to stay in the region. The Bolsheviks thus faced strong challenges from both their left and right flanks in their efforts to gain control of the soviet but, nevertheless, succeeded in doing so in December. Having little armed strength, they left what remained of real authority in the city in the hands of the old duma or city council.[100]

All the Allies were obviously concerned about the situation because of the huge depot of supplies, mostly from the United States, and because of Vladivostok's importance as the safest and most reliable entrance and exit point. Japan had another serious concern, as the closest of the Allied powers and actually neighboring on Russia. The Japanese sphere of imperial interest included Korea and Manchuria. Consequently, that country now had a long land frontier with an unsettled and increasingly radical country. Naturally some Japanese leaders, mostly identified with the army and navy, saw an opportunity to increase Japanese influence by armed presence, while other isolationist circles thought any involvement was dangerous and inimical to long-term Japanese traditions.

98. Caldwell to Lansing, 4 October 1917, AE Russia 1917, DPR 425, RG 84, NA.
99. Caldwell to Lansing, 12 December 1917, copy in f. 5, box 712, WA-6, RG 45, NA.
100. James William Morley, *The Japanese Thrust into Siberia, 1918* (New York: Columbia University Press, 1957), 37-40.

The Japanese foreign minister, Ichira Motono, a former ambassador to Russia, thought that Japan had an obligation to pacify the region, if not for a permanant acquisition, at least to hold in trust for a compatible Russian government and as a card to play at the eventual peace conferences. An important factor known by everyone at the time was that Japan had plenty of troops and naval vessels to spare, and that the other Allies did not. Prior to any use of them, however, Motono wanted approval by the Allies to appease opposition in Japan.[101]

The initiation of a Japanese plan for intervention by sending ships to Vladivostok in early November was at first rejected by the British, who said that the supplies there were an American responsibility. But with unrest rising and Brest-Litovsk looming on the horizon, by the end of December the British and French shifted to the support of intervention but not by Japan alone, because that would likely be misunderstood by the Russians. They instead favored a joint Allied intervention with a substantial Japanese force but with token units from the other Allies. Japan was reluctant to agree because this plan seemed an obvious show of distrust in Japanese intentions, and it went against a long-standing Japanese goal of getting the West out of the Far East.

The United States and Japan clearly had the greatest interest in the area. American interest can be traced back to the late eighteenth-century China trade but more especially to Russian expansion and development in the Maritime Provinces that coincided with the purchase of Alaska. Subsequently, the building of the Trans-Siberian Railroad provoked much public interest but also some alarm at Russian imperial expansionism, as it did in Japan. Thus American sentiment was very pro-Japanese at the beginning of the Russo-Japanese War, only to shift back again after major Japanese victories.

American concerns for the stability of the region rose considerably in 1917, due to the strategic importance of the port of Vladivostok and the Trans-Siberian Railroad as the main route to European Russia, as well as the fear of the spread of Bolshevik revolution into Asia and, even more, of the potential damage that thousands of released German and Austrian prisoners of war could do in the area. Supporters of using Japanese military forces to stabilize the area ranged from those, such as George Kennan, who were strongly in favor to those who were adamantly opposed to allowing a greatly enlarged Japanese presence on the mainland of Asia.

Although wavering and inconsistent, the latter opinion prevailed in Washington circles, at least for the first half of 1918. The strongest voice of opposi-

101. Ibid., 136-43.

tion came from quarters, such as that of Raymond Robins, that condemned any kind of intervention as destroying hopes for closer relations with the Soviet government and the people of Russia. Colonel House so strongly opposed Japanese intervention that he cabled directly to Arthur Balfour, British foreign secretary, with the president's approval, "I feel this action will mean a serious lowering, if not actual loss, of our moral position in the eyes of our own peoples and of the whole world, and a dulling of the high enthusiasm of the American people for a righteous cause." The State Department's William Bullitt also took a strong anti-Japanese position on the grounds that all the excuses for any substantial Japanese presence were "simply dust for the eyes of the ignorant."[102]

While sending mixed signals in March and April, President Wilson generally retained an anti-Japanese bias, while the main concern of others was fear of a Russian anti-Allied backlash that would play into German hands. Indeed, Ambassador Bakhmeteff and other Russians warned of the harm to Allied interests in Russia by allowing a major Japanese intervention that was certain to provoke an intense Russian reaction. If intervention was necessary—to avoid a complete Bolshevik or German takeover—he counseled that a joint one was essential, with the number of American troops equal to those of the Japanese.

Meanwhile, events were taking an unsteady and crooked course for actual intervention. On 1 March, Admiral Austin Knight, commander of the American Pacific Squadron, returned to Vladivostok aboard the *Brooklyn*. Also that month, about half of the railway technical service corps of over 300, organized by John Stevens, landed and proceeded to set up headquarters in Harbin.[103] In a sense this could be considered a form of intervention on the scale of that of the Japanese in April, since the corps' members were armed (for their own protection) and wore military-style uniforms. To the Japanese, for whom they were rivals (and intruders) from the beginning, they were probably considered an American military unit. On the other hand, their mission to reorganize and improve operations on the Trans-Siberian was not specifically military, nor did they come under a military command jurisdiction, at least until intervention was

---

102. House to Balfour, 4 March 1918, in *The Intimate Papers of Colonel House*, vol. 3, *Into the World War*, ed. Charles Seymour (Boston: Houghton Mifflin, 1928), 395; Bullitt to Polk, 2 March 1918, f. 675, box 33, Polk Papers, Yale-Sterling.

103. Butler Wright, having spent twenty-seven days in reaching Vladivostok from Vologda, was reporting to Stevens in Harbin about the chaos on the Trans-Siberian at the time of the Japanese landing. He thought the "immorality and intrigue" in Harbin to be the worst in the world, even though it was relatively free from Bolshevik agitation and prisoners of war. Diary, 3 April 1918, box 2, Wright Papers, Princeton-Mudd.

well under way. Interestingly, most of the corps' expenses were paid by the Russian embassy in Washington from American loans to the Provisional Government.[104]

Another sign of a growing American involvement was the dispatch of an army intelligence officer in the Far East, Major David Barrows, from his base in Manila to Harbin, where he arrived at the end of March.[105] There he conferred with the local Russian commander (General Dmitri Horvat), George Emerson, and Consul Charles Moser and met Butler Wright and James Bailey, traveling through from Vologda. They were all convinced that sooner or later the United States should intervene in a substantial way: "The whole difficutly is getting Wilson to see it."[106]

The Japanese landing in April was front-page news in many newspapers and indeed provoked a furor in certain places, especially Moscow, where Soviet leaders demanded an explanation from Allied representatives. Francis, of course, knew nothing about it, nor was he able to find out much, while the Bolsheviks thought he was being evasive.[107] The State Department was alarmed at the unilateral action, that Japan had not consulted its allies, though it was also learned that the British had sent in fifty marines on 6 April to protect their consulate.

While both Francis and Robins, on the basis of what they knew about American policy, publicly condemned the Japanese action in response to strong Soviet protests,[108] Admiral Knight on the scene fully approved of the land-

104. Polk to Bakhmeteff, 14 March; Bakhmeteff to Ughet, 6 May; Bakhmeteff to S. M. Felton (Director General Military Railways), 6 May 1918, f. 170, op. 512/4, d. 43, AVPR.

Just whose jurisdiction the corps was under is a problem. The State Department had more authority over the mission than any other agency, but in its independent status the corps functioned more like the Committee on Public Information in the field. The National Archives was correct in designating a separate record group for its files. Many years later, however, survivors were able to gain a favorable court decision on their right to military service pensions. This ruling may unwittingly have given the United States the distinction of being the first military "interventionist" in Siberia, except that the initial focus was on the Russian interests in Manchuria.

105. Barrows to his wife, 31 March 1918, f. May 1917 to November 1918, box 2, Barrows Papers, UCB.

106. Ibid.

107. A month earlier, 130 British marines had landed at Murmansk with little fanfare or attention, but this was by invitation of the local soviet, which had received clearance from Trotsky "that all necessary aid should be accepted." And the ship involved, the battleship *Glory*, fired a salute to the local flag, a red one. Thomas Thacher statement to intelligence officer, USS *Melville*, 11 April 118, f. 1, box 706, WA-6, RG 45, NA.

108. Francis was not pleased that Robins stole the show, being cited in Moscow newspapers: "American representative emphatically announced that his government is opposed to Japanese intervention in Siberia." Francis to Long, 7 April 1918, box 186, Long Papers, MD, LC. He also accused Robins of having an anti-Japanese bias. Francis to Roland Morris (Tokyo), 26 May 1918, box 4, Morris Papers, MD, LC.

ing.[109] American concern subsided when the operation seemed successful and strictly limited to a police role.[110] The Japanese force, however, did not withdraw and soon became another source of tension for the Allies with both local authorities and the Soviet leadership in Moscow.[111] In the meantime, there was a new complication. Czecho-Slovak units that had been formed from Austro-Hungarian prisoners of war were on their way out of Russia for deployment on the Western Front. They began arriving at Vladivostok on 27 April and had reached 6,000 on 1 May, with 2,000 more coming in daily, adding another major strain to an unstable situation.[112]

The value of having an observation ship in Vladivostok registered with the Navy Department; on 19 April the chief of naval operations issued sailing orders for the USS Olympia, an old but well-known battle cruiser (Admiral Dewey's flagship at the Battle of Manila Bay), to go to Archangel.[113] Carrying Frederick Poole, the British general assigned to command in the area, and his staff of officers, it arrived at Murmansk on 26 May.[114] By this time in May the United States was viewing the two interventions separately and the one in north Russia more favorably. The Allied War Council in Paris was thus able to call formally for sending military forces to Murmansk and Archangel on 3 June.[115]

Meanwhile, another dimension of the Siberian situation was setting the stage for a broader Japanese intervention. Grigori Semenov, a young (twenty-seven), ambitious Ussuri Cossack officer, born in a village not far from Chita, was already on the scene. Having commanded Siberian Cossack units on the Southwestern Front and then in the Caucasus, he returned to Siberia in 1917 to resurrect an old plan to raise a large army from among the Mongol-Buriat people to save the tsar—and then Kerensky. With the backing of a Baltic German of-

109. Morley, *Japanese Thrust into Siberia*, 146–47. Knight apologized to Francis for the lack of coordination, blaming communication difficulties but also complaining that telegraphic messages to and from Francis that passed through Vladivostok could not be deciphered. Knight to Francis, 21 April 1918, reel 9, Francis Papers, MoHS.

110. Admiral Knight reports, 5–15 April 1918, box 613, WA-6, RG 45, NA.

111. Knight to Francis, 21 April 1918, reel 9, Francis Papers, MoHS.

112. Intelligence reports, USS *Brooklyn*, 27 April and 1 May 1918, box 613, RG 45, NA.

113. Admiral William Benson, 19 April 1918, with instruction "Guard this as confidential," f. 9, box 706, WA-6, RG 45. Interestingly, the orders specified Archangel, which would be closed by ice for another two months, rather than Murmansk, where the British were concentrated.

114. Admiral Sims to CNO, 2 May 1918, and Capt. V. A. Longhope (*Olympia*) to CNO, 26 May 1918, box 708, WA-6, RG 45, NA.

115. For more details and analysis, see John W. Long, "American Intervention in Russia: The North Russian Expedition, 1918–19," *Diplomatic History* 6, no. 1 (winter 1982): 49–57.

ficer, Baron Fedor Ungern-Sternberg, he gained authorization from Kerensky to organize a "volunteer army" in Siberia. After the latter's fall, Semenov convinced local soviets to support him, and by the end of 1917 he commanded a motley army of Mongols, Cossacks, and German and Turkish prisoners of war. Needing arms and political leverage, he saw Japan as a potential ally, and in mid-February 1918 Japan agreed to send some limited aid.[116]

Barrows, who visited Semenov at his headquarters at Manchuli in northern Manchuria in April, was quite impressed by his patriotism and determination but not with his assortment of 2,000 staff officers and men that included a Serbian company and a number of untrained Chinese. He noted that their Japanese carbines were antiquated and the artillery consisted of an awkward variety of calibers. He predicted, however, that Semenov would be able to seize a section of the Trans-Siberian and hoped that he could be convinced to turn it over to the American railway corps.[117]

Rivals to Semenov quickly appeared. General Horvat, as director of the Chinese Eastern Railway, with his headquarters in Harbin, occupied a strategic position in control of vital telegraphic and rail communications. A polished elderly Russian gentleman, he naturally gained the support of local Allied representatives in the interests of having access to crucial transportation into Russia and courted American assistance.[118] Horvat lacked, however, the troops, charisma, and Siberian base of Semenov. He was also tinged with the reputation of being inefficient and quasi-corrupt, typifying the old tsarist administration.

Admiral Alexander Kolchak, stranded in the United States by the Bolshevik revolution, was sent by Ambassador Bakhmeteff on an intelligence mission to China in December 1917. There he soon became the center of a third option for Russians and others, who considered both imperial Horvat and renegade Semenov as poor prospects for leading a viable anti-Bolshevik movement in Siberia. He also claimed the important financial backing of banker and Russian consul general in China Aleksei Putilov and had the advantage of being known and respected in American circles. For now, however, he lacked an army. In early 1918, Japanese agents in the field leaned toward Semenov, since he actually had an army of sorts, needed their support most, and, unlike Kolchak, was not tainted by close American connections.

116. Morley, *Japanese Thrust into Siberia*, 46–47, 97–98.
117. Barrows (Harbin) to Admiral Knight, 23 April 1918, and to Chief Army Intelligence, General Staff (Washington), 25 April 1918, f. 1917–1918, box 2, Barrows Papers, UCB. Barrows traveled with an interpreter companion from Manila by the name of Romanov and with Frank Cole, a railroad corps member.
118. Moser (Harbin) to Long, 4 April 1918, box 186, Long Papers, MD, LC.

To further complicate the situation, another Cossack officer, Ivan Kalmykov, returned from the Caucasian front to lay claim to Siberian leadership and received some British funding and Japanese encouragement. Because he had a more liberal reputation, local Socialist Revolutionaries saw him as the best alternative to the Bolsheviks. Like Semenov, he had an adroit Baltic German adviser, but he ultimately failed to raise much of an army in competition with the other Russian would-be Siberian potentates.[119] From the beginning, and throughout most of the chaos and confusion of civil war and intervention in Siberia, the big problem was the inability of any Russian leader to obtain real credibility, assert authority, and gain the support of both the Siberian people and the Allies.

"May Day"

All the major Allied governments in Russia had their left and right wings, agents who were in regular contact and others, including the French and American ambassadors, who remained aloof in a stance of as complete nonrecognition as could be achieved, but neutral and waiting to see. The former were represented by Robins, Lockhart, and Sadoul. French ambassador Joseph Noulens broke this "accord" in late April by issuing a statement of clear hostility toward the Soviet government.

Most of the French diplomatic personnel had left Russia along with the British through Finland in February, but Noulens became stranded in Finland and, fearing possible capture by the Germans, gained permission to return with part of his staff to Russia and join Francis at Vologda, where he arrived at the end of March. A constant and inveterate foe of radical revolution, he did not hide his support for uninvited Allied intervention. On 23 April, at a meeting with representatives of non-Bolshevik newspapers, he issued a thinly veiled call to overthrow the Bolshevik revolution and defended the right of the Japanese, or any other ally, to intervene directly in Russia.[120]

The timing, either deliberate or coincidental, was on the very day of the arrival of the new German ambassador, Count Wilhelm von Mirbach, adding to

---

119. Morley, *Japanese Thrust into Siberia*, 95-97, 166-67.
120. Debo, *Revolution and Survival*, 245-53; Noulens, *Mon ambassade en Russie soviétique*, 2:51-63. Francis could now proudly report, "Vologda is now the Diplomatic Capital of Russia. Today a photograph was taken of the Chiefs of Allied Missions here and they numbered eight—American, French, Italian, Serbian, Siamese, Brazilian, Japanese and Chinese." To Basil Miles, 8 April 1918, reel 9, Francis Papers, MoHS.

the sensation.[121] Although Soviet leaders were increasingly frustrated about any substantial aid or recognition coming from the Allied governments, the Noulens publication seemed to reinforce that conclusion as well as pose a direct threat to Soviet power, especially since there was no subsequent attempt to temper the message. It also severely damaged the Robins-Lockhart-Sadoul initiatives.[122] Noulens had apparently not consulted Francis, the recognized dean of Allied diplomats, who was indeed very ill at the time, despite a general agreement that such matters be subject to review and consultation by all the Allied representatives. This all had a direct impact on Francis, who, having suddenly recovered his health, sent his strong plea for Allied intervention to Washington on 2 May.[123] Nearly the last shot for the cause of recognition was taken on the same date by William Webster, Robins's Red Cross associate, who may have known of Francis's decision.[124]

By the end of April, Bullard in Moscow proudly boasted of his accomplishments in reaching so many more people with press releases—verified by receiving 200 to 300 letters of appreciation per day—without any government interference and planned a new campaign along the Volga.[125] His Petrograd assistant, Graham Taylor, while watching a long, relatively quiet May Day parade from his storefront office on Nevsky Prospect, complained of the routine material coming from America that did not fit the Russian situation. Expecting Sisson to have reached Washington, he wrote Bullard, "I cannot understand why the service has not bucked up considerably."[126]

That same day Bullard was shocked to receive a partly garbled cable from Creel ordering all American publicity personnel to leave Bolshevik-held territory by

121. Fate added insult to injury for all concerned by locating the German embassy and consulate across the street and next door to buildings housing the French mission in Moscow. Sadoul, *Notes sur la révolution*, 319.

122. Ibid., 423-34; Lockhart, *Memoirs of a British Agent*, 270-74.

123. Francis to Lansing, 2 May 1918, *FRUS 1918: Russia* 1:519-21. Lansing answered with a strong assertion of nonintervention. Lansing to Francis, 8 May 1918, *DSAR* 1:53-54. Although there is not a specific reference to the Francis message, it was received at the State Department on that date.

124. Webster, "Reasons Pro and Con for Allied Recognition of the Soviet Form of Government," AE Russia, DPR 344, RG 84, NA. As if Robins himself needed further convincing, Lockhart, as late as 5 May, listed six reasons why Trotsky could be counted on to work with the Allies, the last being his agreement that day to allow the Allies "to retain those stores which we require for ourselves" at Archangel. Lockhart to Robins, 5 May 1918, f. May 1918, box 14, Robins Papers, SHSW.

125. Russian CPI Report for May 1918, box 6, Bullard Papers, Princeton-Mudd.

126. Taylor to Bullard, 1 May 1918 (2 messages), ibid.

5 May.[127] He made a quick trip to Vologda to seek explanation, but Francis, too, was baffled by the sudden recall.[128] Since no reason was given, Bullard had no way of knowing that the cause was a cable from Sisson in Norway to Creel on 22 April to "instruct Bullard that he and his American men are ordered out of Bolshevik area of Russia by two weeks from date." In the belief that the material he was bringing home "proving" leading Bolsheviks were German agents would be immediately published, Sisson feared a reaction against operations there.[129] Captain Riggs sensed impending doom. "We are still hanging on the brink and the Maximalists haven't fired us out of Russia yet! I wish they would!"[130]

Packing belongings and records and getting Taylor out of Petrograd took time, and the sudden death of Summers added more complications. Bullard finally transferred his remaining funds to Poole and the unfinished business to Boris Lebedev and other Russian employees.[131] The last straw was a fight with Robins and Gumberg at the Yaroslav station over space on a train heading north and an exchange of words over the authenticity of Sisson's documents.[132] As usual, Bullard did not disclose to them anything relative to his own destination.

Finding no decent rooms available in Archangel, Bullard and his five American subordinates found temporary refuge on an old British-manned cruiser that was icebound fifteen miles downstream. They still hoped to resume business in Moscow and tried to direct things as best they could from afar.[133] It was still quite a blow to dedicated enthusiasts such as Taylor, who was still wondering why they were "dumped up here" three weeks later: "It is the very devil to have my work all shot to pieces, needlessly as it seems to me."[134]

The death of Maddin Summers was a severe blow to American operations in Soviet Russia. While adamantly anti-Bolshevik, he was a diligent public servant

127. The garbling had caused a few days' delay in transmitting the message from Vologda through Riggs to Bullard. Bullard (Archangel) to Creel, 9 May 1918, ibid.

128. Francis to Summers, 3 May 1918, reel 9, Francis Papers, MoHS.

129. Sisson, *One Hundred Red Days*, 426.

130. Riggs to Aunt Jane, 6 May 1918, box 124, Riggs Family Papers, MD, LC.

131. Bullard to Poole and to Lebedev, 5 May 1918, reel 9, Francis Papers, MoHS. Lebedev was a son-in-law of Prince Peter Kropotkin.

132. In describing the scene, he converted it into a short three-act play. Bullard (en route) to Poole, 6 May 1918, ibid. The Creel people clearly resented Robins's superior demeanor and his throwing his weight around by wearing fancy uniforms and cruising around Moscow in a luxury car.

133. Bullard to Creel, 9 May 1918, and to Lebedev and to Francis, 22 May 1918, ibid. He expressed his regrets to Poole: "My get away was disgusting and needlessly quick—and besides we were all too shot up by Summer's death for any proper farewell arrangements." 1 June 1918, ibid.

134. To Imbrie, 22 May 1918, box 4, Petrograd consulate, RG 84, NA.

who fully served the interests of his country, even when they required cooperation with Soviet authorities. And though Americans at the time were constantly
bickering with each other, few found fault with Summers. He served a vital role
as mediator and communications center, especially with Francis and the embassy
marooned in Vologda, and in condoning and coordinating the contacts of his
staff and other Americans with Soviet officials. Bullard left a sincere tribute:

> I never knew anyone who could really agree to disagree as he could. On a
> whole lot of important things we disagreed fundamentally. But he never let
> this interfere with the working agreement we had on the job. I feel that it
> has been a real privilege to have known him and his loss is a real personal
> pain. . . .
>   I was looking forward to a long talk with him on the best way to save
> something out of the wreckage [of CPI work]. I missed his advice very much.

Then he added pointedly, "How I wish the Ambassador had some of his fine
qualities! Somehow one learns not to ask the Ambassador's advice."[135]

Francis also greatly appreciated the advice of Summers and deeply regretted
his passing. He went to Moscow for his first—and only—appearance in the new
Soviet capital for Summers's funeral and delivered a fitting elegy, comparing his
death to a battlefield casualty.[136] While there, he talked with a number of Americans and Allied consuls who attended the ceremony and met face-to-face with
Vosnesensky, Chicherin's assistant in the Commissariat of Foreign Affairs. They
agreed that more regular communication should be established. Poole then arranged to meet with Chicherin every Monday and Thursday.[137] One result of
more regular contact was the lifting of the ban on telegraphic messages in code.

Poole not only took over direction of the vast work of the American consulate
general but also filled another void, maintaining communications with Soviet
officials, that resulted from the departure of Robins, whose tenure had been an
on-again, off-again affair since early in the year. The matter came to a head in
late April from at least two sources: Summers and Sisson. The former had made

135. Bullard to Poole, 6 May 1918, reel 9, Francis Papers, MoHS.
136. "Maddin Summers yielded his life in his country's service and did so as effectually
as if he had been taken off by the enemy in ambush and as couragiously [sic] as if he had
fallen in attack on the enemy's works. He realized as fully as does an officer leading his
troops in a battle that his very life was in jeopardy and that realization nerved him to renewed effort." "Address of American Ambassador David R. Francis over body of Maddin
Summers, Consul General, May 8, 1918," reel 9, Francis Papers, MoHS.
137. Francis diary, 9 May 1918, reel 11, and Poole to Francis, 14 May 1918, reel 9,
Francis Papers, MoHS.

Arthur Bullard (American Red Cross) in middle, flanked by British sailors, Archangel harbor, June 1918, couresy of the Princeton University Libraries

clear to Francis and directly to the State Department that his request for transfer involved a jurisdictional dispute with Robins. Sisson, in recommending the removal of the Creel committee men, had also advised that Red Cross personnel be withdrawn.[138]

An official recall of Robins was sent the same day, 24 April, as the one to Bullard, but it, too, was ambiguous, especially since it was followed by a communication from Thacher in New York informing him that Davison (executive secretary of the American Red Cross) desired him to remain in Russia for the time being.[139] Robins had his own personal reasons for leaving: he had failed to convince Francis to recommend recognition of the Bolsheviks, and he thought that he might have a better chance of influencing American policy in Washington than in Moscow. The arrival of Count Mirbach as German ambassador at the end of April may have been decisive. Still, after informing Francis of his

138. Salzman, *Reform and Revolution*, 264–68; Sisson, *One Hundred Red Days*, 426; Francis to Summers, 3 May 1918, reel 9, Francis Papers, MoHS.
139. Francis, describing his conversation with Robins at the Vologda station, to Poole, 15 May 1918, reel 9, Francis Papers, MoHS.

plans to depart on 3 May, he remained for several more days. On 13 May he made his farewell calls on Lenin, Trotsky, Chicherin, and other Bolshevik leaders, and the next day he and Gumberg boarded the well-traveled Red Cross railway car for the long journey home through Vologda and Siberia.[140]

Also leaving European Russia about this time was Albert Rhys Williams, who stayed behind after Reed left to do some of his own personal intervention, enlisting in a small International Legion to help protect Petrograd from the Germans in February. There he met another lost soul, a German-American scholar by the name of Charles Kuntz. They left Moscow together, debating Lenin and the revolution all the way across Siberia, according to Williams.[141]

The Home Front

While the departures of Bullard, Sisson, Reed, Williams, Robins, and others may have had a calming effect on the remaining members of the American colony in Russia, the return of people with such diverse views would increase the tension and fuel the debate about Russia at home. All of them, however, faced delays in getting back and then in getting their materials before the public. None seemed to find home much more inviting than Russia. At least Robins had a laugh at the expense of Sisson and Bullard.

> I have built several fires under S. [Sisson] and one or two of them threatened a very decent little conflagration. If a story could be written that pictured Compub activities in Russia, the wild departure of S. on the 4th of March claiming that everything had gone to Hell, his rusticating for three weeks in Finland and arrival in London only to find that his great story was as stale as a last year's bird's nest, and then to picture Father Time [Bullard] fleeing from Moscow with a date of doom that he had to beat by escaping from Soviet Russia, and his rusticating on the ice-breaker in Archangel and then arrival here it would be worth doing.[142]

Sisson's expectations of the prompt publication of the sizable number of documents he had procured were disappointed. Their existence was widely

---

140. Salzman, *Reform and Revolution*, 267–70. Francis wired his counterpart in Tokyo of Robins's impending arrival and of his dislike of Japanese, which he attributed to a long residence in California. To Roland Morris, 26 May 1918, box 3, Morris Papers, MD, LC.
141. Williams, *Journey into Revolution*, 249–51, 287–92.
142. Robins to Gumberg, 19 July 1918, f. July/August, box 14, Robins Papers, SHSW.

known, since both he and Robins had discussed both sides of their authenticity. Robins, though returning a couple of months later, outmaneuvered Sisson by having his journalist friend, Louis Edgar Browne, publish and cast doubt on several of the documents, which indeed were translated (from German to Russian) copies containing quite a few obvious typographical and other errors of spelling and translation.[143]

Once the documents—and others sent by Bullard and Francis—were safely in the hands of Creel, they were properly considered to be government property, purchased with government funds.[144] Although Creel personally gave them an enthusiastic stamp of approval,[145] Bullard, who had been involved in collecting them, had doubts and "thought there was a strong possibility of chaff being mixed up with the wheat." He wrote Sisson,

> I . . . would not be at all surprised if the second batch of "documents" sold to the Embassy after you had left were all fakes. I had half an hour to look at them in Vologda—but what good was that. I can't read Russian, I'm not a handwriting expert, I could not even swear that it was the same kind of paper. There was an obvious temptation for a gang of crooks to sell a gold brick.[146]

The documents' formal release was further delayed by political considerations, since at this time in May and June, Wilson was hesitating about intervention and knew that they would create a sensation and damage what relations remained with the Bolsheviks. More time was also needed to have them thoroughly examined by experts. For the latter, Creel recruited a team consisting of J. Franklin Jameson, editor of the *American Historical Review*, and Samuel Harper. In due course and while expressing some doubts and noting discrepancies, they declared that most of them were genuine. Sixty-eight documents finally appeared in a special

143. C. H. Dennis (*Chicago Daily News*) to Harper, f. 4, box 5, Harper Papers, UC.
Bullard was quite upset about Browne sending articles and information about the documents out of Russia in the clear (and perhaps with Soviet connivance) and thought it would endanger his work. Bullard to Creel in Summers to Lansing, 20 April 1918, AE Russia 1918, DPR 314, RG 84, NA.
144. Imbrie to Francis, 24 April 1918, AE Russia, DPR 344, and 8 May 1918, box 4, Petrograd Consulate, RG 84, NA.
145. Creel assured the president on 9 May: "I spent most of the night going over his [Sisson's] papers, particularly the original documents taken from the files at Smolny Institute. They are absolutely conclusive, and contribute the most amazing record of double-dealing and corruption." Vol. 2, Creel Papers, MD, LC.
146. Bullard to Sisson, n.d. [June 1918], box 6, Bullard Papers, Princeton-Mudd.

pamphlet of the Committee on Public Information in late October, after intervention was well under way and all contact broken with the Soviet government.[147]

At the opposite end of the spectrum, John Reed endured similar delays, owing to Sisson's influence. Having also been held up in transit for a late May arrival, his papers were seized at customs and retained by the State Department for several months. Despite the sympathetic efforts of William Bullitt and others,[148] they were not released until August, at which time Reed began feverishly writing his epic memoir of the revolution. He also spoke publicly, defending the revolution. One lecture in early September resulted in a brief arrest, which he attributed to the tension arising over the release of the Sisson documents.[149]

The two military attachés returning from Russia gave contradictory advice in both private and official communications. Brigadier General William Judson reached Washington in March, hopeful of reinforcing a moderate interventionist American course, but he was disappointed in being ignored and quickly relegated to a remote training camp.[150] He reappraised the mistakes of 1917 as (1) the expectation that Russia could stay in the war; (2) failure to back Kornilov and put pressure on Kerensky to submit; (3) not sending good, small units of troops; and (4) allowing Russia to attempt to mount an offensive. "Tereshchenko always told the allied diplomats what he thought they wished to hear and the diplomats always believed what T. told them. Thus some of us lived in a fool's paradise until the early days of November 1917."[151]

Captain Walter Crosley finally reached London at the end of April, after the long delay in Finland, bitter and dejected about Russia. He recommended to the Navy Department that a force of 100,000 Japanese be sent immediately to Siberia, but he had no confidence that a stable government could be sustained by the Russians themselves for very long.[152] He also pressed this position in Paris, where he had to be reprimanded for diverging from American policy without authorization.

---

147. A facsimile is included as an appendix in Sisson, *One Hundred Red Days*.

148. Bullitt to Reed, 23 May and 22 July 1918, f. 311–13, and Polk to Bryant, 13 June 1918, f. 977–80, Reed-Bryant Papers, Harvard-Houghton. Part of the problem was that Frank Polk, who finally secured their release, was resting from exhaustion for six weeks during the summer.

149. Reed to Mrs. Robins, 15 September 1918, asking for Raymond's support, f. September–October 1918, Robins Papers, SHSW.

150. Judson (Camp Shelby, Mississippi) to Bryant, 28 March 1918, f. 1012, ibid.

151. Judson report to Chief Intelligence Section, General Staff, 16 March 1918, roll 3, M 1443, RG 165, NA.

152. He was also dismayed by what he sensed was a lack of interest in Russia in London and Paris. Crosley to DNI, 12 May 1918, f. 7, box 706, WA-6, RG 45, NA.

Public Perspectives

Meanwhile, the most active members of the former Root mission were trying to get something privately accomplished in the way of Russian-American communication. Charles Russell took the initiative back in January, proposing the establishment of an additional press bureau that, unlike the Committee on Public Information, would be privately funded and operated. He believed that $50,000 could go a long way toward an independent operation that would prepare articles to be sent by mail to Russian newspapers and provide films to be shown through the facilities of the YMCA. He asked Cyrus McCormick to furnish half of the money and argued this would be more effective in Russia than the efforts of an agency tied to government funding.[153]

Matters moved slowly due to the pressure of time upon business and professional men in wartime and because of advice directly from the president and Lansing to maintain a low visibility. "The New York men" (Root, Mott, Crane, and Bertron) and Basil Miles of the State Department, nevertheless, met on 9 February at Root's apartment to discuss what could be done.[154] Although McCormick was unable to attend, he sent a memorandum that proposed a "quasi-recognition" of the Bolsheviks and sending a member of the mission (suggesting Crane) to negotiate with them. He also recommended that Francis be withdrawn and that a senior diplomat such as William Sharp, current ambassador to France, replace him.[155] The consensus of the meeting, however, was "to concentrate on strengthening the hands of Creel and not working apart from him."[156]

Russell, having contributed comments on the memorandum, came to the same conclusion; he soon volunteered to serve Creel's propaganda machine and was sent to Britain. His parting shot was a proposal that various branches of American organized labor send assistance directly to comparable groups in Russia. He suggested specifically that the American Federation of Labor ship 5 million pairs of shoes to the railroad workers of Russia.[157] Although nothing came of it, the effect of such proposals of assistance was to strengthen the "wait-and-see" attitude toward Soviet Russia and tolerance of the Robins effort at dialogue or quasi-

---

153. Russell to McCormick, 4 January 1918, and Judge P. S. Post Memorandum, 26 January 1918, f. Department of Commerce, box 115, 2C, McCormick Papers, SHSW.

154. McCormick to Russell, 8 February 1918, vol. 8, Russell Papers, MD, LC.

155. McCormick Memorandum, 6 February 1918, f. 20, box 4, Harper Papers, UC.

156. Mott to Harper, 11 February 1918, ibid.

157. Russell to McCormick, 26 March and 5 April 1918, box 118, 2C, McCormick Papers, SHSW.

recognition in Washington.[158] The Root people also opposed the Japanese intervention in Vladivostok and supported another important voice of moderation that emanated from New York, the American League to Aid and Cooperate with Russia, which advocated understanding and sympathy toward all of Russia under whatever government. Led by prominent businessmen Herbert Carpenter, Charles Boynton, and E. Chappell Porter, this organization was an offshoot of the American-Russian Chamber of Commerce.[159]

In the first point of its eleven-point program, adopted at a meeting in the office of Senator (from Oklahoma) Robert Owen in Washington, the League recommended "the creating of an official division of the Government on Russian affairs." Other points dealt with obtaining knowledge of Russia, encouraging universities to expand Russia-related courses, and circulating "a Russian weekly publication." Above all, it called for sanity, sympathy, and understanding toward Russia. The League also brought back to the foreground the idea of sending another special commission to Russia. It suffered, however, from being broadly conceived; including Boyce Thompson as one of the officers caused some initially to mistrust it.[160] On the other hand, Chappell Porter, executive secretary of the American-Russian Chamber of Commerce, hoped to steer the League more toward an anti-Bolshevik stance and thought that Arkady Sack's book, *The Birth of Russian Democracy*, to be issued by the Russian Information Bureau in late May, would help.[161]

Samuel Harper supported most of the program, especially the idea of a clearer government focus on Russia. Exasperated by a fruitless search for Russian newspapers that had been sent to the State Department, Harper complained to House's secretary that things just seemed to get lost there, then discovered that they had been put in storage until after the war. "The trouble is that there is no single man, of force and vision, giving all his thought and energy to the Russian situa-

158. Letter of introduction of Newton Baker, 19 April 1918, vol. 9, Russell Papers, MD, LC.

159. Harper was in close contact with members of this group, but he worried that they and the president were being too cautious: "I believe he is very wise in going cautiously. But too much caution may mean . . . too late." To Mott, 27 May 1918, box 4, Harper Papers, UC.

160. Hayden Eames to Carpenter, 7 May 1918, f. 6, box 5, Harper Papers, UC. After seeing Eames's letter, Harper responded, "I also am a bit afraid of Thompson, but he is a force, and he is interested in Russia." Harper to Eames, 9 May 1918, ibid. Frederick Corse was another returning Russia veteran who questioned the agenda of the League. Corse to Harper, 7 May 1918, ibid.

161. Porter to Harper, 25 April 1918, f. 5, box 5, Harper Papers, UC. Sack sent Harper a copy on 29 May. Sack to Harper, 29 May, f. 8, ibid.

tion, and our possible action and policy. . . . When it comes to definite action we are still groping."[162] He noted that Berlin had a special division on Russian affairs and that Washington should have the same.

The department's own William Bullitt also had this in mind when he complained privately to House about the lack of expertise on Russia:

> After all, isn't indecision the keynote of our Russian policy just now?
> . . . At present Basil Miles is vaguely responsible for our general policy. Miles is an excellent diplomatist, really excellent, but he is not an expert on military, economic and financial matters. And one man with two stenographers can not handle the problem presented by Russia.[163]

He urged the establishment of a separate Russian Board in Washington—and a counterpart in Russia—with representatives from various agencies (including Miles from the State Department) and suggested Justice Louis Brandeis to head it. In the absence of such an organization, the president would continue to be besieged from all directions with contradictory advice on what to do about Russia.

The State Department responded halfway to these suggestions, welcoming back J. Butler Wright from his long return voyage through Siberia from Vologda into its inner sanctum to join and really run its Russian Bureau, nominally headed by Miles. Then, in early June, it brought in Jerome Landfield, a history instructor from the University of California who had spent considerable time in Russia before the war, mostly in gold mining in Siberia. He knew Russian and was married to a member of the old aristocracy (Liuba Lobanov-Rostovskaya)—in Paris in 1907.[164] From the beginning, he was a strong advocate of intervention. Harper, who met Landfield when he passed through Chicago, was unenthusiastic and thought he was not the man for the job.[165] He welcomed, however, the department's recruiting of Archibald Cary Coolidge, a pioneer of academic Russian studies at Harvard, for a fact-finding trip to

---

162. To Walter Lippmann, 7 May 1918, f. 5, box 5, Harper Papers, UC. To another interested party, Harper commented on a similar matter: "They are the worst lot of routine bureaucrats at the State Dept." To Ven Svarc, 3 June 1918, f. 9, ibid.

163. Bullitt to House, 20 May 1918, in House to Wilson, 24 May 1918, *PWW* 48:145.

164. Landfield, "'Operation Kaleidoscope': A Melange of Personal Recollections," typescript, UCB. Unfortunately, this memoir reaches only 1914.

165. Harper to R. Crane, 11 June 1918, and to Coolidge, 8 June, f. 9, box 5, Harper Papers, UC.

To Porter, Harper complained that he "had never thought of Landfield as a serious man, and he has not been in Russia for ten years"; n.d. [June 1918], ibid. Perhaps the Chicago professor was a bit jealous that he had not been asked.

Russia.[166] Harper obviously wanted to be included himself, but Charles Crane had urged Harper to remain independent, and that was probably known in the State Department. Mott, for one, thought Harper would still be asked to head a new, even larger Russian division.[167]

The Russian Embassy

Although at times David Francis felt isolated in Vologda, launching messages into space and getting virtually nothing in return, Boris Bakhmeteff in Washington was in an even more precarious situation. No longer having any authority from a government in Russia, the Russian embassy had in fact become a quasi-agency of the American government and reported to it, thus placed ironically in a position of filling a void of expertise on Russia. The relationship was uncomfortable from both sides; it also caused dissension within the embassy staff.

The Russian personnel certainly had plenty to do in sorting out, canceling, and arbitrating the large number of contracts and obligations of the former Provisional Government in the United States. One involved the resale to the United States government of $25 million worth of steel rails ready for shipment to Russia but now much needed in the United States. The problem was that $14 million of the amount had come from gold shipped by the Provisional Government. Georgi Lomonosov, in charge of the Russian Transport Mission since his arrival the previous June, thought that the income from the sale should be put into a separate Russian account rather than going directly to the U.S. Treasury, which controlled the balance of remaining credits to Russia.[168] His disagreement with Bakhmeteff over this affair led to Lomonosov's ouster and his becoming a bitter opponent of the ambassador.[169]

Very likely Lomonosov and Bakhmeteff already disagreed over intervention policy, since immediately after his dismissal the former became an ardent and effective spokesman (though he still did not know English) for the pro-Soviet

166. Coolidge to Harper, 3 June, and Harper to Coolidge, 9 June, ibid. He had already reached Paris by 22 June on his way to Stockholm. Hugh Gibson diary, 22 June 1918, typescript, Gibson Papers, HPL.

Coolidge's recruitment may have been initiated by House, since he took a particular interest in how he was doing. House to Long, 1 August 1918, box 35, Long Papers, MD, LC.

167. Mott to Harper, 2 July 1918, f. 10, box 5, Harper Papers, UC.

168. Lomonosov to Bakhmeteff, 18 April, and Ughet to Norman Davis (Treasury Department), 18 April 1918, f. 170, op. 512/4, d. 61 (1918), AVPR.

169. Bakhmeteff circular, 18 June 1918, ibid.

line, while Bakhmeteff and Sack leaned more definitely in favor of increased armed intervention.[170] A central issue was whether one could work through the soviet and cooperative organizations *against* the Bolsheviks. Lomonosov argued in favor of this, insisting that Bolshevik control over them was waning.[171] Disagreement and disunity among Russian representatives certainly added to the American confusion about Russian policies.

Bakhmeteff's position strengthened in June owing to the arrival of two prominent officials of the former Provisional Government, Aleksandr Konovalov, minister of commerce and industry under both Miliukov/Lvov and Kerensky, and Sergei Korff, a professor of law at the University of Helsinki who had served as assistant governor-general of Finland in 1917. With the help of Bakhmeteff, his old protégé, Konovalov managed to see both Lansing and House in late June and have his argument that Allied intervention would serve as a rallying cry for anti-Bolshevik Russians read by the president.[172] When asked by Lansing about Russian reaction to a Japanese armed presence in Siberia, Konovalov wanted to consult with Bakhmeteff before answering. He then replied that he had been much opposed to the idea before but now would consider it appropriate as long as it was part of an inter-Allied force that was not under Japanese command.[173]

"Baron" Korff, married to an American and well known in American Russian circles as a friend of Crane, Harper, and Kennan, wrote strategically timed articles condemning the Bolsheviks. Another refugee from the Provisional Government, Aleksandr Bublikov, an engineer who was briefly minister of transportation, like Korff, had the advantage of a knowledge of English.[174] But perhaps the most influential in the media campaign in favor of intervention from among the Russians was the Constitutional Democrat leader Ariadna Tyrkova-Williams, who, though still in Britain, managed to get her message across through Samuel Harper in the pages of the *Christian Science Monitor*.[175]

170. Harper to Carpenter, 25 June 1918, and to Richard Crane, 30 June 1918, recounting his conversations with Bakhmeteff in Washington, f. 9, box 5, Harper Papers, UC.

171. A more detailed summary of Lomonosov's position is found in "America and Russia," *The Public: A Journal of Democracy*, 29 June 1918, 813–15.

172. Konovalov statement, 24 June 1918, enclosed in Lansing to Wilson, 24 June, *PWW* 48:406–8. Konovalov's entrée in Washington was no doubt facilitated by Bakhmeteff, who briefly served under him before being sent to Washington.

173. Konovalov to Lansing, 26 June 1918, copy in f. State Dept. 3, box 21, Bakhmeteff Papers, BA, CU.

174. Bublikov to Kennan, 28 May 1918, f. 1918, box 4, Kennan Papers, MD, LC. Sack thought Bublikov was too much of a whiner, always critical of the Provisional Government. Sack to Kennan, 3 June 1918, ibid.

175. Harper to Dixon (*Christian Science Monitor*), 2 July 1918, f. 11, box 5, Harper Papers, UC.

These Russian voices were still muted by the general lack of sympathy in America for anyone associated with the Provisional Government, which, most Americans believed, had failed Russia so miserably. Even Harper was dismayed by the divisions among the Kadets, who might have been the "party of America's hope." Constantine Nabokov, uncle of the author and Bakhmeteff's equivalent in London though formally only chargé d'affaires, believed that Russia should settle its own problems: "All of my hopes are now centered on Russia, on salvation and regeneration within. The less we are helped the better."[176] And the Russian ambassador to France, the "erratic and temperamental" Vasilii Maklakov, made matters worse by spending much of his time attacking Miliukov.[177]

Alexander Kerensky surfaced in Paris in July with serious but spurned attempts to see the top American officials—Pershing and Ambassador William Sharp.[178] He did manage to present lower-level Americans with another plea for intervention, hopefully purely American. He understood that an Allied intervention was more feasible but was more doubtful about its acceptance by the Russian people. He indicated that "any form of intervention is preferable to one of a purely Japanese character" and insisted that action must come soon, that September would be too late.[179]

Although Kerensky was able to meet with Clemenceau twice, on the second occasion he was shown a cable from Lansing stating that a proposed visit to the United States was "undesirable," and a French invitation to participate in the Bastille Day celebrations was suddenly withdrawn. When Kerensky objected, Clemenceau responded, "Russia is a neutral country, which has concluded peace with our enemies. The friends of our enemies are our enemies."[180] Kerensky continued to make himself obnoxious in Paris by circulating wild stories of Bolshevik-German military collaboration.[181]

Meanwhile, financial matters consumed most of the time of the Russian ambassador and his staff in Washington, with the primary burden falling first on Lomonosov and then on Sergei Ughet, commercial attaché of the embassy.

176. Nabokov to Mrs. de Peterson, 2 February 1918, in f. "Nabokoff, Constantine," box 102, Leland Harrison Papers, MD, LC.

177. Harper to Carpenter, 11 June 1918, box 5, Harper Papers, UC.

178. Hugh Gibson diary, 10 July 1918, typescript copy, Gibson Papers, HPL.

179. Gibson confidential memorandum, 10 July 1918, ibid.

180. As quoted in Abraham, *Alexander Kerensky*, 341. Kerensky admitted his surprise at these rebuffs but claimed he had no intention of visiting the United States. He blamed supporters of his old nemesis, Kornilov, for an Allied decision to back Kolchak as an alternative to Kerensky. See Kerensky, *Russia and History's Turning Point*, 494-99.

181. Gibson diary, 19 July 1918, Gibson Papers, HPL.

Bakhmeteff was also bothered by exiles from the Provisional Government concentrated in France who were anxious to gain American support for a resurrected, non-Bolshevik Russia and especially access to the American credits still earmarked for Russia. But most of these tragic and somewhat depressed figures stayed in Europe—to be close for an anticipated return—where they were at a disadvantage in pleading for assistance from Allied representatives who were facing the continually escalating demands of the war.

Paths to Intervention

From late May through June, more and more pressure was building for direct American military intervention in Russia. The main reasons were to safeguard supplies in the ports of Murmansk, Archangel, and Vladivostok; to act in unity with allies, especially Britain and Japan; to assure exit routes for remaining Americans and for Czech and Serb former prisoners of war; and to rally the Russian people against Bolshevism. With a few exceptions, most of the proposals were tentative and limited, but pressure was mounting from both Britain and France for an inter-Allied expedition to Siberia. Sources in London and Paris saw American resistance to Japanese intervention weakening.[182] But on 23 May the president still resisted, arguing that the time was inopportune and that shipping could only be found by subtracting from that committed to supplying Europe.[183]

Samuel Harper maintained a firm commitment to the program of "no recognition, no intervention" until 21 May, when he received a cable from his old mentor at the Sorbonne, Paul Boyer, who was now advising the French government on Russian affairs. Boyer stressed that Russians now wanted Japanese intervention and that America should support it in the cause of Allied unity.[184] While expressing words of caution, Harper was evidently swayed and imme-

182. This was in reference to Wilson's offhand assertion in an American Red Cross fund-raising speech that America would "stand by Russia" as much as by Britain and France. The State Department's informal representative in London, Ray Stannard Baker, noted, "Mr. Wilson's watchword, 'stand by Russia,' becomes suddenly,—not at all for idealistic or democratic reasons, but for imperialistic and military reasons—a new policy to be eagerly seized upon." Baker to Polk, 28 May 1918, reel 29, Baker Papers, MD, LC.
183. Reading to Balfour, 23 May 1918, *PWW* 48:133–34.
184. Boyer to Harper, 21 May 1918, f. 6, box 5, Harper Papers, UC. At the same time, similar advice came from General Tasker Bliss, the War Department's representative on the Supreme War Council in Paris. Bliss to Baker, 26 May 1918, enclosure in Baker to Wilson, 28 May 1918, *PWW* 48:179–81.

diately passed Boyer's message on to friends in influential places.[185] To Richard Crane, Lansing's personal secretary, Harper emphasized that Boyer wanted Wilson to be convinced of the necessity of Japanese intervention as part of an Allied effort.[186] At the same time, Harper regretted the departure of Robins from Russia: "I am sorry to hear this, because I believe he was just the man for the delicate and difficult job over there."[187]

Trying to find, or define, an alternative to a Soviet-ruled Russia was a dilemma for many Americans, including Harper, and probably the president. While agreeing with much of the condemnation and criticism of the Bolsheviks, they still considered trying to save the Soviet structure as the most effective way of combating German advances, soviets without Bolsheviks. The question was: "Have the Bolsheviki by their methods of the last months discredited the Soviet idea?"[188]

In late May, George Kennan also weighed in with a clear and detailed recommendation for intervention in Siberia in a letter to Lansing that repeated his earlier plea for using Japanese forces. He argued that the anti-Bolshevik forces there were strong, but at the same time the threat of German control of the region was quite real. "The danger that Germany will acquire economic domination in Siberia—the richest part of the old Empire that is still left intact—seems to me very great."[189] He also argued in sharp disagreement with the League to Aid and Cooperate with Russia that no assistance should ever be contemplated to any Soviet agencies, "even if they make a show of fighting Germany."

They are usurpers pure and simple; . . . they obtained what power they have by criminal violence, and they are retaining it by a system of terrorism which prevents the majority of the nation from giving expression to its will.[190]

185. Harper to Lippmann and to Carpenter, 21 May 1918, f. 8, ibid. Probably about this time Chapin Huntington's message of 28 April from Irkutsk reached Harper. From this vantage point, Huntington foresaw "that the Allies will be forced to intervene here" and "that the best and the most of Siberians would welcome it." Huntington report, 28 April 1918, f. 5, ibid.

186. Harper to C. Crane, 1 May [sic; 21 May] 1918, f. 6, ibid. Since the letter refers to Boyer's cablegram of 21 May, the file copy is obviously misdated.

187. Harper to R. Crane, 30 May 1918, f. 8, box 5, Harper Papers, UC.

188. Harper to Mott, 2 July 1918, f. 11, box 5, Harper Papers, UC.

189. Kennan to Lansing, 26 May 1918, enclosure in Lansing to Wilson, 28 May 1918, *PWW* 48:185. To his wife, Kennan wrote that he had sent to Lansing a long letter "about the Russian situation and the necessity of doing something to help overthrow the Bolsheviks and to prevent the Germans from getting economic, if not military, domination in Siberia. It is a pretty solid letter and I hope that it will make some impression on him." Kennan to wife, n.d., box 15, Kennan Papers, MD, LC.

190. Ibid.; also in box 8 (Letters sent), Kennan Papers, MD, LC.

Lansing immediately informed Kennan that he would present his communication to Wilson, but he voiced some reservations:

> I have read the letter with special interest because it comes from the highest authority in America on Russia. . . . I am not so sure of the wisdom of intervention in Siberia but I can assure you that the subject is receiving very careful consideration.[191]

A serious problem, he noted, was the lack of shipping in the Pacific. What Kennan clearly had in mind, however, was a stabilization of eastern (Trans-Baikal) Siberia, with no Allied forces to be committed farther west than Irkutsk.

President Wilson continued to resist various prods toward a major military intervention. In remarks to Mexican newsmen on 7 June, he seemed to recant the interpretation that had been put on his "stand by Russia" remark and indicated his amazement at its popularity:

> We cannot make anything out of our standing by Russia at this time—the remotest of European nations, so far as we are concerned, the one with which we have had the least connections in trade and advantage—and yet the people of the United States rose to that suggestion as to no other that I made in that address.[192]

At the same time he had already approved the sending of troops to north Russia.

Elihu Root, who had earlier urged funding for a massive propaganda campaign, was one of a number of influential political figures who moved toward favoring military intervention in June, but he believed that first it should be known "what specific concrete things can they and will they do towards the organization of an Army and towards uniting patriotic elements?"

> When that point is reached (and I hope it has now been reached) the course of the Allies seems to me quite clear to send Allied forces into Siberia to form a firm and indissoluble nucleus around which a Russian force could be gathered to furnish supplies to that force. . . .
>
> I have very great hope that the opportunity for the Allies to follow such a course is here, or nearly here, and I hope they will avail themselves of the opportunity promptly and effectively.[193]

191. Lansing to Kennan, 28 May 1918, vol. 35, Lansing Papers, MD, LC.
192. PWW 48:257; printed in New York World, 11 June 1918.
193. Root to Russell, 26 June 1918, vol. 9, Russell Papers, MD, LC.

From London, Russell sent the president on 21 June a copy of a memorial, "To all British friends of Russia: A Clear Call," which argued that Russia alone could not suppress anarchy. The "call" emphasized that "intervention be not Japanese-Chinese intervention, but be strictly an inter-allied enterprise, that this be so is of paramount importance."[194] It was signed by a number of prominent British correspondents and politicians and by leading Russian exiles. Apparently, Wilson received and read the memorial around 1 July, since he replied to Russell on 3 July, "I have read it with great interest and am trying hard to think out a practicable method of assisting Russia."[195]

The anti-intervention forces were still quite strong and vocal and cut across party lines. The grounds for opposition were varied but centered on the view that working with the Bolsheviks was a better alternative in meeting the German threat, opposition to dispersion of military forces away from winning the war on the Western Front, and reluctance to allowing Japan a strong foothold in Siberia. Unfortunately for the nonintervention cause, some of the most active spokesmen, such as Boyce Thompson, were dismissed by many as cranks. In the interval Thomas Thacher carried the ball with the pamphlet "Russia and the War," which argued that the Allies could oppose Germany in Russia most effectively by working with the Soviet government and that any direct intervention would antagonize not only the government but also the Russian people in general.[196] Although its distribution in early June was openly financed by Thompson, it received due respect as a strong statement for an alternative course that would include the sending of a high-level economic aid commission to Russia.[197] Thacher also corresponded with influential newspapermen, such as William Allen White, in an effort to get them to withhold any support for intervention until Robins's return.[198]

After traveling the long, tiresome journey across Siberia and the Pacific, Robins reached Seattle on 19 June and, after a brief rest at home and meeting with Thompson in Chicago, entered the Washington fray for an interview on 26 June with Lansing, who put him off in the usual way by requesting a statement in writing. Although the president had already decided not to see Robins, he was

194. Russell to Wilson, 20 June 1918, *PWW* 48:375–76; quotation from copy in vol. 9, Russell Papers, MD, LC.
195. Wilson to Russell, 3 July 1918, vol. 9, Russell Papers, MD, LC.
196. A copy, dated 4 June 1918, is in f. 4 (Schossberg-Trachtenberg), box 1, Rand School Papers, MD, NYPL.
197. Harper to Lippmann, 11 June, and Lippmann to Harper, 12 June 1918, f. 9, box 5, Harper Papers, UC.
198. Thacher to White, 12 June 1918, box C47, White Papers, MD, LC.

impressed with his written observations, duly forwarded by Lansing. Robins stressed that any intervention must be welcomed by the masses of Russians and coupled with economic cooperation and assistance. The president thought these ideas were "much more sensible than I thought the author of them capable of. I differ from them only in practical details."[199]

Although the Bolshevik-leaning Robins-Thompson-Reed group might be dismissed by many in Washington as cranks, Norman Hapgood remained a respected voice of Wilsonian internationalism. On 21 June he wrote to Ray Stannard Baker in London, "From this end, diplomatically, Russia is the big problem. The danger is that nervousness, private interests, and material national interests may bring about Japanese intervention (disguised as joint allied intervention). If so, goodbye!"[200] In general, however, the anti-intervention forces were on the defensive and disrupted by government interference. Bessie Beatty cited several instances of having her mail and telegrams delayed or undelivered.[201] Others weighed in too late. Lincoln Colcord, another Wilsonian internationalist, forcefully insisted to the president on 7 July: "If the allies intervene in Russia in support of any counter-revolution whatsoever, there will be a wrong peace compacted with the imperial German Government this fall, and Russia will be the spoils of the world. If America cannot stop them now, she cannot stop them then."[202]

Wilson had made a commitment to intervention the day before. An even stronger pro-Soviet, anti-intervention missive to the president came on 11 July from Wisconsin sociologist Edward Ross through Charles Crane.[203] These late efforts to head off intervention may have contributed to the hesitation that was so evident in July.

A variety of factors were pressing for concrete military action in Russia by the end of June, chief among them being the addition of Landfield and Wright to what could now be truly designated a Russian Bureau in the State Department, the influence of the Allies, new input from Russian sources such as Konovalov, Korff, and Bochkareva, and a sense of fait accompli. John Caldwell cabled from Vladivostok on 29 June that with a Bolshevik takeover imminent, more Japanese and British marines had landed, with the addition this time of twenty Americans to protect the consulate. The real force for maintaining order, however, was several thousand Czecho-Slovaks. This was confirmed a few days later

199. Wilson to Lansing, 3 July 1918, *PWW* 48:489.
200. Hapgood to Baker, 21 June 1918, reel 29, Baker Papers, MD, LC.
201. Beatty to Robins, 22 June 1918, f. June 1918, box 14, Robins Papers, SHSW.
202. *PWW* 48:547; copy also in f. July/August 1918, box 14, Robins Papers, SHSW.
203. Ross memorandum, "Notes on Methods of Helping Russia," and Wilson to Crane, 11 July 1918, *PWW* 48:570–73, 590.

by Admiral Knight, with the added note that their presence was welcomed by the population.[204] And from Vologda by direct cable came another plea for action from Francis: "Russian people confidently expecting Allied intervention and will welcome it. . . . Their patriotic pride is touched and they are becoming sensitive concerning Russia's position among nations."[205]

The Allied War Council in Paris, receiving similar information, committed itself to a large-scale intervention in Siberia, but the parameters and details were not yet forthcoming. As reported by the American military observer General Tasker Bliss, the discussion was vague and contradictory, mentioning in one place the need for 100,000, in another for 600,000 men, the great bulk of which were to be Japanese, but the terminology of "considerable" forces was changed to "adequate" forces, so as not to alarm Washington.[206] Coupling a Siberian expedition with the arrival of 100 American divisions in France by August 1919 seemed to remove any sense of urgency, or at least so it could be interpreted in Washington.[207] But the intent was that some forces should be sent "immediately."

The Czecho-Slovak Legion

A large number of Czech and Slovak deserters and prisoners of war from the Austro-Hungarian army, as many as 80,000 to 90,000, had been constituted into regiments to fight with the Russian army on the Eastern Front, as the shortest and easiest route to the liberation of their homeland. Thanks to Thomas Masaryk, the influential promoter of an independent Czechoslovakia, and his friend and supporter Charles Crane, these forces received much attention and sympathy in the United States. The Allies hoped they would be key to the maintainance of the Eastern Front in 1917, and late that year plans were afoot to combine them with remnants of the Russian army in the Don region. The failure of that movement to develop and the signing of the Treaty of Brest-Litovsk formally ending Russia's war left this sizable and capable army stranded in Russia. Always in

204. Caldwell report, 29 June, and Knight report to Secretary of Navy, 3 July 1918, f. Knight reports, box 613, WA-6, RG 45, NA. A note indicates that copies of all these reports go to the president.

205. Francis to Lansing, 22 June 1918, reel 8, Francis Papers, MoHS.

206. Bliss report of 2 July 1918, enclosed in March to Wilson, 3 July 1918, *PWW* 48:503-6.

207. For an interpretation that the United States rejected the Allied proposal for an expeditionary force of 600,000 and thus condemned Russia to seventy-five years of disaster under communism, see Fic, *The Collapse of American Policy*, 130 and passim.

need of more troops for the Western Front, the Allies now decided to bring them out of Russia to that area.

Two similar "armies" of 18,000 Serbs and Croats had already left Russia to join the bulk of the Serbian army deployed on the Salonika Front, the first by way of Archangel in 1917 and the other through Siberia. The latter passed along the Trans-Siberian Railroad without incident during the winter of 1917-18 and embarked at Port Arthur. It reached Greece by March 1918 and played a key role in the successful late summer offensive against the Turks, Bulgarians, and Austro-Hungarians.[208]

The Czechs and Slovaks would have a different fate for several reasons. First, they represented the only substantial armed force of what was expected to be a new, independent, democratic state, especially after the collapse of secret French-Austro-Hungarian negotiations in April. Second, they had taken advantage of the disintegration of most of the Russian army to become "armed to the teeth" with weapons that, it could be argued, did not belong to them. Third, indecision and wavering on the part of both Bolsheviks and Allies on the route of evacuation caused delays, confusion, and conflict. Going north through Archangel would clearly be the shortest way west, but the port would not be open until June, and transport was scarce and needed for other Allied and Bolshevik purposes; it could also disrupt the ongoing Soviet extrication of military supplies from there.

The Czecho-Slovak problem in Russia was further complicated by logistics (transport and basic support) and by politics (subordination to the Czecho-Slovak National Council). Finally, by May both the Entente and the Central Powers saw reason to keep the Czecho-Slovaks in Russia, the first to assist the formation of a loyal (anti-Bolshevik) Russian force in Siberia or elsewhere to depose the Bolsheviks, the latter to forestall their deployment on the Western Front.[209]

American Decision to Intervene

In the middle of June, pressure mounted further on the president to commit armed forces to Russia, mainly from the French and British military missions acting in consort. Both General George Tom Molesworth Bridges and General

---

208. See Alan Palmer, *The Gardeners of Salonika: The Macedonian Campaign, 1915–1918* (London: Andre Deutsch, 1965), 172ff.

209. For more details and expert analysis, see Betty Miller Unterberger, *The United States, Revolutionary Russia, and the Rise of Czechoslovakia* (Chapel Hill: University of North Carolina Press, 1989).

Henri Berthelot were bolstered by fresh reinforcements: Colonel Maitland Edwards, formerly of the British military mission in Russia; Marcel Delanney, the new French ambassador to Japan, bringing a special message from Clemenceau; and Henri Bergson as a special agent of the French foreign ministry. Berthelot and Delanney, accompanied by Ambassador Jusserand, saw the president on 17 June. They argued the case for an expeditionary force of 30,000 Americans, 60,000 Japanese, and small British and French contingents, to deny the food and other resources of Siberia, including the Urals, to the Germans.[210] The president was also swayed by a cable from Paul Reinsch, his ambassador in China, that the Czech forces should be kept in Siberia: "With only slight countenance and support they could control all of Siberia against the Germans. They are sympathetic to the Russian population, eager to be accessories to the allied cause."[211]

At the behest of Charles Crane, Wilson saw Thomas Masaryk late the next day to discuss this proposal and seek his cooperation. Admitting that he had only vague details about intervention plans, the Czech leader told the president that he thought at least a million men would be needed and that the Japanese would have to be paid, not only for their expenses but also with territory.[212] Moreover, the president still had to contend with strong voices of opposition to intervention within the administration, chiefly Secretary of War Baker, because of his belief that a large force would ultimately be required and that would necessarily draw away from the primary commitment to the Western Front, because of its cost and the likelihood of failure.[213] Bergson countered with a persuasive interview on 26 June, dismissing the idea that Japan would seek territory and emphasizing that the key to the control of Siberia, as the Czechs had shown, was the Trans-Siberian.[214]

---

210. Bridges to Lord Reading, 18 June 1918, *PWW* 48:352–54, and n. 3, 354. Bridges had dined with the Jusserands that evening. Jusserand to Foreign Ministry, n.d. (received 18 June), ibid., 355–56.

211. Enclosure, dated Peking 13 June, in Wilson to Lansing, 17 June 1918, in which the president saw a "shadow of a plan that might be worked." *PWW* 48:335.

212. Wilson to Crane, 11 June 1918, *PWW* 48:283; and to Lansing, 19 June 1918, ibid., 358; Victor S. Mamatey, *The United States and East Central Europe, 1914–1918: A Study in Wilsonian Diplomacy and Propaganda* (Princeton, N.J.: Princeton University Press, 1957), 285–86. The British and French certainly erred in not attempting to inform and convince Masaryk of their plans.

213. Baker was still open to discussion at this time. "Colonel Edwards was sent for by Mr. Baker . . . and had a long conversation on conditions in Russia and Mr. Baker appeared much interested and said he was going to send for him again." Bridges to Lord Reading, 18 June 1918, ibid., 354.

214. Bergson to Pinchot, 26 June 1918, *PWW* 48:441–43.

Conversations about Russia filled lunch, tea, and dinner conversations around Washington in June, partly due to the presence of Bergson, Edwards, Bridges, and others with Russian intervention on their agenda.[215] A special center of attention was Colonel Maria Bochkareva, former commander of the women's battalion of death, who arrived in Washington on 23 June, having toured the country with much fanfare. She and her interpreter stayed with Florence Harriman, who was active in various Washington organizations, such as the Red Cross, and was a personal friend of the president. Mrs. Harriman took her to the surgeon general to have some war wounds inspected and arranged an interview with the president.

The situation regarding the disposition of the Czecho-Slovak military units in Siberia was an important factor that committed the United States to military intervention in the Far East. Behind this was the hope that they could rally loyal Russian forces to the cause. The final decision came on Saturday afternoon, 6 July, at a conference of President Wilson with Lansing, Baker, Secretary of Navy Daniels, Chief of Staff Peyton March, and Admiral William Benson (chief of naval operations).[216] Breckinridge Long, away on vacation since late June, was informed a few days later by his secretary that

> it was decided that in view of present—and apparently future—conditions in Russia we are to send 7,000 troops; Japan is to send a like number, and France and England are to send as many as possible. These armed forces are to be sent to Vladivostok to protect the supplies and communications and give aid to the Czecho-Slovaks.[217]

Colonel Bochkareva may have placed a seal on this determination a few days later (late afternoon of 10 July) in an emotional interview with the president, during which she fell to her knees before him while pleading for assistance and brought him to tears.[218] Florence Harriman described the scene as she remembered hearing about it immediately afterward:

215. Harriman, *From Pinafores to Politics,* 278–81.
216. Lansing memorandum, 6 July 1918, *PWW* 48:542–43.
217. Mildred Cunningham to Long, 10 July 1918, box 32, Long Papers, MD, LC.
218. Landfield to Long, 13 July 1918, Box 38, Long Papers, MD, LC. Landfield quoted her as saying:

> You know, Mr. President, that Russia was a great and brave country. When the revolution came we all rejoiced. . . . Now they realize they have been fooled and that Russia has been dragged in the dirt. All they ask is an opportunity to redeem themselves and they will fight to the last drop of blood for their native land, and they will fight

Maria Bochkareva and "fellow" soldier. From Thompson, Blood Stained Russia

The Batchkarova [*sic*] interview was intensely dramatic. Beside her own interpreter, there was another one from the State Department [Landfield] to check up. Batchkarova started off her story in a fairly matter-of-fact way; then suddenly she began to tell the tale of the sufferings of her people and her tongue went like a runaway horse. She would hardly wait for her interpreter

---

with understanding. But there is no one to lead them, for they are afraid of parties and partisans and the Soviets have ruined the country. Therefore they appeal to you for military aid. If the Allies will come, even with a small force, with the Americans in the lead, they will flock around them by the hundreds of thousands. They are only waiting for this to form a great army with iron discipline.

Harper, however, resented the fact that "the chief" would not see him but saw a woman colonel, "who could give him some of the atmosphere, which is important, but not much more." To Mott, 30 July 1918, f. 14, box 5, Harper Papers, UC.

to put what she was saying into English. Her face worked. Suddenly she threw herself on the floor and clasped her arms about the President's knees begging him for help, for food, for troops to intervene against the Bolsheviki. The President sat with tears streaming down his cheeks, and assured her of his sympathy. The little party finally got away from the White House, all very much shaken.[219]

Russians would welcome especially an American presence, she insisted. In fact, the president was already aware of the thrust of Bochkareva's appeal and had discussed it with the French ambassador.[220] So from Vladivostok directly and from Bochkareva personally, the president seemed to have received the invitation from the Russian people that he was waiting for.

Coincidentally, Austin Knight took the initiative in Vladivostok to organize an Allied command over the city that was instituted formally on 6 July with the following proclamation:

This action is taken in sympathetic friendship for the Russian people without reference to any political faction or party and in the hope that the period of tranquility which will result may permit the reconciling of all factions and their cooperation in a harmonious and patriotic effort for the establishment of a stable and permanent government and for throwing off the yoke of tyrannical dictation which the Austro-German Powers are endeavoring to fasten permanently upon the Russian people.[221]

With Lansing and Long on vacation, Frank Polk and Landfield ironed out the details of intervention during July, with the only significant change being to allow Japan an unspecified larger share on the insistence of the Japanese ambassador that "the Japanese people would view it [the 7,000 limit] as lack of confidence."[222] Kukujiro Ishii assured the State Department that only one division

219. Harriman, *From Pinafores to Politics*, 280–81. Bochkareva left suddenly for Russia in mid-July, leaving behind her fifteen-year-old sister in Mrs. Harriman's care.

220. Jusserand to Wilson, 30 June 1918, and Wilson to Jusserand, 1 July 1918, *PWW* 48:469, 473.

221. Logbook, USS *Brooklyn*, 6 July 1918, RG 24, NA. In the list of signatures to the proclamation, Knight's name came first.

Consul Caldwell noted with some humor that local Red Guards had interpreted the decking out of the *Brooklyn* on the Fourth of July as a demonstration on their behalf. Caldwell to Roland Morris, 7 July 1918, box 3, Morris Papers, MD, LC.

222. Polk to Lansing, 24 July 1918, vol. 37, Lansing Papers, MD, LC.

on a peace footing was planned, "in order to create the proper impression on the Russian mind."[223] Lansing agreed but thought it was especially unfortunate that Britain and France were also sending troops. "The participation of those two Governments will give the enterprise the character of interference with the domestic affairs of Russia and create the impression that the underlying purpose is to set up a new pro-Ally Government in Siberia if not in Russia."[224] In a document dated 11 July, apparently intended as a policy announcement, Landfield listed three reasons for intervention: (1) to assist Czecho-Slovaks; (2) because Bolshevik weakness threatens to produce a German occupation; and (3) to win the war in 1919.[225] Unstated but obviously a factor was an opportunity to take advantage of "Bolshevik weakness" to establish a more congenial political environment in Russia.

The 7,000-troop commitment to Siberia was based on calculations on what manpower could be spared, transport and support facilities, and the reluctance of Baker and March to send even that many. No objections were raised by any of the Washington pro-interventionists, such as Landfield, that this was inadequate or that a much larger diversion of forces to Siberia was essential.[226] No one thought about preparing supplies for a larger force; it seemed to be thought of as something of an experiment. Nor did there seem to be any rush to effect the new policy. An "aide memoire" announcing the American policy to Allied representatives appeared only on 17 July.

Another major reason for not considering a larger force was the state of railroads in the region. The Russian Railway Service Corps sent by the United States had encountered endless difficulties and obstacles. Russians opposed the reorganization of lines for more efficient operations in February, Chinese workers were striking in March, and Emerson was still in the stage of initial negotiations in April.[227] An officer in the War College Division recommended that no work be done on the Trans-Siberian because it would be too costly in salaries to en-

223. Polk to Morris (Tokyo), 27 July 1918, copy in box 187 "Siberia," Long Papers, MD, LC.
224. Lansing to Polk, 3 August 1918, ibid.
225. "Allied Intervention in Siberia and Russia," 11 July 1918, f. 10, box 706, WA-6, RG 45, NA.
226. In a separate memorandum, dated July 1918, found in the files of the chief of naval operations, Landfield made this clear: "An expedition of moderate size is better than a very large expedition. If the Russian soldiers rally and form an army, intervention is feasible; if they do not do so, no form of intervention will avail. The consensus of testimony at the present is that they will." Box 606, WA-6, RG 45, NA.
227. Emerson reports from Harbin, 23 February, 14 March, and 28 March 1918, box 1, Emerson Papers, HIA.

gineers and too dangerous, unless the line was guarded by a large inter-Allied force.[228]

Most discouraging of all was the situation in Vladivostok, where labor unrest was the worst. In May, Emerson lamented to Stevens that the assembling of locomotives shipped from America seemed impossible and that the repair shops that normally employed 3,500 workers now had only 800 and might be capable of repairing, at most, twenty-four locomotives in a year, instead of that number in a month as before. "Personally I am satisfied that nothing can be done on the Chinese Eastern Railway as the powers in control are not at all in sympathy with our mission."[229]

Hiatus

In retrospect the meeting of 6 July marks a turning point in the direction of intervention, but at the time it did not seem so, and perhaps was not even in the president's mind. First of all, the "decision" to send troops to Siberia was not announced publicly, and some of those who did know remained skeptical. Samuel Harper, who was in and out of Washington in June and July and saw a variety of officials, gained the impression that the president was on the verge of a decision at the beginning of the month but that everything was still in suspense, that the president was still considering recognition of the Soviet government, three weeks later.[230] On 20 July, Chapell Porter aptly observed:

> Anxious waiting seems to be the chief occupation of many of those who are interested in Russia just at present. . . . For our [American Russian Chamber of Commerce] we are emphasizing, where ever it is possible, the fact that the first step in any procedure is to secure a high-class committee of four or five real organizers directly responsible to the President

228. Colonel D. W. Ketcham memorandum summary, 26 April 1918, box 13, record cards, RG 165, NA. Many papers of this period were destroyed, with only file card notations remaining.

229. Emerson (Vladivostok) to Stevens, 9 May 1918, ibid. His engineer colleague, Benjamin Johnson, painted an even more depressing picture in retropect. "The Trans-Siberian Railway," *Journal of the Worcester Polytechnic Institute* 26, no. 4 (July 1923): 179–85, in Johnson Papers, HIA.

230. Harper to Tyrkova-Williams, 2 July, f. 11, and Harper to Graham Taylor, 14 July, and to Mott, 15 July 1918, f. 12, box 5, Harper Papers, UC.

with full authority to go ahead and work out the details of the plan but we have received no definite word of any fulfillment of this suggestion.[231]

Another Commission for Russia?

During all the debate pro and con, action and inaction, regarding intervention, an idea of the League to Aid and Cooperate of sending a commission to Russia remained on the agenda. Colonel House sounded out Norman Hapgood in mid-June about sending Herbert Hoover at the head of a "Russian Relief Commission, . . . and let him take charge of the Russian situation for the time being." He asked him to keep this confidential because no one knew of the plan except the president, Lansing, and Hoover.[232] Two weeks later, House reported that the president still had this under advisement:

> The Russian situation is so confused that it is hard to come to a satisfying conclusion. The advice that one gets from those directly from Russia is absolutely contradictory. . . .
> I am quite clear, however, if Hoover is sent in the right way, there are more chances for a successful outcome than in any other plan that has been suggested. There is some danger of the situation slipping out of the President's hands and this I would regard as most unfortunate.[233]

Through July, discussion continued about who might be involved in a commission. John Mott, who saw the president three times early that month, believed he was seriously considering this project, perhaps as a kind of carrot to go along with the stick of military intervention, or as yet an alternative policy.[234]

---

231. Porter to Harper, 20 July 1918, box 5, Harper Papers, UC. Senator Hiram Johnson repeated this refrain to Robins: "I am waiting anxiously to see what the decision of the President is regarding Russia. I have about reached the conclusion that his decision will be like most decisions that have been rendered by him and by our Allies—too late." To Raymond Robins, 24 July 1918, f. July–August 1918, Robins Papers, SHSW.
232. House to Hapgood, 15 June 1918, f. Edward House, box 9, Hapgood-Reynolds Papers, MD, LC. As usual in Washington, few secrets were really kept. British agent Sir William Wiseman knew all about it and approved of it, because Hoover "knows Siberia, having spent some time there as an engineer." "The president would, I think be very largely guided by Hoover's advice, and if he told the U. S. G. armed intervention (even mainly Japanese) would be acceptable to the Russian people, the President would probably support the proposal." Wiseman to Sir Eric Drummond, 14 June 1918, *PWW* 48:316.
233. House to Hapgood, 29 June 1918, ibid.
234. Mott (Quebec) to Harper, 17 July 1918, f. 12, box 5, Harper Papers, UC.

Mott recommended that Secretary of Interior Franklin Lane head the delegation, while Charles Crane suggested Mott himself. Both felt Wilson was still taking his time before acting on Russia.[235] Harper suggested John Stevens as leader, with the inclusion of Justice Brandeis and Butler Wright, "the most energetic and authoritative person on the Russian problem,"[236] but he advised against including Thompson, who had "used himself up," or Francis. He added that it was "too bad we do not have an Arthur Henderson."[237]

Many who were puzzled about Washington's inaction feared that Raymond Robins had finally won over the president and might yet take charge of American policy toward Russia. Korff attributed the delay to "Brandeis and his small group of Jews," influenced by the Robins clique. He wrote to Kennan, "You cannot imagine how much harm these men have done to Russia with their obnoxious propaganda for the Bolsheviki."[238] Frederick Corse strongly seconded this opinion:

> I saw how the leaders of this government, the chosen representatives of the Soviets, repudiated the public debt, wrecked the private banks, concluded the treaty of peace with the Allies' enemies, and prevented with bloodshed the meeting of the Constituent Assembly. I saw, in that four months' time, all the machinery of civilized life broken down.[239]

At the end of the month, a mood of drift and hesitation still prevailed. Charles Crane saw an advantage in doing nothing and advised the president "to be as steady and as patient as you have been with Mexico."[240] But George Kennan expressed frustration from his summer home in Nova Scotia that his recommendation in May had resulted in so little "for aiding the sane and patriotic Russians there in their fight against the Bolsheviks and the Germans."[241] Even

235. Crane to Wilson, 23 July, and Mott to Wilson, 24 July 1918, PWW 48:62–63, 77–79; Mott draft in f. 1762, box 75, Mott Papers, DSA.

236. Harper to Charles Crane, 17 July 1918, f. 13, box 5, Harper Papers, UC.

237. Harper to Mott, 23 July 1918, ibid. Harper may also have convinced McCormick, who had influence in the Red Cross: "I believe it would be most unfortunate for Mr. Thompson to be chosen for such work as this." McCormick to Henry Davison, 29 July 1918, f. Crane, box 116, 2C, McC (McCormick Papers), SHSW.

238. Korff to Kennan, 19 July 1918, box 1, Kennan Papers, MD, NYPL.

239. Corse to Alexander Legge, 20 July 1918 (c), f. Corse, 2C, box 115, McCormick Papers, SHSW. Legge was on leave from his post as managing director of International Harvester to help direct the mobilization of the economy in Washington.

240. Crane to Wilson, 1 August 1918, PWW 49:154.

241. Kennan to Joseph Price, 5 August 1918, enclosed in Kennan to Lansing, 6 August 1917 [sic; 1918], vol. 37, Lansing Papers, MD, LC.

Admiral Knight on the *Brooklyn* was in the dark, writing on 31 July that if American troops are to be sent it ought to be soon: "If it is true that Allied Forces other than eight hundred British are to be sent here, it is urged that they arrive at earliest possible date."[242]

Finally, exactly four weeks after the "decision" of 6 July, on 3 August Major General William Graves, who had just taken charge of the Eighth Infantry Division in training at Palo Alto, California, was summoned to Kansas City to meet with Secretary Baker.[243] There he was handed the aide-mémoire, dated 17 July, that had been typed by the president himself for distribution to the Washington diplomatic corps. It spelled out the parameters of his new mission:

> For helping the Czecho-Slovaks there is immediate necessity and sufficient justification. . . .
>
> It [the U.S. government] hopes to carry out the plans for safeguarding the rear of the Czecho-Slovaks operating from Vladivostok in a way that will place it and keep it in close cooperation with a small military force like its own from Japan, and if necessary from the other Allies, and that will assure it of the cordial accord of all the allied powers.[244]

But the document also specified a duty "to guard military stores which may subsequently be needed by Russian forces."

The ambiguity of American policy in Russia was also evident, because the aide-mémoire insisted that this was not military intervention:

> It is the clear and fixed judgment of the Government of the United States, arrived at after repeated and very searching reconsiderations of the whole situation in Russia, that military intervention there would add to the present sad confusion in Russia rather than cure it, injure her rather than help her, and that it would be of no advantage in the prosecution of our main design, to win the war against Germany.[245]

What had caused the sudden action in early August was the announcement by Ambassador Ishii on Saturday morning, 3 August (to the disgust of many in Washington, emergencies often came on the weekends), of the Japanese land-

---

242. Knight report to CNO, USS *Brooklyn*, 31 July 1918, box 613, WA-6, RG 45, NA.
243. Graves remembers the date as 2 August but probably is in error in light of below.
244. William S. Graves, *America's Siberian Adventure, 1918–1920* (New York: Jonathan Cape and Harrison Smith, 1931), 8-9.
245. Ibid., 7.

ing at Vladivostok of a substantial force, now estimated at 12,000, rather than the 7,000 initially anticipated. Wilson, clearly upset and indignant, went immediately to the State Department to confer with Polk (in Lansing's absence) and Baker. Phillips recorded in his diary:

> Ishii brought a copy of the announcement this morning; but just previous Japanese troops were sent to Siberia. We do not know how many—probably about 12,000. The Japanese have moved in circles all around us. They have beaten us out everywhere. Not only have they secured our consent to a Japanese command, but their troops have entered Siberia before ours even began to move. This is not the way it should have been—in fact it is just the opposite of the way the President intended it. The result of indecision and playing the lone hand![246]

Polk should have noted that the Japanese were as mystified as some Americans about Washington's inaction. At any rate, the panic button was hit, and hasty preparations were immediately under way to get American troops on the scene in Siberia. The United States was going much farther "over there" than had been anticipated when it entered the war.

Preventive Maintenance

In the meantime, another, more secretive kind of intervention was winding up. A high-priority task for the American staff in Russia just before and all during the Vologda days was the securing of Russian strategic metals and other supplies that might fall into German hands through direct seizure, through purchase by third (mainly Swedish) parties, or by agreement with the Soviet government. The immediate concern was the Petrograd area, where a variety of independent agents were at work, mostly with the aim of selling goods in demand to hard-pressed Germany at considerable profit. A hastily organized Inter-Allied Trade Board, an Anglo-Franco-American coordinating group, backed mainly by American money with at least $1 million funneled through New York City Bank offices in March and April, managed to obtain a large quantity of nickel, copper, platinum, furs, sunflower seed oil, food stocks, and so on, and ship them to safer points inland or abroad.[247] Major Henry Emery, special military agent, and R. R.

---

246. Phillips diary, 3 August 1918, *PWW* 49:178.

247. Tredwell to State, 20 February 1918, DPR Petrograd consulate 1918, box 2, RG 84, NA; Huntington to Francis, 17 May 1918, DPR 314, ibid.

Stevens, head of the New York City Bank branch in Russia, were the key facilitators of the initial operation.[248]

Details are obscure in regard to how much was expended or how much of what was purchased or remained more safely in Soviet hands. Nor is it clear how much money was paid to Soviet authorities, either individually or collectively in the process. A June list compiled by Imbrie cited the removal by waterways from Petrograd of 500,000 *pud* of copper, 36,000 of lead, 35,000 of nickel, 20,000 of high-quality steel, 13,000 of raw rubber, and 28,000 of telephone wire, as well as 20,000 cartridge cases, 3 million aluminum cartridge caps, and a number of field and naval guns, much of which probably ended up in Soviet hands. The Putilov combination of enterprises, the largest in the city, was reported to be entirely stripped.[249]

In June, Allied purchases increased considerably, now centralized under Francis's control with Huntington directing. Another $5 million was authorizied and expended. At least one carload of platinum (at $104 an ounce) was purchased with the permission of the Soviet government and safely escorted across Siberia and eventually to the United States. As Huntington noted, for the Bolsheviks this was "an excellent opportunity for obtaining large sums of money, which they need, as well as much personal graft."[250]

The main purpose, preventing a wholesale acquisition by Germany of Russian materials, was apparently successful, though the operation probably aggravated the already precarious situation of Petrograd's food and fuel supply and manufacturing capability.[251] The illness of the ambassador in April, disruptions in May, such as the death of Maddin Summers, who played a key role in directing the effort, and exhaustion of funds caused problems in the continuity of operations. Another difficulty was that freight cars were becoming scarcer by the week. Norman Armour tried to bring in 500,000 pairs of shoes from the Far East in June to facilitate obtaining rolling stock. "They would prove most useful in oiling the wheels in getting the wagons."[252]

248. Tredwell to Lansing, 20 February 1918, box 2, Petrograd consulate, RG 84, NA, thanking him for the million-dollar credit.

249. Imbrie to Poole, 15 June 1918, DPR, Petrograd consulate, box 4 (letters to consul general), RG 84, NA.

250. Huntington (Moscow) to Francis, 20 June 1918, AE Russia 1918, DPR 314, RG 84, NA. Arthur Bullard, however, thought that the Left Socialist Revolutionaries were involved in the platinum deal—in order to purchase arms. Bullard, "Dealing with the Bolsheviks," June 1918, box 6, Bullard Papers, Princeton-Mudd.

251. Lieutenant Bukowski summed up the operation as preventing crucial supplies from going to Germany during the late spring and summer of 1918. Bukowski to Ruggles, 5 October 1918, box 41, Riggs Papers, BA, CU.

252. Armour to Imbrie, 15 May 1918 (confidential), Petrograd Consulate, box 4, RG 84, NA.

From the records available it appears that much of the time of the American consular and military staff—Poole, Riggs, Armour, Ruggles, Huntington, and Imbrie—as well as local American business recruits was spent in bribing local officials, perhaps little more than normal for Russia. John Lehrs and Eugene Prince employed their skills and contacts, while Stevens of New York City Bank was in charge of credits and exchanges. Francis devoted much time to this matter during his visit to Moscow and turned up the operation a notch in mid-May by assigning two additional subordinates, Lieutenant Peter Bukovski and Frederick Mason, to Petrograd "to urge all possible haste in such evacuation."[253]

Petrograd was not the only point of concern, however. Francis authorized the purchase of 15,000 pud of glycerine at Rostov on Don, not because it was of any use to the Allies "but to prevent the glycerine from falling into the hands of the Germans who need it badly."[254] At the same time he was alarmed that some cooperation with local Soviet authorities was getting out of control, especially in the transportation of arms and other supplies from Archangel to Vologda and Moscow. The ambassador was also aware that any coordination with Soviet officials could be misconstrued and instructed Huntington as follows:

> While I wish Poole and yourself to maintain pleasant relations with the Soviet Government at the same time desire to caution you against placing yourselves under obligations to it or doing anything that can be construed as (by them) committing our government or myself to support or to non-intervention— of course I have never thought of recommending their recognition.[255]

Francis went to Petrograd himself in early June to promote the cause, but much of the real work in the field was done by Huntington (in charge of the operation after Summers's death) and freelance agent Xenophon Kalamatiano, a somewhat enigmatic person of Russian immigrant background with a degree from the University of Chicago, who had primary responsibility for southern Russia. All these agents, especially Kalamatiano, gathered information about conditions in and outside of Soviet-controlled Russia.[256] Much responsibility for coordination on the American side fell to Robert Imbrie, who colorfully described his office overlooking Nevsky Prospect on the sixth floor of the Singer building:

253. Francis to Imbrie, 15 May 1918, reel 9, Francis Papers, MoHS.
254. Francis to Summers, 1 May 1918, ibid.
255. Francis to Huntington, 20 May 1918, ibid.
256. Huntington noted, "Kalamatiano has been doing useful work in his quiet way and gathers much valuable information." To Francis, 17 May 1918, DPR 314 (Russia 1918), RG 84, NA.

The Consulate, thanks to the untiring efforts of the Embassy, Consulate General, the Red Cross, Dr. Simons, . . . and thirty as hopeless Americans as ever misused a passport, has managed to keep busy. The paper in my sanctuary has peeled off the wall in many places owing to the sulphuric language which this condition of affairs has compelled me to indulge in. Give me one month more and the furniture will be seared.[257]

Connected with this complex enterprise was a simultaneous effort to reduce German influence and control and win friends by providing food and other supplies. Some of this was being done through charitable auspices (such as the Red Cross, Society of Friends, and YMCA) without much regard for who were the actual beneficiaries.[258] The prevailing sentiment at the time, just before American troops would land in Russia, was that it was better to strengthen Bolsheviks than to let critical supplies fall into the hands of the Germans.

The Czecho-Slovak Revolt

Whatever arms and other supplies reached Moscow, the Bolshevik-led Soviet government did not appear to strengthen. In fact, it seemed to weaken. One demonstration of this was a series of incidents involving the Czecho-Slovak "legion" that by the end of May was scattered across Siberia in some sixty trains, tying up much of the rolling stock and other facilities of the Trans-Siberian Railroad. Spread out over thousands of miles, the Czechs naturally felt vulnerable and threatened, especially when the Bolsheviks tried to detain and disarm them.

Clashes occurred in late May and June between the Czech forces and those of local soviets that in some cases included former Austrian and German prisoners of war. The result of their superiority was that the Czechs quickly found themselves in temporary control of several key points along the rail line from Samara on the Volga, through Chelyabinsk in the Urals and Omsk, the largest city in western Siberia, to Irkutsk, and finally to Vladivostok. Their successes not only demonstrated Bolshevik weakness in the countryside but also raised Allied

257. Armour to Imbrie, 15 May 1918, and Imbrie to Taylor, 5 June 1918, DPR Petrograd Consulate 1918, box 4, RG 84, NA.
258. The Red Cross Commission, headed by Thompson, Robins, and then Allen Wardwell, dispensed $666,000 worth of aid up to 30 June 1918, mostly in the form of drugs and medical supplies ($283,000) and food ($294,000). Commission for Russia expense report, 30 June 1918, box 866, RG 200, NA.

hopes that they might form the nucleus of a new Russian opposition to the Bolsheviks that might overthrow the Soviet government or force it back into the war.

Moreover, the situation disrupted communications and other traffic through-out much of the former empire and placed in serious doubt the possibility of a Siberian escape route for the remaining Allied diplomats and agents. George Emerson, head of the American railway corps in Manchuria, tried to make his way through from Harbin to Vologda and failed. Spearheaded by a Czech ar-mored train, the American engineers, setting out from Harbin on 3 May, com-mandeered locomotives and repaired bridges blown up by retreating Bolshevik units as they went, a slow and laborious process considering the distance involved.[259]

Allied capitals awakened to a concern of danger to the Czechs from released prisoners of war and the need for greater assistance either to bolster them as an anti-Soviet force or to quickly rescue them for deployment on the Western Front. On the other side, the Bolshevik leadership was shocked by this display of their own weakness and vulnerability, while their German ally suddenly and belatedly was equally alarmed about a possible disintegration of Soviet power and a re-vival of an Eastern Front, at least by the spring of 1919.

Lacking instructions from Washington, Americans on the scene were in a quandary about what to say to Czechs seeking their advice. Ernest Harris, the consul general for Siberia, did his best to solve some of the local conflicts and achieve a working arrangement between Czechs and local soviets, but his efforts were resented by the Czechs for being pro-Soviet. From Moscow Poole suggested to the Czechs that they hold Samara, but then he reconsidered, thinking he had exceeded his authority and had not followed correct policy.[260]

Still, at the beginning of July in both the United States and Russia, a sense of drift, not immediate crisis, prevailed. The Fourth of July passed quite calmly. Francis, enjoying perhaps his last pleasant social occasion for some time, boasted proudly of accommodating over a hundred at the embassy reception in Vologda. Chicherin even remembered to send appropriate greetings for the occasion. In Moscow, the "Y" people organized festivities that highlighted a baseball game between them and a team made up from consulate, Red Cross, and International

259. Lansing to Francis, 8 May 1918, *DSAR* 1:53–54. Apparently intentionally, only minor damage was usually inflicted. The best description is in a letter of Benjamin Johnson to Walter Bradford (a friend in Montana), 28 July 1918, box 1, Johnson Papers, HIA.

260. Poole to Francis, 21 June 1918, reel 10, Francis Papers, MoHS.

YMCA/YWCA on summer holiday at the Usava dacha outside Moscow, June 1918. Sitting, from left to right: Maria Luboslinski, Anna Usava, Clara Taylor, Helen Ogden; standing: Mme. Usava, center, and to her left Olmstead, Crawford Wheeler, Donald Lowrie, Somerville, Penningroth, others unknown, courtesy of the Donald Lowrie Papers, University of Illinois Archives

Harvester men. One of them proudly noted that the evening featured "a real American supper," served by "a real American colored lady."[261]

But there were already signs of a storm brewing. On 27 June, John Lehrs, as an assistant to Poole in Moscow, had a very disagreeable encounter with Karl Radek in the Foreign Affairs Commissariat over permission for consular personnel to be armed, after which Poole thought it wise to send Lehrs out of town to Vologda.[262] At the same time, Chicherin dispatched Vosnesensky to Vologoda to annoy Francis for three days about what he knew about intervention.[263]

261. Donald Lowrie to Folks, 16 July 1918, f. 1918, July–Sept., box 1, Lowrie Papers, UIA.

262. Lehrs to Poole, 29 June 1918, and Poole to Francis, 1 July 1918, reel 9, Francis Papers, MoHS.

263. Francis to Poole, 1 July 1918, ibid.

Exit

While trying to find a way to save face and reestablish authority along the Trans-
Siberian, the Bolsheviks also were challenged at home in the center of the capital. The Left Socialist Revolutionaries, who had supported the seizure of power
in October and provided crucial support in the initial Soviet government, had
opposed the peace settlement at Brest-Litovsk and the growing Soviet connection with Germany. Although their popular appeal seemed to be growing as a
credible opposition party to the Bolsheviks, they faced more and more isolation
and removal from offices. The Left SRs, however, were still powerful in the growing state police force of the revolution, the Cheka. In this situation it is not
surprising that they reverted to the tactics of their direct antecedents, the terror-
ist wing of the prewar Socialist Revolutionary Party.

On 6 July, ironically on the very day of Wilson's intervention decision, Left
SRs successfully invaded the German embassy and assassinated the ambassador, Wilhelm von Mirbach. This created a sensation and virtual panic in the
capital, as the Bolsheviks immediately moved to suppress the opposition from
the left, which had organized an armed militia that also seized the Cheka headquarters. Trotsky quickly ordered recently formed and well-armed Red Army units
into action, and the short-lived rebellion was brought quickly to a close.

There was also a fear that German reaction would precipitate military action
and possible German occupation of the city. Although issuing a strong protest,
Germany wisely stayed clear of getting any deeper in the Russian mess. The atmosphere had definitely changed, however. Donald Lowrie, who was sitting in
his "Y" office around the corner when the bomb exploded, wrote home about
his relatively normal day-to-day life in Moscow: "Then came the murder of
Mirbach. . . . The trouble with the Czecho-Slovaks in the east is not yet finished,
and now there is a good deal of dissatisfaction on the part of the present government with the conduct of certain of the Allied military missions."[264]

An immediate problem that the embassy faced was reponse to an intensive
Soviet effort to get the embassy to move to Moscow, which Robins had earlier
recommended and supported.[265] On 11 July, Chicherin telegraphed the Allied
missions in Vologda that the Commissariat of Foreign Affairs "considers it
necessary that the Diplomatic Corps should move from Vologda to Moscow."
He explained crisply that they were no longer safe in Vologda. After consulting

264. Lowrie to Folks, 16 July 1918, box 1, Lowrie Papers, UIA.
265. Huntington to Francis, May 17, 1918, DPR, vol. 314 (Russia 1918), RG 84, NA.
Huntington saw Robins at the ballet in Moscow: "He said, 'Why can't you persuade the
Embassy to move down to Moscow? Its just as safe as Vologda.'"

with the other missions, Francis responded, "I am requested by them to ask you why you think our remaining in Vologda unsafe or inadvisable. We have no fear of the Russian People whom we have always befriended and whom we consider our Allies and we have full confidence in the population of Vologda."[266]

At the same time Francis complicated the matter by releasing the texts of both telegrams to the press and wiring the British commanders at Murmansk requesting an immediate occupation of Archangel.[267] Chicherin responded by sending the hotheaded Karl Radek to Vologda, who argued with Francis at length on the relative safety of Moscow and Vologda. Much of their conversation pertained to German prisoners of war, who Francis thought were guarding the German embassy and would pose a threat to any Allied diplomats in the capital. Radek responded that there were more in the vicinity of Vologda than in Moscow and insisted on a categorical answer to his demand that the embassy move to Moscow.[268]

When Francis still refused to budge, Radek ordered the local Cheka to guard the Allied missions and screen anyone arriving and departing for their own safety, which Francis protested was house arrest. The Soviet commissar responded that this was only for their own protection and assured Francis that a move to Moscow would not be interpreted as a change of policy—toward recognition.[269] Forced to return to Moscow on 17 July, Radek bade farewell more diplomatically by trying to blame the whole problem on the English landing of troops at Murmansk: "It is very disagreeable to us that your idyllic sojourn in Vologda has to lend its place to a more regulated mode of living, but war has made such regulations necessary also in your countries; as to us in Russia, we are in a continuous state of war on all fronts."[270]

The more Francis resisted, the more Soviet pressure was applied. As he reported on July 14, "I have just received a letter from Radek demanding a categorical reply whether we will go or not; that reply will be given tomorrow and of course will be a negative one."[271] But after Francis requested trains and prepared

266. Francis to Chicherin, 11 July 1918, reel 10, Francis Papers, MoHS.

267. Francis to Cole, 11 July 1918, ibid.

268. Francis to Imbrie (Petrograd), 14 July 1918, DPR Petrograd Consulate, box 4, RG 84, NA. Adding his own two cents worth to the July melee in Vologda was British agent Sidney Reilly, who was serving as courier between Petrograd and that city. Armour to Imbrie, 20 and 24 July 1918, ibid.

269. Record of interview of 13 July, and Radek to Francis, 14 and 15 July 1918, ibid.

270. Radek to Francis, 17 July 1918 (translated copy), reel 11, Francis Papers, MoHS. Radek also offered to forward any communications that Francis wished to send by wireless from Moscow.

271. Francis to Imbrie, 14 July 1918, DPR, Petrograd consulate 1918, box 4, RG 84, NA.

to depart for the north, Chicherin tried a much softer approach, arguing that Archangel was not a fit residence for an ambassador and that Moscow was "a city with splendid villas and peaceful gay suburbs, an appropriate abode which our government deliberately proposes to the Ambassador of friendly America. We must at any cost avoid the danger of your departure being misinterpreted in the eyes of our great masses and of American public opinion."[272]

News of the execution of the tsar reached Vologda on 20 July, followed immediately by the removal of several grand dukes from confinement in Vologda. This development may have been decisive in the decision to evacuate the city, but while most of the missions hurriedly boarded trains, Francis dallied at his residence for a few more games of poker, much to the chagrin of the French, who were left to face a nasty encounter with Red Guards.[273] Finally, on the evening of the twenty-fourth, one very long train, containing the several missions, an immense amount of baggage, and a carload of Red Guards for "protection," headed north out of Vologda.[274] Francis and most of his remaining staff were already aboard a train by the twenty-fifth, facing one remaining obstacle—the lack of a locomotive. Chicherin finally and personally provided one along with one last message hoping that it would head south rather than north.

Once the direction of the train was known, Chicherin still hoped to appease the Allied missions and provided Poole with radio access and a personal message to send out: "He then requested me to inform American Government that insistence upon removal of the Ambassador to Moscow results from circumstances not within control of Soviets, that is, impending White Guard rising at Vologda . . . and hopes that the American Government will not regard this as affecting friendly relations."[275]

Soviet defeat on this issue was assured by three factors: inability to ensure law and order in Moscow, owing to the revolt of Left Socialist Revolutionaries and anarchists, and the growing commitment of the Allies to military intervention. Finally, Francis's weariness, bad humor, and poor health weighed in the decision to abandon Vologda and go north. A few secretaries were left behind to complete the evacuation and arrived in Moscow about a week later. Chicherin took some satisfaction from the fact that Vologda had been abandoned, that some of the embassy staff came to Moscow, and that nothing dire had happened to

---

272. Chicherin to Francis, 24 July 1918, ibid.
273. Robien, *The Diary of a Diplomat*, 21 and 22 July 1918, 280–83.
274. Ibid. (24 July), 286. Robien thought the whole operation was risky because Soviet authorities could easily have attached engines to the other end and pulled the whole outfit to Moscow.
275. Poole radiogram to Paris, 25 July 1918, copy in box 707, WA-6, RG 45, NA.

them, "in view of the present state of mind of the popular masses."[276] Reacting to these uncertainties, the American YMCA personnel prepared to pull out of Moscow. Anderson recommended that the organization concentrate on Siberia instead.[277] The American Red Cross Commission that had come almost exactly a year before prepared to follow suit, having expended $666,000 in relief, not counting what Thompson and others may have dispersed personally.[278]

Civil war and intervention could not have been prevented in 1918, given the continuation of war on the Western Front into November. For some, and in varying degrees, the war was actually an excuse for an ideological crusade against Bolshevism. But more carefully thought out, better-led, and more objective considerations of the Russian problem might have considerably reduced the scope of both civil war and intervention and saved millions of lives from war and famine. Failure to solve the Russian problem damaged severely any hopes to realize the American Wilsonian goal of a democratic world protected by a powerful League of Nations. The legacy of this failure would shape much of the international history of the twentieth century.

276. Chicherin to Poole, 8 August 1918, ibid.
277. Anderson to Harte, 13 and 18 July 1918, f. 701, box 38, Mott Papers, DSA.
278. Totals through June 1918 were divided as follows: $283,000 for drugs and medical supplies, $294,000 for foodstuffs, $69,000 for an ambulance unit, and $20,000 for destitute relief. Commission for Russia expense account, box 866, RG 200, NA.

6

Intervention

August and September 1918 formed a crossroads in Russian-American relations. The quasi recognition of the Soviet/Bolshevik government came to an end with the retreat of Ambassador Francis to Archangel and Murmansk, followed a few weeks later by the departures of other official military and consular representatives from Bolshevik-controlled territory. These moves corresponded to military initiatives in the north and in the Far East and an escalation in tension and hostility by the arrest of a number of Allied officials and private citizens in Moscow.

Although President Wilson was not, in general, averse to the idea of intervention in the affairs of other countries—and had established ample precedent for such actions in Mexico—he had still been reluctant to commit armed forces to Russia. The main reason was a conviction that America should deploy all its military and economic potential on the Western Front, to assure a strong American position in the making of peace. He was also constrained by a small but vocal element of the population that strongly opposed interference in Russia, even sympathizing with Russia's radical socialist direction. In a resulting policy of caution regarding Russia, he was supported by most of his military and political advisers. He also responded to important public pressure coming from people he trusted, such as Charles Crane, John Mott, Cyrus McCormick, and Norman Hapgood, who favored economic aid but believed that a military presence was not the answer, at least in the light of seeing no clear alternative to Bolshevik rule.

One danger of military intervention was that Russia would be broken up into a number of separate states that would become fiefs of the Allied powers, namely, Britain and France, and of Japan. The United States clearly supported the integrity of Russia, of maintaining that former empire, except for Poland and Finland, as a republic, an element of consistency in an otherwise vague and confused policy toward the new Russia. By July 1918, however, the president's mind shifted, and he initiated a new strategy, tentative though it was. He was influenced by extensive pressure from France and Britain for a more proactive role in Russia over several months, a concern for protecting the Czechoslovak forces in Siberia and the possibility of using them to consolidate a non-Bolshevik control instead of for duty on the Western Front, and, finally, a sense of having an invitation from "the Russian people" that he had been waiting for. Allied unity on a policy for Russia was deemed necessary for winning the war and controlling the peace. Perhaps he and other Americans also began to see, as George Kennan argued, that preserving the Russian Empire and fostering an American-type federal republic were incompatible, at least for the near future.

Among the Americans in Russia who could observe the situation at close hand, a balance existed between intervention and recognition, with a number of moderates in the middle, during the first six months of Soviet rule. By May 1918, however, the tide turned in favor of intervention. Ambassador Francis, under increased pressure from staff members such as Maddin Summers and from Ambassador Noulens of France finally made a strong plea for intervention in early May. With the withdrawal of Robins that month, American votes for intervention clearly dominated both in Russia and among those such as Sisson and Corse who had returned to the United States.

One lone but clear warning against armed intervention but in favor of food shipments instead was that of Felix Cole, consul in Archangel. His sharp opposition to the growing trend for intervention sent to Francis on 1 June was passed on for review to Consul General Poole and did not reach Washington until six weeks later, well after the course for intervention was set. Not only were Cole's efforts thwarted to have an alternative American plan for Russia considered; he was also kept ignorant of steps being taken toward intervention in his particular area of jurisdiction.[1]

Ironically, many of the official reasons for intervention were evaporating during the summer of 1918. The German menace to Russia, if it ever really existed, was definitely waning; the supply depots at Murmansk, Archangel, and Vladivostok were no longer threatened. In fact, at Archangel, where American troops would first land, few military supplies were left to guard, since most of them had been moved inland under Bolshevik control.[2] Nor had the Bolshevik leaders

---

1. For a detailed review of the "Cole affair," see Allison, *American Diplomats in Russia*, 129-40.

2. A number of witnesses attest to this, for example, Bullard to Creel, 26 August 1918, f. CPI, box 6, Bullard Papers, Princeton-Mudd.

turned out to be totally hostile; weak and disorganized, they were actually seeking, though clumsily, a modus vivendi with the Allies and would continue to do so. Certainly, no clear alternative for Russia was discernible. Those, such as the French, who despised the Bolsheviks most for their economic and social programs had been much disappointed by the repeated failures to find viable resistance movements. They would, with mixed success, try to invent such centers to justify intervention.

Finally, American units were being sent to Siberia to secure the withdrawal of the Czecho-Slovak forces that were strung out precariously along 5,000 miles of the Trans-Siberian Railroad. But at that very time, a number of these units were moving west and north to seize Bolshevik-controlled areas rather than east for embarkment. These factors were not lost on the administration in Washington. In fact, the decision for military intervention coincided with another public statement against intervention, essentially a summary of the July aide-mémoire.

> In the judgement of the Government of the United States,—a judgement arrived at after repeated and very searching considerations of the whole situation,—military intervention in Russia would be more likely to add to the present sad confusion there than to cure it and would injure Russia rather than help her out of her distresses. Such military intervention as has been most frequently proposed even supposing it to be efficacious in its immediate object of delivering an attack upon Germany from the east would, in its judgement, be more likely to turn out to be merely a method of making use of Russia than to be a method of serving her.[3]

The document then explained the mission of the American forces: to safeguard military supplies, to aid local Russian governments that ask for assistance, and to protect the exit of Czecho-Slovaks. There is no mention in this rather lengthy document for public consumption about intervention against Bolsheviks or Soviets. Clearly, Washington wanted to leave the impression that intervention was strictly limited to ports, supply dumps, and Czechs–and to limited amounts of material and funds for viable anti-Bolshevik forces.

The American consul in Irkutsk recommended a modified strategy, which came close to being what the United States actually did in Siberia:

---

3. "A Press Release," *PWW* 49:170. Although directed to all Allied missions in Washington, it seems to have been meant mainly for the Japanese. Polk to Roland Morris (Tokyo), 3 August 1918, quoting a message delivered to the Japanese ambassador in Washington, box 4, Morris Papers, MD, LC.

As it may not be practicable for America to send troops here [Irkutsk] and in view of the changed situation in France, suggest the following formula: America cannot recognize present all Russian Government [in Omsk] as it does not represent European Russia. America is heartily in sympathy with efforts of present [Omsk] Russian Government to reestablish law and order in Russia and will therefore immediately send money, equipment, clothing and supplies for one hundred thousand Russian soldiers providing American authorities can control railroad for time being.[4]

Archangel

The confused scene at Russia's White Sea port at the end of July proved Commissar of Foreign Affairs Chicherin's point that it was no fit residence for diplomats. A Bolshevik commission with the support of around a thousand Red Army men was hastily preparing to evacuate as much of the remaining supplies as possible. The diplomatic train from Vologda arrived around noon on 26 July. After frustrating negotiations with local Bolshevik leaders, who were preparing to abandon Archangel for Vologda and probably needed the train, most of the 150 members of the diplomatic missions and a number of local British and French residents scrambled aboard ships on 28 July and headed for safer quarters.[5] Reaching the safety of Kandalaksha across the White Sea and after a miserable boxcar journey to Murmansk,[6] Francis found refuge on the *Olympia* and immediately requested of the new British commander in the area, General Frederick C. Poole, an immediate occupation of Archangel.[7] This, in fact, was already under way.

On 30 July a squadron of mostly British ships but including a French cruiser departed Murmansk under the command of Rear Admiral Thomas Kemp. Transports following in its wake carried a motley assortment of 1,200 troops—a royal

4. Alfred Thomson to Reinsch, 19 November 1918, box 707, WA-6, RG 45, NA.

5. Francis to Tom West (a St. Louis friend), 26 August 1918, reel 10, Francis Papers, MoHS.

6. Jordan to Mrs. Francis, 8 September 1918, reel 10, Francis Papers, MoHS. Jordan reported that Francis occupied the same quarters as Admiral Dewey on the *Olympia,* and that they had good meals, accompanied by a twenty-piece band (which must have made conversation difficult). But he also specially requested from home roach powder and rat poison. Ibid.

7. Francis found plenty to occupy himself in Murmansk, as a courier with forty-two pouches of embassy mail had been stranded there for two months. Francis to McCully, 4 August 1918, reel 10, Francis Papers, MoHS.

Scottish brigade, a Canadian artillery brigade, a French colonial battalion, a Serbian infantry company, and fifty-one sailors and three officers from the USS *Olympia*, all commanded by Poole, who had only some experience with the British military mission in Petrograd and service in the Boer War to commend him.[8] The first true Allied invasion of Russia occurred on 2 August after a British-inspired coup had deposed existing authority and forced all remaining "Reds" to abandon the city. Poole and his "army" were greeted by most of the middle-class townspeople as liberators, and they proceeded to behave as conquerors.[9]

Although Poole and his officers made clear from the beginning that they were in charge, the first "action" on 3 August involved a small contingent of American sailors who, assigned to guard supply depots, ended up chasing some Bolsheviks down the railroad and exchanging shots. Ensign Donald Hicks, who was in charge, took one in the leg, making him the first recorded American casualty of the intervention.[10] The wound turned out to be superficial, fitting the scope of the American intervention.

With his base firmly established in Archangel, Poole bowed to local pressure and allowed the reinstatement of a "Soviet" government under Captain George Chaplin, instigator of an uprising in the guise of a British naval officer. Nikolai Chaikovskii, who had the advantages of being an elder statesman of the non-Bolshevik moderate socialist movement, represented by the right wing of the Socialist Revolutionary Party, was briefly deposed, but a popular outcry brought him back. He had an excellent knowledge of English from an exile residence of several years in the United States and Britain. Poole further alienated much of the local population by demanding the removal from buildings of red flags, a treasured symbol of the revolution, and exercising veto power over local Russian authorities.[11]

Admitting the weakness of his forces, Poole nevertheless pressed an advance along two fronts, the rail line to Vologda and along the Dvina River. The goal

8. Weekly report, USS *Olympia*, 3 August 1918, f. 1, box 719, RG 45, NA.

9. In his official report, Poole simply said, "I occupied Archangel today with Allied troops." Poole to War Office, 4 August 1918, copy in f. 1 (Russia–Murmansk, Archangel and White Sea Operations, Sept.–Oct. 1918), box 709, WA-6, RG 45, NA.

10. Richard Goldhurst, *The Midnight War: The American Intervention in Russia, 1918–1920* (New York: McGraw-Hill, 1978), 94–95. For a compendium of recollections, see Dennis Gordon, ed., *Quartered in Hell: The Story of the American North Russia Expeditionary Force* (Missoula, Mont.: Doughboy Historical Society, 1982).

11. DeWitt Poole later could not recall whether Chaikovskii was formally a socialist, "but his deepest motivation was hatred of the social inequities. This resentment was immersed in an extraordinarily sweet nature and came to the surface only in good acts and in his beard, which his sub-conscious mind kept always a bit moth-eaten as protest against the well groomed." "Chaikovsky," f. 26 (Archangel), box 7, Poole Papers, SHSW.

was to occupy strategic stations on the Trans-Siberian and make contact with other resisting forces, especially the Czechs at Samara. After initial easy advances, they soon met stiff resistance, which Poole credited to the "Bolos" being commanded by German officers.[12] They dug in to await the expected American reinforcements. Meanwhile, Poole's role as dictator of Archangel was complicated by the return on 9 August of the diplomatic missions from Murmansk. The result was a three-way struggle for authority between Poole and his military command, the diplomats, and Chaikovskii and his supporters. Poole definitely won out initially, to the resentment of the others.

Francis, battling an increasingly debilitating illness, attempted to establish working arrangements. With the aid of Harvard historian Archibald Coolidge, who arrived in Archangel on 26 August, he presided over a two-hour conference of diplomats and local leaders and thought he did some good. Although he heartily disliked the arrogant British commander, to appease General Poole, he sent Riggs to Paris to beg for reinforcements. This was to no avail, as House reflected after meeting the military attaché there:

> I have tried to impress upon Major Riggs that so long as the Government in Washington holds its present view (and I agree in its present view) his time would be wasted in trying to impress upon American officers the necessity of sending reinforcements to the Northern Ports of Russia, but that he should devote his time to persuading the British and French Governments to do so. . . . All Americans are agreed that there is only one place where the American effort can be most promptly and most effectively brought to bear, and that is here on the Western Front in France.[13]

To Charles Crane, Francis wrote a long letter of explanation, including, "I have been endeavoring to maintain harmony between the military and civil authorities, . . . but it is by no means an easy task as the British are very difficult, being accustomed to colonize uncivilised countries and the French are impetuous and voluble."[14] Left largely in the dark as far as policy and strategy were concerned, Francis did learn of the fate of the tsar–his corpse burned in a mine

---

12. Benjamin D. Rhodes, *The Anglo-American Winter War with Russia, 1918–1919: A Diplomatic and Military Tragicomedy* (New York: Greenwood Press, 1988), 27–29; John Cudahy, *Archangel: The American War with Russia by a Chronicler* (Chicago: A. C. McClurg, 1924), 56–59.

13. House to Francis, 3 October 1918, reel 10, Francis Papers, MoHS.

14. Francis to Crane, 29 August 1918 (o), in f. 20, box 5, Harper Papers, UC.

shaft—from a Czech courier from Ekaterinberg.[15] Clemenceau's request for an additional five American battalions for north Russia was quietly sabotaged by Marshal Ferdinand Foch, who had no more desire than Tasker Bliss or House to see any more American forces diverted.[16]

The promised American forces for north Russia arrived a month after the occupation of Archangel. Hastily assembled and assigned to Russia while undergoing basic training in Britain, they consisted of the 339th Infantry Regiment, mostly recently recruited from Michigan ("Detroit's Own"), with some from Wisconsin, about 4,600 altogether, and several support units—the 310th Engineer Battalion from Wisconsin, the 337th Field Hospital, and the 337th Ambulance Company. Apparently the choice assumed the value of familiarity with northern lake country and the inclusion of Poles and Finns from the region who could speak Russian. The designated American commander, Colonel George Stewart, likewise had experience with command in Alaska. All had expected to be deployed, after thorough training, in France, but they knew something different was in store when they were suddenly issued winter coats (during the heat of July), British Shackleton snow boots, and new rifles that, though made by Westinghouse, were manufactured according to Russian specifications with permanently fixed bayonets and were considered notoriously unreliable.[17]

The American units went directly to Archangel on crowded British transports, on which they began their accommodation to the British rations they would endure for the duration of their stay in Russia. Their Russian experience began badly, with many of the men arriving quite ill with Spanish influenza, for which existing medical facilities were sorely inadequate; at least seventy-two Americans died of the flu without seeing action. Healthy infantry units of company size were sent forward by the British command almost immediately to the rail and river fronts. Arriving late in the short summer season, they were quite unprepared for the weather and terrain.

The American warriors in Russia met swarms of mosquitoes, cold and damp weather, and small but well-armed and well-disciplined Bolshevik forces. On the rail line, the advance was slowed by the Bolshevik units blowing up some of the many bridges, while efforts to outflank the enemy through the surrounding swamp were futile. The freezing and thawing of autumn, and then the snow and ice of winter, soon upon them, proved the Shackleton boots particularly inade-

15. Francis to Crane, 29 August 1918, reel 10, Francis Papers, MoHS.

16. "Bliss says Foch consents only out of deference for Clemenceau and will not misunderstand your declining." Newton Baker for President, in Page to Lansing, 15 September 1918, enclosed in Lansing to Wilson, 16 September 1918, *PWW* 51:17.

17. Rhodes, *Anglo-American Winter War*, 33-34.

quate for the conditions. Greater success was obtained on the river, but conditions were even worse, with four American companies crowded on coal barges and forced to sleep on the damp, bare floors covered with coal dust ("Our faces and uniforms are black with moist coal dust"). Several Americans died not in battle but from such "circumstances."[18]

During the first three months of the campaign in north Russia, it would be difficult to find a happy soldier—or diplomat. Complaints filled letters home and the pages of the *American Sentinel*, a locally published newsletter: "Up here in this tough town there are 269,831 inhabitants, of which 61,329 are human beings and 208,502 are dogs. . . . The wind whistles across the Dvina River like the Twentieth Century Limited passing Podunk." Sanitation services, already in bad condition from neglect, broke down completely under the strain of increased service population ("It [Archangel] can be smelled for quite a distance"). The engineer battalion tackled this problem with some success. It also rendered critical assistance in maintaining utility and urban transport services and policing the streets during a general strike in protest of Poole's interfering with local administration, but this was not the service that most American soldiers expected to perform.[19] The little Russian support they received was disappointing and demoralizing; this placed the whole campaign on the defensive. Already in September, President Wilson instructed that Francis be told that, "it being in our view plain that no gathering of any effective force by the Russians is to be hoped for, we shall insist . . . that all military effort in that part of Russia be given up except the guarding of the ports."[20]

As if to provide some relief to the surroundings and the tedium, the American regimental and cruiser bands marched through the streets.

The "band" from the *Olympia*, which is rampaging round since our arrival in Archangel is going to constitute a danger to our ear-drums.

. . . There is nothing more comical than to see them in their little white straw clown's hats struggling with their big drums and their cymbals, while

18. Ibid., 38–39. Another excellent account of the intervention in north Russia is by Leonid I. Strakhovsky, *Intervention at Archangel: The Story of Allied Intervention and Russian Counter-revolution in North Russia, 1918–1920* (Princeton, N.J.: Princeton University Press, 1944). Although in part based on personal experiences at the scene, it is well researched.

19. Quotations from Rhodes, *Anglo-American Winter Wars*, 35. At least American humor survived the north Russian ordeal.

For strongly critical contemporary accounts of Americans "fighting in nowhere for nothing," see Cudahy, *Archangel*; and Ralph Albertson, *Fighting Without a War: An Account of Military Intervention in North Russia* (New York: Harcourt, Brace and Howe, 1920).

20. Wilson to Lansing, 26 September 1918, f. Woodrow Wilson 1918 Aug–Sept., box 41, Long Papers, MD, LC.

the slide-trombones are manoeuvred by athletic arms into letting out deep bellowings! The favourite tune *Teasing the Cat* . . . is a sort of solo on the big drums, accompanied by the slide-trombones, which could "tease" not just a "cat," but a hippopotamus![21]

From afar William Judson tried to cheer the ambassador with reflections on an unreal year, "so momentous in the world's history. [People who were not there had no idea how we managed with] the intricacies of the six card draw and the double deal. I realize that they have never played golf in a hay field or putted into cow dung, or been chased off the 'links' by Bolshevik farmers."[22]

Under the circumstances, the Allied military and diplomatic officers were hardly a congenial group. General Poole made public references to the incompetence of American soldiers, while Francis challenged Poole and backed the elderly but congenial Chaikovskii and wooed his allegiance against the British.[23] Probably probed by Francis, the latter wrote letters to American "authorities," such as Wilson and Kennan, pleading for more support.[24] Both the martinet Poole and the invalid Francis, however, were soon to leave the scene. In mid-October, after complaints had reached Washington and then were relayed to London about Poole's abrasive behavior and abuses of power, such as his support of the Chaplin coup, he was recalled and replaced by his second in command, General Edmund Ironside, who at least displayed more political tact in dealing with local authorities, while continuing to harp about American inaction. Under orders to exercise caution, Ironside concentrated on building up defen-

---

21. Robien, *The Diary of a Diplomat* (4 September 1918), 287.
22. Judson to Francis, 1 September 1918, reel 10, Francis Papers, MoHS.
23. Francis admitted that British and French support for Chaikovskii was grudging and much regretted it:

> The new Government is menaced not only by the Bolsheviks but by the Monarchists also and there are many among the British and French and a few among the Americans here . . . ; the British who are colonizers by instinct and practice and who have had control of Archangel harbor since the war began are disposed to look contemptuously on the new Government which is professedly socialistic, but not damn fool socialist like the Bolsheviks.

Francis to son William, 4 September 1918, reel 10, Francis Papers, MoSH.
24. See, for example, Chaikovskii to "Mr. Cannon" [sic], 22 October 1918, box 1, Kennan Papers, MD, NYPL, expressing his hopes that he could help "deepen the sympathies toward our Russian democracy." Although the Archangel socialist leader had difficulty with written English, by all accounts his speaking ability was quite fluent. The most impressive thing about Chaikovskii was his beard, which Poole described as "mild as his politics . . . , such a beard that a child might play with." Poole notes, f. 26 Archangel, box 7, Poole Papers, SHSW.

sive positions on the lines, while achieving limited success in recruiting and training Russian reinforcements.

Another problem that the lame-duck ambassador faced in Archangel was isolation from what was really going on in Russia, in Moscow and elsewhere. As a result, the State Department was turning more and more to its two Morris envoys: Ira Morris in Stockholm and Roland Morris in Tokyo. While the latter was the highest-ranking diplomat near the new Siberian "front" and, of course, vital to relations with Japan, Ira Morris had for some time acted as a second ambassador to Russia, reporting regularly on news he could obtain, which was not inconsiderable.[25] In late 1918 his ambition to be the chief informant was augmented by the assignment to his staff of Petrograd veterans Sheldon Whitehouse and Norman Armour. Paul Reinsch, ambassador to China, felt left on the fringe: "I have the feeling that America does not sufficiently realize the critical importance for our own future welfare, and safety, of decisions to be made with respect to the Far East. Unless these decisions are right, we shall not be able to live in Peace."[26] A fitting eulogy; perhaps it was fortunate that Francis, afflicted with prostate trouble, was forced to retire from Russia in early November to the *Olympia* for better medical care and eventual surgery in Britain.[27] Francis wrote a typically homey epitaph for American diplomatic presence in Soviet Russia: "The situation here is as a shoemaker described it in Springfield, Mo, when going to his shop one morning and finding his floor covered by three or four feet of water, closed his establishment and put a notice on the door 'Closed.'"[28] So the American diplomatic presence in Russia, continuous since 1809, closed not with a bang but with a whimper. In convalescence in Scotland, Francis seemed happy to have his son and daughter-in-law present and mellowed in regard to

25. The Morrises were not related. Ira was a businessman (meatpacking) from Chicago; Roland, a Philadelphia attorney, later a long-term chaired professor at the University of Pennsylvania Law School.

26. Reinsch (Peking) to Long, 7 December 1918, f. 1918 P-S, box 36, Long Papers, MD, LC.

27. Francis, *Russia from the American Embassy*, 290–93. Although Francis insisted on an operation to remove his prostate, British and American doctors agreed that it was unwise to attempt surgery in Archangel. In a letter of 28 October, he described his illness as requiring only a catheter to empty his bladder twice a day, which Philip Jordan could do. Francis to Whitehouse (Stockholm), reel 10, Francis Papers, MoHS.

Francis cleared Murmansk for Britain just after learning that the Armistice had been signed. Francis to Poole, 11 November 1918, reel 10, ibid. For excruciating detail of the early stages of his illness, and his brave determination to stay the course in Archangel, see Francis to son Perry, 26 August 1918, ibid.

28. Francis to Whitehouse, 28 October 1918, ibid. Typically, Francis also wondered if his illness was not a British plot. To Poole, 11 November 1918, ibid.

his prior associates and to Russia in general.[29] The old Russia for so many would become a nostalgic remembrance.

After the somewhat embarrassing withdrawal of Francis, Colonel Ruggles and Consul General Poole, the latter arriving from Moscow through Sweden on 2 November, remained in charge of what was left of American affairs in Archangel. They were bolstered by the timely arrival on 28 October, just before Francis's health took a turn for the worse, of Rear Admiral Newton McCully, an American with much Russian experience, and by consular agent Hooker Doolittle. McCully was designated not only as naval attaché again but also as commander of American naval forces in north Russia.[30] His first report concerned the latter—the old *Olympia* was in good shape, but the crew needed rest.[31]

Ambassador Noulens of France finally, but to his chagrin much too late to have much effect on events, assumed the leadership of the rump diplomatic missions remaining in Archangel. Although never fond of Francis, especially his partiality for Chaikovskii, Noulens had no more respect for the British command than did the Americans.[32] After 11 November every diplomat wanted to be in Paris, Noulens and Francis certainly included; they would be quite happy to leave intervention in the hands of the generals and admirals.

Before his departure and well before news of the Armistice, Francis became concerned about the morale of American soldiers from a series of letters beginning in mid-October from Major J. Brooks Nichols, in command of the battalion on the railroad front. He reported increasing disaffection among his troops that he blamed especially on association with a French unit that was in a state of near mutiny. They were in an exposed condition with few men and under a poor and much-despised British commander, and "our policy was not clear to either American officers or men."[33] The visits of Colonel Ruggles and Lieutenant Peter Bukovsky had little effect in lifting morale. One veteran felt, condescendingly, that "the war with Russia was a typical British show." He may have exaggerated, but he reflected local American opinion in claiming that the British brought 600 surplus officers, unfit for duty in France, along with 40,000 cases of Scotch whiskey to keep them content.[34] He was relieved that the varied mili-

29. Francis to Miles, 29 November 1918, reel 11, Francis Papers, MoHS.

30. Lansing to Daniels, 8 October 1918, f. 8, box 706, WA-6, RG 45, NA.

31. McCully to Force Commander, 26 October 1918, f. 4 (Misc.), box 709, WA-6, RG 45, NA.

32. Noulens, *Mon ambassade en Russie soviétique*, 2:242–48.

33. Francis to Lansing, 12 November 1918, reel 11, Francis Papers, MoHS.

34. Cudahy, *Archangel*, 75–76. The 40,000 cases of whiskey for British officers became a regular refrain in American complaints. See Henry White memorandum to Lansing of a conversation with Hooker Doolittle, 22 February 1919, vol. 41, Lansing Papers, MD, LC.

A north Russian American supply train, winter 1919, courtesy of the U.S. Army Signal Corps, Photographs Division, National Archives

tary components "were having a rather unique and amusing time of it in jaunty ... Archangel, and none of the impassive Slavs there seemed agitated or even interested in this war."[35] He highlighted two important problems of a coherent policy for Russia: disunity among the Allies and the lack of direction among the Russian population.

DeWitt Poole, left to deal with the depressing situation in Archangel, acknowledged (!) that "the American military expedition to North Russia had to accommodate itself to a rather awkward situation." Noting that the virtually defunct American senior officer was in a difficult position with his command broken into small units under British officers, he advised Frank Polk privately that Stewart's negative attitude was becoming contagious. "Unfortunately, in the view of those most competent to judge, Colonel Stewart has not proved adequate to the situation. . . . He seems to have neither the strength of character nor worldly experience to cope with the delicate problem which has confronted him. . . . He

35. Cudahy, Archangel, 97–98.

is simply a square peg in a round hole."[36] The same might be said about most Americans in north Russia at the end of 1918.

In one of the rare real battles on the Northern Front at Kodish that began on 29 December and continued through the first two weeks of 1919, American soldiers fought their largest battle on Russian territory in assaults and counterattacks against a Bolshevik stronghold. Several Americans were killed, and others suffered from frostbite from exposed positions in subzero temperatures. Captain Prince was pleased at the performances he witnessed, but general bitterness toward the British increased for their failure to bring up reinforcements and from the drunken appearances of their officers who came forward on reconnaissance.[37] Even the British command, after an investigation by Ironside, acknowledged that its performance was a disgrace. This was par for the course for intervention in north Russia.

Vladivostok

The Archangel of the East was not faring much better under Allied assault. Both cities were about the same size, with a population of around 75,000, but that of the Far Eastern port was quite cosmopolitan, with 25,000 Chinese and Korean and 3,000 Japanese residents. An American report also noted that quite a few of the Russians were Jewish.[38] A hasty scrambling for a presence of military contingents resulted in a British battalion from Hong Kong landing first, on 3 August. It consisted of 800 men considered unfit for service on the Western Front, none of whom could speak Russian nor had any experience in the area.[39] A few days later a token French colonial battalion of Vietnamese under French officers arrived. These were soon dwarfed by a massive Japanese invasion of over 50,000 men who arrived over several days and were immediately deployed inland. The numbers were not certain at the beginning, since, of the first three Japanese divisions, one landed at Port Arthur and moved north to Harbin, another entered overland from Korea, and one disembarked at Vladivostok.[40] Technically,

36. Poole to Polk, 9 December 1918, box 345, DPR Russia 1918-19, RG 84, NA.

37. Rhodes, *Anglo-American Winter War*, 79-81; for graphic details by a participant, see Donald E. Carey, *Fighting the Bolsheviks: The Russian War Memoirs of Private First Class Donald E. Carey, U.S. Army, 1918-19*, ed. Neil G. Carey (Novato, Calif.: Presidio Press, 1997), 104-27.

38. USS *Brooklyn* report, 4 November 1918, box 713, WA-6, RG 45, NA.

39. For an account by its commander, see Colonel John Ward, *With the "Die-Hards" in Siberia* (New York: George H. Doran, 1920).

40. USS *Brooklyn* reports, 3, 10, and 13 August 1918, box 613, WA-6, RG 45, NA; Barrows to Capt. Straughn, 16 October 1918, box 2, Barrows Papers, UCB.

the Japanese could argue that the extent of their "intervention in Russia" was exaggerated, since a substantial number of troops remained in Manchuria.

Major General William S. Graves, who had recently assumed command of the newly formed 8th Infantry Division at Camp Fremont, California, met Secretary of War Newton Baker in a secret rendezvous at Union Station in Kansas City on the night of 3 August to receive new orders to command a special American expeditionary force for Siberia. He was given a sealed envelope, which he opened afterward at his hotel. It contained only the aide-mémoire of 17 July, which vaguely confined American intervention in the Russian Far East to extricating the Czecho-Slovaks.[41] In Washington, Long understood from Lansing that the president's policy was simple: "Aid Czechs and hold supplies."[42]

At Fort McKinley in the Philippines, the 27th and 31st Infantry Regiments were alerted on 9 August. Private Verne Bright from Kansas wrote home, "When ye get this maybe I'll be pitchin Bolsheviks like a farmer pitchin hayski." His unit landed at Vladivostok on 21 August, greeted by the USS *Brooklyn* band playing "Hail, Hail, the Gang's All Here."[43] Bright was duly impressed by his new post: "This is *some* place. I've seen more kinds o' people in one day here than I saw all the rest o' my adventurous life."[44]

When General Graves reached Vladivostok with about 5,000 troops from the California 8th Division on 1 September, he combined them with the Philippine regiments, for a total command of around 9,000, while the Japanese had already landed several times that number and were requesting considerable reinforcements. From the beginning Graves was in an awkward position: "Due, in part at least, to my ignorance of the conditions, I landed in Vladivostok without any preconceived ideas as to what should or should not be done. I had no prejudice against any Russian faction and anticipated I would be able to work harmoniously and in a cooperative spirit with all the Allies."[45] He would quickly be cured of this naive view. In his first meeting with the Japanese commander, General Kuzuki Otani, on 2 September, he was shocked to learn that Otani expected

41. Graves, *America's Siberian Adventure*, 4. In the brief exchange at the station, Baker told Graves, "If in the future you want to cuss anybody for sending you to Siberia I am the man," to which he added, "Watch your step; you will be walking on eggs loaded with dynamite." Although Graves may have had good reasons to curse Baker for getting him involved in the Siberian explosive mess, he, interestingly, dedicated his book to him, no doubt because they were in agreement that this was a cautious, experimental project, not a serious military campaign.

42. Long diary, 5 September 1918, box 1, Long Papers, MD, LC.

43. Bright to mother, 11 August 1918, box 1, Bright Papers, UOA.

44. Ibid., 27 August 1918.

45. Graves, *America's Siberian Adventure*, 56.

Vladivostok harbor (the "Golden Horn") with USS Brooklyn on the left, courtsey of the U.S. Army Signal Corps, Photographs Division, National Archives

him to turn over command of the American force and merge it with his own, as Poole was doing at Archangel.[46]

With little briefing and no experience in the area, Graves relied from the beginning on the advice and support of those who preceded him—Admiral Austin Knight, Consul John Caldwell, and ambassador to Japan Roland Morris, and upon his chief intelligence adviser, Colonel Robert Eichelberger.[47] They all agreed that Japan had set a course to dominate the region, but they were perplexed about what to do about it, given the size of the American presence. At least, and in contrast to north Russia, American forces would not be placed under another nation's command and would be concentrated in the Vladivostok area. Various detachments would be sent out to Khabarovsk and as far west as Verkhneudinsk, just east of Lake Baikal. The result was no overall command jurisdiction for the Allied Siberian operation, resentment by the Japanese for apparent mistrust, and considerable confusion on all sides about policy and goals. Graves was clearly

46. Ibid., 57–58.
47. Ibid., 276, 296.

frustrated, reporting that Semenov was in the pay of the Japanese, that his and Horvat's armies were committing atrocities, and that he was reduced only to enumerating the number of prostitutes in Vladivostok.[48] Even a face-to-face conference with Semenov on board the *Brooklyn* did not seem to help.[49]

From the top floor of his headquarters in the building of the German Mercantile Company in central Vladivostok, Graves looked out on Siberia, a territory the size of all of North America, torn into a number of shifting and varied political jurisdictions, not counting a formal but weak Chinese suzerainty over Manchuria. Siberia was not really Russia but an extension of it, as Alaska and Hawaii were to the continental United States. It had a long tradition of greater independence and freedom, despite its reputation as a depository for political and real criminals. Although Siberia fascinated Americans, few of them ever understood its dynamics. For example, somewhat like Finland, the two Marxist political parties, Bolsheviks and Mensheviks, were much closer together in Siberia than in European Russia.[50] This solidified and strengthened the radical political agenda in the civil population, weak as it was militarily.

During the decline of the Provisional Government's central authority in 1917, a Siberian separatist movement gained momentum, led by Socialist Revolutionaries but including local Mensheviks and Bolsheviks. A regional congress that met in Tomsk in December and a separate Siberian Constitutent Assembly in January 1918 established the Siberian Regional Duma. Withdrawal of the Marxists and an influx of anti-Bolshevik remnants of the Provisional Government led to a declaration of opposition to Bolshevik central power and nominal independence. Internal divisions, such as trying to settle the thorny issue of the extent that Siberia should be independent or united with a new Russia, and the general economic problems of Russia as a whole spawned several separate governments in the vast territory.[51]

An uneasy consolidation was finally effected by June 1918 in the Omsk Provisional Siberian Government. In its favor during that summer was the presence of the Czech-Slovak army that helped it consolidate its authority over a vast region that at times extended beyond the Urals into European Russia. Several problems remained and were coming to a head about the time that American forces landed in Vladivostok: withstanding the growing capability of Trotsky's

48. Graves's reports, 14 September and 1 October 1918, roll 1 (M 917), RG 395, NA.
49. Logbook, USS *Brooklyn*, 23 September 1918, RG 24.
50. Norman G. O. Pereira, "Regional Consciousness in Siberia Before and After October 1917," *Canadian Slavonic Papers* 30, no. 1 (March 1988): 118–22.
51. Ibid.; and Pereira, "The 'Democratic Counterrevolution' in Siberia during 1918," *Nationalities Papers* 16, no. 1 (spring 1988): 71–93.

Red Army; retaining Czech support or replacing it with a viable army of its own; having stable leadership; gaining the allegiance of the already established "warlords" of eastern Siberia (Horvat, Semenov, and Kalmykov); and obtaining Allied recognition and aid. Not a simple agenda, especially with the complications of a large Japanese presence and a failing transportation system.

Except for Vladivostok, various right-wing groups found refuge in eastern Siberia and were able strategically to command important positions on behalf of vague but clearly anti-Bolshevik crusades. Unfortunately, they competed and actually fought against each other. General Dmitri Horvat "commanded" the Chinese Eastern that including much of Manchuria; Cossack General Grigori Semenov butchered his way to power in the area of Chita,[52] a strategically important intersection on the Trans-Siberian; Ivan Kalmykov acted as usual like a nasty bandit at Khabarovsk, dangerously near Vladivostok; then, finally, Admiral Kolchak seized control of the Omsk government in mid-November and emerged as the new anti-Bolshevik "savior." In contrast to the others, he at least had some moral dignity and respect.

Meanwhile, the Czechs were scattered awkwardly along with the Japanese through much of Siberia, posing complicated local and international problems. This situation would have defeated the best Eisenhower of the times. Faulted by many for inaction, Graves at least had the courage to stand up successfully against a stream of bullying efforts by Japanese commanders. These Japanese forces were on the ascendant, however. Over American objections, they took over running the trains on the Chinese Eastern and on parts of the Trans-Siberian. Graves, relying on information from Barrows and Eichelberger, reported regularly on his difficult relations with the superior ally, but one of his staff attributed some of this to German schemes.[53] A cable relating more problems elicited a somewhat incoherent handwritten note from the president: "It looks as if Japanese had the best of this argument. Can we object if regular former administration is continued and our men continue to function *as formerly?*"[54] By November the Japanese army probably numbered over 72,000 in Siberia and Manchuria.[55] Bolstering the comparatively meager American contingent was only

---

52. By all accounts, the area around Chita, a vital link on the Trans-Siberian, posed a real problem for everyone, because of Semenov's presence, volatility, unpredictability, and extreme brutality. Report of Consul J. P. Jameson (Chita), 16 September 1918, box 1, Harris Papers, HIA.

53. Report of Captain T. W. King, 18 September 1918, ibid.

54. Wilson to Long, 20 September 1918, box 187, Long Papers, MD, LC.

55. Having little precise information, General Graves estimated the Japanese forces toward the end of October at 40,000 in Siberia and 20,000 in Manchuria. Graves to Adjutant General Peter Harris, 25 October 1918, *PWW* 51:449.

Eastern Siberia and Manchuria. From World's Work, *October 1918*

a small unit of intelligence officers and clerks, its primary mission being to infiltrate and observe the American soldiers in order to detect any Bolshevik sympathizers. None could be found, so most of their time was spent in elaborating various rumors and in arguing among themselves.[56]

Graves was under orders from Washington not to send any of his forces to Omsk, nor to attempt to support activities against Red forces on the Volga. President Wilson himself advised that "it is the unqualified judgement of our military authorities that to attempt that is to attempt the impossible."[57] Under the circumstances, Graves had to be content with his Vladivostok realm, except for detachments sent along the railroad to maintain communications and to protect YMCA and Red Cross units.

When questioned in November, the Japanese embassy in Washington reported that their deployment in Siberia had been reduced from 44,700 combatants and 27,700 (?) noncombatants to 42,200 and 16,400, respectively. The president's simple arithmetic in the margin: 58,600. Enclosure in Lansing to Wilson, 20 November 1918, *PWW* 53:145.

56. The unit consisted of sixteen officers and fifteen clerks. Eichelberger report, 15 August 1918, roll 1, RG 395, NA.

57. Wilson to Lansing, 26 September 1918, f. Woodrow Wilson, box 41, Lansing Papers, MD, LC.

Although the economic and political stability of Vladivostok was no better than Archangel, the population was more accustomed to foreign presences and, in fact, was quite diversified, including large minorities of Chinese, Japanese, and Koreans. Like Archangel, Vladivostok was a vital entrée into Russia proper. The American Expeditionary Force (AEF) in Siberia, in contrast with that in north Russia, was larger, more professional (regular army units), and directly under American command. Although it actually did practically nothing in terms of Siberian military intervention, the potential clearly existed.

An American Siberia

For sustaining morale and extending the American presence, Graves also inherited well-established and experienced networks of YMCA and Red Cross units in Siberia. The YMCA especially was much in evidence already in 1918, coming from two directions. A number of American secretaries from European Russia left during the year through Siberia, where they found the various Czech units and many groups of prisoners of war who needed and welcomed their assistance. Samara on the Volga was an important waystation:

> The coming of the Czecho-Slovak soldiers and the organization of the new Russian National Army made it very evident that the number of soldiers who could be served in the city were quite numerous and would be continually increasing. . . . A vacant space at the end of the halls was used as a barber-shop but it quickly became evident that this would not serve as two barbers were needed to meet the demand. . . . The night of the opening was interesting. Several Russian priests came to the building carrying their incense, golden crosses, and wearing their golden and yellow robes. . . . The matter of furnishing the clubs has been of little trouble because the officers themselves offered to furnish stools, tables, mirrors for the barber-shop, and other necessary pieces.[58]

Additional support was readily provided by YMCA base headquarters in China and Japan, areas of concentration of the organization before the war.[59] The con-

58. "A Survey of the Samara Association Activities," 21 September 1918, box 5, Anderson Papers, UIA.
59. George S. Phelps, "Activities of Red Triangle in Siberia Since Foundation," typescript, f. Siberia General, box 57, YMCA Papers, HIA.

tinuation and expansion of this work during the civil war in Siberia would be among the YMCA's most difficult assignments.

Finally, the United States held a vital trump card in Siberia, the railway advisory corps under Stevens and Emerson that had arrived in early 1918, before any foreign military units, and that possessed a clear, high-priority mandate for improving and maintaining a vital transportation system, a goal that should have been in everybody's interest. But civil conflict led to much disruption and destruction on the line by all sides. Stevens became so fed up with political and economic obstacles and the failure of his repeated efforts to obtain substantial military protection for his technical mission that he was ready to abandon ship in November.[60]

Most complicated of all was the position of the Czecho-Slovak units, whom the Americans had been sent to rescue. Having been instructed to take up holding positions until the arrival of Allied forces, the Czechs, with French encouragement and confronting disorganized Bolshevik resistance, advanced north in July to seize the important Volga River port of Kazan, thus cutting a vital line of communications in European Russia, and then occupied Ekaterinburg in the Urals, another key point, just after the murder of the Romanov family. Another major military success was the capture of Irkutsk on 11 July and the critical stretch of the Trans-Siberian along Lake Baikal with its many tunnels vulnerable to explosives.[61]

This successful July offensive by the Czechs, before any substantial Allied units had reached Russia, had several important results that would shape the intervention and civil war to come. First of all, it shocked and panicked the Bolsheviks into a major mobilization effort that would soon make Trotsky's fledgling Red Army a military reality. Second, it encouraged the formation of anti-Bolshevik centers at Samara, Ufa, Chelyabinsk, then Omsk, in western Siberia. Third, it encouraged the Allies to provide military and logistic support, that is, direct intervention. But the region was still a cauldron of political rivalries.

60. For example, Stevens (Harbin) to Lansing, 12 August 1918, in Roland Morris Papers, 12 August 1918, box 4, Morris Papers, MD, LC. He was even more depressed by the situation in November: "As situation now exists, complicated by Russian helplessness and venality, not only would failure result, but owing to high handed interference and autocratic methods practiced by Japanese in Russian railway affairs serious troubles would be inevitable which might produce international complications." Stevens to Lansing, 8 November 1918, box 1, RG 43, NA.

61. Benjamin Johnson (Irkutsk) to Walter Brumfield, 28 July 1918, box 1, Johnson Papers, HIA.

Czech military successes created hero-commanders such as Rudolph Gajda, an especially young, dynamic, and ambitious officer, and political and allegiance divisions within their forces. To encourage and sustain this filling of a vacuum of power in western Siberia, the French and other Allied agents in the area promised major military support in the form of money, supplies, and reinforcements. The July events in the Volga and Urals regions also misled Poole in the north to believe the road was open for his relatively small and inexperienced command to rendezvous with the Czechs somewhere south of Vologda, perhaps even in Moscow!

Unlike their comrades in north Russia, who were forced to wade through frigid bogs and deep snow on patrols 150 miles into the hinterland from Archangel, the men of the Siberian Expeditionary Force, with the exception of guard units sent inland along the railroad, remained encamped in and around Vladivostok during the fall and winter, accessible only to what amenities the "Lord of the East" could offer. They had the advantage of already established YMCA and American Red Cross facilities ready to serve them. Most were quite relieved to be stationary from observing the appalling conditions on the packed boxcars of departing Japanese and arriving Czech trains. They were regularly amused at "Y" dances, films, lectures, traveling vaudeville shows, and other entertainments, but after November 1918, they grew increasingly impatient to be home. Verne Bright recalled a verse from a local minstrel show:

> We steam into Hakodate,
>   Couldn't see no Fritzes anywhere,
> Got our skins so full of saki,
>   Bet your life we didn't care,
> Then we came into Siberia
>   (Gee, ay wish ay not been born)
> The boys from the Phillipines [sic] had the Yermans,
>   All lined up along the Golden Horn.[62]

Another extracurricular activity to pass the time was taking pictures and sending them home, though Bright warned that Vladivostok looked better in pictures than it was, "and then besides the 'smell' ain't in the pictures or it m'it be 'good night' when you opened the letter that contained em."[63] Apparently the city could cope no better than Archangel with the pressure on its facilities from Allied "occupation" forces.

62. To mother, 5 February 1919, box 1, Bright Papers, UOA.
63. Ibid., 18 March 1919.

The Red Cross, however, had two agendas—to provide what aid it could and keep out of the increasingly complex politics—and this was not easy. The head-quarters in Kyoto advised its field agent in Siberia:

> I agree thoroughly with what you say as to the need for caution in extend-ing the scope of our work and as to the advisability of limiting its duration. Indeed, if I accomplished anything in my trip to West Siberia, it was chiefly in keeping the Red Cross out of a very extended refugee program which would have involved a great expense and a large force of workers, and which to my mind would have done more harm than good, both to the refugees and to the Russians in general.[64]

Acting on instructions from the State Department, Morris arrived from Tokyo in September to confer with Knight and Graves about subsequent steps. Despite a clear statement of very limited intervention from Lansing,[65] they agreed on recom-mending that the American forces be deployed immediately to Omsk, citing four advantages: (1) to provide much-needed and timely support to the Czechs, (2) to assure protection and improvement of the railroad and future economic develop-ment, (3) to have a moral effect on the Russian population, and (4) to allow a greater range of options in the use of American troops during the winter. Morris admitted a major drawback to be that the move would convey to the Czechs and Russians that the United States would be more actively involved in intervention than was intended and suggested that a clear statement be made in regard to American limitations.[66] Graves seemed perplexed about how to help the Russians form a stable government, especially since most of them he could find were ignor-ing the Americans and seeking Japanese assistance.[67]

Going any deeper into Siberia was discouraged by other incoming reports, before Kolchak's "seizure" of the Omsk government in mid-November. The State Department made it clear to Morris that "your suggestion that General Graves establish himself at Omsk or any other point in the far interior must be dis-approved . . . , strongly as our sympathies constrain us to make every possible sacrifice to keep the country on the Volga front out of the hands of the Merci-less Red Guards."[68] Given the small size of the American expeditionary forces

64. Tucker to Scudder, 17 December 1918, box 915, RG 200, NA.
65. Lansing to Morris, 9 September 1918, box 4, Morris Papers, MD, LC.
66. Morris to Lansing, 23 September 1918, FRUS 1918: Russia 2:388-89.
67. Graves to Adjutant General, 1 October 1918, roll 1 (M 917), RG 395, NA.
68. Lansing to Caldwell for Morris (draft copy), 26 September 1918, box 187, Long Papers, MD, LC; and in FRUS 1918: Russia 2:392-94. But he did authorize him to move to Harbin if deemed necessary and approved by Chinese.

in Siberia, they could really have little impact on the situation anywhere and might get into such a position that would require a major expedition to extract them—and that had already been ruled out. Sending any sizable American forces west was impossible in any event during the winter, Graves reported, "as the Japanese have practically filled all empty barracks east of Lake Baikal," and their flags were flying from all railway stations.[69]

John Stevens, still superintending the railway commission, wrote from Harbin of the confusion created on the disintegrating Trans-Siberian by the movement through and back of Japanese and Czech forces. He bemoaned the paralysis of the repair facilities there and in Vladivostok: "It's a hell of a mixup & God only knows the outcome."[70] An American consul's description in September of the four-way struggle for authority in Chita between Semenov's Cossacks, the Japanese, the Czechs, and the Bolsheviks would certainly not encourage anyone to travel through that vital rail center.[71] Even after Kolchak's coup at Omsk, official intelligence reports were certainly not encouraging: Kolchak weak and disorganized, Czechs exhausted with very low morale, expecting the American forces to come to their rescue, and Semenov at loggerheads with Kolchak, leading to armed clashes between the two White forces.[72] One intelligence officer was appalled by the brutality inflicted by Colonel Shemelin in Blagoveshchensk at the end of November.[73]

Another dimension of the situation, known in Washington, was that the Czech political leader, Thomas Masaryk, had a grandiose vision of saving Russia: "If

69. Graves to Harris, 25 October 1918, *PWW* 51:449.

70. Stevens to Emerson, 21 August 1918, f. 8, Emerson Papers, HIA. At least Stevens had time to write reports. One of 28 September summarizing the activities of his mission— or rather the obstacles to getting anything done—was seventy pages. F. 18, ibid.

71. Jameson to Harris, 16 September 1918, box 1, Harris Papers, HIA. The Japanese foreign minister's pledge to Morris that Stevens would be in charge of the Trans-Siberian seems to have been a delusion, at best. Morris to Lansing, 20 September 1918, Morris Papers, MD, LC. Stevens noted, "I find the question of transportation even more serious than I anticipated. It should be solved promptly or all our efforts to aid Russia during the coming winter will be useless." Ibid.

72. Barrows intelligence summary, no. 36, 30 November, and no. 40, 4 December 1918, roll 3, RG 395 (AEF Siberia), NA. *New York Times* correspondent Carl Ackerman claimed that the Czechoslovak leaders were misled by Consul General Ernest Harris and by Red Cross director Rudolf Teusler into believing that they could count on substantial American military assistance in western Siberia. He quoted Teusler: "I am convinced that if the Czechs shout loud enough for American help that it will come." Ackerman telegram from Chelyabinsk to Roland Morris, 25 January 1919, box 140, Ackerman Papers, MD, LC. Teusler carried weight because he boasted about being a first cousin of the president's wife, with ready access to the White House.

73. Eichelburger intelligence summary, 10 December 1918, roll 3 (M 917), RG 395, NA.

we can hold Siberia, that should have the political effect of placing the whole of Siberia under one government and enabling the Russians there to organize an army."[74] Respect for the Czech leader at the highest levels in Washington enhanced the delusion of a Siberian salvation for Russia. A definite ambivalence prevailed over the Siberian landscape as it headed into a long winter. At the very end of December, however, an Inter-Allied Technical Board was finally established by agreement with Japan (and the other Allies), with Stevens in charge, raising further hopes that the crucial transportation situation might be improved.[75]

One more expert on the old Russia, Montgomery Schuyler, on a special commission to Siberia, was distressed by the confused and terrible conditions of the German POWs and the ascendancy of Japanese authority in Omsk. He also found considerable resentment that the United States AEF had not come to their rescue.[76] The political situation was crystallizing into a struggle of ascendancy between the Japanese and the French-backed Czechs. Acting as a temporary American liaison with Kolchak's headquarters, Schuyler reported from Omsk in December that the White leader was quite annoyed at the interference of French General Pierre Janin, who had been sent to aid and advise the Czechs. Schuyler found utter confusion in regard to what Russians expected from their erstwhile allies. "I am constantly asked for advice by all parties but I give none at all."[77] The leading American field intelligence officer in Siberia, Barrows, strongly supported Semenov and advised against having anything to do with Kolchak because of his gross incompetence.[78]

The AEF prided itself on its intelligence unit that, besides Eichelberger and Barrows, included the newly arrived Schuyler, who was in charge of contact with Kolchak, John Powell, Kenneth Roberts, Robert Scovell, and Laurence Richmond. Unlike the rest of the American forces, they traveled extensively along the Trans-Siberian and filed many reports on what they found.[79] They were certainly diligent in their duty, writing reports of up to 114 pages on conditions in Siberia, which stressed the violations of Japan, and also Britain and France, to the agreements on intervention and were very critical of the

74. Paragraph 9, Masaryk agreement with General Janin, 21 September 1918, copy in box 187, Long Papers, MD, LC.

75. R. Morris (Tokio) to Lansing, 27 December 1918, box 707, WA-6, RG 45, NA.

76. Schuyler (Omsk) to Caldwell and Graves, 12 and 27 December 1918, ibid.

77. Schuyler (Omsk) to Barrows (Intelligence Office, Vladivostok), 19 December 1918, roll 4, ibid.

78. Barrows to Eichelberger, 21 December 1918, roll 4 (M 917), RG 395, NA. But Semenov was also in a precarious condition and "wondered how he would support forces." Eichelberger was the chief of intelligence on Graves's staff. Barrows reported to him.

79. Intelligence reports for August–September, roll 1 (M 917), RG 395, NA.

Kolchak "dictatorship" at Omsk that was described variously as under French or Japanese control.[80]

In an intelligence summary of 30 November, Barrows described the Czechs as worn-out, with bad morale, and with few fresh troops. The unit also kept tabs on the local press, circulating weekly press summaries. Despite the details of atrocities committed by Semenov's bands, Barrows still supported him and reported in December that Semenov would bow to Kolchak, if Kolchak would recognize the supremacy of General Anton Deniken.[81] But, Barrows reported, Semenov harbored deep resentment against Kolchak, whom he accused of preventing him from getting arms when he most needed them.[82] Schuyler in Omsk was one of the few Americans in Siberia, along with Consul General Ernest Harris, who had any respect for Kolchak, and that was lukewarm. After a long talk with a Kolchak staff member, General Syromiatnikov, he concluded that there was much confusion and resentment regarding expected American aid. Before anything could be done in this regard, the railroad situation had to be remedied.[83] Syromiatnikov also complained vociferously about Japanese support of Semenov. He claimed that Japan was the main obstacle to defeating the Bolsheviks.

The State Department was appalled by the turn of events in Siberia: "The United States has viewed with surprise the presence of the very large number of Japanese troops now in North Manchuria and Eastern Siberia. Reliable information indicated the number of these troops to be so great as to constitute a definite departure from the express understanding for cooperation between Japan the United States."[84] But some unidentified American officers on the scene had a logical plan that included them. They determined the goals of their mission as simply (1) to aid Russia, (2) to form a new Eastern Front, and (3) to deny resources of Russia to Germany. To accomplish this required a secure base at Chelyabinsk, protected by a force of 100,000: two Anglo-French-American divisions, two Czech divisions, and the remainder Japanese, "who would form the

80. Ibid. "It became clear, of course, as soon as the allies were represented in force in Vladivostok and elsewhere, that France, Japan, and Britain had particular interests, which they desired to push, even in contradiction of their formal announcements, and certainly in opposition to those of the United States." Ibid.

81. Barrows to Eichelberger, 19 December 1918, roll 3, ibid.

82. Ibid., 21 December 1918. His main concern was that "the Japanese have taken full advantage of America's unpopularity and are strengthening their own position at our expense." To General Churchill, 29 August 1919, f. Aug–Dec 1919, box 3, Barrows Papers, UCB.

83. Schuyler report, 12 December 1918, roll 4 (M 917), RG 395, NA.

84. Lansing to Page (London), 16 November 1918, ibid.

shock troops of the revolution." The plan stressed that all this must be in place before winter set in.[85] This was clearly impossible.

Peace in Europe and winter in Siberia brought much longing of Americans to return home. Private Elliott Reynolds of the Ordnance Depot Company found little to do but study Russian and French and attend lectures and entertainments. The only "enemy" Germans they had found were 200 stranded prisoners of war whom they employed to do the heavy work in the warehouse. "I would be perfectly contented were it not for the feeling that, now that the Big Show is over, and I am of no apparent use here, I should be home and making money again."[86] Many of the Czechs and Slovaks wanted to leave for their emerging new country to be on the ground floor of building its political and military institutions. Kolchak, however, persuaded General Gajda to command his new Siberian army, bringing some of the Czech units with him as mercenaries, causing further division among the Czechs, since many of them were inclined toward social democracy and viewed Kolchak and his retinue as reactionaries.[87] However, Gajda's forces —and British and French moral and monetary support—afforded the anti-Bolshevik forces in the Omsk region an illusory sense of unity and strength.[88]

Peace also heightened American suspicions of Japanese intentions and revived fears of British imperialist ambitions, casting a different light on intervention proceedings. In an internal State Department memorandum to William Phillips, Breckinridge Long revealed this new concern: "A great part of England's influence in the Far Eastern matters is a reflected one and now exists largely because of her understanding with the Japanese who really have the influence."[89] Lansing was especially alarmed about the Japanese buildup in violation of the mutual agreement, and he solicited Morris's advice again in mid-November about whether American forces there should become more active and go to Omsk or be completely withdrawn, including the Railway Service Corps, "as evidence of our unwillingness to be associated with a policy so contrary to our declared

85. "Technical Memorandum Relating to Allied Military Operations in Siberia," n.d., roll 1 (M 917), RG 395, NA.

86. To Miss Sutleff, 30 December 1918, Reynolds folder, HIA.

87. Unterberger, *The United States, Revolutionary Russia, and the Rise of Czechoslovakia,* 333-34.

88. Fedotoff White, who was on Kolchak's staff, claimed many years later that the admiral could have accomplished very little on his own. "I was able to judge the situation from information on the spot and I doubt very much that any measure of success should have been obtained without the help of the Czechs both on the Volga and in Siberia. They were the organizing nucleus that catalyzed the rather disorganized movements that were going on in those places." White to Michael Karpovich, 10 January 1946, f. Karpovich, box 1, Fedotoff White Papers, BA, CU.

89. Long to Phillips, 21 December 1918, box 36, Long Papers, MD, LC.

General Graves and Ataman Grigori Semenov, courtesy of the Stanley Partridge Papers, Hoover Institution Archives

purpose regarding Russia."[90] Washington was clearly exasperated by the Japanese strategy of displaying a huge military presence and playing off one Russian center against another to cripple all and take over control: "They are apparently supporting each of the factions, Semenoff, Kolchak, etc.–and instigating them against each other. . . . They are playing a dangerous game and one that will lead us into trouble with them, if they pursue the present policy."[91] Although still strongly anti-Soviet at the end of 1918, many in Washington thought a conflict with Japan was more likely in the Far East than one with Soviet Russia.

The situation for people caught up in the civil war in Siberia was especially difficult. A huge tide of refugees (estimated by Carl Ackerman at over 7 million), weak and divided civil and military authority, and the virtual collapse of rail transportation, at least for ordinary people, added to the miseries. The large number

90. Lansing to Morris, 16 November 1918, *FRUS 1918: Russia* 2:434–35; box 4, Morris Papers, MD, LC.
91. Long diary, 21 December 1918, box 1, Long Papers, MD, LC.

of abandoned boxcars provided very basic shelter for many, but the result of living in such cramped, temporary housing was a serious typhus epidemic. The several foreign army units, as well as Russian and Cossack, provided some subsistence, often at a debasing price, and they were liable to be caught in the middle of armed conflict. The American Red Cross and YMCA did what they could to alleviate the hardships, but the territory was vast, and security was slim. Much of the food and medicine that they could provide ended up in the hands of the warring factions. For those real refugees who managed to reach Vladivostok and Harbin, opportunities improved from the widespread pilfering of stored provisions and materials.

Moscow

Given the refusal of the Allied diplomatic missions to move from Vologda to Moscow as requested, but instead to escape to what was soon to become occupied territory, and the military invasions that followed, the Bolshevik leadership naturally became more hostile. The Czecho-Slovak advances in the Urals and on the Volga severed regular communications with Siberia, followed by the occupation of Archangel, only a few hundred miles north of the capital. Landings in Vladivostok were too far away to pose much of a threat, especially considering the chaos and confusion that lay in the vast territory between it and Moscow. Meanwhile, terror and counterterror reigned in the Soviet capital. The Bolshevik regime struggled for its life, especially after the nearly successful attempt to assassinate Lenin at the end of August. He spent several weeks convalescing from a serious face wound.

Thomas Martin, making an inspection survey for the YMCA from Vladivostok to Moscow and Vologda and back in August, returned very discouraged by what he had seen. He wrote Frederick Jackson Turner, "They [the Russians] are singularly lacking in political ability for self-government; and they show amazing tolerance to enemies and indifference, not to say aversion, to friends. They invariably admire the man with the big stick who is in a position to wield it over their heads."[92] He then argued that intervention was required to teach them order and self-government, that it was America's duty to civilize this eastern frontier.

Francis left Norman Armour behind in Vologda to care for around twenty Americans (fifteen National City Bank employees, a few YMCA secretaries, and a stranded member of a forestry commission). This was not an easy task, espe-

92. Martin (Honolulu) to Turner, 9 September 1918, Turner Papers, Huntington Library.

cially after he was forcibly removed from the embassy quarters by a Bolshevik guard on 2 August to a train departing for Moscow. He was allowed, however, to stop for three days at Danilov between Vologda and Moscow until all his charges had passed through. Arriving with the remnants of the other missions, he found Moscow as confused as everywhere else in Russia. "The Bolsheviks have gone quite mad. They are on their last legs and know it, but unfortunately there seems to be no one or no party to take their place if they should fall, so this state of affairs may drag on indefinitely and personally I should not be surprised to see them still in the saddle next spring."[93]

After the British landing at Archangel, Moscow was in a state of panic, since initial reports exaggerated the numbers to as many as 100,000.[94] At least Armour, Consul General Poole, and their small staffs fared better than their British and French colleagues, who, along with as many as 200 or more compatriot residents, spent several days under arrest in early August before being released, when the size of the Allied Archangel expedition turned out to be quite small. Surprisingly, life for the remaining foreign diplomats and other foreign residents returned to near normalcy for a couple of weeks in August. They met regularly at the offices of the American consul general to discuss affairs, played football (soccer), socialized with friends, and even continued to move funds south into anti-Bolshevik hands for the purchase of strategic supplies.[95]

Chicherin, somewhat peevishly, but in contrast to his assistant Lev Karakhan's more aggressive stance, wrote DeWitt Poole, "We have done nothing to provoke this aggression, our people want nothing else but to remain in peace and friendship with all the toiling masses of all other countries."[96] More bad news came from Petrograd. Consul Imbrie urgently requested more merchandise and food: "Cannot emphasize too strongly relapse of economic life of former great nation to primitive condition, money has limited use."[97]

For other Americans it was a day-to-day existence. Helen Ogden and her fellow "Y" men and women were advised by Poole on 1 August to prepare to leave immediately, but they continued scaled-down operations in Moscow for two more weeks. She reported to her family:

93. Armour to Whitehouse, 19 August 1918, Armour Papers, Princeton-Mudd. He added a postscript in his own hand: "If you have the slightest idea of what the Dept's plans are for G——'s sake let us know—as they have sent no word for ages."

94. Lockhart, *Memoirs of a British Agent*, 308–9. Lockhart was disappointed that the invading force turned out to be so small. "It was a blunder comparable with the worst mistakes of the Crimean War." Ibid., 311.

95. Ibid., 312–14.

96. Chicherin to Poole, 5 August 1918, copy in box 707, WA-6, RG 45, NA.

97. Imbrie to Lansing, 11 August 1918, ibid.

It is certainly an interesting life with no monotony and I'm afraid I'll never be able to get along again with less than a revolution a week. If you could only see me peacefully attending to my housekeeping, going on picnics, washing my hair, darning stockings, reading in bed, in fact doing all the most ordinary things, I'm sure you would feel more comfortable about me. For in spite of a continual undercurrent of excitement and tenseness, life runs along very smoothly in much the same grooves as it does at home.[98]

Soon they were on the move, their building in Moscow having been "requisitioned," to Nizhni Novgorod, where they lodged on their train, not knowing what would happen next but expecting somehow to exit to the east. They passed time sightseeing through the renowned but totally deserted fairgrounds. During the two weeks spent in the Volga city, they had an exciting skirmish and "arrest" by local Red Guards and were held for questioning for several hours at the station. But in general they enjoyed relaxed time for reading and good food.[99] The main problem was that their venerable chief, Ethan Colton, was seriously afflicted with rheumatism.[100]

Then at the end of the month, to their surprise, Poole summoned them back to Moscow to board a special train for Finland and Sweden.[101] They managed to carry out a lot of baggage, including many valuable souvenirs.[102] The "Y" personnel were treated especially well by the Bolsheviks at this time, probably because of the service they performed in caring for returning Russian prisoners of war. But with the departure of this train from Moscow, most American contact with Russia was confined to the non-Bolshevik regions. Finally, the Cheka, from its Lubianka headquarters, officially shut down the YMCA on Bolshevik territory: "*Association to be closed, property to be Confiscated.* Persons employed as couriers . . . *to be sent abroad or to be kept in concentration camps.*"[103]

Businessmen were reluctant to leave the scene of much of their time and investment but eventually had to face the reality, not so much of a Bolshevik socialist government but of a collapsing economy. With their Moscow suburb plant

98. Ogden to family, 13-14 August 1918, f. Ogden Corresp. July–Aug. 1918, box 3, Lowrie/Ogden Papers, UIA.

99. Donald Lowrie to Folks, letter 53, 6 September 1918, f. July–Sept. 1918, box 1, ibid.

100. Colton memorandum, 26 August 1918, f. YMCA Inter. Comm., box 5, Anderson Papers, UIA.

101. Lowrie to Folks, letter 55, 6 September 1918 [same date as above], ibid.

102. See list in ibid., 10 September 1918.

103. Peters (All Russian Extraordinary [*sic*] Commission for Combatting Counter-Revolution) to YMCA, 25 October 1918, f. YMCA Russia, box 5, Anderson Papers, UIA; emphasis in original.

practically closed, Singer managers found relief in somehow forwarding much of its substantial inventory to the south, where they continued to operate with profit, because of demand for machines to sew new uniforms for the fledgling White armies in Ukraine and Siberia, but they also had to contend with shops being expropriated by assorted armed forces and self-styled militias. In mid-November Singer still had 250 shops with 2,000 employees functioning in the south of Russia.[104] Otar Myslik reported that the factory was still intact with a skeleton workforce and estimated the inventory held there at 80,000 family machines and 30,000 commercial. Under the direction of company engineer Aleksei Miliukov (brother of Paul Miliukov!), one section of the plant was being re-equipped as a railway repair shop.[105] And even in the Moscow area, sales in late 1918 and early 1919 were over 2,500 units. Despite revolution and civil war, some Russian-American commerce and industry persisted.[106]

The American insurance companies in Russia did not have plants to try to keep operating but were left with many policies in abeyance. The Soviet government basically ignored them and let them stew in legal controversy for the next fifty years. Frederick Corse of New York Life commented, "It seems that the insurance business is practically the only business which the Bolsheviks did not nationalize."[107] It would have been better if they had, considering the high legal fees the companies faced.

On the diplomatic side, Chicherin and his staff were clearly as perplexed as their Washington counterparts in dealing with the situation. Besides carrying on an awkward discourse with Poole on various matters through September, the commissar also commiserated with Allan Wardwell, left in charge of the remnants of the American Red Cross mission to Russia. In response to Wardwell's protest about the "Red Terror" in Moscow, Chicherin complained that the Red Cross did not acknowledge the atrocities on the other side. In one letter in his own hand in English, Chicherin berated Wardwell's "intervention as a displaced inmixtion [sic] in the affairs of a foreign state."[108] He was bitter about the failure of the Red Cross to protest intervention. "I would be glad to learn what the American Red Cross has done in order to publicly brand these atrocities, the every-day work of our enemies, everywhere practiced by them upon our

104. Myslik (Odessa) to Alexander (New York), 16 November and 5 and 6 December 1918, box 156, Singer Papers, SHSW.

105. Myslik to Alexander, 8 December 1918, ibid.

106. Myslik to Alexander, 25 March 1919, ibid.

107. Corse to Francis, 7 November 1918, reel 11, Francis Papers, MoHS.

108. Wardwell-Chicherin correspondence notes, September 1918, f. commission file, box 866, RG 200, NA.

friends when they have the power to do it."[109] But Bolshevik confidence grew somewhat in late September after a victory over the Czechs at Kazan and a sense that Allied intervention was quite limited.

Other less connected Americans did the best they could wherever they were. Karin Sante, still superintending the vacant embassy building in Petrograd, reported that she was managing despite a severe food shortage: "Everything is perfectly all right and in good order. Is just being washed and cleaned for the winter."[110] Even the ambassador's old friend, Matilda de Cram, surfaced to report her ability to survive—but with considerable difficulty: "Myself without money. Impossible to find any employment. Country house furniture requested. Prohibited any sale. . . . Body weak. Spirit still strong. Sons alive."[111] Zenaida Ragozin, choosing to stay behind in semipoverty and destitution because of an arthritic disability, related a similar scenario but was proud that what was left of the American community had rallied for a gala occasion to celebrate her eighty-fifth birthday. Alexis Babin, another displaced American of Russian origin, trapped in Russia, recounted in his diary the difficulty of surviving through the terror of the fall and winter of 1918–19 in the Volga region. With the family estate in ruins in Ukraine, Julia Cantacuzene-Speransky found temporary refuge in Crimea. The same fortitude was displayed by many others of that class and generation.

Washington

The public discussion of American intervention in Russia varied across the spectrum from enthusiasm to hostility, from "about time," to "what is the purpose," to "not enough," to "hands off Russia." Kennan was quick to congratulate Lansing on finally following his advice: "If the sane and patriotic Russians in the trans-Baikal are properly supported, and are furnished with arms, ammunition and much needed supplies, they will soon put an end to the domination of the Bolsheviki and the Germans."[112] Lansing's response was more hesitant: "I hope your prediction as to the friendly welcome of our troops will be realized."[113] Raymond Robins expressed some of the frustration outside Washington at the muddle there concerning Russia:

109. Chicherin to Wardwell, 11 September 1918, box 707, WA-6, RG 45, NA.
110. Schmedeman (Christiania) to Francis, quoting letters, 27 November 1918, reel 11, Francis Papers, MoHS.
111. Ibid.
112. Kennan to Lansing, 9 August 1918, vol. 37, Lansing Papers, MD, LC.
113. Lansing to Kennan, 15 August 1918, vol. 38, ibid.

Two clear policies were open in the Russian situation-one, definite opposition to the Soviet power, which should have been clearly stated and then followed by a sufficient armed force to intervene effectively in Siberia and to inspire the opposition to the Soviets with the hope of speedy success; the other, co-operation with the Soviets in rebuilding the economic life of Russia and organizing a revolutionary army, thus establishing a fighting front against the Central Powers in the only way such a front can be established by the Russia of this hour. The President has adopted neither policy. He stands feebly by the Czecho Slovaks, who are alien soldiers at war with the Soviet power, and yet talks of an Economic Commission to the Russian people and says he is against armed intervention.[114]

Robins apparently did not understand that his own forceful presentation of the case for the latter policy during the first half of 1918 had contributed to the indecision.

The American government in August and September was still concentrating on winning the war on the Western Front—and that was indeed being accomplished. In the meantime, consideration was again raised on sending a special mission as a civil gesture to mollify the effects of the military presence. There was an abundance of recommendations on its composition. George Kennan, emphasizing the failure of the Root mission, "that did not understand what was going on around it" and "did not influence the course of events in Russia in the slightest degree," advised careful consideration of "the mixture of air and gas in the carburetor [as] the American air and the Russian gas did not mix at all—they did not even get in contact." His solution was to detach Franklin Lane from his post at the Department of the Interior to head such a mission, because he "knows what Socialism can and cannot do. He is also accustomed to deal [sic] with big affairs and to look at things in a broad way."[115] In recommending advisers for the commission, Kennan cited his Russian friends Konovalov, Korff, and, interestingly, Nicholas Russel, a Russian physician and revolutionary exile who had achieved a certain notoriety in San Francisco in the 1880s but was now practicing medicine in Japan.[116]

114. To Theodore Roosevelt, 24 August 1918, f. July–August, box 14, Robins Papers, SHSW.

115. Kennan to Lansing, 18 August 1918, box 4, Kennan Papers, MD, LC.

116. Ibid. Kennan's relationship with Russel began with his sojourn in Japan during the Russo-Japanese War. For more on Russel's exotic career, see Terence Emmons, *Alleged Sex and Threatened Violence: Doctor Russel, Bishop Vladimir, and the Russians in San Francisco, 1887–1892* (Stanford, Calif.: Stanford University Press, 1997).

Just who could be spared was one problem; another was to avoid a repetition of the Root "fiasco." Learning of the prospect of a new mission in Archangel, Francis could think of no American knowledgeable about Russia, of all those he had known during his tenure, to recommend except his old friends Corse and Crane.[117] Crane was on his way to China, while Corse hesitated about Lane and thought the situation called for someone of the stature of William Howard Taft or Theodore Roosevelt. He especially feared the choice of Louis Brandeis, "feeling that [he] had been much influenced by Robbins [sic] and was more or less sympathetic with the point of view taken by the New Republic."[118]

The Russian Bureau and Batolin

While the project of a special mission to Russia floundered, another idea gained the support of the president. This was to establish a special agency, dubbed "the Russian Bureau," to coordinate and increase trade with Russia and to act as a conduit for aid to the Czechs and other parties under the administration of Vance McCormick and the War Trade Board.[119] This may have been partly inspired by the activities of Petr Batolin, as well as a desire to head off an effort by the Department of Commerce and Secretary William Redfield to get into Russian affairs. Harper, Batolin's initial chaperone in Washington, reported, "I was told that he gave the impulse to the economic side of our Russian program."[120] Harper was quite enthusiastic about Batolin at first, writing Mott, "I consider him the best if not the only medium through which to start the program of economic assistance."[121] But many were disappointed at the results: "The general ignorance in this country on certain phases of the Russian situation is nothing less than appalling."[122]

The Russian Bureau seems to have been inspired by State Department officials Long, Polk, and Gordon Auchincloss in their continuing rivalry with the Department of Commerce. Auchincloss was a confidant of both House and the president, and the idea of using Batolin as an entrée into Siberian economic

---

117. Francis to Crane, 29 August 1918, reel 10, Francis Papers, MoHS.
118. Corse to Harper, 2 August 1918, f. 15, box 5, Harper Papers, UC.
119. For a detailed and critical appraisal, see Linda Killen, *The Russian Bureau: A Case Study in Wilsonian Diplomacy* (Lexington: University Press of Kentucky, 1983).
120. Harper to Roger Williams, 18 October 1918, reel 2, Crane Papers, BA, CU.
121. Harper to Mott, 17 August 1918, f. 18, box 5, Harper Papers, UC.
122. Graham Taylor to Harper, 24 August 1918, f. 19, ibid.

affairs received the blessings of Lansing.[123] According to Basil Miles, this was the result of a hasty compromise to present to the president "some general scheme for Russia which he could approve."[124] Having conceived the notion of an independent Russian Bureau, the State Department found that it had created a rival and took a dim view of the enterprise from the beginning to the end.

Batolin reached Washington in August, posing as a self-styled Siberian millionaire of peasant origins—a male counterpart to Bochkareva. Although speaking hardly a word of English, he impressed almost everyone he met, which included J. P. Morgan, Cyrus McCormick, Robert Lansing, Thomas Masaryk, Charles Schwab, Charles Crane, and especially Edward House.[125] Through the assistance of Samuel Harper, with whom he lived for a month, the American political and business communities were at his service, up to, but not including, the president and John D. Rockefeller.[126] Colonel House was especially impressed: "I think Russian matters will move faster now and that Mr. Batolin will soon begin to see the good effect of his visit."[127] Bakhmeteff, while supporting Batolin, lobbied ineffectively for more American support for the fledgling "government" in Omsk. Breckinridge Long, after a three-hour conference with Batolin, Bakhmeteff, Landfield, and Harper,[128] noted in his diary, "I told him [Bakhmeteff] that we could send supplies and lend men to the Czechs because we recognized them as a nation, but that there was no Government in Russia which we could recognize."[129]

Harper was disappointed that Batolin did not get to see the "Chief."[130] By late November he had definitely overextended his stay, and Washington's

123. Lansing to Wilson, 9 September 1918, *PWW* 49:491–93; Richard Crane to Charles Crane, 24 October 1918, reel 2, Crane Papers, BA, CU. This new agency for Russian aid was, in fact, coordinated with what Wilson termed his "little war board." Long diary, 8 September 1918, box 1, Long Papers, MD, LC.

124. Miles to Francis, 1 November 1918, reel 11, Francis Papers, MoHS.

125. Harper to House, 28 August 1918, f. 20, box 5, Harper Papers, UC; "Memorandum on Batolin," box 1, Roland Morris Papers, MD, LC. The State Department was asking Morris to assist Batolin on a return to Siberia mission.

126. Rockefeller to Harper, 9 September 1918, f. 21, box 5, Harper Papers, UC.

127. House to Harper, 9 September 1918, ibid.

128. Long diary, 7 September 1918, box 1, Long Papers, MD, LC. Harper continued to be impressed by Batolin's down-to-earth performance: "It was a great education to be closely associated with that most 'real' man, of peasant origin, and direct and keen." Harper to Roger Williams, 18 October 1918, f. 3, box 6, Harper Papers, UC.

129. Long, memorandum of conversation, 17 September 1918, box 187, and Diary, box 1, Long Papers, MD, LC.

130. Harper to Mott, 3 October 1918, f. 24, box 5, Harper Papers, UC. Exactly what eventually happened to this mysterious Batolin is not clear. He was passed back and forth between Chicago and New York and various Russian-interested business groups. Harper found too much intrigue involved. Harper to Porter, 26 October 1918, f. 2, box 6, ibid.

patience had worn thin. Harper was surprised that he had been left out of the formation of the Russian Bureau of the War Trade Board.[131] Harper, at a loss over what to do next regretted that Colonel House (in Europe) was no longer available; he hoped that Batolin would simply return to Russia.[132] Landfield interviewed Batolin again on 29 November with Frank Polk. "The only thing I gathered from Batolin himself was his inordinate conceit. I certainly have lost all belief in his humanitarian professions."[133] This simple Russian with the charisma of a Rasputin obviously struck some chords among the American political and economic establishment, but its effect was no more than a distracting fly in the sticky Russian ointment.

Another prominent Russian with much talk and little substance, Prince Georgi Lvov, the first actual head of the Provisional Government, arrived on the Washington scene belatedly in November as a representative of the Omsk government. Unfortunately for him, that government underwent considerable change while he was in transit, and he seemed somewhat baffled about what to do. Landfield lamented, "I had hoped that his experiences might have taught him something and he might be more forceful and practical. But alas, there is no evidence of this and he remains the same kindly charming and impotent man."[134] Despite this honest appraisal, Lvov rated a rare interview with the president. Like Landfield, most American officials were clearly frustrated by the inability to find a Russian to lead Russia on an American path.[135] The too few Miliukovs had already fallen along that road.

Nonetheless, the Russian Bureau was allocated $5 million to help subsidize trade with Russia. Not surprisingly, it got off to a slow start, partly because it was staffed with personnel from the War Trade Board who knew nothing about Russia and had other duties. The big problem was finding the facility for expanding commerce on the Russian side. It drafted August Heid, an experienced International Harvester representative in Siberia, as its agent for Vladivostok[136] and Consul Felix Cole for Archangel, thus covering two main access points. After arriving at the latter place in November 1918, DeWitt Poole was quite

131. Landfield to Harper, 22 November 1918, f. 7, ibid.
132. Harper to Landfield, 26 November 1918, ibid.
133. Landfield to Harper, 29 November 1918, ibid.
134. Ibid.
135. Harper passed this and other Landfield letters on to McCormick and Mott with his endorsement: "Landfield is the closest to what is going on in Russia, and in Washington also. I have confidence in his judgement. I tell him that he is not very much of a Liberal, and he tells me to be a bit more practical." Harper to McCormick, 27 November 1918, f. 4, box 6, ibid.
136. Lansing to Morris, 23 September 1918, box 4, Roland Morris Papers, MD, LC.

pessimistic, writing diplomatically that he would not want to give the impression that great economic opportunities existed there: "I am constrained to say, and Mr. Cole agrees with me, that unless the general situation in Russia undergoes a radical change before next spring, private enterprise will have relatively limited scope in this region, and will probably find this market much less attractive than many others."[137] That was putting it mildly. One of the first commendable actions of the bureau was to seek available young men of good character who could speak Russian.[138] Good luck! The Russian Bureau, such as it was, set forth goals to expand trade and foster capital investments—in short, to "promote such trade with Russia as will assist in the rehabilitation of her economic life."[139]

A Saga of Dilemma

Those Americans, like Robins, who were keenly interested in Russia were quite disappointed by these halfway measures. Corse complained to Harper that "the administration does not accept kindly any suggestion relating to Russian relief, intimating that the action now taken by the War Trade Board, in sending some goods to Russia, is all that public opinion calls for." But he also blamed his own community: "Very few business people in this country are keen on Russian business."[140] Vance McCormick admitted that the bureau's main purpose was basically limited to sending relief supplies for the Czechs,[141] while Jerome Landfield was so upset by the bypass of his expertise in the State Department that he resigned his short-lived tenure as an expert on Russian affairs.[142] Russia

137. Poole to Lansing, 11 December 1918, DPR 335, Russia 1918, RG 84, NA. One of later fame was John Foster Dulles, who served as secretary.

138. War Trade Board to Harper, 1 October 1918, f. 25, box 5, Harper Papers, UC.

139. Vance McCormick memorandum, War Trade Board, 30 November 1918, f. War Trade Board, McC, 2C, box 116, McCormick Papers, SHSW. The Russian Bureau's board of directors included no one with any Russian expertise and no person of any note, except perhaps John Foster Dulles as secretary-treasurer.

140. Corse to Harper, 4 December 1918, f. 8, box 6, Harper Papers, UC.

141. Vance McCormick to Cyrus McCormick, 5 October 1918, f. War Trade Board, box 116, McC, 2C, McCormick Papers, SHSW. In his response, Cyrus McCormick regretted the obsession with the Western Front in Washington: "Just now the thoughts of every one are centered upon the Western front. . . . Tho I do not suppose for a moment that we can expect Russia to get much attention, I will make it a point to see you the next time I am in Washington."

142. Landfield to Harper, 4 and 6 December 1918, f. 8, box 6, Harper papers, UC. Already at the end of October, he informed Harper, "I do not see that I can do much more

as a "promised land" for increased American business was now displaced by the new Europe of the peacemakers. Harper regretted that Chapin Huntington, another real expert, was ignored in setting up the Russian Bureau.[143]

For its part, the State Department was literally laid low: Lansing was on the outs with nearly everyone; Phillips wanted nothing to do with the Russian mess; Polk was exhausted and out of the office most of the time; and, in the crucial month of October, Long came down with the Spanish flu, incapacitated for over three weeks. America's Russian problem may simply have been lost to exhaustion and disease.[144] Louis Brandeis, when queried by Straus about reports of aid being sent to Russia, replied that it would be a serious mistake to make "American relief conditional upon some political undertaking of the Bolshevik government."[145]

Landfield saw clearly the dilemma of American support for one or another Russian cause: "What I do fear is this. It is not only the class of large land owners that has been restored to possession and maintained in the Ukraine and the Baltic Provinces by German bayonets, but all the smaller bourgeoisie there owe their existence to the same support."[146] Cyrus McCormick also thought that, amid all the concentration on events in France, a boat was being missed in regard to Russia. "I feel greatly the need of doing something for poor Russia," he commented, but like others he did not know what.[147] Landfield reflected philosophically on departing government service:

> To me all that has gone on in the past two years seems like waves on the surface of the deep sea. The nature, the beliefs, and the psychology of the

here, ... I am anxious for active service, and am considering the possibility of getting a commission and going to Siberia for Military Intelligence, after which perhaps the War Trade Board may make use of me. . . . It might be better to go back to San Francisco as a private citizen, and devote myself to influencing public opinion on the Pacific Coast toward assistance to Russia." Landfield to Harper, 31 October 1918, box 5, ibid. Frustrations abound!

143. Harper to Huntington, 28 October 1918, f. 2, box 6, Harper Papers, UC.

144. Long, the person in Washington most directly responsible for Russian policy, frequently complained of the work burden, for example, in a diary entry for 20 August 1919: "I had appointments with and saw 18 different people . . . [and] left the office disgusted with the system which prevents an executive officer in charge of policy from having time enough to think about any one thing for more than thirty seconds without interruption." And then he cryptically recorded the worsening state of affairs: 1 October—Polk ill, hair gray; 8 October—has flu, raging here; October 20—all public meetings prohibited; 4 November—weight 129 pounds. Diary, box 1, Long Papers, MD, LC.

145. Straus to Hoover, 15 November 1918, f. Russia, ARA Europe, Paris File, HIA.

146. Landfield to Harper, 2 November 1918, f. 3, box 6, Harper Papers, UC.

147. McCormick to Vance McCormick, 7 December 1918, f. War Trade Board, box 116, McC, 2C, McCormick Papers, SHSW.

Russian people have not changed. There is the same inertia, the same depth of religious feeling, the same fundamental aspirations. The agitation and interplay of politicians may go on for some time as a sort of rash on the body politic and interfere seriously with economic health.

His parting shot: "The government is sensitive only to public opinion and as long as the Russian question is not put forward strongly it will continue to be shunted aside by questions of far less importance."[148] Indeed, the administration was under increasing criticism from conservative Republicans for its ambiguous Russian policy.

The real problem, however, was that the White House was focused on armistice terms with the Central Powers and the peace negotiations that would follow. Very little mention of Russia can be found in any correspondence or conference memorandums for the months of October and November, while American forces in north Russia and Siberia were wondering why they were there and what to do. When Sir William Wiseman queried him about Russia on 16 October, Wilson responded,

> My policy regarding Russia is very similar to my Mexican policy. I believe in letting them work out their own salvation, even though they wallow in anarchy for a while. I visualize it like this: A lot of impossible folk, fighting among themselves. You cannot do business with them, so you shut them all up in a room and lock the door and tell them that when they have settled matters among themselves you will unlock the door and do business.[149]

"The question of Russia, he thought, should be left to the Peace Conference."[150]

Adding to the confusion on Russia, a new broadly based organization was formed as a Washington lobby, the American-Russian League, formally "An American League to Aid and Cooperate with Russia," a revival of earlier cooperative efforts. It included a who's who of the American liberal establishment, loosely defined. Its letterhead listed around a hundred names, headed by Frank Goodnow as president and an unlikely trio of William Boyce Thompson, Oscar Straus, and James Duncan (the silent labor member of the Root mission)

---

148. Landfield to Harper, 4 December 1918, f. 5, box 6, Harper Papers, UC. He joined the publicity campaign of the American-Russian Chamber of Commerce. Porter to Harper, 10 December 1918, ibid.

149. As quoted by Wiseman, memorandum of interview of 16 October 1918, *PWW* 51:350.

150. Ibid., 351.

among the vice presidents. The real moving force was Herbert Carpenter of the American-Russian Chamber of Commerce as chairman of the executive committee.[151] Because of its wide range and the other occupations of most of its members, this organization, like many previous ones, had very limited, if any, influence over the course of events in the late fall of 1918.

Harper, meanwhile, became more and more discouraged at the administration's lack of attention to Russia in late 1918, as "the chief" and his closest advisers were totally engrossed in the approaching peace negotiations. He was especially disappointed that the president could not find time to hear Chapin Huntington, probably the leading expert on Russia at this time. "I wished he had, for he gives a very clear statement. Why will not the chief see men like Huntington, yet spend hours talking the Russian situation with such men as Weyl and Brandeis?"[152] Harper consoled himself that a successful negotiation in Paris might lend weight to solving the Russia problem.

On the somewhat muted left wing of American opinion, a major battle was brewing over the Sisson documents that were finally released to the press and published officially in a government pamphlet in September. When challenged by Louise Bryant, incidentally an old friend, Creel adamantly proclaimed the documents' authenticity: "Absolutely cannot be fakes. Your position is only one of faith in Lenin. Every happening in Russia has been an indictment of these creatures."[153] Sisson and Creel charged on, oblivious to any sense of decent responsibility, despite the fact that most credible authorities doubted the documents' authenticity. "Breck" Long was upset that the State Department was never consulted about them and that their release could jeopardize the safety of Poole and others still in Moscow.[154] He labeled the "so-called Sisson Story" an "anti-Bolshevic [sic] document propaganda. . . . We had not been consulted. The effect on Poole, who is still at Moscow with a few Americans, will be to put him and them in a hazardous position."[155] The obvious irresponsibility of Sisson and Creel harmed their quite legitimate cause and permanently damaged their reputations. Raymond Robins, Sisson's old foe, was approached by John Reed,

151. Carpenter to Harper, 5 October 1918, f. 22, box 5, Harper Papers, UC.
152. Harper to Mott, 4 December 1918, ibid.
153. Creel to Bryant, 20 September 1918, Reed/Bryant Papers, Harvard-Houghton.
154. Long diary, 15 September 1918, box 1, Long Papers, MD, LC.
155. Ibid. Even Harper, who had helped authenticate them, thought that some were in doubt and agreed with Long. "I have been a bit skeptical, for between us, no consultation with the State Department. Each place runs its own show independent down here." Harper to Corse, 18 September 1918, f. 22, box 5, Harper Papers, UC. See also Harper to Roger Williams, 27 October 1918, reel 2, Crane Papers, BA, CU.

Herbert Croly, editor of *New Republic*, and others to write a rebuttal. Little should have been needed.

Samuel Harper, embarrassed by his role as an authenticator in the affair, asked, belatedly, to see the originals or at least facsimiles thereof, having seen only typewritten copies.[156] After seeing some of these, and despite Corse's declaration of their genuineness, he toned down his verification to a cautious acceptance.[157] He also lamented to Vance McCormick that there were so few Americans who knew Russian and who could be trusted.[158] But he was deeply hurt by the *Nation*'s personal criticism of his and Jameson's roles in the affair.[159]

The war news from France heralded triumphant victories and for a few weeks drowned out the Left's cry for their Russian cause. Harper could assure Chapin Huntington upon his return to the United States, "Don't worry over Raymond Robbins [sic]—he is out of the running completely. I cannot make out just where WBT [William Boyce Thompson] comes in now, or what he is doing. Albert Rhys Williams is back, talking very loose and wild, in my opinion."[160] And down went the pro-recognition lobby, much to their own blame. Harper then posed the universal Russian question to his friend Corse, "Chto dyelat?"—What is to be done?[161] He questioned why no one seemed to understand that "now was the time for all good Eastern Fronters to rise to the call." He thought, correctly, that the concentration on the Western Front was leaving the East in the dust.[162]

But if recognition was only simmering on the back burner, intervention was not faring much better. Robert Lansing, regaining some stature in the Washington power picture, wrote an eloquent statement for intervention, a cry in the dark, to Elihu Root in October:

> There are two great evils at work in the world today, Absolutism, the power of which is waning, and Bolshevism, the power of which is increasing. We have seen the hideous consequences of Bolshevik rule in Russia and we know that the doctrine is spreading westward. The possibility of a proletariat despotism over Central Europe is terrible to contemplate.

156. Harper to Sisson, 1 October 1918, f. 25, box 5, Harper Papers, UC.
157. Corse to Harper, 21 October, and Harper to Jameson, 30 October 1918, f. 3, box 6, ibid.
158. Harper to V. McCormick, 3 October 1918, ibid.
159. Editorial, "The Sisson Documents," *Nation* 107 (23 November 1918): 616-17; Jameson to Harper, 30 November 1918, f. 7, box 6, Harper Papers, UC.
160. Harper to Huntington, 11 October 1918, f. 1, box 6, ibid.
161. Harper to Corse, 14 October 1918, ibid.
162. Harper to Porter, 17 October 1918, f. 3, ibid.

Democracy *without* education and Autocracy *with* education are the great
enemies we have to face today. But I believe the former is the greater evil
since it is destructive of law and order. How can we best utilize the hostility
of these two principles, which are at opposite poles of political thought, so
that both will be weakened?[163]

Others who favored a smart, quick intervention were dismayed by Washington's
slowness and methods. Harper still had little confidence in the War Trade Board
initiative of a Russian Bureau. Corse seconded his view: "It will be a long time
before America can think of going into Russia with capital. . . . I am trying to
get a coterie of bankers organized, representing much bigger capital than the
National City who would take hold of Russia in a large way," but he had little
leverage with the eastern financial establishment.[164]

The end of the war in Europe naturally caused reevaluations of an American
presence in Russia. Newton Baker reflected that we were in Murmansk and
Archangel to protect supplies and in Vladivostok to assist the Czechs. "Neither military expedition was in theory hostile either to Russia or to any faction
or party in Russia."[165] The only reason for staying in Russia, he concluded,
was the large Japanese presence there. In response to an effort of Cyrus
McCormick to get reinforcements sent, Baker voiced a new pragmatism on
the Russian situation:

I don't know that I rightly understand Bolshevikism [*sic*]. So much of it as
I do understand I don't like, but I have a feeling that if the Russians do
like it, they are entitled to have it and that it does not lie with us to say that
only ten percent of the Russian people are Bolsheviks and that therefore
we will assist the other ninety percent in resisting it, which is the case as
Mr. Cyrus McCormick states it.[166]

Chapin Huntington returned from Russia in mid-November and was appalled
at the conflicting information circulating about Russia, but his effort to clarify
matters by casting the problem in broad historical terms fell on deaf ears, in part
because his agency, the Department of Commerce, no longer had a voice on
Russian affairs:

163. Lansing to Root, 28 October 1918, box 136, Root Papers, MD, LC.
164. Corse to Harper, 16 October 1918, f. 3, box 6, Harper Papers, UC.
165. Baker, Memorandum on Siberia, 27 November 1918, copy in f. Baker, box 1, Pre-
Commerce, HPL; and in *PWW* 53:227, with slightly different wording.
166. Ibid.

In considering political Russia it is not hard to understand how under the constant tragedy of contrast and tyranny, radicalism should be most natural. It became, and is, the dominant note in Russian political life. It is not strange that the Russian Radicals, looking to the Western countries for experience, and conceding their superiority, should have imported Socialism, one brand for the industrial workmen in the cities and another for the peasants.[167]

In short, Washington seemed totally confused about what to do about Russia on the eve of the peace negotiations in Paris.

Russian Studies

As during and after World War II, the Russian Revolution promoted new specialized studies centers on Russia at Chicago, Harvard, Dartmouth, and elsewhere. Samuel Harper was especially under the gun and had to drop his regular course in Russian culture to give a series of general lectures on Russia, but this was a popular-level "war aims" course. His regular elementary Russian language course drew the lowest level yet, only three students. He also felt pressure to respond to public demand and give many public lectures not only on Russia but also on the eastern European situation in general. Harper felt especially obligated to serve these demands and responded to them, even when they required additional research, until the flu quarantine in August canceled public gatherings in the city. But he still went elsewhere and appealed to the "Crane Foundation" for funds to cover his out-of-town expenses for appearances, though Batolin, somehow, paid part of them.[168]

The situation in Russia, such a surprise to so many Americans, naturally caused some reflection and reevaluation. Arthur Bullard, on his way home from Russia, wrote Creel, "It was really appalling to see the old Imperial Lies crumbling to pieces. So very many things we had carefully been taught to believe about Russia, simply aren't so. Russia isn't a nation, it's a continent with quite as many animosities and clashing interests as the rest of Europe."[169] This American befuddlement with the new Russia echoed a similar refrain on the left. Upton Sinclair wrote Reed that he was trying to see both sides but that the problem "is

---

167. Huntington, "Memorandum on the Russian Situation," 22 November 1918, copy in f. Dept. of Commerce, box 115, McC, 2C, McCormick Papers, SHSW.

168. Harper to Williams, 10 October 1918, box 6, Harper Papers, UC. Harper kept meticulous accounts, barely covering expenses on his local and distant lectures.

169. Bullard to Creel, 26 August 1918, Bullard Papers, Princeton-Mudd.

the most complicated in history."[170] After Reed in response acclaimed the simplicity and "splendor of the Bolshevik dream," Sinclair rebutted: "And some of my American friends who have been to Russia expect me to sympathize with the forces that have thrown Kropotkin into jail, and not find it the least bit complicated and distressing!"[171] Reed himself was busy working on his book on the revolution, while his spouse, Louise Bryant, toured the country speaking, mainly to pay their expenses.[172]

But left-wing socialists were not the only ones who were inclined to seek a reconciliation with Russia, no matter what government it might have. A number of Russophiles, including journalists such as Eugene Lyons and William Henry Chamberlin and "academics" like Samuel Cross, Edward Ross, and even Harper, hoped to salvage cultural contacts. And they had the support of a number of people in the business community. Above all, in this period Russia was attracting considerable public attention in articles, editorials, and public forums. Russia, as after World War II, became a matter of high-priority intelligence.

The army sent a number of men for "special training" for the fall semester of 1918 at Dartmouth, where Elizabeth Hapgood had been hired the previous spring to establish a Russian language department (and incidentally to become its first woman faculty member).[173] Overwhelmed by ninety enrollees in her fledgling Russian program, she sought an assistant. To Harper, her old friend and now rival, she appealed for a "university man" who could also give lectures in history and politics and "was free from propaganda." She emphasized that Dartmouth wanted to get the job done, and "so will pay."[174] In their spare time, Harper, Hapgood, and many others with some credentials or knowledge of Russia were involved in public education: lectures, forums, meetings. Unlike after World War II, this interest would be fleeting and transitory.

Preparing for Peace

The cessation of the war in most of Europe, rather suddenly in November, reoriented much of the thinking on the Russian situation. Unfortunately, much of it

---

170. Sinclair to Reed, 4 October 1918, f. 780–84, Reed/Bryant Papers, Harvard-Houghton.

171. Sinclair to Reed, 22 October 1918, ibid. Sinclair would later refer to Reed, jokingly, as "the playboy of the socialist revolution," a name that stuck. To Reed, 14 May 1919, ibid.

172. There are a number of references in their correspondence during this period to financial difficulties. Obviously, they had received nothing from their Bolshevik friends.

173. Elizabeth Hapgood to Norman Hapgood, 22 March 1918, box 16, Hapgood-Reynolds Papers, MD, LC.

174. E. Reynolds Hapgood to Harper, 17 October 1918, f. 3, box 6, Harper Papers, UC.

was distracted by the geopolitics of remapping Europe. Still, a call for reassessment of Russia was in the background as a ghost or shadow over Versailles. Norman Hapgood wrote Frank Polk at the end of December, "Of course I know there is terrific hostility in all the Western world to such an experiment as Lenin is making, but I do believe he is beginning to gain strength, and I also believe it is up to Russia and not up to us to decide whether his experiments shall go on and be modified by the natural course of events or dictated by the western forces."[175] Polk responded with a simple parable: "A man who worked with Lenine said that Lenine recognized his own shortcomings as his mission was to destroy and now that he had destroyed, he was considerably embarrassed by the fact that he had no creative faculties."[176] One viewpoint that thus gained ground was that the Bolsheviks could be shaped, cajoled, molded (bought?) to fit into the great new postwar world.

But there was also a more pessimistic view, that a peace would be made in Paris without a real peace. William Allen White, the sage of Emporia, was among the first to perceive an approaching division of the world:

Bolshevism is a real danger for the next few years. . . . It can never take hold in a community where a majority of the laboring men own their homes and a majority of farmers own their land. It appeals to the landless and homeless. The most stabilizing influence in any country is the ownership of a bit of ground. The wisest statesmanship is that which will enable every individual to have that stake, that little possession.[177]

But a difference was evident still in what to do about it. Some, like White, argued that there was nothing the United States could do, morally and legally, while others saw a mission to fulfill in assuring that the world was really left safe for democracy, American-style.

All indications are that Russia was very much on the president's mind on the eve of his departure for Paris. He certainly continued to be besieged by interested parties. Rabbi Stephen Wise told George Kennan that he had finally been able to see Wilson expressly to plead the cause of greater intervention, but he thought without success, because Wilson was under the "influence of Walter Lippmann of *New Republic* and other Bolsheviks."[178] If anything the anti-

175. N. Hapgood to Polk, 26 December 1918, f. 232 (Hapgood), box 7, Polk Papers, Yale-Sterling.

176. Polk to Hapgood, 31 December 1918, ibid.

177. To T. Dumont Smith (attorney, Hutchinson, Kansas), 21 November 1918, C47, 1918 (S-W), White Papers, MD, LC.

178. Kennan 1919 diary, 10 February, box 14, Kennan Papers, MD, LC.

intervention forces seemed to strengthen as a result of the approach of peace negotiations. Maybe, after all, everything could be sorted out in Paris.

In the midst of the preparations for peace, one of the great American warrior-presidents, Theodore Roosevelt, died in January. Raymond Robins was stunned, as he had counted on his hero to lead the Republican Party to victory in 1920 and to a reconciliation with Soviet Russia.[179] In a way, his baton was passed to an old Russian revolutionary warrior, Ekaterina Breshko-Breshkovskaya, the "babushka" of the Russian Revolution, campaigning for an anti-Bolshevik crusade. She toured the country with her down-to-earth soliloquies on the genuine goodness of Russia, while the diplomats in Paris tangled with making a just peace. Neither was very close to reality.

Emotion was still an important part of the idyllic hope for a new Russia. On 29 January 1919, Breshkovskaya embraced George Kennan with three kisses at the Henry Street Settlement House to the applause of 100 to 150 enthusiasts present, including Raymond Robins, Albert Williams (where was John Reed?), the Reverend George Simons, Rose Strunsky, Alice Stone Blackwell, and Jerome Davis, a group that Kennan was only slightly embarrassed to be a part of.[180] The dream of a great, new Russia somehow materializing would not die easily, but it was torn between those who saw it in an American image and those who believed in a national *Russian* renaissance. Most members of the growing Russian refugee influx to America regretted most of all a fragmented and weak Russia. Mikhail Perovskii expressed a typical Russian response in being profoundly unhappy about "dismembered, dishonored and ruined Russia."[181]

Paris

The winter of 1918 and 1919 witnessed a great exodus of Americans of all political stripes and journalistic endeavors, with their socialite conference followers, to the center of the European cultural world and now the fortuitous capital for delivering the consequences of the peace, as the result of an armistice forced upon the Central Powers on 11 November 1918. Many broad issues and a multitude of technicalities were yet to be resolved in the redrawing of the map of Europe. The victors, to be sure, were the dominant voices, but they were muted

---

179. Robins to W. A. White, 13 January 1919, f. Jan–May 1919, Box 15, Robins Papers, SHSW.

180. Kennan 1919 diary, 29 January, box 14, Kennan Papers, MD, LC.

181. To Isabel Hapgood, 3 February 1919, box 3, Hapgood Papers, NYPL.

by the turmoil that continued, especially that in eastern Europe and the Middle East. The collapse of four empires—German, Austro-Hungarian, Ottoman, and Russian—wreaked havoc upon the continent. And the contests for power in Siberia, north Russia, and the Caucasus that would soon to spread to Ukraine, south Russia, and eastern Europe were yet unresolved. President Wilson seemed to believe that with the war won quite victoriously for the sake of democracy, he was handed a golden opportunity to redraw the map of Europe along lines of national self-determination, and that the problems of Russia would somehow sort themselves out by peaceful negotiation. Others had settlement by force in mind, believing now that the big war was over, the Allies might concentrate their military power against the Bolsheviks.

What to do about Russia, everyone agreed, was a thorny question. There were almost as many answers as there were politicians in Paris, or Russians on hand. Many also believed that Russia, a major participant in most of the war, should be represented in the peace talks, but the problem was who, among the several claimants, could be the voice of Russia. These ranged from conservatives such as Sergei Sazonov, the imperial foreign minister for much of the time that Russia participated in the war; to the middle ground of ambassadors of the Provisional Government represented by Bakhmeteff and Maklakov; to the flamboyant Boris Savinkov, who claimed to represent the Kolchak government; to Nikolai Chaikovskii, the old socialist who actually headed, at least nominally, a government in Russia but whose jurisdiction was mostly a northern wasteland; to the upstarts Kolchak and Denikin; to those who controlled most of Central Russia, the Bolsheviks. Neither Kolchak in Siberia, Denikin in the south, nor the Bolsheviks in Moscow were happy about the prospect of "Paris Russians" deciding the fate of their part or all of the country.

No wonder there was a real ostrichlike ambivalence about Russia in the minds of the American negotiators. Wilson spent several days in London on his way to Paris. Ambassador Francis, recovering rapidly from his prostate surgery, tried hard to see him, but the president could not find time, much to the ambassador's dismay, because he had wanted to present his view on Russia, "which, to use a mild term, is appalling."[182] The American diplomatic crossing of the Atlantic seemed to leave Russia even farther behind in the mist.

Paul Miliukov came to Paris late, in December, with Denikin's blessings and should have been an obvious compromise leader for the Russian quasi-democratic and anti-Bolshevik forces. But his misguided negotiations with the Germans for a separate peace during the summer of 1918 had infuriated the

---

182. Francis to Lansing, 1 January 1919, vol. 39, Lansing Papers, MD, LC.

Allied leaders. Similarly, Kerensky, also present in Paris, had little shred of respect left in the camp of the victors. Under the leadership of Ambassadors Maklakov (to France) and Bakhmeteff, diverse Russian parties nevertheless held a Political Conference in December to try to sort things out. They agreed on a "delegation" of four—Lvov (Omsk government), Sazonov, Maklakov, and Chaikovskii (Boris Savinkov later added)—to represent Russia.[183] This was a strange combination of former revolutionaries, imperial servants, and erstwhile liberal democrats.

While this "Russian conference" was being formed, Wilson was approached by Lvov and Bakhmeteff for his support. He in turn consulted Lansing: "Is it feasible, in view of the present at least temporary disintegration of Russia into at least five parts . . . to have Russia represented at the peace table, or to admit a part of her by recognizing and receiving delegates from the Omsk government?"[184] The response was that only delegates from a "democratic" Russia should be recognized at Paris. This would revive another debate on definition. In general, however, the Russians in Paris were quite divided and quarrelsome, and this lack of unity hurt their cause.

Konstantin Nabokov, attached to the embassy in Washington when the war started, was now the "Bakhmeteff of London," where sentiment wavered wildly from the extremes of substantially increased intervention to full recognition of the Soviet government. By late December the trend turned, however, toward including the Bolsheviks in the peace settlement in Paris in some way. Lloyd George thus became the main proponent of the idea of bringing all Russian parties together to thrash out their differences at a neutral location.[185] But the French strongly opposed any meeting that would include Bolshevik representatives.

Colonel Edward House, early on the scene in Paris, became more and more opposed to intervention and in favor of any moderate program. He urged American support for discussion and compromise:

> I cannot make anyone realize some situations as I see them. For instance, Bolshevism is steadily creeping westward. Intervention would only aggravate it. We have had too much of that already. Not only would it aggravate it, but it is so interlocked with other questions that it would be impossible to realize even if it were advisable and just.

183. For a fuller treatment, see John M. Thompson, *Russia, Bolshevism, and the Versailles Peace* (Princeton, N.J.: Princeton University Press, 1966), 66–81.

184. As quoted in ibid., 79.

185. For more details on Prinkipo, see ibid., 82–103; and David M. McFadden, *Alternative Paths: Soviets and Americans, 1917–1920* (New York: Oxford University Press, 1993), 191–217.

And then he came to the crux of the whole Russian problem:

> There is not a Western country that could safely send troops into Russia
> without creating labor troubles at home. It seems to me therefore that a
> barrier should be raised by helping the Central Powers bring about stable,
> *democratic* governments of the right sort. To do this it is necessary to send
> food there and lift the blockade and other restrictions.[186]

Definitely, concern for the domestic impact of Russian decisions was much
thought in private but little voiced in public.

A Soviet Initiative

Realizing that the wave of terror in August and September, after the assassination of Mirbach and the attempt on the life of Lenin and several others, had
resulted in isolation and renewed intervention, the Soviet leadership commenced
a peace offensive. The goals were to obtain a withdrawal of Allied forces and a
cease-fire on the three main fronts in Siberia, Ukraine, and North Russia. Overtures involved resolving a protracted military conflict, a willingness to negotiate
on the debt obligations, a recognition of other Russian political centers, and
opening Russia to trade.

Maxim Litvinov, who had emerged as a much-needed informed and experienced Soviet foreign spokesman, came on a special mission to negotiate with
Russia's former allies and perhaps play a role in Paris. He arrived in neutral
Stockholm in mid-December, with authorization personally from Lenin and on
the eve of the Paris peace negotiations.[187] Since the French were adamant that
no Bolsheviks be allowed to present themselves in Paris, Litvinov was left stranded
in Sweden, but he made the most of it. On 23 December 1918 he sent an appeal to negotiate directly with President Wilson, who showed it to Lloyd George.
They agreed very generally that something should be done in response.[188]

William Buckler, a trained archaeologist and left-leaning wartime secretary of
the American embassy in London with no knowledge or experience of Russia,
was quickly dispatched to Stockholm to confer with Litvinov in mid-January.

---

186. House to Hapgood, 6 January 1919, f. Special correspondence, box 9, Hapgood-
Reynolds Papers, MD, LC.
187. Zinovy Sheinis, *Maxim Litvinov* (Moscow: Progress Publishers, 1989), 120–22.
188. Thompson, *Russia, Bolshevism, and the Versailles Peace*, 90–93.

His important prerequisites were a close connection to Colonel House and a chance meeting with Litvinov a year earlier in London. He and Litvinov discussed intensively Soviet-American relations in long sessions for three days. Litvinov stressed that the devastation of Russia from the war required Western assistance. A main point was a promise that the Soviet government would practice no more revolutionary propaganda in "friendly" countries.[189] Litvinov's message to Buckler was that the Soviet government was ready to negotiate on any and all differences. The idea of a general conference of Russian parties on neutral ground thus materialized.

As part of this Soviet "peace offensive," a mission in America was formed in early 1919 with the goals of launching a propaganda offensive and achieving closer economic and political ties. It was led by Ludwig Martens, for several years resident in the country, and Santeri Nuorteva, a Finnish Marxist, who was first concerned with obtaining American backing for the Red, anti-German movement in Finland and set up a Finnish Information Bureau that became the model for a Soviet one. With instructions and funds from Moscow they quickly established contacts with other Bolshevik sympathizers in the left-wing socialist movement and became both a semiofficial Soviet delegation to the United States and a conduit for the spread of revolutionary propaganda.[190]

Prinkipo

Woodrow Wilson, reporting on the conciliatory meeting of William Buckler with Litvinov before the Council of Ten in late January, seconded Lloyd George's plan for placing more emphasis on relief and bringing all the Russian parties together to try to settle their differences, but he did so without much enthusiasm. The Soviet conciliatory peace initiative, spearheaded by Litvinov, was in fact a catalyst for the Lloyd George move. The French, already morally and financially invested in the anti-Bolshevik White army crusades, were willing to see Russia disintegrate rather than bolshevized and were adamant in not allowing any Soviet representatives in Paris. Given the situation at the time—with a multifront civil war going on—resolution in the form of a Russian "rodeo" was a practically hopeless undertaking from the beginning. Also, staging this in Paris, already congested with people, meetings, and diplomatic lobbyists, was considered by

189. For an excellent description of Buckler's mission, see McFadden, *Alternative Paths,* 182–89.
190. For details, see ibid., 271–75.

all parties as unwise. Perhaps to some the prospect of getting rid of the Russians who were already there was appealing.

In the announcement of 22 January 1919, all Russian factions were invited to send delegates to a conference at Prinkipo, one of the Princes Islands, off the coast of Constantinople in the Sea of Marmora, as if the whole Russian morass could be relegated to a remote island. Actually the selection was determined over other possibilities by the availability of hotel space and nearness to Russia.[191] And it certainly agreed with Wilson's October dictum that the Russians should be put in a corral and forced to sort things out for themselves before being let out to pasture. But it was not clear what they were to do there. Perhaps to add to the comic relief, President Wilson designated as American "observers" to this meeting the unlikely pair of an eccentric philosophical socialist, George Herron, who had been dabbling in surreptitious contacts with German democratic elements from his post in Switzerland during the war, and a popular, homespun American journalist from Emporia, Kansas, William Allen White.

On closer examination this made sense. Herron had met with a number of Russian political refugees in 1918 and relayed information to the State Department, including such prescient observations as "These Russians urge that, unless there is a very early shrift made of the Lenin Government, Russia will soon be past saving."[192] White and Samuel Harper had returned from Europe in 1917 on the same ship and spent much time together. Both were renowned as avid talkers, but apparently they listened as well. White subsequently arranged a speaking tour for Harper in early 1918 through Middle America that included Emporia, and he kept up a fascination with Russian affairs that he had caught from Harper. White was also in regular communication with Walter Lippmann, who was close to House, and others of the eastern journalistic establishment.[193] As he would have put it, he knew the wheat from the chaff.

Both Herron and White took their prospective jobs seriously and canvassed the Paris environs extensively for a couple of weeks seeking advice about Russia and naturally received plenty. They at least knew something about the problems

---

191. Richard Ullman, *Anglo-Soviet Relations, 1917–1921*, vol. 2, *Britain and the Russian Civil War, November 1918–February 1920* (Princeton, N.J.: Princeton University Press, 1968), 107–10.

192. Herron to Lansing, 20 November 1918, vol. 10, Herron Papers, HIA. He later claimed to have developed an attachment for Russia as a student of Kropotkin's at the London School of Economics. Herron to Norman Thomas, 27 April 1920, ibid.

193. Another reason for designating White was that Wilson at the time was under fire and receiving criticism for ignoring the American press corps.

from prior exposure to experts on the subject,[194] but their sincere dedication to the task was in vain. The Bolsheviks, learning indirectly of the plan through Litvinov in Stockholm, quickly sent an acceptance (on the proviso that they receive a direct invitation) and indicated a willingness to grant concessions,[195] but other Russian parties in Paris and Russia would have nothing to do with a plan that involved the Bolsheviks, especially since they had not been consulted beforehand. The Russian Political Conference, now moving toward firm support of Kolchak and supported by the French with promises of aid, rejected and doomed the Prinkipo proposal. Most of the separate Russian political entities wanted to control the whole, not share or compromise on it. The idea of negotiating the Russian question still appealed to some in the Allied camp, who were hopeful of an idealistic solution to the Russian question, but most grew increasingly exasperated and despairing in regard to dealing with any Russians, as divided and weak as they had shown themselves.

Dejected about the Prinkipo failure, Herron concluded, "So far as the Peace Conference is concerned, it has wasted its last hour of grace. Europe is lost to the German and the Bolshevik."[196] White was also bitter about the French torpedoing of the conference and viewed it as "the story of a great Nation drunk with victory, turned reactionary, blind with materialistic philosophy, and going to hell in a handcar."[197] He then became one of the strongest and most influential voices in America against intervention in Russia. "It would take a million American soldiers to forcibly restore order in Russia. And probably we would shed as much blood in doing it as would be shed inevitably."[198] He was one of many who believed that if we let Bolshevism alone it would fail.[199] To Cyrus McCormick, he wrote, "American participation in the Kolchak conquest of Russia is an inexcusable folly. . . . The thing for America to do is to get out of Russia and let bolshevism hang itself with its own rope."[200] The overwhelming majority of the readers of his syndicated columns seemed to agree.

In Paris, American sentiment turned decidedly anti-French over Prinkipo and contributed to American revulsion against everything that happened there. After

194. White and Samuel Harper had met on board ship, returning to America in 1917, conversed at length about Russia, and maintained an active correspondence.

195. Chicherin to Lansing, by wireless, 4 February 1919, vol. 41, Lansing Papers, MD, LC.

196. Herron to Walter Kruessi, 25 April 1919, vol. 10, Herron Papers, HIA.

197. To Upton Sinclair, series B, vol. 38, White Papers, MD, LC.

198. To A. M. Holt (Cyrus McCormick's secretary), 21 October 1919, vol. 39, ibid.

199. William Allen White, *The Autobiography of William Allen White* (New York: Macmillan, 1946).

200. To McCormick, 29 September 1919, series C, box 48, White Papers, MD, LC.

this, France could not count on anything but token American support for any interventionist programs in Russia. The French had definitely played their cards wrong. But Russian opinion in the Far East also turned anti-American and pro-Japanese over Prinkipo, as the Japanese renounced it, winning unusual support from the Russians "because," according to Polk, "they are looking for someone to fight at the front rather than do it themselves."[201]

The Bullitt Mission

Among those going to Paris in the official party was a young Yale graduate, William Bullitt, who had joined the State Department in 1917 as a fledgling assistant and was included in the staff for the conference. On his cabin door going over with the president was a sign, "Attached to the American Delegation," which accurately described his role. But he had one big advantage over many others in the Paris cauldron: he was a protégé of Colonel House, who arranged for him to be one of the several secretaries for the American mission.[202]

After the failure of the Prinkipo project, Wilson acquiesced to House for an appeal directly to the Soviet government by sending a special mission to Moscow in March 1919. The idea actually originated with Lloyd George in mid-February, when the president was leaving for America, with hopes of finding a middle ground on the Russian question. The main issues were a cease-fire of the warring parties in Russia, an acknowledgment of responsibility for past debts, and amnesty for opposition groups. The idea of another "Root" mission had been brewing for a long time, but this was no comparison. The timing was not propitious with the war over and the peace conference already fully under way. The inexperienced Bullitt, provided with vague instructions from Lloyd George's secretary, was overly optimistic on what he could accomplish. But there was yet an honest wish to know just what the Bolsheviks wanted.

So a low-level diplomatic staff member, knowing very little about Russia and completely unknown there, was singled out by House for a mission to Russia. It was thought that a higher-level emissary might attract too much attention, since the mission was supposedly secret. A well-known person would probably have elicited a French veto. To add to the incongruity, Lincoln Steffens, whom House

---

201. Polk to Lansing, 20 March 1919, copy in box 106, Leland Harrison Papers, MD, LC.
202. Beatrice Farnsworth, *William C. Bullitt and the Soviet Union* (Bloomington: Indiana University Press, 1967), 32–35.

believed to be trusted by the Bolsheviks, was assigned to go along, riding shotgun, no more successfully than he did with Charles Crane in 1917. He watched with benign amusement while Bullitt wrestled with a couple of accompanying military attachés in the train's corridor.[203] Like white men encountering Indians, they brought diplomatic pouches filled with cheap but much-welcomed canned goods and received heaps of caviar and box tickets to the ballet in return.[204] Arriving unannounced in Petrograd as low-level Allied negotiators, at first they baffled Soviet authorities. Chicherin finally came to see what they wanted and politely invited them to come on to Moscow. In fact, they had no real authority to negotiate anything.

They went to Moscow, they saw Chicherin a few times, met briefly with Lenin, but they did not conquer. The timing was bad, arriving just a few days after the conclusion of the First Congress of the (Third) Communist International, which was full of rhetoric about a world socialist revolution, inspired by the end of the war and the almost miraculous survival of the Soviet regime. Steffens managed to obtain an interview with Lenin, later recounting that he was impressed by the Soviet leader's admission to his miscalculations but confident that they would soon be back on the right path.[205] After a few days in Moscow with the perplexed Bolsheviks, the American party returned to Paris from their reconnaissance raid into Russia with some vague statements from the Bolsheviks, which promised a willingness to compromise and negotiate that included recognizing some foreign debts, too late in any event to affect the peace settlements or the ongoing civil war. Colonel House was happy to have the information. Mission accomplished. What other avenues might rashly and incompetently be explored on the Russian question?

Part of the reason for this haphazard diplomacy with the Bolsheviks was that any contact was strongly opposed by Winston Churchill, emerging once again as a major voice as head of the War Office, and by the conservative branch of the British press, headed by Lord Northcliffe and the *Times*. Churchill, who believed that the Bolsheviks were taking advantage of the Prinkipo confusion to score military victories, proposed an opposite course: issuing an ultimatum to Bolsheviks to cease fighting at once and then, once they had refused as he expected, to launch massive military intervention on all fronts.[206]

Some authors view Churchill's February 1919 proposal as the West's lost opportunity, but it was considered for only a few days and promptly vetoed by

203. Steffens, *Autobiography*, 791–93.
204. Farnsworth, *Bullitt*, 39–42.
205. Steffens, *Autobiography*, 797–99.
206. For an excellent summary by a Paris eyewitness, see f. 1 (Russia), box 18, Ray Stannard Baker Papers, Princeton-Mudd.

House and Wilson (in midocean) and by Lloyd George and most of the rest of the British cabinet, who were reluctant to undertake such a large, expensive war. Even Balfour, the foreign secretary, was knocked off his fence-straddling position to support nonintervention. In any event, Lloyd George pursued another tactic: tiptoeing into Russia to find a miracle of a resolution but only to see a mirage. The American side did not help, despite House's good intentions, in part because of the timing of Wilson's forays back and forth to America, where he found the sentiment changing sharply against the peace and his goal of a world organization.

The Hapgood Alternative

Norman Hapgood, still faithful to his liberal internationalism and opposition to intervention in Russia, was one of the most visible Americans in London and Paris on the eve of, and during, the peace deliberations. As a former editor of *Collier's* and *Harper's Weekly*, before the latter's merger with the *Independent* in May 1916, and a friend of Charles Crane, Walter Lippmann, Edward House, and many other Wilsonian stalwarts, he represented in many ways Wilson's alter ego, what he might have been if he were not a temporizing, indecisive president. Possessing some of the same moralistic concerns and idealist vision on world issues as the president, Hapgood was free from the responsibility for them. He also had a connection with the left wing of American socialism through his younger brother, Hutchins Hapgood, who was a close friend of John Reed. His direct approach, opposed to that of so many ostrichlike officials in Washington, was refreshing and won him support; for example, he elicited from House, "There is not a Western country that could safely send troops to Russia without creating labor troubles at home."[207] This would not endear him with the more conservative elements, deeply rooted in the State Department.

Hapgood had spent most of 1917 in Europe with his wife and returned to Europe, like so many others, in late 1918. Thanks to the support of Charles Crane and Walter Lippmann, who, of course, were also in Paris, he was well enough known to be able to have lunch, just by chance and separately, with Winston Churchill and Herbert Hoover in mid-December expressly to discuss Russian affairs.[208] He also had excellent social and political connections in Paris

207. House to Hapgood, 6 June 1919, f. 1733, box 55, House Papers, Yale-Sterling.
208. Hapgood to Elizabeth, 11 December 1918, f. Oct.–Dec. 1918, box 16, Hapgood-Reynolds Papers, MD, LC.

that included a resident American socialite and close friend of his wife, Beatrice Woods.[209] His interest in Russia and especially his wife's were well known in Washington, London, and Paris—and probably in Moscow.[210]

As early as May 1918 he was being considered for a diplomatic post.[211] This finally materialized in early 1919 with an offer of an appointment as minister to Denmark. Frank Polk, not known for a desire for accommodation with the Soviet government, wrote, "Hope earnestly the offer made to you will be accepted. Feel confident you can do much at Copenhagen to help us find solution of Russian problem, and I believe that emergency demands acceptance of important task tendered you."[212] His written and verbal instructions from Wilson and House also made clear that the central part of his mission was to establish a sounding board, or "listening post," for Communist Russia. The president wrote personally, "I am glad that you are keeping your eye and your thought on the Russian situation. It is the most difficult now insight, and the direct lights and sidelights you throw on it in your dispatches are very welcome."[213] And signals were floated over the east European clothesline that if messages needed to be relayed or information passed, Hapgood was there.

Unfortunately, Hapgood had been indiscreet in a meeting with New York businessmen before his departure for Copenhagen, allegedly suggesting that U.S. bankers propose loans to Soviet Russia. Although he categorically denied this, the report fomented a move in the Senate to reject his nomination, simply because, he noted, "I am a dangerous and foulish Bolchevik."[214] He retained the support of J. P. Morgan, who was present at the meeting. The State Department was obviously in a quandary about what to do about this "loose cannon" in the heart of Europe.[215] As with the Prinkipo initiative and the Bullitt mission, very little really came of this, in part because Stockholm and then Riga were much better situated for any contacts, but Hapgood, his wife, and their two children enjoyed an idyllic summer in Copenhagen, before the Senate refused to sanc-

209. Hapgood to Elizabeth, 8 January 1919, f. Jan–April 1919, ibid. "Bice," in correspondence, then a dress designer, later a renowned potter, was residing over eighty years later in Ojai, California.

210. His interest in Russia actually predated his acquaintance with Elizabeth. He was a freelance drama critic before the war and became interested in Konstantin Stanislavskii and his Moscow Art Theater and had even arranged for a New York tour, which was canceled because of the war.

211. House to Tumulty, 25 May 1918, box 44, Tumulty Papers, MD, LC.

212. Polk to Hapgood, 14 February 1919, box 9, Hapgood-Reynolds Papers, MD, LC.

213. Wilson to Hapgood, 1 August 1919, ibid.

214. Hapgood to Polk, 5 November 1919, ibid.

215. Phillips to Long (c), 10 September 1919, ibid.

Norman and Elizabeth Reynolds Hapgood, with their first child, Elizabeth (Benny), and her grandmother Margaret Reynolds, in Copenhagen, Easter 1919, courtesy of the Prints and Photographs Division Hapgood-Reynolds Papers, Library of Congress

tion his appointment, and they were forced to return home. Yet one more Wilsonian straw in the wind crumbled.

Hapgood continued to fight for a more moderate, understanding view of the new Russia, complaining to Lansing's successor that "Bakhmeteff and the émigré atmosphere has had a strangle hold in the department." He still had some support from the State Department. Frank Polk, stalwartly remaining to the end in Paris, tried to keep Russia out of the proceedings: "I feel the State Department should handle it through regular diplomatic channels, but in spite of my best efforts the 'old bird will come home to roost.'" And like Hapgood he opposed the blockade of Russia: "I have been trying to get them to forget it, but the British and French would have it."[216]

216. Hapgood to Colby, 4 November 1920, box 3B, Colby Papers, MD, LC; Polk to Hapgood, 23 October 1919, box 13, Hapgood-Reynolds Papers, MD, LC.

The Fronts

Meanwhile, back on the remaining—and seemingly endless—World War I eastern battlegrounds, a misery compared to France in 1917, but different, prevailed during the 1918-19 winter in Russia. In a dispatch dated 20 December from Vladivostok, veteran Russian correspondent Carl Ackerman reported to the *New York Times*, "Chaos rules Russia today with greater power than the Czars possessed in their sublimest days, for not only is Russia at the mercy of universal disorder, but the Allies are seemingly powerless." He listed the conflicting options: leave Russia alone or intervene; keep the Japanese out or let them in; render substantial aid but keep all foreigners out; above all, do not give Russia to Germany, but some nation will come in if the Allies do not.[217] He described in detail the tremendous difficulty he had in traveling by train—on the fastest express from Vladivostok to Irkutsk—that took over ten days. Ackerman also wrote privately to the State Department after his departure from Siberia, emphasizing that the help the Czechs expected from America was not sent, and that there was no united policy. On the other hand, he still found the Kolchak government completely unsupportable.[218] The dilemma of whom to support remained.

The situation in Siberia resembled an Antarctic expedition, except that there were many people involved, and a number of them were dying. Edward Taylor, a tropical herpetologist from Kansas, recruited in the Philippines to lead a Red Cross typhus expedition into Siberia, reported his impressions of the extreme sixty degree below zero winter at Omsk while living in a second-class passenger car on a siding for several weeks. He was appalled by the conditions he found, especially among the refugees from European Russia, with up to twelve families trying to exist in one room. "Things are certainly uneasy" under "dictator Koltchack [*sic*]."[219] In February he expected "the lid to blow off in a rather terrific explosion" and felt fortunate to be living in the railroad car, "so that if things get too bad we can make a quick getaway."[220]

The Committee on Public Information was also getting its boots covered with Siberian snow with an ambitious propaganda project. Arthur Bullard, after his exciting turn as Sisson's assistant and replacement in European Russia in 1918, arrived in December, game for more, but he succumbed to a physical

217. Ackerman, *New York Times*, 20 December 1918.

218. Ackerman (Peking) to State Department, 2 January 1919, f. Siberia, box 187, Long Papers, MD, LC.

219. Taylor (Omsk) to Family, 12 February 1919, box 34, Taylor Papers, University of Kansas Archives.

220. Ibid.

ailment that required immediate surgery and a long convalescence. He still managed to write an eleven-page Christmas Day letter of instructions from his hospital bed:

> It all boils down pretty well to my slogan that our job is to raise the political standard of living of these people. When immigrants from Russia come to America we very quickly raise their economic standard of living, teach them to demand bath tubs in their tenements. . . . Our job here is similar, if we put it in political terms, these poor devils don't know what to demand of their government. They don't know what a "good road" is and never dream of expecting the Government to furnish them.[221]

The major CPI accomplishment in this direction was the publication of a weekly newspaper, *Druzheskoe Slovo* (Friendly Word), beginning 1 December. Edited by Malcolm Davis and Graham Taylor, it attained a circulation of 50,000 by February with the chief targets being Omsk and Irkutsk, with over 10,000 copies each. The covers featured familiar scenes (Fifth Avenue, Independence Hall, and the Capitol) and personalities (Lincoln, Wilson, and House).[222] Taylor was again disappointed, as he had been in Petrograd in 1918, about having this promising project suddenly canceled in March 1919: "There will be a great need for a long time to come for an interpretive and informational service from America to Russia. . . . American relations to Russia are about the most social service job I know anything about."[223]

From Siberia and a hospital in Japan, Bullard wrote regular letters to Colonel House in Paris with detailed information collected from various sources. In an early thirty-two-page letter, he concluded that people at home "do not realize the extent and degree of chaos here." He strongly recommended intervention in the form of a 50,000-man international police force but emphatically opposed recognition of the Kolchak government.[224] Davis concurred, describing the factions there as the pro-Semenov, anti-Semenov, pro-Kolchak, anti-Kolchak, radicals, conservatives, property owners, socialists, peasants and Cossacks, and many political parties "intermingled with the influences of the

---

221. Bullard to Norton, 25 December 1918, f. CPI files, box 7, Bullard Papers, Princeton-Mudd.
222. A complete file is in box 2, Graham Taylor Papers, BA, CU.
223. Taylor to Newton Baker, box 1, ibid.
224. Bullard to House, 28 November 1918, box 9, Bullard Papers, Princeton-Mudd. His recommendation against Kolchak was repeated on 25 January 1919, and he stressed that Ambassador Morris agreed. Ibid.

Czech (on left) and American troop trains passing on the Trans-Siberian, 1918–note difference in class of travel, courtesy of the Stanley Partridge Collection, Hoover Institution Archives

various allied nations and the reaction to them, creates a rather subtly confused situation."[225] This was to say the least. Consul Alfred Thomson in Omsk again cautioned that the United States should not recognize the Kolchak government "as it does not represent European Russia."[226] Most other Americans agreed, especially after the promising Kolchak advance during the summer of 1919 faltered and crumbled.[227]

At Archangel, Admiral Newton McCully, one of America's best observers of the complex Russian scene, was firmly converted to the cause of relief, not war. "Conditions in Russia," he asserted, "have reached a stage so distressing that it does not seem necessary to prove that it exists, or to give harrowing incidents. Bad as the conditions are now they will become progressively worse, and probably reach a climax in April and May 1919."[228] He stressed that this condition

225. Malcolm Davis, "Estimate of Public Opinion," 29 January 1919, box 1, Graham Taylor Papers, BA, CU.

226. Thompson to Eichelberger, 19 November 1918, box 707, WA-6, RG 45, NA.

227. For the most complete description of the complexities of the Kolchak government and its fate, see Jon Smele, *Civil War in Siberia: The Anti-Bolshevik Government of Admiral Kolchak, 1918–1920* (Cambridge: Cambridge University Press, 1996).

228. McCully report, 18 December 1918, box 711, WA-6, RG 45, NA.

existed over all of European Russia. He waxed even more eloquent in a report a week earlier:

> Russia is now mad, sick and starving. To use force alone at this time on such an organism, to try to compel it to act with due observance of all the proprieties, to act reasonably, to pay its debts, or even to keep a clean bed, will hardly benefit the patient, and may imperil the Doctor, as the disease is communicable.
>
> Russia is too great a country, and has too much national Slav spirit to even reconcile to the domination of any other power. There cannot be foreseen any reason for serious conflict of interests in the future between Russia and the United States, but there are possibilities that in time Russia will be a friend, if we can make and keep her so, of whom the United States will be much in need.[229]

Morale was very bad, McCully emphasized, beginning with the lowest, the French units, and in the following ascending order: American, British, Italian, and Serb. "To the soldiers the question 'Why are we here?' was never satisfactorily answered."[230] What has been needed, he asserted, was a clear message that what was at stake was "the Good of Russia at heart and only the Good of Russia."[231] But could Russians ever buy such generalities?

The arrival at Murmansk of the USS *Yankton* in March, with supplies, motorboats, and a high-powered radio station, lifted morale briefly, as it was a sign of at least some Americans' concern about the fate of their "forgotten" warriors. Captain Bierer, a rare American officer who really had a command in north Russia, the hallowed cruiser *Olympia*, assessed his "impressions and observations after finishing a tour of duty in North Russian waters. . . . Both the British and the French are taking especial interest in this region and these waters, especially the British [who] hope that conditions may so shape themselves or that they may be able to so shape circumstances, so that this region as well as the waters, may come under their control or domination."[232]

Meanwhile, in small ways, the YMCA secretaries were out in the field to alleviate distress. Ernest Ropes, a fourth-generation American-Russian, arrived at Murmansk on 1 April 1919 and immediately went to the "front" area, at Oberskaya, south of Archangel, to establish a "Y" base. The main problem,

229. McCully to CNO, 10 December 1918, ibid.
230. McCully North Russian Report, 9 July 1919, box 706, ibid.
231. Ibid.
232. Bierer to ONI, 31 March 1919, f. 1, box 710, WA-6, RG 45, NA.

he noted in a diary, was the Russian soldiers, who were "unsatisfiable in their demands, and would buy the canteen out daily if allowed."[233] He had an advantage—or disadvantage—in being fully conversant in Russian and able to bring more Russians under YMCA auspices. Another "Y" veteran, Helen Ogden, came from recent service in Moscow to north Russia and encountered once again her future husband, Donald Lowrie. She described to her family how they trudged two miles along a railroad track, he with a phonograph and she with a pail of flour and baking powder used in making pancakes. The men they served constantly wanted to know when they could go home; that was the only thing that interested them.[234] Ropes, meanwhile, was as proud of a wooden tennis court he built as Ogden was of an arena for basketball she opened, but by the time these were ready in June, most of the Americans had left.[235]

The fight against Bolshevism was strongest and most promising in south Russia, where organized units of the old army and local Cossacks were already in place and actively supported with funds, material, and reinforcements by the Allies. The latter were token efforts numbering only in the hundreds of unhappy and untrustworthy soldiers. Unfortunately, "White" leadership was unstable because of changes of command (unexpected deaths of Kaledin and Kornilov) and the influx of a large number of refugee Russian officers from other areas who wanted to fight against the Bolsheviks—and, of course, to retain their privileged status in Russian society. The "Volunteer Army" thus retained a potential through 1919 to keep alive the idea of a restoration of a traditional, conservative Russian government. Their goals were enhanced by the opening up of communications into the Black Sea in 1919, and the addition of some small British and French units that were shifted to this region, but no American land forces would follow.

The United States, nevertheless, was represented in the region by a number of modern warships, manned by skilled and experienced officers and seamen and with exemplary morale and discipline. Part of the credit for this must go to Admiral Mark Bristol, who commanded the American Eastern Mediterranean Squadron. By early January 1919 he had established his headquarters in Constantinople.

233. Ropes diary, 25 April 1919, Ropes Papers, BA, CU. Ropes was a fourth-generation Russian-American, born and educated in St. Petersburg but also the recipient of a Columbia University degree. Ropes, "The Russia I have Known," typescript memoir, ibid.

234. Ogden to Family, 4 and 19 March 1919, f. Ogden Corresp., box 3, Lowrie Papers, UIA.

235. Ropes diary, 4 and 31 May 1919, Ropes Papers, BA, CU.

Rock Creek

Meanwhile, back in Washington, unhappy congressmen and overworked bureaucrats were left scrambling in an abyss, out of the Paris limelight. Upon his return for a brief visit in February, President Wilson found opposition growing to his international and peace programs. Few seemed ready or willing to carry on the crusade. Breckinridge Long, faithfully manning his desk in the virtually deserted State Department, was "mentally and nervously tired out."[236]

With Bakhmeteff still in Paris, the Russian embassy pressed for money and arms for Kolchak's government, with little result. Sergei Ughet offered to sell railroad equipment that was ready to send for stockpiled Remington rifles made to Russian specifications.[237] What he got was counterfeit rubles that proved an embarrassment to Omsk—not entirely, though, since many of the large loans to the Provisional Government were still available, kept safely in the United States Treasury, but released on application of the embassy and the approval of the State Department. In fact, many orders, placed earlier, were now available for shipment to anti-Bolshevik forces.

Long complained about the enormous backlog of work in the State Department at the end of May 1919 with Lansing, Phillips, Polk, and Adee all still away. He had lunch with a depressed Lansing after his return from Paris: "He told me he would turn Russia over to me to manage. He thinks Turkey, Russia . . . and the Far East are the three outstanding places of importance. . . . See how I get along with Lenin."[238] Samuel Harper felt especially depressed after a bout with the flu in December and January. He turned down an offer by Crane for him to go to Paris but insisted that he was obliged to "continue my efforts to counteract Bolshevist propaganda, which is getting enormous headway."[239]

Withdrawal

Intervention in Russia became a major political issue during the president's absence in Paris. While Acting Secretary of State Polk and General March urged withdrawal as soon as practical, public sentiment was growing in Congress and the country against the Bolsheviks, abetted by the publication of the Sisson

236. Diary, 7 April 1919, box 2, Long Papers, MD, LC.
237. Ughet to Polk, 10 April 1919, and Polk to Ughet, 15 April 1919, box 1, Russia Posolstvo, HIA.
238. Ibid., 29 July 1919.
239. Harper to Crane, 23 January 1919, f. 8, box 6, Harper Papers, UC.

documents and threatening labor troubles. A brief window of opportunity may have existed in early 1919 for increasing armed pressure against the Bolsheviks in the immediate wake of winning the war, but it was short-lived and obscured by the Prinkipo and Bullitt ventures. In the meantime, the cry to bring them home was gaining momentum at the grassroots level and among certain congressmen with their ears to the ground. By May 1919, with opposition escalating against Wilson, the League, and the peace, continued American intervention was doomed. Robins, with the substantial support of influential congressmen such as Senator Hiram Johnson, waged an effective public campaign against the government's military escapades in Russia.

Although most Americans in north Russia could not wait to get home, at least one anonymous officer regretted the withdrawal. "It is deserting good friends to the danger of starvation and a hideous orgy of rape and massacre by the Bolsheviks." He noted that the Russians "trusted us and we were the first to go out." This abandonment would release 60,000 of the Red Army to fight against Kolchak and Denikin and would increase Bolshevik strength enormously.[240] On 2 June, just after breakfast, the men of the 339th Infantry rolled their bags for departure. General Ironside ceremoniously reviewed this main body of the American contingent in north Russia before it boarded the *Czar,* fittingly named for its swan dive into the Arctic Ocean. American military intervention in north Russia had lasted barely nine months. Only a few token remnants remained in housecleaning capacity.

In Siberia the situation was different. The British were left to stew in their own juices in impoverished and faction-ridden north Russia, but the much larger Japanese forces in Siberia were seen by internationally sensitive Americans as California forty-niners, staking out rich territory for future exploitation, and they had to be watched and contained. So the American AEF in Siberia, after a confusing premature withdrawal order in January, were left to their own devices, lingering month after month on the Asian fringe of Russia.[241] The number one problem remained transportation. "The traffic situation throughout thousands of miles of railroad has become so desperate, that nearly everybody realizes that there is nothing else to be done; trains have almost ceased running."[242]

---

240. An officer to his brother, 9 August 1919, carbon copy enclosed in Cyrus McCormick to William Allen White, 29 September 1919, series C, box 48, White Papers, MD, LC.

241. Intelligence officer Barrows reflected the confusion: "We are still in the dark as to whether anything further will be required of us, or whether we will be called home." Barrows to General Evans, 22 January 1919, f. Dec. 1918-Feb. 1919, box 2, Barrows Papers, UCB.

242. Ibid. Barrows wrote his wife on 24 January, "I think political and military prospects in Russia and Siberia are worse than at any time."

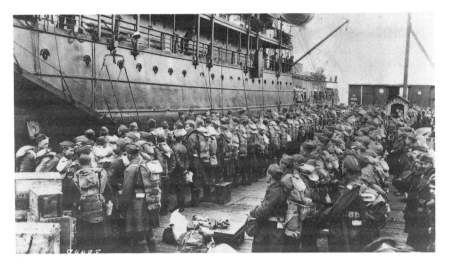

Evacuation from north Russia, spring 1919, courtesy of the U.S. Army Signal Corps, Photographs Division, National Archives

Anglo-American Discord

One reason for the failure of the anti-Bolshevik cause and of a lack of coordinated effort in intervention was American suspicion of British motives. This was partly due to a lack of sympathy with British personal commitment to intervention. For example, Commander Thomas Kemp, chief of naval operations in north Russia, was a close friend of submarine squadron commander Francis Cromie, who was killed by the Bolsheviks defending the British embassy in Petrograd at the end of August 1918. Kemp insisted that "interest and honour alike forbid any withdrawal of Allied Forces from Russia, which would subject those who have been loyal to the Allied cause to savage reprisals," and added that all Bolsheviks must be conquered for murdering his friend.[243]

All major American officers in the field—Stewart, Graves, McCully, Bristol—as well as almost all other Americans such as regular soldiers, Red Cross, and YMCA personnel complained bitterly of British interference, attitude, and opposition. After the conclusion of his Siberian adventure and relegated to the Philippines, General Graves blamed the connivance of the British and French with "the reactionary Kolchak crowd, which included Siminoff [sic], Kalmikoff," and a Japanese inspired virulently anti-American press for attempting to relieve

243. Kemp, "A Defense of Intervention," n.d., f. 1, box 710, WA-6, RG 45, NA.

him and for undermining American efforts to maintain peace. He claimed to have obeyed his strict orders not to involve American troops in these "sordid affairs."[244]

From the south, Mark Bristol described the situation at the end of 1920 to Charles Crane in China, noting that "matters have steadily drifted from bad to worse, and at the present time the situation is such a mess that the best informed cannot foresee a reasonable solution of the problem." He summed up the civil war in the south of Russia:

> England started out with France to support Denekin [sic] against the Bolsheviks. Denekin, and those around him more especially, were reactionaries that were not equal to the task of either defeating Bolshevism, or setting such an example that the adherents of Lenine and Trotsky would desert them for Denekin's cause. Therefore, Denekin lost. Wrangel, the successor of Denekin, is a man a generation ahead of his time, but those around him belong to the old reactionary class and Wrangel could not carry the load by himself, and he was defeated.[245]

In many of his dispatches to both the Navy and State Departments he reiterated his concern about the British domination of the Middle East at the expense of the Turks and American interests. The American consensus from the scene was to not trust the British and get out of Russia. But getting out was not that easy.

Felix Cole, who was left to man the last rampart of American diplomatic representation in north Russia, saw the dilemma. Although he had initially opposed American intervention, he now objected to ending it:

> The withdrawal of American forces . . . would be used by the Bolsheviks as propaganda in two directions, as is being done already. First, Bolsheviks assert to loyal Russians that their friends have abandoned them and that they should desert across the Bolshevik front. . . . Second, it is stated that the withdrawals prove that America, the most democratic and liberal of the Associated Powers, disapproves of the "monarchist and reactionary" Provisional Government. The rapidity with which the withdrawals follow one another strengthen this propaganda.[246]

244. Graves to Col. A. J. Galen, 20 August 1920 (c), f. June–Oct. 1920, box 16, Robins Papers, SHSW.

245. Bristol to C. R. Crane, 14 January 1921, f. Jan. 1921, box 33, Bristol Papers, MD, LC.

246. Cole to Lansing, 11 July 1919 (c), f. 1, box 713, WA-6, RG 45, NA.

Colonel Ruggles also regretted the withdrawal of American forces: "It is deserting good friends to the danger of starvation and a hideous orgy of rape and massacre by the Bolsheviks. It will release close to 60,000 men to send against General Denniken [sic] in the S.E. and Kolchak in the East."[247]

Anti-Bolshevik centers still existed and might yet form a viable alternative for Russia. The main one under Kolchak, however, seemed to be in continual fluctuation. Initial enthusiasm for the successful Kolchak advance in the spring of 1919 quickly faded with its retreat. The others—Semenov, Kalmykov, Horvat— were totally distasteful to the Americans for their pro-Japanese stances, complete lack of unity, and the many atrocities committed against prisoners and civilian populations. The Americans also had a comparatively secure and comfortable base in Vladivostok, which had assumed a character for Americans in Siberia similar to Vologda in 1918, a very temporary residence.

The American military units remained in Siberia for a number of months beyond that of north Russia for several reasons. The Kolchak government in Omsk was weakening fast, but it was thought imprudent to abandon it completely. And the Czechs still needed a rear guard for their departure. Concern about the considerable Japanese entrenchment remained. There were a number of Red Cross, YMCA, and other search and rescue missions going on that needed at least a morale boost from American armed forces in the area and seemed important for the cause of humanity.

But the tide definitely turned in late 1919 with the collapse of Kolchak, the disgust with any alternative, and increasing pressure from home. The first withdrawal of units occurred in late 1919 and early 1920, with the last American military "occupation" of Russian territory ending in April 1920. Intervention— at least the American military side of it—came to a close.

247. Ruggles to brother, 9 August 1919, f. 5, box 6, Harper Papers, UC.

7

Relief

Trying to rearrange the political and social structure of Russia was definitely on the agenda of many countries and individuals both before and after the Russian revolutions. Several results were direct and indirect political pressures, military interference, and financial leverage from a variety of interested parties. Another approach was simply to supply humanitarian aid to a country and people in great distress, who were going through tumultuous times beyond their control or ability to cope. Humanitarian intentions and political motives were mixed, as relief was seen by many as a means to win support of the population and lessen its dependence on the Bolshevik government and by others as a means of supporting that regime. At least the United States had considerable experience in providing relief to Russia in earlier desperate circumstances, such as in 1893. While the campaign for, and interest in, intervention waned, conditions within the country worsened, and the need for relief became more crucial.

The transition from military intervention to relief was a long one and very much intertwined with political agendas, especially in Siberia and the south of Russia. Assistance went hand in hand with intervention, since, beyond humanitarian desires, there was the goal of winning the support of local populations and bolstering the morale of anti-Bolshevik Russian and Czech units. In north Russia direct aid was provided mainly by the American YMCA as an extension of its work in Russia proper in 1917–18 and by the casual and indirect dispersal of the remaining supply dumps at Murmansk and Archangel. After the withdrawal of the main American forces in June 1919, the organization continued to serve Allied and Russian units and some of the civilian population for a few more months. The situation was less desperate than in other areas, simply because of the remoteness, smaller size of surviving depots, and the low population base of the region. But still, the refrain "When are we going home?" prevailed everywhere Americans could be found in Russia.[1]

1. Ernest Ropes diary, 26 April 1919, box 1, Ropes Papers, BA, CU.

European Relief

The aftermath of war left much of the European continent in shambles, economically as well as politically. The situation resembled Europe after World
War II but without the massive physical destruction of major cities and the
genocidal aspects. Obviously something had to be done in the wake of all this
disruption of people and nations. In the forefront, in pressing for humanitarian
aid regardless of political or ideological boundaries, was Fridtjof Nansen, the
Norwegian explorer, philanthropist, and relief advocate. He addressed President
Wilson in April 1919 directly about Russia's desperation for food and the folly
of the Allied blockade.

Nansen was seconded by the powerful voice of "Mr. European Relief," Herbert
Hoover, who stressed the importance of immediate aid especially for any territory that could now be reached, such as the Baltic States, Poland, the rest of the
new eastern Europe, Finland, and south Russia.[2] At about the same time Gordon
Auchincloss and Vance McCormick hatched a similar plan and found Colonel
House a willing adherent. Thus relief and intervention, food and arms, political
agendas and humanitarian ideals, found themselves uncomfortable bedfellows
in the Russia and America of 1919. Herbert Hoover wrote the president about
the Bolshevik threat, "I have the feeling that revolution in Europe is by no means
over. The social wrongs in these countries are far from solution and the tempest
must blow itself out, probably with enormous violence. Our people are not
prepared for us to undertake the military policy of Europe while it boils out its
social wrongs."[3]

The main thrust of these initial projects was to exchange a major relief program in Russia for a cessation of all hostilities. Balfour, for Great Britain, backed
the effort, but Clemenceau wanted any such aid limited to the non-Bolshevik
areas of Russia, which basically guaranteed a continuation of the fighting.[4] Nevertheless, the appeals touched directly upon the president's interest in eastern
Europe, and American funds were soon forthcoming for those areas in central
Europe that were the immediate fallout from the demise of the Russian and Austro-
Hungarian empires, chiefly in the reconstituted Poland and the new Czechoslovakia, where Charles Crane's son and Lansing's recent secretary was named first
American ambassador. By June 1919, Herbert Hoover sensed that he was now

2. Nansen to Wilson, 3 April 1919, and Hoover to Wilson, 11 and 26 April and 7 May
1919, Pre-Commerce, box 20, Hoover Papers, HPL. A practical man, Hoover emphasized
that the main obstacle to relief was shipping. To Wilson, 9 April 1919, box 60, ibid.
    3. Hoover to Wilson, 11 April 1919, ibid.
    4. For a full treatment, see McFadden, *Alternative Paths*, 244–63.

free from his duty as wartime food tsar to devote his attention to relief: "The Food Administration has ended, except in the sense that the Relief of Europe represents its final phase."[5] But time moved slowly—or fast if you were starving. As late as September 1919, Bertron wrote Francis about his "very interesting talks with Mr. Hoover today." "I might say that he is very sympathetic, his idea of a program, as expressed by him, coincides very much with our own, and he would be glad to be of help later on."[6]

The pace of the language corresponded to that of more relief. The idealism of relief remained in evidence, commendably, on all sides of the American political arena: "We [advocates for Russian relief] are advised that the Administration would not object to the Republicans proposing a measure for constructive and economic relief to Russia, and we are endeavoring to arrange that they should do this."[7] Unfortunately, the cause of genuine relief would become a victim of the growing opposition to the administration's peace projects, centered on the League of Nations. Basic, ground-level assistance to Russia was thus sidetracked by grander, more sophisticated schemes for a higher world order.

Others sitting in the grandstands of the three-ring peace circus in Paris, perhaps in boredom, reflected back on the humanitarian aspects of ending the war, especially with "the rape of Belgium" in mind that began the war. After that precedent, the situation in Russia and eastern Europe could not be ignored because of so many direct and intimate connections with America, and in hopes of rescuing something from the general disillusionment with the peace process. In a revealing comment, Charles Crane lamented to his daughter, "I sometimes think that most of the best of the world has been killed off and spent its inspiration in the war, leaving the peace settlement to the profiteers and stay-at-homes."[8] British writers such as Siegfried Sassoon might describe the scene more eloquently but no more succinctly. Others would express the same sentiments in different ways, but such discouraging notes of despair may have slowed what relief should have come immediately to east-central Europe and Russia.

A major obstacle to genuine assistance and the possibility of any political accommodation to those who really needed it was an Allied economic blockade of Soviet Russia. Due mainly to French and British pressure in Paris, after the Prinkipo and Bullitt follies, a blockade was declared on Bolshevik Russia in 1919 in support especially of the more active and mainly French-sponsored interven-

5. Hoover to Wilson, 24 June 1919, Pre-Commerce, box 60, Hoover Papers, HPL.
6. Bertron to Francis, 17 September 1919, f. Francis, Pre-Commerce, HPL.
7. Bertron to McCormick, 16 September 1919, f. Misc., 2C, box 115, McC, SHSW.
8. Crane to Josephine Crane, 10 May 1919, reel 1, Crane Papers, BA, CU.

tion in the south of Russia and in Poland that did not involve the United States directly. The United States acquiesced and supported the policy. This boycott was a foolhardy and largely symbolic measure, as Soviet Russia was already virtually isolated from the rest of the world commercially, but any transactions that were considered high priority by either side, such as shipments of gold through Sweden or platinum through Siberia to pay for surplus Western munitions, went through easily in any case. The Soviet government transferred large amounts of its gold stockpile, inherited from the imperial regime and acquired by seizure of private and church property, to Swedish banks for laundering into nondescript gold bars, most of which ended up in Fort Knox, after paying for large quantities of imported military supplies for the Red Army.[9] Not all these transactions can be fully and authentically documented, but it is clear that the United States, Britain, and to a lesser degree France—and probably Germany—bought sizable amounts of platinum and gold from Soviet Russia for their own immediate wartime needs, mostly from the Soviet government in 1918 and 1919, amounting to many millions of dollars that helped finance the Soviet side of the civil war.[10]

The United States and Charity

A boost for the cause of relief came from a number of exiled Russians and from Americans returning from Russia, as well as a substantial and revived sentiment of many Americans to share their wealth with the unfortunate and downtrodden, a spirit that was behind many of the international operations of the Red Cross, YMCA, Society of Friends, and other relief organizations.[11] Divided as they may have been over military intervention, most favored humanitarian assistance of some kind to the Russian people, especially if the efforts could be headed by people of respect. Even David Francis, who had metamorphosed in 1918 from regular diplomatic dealings with the Bolsheviks to ardent intervention, from his hospital bed at the beginning of the new year recommended to Lansing privately the sending of a special food mission, with political strings attached, to Soviet Russia.[12]

9. For what is now known about these transactions, see Christine White, *British and American Commercial Relations with Soviet Russia, 1918–1924* (Chapel Hill: University of North Carolina Press, 1992).

10. Ibid., 157–65.

11. American aid to Russia followed precedents established in the nineteenth century.

12. Francis to Lansing, 1 January 1919, vol. 39, Lansing Papers, MD, LC.

The colorful and grandmotherly Ekaterina Breshko-Breshkovskaia,[13] having been rescued by the Czechs from the clutches of the Bolsheviks in western Siberia, reached Seattle in January 1919, just after her seventy-fifth birthday. She came to "find warm hearts who will pity and succor the four million orphans in Russia,"[14] and she immediately launched a program on their behalf. Well-known from previous speaking tours in the United States, she received an emotional home-coming at the Henry Street Settlement House in New York on 29 January. The audience included a wide array of American well-wishers of Russia, among them Jerome Davis, Albert Rhys Williams, Leroy Scott, Raymond Robins, Rose Strunsky, George Simons, and Breshkovskaya's closest American friends, Alice Stone Blackwell and George Kennan. According to the latter, she ceremoniously embraced him and gave him three kisses, to the delight of all assembled but to his own embarrassment.[15] Breshkovskaya advocated increased intervention and continued to attack Bolshevism, but after the call for the Prinkipo conference, she concluded that military opposition was only causing more misery and shifted her focus to repairing the damage.[16] Breshkovskaya's cause was hurt by her unflagging support of Kerensky, who had already been cast by almost all Americans into Trotsky's proverbial "dustbin of history," and by her constant refrain that the Bolsheviks were German agents. She was baffled by the American sympathy she found for the Bolsheviks.[17]

At a testimonial evening for Breshkovskaya at Carnegie Hall on 10 February, a Russian orphanage fund in her name was launched. The initial promoters were Kennan, Blackwell, Arkady Sack, Simons, Lillian Wald, Frederick Corse, and Dr. Edward Egbert, who had served the American Red Cross in Russia during the war. Corse, Kennan, Lyman Abbott, and Florence Harper were soon framing a more general "American-Russian Relief" drive.[18] Abbott offered space at his *Outlook* editorial offices for coordinating the campaign. Almost immediately there were divisions and quarrels between the socialists, the Jews, and the

13. This is a direct transliteration, but, as for many Russians familiar to Americans, the name is spelled in a variety of ways. She signed her name "Catherine Breshkovsky" in correspondence in English. Hereafter I will use "Breshkovskaya."

14. *New York Times*, 19 January 1919.

15. 1919 diary, 29 January 1919, box 14, Kennan Papers, MD, LC.

16. Breshkovskaya to Edward Egbert, 6 February 1919, f. A, box 1, Egbert Papers, HIA. She appealed for a "free, strong, united Russia"—and for aid funds—in printed form letters. For an example, Breshkovskaya to Anthony Griffin, 22 March 1919, box 2, Griffin Papers, MD, NYPL.

17. Jane E. Good and David R. Jones, *Babushka: The Life of the Russian Revolutionary Ekaterina K. Breshko-Breshkovskaia (1844–1934)* (Newtonville, Mass.: Oriental Research Partners, 1991), 166–68.

18. 1919 diary, February entries, box 14, Kennan Papers, MD, LC.

more conservative Russianites over the management of relief that caused Kennan—
and probably others—sleepless nights.[19] Kennan was frustrated with the senti-
mental, endearing Breshkovskaya: "It is difficult to get her to decide on the
practical measures that are needed here."[20] She herself was discouraged
by the "thin" results of her appearances at benefits in the East and Midwest.[21]
Henry Morgenthau, recruited from the New York business community to raise
funds, confirmed that what they were doing was "only a drop of water on a hot
stove" and he could only come up with $10,000 for administration, $3,000 of
which went to Egbert for his secretarial duties.[22]

To her credit, and despite ill health in early 1921 that confined her to a sanatorium near Paris, Breshkovskaya valiantly preached the cause for a desperate
need for relief for Russia: "This frightful calamity was foreseen and predicted by
those who knew the truth about Russia. The management of state's affairs were
of unimaginable sadness, corruption and foolishness, so that no wonder such
results."[23] Unfortunately, it was difficult for her to broaden the focus beyond
the narrow "little Carpatorussia regeneration."[24] She would spend most of the
rest of her life tending to a few hundred orphans in this far eastern section of
the new Czechoslovakia.

It was indeed a mixed lot of Russian relief companions in the United States.
As Kennan described Sack, who was still handling publicity for the Provisional
Government embassy in Washington, "He impressed me . . . as theorizing in
the air—as all Russians do—without proposing any concrete practical remedies
for existing evils."[25] Another supporter of the Breshkovskaya effort, Methodist
minister George Simons, separated from his long-standing Petrograd parish, wrote
a long report for the American Red Cross that concluded with a plea for the
support and recognition of Kolchak, since, he argued, aid could be effectively
administered only under a stable regime, and he was the best alternative.[26] Relief was almost always connected to politics, at least as far as Russia was con-

19. Ibid., 23 February.

20. Ibid., 28 February.

21. Breshkovskaya to Blackwell, 4 May 1919, reel 10, Blackwell Papers, MD, LC.

22. Ibid., 7 March.

23. Breshkovskaya to Blackwell, 16 July 1921, reel 11 (cont. 11), Blackwell Papers, MD,
LC.

24. To Blackwell, 10 April 1921, ibid. She was also exasperated by American "tolerance"
of Bolshevism, putting most of the blame on Trotsky's manipulative skills.

25. Ibid., 4 December.

26. Simons, "General Political Situation in Siberia," 20 May 1919, box 916, RG 200,
NA. This long and somewhat rambling report by a man with much Russian experience is
worth more study.

cerned. The Breshkovskaya relief transformed into another committee, headed by Kennan, Corse, Egbert, Lyman Abbott of *Outlook*, and Nicholas Murray Butler of Columbia University.

By April, Egbert was employed officially as the coordinating secretary of the Catherine Breshkovsky Russian Relief Fund, with Butler, Kennan, and Charles Evans Hughes listed on the advisory committee.[27] A number of prominent Americans were willing to lend their names to Russian aid. After an exhausting western tour, the lady herself went to Paris in June and then to Prague in September to search for people to relieve. She had no difficulty finding them. Unfortunately, neither Breshkovskaya nor Egbert was a skilled organizer.[28] In December, Egbert reported that materials valued at (only?) $50,000 to $60,000 had been collected and shipped to outfit and operate an orphanage for 200 children planned for the "Ruthenian" (Ukrainian) area of Czechoslovakia, and that an additional $36,000 had been transferred to the American Central Committee for Russian Relief.[29] This was obviously little more than a token effort, since Breshkovskaya had earlier numbered the orphans in the former empire in the "several millions."[30] Early Russian relief efforts were well-meaning but half-hearted, tiptoeing along party and ideological lines.

Fitting her image, Breshkovskaya tried to withdraw from the political aspects of relief to become the matron of a relatively small Russian children's orphanage, beginning with 24 children at Mukechevo, near Uzhorod, the provincial center of Ruthenia in the far eastern part of the new Czechoslovakia.[31] This soon grew to annexes nearby to house a total of about 100 boarders. Egbert and other friends, especially Alice Blackwell, solicited funds to maintain Breshkovskaya's modest mission through the worst of times in eastern Europe, and she constantly appealed for more help in whimsical handwritten letters in uncorrected English. But she probably did not aid her cause by revealing typical Russian biases, for example, that "only the Jews are clothed and fat." Soon she had satellite houses

27. Egbert to Breshkovskaya, 28 October 1919, box 1, Egbert Papers, HIA. These occasions did not always come off well. Breshkovskaya, fitting her grandmotherly image, usually spoke softly in broken English, which sometimes turned off audiences. She was also growing increasingly deaf, which made audience communication difficult. In contrast, Raymond Robins was an experienced lecturer who could easily sway an audience or at least create excitement. Landfield to Harper, 11 February 1919, f. 14, and 26 March 1919, box 6, Harper Papers, UC.

28. She wrote Lyman Abbott from Prague that she had not heard from Egbert in some time. Breshkovskaya to Abbott, 14 September 1919, f. A, box 1, Egbert Papers, HIA.

29. Egbert to fellow members, 29 December 1919, f. H, ibid.

30. BB (Chelyabinsk) to Arthur Bullard, 17 October 1918, Blackwell Papers, reel 10 (box 11), MD, LC.

31. Breshkovskaya to Egbert, 4 October 1920, f. A, box 1, Egbert Papers, HIA.

for Russian orphans in other parts of Czechoslovakia, the plan of limiting each to 25 to 30 children being a compassionate and realistic one. Her contribution was much broader than that, since the American Relief Administration, well apprised of her pioneer efforts, sent additional support, mostly in kind, to dispense as she wished.[32]

Although the relief she directly administered was a relative "drop in the bucket" of what was needed and soon to come, she was an important symbol of a dignified "American-style" philanthropic activism that galvanized much more American assistance to a variety of Russian causes. Breshkovskaya's wonderful way of scrambling the English language while getting her message across endured her to many Americans. In reference to her orphan charges, for example, she said, "Our future, world's future lie into their souls and bodies."[33] In regard to that region, "Austria was a wicked teacher, vary malicious."[34] And for the Bolsheviks, she attacked "their 'hyperving' [sic; wonderful word] and absence of any conscience of the evil they bring to the whole of humanity."[35] Unfortunately, she collapsed from mental strain and physical exhaustion and spent several months more or less isolated in a sanatorium near Paris in early 1921. She could yet provide a suitable epitaph for this and other work on behalf of Russian-American relations at the time: "What beautiful alliance it would be when Russia and America stand together to work and to watch the peace and justice over the world. . . . We have nothing to envie [sic] each other, nothing to quarelle [sic] and dispute."[36]

During the momentous summer of 1919, perhaps the most decisive of the twentieth century, Julia Grant Cantacuzene-Speransky, herself now a refugee from Russia but possessing a unique combination of illustrious American heritage and acquired Russian nobility, spearheaded another relief effort. This focused on misfortunate but "professional" refugees, who she believed could contribute to her campaign to save Russian culture, or at least be beneficiaries of it. Both hers and Breshkovskaya's causes would endure but remain relatively small and private, one directed toward a small number of refugee children, the other toward the expatriate Russian intelligentsia. After soliciting her old friend David Francis for advice, Cantacuzene-Speransky managed to assemble quite an impressive group of backers that included Charles Eliot as honorary president, Elihu Root, Samuel Gompers, John Mott, Charles Evans Hughes, and Cyrus

32. Ibid., 25 June 1920.
33. Ibid., 27 February 1920.
34. Ibid., 4 May 1920.
35. Ibid.
36. Ibid., 9 February 1921.

McCormick as vice presidents, with Montgomery Schuyler, having returned from a brief mission to Siberia, as secretary.[37] But some soon perceived a conservative, aristocratic agenda in her cause and withdrew their support.[38]

Yet another displaced Russian in the United States, Konstantin Oberuchev (Oberoutcheff), began a similar relief effort as early as June 1919 that was targeted even more directly at scholars, the Fund for the Relief of Men of Letters and Scientists in Russia, but it got off to a slow start.[39] Oberuchev, too, aimed to salvage the history and culture of the old non-Soviet Russia. The ubiquitous Sack was again a member of the executive committee of this organization.[40] Narrowly conceived, it would still have a longer life than many such relief efforts, because new American restrictions on immigration left loopholes for professional scholars. Separate and competing Russian relief funds, however, were confusing to potential donors and probably counterproductive in comparison with a united effort.

A large number of Imperial and/or Provisional Government minor and major officials were left virtually without means, having lost whatever fortune they had in the revolution—and now their jobs as well. For example, Adolf Schlippenbach, former Russian consul in Chicago, offered a Gainsborough, a couple of Vereshchagins, and other art objects to Charles Crane in exchange for his basic survival needs at a refuge in Switzerland.[41] Bakhmeteff doled out small grants from his slush fund, courtesy of the U.S. Treasury, to support this worthwhile cause. Unfortunately, most of these spontaneous relief efforts—though well-intentioned—had drawbacks and limitations.

Among several other prominent America voices against intervention and for relief was William Allen White. In his syndicated columns and in a flood of daily correspondence emanating from his *Emporia Gazette* office, he castigated those who would continue a hopeless war in Russia. To David Starr Jordan he wrote, "French military missions in red pants are making nuisances of themselves all over the Slovak [Slavic] country, from the Adriatic to Archangel."[42] And to Upton Sinclair, he blasted France even more, "It is a very interesting story. The story of a great Nation drunk with victory, turned reactionary, blind

37. Julia C.-S. to Francis, 21 September 1919, box 49, MoHS; Frederick Keppel, 27 September 1920, box 874, ARC 1917-34, RG 200, NA.
38. Eliot to Hapgood, 7 August 1920, Hapgood-Reynolds Papers, box 11, MD, LC.
39. Harper to Oberuchev, 6 June 1919, f. 22, box 6, Harper Papers, UC.
40. Letterhead in English, text in Russian, Oberuchev to Kennan, 21 December 1919, box 4, Kennan Papers, MD, LC.
41. Schlippinbach to Crane (received 25 June 1919), reel 2, Crane Papers, BA, CU.
42. White to Jordan, 6 August 1919, series B, vol. 38, White Papers, MD, LC.

with materialistic philosophy, and going to hell in a handcar."[43] He, along with Walter Lippmann, urged Herbert Hoover to take the matter in hand, while Simons advised that immediate action be taken instead to support Kolchak as the best way to extend relief:

> Russia's first great need is stable government. Admitting that the Omsk government is not ideal, that it may not be the permanent controlling force, it is still the only power definitely arrayed against Bolshevism, hers is the only army struggling to regain Russia from the Red terrorism that is endeavoring, through her to get a grip on the throat of the world. It is no time to quibble over niceties of political complexion. That can wait. But in the immediate future will be decided the momentous question as to whether Bolshevism or civilization shall be the world's guiding influence. And so the Army of Kolchak *must be supported by every right thinking nation and the support must be immediate and extensive to be effective.*[44]

Clearly, one of the problems with American relief to Russia in 1919 was disunity over methods, divergent political views, and varied social backgrounds. A more militantly anti-Bolshevik organization with antecedents traced to the American-Russian Chamber of Commerce was the Russian Economic League, with Alexander Behr as acting president and Jerome Landfield as the moving force behind it.[45] They launched an anti-Bolshevik propaganda campaign combined with encouragement for, and subsidies of, commerce with the non-Bolshevik areas of Russia. Their message was sharply defined: give aid for needy Russians, develop business ties, and help defeat the Bolsheviks.

43. White to Sinclair, 29 July 1919, ibid.

44. Simons, "General Political Situation in Siberia," 20 May 1919, box 916, RG 200, NA.

45. Landfield in New York was involved in a number of anti-Bolshevik organizations. He served as a communications center for various organizations and as a conduit to the State Department and to Harper in Chicago and worked closely with Bakhmeteff. Because of this, the latter thought Landfield should not be trusted with confidential information because he would leak it. Bakhmeteff to Landfield, 23 October 1919, f. Landfield, box 19, Bakhmeteff Papers, BA, CU. Harper to Poole, 8 December 1919, f. 9, box 7, Harper Papers, UC. But Felix Cole, temporarily assigned to the State Department, thought that Bakhmeteff was the biggest leak over the long run. Cole to Harper, 13 November 1920, f. 15, box 8, Harper Papers, UC.

Prisoners of War

One major problem that was apparent soon after the Armistice was the desperate situation of Russian prisoners of war who were still in Germany or Austria-Hungary and had no easy means of returning home due to the nonrecognition and blockade policies and civil wars. They initially numbered around 1.5 million, and their plight continued to deteriorate as they became a political issue. The French wanted to delay any repatriation for the possibility of rearming them as a formidable anti-Bolshevik Russian arm—or at least to prevent them from being merged into the Red Army, but France could not afford to feed and maintain them any better than Germany. This was left to American aid. Already on Christmas Day, 1918, Herbert Hoover reported to the State Department, "It is my view that the most suffering in Europe today is that of the Russian prisoners in Germany and Austria and en route home. They are dying wholesale from neglect. . . . It would seem to me a proper work for the American Red Cross."[46] After the Red Cross advised that it did not have the resources, Hoover turned to the president in February 1919 with an appeal for direct government subsistence of the Russian prisoners—to prevent them from returning to Russia and becoming a source of added strength for the Red Army.[47] Thus, the beginning of major American postwar relief in Europe pertained directly to a particular situation created by the Bolshevik revolution and involving Russians and was politically motivated.

The Nansen Committee focused on this problem and, meeting with American Red Cross officials in Paris at the end July 1920, formed a plan to exchange remaining German prisoners in Siberia for Russian prisoners in Germany who lived in Siberia. The first ship sent under the auspices of the League of Nations would initiate this exchange in July 1920.[48] It was composed of prisoners of 1914 from all parts of the former empire. Since the YMCA had been providing what services they could in the German camps, some accompanied them for their long-delayed repatriation. Donald Lowrie was aboard and described the

46. As quoted in Edward F. Willis, *Herbert Hoover and the Russian Prisoners of World War I: A Study in Diplomacy and Relief, 1918–1919* (Stanford, Calif.: Stanford University Press, 1951), 22.

47. Ibid., 25–52; see also Eugene P. Trani, "Herbert Hoover and the Russian Revolution, 1917–20," in *Herbert Hoover: The Great War and Its Aftermath, 1914–23*, ed. Lawrence F. Gelfand (Iowa City: University of Iowa Press, 1979), 127–34.

48. Olds memorandum, 29 July 1920, f. German Prisoners, 1920, box 188, ARC Papers, HIA.

miserable trip from Stettin to Revel for the Russians, most of whom had never been at sea but now were stranded on a

> dirty, little steamer, with proper accommodations for nine hundred men at a pinch, [but] we had twelve hundred aboard. . . . Sanitation was attended to as well as it could be, conveniently, and I found no worse experiences than some very bad smells and some equally vicious fleas. By the end of the trip, most of us looked like a map of Russia with every bolshevik marked in red! The sea was none too smooth, and our little steamer rolled considerably, and most of our passengers were making their first trip on water, so you may imagine we had a journey whose most joyful spot was the finish.[49]

There was still at least one high point, when members of a randomly selected male choir serenaded their fellow voyagers at sunset, as Lowrie emotionally recorded:

> The picture of that little group of men, in clothes of all descriptions, simply pouring out the soul of Russia in song for a thousand of their comrades, is one I shall often like to think about. The crimson and flame-color of sunset in these northern waters lasts for hours, and the music was as gorgeously solemn as the sky. Our boat slipped evenly along a mirror-like ocean, and men sang what was in their hearts as they returned from six years of exile to what they once called home. It was like a dream, where deep feeling moves one to tears.[50]

Once in a Baltic port, the Russian (former) prisoners were transferred to barges and then to railheads for the journey back to Russia. They often had to wait for many hours or a day or two without food or shelter. Again the YMCA came to the rescue with tents, food and drink, and even reading and writing materials. "The only water available was in roadside ditches and so the first thing we did was to set up a couple of field-kitchens, arrange for a water-supply, and serve teas to all comers. Since then we have enlarged our equipment by putting up a small tent for reading and writing, and by beginning the issue of cigarettes and chocolate."[51]

49. Lowrie (Narva) to Folks, 18 July 1920, f. May–July 1920, box 1, Lowrie Papers, UIA.
50. Ibid.
51. Ibid.

But much of the work there was concentrated on the returning German and Austrian prisoners, coming through the much longer reverse channel but on the same tracks. Special rations included cigarettes and chocolate ("It is a never ending source of interest to see the childish delight on the face of some grizzled old Austrian or Hungarian prisoner at the receipt of a tiny square of chocolate").[52] But most welcome were water heaters, bathtubs, laundry soap, and clotheslines. What was different about those returning from Russia (mostly of the various nationalities of Austria-Hungary) was that many brought wives and children, since they had been essentially loose (but marooned in Russia) for two years, and this obviously presented additional relief problems.[53] In the meantime, the most fortunate of the remaining German prisoners in Russia in the Far East performed KP, latrine, and supply details for the AEF in and around Vladivostok. They also provided support services for the Red Cross and YMCA detachments throughout Siberia and benefited from them.[54]

Most of central and eastern Europe was in desperate condition. From his "food office" in Washington and then in Europe, Herbert Hoover hoped to resolve these problems by channeling food and medicine to areas that desperately needed them through already established neutral agencies, such as the American Red Cross. A primary purpose, however, was to stabilize this region against Bolshevism. And with his organizational skills and supply reserves, this was quickly under way in the summer of 1919. It soon became apparent that the scope of the problem was beyond the capability of even this large and experienced organization. Almost by default, then, Hoover took charge, as he had earlier in Belgium, and by the summer of 1919 the American Relief Administration came into existence. Its first goal was feeding children, but then it saw the necessity of extending assistance to their parents. This centralized office supported the efforts of other relief agencies with available American government reserves of food and medicine, especially in regard to displaced Russian prisoners of war who could not return home, but also tried to bring them under central control. By the end of November 1920, thanks to the end of the civil war, many succeeded in returning, but almost 200,000 remained, including an addition of 47,000 Red Army personnel captured in the Soviet-Polish War. A YMCA report found them frightfully homesick and unhappy. "They wanted to go back to Russia and

---

52. Ibid.
53. "We have had as many as 250 children and women in camp at once. For the Children we have a professional play director who comes each day to take charge of their youthful part of the camp population." Ibid.
54. Bessie Lyon to "Jim," 12 April 1920, Lyon Papers, box 1, HIA.

didn't care whether the Tzar Nikolas [sic] or Lenin ruled; they wanted to be with their wives and fathers and children again."[55] Some had been away over seven years.

Soviet Initiatives

Following a similar aggressive approach as the YMCA in Russia, Soviet agents in the United States, Santeri Nuorteva and especially Ludwig Martens, the official Bolshevik representative in the United States, capitalized on the rising humanitarian spirit in America and growing disillusionment with intervention— and international affairs in general—to argue more convincingly that the blockade of Soviet Russia and the targeting of aid to non-Soviet areas was not only unfair but poor business. They insisted that for such aid and business to succeed, recognition of the Soviet government was essential. The stigma attached to their strangely non-Russian, foreign, and German-sounding names, which hampered their initial efforts, had worn off, and they had established ties and received support from a broader pro-Soviet constituency that included Alexander Trachtenberg, Harold Kellock, John Reed, Raymond Robins, and many others.[56] At a noisy rally in Madison Square Garden on 11 June, the formation of the Soviet Russian Recognition League was announced, soon to be transformed into the Soviet Russian Information Bureau.[57]

This cause was also aided by reports filtering out of Russia that described the increasing misery and desperation in most of the region. Unfortunately, political activists in this pro-Soviet crowd, inspired in part by the Seattle general strike of February 1919 and the rhetoric of the founding congress of the Third (Communist) International in March, set out to obtain more extreme political goals. One result was the formation of the American Communist Party and the espousing of Soviet-led revolutions everywhere by a radical element of American society. Popular and official reaction to the "Red Scare" of 1919 featured sensational investigations, beginning with a committee headed by State Senator Clayton Lusk, into the activities of Martens and other Soviet supporters in New York

55. "Russian Prisoners of War," unsigned, undated memorandum, f. Russian Work, box 5, Anderson Papers, UIA. It also stressed the lack of success of Denikin and Wrangel's recruiting efforts among them.
56. John Reed, naturally, was optimistic about Martens's mission: "It is kicking up quite a fuss around here . . . [and] will do more than any thing else to get recognition for Russia." Reed to Bryant, 21 March 1919, f. 94–98, Reed Papers, Harvard-Houghton.
57. McFadden, *Alternative Paths*, 272–73.

City. They employed high-handed and often brutal police methods, aided and abetted by the virulently anti-Bolshevik Russian community there, to obtain and manufacture evidence of seditious activities. The reaction was not only political but also ethnic, as so many of the social troublemakers were of foreign origin.

Not to be outdone by a state committee, Senator Lee Overman of North Carolina, chairman of the Senate Judiciary Committee, began his own investigations with the help of a dynamic new attorney general, A. Mitchell Palmer, and his ambitious assistant, J. Edgar Hoover, who conducted raids on Russian and leftist centers, especially in Detroit and Bridgeport, Connecticut.[58] Of the large number of people arrested in November 1919, over a hundred were processed for deportation.[59] More followed. The end result was an embarrassing number of arrests and deportations of many foreign nationals who had Russian or east European roots in these ruthless and arbitrary "Palmer raids." Among others they netted was Emma Goldman, an acute and prolific champion of the socialist cause, who was forced to endure very primitive conditions aboard a ship that she described as "a floating prison." But she was still looking forward to seeing the Soviet miracle and upon landing found that "Russia is marvelous but painfully confused," putting it mildly.[60] The negative reaction and public sympathy for these hapless supporters of the idealism of revolution, or simple victims of random persecution, benefited the Bolshevik cause.

Unlike most of them, however, Martens at least had a hearing before Overman's committee, in which he convincingly defended his activities as nonpolitical. But he, too, was forced to leave the country, virtually closing down the "Soviet mission" and seriously damaging and definitely postponing any case to be made for aid through recognition. The tragedy was that in all of the publicity and justifications surrounding such repressions, the political gulf widened between sympathizers and opponents of Soviet Russia, any rational treatment of the question of recognition was made more difficult, and millions of Russians would starve to death before any American aid could reach them. This political climate, though having little effect on increasing a direct American commitment to active intervention in Russia, may have stiffened British and French unwillingness to end it. A new-found American isolationism was torn between withdrawal from direct military involvement and the need for humanitarian assistance.

58. This followed the precedents during the war of investigating alleged seditious or disloyal activities that had landed such mainstream socialists as Norman Thomas and Eugene Debs in jail.

59. A. Trachtenberg to William Feigenbaum, 20 October 1920, f. 3, box 1, Rand School Papers, NYPL.

60. Goldman to Harris, 16 and 26 January 1920, in box 187, Long Papers, MD, LC.

Washington Drifts

The overburdened and virtually collapsed State Department, owing to exhaustion, disaffection, illness, and the considerable drainage of staff and leadership to Paris in 1919, drafted Samuel Harper as an emergency replacement for Jerome Landfield in April and slowly began to accumulate a small arsenal of Russian expertise.[61] Harper could not abandon his post in Chicago, so his job was mainly to examine the Soviet press sent to him by Dorothy Read (until her departure for China in March 1920) for any relevant information. His work, however, was mainly translation—"It was definitely understood that I was not to be associated with policy."[62] But he naturally largely determined the selection and interpreted the meanings of the translations and gradually began to add his own memorandums.

Harper was assisted on the Washington end by another new member of the State Department staff, attorney Allan Carter, who was involved with Russian affairs beginning in May 1919. From Chicago, previously known and recommended by Harper, he tried valiantly but unsuccessfully to create reason out of chaos, substance out of vacuum, and frequently complained to Harper about the Washington bureaucracy. Carter's correspondence with Harper reveals much about the State Department at this time. Another valuable addition in early 1920 was Felix Cole, most recently consul at Archangel and a former vocal opponent of intervention. But within a few months he was transferred out to the consulate in Bucharest and, on the way, to assist McCully in Crimea.[63] Arthur Bullard came in and out, causing more inconsistency in late 1920, until he finally resigned on 4 March 1921 (change of administration).[64] All this rotation, however, appeared rather makeshift and temporary. No one seemed to know who was in charge of Russian policy.

A major problem for American policy toward Russia was thus a lack of clear direction from the State Department, some of it accidental or fortuitous, due to illness and absence, or otherwise simply from happenstance or neglect. Basil Miles, one of the soundest voices on Russian matters, seemed to have developed psychological (in addition to physical) problems and resigned at the end of September 1919.[65] He was replaced by DeWitt Clinton Poole, a veteran of much

61. Miles to Harper, 4 March 1919, f. 15, box 6, Harper Papers, UC.
62. Harper to Roger Williams, 22 May 1919, f. 20, ibid.
63. McCully to Bristol, 26 March 1920, f. March 1920, box 32, Bristol Papers, MD, LC.
64. Cole to Harper, 23 November 1920, and Bullard to Harper, 3 December 1920, f. 16, box 8, Harper Papers, UC; Bullard to Harper, 7 March 1921, f. 3, box 9, ibid.
65. A few years later he committed suicide.

of the Russian turmoil of 1917-19 in Moscow and Archangel, but he, too, was afflicted by illness at critical times. He followed the general line of Miles and Landfield in being mildly supportive of intervention but adamantly opposed to recognition. Sheldon Whitehouse was back from Sweden as a consultant, and Mrs. Maddin Summers, in consideration of the service of her husband, came aboard as a translator.[66] And on Harper's recommendation, Leo Pasvolsky, a trained economist (Columbia University) and editor (*Russian Review; Russkoe Slovo*) was hired as a consultant on Russian economic affairs.[67] Despite this expansion of Russian expertise and the advent of new and sharper anti-Bolshevik voices in the State Department, the mood for intervention definitely waned during the summer of 1919. Harper confessed to Landfield in June that he had been an advocate for recognition of Kolchak's government five months before but now thought it was too late, that we "should not back a falling man."[68] Despite the instability in personnel, the State Department was consistent in following a program of nonrecognition and quasi intervention in the form of material and financial support for anti-Bolshevik forces.

Breckinridge Long, one of the few constants in the State Department and an opponent of intervention, reflected at the end of 1919 his disappointment in Lansing turning against the peace and Wilson and the absence of Phillips, but he welcomed the return of Frank Polk from a long and needed rest and the recruitment of Bullard to assist Poole with publicity (with the demise of the Committee on Public Information). Partially replacing the earlier misadventure of the separate Russian Bureau under the War Trade Council was a Russian Division in the Bureau of Foreign Trade and Domestic Commerce under Chapin Huntington, which, however, got off to a poor and unimpressive start.[69] There was by now a Division of Russian Affairs in the State Department, but it was practically devoid of leadership, though Poole finally took charge in April 1920 amid rumors that Butler Wright would soon succeed him.[70] The various agencies seemed to be in competition and unaware of what one another was doing. All suffered from lack of funds. To economize on the multiplicity of Russian

66. Carter to Harper, 18 August 1919, f. 1, box 7, Harper Papers, UC. A secretary referred to this new Russian clique in the State Department as "Our little Bolshevist 'chamber of horrors.'" Read to Harper, 1 October 1919, f. 2, ibid.

67. CV of Pasvolsky, f. 10, box 8, ibid. Pasvolsky's tenure was a short one, like so many others, ending in October 1920. Pasvolsky to Harper, 15 October 1920, f. 12, box 8, ibid.

68. Harper to Landfield, 10 June 1919, f. 22, box 6, ibid.

69. Huntington to Harper, 29 September 1919, f. 2, box 7, ibid.

70. Carter to Harper, 26 and 28 April 1921, and Harper to Carter, 8 May 1921, f. 9, box 9, ibid.

quasi agencies, it was decided to abolish the one in Stockholm under Ira Morris and Sheldon Whitehouse.[71]

The State Department lacked stability. After Carter resigned in May, Poole lamented to Harper, "Bear in mind that the watchword of the moment is economy and that we cannot expect to have an organization of ideal dimension."[72] Carter had hoped "that our skeleton organization here in the Russian Division might be expanded into a larger unit working on the whole Communist program along the lines of the group now functioning in Berlin and doubtless in other world capitals!"[73] Roger Williams, the voice of Charles Crane during his absence, expressed his appreciation that Harper had stayed away from Paris to do noble duty at home: "Those there have been in such a turmoil that I believe very few of them have succeeded in keeping an even poise."[74] But Harper himself pulled up roots in June.

In Denmark, Norman Hapgood tried to mend fences between the West and Soviet Russia but to no avail. He felt that he was definitely handicapped by an absence of direction—and also by the Senate's refusal to confirm his appointment as minister.[75] His friend Frank Polk, left in Paris to supervise the tedious cleanup business of the peace conference, warned him:

> I am afraid you are going to be a little too charitable in regard to the extremists. I suppose most of us have been listening to conservatives on the Russian situation. For heaven's sake, don't listen to [Isaac Don] Levine. That is, listen to him, but don't take all he says as gospel. I have great sympathy for the people of Russia, and I feel we should do all we can to assist them. I am not prepared to believe that Trotsky and Lenine are in the same class with William Jay Shieffelin and Norman Hapgood. Perhaps I should apologize for classing you with Shieffelin.[76]

The other end of the spectrum also gained the offensive in early 1919, as the leading wedge of the Red panic in America made headway. Louise Bryant and Sinclair Lewis concentrated on lecturing together and separately to receptive

71. Carter to Harper, 3 December 1919, f. 9, ibid.

72. Poole to Harper, 7 May 1921, ibid. Carter had no regrets: "I'm glad to be getting away from such petty inside intriguing and peanut politics." Carter to Harper, 12 May 1921, ibid.

73. Memorandum to Poole, 19 May 1921, f. 11, ibid.

74. Williams to Harper, 26 May 1919, f. 21, box 6, ibid.

75. Hapgood to Wilson, 16 September 1919, box 13, Hapgood-Reynolds Papers, MD, LC.

76. Polk to Hapgood, 9 July 1919, box 9, ibid.

audiences in Seattle and Portland. Bryant became increasingly convinced in favor of the Russian socialist crusade and more effective as an enthusiastic campaigner against intervention. She wrote home to her husband in New York, "*I believe* in my whole heart it is wrong to have troops in Russia. I want to write it *once*, say it *once*, but I *have* to do *both* a *million times*." She complained that her book on the revolution in Russia was constantly being sold out and she could not get enough copies.[77] In the meantime, Reed's own story, *Ten Days That Shook the World*, came out in March and was an immediate sensation, in itself affecting and complicating public opinion in regard to America's involvement with Russia. It spurred a new wave of opposition to intervention: Why should Americans be fighting against a good, just, experimental cause, filled with the quirky but "adorable" Jack Londonish heroes he portrayed? To many Americans it was an imaginative revelation from the other side of the moon, or the settlement houses' dream fulfilled.

Siberia, the Great White Hope

The vastness of Siberia, the number of separate political and military centers, and the dependence of the United States on a base of operations in Vladivostok on the extreme Asian fringe continued to complicate relief service and decision making. The American Red Cross, complemented by the YMCA, was the main agency for relief, providing especially important medical services to anti-Bolshevik forces and to the local population. Need was acute because of the large number of refugees from European Russia hoboing along the Trans-Siberian and the continuing breakdown of transportation and communication. An additional mission of the AEF was now to protect a possible extension and expansion of this aid from its base in Vladivostok.

A major unresolved issue was the status of relations with the Kolchak regime in Omsk that had received token recognition from Britain and France and belated financial and military support from the United States. Ambassador Roland Morris and General William Graves, accompanied by William Donovan, journeyed to Omsk in July to observe the situation there at close hand.[78] Morris met

77. Bryant (Seattle) to Reed, 23 March 1919, f. 278–82, Reed-Bryant Papers, Harvard-Houghton.

78. According to one biographer, Donovan was on a secret intelligence mission for President Wilson under the cover of a honeymoon trip to Japan with his wife. If so, it was the first of many for the future head of the Office of Strategic Services during World War II. He supported Morris and Graves on a recommendation to withdraw American forces in his

A mission to Omsk, 1919. From left to right: Ambassador Morris, General Graves, Colonel Lantry (Railway Service Corps), and William Donovan, courtesy of the Partridge Collection, Hoover Institution Archives

first with Acting Minister of Foreign Affairs Sukin, formerly with the Russian embassy in Washington. He unwisely stressed the bitter resentment against America among the Russian population for not giving Kolchak full support. Morris expressed his regret that hostility of the Omsk government had forced the American Red Cross to cease its activities there, but, learning of many thousand refugees headed east from Ekaterinburg and Cheliabinsk, he asked that fifty Red Cross nurses be sent to meet them.[79] From a conference with Generals Janin and Knox, he learned that "army staff and supply departments were completely disorganized, inefficient, corrupt, and unsettled." Morris summed up his impressions:

> Admiral Kolchak is, in my judgment, an honest and courageous man of very limited experience in public affairs, of narrow views and small administrative ability. He is dictator in name but exercises little influence on the

---

personal report to Newton Baker (due to the president's illness). But the author's source for this account was apparently only Donovan himself. Richard Dunlop, *Donovan, America's Master Spy* (Chicago: Rand McNally, 1882), 117–29.

79. Morris to Lansing, 24 July 1919, box 187, Long Papers, MD, LC; Morris to Lansing, 22 July 1919, ibid.

council of ministers. His intentions are good, but he seems to have had no appreciation until recently of the political and economic dangers which threaten the Government. He has no military knowledge or experience.[80]

This stinging indictment provided considerable detail against Kolchak and concluded, "The [Omsk] military leaders have lost much of their influence because of their obvious failure in army organization and in civil administration." Morris was also annoyed about receiving a "laundry list" of "requirements" from the United States that included 600,000 pairs of boots, 400,000 rifles, 500 million cartridges, and 3,000 machine guns. He estimated that a proposed credit of $75 million would cover less than a third of it.[81]

Kolchak admitted to Morris in another interview on 18 August that in the spring he had concentrated on military operations over economic and financial problems in the belief that the Bolsheviks would soon collapse, but that now he was revamping his policies and hoping for Allied support. It all seemed very vague and unconvincing to the Americans. In a tour of military camps, moreover, Graves found total disorganization.[82] At the same time, John Stevens reported from Harbin that "the Siberian army was collapsing."[83] As if to add another nail to Kolchak's coffin, Morris reported that in regard to dealing with the Kolchak "ministers," "Stevens seems to have reached the limit of his patience."[84] While he stayed on, discouraged, as "president" of the virtually powerless Inter-Allied Technical Board, his highly valued chief assistant, Colonel George Emerson, resigned and went home. Stevens sympathized:

Personally, I am tired beyond words of all the mess, and if I felt that I could, without leaving our Government in the air (more than they apparently are), I would pull out for good and all. But this I cannot do as I must hold on in the hope that Washington will find some way out of the muddle. . . .

The failure of the Allies to put up the money we asked for has complicated the situation. If we had a reasonable amount of funds I would be in favor of putting Allied men directly in charge of each Railway, taking over absolute control of all operation and of all income, and then if the Russian staff did not come across, to tell such of them as needed it, that they were dismissed and their pay stopped. I know that is the only solution, but I

80. Morris to Lansing, 4 August 1919, ibid.
81. Morris to Lansing, 4 and 8 August 1919, ibid.
82. Morris to State, 18 August 1919, box 187, ibid.
83. Stevens to Lansing, 15 August 1919, ibid.
84. Morris to State, 20 August 1919, ibid.

would feel more certain of success if we had fifty to seventy-five thousand troops over here, which I know we cannot get. Neither do I believe we can get the money. So far the United States has put up $4,000,000, the Chinese $500,000 and that is all. We should have $20,000,000 now in hand and at least $30,000,000 more assured.[85]

He recalled several years later that his greatest accomplishment after more than six years devoted to railroad improvement in Russia was not specifically about the technicalities of transportation but in helping to extract the Czecho-Slovak forces.[86]

Other personnel of the railroad service corps repeatedly recommended withdrawal from Russia and were universally and consistently opposed to Kolchak.[87] All of this naturally affected the morale of those who remained and those trying to administer relief under increasingly difficult conditions. Reading all these negative reports, Lansing felt caught in a Catch-22.

The Bolsheviks already thoroughly mistrust us for the so-called Bullitt episode and rejected proposals; every loyal Russian on the other side will distrust us for the impending Kolchak incident.

If we attempt to shoulder onto Japan the blame for our withdrawal before we have properly safeguarded the Kolchak interests which we publicly announced we would further, we certainly fail.[88]

Breckinridge Long, who was in charge of the Siberian "desk," if it could be called that, reflected in a long diary entry:

I am studying Morris' reports from Omsk, with great care, and am entering a period of general survey of the whole situation. I am going to bring order out of that chaos, if possible, if policy on our part will help any. There must be something that can be *done*—some aggressive policy, some constructive action—in order to promote the return of order.[89]

---

85. Stevens to Emerson, 29 September 1919, Emerson Papers, HIA. Systemwide, barely 4,500 locomotives were in serviceable condition, compared with 15,000 in 1917. Captain George Williams, ONI to OPNAV, 25 March 1919, box 713, WA-6, RG 45, NA.

86. Stevens Memoir, n.d., Stevens Papers, HIA.

87. For examples, Colonel Lantry to Emerson, 13 August 1919, box 9, Roland Morris Papers, MD, LC; and Benjamin Johnson to Emerson, 25 November 1919, Emerson Papers, HIA.

88. Lansing memorandum for Long, 26 August 1919, box 187, Long Papers, MD, LC.

89. Long diary, 1 August 1919, box 2, ibid.

Vladivostok, 1919. Some unfortunate Americans returning home, with the assistance of former German prisoners of war, courtesy of the U.S. Army Signal Corps, Photographs Division, National Archives

He was confounded by "60,000 dissatisfied Czech troops who want repatriation and are a disturbing element in their present frame of mind; 200,000 or more German and Austrian prisoners in a sad and neglected plight."[90] Montgomery Schuyler, veteran of many Russian ventures, reported back from a special mission to Siberia on Graves's "lack of decision and unforceful character" but also on Kolchak's "lack of political experience. . . . The consequence is a weak authority and a tottering regime," which had become practically a universal American refrain.[91] It would be difficult to find an American in Siberia or elsewhere who had a good word for Kolchak or any of his entourage, except perhaps his "foreign minister," Sukin. Siberia was left to drift on its shifting and anarchic permafrost.

90. Ibid.
91. Ibid., 7 August 1919.

Washington and Siberia

The State Department official most responsible for guiding America's Siberian affairs was Breckinridge Long. Soon after his doctor advised extensive rest for mental and physical exhaustion, Long noted that he had become "acting Secretary of State," owing to Lansing being in Paris and Polk and Phillips on leave.[92] He dined with the Lansings, soon after their return at the end of July 1919, and received a shock: "He told me he would turn Russia over to me to manage."[93] One of his first private comments on studying that situation was, "Kolchak is between the upper and nether millstones. . . . I don't see how he can survive long. Nor do I see how we can help."[94] Long, like so many others, was perplexed by the Russian situation: "I am wrestling with Russia, assiduously, but get no where yet. The questions of this day are so vast and deep they baffle casual treatment. I will have evolved some policy before long though."[95] Good luck, especially with the oppressive heat of Washington in August adding an additional obstacle to rational thinking on anything relating to Russia. In December 1919, Long reflected that

> the policy in the past seemed only to have helped the Bolsheviki, that partial support had been given at various times to each of the Anti-Bolshevik elements, but only in sufficient quantity to permit the Bolsheviki to advertise that the allies were opposing them, and to gain great credit by defeating the comparatively small contingents opposing them on various fronts, thereby strengthening the prestige of the Soviet Power and consolidating their ranks.[96]

Upon returning to Vladivostok from Omsk, Morris strongly urged the need for greatly increased American relief assistance to the people of Siberia, because Kolchak was totally incapable of dealing with the problem. For this he asked for an emergency credit of $20 million and another long-term credit of $70 million, an agreement with Japan to ensure coordination, and the reinforcement of the army units under Graves with an additional battalion of field artillery. With Czech forces leaving and White forces disintegrating, the

92. Ibid., 7 April and 31 May 1919.
93. Ibid., 29 July.
94. Ibid., 30 July.
95. Ibid., 5 August.
96. Long, Memorandum of conversation with Russian ambassador, 9 December 1919, f. Russia 1919–20, box 182, ibid.

only rationales left for intervention were to provide relief and to watch the Japanese.[97] Still, there were optimistic challenges to the general dismal predictions for Kolchak as late as September and October 1919, both in Siberia and in Washington.[98]

The American Red Cross did not, of course, offer to extend its services to the Bolshevik or pro-Bolshevik centers in Siberia. This caused some grumbling among the personnel. For example, Captain F. L. Barnum of Philadelphia complained that if the Red Cross is neutral, why does it give aid to the Omsk government and not to the Bolsheviks? He also thought what they were providing to the "White" side was not appreciated but simply squandered and corrupted away. "The R. C. people don't seem to get it in their thick heads that the Russians don't want us here & are pulling all sorts of obstructions in the way in order to make us get out."[99] He apparently did not receive an answer. Indeed, one of the major features of Red Cross and other relief activities was friction with those whom they were trying to serve. Simply, in a volatile, anarchic situation, the reliefers were often considered a nuisance by local military authorities, especially in regard to access to scarce transport facilities and the better buildings and residences. The fact that the personnel were American carried some weight, but many Russians in the anti-Bolshevik camp thought the "do-gooder" Americans of the Red Cross and YMCA were doing more harm than good. Another problem that the Red Cross field staff in Siberia had to contend with was Colonel Teusler, who was in overall command from Japan, which he seldom left, and who was totally incompetent from all accounts.[100]

Still, with very able and devoted subordinates, such as Riley Allen, the Red Cross prevailed, despite the increasing obstacles of political turmoil and transportation breakdowns. Against odds, two new hospitals were established in the Irkutsk region with a total of 2,000 beds, served by American Red Cross nurses.[101] And Americans had a facility for making do under the circumstances. Verne Bright boasted that his baseball team beat the Canadians but then lost to the sailors of the USS *Albany*. Then he lamented that the Canadians had actually

97. Morris to Lansing, 23 September 1919, copy in box 187, ibid.

98. See, for example, Basil Miles to Long, 12 September 1919, f. Mel–Mil, box 55, ibid. He thought there was still time "to pull the Siberian chestnuts out of the fire." Miles to Long, 8 September 1919, ibid.

99. F. L. Barnum diary, vol. 1, 22 August 1919, BA, CU.

100. Stanley Partridge to Family, 16 November 1919, Partridge Papers, HIA.

101. F. W. Prince to Allen, 13 November 1919, Siberian Commission, box 138, ARC Papers, HIA.

Opening of the baseball season in Vladivostok, summer 1919, courtesy of the U.S. Army Signal Corps, Photographs Division, National Archives

won because they were leaving Siberia: "All want to go home."[102] The Red Cross abandoned Omsk due to the Red Army's advance into that area at the end of October in favor of Irkutsk, with its hospitals, equipment, medicines, and so on, leaving nothing behind for that region.[103] For it the main problem was not the Russians, who had been essentially abandoned to their own fate, but the Czechs, who as late as December 1919 were "still fairly well strung out along the line," though rapidly withdrawing and leaving Kolchak to his fate.[104] Consul John Caldwell, a stalwart at his post in Vladivostok through all the turmoil, reported on the overwhelming support for the relief effort from the resident American community, singling out especially Mr. and Mrs. Frederick Pray, who operated a small sporting goods store for hunters, for commendation.[105]

The YMCA had one of its largest operations abroad in Siberia, with over 100 American secretaries and 200 Czech, Russian, and other assistants. The "inter-

102. Bright to Family, 5 and 11 May 1919, box 1, Bright Papers, UOA. A following letter (22 June) was addressed from "Stick in the Mud, Siberia," describing more of the depressing situation of the "lost" American contingents in Siberia.

103. Red Cross memorandum (Irkutsk), 18 November 1919, ARC Papers, HIA.

104. Report to Livingston Farrand, 4 December 1919, box 916, RG 200, NA.

105. Caldwell memoirs, 39, February 1973, Caldwell Papers, HIA.

national hut" in Vladivostok served over 60,000 soldiers of thirty nationalities in 1919. This included 600 sleeping accommodations; 45,000 served with buffets of sandwiches, cakes, tea, coffee, cocoa, and so on; the mailing of 50,000 letters; and the showing of fifty different moving pictures. Quite an accomplishment.[106] In November 1919 the YMCA still had 102 American secretaries scattered in the region: "17 among the American Expeditionary Forces, 15 in the Czech Army, 20 for Russian work, both Army and Civilian, 10 to the International Hut and other allied units, 2 to the Railway Department, 7 to the Executive Bureau, 12 to the Lecture Bureau (including 8 kino experts), 8 to Finance, 4 to Supply and 7 to the Rural Department," whatever that was. At the micro level the association in Vladivostok had a regular "enlisted" clientele of 1,162 young men and 114 boys on 1 October 1919.[107] This was an excellent foundation for future advancement—in normal times.

The withdrawal of American military forces from Siberia was basically decided by August 1919, announced prematurely by General Graves in September, delayed over the explanation for it and a sensitivity to the Japanese situation, officially declared in October, partially completed in November, and fully effected in April 1920. Graves gave a lavish farewell dance for the American community on 8 November with the bands from the *Brooklyn* and the 31st Regiment providing the music.[108] The reports of Morris and Stevens, advising this course of withdrawal and forecasting the collapse of the Kolchak government, were perhaps the most decisive factors in Washington minds. Long clearly agreed and thought strategy should be "to put onus on Japan for U.S. withdrawal—in fact it is Japan's support of Semenov that makes operations impracticable."[109] The sage of Emporia once again was the wise voice of Middle America in predicting difficult times ahead for Russia:

There is no question but that Russia is in for a long bloody time, no matter what happens. And the blood letting will come, no matter who wins. It is in the Russian people. They have been ruled by an autocracy with cruel tyranny so long that when the autocracy changes from one group of society to another the ruthless, bloody tyranny remains. It would take a million

106. George Phelps, "Activities of Red Triangle in Siberia Since Foundation," November 1919, f. Siberian Division, box 57, YMCA papers, HIA.

107. Report of City Work Department for October and November 1919, ibid.

108. Colonel Fred Bugbee to wife, 9 November 1919, Bugbee Papers, HIA. He also noted another reason for getting out: the refugee influx had swollen the population of Vladivostok from 80,000 to over 300,000.

109. Long memorandum to Colby, 26 August 1920, box 187, Long Papers, MD, LC.

American soldiers to forcibly restore order in Russia. And probably we would shed as much blood in doing it as would be shed inevitably. When Kolchak comes in, he will massacre the Bolshevik to keep them in order, and then there will be a reaction against Kolchak and the Bolshevik will go in and massacre the Kolchak expedition and so the problem will swing year after year. And I cannot see that the presence of our soldiers there is going to help.[110]

There was also sentiment in the United States and in other Allied camps that Siberian affairs were in such a hopeless state and so unpopular that it was better to concentrate forces, money, and public education on the other civil war fronts much closer to Europe.[111] One sentiment was that if the main concern was the spread of Bolshevism in Asia, the Japanese could take care of it, but many others objected to the Japanese being involved at all. This remained the dominant factor in American intervention in Siberia.

The collapse of the Omsk government and Kolchak's military leadership came suddenly but without surprise in October 1919. The Czechoslovaks withdrew their last support to the White cause, took Kolchak hostage, and, according to Stevens, exchanged him to the Bolsheviks for certain death in return for safe passage on the stretch of the Trans-Siberian Railroad around Lake Baikal that had many tunnels and was vulnerable to sabotage. Leaving the remnants of Kolchak's army to their own devices, the American railway men then managed to shepherd over 300 trains (averaging only ten cars each) of Allied troops, American Red Cross and YMCA relief personnel, and as many supplies as could be evacuated in a hasty retreat to the safer environs of Vladivostok and Harbin in November. Stevens considered this a near miracle and the major accomplishment of the corps. Refugees of all kinds fled eastward, many on foot, over the next year.

Stevens and part of his railroad commission remained, caught in the limbo of Siberian anarchy. This was partly due to major personnel changes in Washington with the resignation of Lansing. His replacement, Bainbridge Colby, apologized belatedly, in July 1920, for the department's neglect with lame excuses.[112] Part of the problem of his jurisdiction had already been solved by the

110. White to A. M. Holt (for Cyrus McCormick), 2 October 1919, series B, vol. 39, White Papers, MD, LC.

111. As summed up in Long memorandums to Lansing, 26 and 29 August 1919, box 187, Long Papers, MD, LC.

112. Stevens manuscript autobiography, pp. 253-61, f. 26, box 3, Stevens Papers, GU. Stevens noted that the Czech soldiers were forced to mine coal for locomotive fuel but also carried out much loot, including sixty carloads of flour. This certainly did not help the food situation in Siberia that winter.

establishment of the Inter-Allied Technical Board with Stevens in charge, but this was still dependent on a number of Russian, Japanese, Czech, and other military agencies that performed "guard duty" over various stretches of the Trans-Siberian and charged for their "services." Their closest equivalents were the highwaymen of early England or the train robbers of the American West. They ended up performing more valuable relief assistance to local populations than in the operation of the nearly defunct Siberian railway.

Business as Usual?

With civil war, intervention, and many other disruptions, one would not expect many business transactions with American companies to occur. But where there were goods in periods of shortage there could be profit, or at least the hope for it in the future. The Singer Sewing Machine Company, trying to salvage what it could from its Russian operations, unloaded a sizable inventory during the civil war. In late 1918 and early 1919, 6,233 sewing machines were sold in central Russia, most of them to local and central Soviet government agencies—and to the Red Army.[113] With a reduction to just over 1,000 employees, the factory at Podolsk managed to complete 20,000 machines (many in production before civil war interruptions) in 1919 and was trying, in addition, to fulfill orders for magnetos and cartridges for the Red Army.[114] The business went sharply downhill after this, but American machines definitely sewed the uniforms for the Red Army.

E. L. Friedlander, a manager who stayed with the slowly sinking Singer ship in expectation that the White armies would triumph, reported in September 1920 that "only poor ruins are left of our once proud enterprise."[115] But it was still there. The plant, however, went downhill fast under a new Soviet-supervised administration, Metal Department, Management for the Manufacture and Distribution of Sewing Machines, but a main part of its business was reoriented to railroad equipment repair, understandably. Technically, this was a caretaker arrangement imposed by the government with Singer ownership remaining intact. But by midsummer 1920 the situation was so bad that Aleksei Miliukov

113. Colby to Stevens, 29 July 1920, box 5, RG 43, NA.
114. Myslik to Alexander, 25 March 1919, f. 4, box 157, Singer Papers, SHSW; Miliukov to Alexander, 30 April 1920, f. 5, ibid. Interestingly, the brother of Paul Miliukov remained at the Singer plant in the heart of Bolshevik Russia during this period.
115. E. L. Friedlander to Myslik, 29 September 1920, ibid.

and eventually Friedlander were forced to flee.[116] The name "Singer" was no longer officially in use in Russia (although popularly any sewing machine was a "Zinger" in Russian for many years).

At the ground level, R. Bark described his travels through the countryside around Rostov-on-Don, selling his remaining stock of Singer needles and thread and combating the new regime by forming a small employees' collective. With the gradual exhaustion of supplies, however, the staff at his once-thriving Rostov agency was reduced to five people. He was forced to leave only after being arrested, held for several days, then released, but was proud to report that he had managed to recover property to take with him that had been seized earlier in the revolutionary turmoil.[117] Situations varied from place to place depending on the rapport of agents with the local population and with the new authorities, many of whom realized the value of sewing machine expertise. In a way, this falls in the category of relief, since Singer realized no profits and was obviously taking a loss on future possibilities.

International Harvester agents had a similar experience but on the whole fared better, since the new government—like the old—placed high priority on agricultural improvements. A central office in Kharkov, however, came under fire, literally from several sides. Typewriters were stolen, fixtures ripped out, and premises trashed. But equipment stored in warehouses remained safe, temporarily. "Our success in this respect was due to the fact that I had taken care to get rid of all objectionable employees before the bandits got here, and those remaining on the payroll stood by me throughout."[118] Civil war in the main Harvester sales areas—Ukraine, south Russia, and Siberia—set back agricultural progress many years.

Nevertheless, the main Harvester planter factory just outside Moscow continued operating through the period of civil war under American management, surprisingly, relatively unscathed though at reduced levels and basically cut off from its Chicago direction. When communication with the main office resumed

116. Ibid. His letter to Myslik stressed his financial and personal losses and made a plea for restitution.

117. Reports of 26, 29, and 30 October 1920, ibid.

118. Field agent (Zuber) to Foreign Sales Department, 2 July 1919, M90-048, box 1, IH Papers, SHSW. He continued with gory details of the civil war in Kharkov: "Bodies are being found in various locations in the town, and it is impossible to conjecture how many will yet be unearthed as time goes on; so far we are able to estimate, some two hundred or more have been recovered, of course many of them quite unrecognizable as same are fearfully mutilated, and besides have been too long dead, and are in consequence too much decomposed. Many of these poor men and of course also women, were murdered for the simple reason that they were unable to raise the cash in order to pay the contribution that was assessed against them." Ibid.

in 1920, General Manager George Sandomirsky reported a solid and impressive balance sheet and praised the cooperation of Soviet government officials, especially those of the Commissariat of Food and Supplies (Narkomprod) and its section on agriculture, Glavselkhoz. He admitted that the main reason was the high priority the new regime placed on agricultural improvement and its recognition of Harvester's expertise, as well as its substantial parts inventory. The company recorded on 1 March 1920 a cash balance of 25 million rubles and certificates of deposit totaling more than 70 million.[119] During a four-month period in the worst of economic times, from October 1919 through January 1920, the Lubertsy plant produced 609 Deering mowers and 1,039 McCormick reapers with a quantity of spare parts. Based on this success, on 30 January 1920, the Russian International Harvester Company signed a contract with the Supreme Council of Peoples' Economy to deliver 5,000 Deering mowers and 7,000 McCormick reapers by 1 October of that year. Major additional income came from repair services to existing equipment.[120]

Amazingly, in early 1920 Harvester had on hand enough steel, iron, coke, and wood for most of its anticipated production and its own rail cars for transport and delivery, although the manager complained that only 2,000 mowers met American specifications. Its 1,150-strong workforce, well below its prewar level, was easily among the best provided for in Russia, with its original company school and hospital remaining intact and under Harvester supervision. One brief strike in March 1920 over a minor problem lasted one and a half days. The plant manager summed it up: "Of course we do have troubles, we have them every day so to speak, and now and again we have big difficulties, but we are getting somewhat experienced now in wriggling out of troubles and manage to 'keep our hair on.'"[121] With contacts abroad resuming in 1920, officials of a Soviet mission to Estonia offered to buy with gold deposited to Harvester accounts a substantial amount of equipment—10,000 mowers, 10,000 harrows, 5,000 drills, 60 tractors with three-share plows, 40 with ten-share plows, 5,000 grinders, and so on.[122] Obviously, business could be done with Bolsheviks under the worst of circumstances.

International Harvester officers in Chicago and Europe maintained an active interest in their Russian operations, though they were basically beyond their control. Special efforts to send supplies of medicine, food, and clothing to Lubertsy

119. Sandomirsky (Moscow) to W. V. Couchman (Brussels), 16 March 1920, ibid.
120. Ibid.
121. A. Kruming (Lubertsy) to Couchman, 16 March 1920, ibid.
122. Essy Ehsing (Revel) to Hutmacher (Brussels), 4 April 1920, ibid. Most of this was apparently delivered through Baltic and Scandinavian offices.

were thwarted by Soviet authorities "on the basis that it would be showing partiality to our organization."[123] As soon as the prospects for major American aid improved during the summer of 1921, Harvester planned to send relief as quickly as possible through the American Red Cross.[124]

American Relief Agencies

As the YMCA began to shift more of its efforts away from the withdrawing Czech forces and to the Russians, it also encountered obstacles, especially from the Omsk government. It was accused of proselytizing, employing Jews, being pro-Bolshevik, and in general meddling in Russian affairs. Ethan Colton, a long-time veteran of "Y" service in Russia and now in charge of the remaining Russian program from the New York headquarters, complained bitterly to Bakhmeteff: "The rise and consolidation of the Kolchak government was early marked by the emergence of certain influences manifestly unfriendly to the program of the Y.M.C.A. . . . One of the Ministers whom I could name did express himself rather vehemently against anything so democratic as educational classes for the soldiers in training and base centers."[125] Despite attempts to negotiate and compromise, the organization's customs and transportation privileges were suspended, then made permanent. Colton contrasted the welcome and appreciation received by the YMCA for its services in western Europe and other places with that in Siberia and regretted that, as a result, some workers who had returned home had spoken very critically of the Kolchak government in ways that might be interpreted as sympathizing with the Bolsheviks.[126] It seemed that it consistently found ways to antagonize Americans. This was also true of the American Relief of Russian Women and Children, headed by Florence (Mrs. Graham) Taylor.[127]

Already in 1919 the YMCA was shifting the focus of its Russian work to Europe and concentrating on the burgeoning refugee problems. Bakhmeteff suggested that the "Y" sponsor publication of school textbooks for Bolshevik Russia. This would become a major "Y" enterprise and the nucleus of the first YMCA Press.[128]

123. S. G. McAllister (IH) to Ernest Bicknell (ARC), 15 August 1921, box 187, ARC Papers, HIA.

124. It helped that Bicknell was a personal friend of Cyrus McCormick. McCormick to McAllister, cable from London, 13 August 1921, ibid.

125. Colton to Bakhmeteff, 27 October 1919, reel 2, Bakhmeteff Papers, BA, CU.

126. Ibid.

127. Florence Taylor to Colby, 30 July 1920, f. 8, box 8, ibid.

128. Bakhmeteff to Harper, 1 December 1919, f. 9, box 7, Harper Papers, UC.

By the spring of 1921, a large volume of such works were published by the International Committee of the YMCA in issues of 5,000 and 10,000 copies on subjects such as "Perpetual Motion," "Matter and Its Mysteries," "The Beginning of Beginnings," "Great Words of Life," and many others.[129] The secondary war of, and for, the minds had begun.

By this time dissension was practically the rule in the various Siberian military quarters. Intelligence officer Barrows objected that his reports could not be sent directly to Washington but only to Vladivostok, where they were filed and forgotten. But a subordinate to Colonel Eichelberger wrote personally to Lansing with his own appraisal of how they were welcomed at the beginning and expected to solve all the Russian problems. That did not happen, and the Russians became increasingly disenchanted with the American presence. The Prinkipo proposal aggravated the situation, but, belatedly in October, it was felt to have been the answer. He stressed that cruelty, graft, and corruption dominate the scene in Siberia, but that Russians must be left alone to solve their own problems.[130] In a more distant quarter, the notion of a separate Russian Bureau to rescue an American Russia, though it had some real potential if supported, was abandoned, and its funds transferred to the State Department.[131] As if a leaf had turned, Hoover's urging of shipments of flour for Archangel were suddenly approved.

The Propaganda Campaign: Words Against Arms

The lecture circuit was busy across the United States in 1919 and 1920, with all views being expressed in regard to Russian problems. Jerome Landfield of the independent Russian Economic League and Chapin Huntington of the Commerce Department often found themselves on the same platform attacking Bolshevism, but American radicals and anti-Bolshevik Russian émigrés nearly always showed up to heckle each other. Huntington described one occasion as follows:

> In Philadelphia, instead of a small audience of University people, I found Witherspoon Hall filled with a general and very intelligent high-class audience. The "Governor" [Francis?] did not turn up, and they gave each one

129. Memorandum, J. F. Hecker, 16 May 1921, box 3, Anderson Papers, UIA.
130. Harold Fay to Lansing, 28 October 1919, vol. 47, Lansing Papers, MD, LC.
131. Hoover to Long, 8 August 1919, f. Russia 1918-19, box 182, Long Papers, MD, LC.

of us thirty minutes on Friday evening. I saw Thatcher [*sic*] in the audience, and Robins' former interpreter, Gomburg [*sic*], in the third row, where he and a frowzy haired young lady obtained much amusement from the accent and animated gestures of A. J. Sack. On this occasion Baron Rosen made a sort of an old-fashioned speech, containing a strong measure of truth, but filled with such unfortunate statements as that there would always be rich and poor and there was nothing to be done about it.[132]

Russell Story of the YMCA was his biggest disappointment as a lecturer, while Huntington grew tired of the whole business and planned to go away on an extended vacation for the summer.

Two leading spokesmen of opposite positions, Stanley Washburn and Raymond Robins, were mainly silent through much of this period, largely due to exhaustion, overexposure, and illness. The appearance of Robins at a University of Wisconsin forum caused something of a sensation when returning veterans of the north Russia campaign took issue with his characterization of their opposition. The "Red Scare" campaign of Palmer and J. Edgar Hoover forced many others into retreat. The serious illness of President Wilson in late 1919 punctured an already deflating balloon of an American settlement of the world.

South Russia

Resistance to Bolshevism—or any social liberal program for Russia—was strongest in the south of Russia, where sizeable units of the old imperial army remained in Ukraine after the revolution and the Brest-Litovsk peace. After retreating from advancing German forces to safer ground in the Kuban region, they composed the first real organized resistance to the new Soviet order in late 1917 and in 1918. Geographically isolated and limited by the economic and political upheaval, they managed to survive precariously with British encouragement and monetary support.[133] Unfortunately, Russian "White" leadership was initially unstable because of several changes of command and especially due to Kornilov's death and the influx of a large number of officers from other commands who

132. Huntington to Harper, 7 May 1919, f. 20, box 6, Harper Papers, UC.
133. Winston Churchill was especially supportive of using these forces to overthrow Bolshevism—and extend British imperial presence from the Persian Gulf northward and to finally win "the great game" and control the Caspian oil resources. One could also argue that the funding of this enterprise was largely American, indirectly from the substantial loans to Britain made at this time.

wanted to fight against the Bolsheviks—and for retaining their privileged status in Russian society. But these units of the old army still existed for want of a real alternative and formed the "Volunteer Army," which maintained a military potential through 1918, as well as to keep alive the idea of the restoration of a traditional, conservative Russian government.[134] The situation changed drastically with the end of the war and the opening of communications into the Black Sea. Some French and British units were quickly shifted to the region from their convenient location in Greece, but no American troops would follow (except for a few volunteers in Allied units).

Nonetheless, the United States was represented militarily in the Black Sea–Mediterranean region by a number of modern naval ships manned by skilled, experienced officers and seamen with high morale. This was in contrast to the situation elsewhere on the periphery of Russia, largely thanks to Rear Admiral Mark Bristol, who commanded the American Eastern Mediterranean Squadron and established his headquarters at Constantinople early in January 1919. He soon achieved additional clout when he was designated the Allied "high commissioner" for the former Ottoman Empire, an obvious neutral compromise, to referee rival British and French partitioning of that region. Under his direct command, Bristol had a cruiser as flagship (USS *Galveston*), a flotilla of modern destroyers, several destroyer escorts, and supply ships at his disposal—twenty naval ships and ten cargo ships—that could make regular tours around the Black Sea.[135] Probably the most valuable was a modern "yacht," the USS *Scorpion*, "attached to special service,"[136] with the most modern radio equipment for instant communication with Washington. Uniquely, Bristol served simultaneously as regional fleet commander, naval attaché, and chief Allied representative and thus reported to different departments in Washington.

Perhaps Bristol's most important role, however, was to serve as director of relief in the region, a duty he took on voluntarily and shared with his wife, Helen. He chose to locate his command center on land at his own expense. For this task he benefited from a long historical record of American relief and missionary activity in the Near East and a number of organizations already on the ground

134. See Peter Kenez, *Civil War in South Russia, 1918: The First Year of the Volunteer Army* (Berkeley: University of California Press, 1971); and George A. Brinkley, *The Volunteer Army and Allied Intervention in South Russia, 1917–1921: A Study in the Politics and Diplomacy of the Russian Civil War* (South Bend, Ind.: University of Notre Dame Press, 1966).

135. These movements can be accurately charted from the detailed logbooks of the ships involved, for example, that of the USS *Humphreys*, touring the Black Sea, with a crew of sixty and Captain William Baggaley in command, RG 24, NA.

136. Logbook, USS *Scorpion*, 1920, RG 24, NA.

or soon to be represented. As an illustration of his leadership qualities, one of the first things he did was to request the assignment to his command of an old friend, a fellow rear admiral, and a leading expert on Russia he could trust— Newton McCully.[137]

Bristol soon was receiving a steady stream of reports from diplomatic and military agents in the field, not that this helped him see a clear picture. And he toured the region himself to see it firsthand. On his first visit to Odessa in April, he found "the conditions . . . most deplorable," as another change of authority— to the Soviet side—was under way. Of the initial contingents of French and Greek troops that came there in December, most had been sent home, and the rest would not fight. A hurried evacuation was in progress, and Bristol managed to see that most Americans resident there were safely removed and the consulate secured under Swiss protection. "It was all a terrible indescribable scene. I cannot understand this Bolshevist movement. It is the expression of ignorant beasts. The Soviets cut off the water supply so there was not a drop of water in the city yesterday."[138] His other reports depicted a region in confusion, chaos, and disarray, not one that the United States should be very much involved with.

At the end of the year, Bristol confided to Colonel William Haskell, who headed the Near Eastern Relief Agency's activities in the Caucasus region, "This whole country is like a large mass of jelly, which, if you touch it in one part, it shakes all over. The Caucasus and South Russia belong to this jellied mass."[139] A few months later he observed,

> The conditions in Russia at the present time are peculiar, but as one looks back, not unexpected. The true facts are that everyone in the world is tired of fighting, the Bolshevists as well as the anti-Bolshevists. This retreat of Denikin and his final collapse with the evacuation of the North Caucasus,

137. McCully proceeded to spend most of his time traveling around the Black Sea littoral and writing long personal letters to Bristol describing the scene, a valuable source of information on events in the Bristol Papers, MD, LC. Both Bristol and McCully were "brevet" rear admirals, with Bristol the senior, and would normally revert to lower rank after their war duties were completed. Because of their extraordinary service in the Black Sea region, they would retain their ranks permanently.

138. Bristol draft report, 3 April 1919, box 31, Bristol Papers, MD, LC. Hooker Doolittle verified the poor showing of the small French contingent and that only Russians could be found to fight on the front: "The same bad feeling exists between the Volunteer Army and the French and at the same time the French soldiers are not very anxious to do any actual fighting"; he stressed "the regular futile and silly experiment of about three kinds of governments, all supreme." Doolittle to Jenkins, 2 April 1919, Odessa Consulate reports, RG 84, NA.

139. 23 December 1919, f. 1 (relief), box 711, WA-6, RG 45, NA.

through Novorossisk to the Crimea, has all been simply a breaking up of the Volunteers."[140]

Almost without exception, American reports on the anti-Bolshevik side of the civil war in the south were totally negative. Hooker Doolittle, yet another transfer from the north of Russia, also found the situation abysmal: "Denikin holds himself coldly aloof and apparently has refused any aid to territories where the command is technically French. The Volunteer Army is not in particularly good favor among the general populace." He described an encounter with the head of the army in Sevastopol, "who blames or tries to, the Allies for all the evils of Russia. Such seems to be the attitude of the V.A. in general. . . . Hope you are well and that the Bolshies don't get you."[141] This was actually one of the least negative American reports on the White forces in the south of Russia. None can be found that were favorable. Vice Consul Alfred Burri wrote Bristol from Odessa on 21 April 1919:

> The Odessa local government was weak. The so-called Volunteer Army government was a myth. . . . The French committed a series of blunders, mostly avoidable [but] . . . the original French expedition was more of a scouting expedition than an army. . . . The Odessa situation brings home again the fact that an incomplete and planless intervention in Russia against the Bolsheviks is futile. Either the Allies should come in with the serious intention of undertaking absolutely alone the task of putting the Bolsheviks out of business, or they should formulate a plan for doing business with them.[142]

Coming from a minor American official, this crystallized the dilemma.

The Caucasus was, if anything, in an even worse state of turmoil than the rest of Russia because of the various national entities scrambling for territory and divided among a number of political causes. After spending two weeks touring that area in June, Bristol reported, "The three republics, Azerbaijan, Georgia, and Armenia that have been formed in the Caucasus, are brilliant examples of political anarchy."[143] In the absence of the longtime Russian central political and military authority that, though repressive of independent movements, never-

140. Bristol to Knapp, f. March 1920, box 32, MD, LC.
141. Doolittle to Jenkins, 2 April 1920, Odessa reports, RG 84, NA.
142. Burri to Bristol, 21 April 1920, ibid. Burri had been a clerk in the consul general office in Moscow in 1918.
143. Report of trip, ending 22 June 1919, box 1, Bristol Papers, MD, LC.

theless maintained law and order among rival nationalities, various protogovernments vied with each other in creating as much misery for each other's people as possible. The main goal of the head of the Armenian government, Bristol reported, was to acquire as much Turkish territory as possible, and the Georgians seemed oblivious to the plight of the thousands of refugees who swarmed into Tiflis (Tbilisi).[144] Bristol reacted negatively to this kind of nearsightedness, sympathizing more with the especially oppressed Muslim population and recommending increased American assistance for them.[145]

The region remained a cauldron of socialist revolutionary and national independence movements. This was obviously a complex situation for the United States and other foreign interests. In the midst of this state of nearly total confusion, veteran American consul Charles Moser, who had been transferred from Harbin to Tiflis (from the frying pan into the skillet), advised, with some convolution, "I have slowly reached the opinion that recognition of Georgia, Azerbaidjan and Armenia as *temporary de facto* governments, without reference to political or territorial aspiration in future, would not be inadvisable."[146] William Dunn, Bristol's special agent in the Caucasus, reported in May 1920 that the "Red" forces in the area had grown to 60,000 and that there was not much left to challenge them, due to so much wasted infighting, especially between Armenians and Azeris, and between Georgians, Ossetians, and Chechens. He did not have much use for the Haskell relief men and their rather sudden abandonment of a totally confused situation, leaving everyone squabbling.[147] Behind the scenes were some freebooting Americans—and many others—dealing in Oriental rugs and other scavenger hunts.

Denikin's setbacks in late 1918 and early 1919, at the very time that the Allied presence was really being felt, were especially frustrating to all observers and participants. Admiral H. S. Knapp, Bristol's immediate superior, wondered about the wisdom of sending McCully, "in view of the tremendous setback that Denikin has had." But he quickly revealed the common hostility and frustration of inaction that nearly all Allied officers had toward Bolshevism:

> The whole Bolshevist situation looks pretty bad to me and I very frankly confess I do not understand the attitude of the Allies towards Bolshevism. I am very much inclined to think that Lloyd George and Clemenceau are

144. Haskell reported from Tbilisi in April 1920 that he was feeding 47,000 children daily. To Bristol, 24 April 1920, box 68, Bristol Papers, MD, LC.
145. Bristol to Lansing, 3 November 1919, ibid.
146. Moser to Bristol, 26 February 1920, f. 2, box 510, WA-6, RG 45.
147. Dunn (Tiflis) to Bristol, 13 May 1920, ibid.

both afraid of their own horses and are fearful of stirring up opposition from the labor element. . . . My own view of the matter is that the solution of the question as far as the Allies are concerned lies in the answer to a very simple question and that is, whether Bolshevism is or is not a danger to the world. . . . If, however, Bolshevism is a danger to the world, and I personally believe it is, then I must say that I feel the measures that have been taken have been so halting that they have gotten no further than they have.[148]

He was not alone in seeing the quandary of which horse to back and how much. The commander of the USS *Tattnall* reported from Theodosia in Crimea in February 1919, "There is an indirect indication among all the higher [Russian] officers that the 'game is finished,' and though they maintain a half bold front they seize eagerly upon suggestion of outside help in any possible evacuation. . . . I have never seen such a morbid, pathetic, yet disgusting element amongst all mankind as these V.A. [Volunteer Army] officers."[149] Such negative reports—and there were many others—forwarded to Washington from knowledgeable people in the field, supported the view that intervention in south Russia should be put in deep freeze during the critical summer of 1919. Why be involved in a costly, retrograde, nonproductive project, especially since the Bolsheviks were sending accommodating signals through Litvinov in Stockholm and Copenhagen, Krassin in London, Martens in New York, and Radek in Berlin? Nevertheless, aid set in place continued to flow to Denikin, and even more to Wrangel.

On the advice of McCully and Bristol and during a more promising White Russian offensive and a French occupation of Odessa in late 1919, the official American office there was reopened by Evan Young as a consul generalship. But this semblance of reestablishment waned quickly with the Denikin retreats. By coincidence an American YMCA and Red Cross mission, headed by Franklin Gaylord, was visiting Odessa on the eve of the panic of another evacuation in February 1920. Learning that 10,000 White supporters were clambering aboard vessels in the harbor, McCully radioed Bristol for his squadron there: "Urge with all possible that duty to humanity require us to help these unhappy people."[150] Brackett Lewis recorded in detail the confusion in a city left without

148. Knapp to Bristol, 8 January 1919, f. Jan–May 1919, box 31, ibid.
149. Captain Bryan to Bristol, 19 February 1919, ibid.
150. Bristol to Lansing from McCully, 9 February 1920, box 73, Bristol Papers, MD, LC.

fuel or electricity, and with hooligans roaming the streets and pogroms against Jews producing many casualties. Commandeering a section of wharfs and customs sheds, the Americans set up a refugee evacuation program with the sick and families first.

> For the port work we took over berths for three large vessels in the central harbor and cleared their adjacent wharves. For our offices, I requisitioned a whole section of the Customs House, but later took the whole compound of the largest shipping and steamship firm on the docks—offices, sheds, warehouses. I had one large tug and an order for more if necessitated by ice or other conditions. . . . Each of us chiefs had to enlist guards required for his own department. This organization we accomplished as best we could without effective cooperation from the Russian authorities.[151]

A constant refrain in American relief efforts in south Russia was the lack of cooperation of Russian authorities of all description.

Northwest Russia

As confusing and divided as were the situations in Siberia, south Russia, and the Caucasus, things were no better—and perhaps even worse—in the Baltic region, where a number of nationalities struggled with national independence and ideological issues to the accompaniment of Western intervention. First, Finland was going through a bitter civil war, decided by the superior command of antiradical forces under former Russian army officers and backed by Germany and then Britain. The Baltic provinces of Estonia, Latvia, and Lithuania were also taking advantage of the removal of Russian authority to establish their independence.

In Estonia one more anti-Bolshevik Russian army came into existence under the leadership of General Nikolai Iudenich. From a nucleus established by Germans from prisoners of war and refugees from Soviet Russia, this force never numbered more than 6,000, much smaller than the armies of Denikin, Kolchak, and Wrangel. It was a close-knit and ably led force, however, and managed, with British naval support, to launch a surprisingly successful strike along the Gulf of Finland into Soviet territory, reaching almost to the outskirts of Petrograd in

---

151. Brackett Lewis to Bristol, 12 Feburary 1920, copy in f. Jan–April 1920, box 1, Lowrie Papers, UIA.

October 1919, before a Red Army counterattack virtually annihilated it. Iudenich possessed similar flaws as other White generals, a capability of fine military leadership with virtually no political skills. For example, he pulled the rug out from under himself at his Estonian base of operations by insisting that Estonia should be an integral part of "his" Russia. Another common failure was to try to succeed alone without coordination with other anti-Bolshevik fronts.

This northwest Russian offensive still had positive results. It bolstered the ability of Estonia and Latvia to attain independence by keeping the Red Army away, and it brought a definite and permanent American presence to the region in the form of diplomatic and consular offices and relief agencies. The Baltic area also quickly became the hub of American intelligence operations with the establishment of "listening posts" (intelligence service) at Vyborg, Tallinn, Riga, and Helsinki, disguised as consulates, and served by a system of internal couriers and naval ships making regular visits.[152]

An American "Listening Post"

The Vyborg consulate was especially active from late 1919 through 1921 in running agents in and out of Soviet Russia. Founded by Robert Imbrie of Petrograd-Vologda embassy staff experience in 1917–18 and under State Department auspices, it recruited "couriers" to cross the border, typically displaced former Russian naval officers, who knew the waters and land well. They were accompanied by Finnish guides, especially Paul Paju, going to and coming from Petrograd at night (though not with a full moon, nor during white nights), across either Lake Ladoga or the eastern portion of the Gulf of Finland.[153] Much of the information, mostly typed in multiple copies or mimeographed for intragovernment and intraparty communications, was purchased from desperate and hungry low-level Soviet officials and was rather innocuous.[154] The tactical intelligence work was directed by Michael Perts, "our best secret agent,"[155] a Latvian who recruited a number of agents from disaffected (and desperate?) Russians

152. See, for example, logbook, USS *Evans*, 7 July–4 August 1919, RG 24, NA.
153. Perts to Imbrie, 16 April 1920, DPR, vol. 15, Vyborg consulate, RG 84, NA. See especially the report of courier Meshcherskii that involved an exchange of shots, a loss of a horse and baggage, and a failed mission, 12 March 1920, Vyborg consulate, DPR, vol. 9, ibid. Paju was repeatedly praised in dispatches for a "large and useful acquaintance in Petrograd."
154. These documents would usually end up some weeks later on the desk of Samuel Harper at the University of Chicago.
155. Imbrie to State, 18 September 1920, DPR, vol. 18, RG 84, NA.

and continued this role even after Imbrie was replaced by Harold Quarton in June 1920 as consul and intelligence agent. Perts was especially concerned about the psychological problems of his personnel: "I request your urgent consideration, as the mental state of employees, awaiting the decision and the spring season threaten to destroy the service to such an extent that its reconstruction will appear for me impossible."[156]

Quarton praised the service of Captain Pavel Tikhomirov and that of Captain Ryl'ke, a former staff officer of the renowned Semenovsky Regiment, who was well informed on "ways and roads" into Petrograd and "who helped a great deal in choosing the trustworthy and energetic couriers for our service."[157] He reflected on his own experience on the frontiers of American-Soviet intelligence operations: "You feel you are on the edge of civilization and no one cares whether you do good work or not."[158] But Bullard reassured Quarton, "I think you too would be surprised to learn what really close tabs the divisions keep on the work of men in the field."[159]

Imbrie and Quarton—and their "couriers"—also investigated the circumstances of the Americans remaining in Russia in 1920, a total of about forty, who included a wide range of business and other professions, such as African-American dancer Beatrice Anderson; circus performers Thomas and Anna Billing; Samuel Caton and Fred Keyes, horse trainers from Kentucky; Kodak representative Samuel Hopwood; International Harvester manager H. C. Carlson; Dr. Lanby (a dentist); and several Russian wives of Americans: Zenaida Bary, Nora Lehrs, Elizabeth Doty, and Mary Ropes (the latter from a long line of New England merchants in Russia).[160] A number of other women, who may not have been counted, included the venerable Zenaida Ragozin, who celebrated her eightieth birthday in Petrograd in the summer of 1918 with as much American fanfare as could be mustered.[161] She managed to survive, confined to her room by severe arthritis, on black bread, water, and porridge through the worst of the civil war— and on a little money that managed to get to her from Putnam's for her translations of Russian short stories.[162]

156. Perts to Imbrie, 16 April 1920, DPR, vol. 15, ibid.

157. Perts to Imbrie, 25 March 1920, DPR, vol. 15, and Ryl'ke to Imbrie, 12 March 1919, vol. 9, ibid.

158. Imbrie to Bullard, 8 October 1920, DPR, vol. 5, ibid.

159. Bullard to Quarton, 19 November 1920, ibid.

160. Quarton to State, 21 October 1920, DPR, vol. 4 (18), Vyborg Consulate, RG 84, NA.

161. Ragozin, a truly heroic survivor of the best and worst times in Petrograd, outlived Lenin by a few months.

162. Ragozin to Elizabeth Hapgood, 1 April 1921, box 9, Hapgood-Reynolds Papers, MD, LC.

A few Americans remained under arrest for alleged anti-Bolshevik activities, notably Xenophon Kalamatiano, Captain Kilpatrick,[163] businessman and Red Cross agent Royal Keely, and journalist Marguerite Harrison of the *Baltimore Sun*. All of these caused many headaches for the consular office, but the most critical part of its operation was still the running of the courier service. "It is like keeping an intricate machine in order. If one part of the machinery does not operate, the whole machine is out of order."[164] Finnish and Estonian bases also served for rescuing Russian political refugees and stranded Americans such as Emma Ponafidin, widow of a Russian; Ralph Wilmer, a hardware salesman; and Arthur Prince, who had served as an American informant and who was arrested, suffered horribly, but managed to escape in tattered clothing and crippled condition.[165] Emma Goldman was also a reluctant visitor, having been rounded up in Palmer's witch-hunt and deported to Russia. "Russia is marvelous but painfully confused."[166]

The twice-monthly runs into Russia were threatened more by lack of American financing than by Cheka intervention. Again, there was much infighting and competition among the Allies. Perts claimed that his agents were purposefully betrayed by the British to gain ascendancy over intelligence operations.[167] He urged a greatly increased budget for couriers and food relief for agents in Petrograd and Moscow, "as the mental state of employees, awaiting the decision and the spring season threaten to destroy the service to such an extent that its reconstruction will appear for me impossible."[168] The American agents congratulated themselves on the quantity of information (mostly published material and intracommissariat communications) they obtained, especially considering the

163. Red Cross official Dr. Edward Ryan, in charge of the Latvian operations of ARC, complained that the central office had little interest in these prisoners, to which Ernest Bicknell replied, "Ryan naturally cannot fully appreciate the great amount of public interest which exists here with regard to these American prisoners." Bicknell to Olds, 20 June 1921, box 170, Red Cross Papers, HIA.

164. Quarton to Bullard, 8 October 1920, DPR, vol. 4 (18), Vyborg Consulate, RG 84, NA. In comparison with harsh conditions for Kalamatiano, Mrs. Harrison was treated quite well. See her *Marooned in Moscow: The Story of an American Woman Imprisoned in Russia* (New York: Doran, 1921).

165. Prince report to Quarton, 3 August 1920, DPR, vol. 18, RG 84, NA; Quarton to State, 21 October 1920, vol. 9, ibid.

166. Goldman to Julienne, 26 January 1920, copy in box 187, Long Papers, MD, LC.

167. Perts to Imbrie, 16 April 1920, DPR vol. 15, ibid. Bitter resentment of British obstruction was a constant refrain in American intelligence reports.

168. Ibid. According to a financial statement, the consulate was operating on a budget of about $50,000 per year, most of it committed to the courier/intelligence service, including courier service, $10,574.68, and cable expense, $11,696.16. Quarton to State, 21 October 1920, DPR vol. 9, ibid.

much larger commitment of funds by the British. Much of this material, duly forwarded to the State Department, ended up in Chicago under the eyes of Samuel Harper for translation and interpretation.[169] Although the expense was minimal, it was probably not worth the effort, as most of the intelligence data were available in the open media. The service also distributed American propaganda in Russia, usually in the form of old Committee on Public Information accounts, such as "The German-Bolshevik Conspiracy," based on the Sisson papers.[170]

At least relief came along with intelligence. In April 1920 Imbrie ordered and received 900 tons of flour, 50 tons of beans, and 50 tons of bacon for relief of Russian refugees in Estonia and Finland and to oil the wheels of the courier operation.[171] The American Red Cross distributed most of this food on the condition that its personnel also provide what information they could gather.[172] Some of this was smuggled over the border by Quarton himself to "pay" sources and to aid such stalwart American individualists as Zenaida Ragozin and Karin Sante, the latter holding down the fort at the former Petrograd embassy until her arrest in late 1919.[173] In 1921, a combination of the opening of Soviet Russia to the West and American isolationism curtailed the courier service. Secretary of State Charles Hughes informed the Riga office, "The Department is impelled to instruct you to reduce somewhat the length and frequency of your cables on account of lack of funds."[174] But the next year it would be revived, with its center in Riga. The success of the early Vyborg service was an important precedent for a long-term American intelligence-gathering operation in the Baltic region.

Those Strange Americans

If Americans were baffled by the Bolshevik ascendancy over Russia, Lenin, Trotsky, and company were equally mystified by wandering, footloose Americans in the midst of their revolution and civil war. They included gung ho sym-

169. Harper wrote Imbrie that his translations of Imbrie's materials were mimeographed in 100 copies and distributed "in the family." Harper to Imbrie, 20 March 1920, f. 20, box 7, Harper Papers, UC.

170. William Carr (State) to Imbrie, 7 February 1920, DPR, vol. 9, RG 84, NA.

171. Imbrie to State, 28 April 1920, DPR, vol. 19, ibid.

172. See, for example, H. C. Rindge (Terijoki) to Quarton, 22 February 1921, DPR, vol. 5, ibid.

173. Corse to Quarton, 1 February 1921, and Quarton to Corse, 26 April 1921, DPR, vol. 5, ibid. "Mdm. Ragozin is such a kindly old lady that it was a pleasure to me to transmit several letters to the United States for her."

174. Hughes to Young, 2 May 1921, vol. 17, ibid.

pathizers such as John Reed, quasi intelligence agents and adventurers like Kalamatiano, official army intelligence officer W. B. Estes, who had been captured in the north, and a surprising number of other adventurers who are usually unaccounted for. Estes, confined to the notorious Butyrki Prison, thought they were being kept as political hostages.[175] Royal Keeley came in September 1919 on invitation of Georgi Lomonosov to lend his engineering expertise to the Soviet economic agenda and seek trade concessions. After becoming disillusioned with the prospects, he received permission to leave, only to find himself under arrest at the border. He was, however, provided with an attorney and sentenced to only two years "compulsory factory work."[176]

Floyd Ramp from Oregon saw great possibilities in the Russian socialist revolution and arrived in Vladivostok in March 1920 to see for himself:

> At last I have arrived at the place I have long dreamed of—Russia. . . . The struggle will end and Great Russia with her new national and social ideal will be victorious and will teach the world a new idea of civilization, one which will redeem the world from its sorrows, its sins, its poverty, and economic uncertainties. . . . the extremes of life—poverty and riches—will disappear. . . . This ideal is beginning to be a reality in Russia.[177]

He was impressed by the 12 March celebration of the revolution, "a day of proletarian culture." "Anyone who was present on March 12 can have no doubt as to the popularity and support of the Soviets in Vladivostok. . . . Long live the Soviets."[178] He was frustrated, however, in his efforts to penetrate deeper into this new wonderland. Ironically, he ended up on the transport *America,* which was taking 6,000 Czech soldiers westward the hard way through the Suez Canal to Trieste, working his way shoveling coal and washing decks and sleeping in lifeboats overnight.[179]

Other Americans, by circumstance of relief duty, appraised their unfamiliar terrain and came to opposite conclusions. Tom Martin, tiring quickly of YMCA duty in Siberia, wrote his old mentor, Frederick Jackson Turner, about Russians:

175. Estes to ARC, Riga, 21 May 1921, f. prisoner relief, box 187, ARC Papers, HIA.
176. Keeley to ARC, Warsaw, 28 May 1921, ibid. Both Estes and Keeley were able to get letters out through repatriated Polish prisoners.
177. Ramp diary, 6 March 1920, f. 189/7, Ramp Papers, UOA. His initial impression of Vladivostok was that it was very crowded, with a lot of long-haired men and short-haired women. Ibid.
178. Ibid., 13 March.
179. Ibid., 6 May.

"They are singularly lacking in political ability for self-government; and they show amazing tolerance to enemies and indifference, not to say aversion, to friends. They invariably admire the man with the big stick who is in a position to wield it over their heads."[180]

Jack Reed, returning in November 1919, was the most visible American not only because of the fame of his *Ten Days That Shook the World* and his renewed activism on behalf of Soviet Russia as a delegate to the Baku Congress of Peoples of the East in 1920 and the Comintern congress but also because of the publicity concerning his dedication to the Communist cause in America and his imprisonment in Finland upon leaving Russia in May 1920.[181] His protracted suffering there and his death from typhus back in Russia lent an undying romantic aura to this "American" affiliation with the cause of world revolution.

Reed was far from being alone in pursuing a new world order through the Russian Revolution. Isaac Don Levine became an unofficial journalistic courier for the Bolshevik regime for the *Chicago Daily News*. Harold Fay, abandoning his army intelligence job in Siberia to join the *New York Tribune*, managed the feat of a tour across Siberia and Russia by Model T Ford in the summer of 1920, much to the surprise and annoyance of both the Soviet government and the State Department.[182] More of a sensation was the much-publicized visit in September 1920 of California engineer Washington Vanderlip, who came with grandiose designs for trade and economic assistance. He impressed Soviet officials, beginning with Litvinov in Copenhagen, who confused him with a prominent American banker. Louise Bryant wrote Lenin on Vanderlip's behalf: "I believe that what they want is the assurance from you that Soviet Russia will not fail to carry out her obligations in regard to contracts and concessions."[183] After subsequent meetings with the top Bolsheviks in Moscow, Vanderlip was "rewarded" with an offer of a dubious mining concession in Kamchatka, nonetheless a harbinger of things to come.

The Last Military Chapter in the South

A new Denikin offensive in the fall of 1919, which through lack of coordination failed to coincide with a Kolchak attack from Siberia in the summer, still raised

---

180. Martin to Turner, 9 September 1918, Turner Papers, Huntington Library.

181. Reed to Bryant, 3, 13, 15 May 1920, Reed-Bryant Papers, Harvard-Houghton.

182. Quarton (Vyborg) to Colby, 12 August 1920, DPR, vol. 9, RG 84, NA. The original of Fay's fourteen-page report on his trip through Russia is in the Vyborg consular records, 8 August 1920, ibid. He especially appealed for help for 200,000 German and Austrian prisoners of war still in Siberia, trapped there by the civil war.

183. Bryant to Lenin, 2 April 1921, f. 5, op. 1, TsKKPSS.

some temporary hopes of a miraculous defeat of the Bolsheviks. But American sympathy for that cause, never very strong and already in decline, waned sharply as it collapsed. Breckinridge Long was very direct in a December 1919 memorandum to Bakhmeteff in regard to major American support for Denikin: "I told him that we could not get any sentiment in this country for fighting the Bolsheviki, and that we could not very well supply them [White armies] with arms unless we were at war with them. I further called attention to the fact that each of the anti-Bolshevik forces was fighting the Bolshevik only a little harder than they were fighting each other."[184] This was the crucial obstacle to any serious American effort to oppose a Bolshevik Russia—no viable, united Russian center of opposition.

The Russian resistance to Bolshevism, weak, disorganized, and poorly led, never gained crucial and full American support. Some have argued that that was the tragedy of the civil war—the missed opportunity. Disorganized and ineffective as it was, the British must shoulder most of the blame. McCully, a true friend of a free Russia, lamented in March 1920, "I am afraid it is all over with poor old Denikin. He has the most remarkable faculty for taking the wrong course—he never misses a chance to do the wrong thing—at the same time [he] is perfectly honest and sincere and you can't help liking him."[185] Although almost everyone had kind words to say for Denikin personally, they could not understand his reliance on one of the most sorry lots of staff officers ever assembled. They personally regretted the tremendous relief problems that their failure produced.

Through the whole period of intervention in the Black Sea, both Bristol and McCully displayed a thorough dislike for, and distrust of, British imperial interests in the region, of which the overly sensitive British, in turn, complained. For example, when Admiral Sims from the Naval War College had cautioned Bristol about his anti-British stance (which Sims agreed with), he replied that "the League of Nations is pretty well shot to pieces" because of the British.

> You state that before 1914 the world was asleep at the switch. I am not so certain that we are not drifting back to the same condition again. The English are certainly reaching out to extend their Empire and to gain commercial control of the world. The extension of the British Empire may be theoretically based on the mandate system but in real practice it is nothing in the

---

184. Long, Memorandum of Conversation with the Russian Ambassador, 2 December 1919, f. Russia 1919–20, box 182, Long Papers, MD, LC.
185. McCully to Bristol, 17 March 1920, box 32, Bristol Papers, MD, LC.

world but an imperial policy. . . . I have been here long enough, taking my experience in the Far East with British methods, to learn that the British are out to get every possible commercial advantage for their people.[186]

This very strong American Anglophobia, reciprocated and probably aggravated by the British, was particularly pronounced among naval officers and had a similar important effect on the failure of intervention in the south in 1920 as it did in north Russia in 1918–19. Discord and hostility among the Allies on all rims of Russia certainly affected the outcome of civil war and intervention, and no one in higher authority seemed to care, perhaps because they harbored the same sentiments. It would be difficult to find any kind words from any official American sources for any British (or French) persons or actions.

The first major relief crisis in south Russia began in February 1920, when Denikin's Volunteer Army retreated into bottlenecks at Novorossisk and Odessa, both important ports on the Black Sea. The scene in both places fully illustrated the tragedy of civil war. McCully, on the scene as usual, lamented the defeats and very basic lack of preparation for evacuation. He agreed with Bristol on the general situation: "Bolshevism as you say is not as strong as it appears—it only seems strong because its opponents are weak."[187] Americans on the scene especially resented the lack of cooperation from Russian officials for the relief work they were trying to accomplish. At Novorossisk, they encountered British and Russian reluctance to cooperate with an evacuation policy that stipulated women and children first. Bristol personally, with McCully aboard, arrived on the USS Galveston to superintend the evacuation of civilians from the port. Marines provided guard duty ashore, perhaps the first and only American soldiers on Russian land in the south. The Red Army shelled the harbor during the evacuation, several falling near the Galveston, fortunately without a hit, and on 27 March it stood out to sea with a number of refugees aboard accompanying destroyers.[188]

Once Russians were safely removed to Constantinople and the island of Proti, problems ensued, "especially with the officers and higher classes who repudiate the idea of being refugees and expect to be treated as royal guests." Americans were especially annoyed that Russian officers claimed they were being treated

186. Bristol to Sims, 1 November 1920, f. Nov 1920, ibid.

187. McCully (Novorossisk) to Bristol, 26 March 1920, f. March 1920, box 32, Bristol Papers, MD, LC. McCully warned Bristol, "Don't let one Russian *General* have a word to say about anything. Be polite to him, or bend to him as you like, but don't give him a chance to butt in or your business will be blocked." Ibid. In general the American staff in the region had the lowest regard for the Russian staff members they encountered.

188. Logbook USS *Galveston*, 22–27 March 1920, RG 24, NA.

*Mark and Helen Bristol in Constantinople, 1919, courtesy of the
Prints and Photographs Division, Library of Congress*

brutally by being asked to carry stretchers of wounded out of the snow.[189] This
was certainly one of the worst hours of the old Russian nobility, which in general
failed to respond to relief needs. In allowance, they were suffering a tremendous
trauma of eviction from long-term landed estates and deprivation of property and
heirlooms; in fact, they found themselves ignobly branded as losers and outcasts.
Much has been and should be written on this chapter of Russian social history.

Dismay about Denikin's political insensitivity heightened in south Russia, but
even Admiral Bristol, one of his sharpest critics, felt some compassion in regard
to universal negative Allied opinion: "It develops into condemnation of Gen-

189. Bristol to McCully, 13 March 1920, ibid.

eral Denikin–which today seems like kicking a man when he is down."[190] Many civilian refugees fleeing from the Denikin disaster in March 1920 descended on Constantinople, though resources were inadequate to accommodate them.[191] This presented an immediate problem for Allied relief agencies. An emergency base to provide for them was established on Princes Islands, where the Russian conference was to have met less than a year earlier. Bristol set up a station on Proti, while the British served others on Prinkipo, but both were supported by contributions, mainly direct from Russian sources but probably indirectly American funds.[192] McCully reported from Crimea that the Russians much preferred the American hospitality, while resenting British efforts to remove them to the island of Lemnos.[193] In the meantime, Admiral Bristol enjoyed a pleasant vacation in Crimea during the summer of 1920 with Whittemore, McCully, and Commander Bryant, inspecting the enormous Massandra wine cellars, touring the imperial palaces, botanical gardens, and churches (all remarkably intact), and staying regally overnight at the Yussupov Palace, arranged by Whittemore with the Tatar servants of the prince. The wine in the imperial cellars was fully stocked, but they lacked coal to steam and coat the casks for the next vintage and bottles for the existing stock.[194] One last Bacchic overture to the old regime?

After suffering such major losses during the unusually severe winter of 1919–20, Denikin was removed from his post in March 1920. He turned over command to one of his staff officers in Crimea, General Baron Petr Wrangel, who managed to inspire a reorganization of what was left of the Volunteer Army that evacuated from Novorossisk to Crimea and then scored some surprising successes in a 1920 summer campaign, thanks at least in part to American support. In general, Americans in the area–McCully, Bristol, and others–welcomed the change and considered Wrangel a much better and more politically astute leader. Additional optimism resulted from the reopening of the American consular office in Odessa.[195] Its superintendent, Hugh Jenkins, was not hopeful of its staying:

190. Bristol to Lansing, 12 January 1920, f. 5, box 716, ibid.

191. Bristol to Lansing, 24 January 1920, box 73, ibid.

192. The largest contributions for relief in November 1920 at Constantinople were (in French francs): Russian embassy, 253,021; Allied ships in harbor, 252,000; Russian Red Cross, 214,580; Jewish Distribution Society, 113,000; and U.S. Navy, including Mrs. Bristol's canteens, 110,000, in a total of 1,300,000. "Summary of Statistical and Narrative Report of the Department General Relief, Constantinople Unit, for the Month of November 1920," box 912, ARC, RG 200, NA.

193. McCully (Kerch) to Bristol (handwritten), 6 May 1920, ibid.

194. Bristol war diary, confidential, 24 July 1920, f. July 1920, box 2, Bristol Papers, MD, LC.

195. Evan Young to Alfred Burri, 20 January 1920, DPR, Odessa, RG 84, NA.

"I really am beginning to become superstitious, as it seems that every place I go to is evacuated sooner or later."[196] Allied disunity and pessimism about Wrangel's ability to succeed—at this late date—and the absence of any coordinated offensive from Siberia reduced his slim chances. Thomas Whittemore, in an interview with Bristol, warned him of the impending disaster and took issue with what he described as McCully's excessive optimism in regard to Wrangel.[197]

Bristol wrote privately about the collapse: "It came very suddenly, and I certainly was disappointed but at the same time the impression had been growing upon me that Wrangel could never succeed, not because of himself but on account of those upon whom he had to depend to help him. . . . The old Russian element are reactionary, and true to the old saying, it is hard to teach an old dog new tricks."[198] McCully agreed: "The primary cause of the Wrangel defeat was failure of his government to win active support of the people. . . . Wrangel's reform laws remained largely on paper only, their execution being blocked by lethargy, and even active opposition of reactionary elements amongst subordinate officials."[199] While carefully recording the dismal military scene in south Russia, both Bristol and McCully had one eye focused on saving humanity.

In this valiant effort they were strongly supported by Bristol's wife, Helen; his aide, Lieutenant Robert Dunn, who seemed to be constantly on tour in unlikely places; and free lance missionary-Byzantinist Thomas Whittemore.[200] The latter, though at odds with McCully politically, shared with him a deep concern about the welfare and education of children. Whittemore resumed the work he was doing in Petrograd in 1917-18 in promoting special education schools and orphanages, more or less on his own and on a shoestring, earning the respect and praise of Admiral Bristol:

> He is a man who does not talk about what he does, but I have seen the results. Then, above all other things, I have heard remarks from many many Russians. I do not believe you could measure Whittemore's activities in dollars and cents. Then too, he has imagination and is looking ahead. He is establishing schools for the children of the present day and working to

196. Jenkins to Poole, 22 April 1919, ibid.

197. Bristol War Diary, 14 September 1920, f. Sept. 1920, box 2, Bristol Papers, MD, LC. Wrangel later boasted to Bristol that he had the allegiance of 800,000 troops at the time of his evacuation, but thanks to limited Allied funding, he had supplies and equipment for only 40,000. Bristol War Diary, interview of 6 February 1921, f. Feb. 1921, ibid.

198. To Roy Stephenson Smith (AP), 22 November 1920, ibid.

199. Bristol to Lansing, from McCully, 20 November 1920, box 708, RG 45, NA.

200. The complete story of this "Grander Game" in the Middle East remains to be told, though much source material can be found in the Bristol Papers.

educate them for the future. . . . He is having thousands of Russian school books printed in Bulgaria and in Dantzig.[201]

The remnants of Wrangel's army were forced to endure a catastrophic retreat through the Crimean Peninsula in late 1920, culminating in a massive evacuation across the Black Sea in November. Captain W. Baggally of the USS *Humphries* recorded the drama of the panic at Yalta on 14 November: "The docks were crowded with people awaiting transportation, many of whom had been there all night."[202] He watched a distinguished Russian woman discharge trunks of belongings into the sea in order to find space aboard a crowded ship. McCully, as usual the Johnny-on-the-spot, was instrumental in bringing some order out of the chaos, especially commandeering the use of American naval vessels as escortguard-rescue ships for the large flotilla that left Crimea. The cruiser USS *St. Louis,* escorted by the destroyer *Long,* rescued a stranded Russian steamer with 5,000 Russian troops aboard but no coal, water, or food and towed it through heavy seas all night to Constantinople.[203] McCully also personally—and permanently—took charge of seven Russian orphans, whom he shepherded out of the turmoil and to America as his adopted children, not a common thing for a bachelor in those days. He clearly demonstrated a unique and personal commitment of Americans to the cause of Russian relief.[204]

The suddenness of the collapse resulted in a massive relief problem, when 120,000 Russian refugees crowded aboard eighty ships descended upon Constantinople in mid-November, catching the relief organizations there by surprise and overwhelming them. It was a wonder that this did not become a major tragedy of the Russian civil war. Thanks to Bristol's quick response and a rare coordination among Allied relief agencies, very few lives were lost. The Constantinople chapter of the American Red Cross took over all direction, placing many of the civilian refugees in quarters on the Princes Islands, one of which, ironically, had been the proposed site for the high-level Russian factions' conference some months earlier. The army units were dispatched to former Ottoman army camps at Gallipoli, while some of the Russian naval ships were diverted to Bizerta. Many of the refugees were sent elsewhere as soon as possible. For example, cargo ships crowded with 8,000 refugees were

201. Bristol to McCully, 31 August 1920, f. August 1920, box 32, Bristol Papers, MD, LC.
202. Baggally report to Bristol, 19 November 1920, box 708, ibid.
203. Logbook, USS *Long,* 16 November 1920, RG 24, NA.
204. Bristol to Lansing, from McCully, 18 November 1920, ibid. For more details, see Weeks, *An American Naval Diplomat in Revolutionary Russia.*

Rear Admiral Newton McCully (rear right), with Secretary of Labor Charles Wilson and McCully's seven adopted Russian orphans and their nurse, 1920, courtesy of the Prints and Photographs Division, Library of Congress

escorted by American destroyers to Cattaro (Kotor) for temporary housing in former Austrian military posts on the Adriatic coast (now in Yugoslav).[205] For all this, Bristol mustered the ships and seamen under his command and used his political office to requisition local credits for housing, food, and supplies. The Red Cross hired many of the refugees themselves as cooks and nurses, to do laundry and cleaning, and so on. In all it was a remarkable salvage operation that would considerably expand the population of "Russia Abroad."[206] A bloody, cruel civil war created massive relief campaigns, first for refugees fleeing it and eventually for much of the population of the land where it was fought.

205. USS *Pittsburgh* to Navy Operations, 21 December 1920, box 713, RG 45, NA.
206. The details are found in the Bristol Papers, MD, LC; the records of the American Red Cross, RG 200, NA; and reports of ship and unit commanders in RG 45, NA. Most of the refugees were eventually resettled in Yugoslavia and Bulgaria, with bounties of five pounds sterling per head furnished by the League of Nations to those countries for their cooperation.

Facing the immediate need in Constantinople, however, American responses were cautious. In forwarding $5,000 from one relief fund, Montgomery Schuyler warned, "I am very much afraid that our collection of funds for these people will be hampered by the political situation."[207] He was referring to the collapse of the White army in Ukraine and the increasing frustration of Americans with resolving the Russian situation.

The Polish-Soviet War

Unfortunately for so many in the region, war and civil suffering were not over. The borderlines of central Europe, beyond the reach of the Versailles mapmakers, were yet to be determined. After the failure of negotiations on determining a boundary between Russia and Poland, a Polish army, backed by French advisers and money, advanced into Ukraine and White Russia in April 1920. The Red Army, buoyed by its success in the south and propelled by its Grand Vizier Trotsky, launched a counterattack on Poland. The Soviet goals were dual: to recover lost imperial territory and to spread revolution deep into Europe. The "born-again" Polish state, with an army formed out of veterans of Austrian, German, and Russian armies—and volunteer legions—under French guidance, however, undertook a stiff defense and counteroffensive, again with mixed motives: to gain as much of the territory of historic Poland as possible and to overthrow Bolshevism.

The American representative in Warsaw, Hugh Gibson, clearly favored the Polish cause, though he wondered "whether the Poles are fighting Bolshevism or Russia."[208] He firmly supported a definition of the Polish border far to the east of the Curzon line discussed at the peace conference. "The territory may not be Polish in blood or even in sentiment, but it certainly is not Russian on either count." But he also wanted international sanction: "The Powers really should send an international body of broad-minded men here and let them study the question on the ground, travel through the eastern districts, interview all the

---

207. Schuyler to Bicknell, 24 November 1920, box 916, RG 200, NA. This was obviously only a drop in the proverbial bucket, and a major American relief organization was reluctant to provide any more. The head of the American Red Cross in Europe advised, "I do not think it would be wise to let the Russians or anybody else know that there is a further reserve of two million dollars which might be drawn upon for Russian relief." Olds to Farrand, 2 November 1920, ibid.

208. Gibson to Allen Dulles, 27 September 1920, box 107, Harrison Papers, MD, LC.

Julia Cantacuzene-Speransky (née Grant). From her
Revolutionary Days

elements of the population, and reach some common sense decision that is based on a knowledge of local conditions."[209]

The result of the 1920 Soviet-Polish War was essentially a victory for the Poles (and many would claim for the West as well, by stopping the Bolshevik penetration of Europe and actually pushing it back). The reasons were clearer—the superior financing and arming of the Poles by the West, the clear sympathy of the Western Allies for the Polish cause, and the exhaustion of Russian military and economic resources. The real result was an East-West truce, formalized by the "Treaty of Riga," which extended Polish boundaries far eastward to include

209. Ibid.

much of White Russia and western Ukraine but at the same time failed to over-throw Bolshevism. In its wake, the conflict left enormous cleanup tasks for relief agencies and the need for major allocations by the American Relief Administration and its Red Cross and YMCA affiliates. Remaining was the enormous problem of determining who was now "Polish"—or Latvian or Lithuanian, and so on—that is, residents of the new states, which included a large part of the former Russian Empire and its diverse population. Many Russians, Jews, and others, who had lived there legitimately, and many others who scurried over the border to claim a new citizenship, produced a subsequent massive rush for emigration to the United States, most of them in desperate condition and dependent on relief.

The natural American sympathy for the Polish cause was evident, but aid to it was a convenient way of containing, if not defeating, the Bolshevik menace. Ignaz Paderewski, the head of the Polish National Committee who was now becoming the president of a newly independent Poland, was well known in America, and, of course, the large Polish-American community was an important lobby. Many of them volunteered their expertise as pilots, engineers, and reliefers to the cause. Moreover, a few Poles visualized their mission as not only stopping *Russian* Bolshevism but hopefully ridding the world of it. The main goal, however, was to stand guard over what Oscar Halecki termed "the border-lands of Western Civilization," and that they did. Long active in the cause of independence (going back at least to 1830), Poles easily won the support of the major Western Allies—France, Britain, and the United States. The money that poured in, mainly from the United States, directly or indirectly, helped build an army and provide relief where it was very much needed—one of the most concentrated war zones—and certainly contributed to the Polish victory over the Red Army in 1920. The American Relief Administration, regardless of its political agenda, did an enormous job in helping stabilize the situation.

The war and shifting boundaries and hordes of displaced people created immense confusion on top of political and economic chaos, as so many tried to leave the region at once. In April 1921, as many as 2,500 people were counted in a line stretching several blocks on any day at the American consulate in Warsaw.[210] There were many charges of falsified papers, bribes taken by Polish officials for resident documents, and Jews who included practically a whole community as their "family." "The charges are freely made that passports are being issued by Polish officials to many Russians for a consideration, the excuse being

210. J. Klair Huddle to Ingram, 20 April 1921, Warsaw consulate, vol. 96, RG 84, NA.

that as the Polish and Russian boundaries are not yet determined it is not possible to say definitely whether or not an applicant is Russian or Polish."[211] One depressing account for the port of Danzig reported that of the 28,500 deloused (for emigration) during the last six months of 1920, 24,000 were from Poland (mainly Jewish and Russian), 1,000 from Czechoslovakia, 760 from Ukraine, and 750 from the Baltic States. Of 13,646 leaving the port in the last two months of 1920, 12,299 departed for the United States.[212] This and a large number of other immigrants flowing in caused a considerable congressional reaction and was a major factor in the movement to limit immigration. The official figures for the first half of 1921 showed a veritable flood of people from Europe to America, despite a long waiting list for steamer space: United Kingdom, 77,206; Germany, 68,039; Italy, 42,021; Russia (including Siberia), 34,247; Poland, 25,800 (mostly Russian). Inclusion of additional numbers from Armenia and Turkey may have put the actual immigrants to the United States from the former Russian Empire in first place.[213] This was not exactly the outcome of the Russian turmoil that the American people expected.

The End of Diplomatic Representation

When Bakhmeteff returned once again to the State Department in late 1919 to press for funding for the Denikin campaign, Long was even more blunt:

> I told him that there were several points of view, and that it seemed there were only two ways to oppose the Bolsheviki. The first by military organization, which would be participated in by the Allied and Associated Powers. Second a withdrawal of military opposition by each and all of the Allied Powers. That the former had proven impracticable, and that this country was not prepared to enter upon a military campaign either with the Allies or alone.[214]

211. Augustus Ingram (Havre) to Leo Keene (Warsaw), 21 April 1921, ibid.
212. Report of William Dawson, Danzig consul, 31 January 1921, ibid.
213. "Act to Limit the Immigration of Aliens into the US," 19 May 1921, in ibid. The American consul in Prague reported that he was besieged by Polish Jews and was issuing over 200 visas a day for entry into the United States. C. S. Winans to Keene, 28 January 1921, ibid.
214. Long, Memorandum of Conversation with the Russian Ambassador, 9 December 1919, ibid.

That same day Long lunched with Poole and Arthur Bullard to discuss an offer
for the latter to join the State Department staff.[215] This would bolster and balance the expertise on Russia and lend it additional continuity, but he worked
there for only a short time. Meanwhile, Long felt increasingly embarrassed about
the persisting strain in the relations between Wilson and Lansing, resulting in
a general atmosphere of impasse in the department and paralysis in the central
administration. He tried to resign twice in February 1920, after Lansing left office, but was rejected, so he valiantly but unenthusiastically stayed the course for
a few more months under Colby, until the arrival of a new administration.[216]

Bakhmeteff lingered on as ambassador, but his days as a Washington diplomat were clearly numbered. In some ways he was the best of Russian representatives at this time, but also the worst. He believed, as did most Russians abroad,
in the integrity of the Russian Empire—with some allowances—and fought bitterly any suggestions of a Siberian separatism or a Denikin south Russia. Perhaps he could claim a real success in winning American support for maintenance
of the empire against various independence movements, but that was already
formally supported by Wilson and others in the American government. Bakhmeteff also resented the rank-oriented Russian émigré political aristocracy that
was attempting to be the dominant voice of Russia in Paris and to a great extent
in New York and Washington. In correspondence with Sazonov, who had been
Nicholas II's foreign minister, he emphasized his fears about "fighting Bolshevism at the expense of Russia."[217] He (though more perceptively) and most of
those beginning to form a permanent "Russia Abroad" wasted much of their
time in infighting and dead-end endeavors to the detriment of their cause of a
Free Russia. Although he remained officially designated as the Russian ambassador, basically for the purpose of settling the outstanding business of the Provisional Government, Bakhmeteff was virtually ignored diplomatically until he
officially tendered his resignation in 1923 and turned over the remaining tedious lawsuits that dragged on for many years to an assistant.

Washington's Hide-and-Seek Russia

One thing that Bakhmeteff, most other Russians, and Lansing and Wilson
agreed on was the integrity of Russia, and they strongly resisted any mention
of plans or forces that would have dismembered it. They were all disgusted

215. Long diary, 9 December 1919, box 2, Long Papers, MD, LC.
216. Ibid., 1, 3, 6 February 1919.
217. Bakhmeteff to Sazonov, 21 January 1919, box 9, BA, CU.

with the dabbling of France and Britain—and Germany—with fractional pieces and feared their dominance over valuable or strategically important pieces. This was the main reason for the refusal of the United States to recognize the Omsk government, actually the only viable alternative to the Soviet one, and then only for a few months. Denikin and Wrangel in the south never really formed a civil government that had any credibility. As Lansing recalled privately to a friend,

> The Allies have wabbled [sic] and changed and experimented and have got nowhere. They now seem disposed to recognize sections of Russia as independent states. I think that is another blunder for two reasons. First, it will induce many Russians with a rudimentary national pride to join the Bolsheviks as the only hope of a Great Russia. Second, Russia cut up into small nationalities will become the prey of German economic control and of German political intrigue. Russia ought to remain with substantially the same frontiers as before the war, the only exception being Finland and the territory within the Polish boundaries. Nothing should be done to encourage the independence of Lithuania, Latvia, Esthonia, Ukrania [sic], Russian Armenia, Georgia, etc. Siberia might possibly be severed from Russia but I doubt the wisdom of so sparsely settled and so vast a territory becoming a sovereign state. It would be too defenseless and vulnerable. Personally, I believe in a Great Russia.[218]

The concluding American negative impression of Denikin was backed by British friends such as Harold Williams, who condemned and much regretted his bad leadership.[219]

Some Americans also believed, as did Norman Hapgood, that if fighting ended and the West opened its doors to all of Russia, Bolshevism would soon die of overexposure. William Allen White reflected this popular, if simplistic, view in a letter to a Kansas friend in trying to explain the failure of the Prinkipo conference a year earlier:

> The conference was abandoned because the French owned so many bonds that they did not want any settlement with the Russians except a military settlement and they thought they could furnish arms and ammunition and money and whip the Bolsheviks, rather than to make peace and let food

218. Lansing to Charles Valentine, 22 January 1920, vol. 40, Lansing Papers, MD, LC.
219. Williams to Harper, 19 June 1920, f. 2, box 8, Harper Papers, UC.

and civilization come into Russia, thereby overcoming the Bolshevik principal [*sic*] with reason rather than force.[220]

There was also a sense that somehow Russia would blunder through:

> Russia is coming along all right in spite of the stupidity which seems to be inspiring the world in dealing with Russia, but the Russian is only suffering the martyrdom of birth which every new idea must suffer in the world, and like every other new idea in the world the Russian idea will be more or less modified by life on this planet in due course, in spite of the malice which greets it now. I have no idea what that place will be. Humanity must react, and the idea of the chemical change is beyond my talent. Whatever is good will be retained and the rest will go.[221]

Was this an American version of the Russian idealistic populism, pronounced by Dmitri Pisarev and others in the 1860s, that led to revolutionary terrorism? From literally out in left field, David Francis, back home in St. Louis but still the official American ambassador to Russia, offered to go back and resume his post somewhere in non-Bolshevik Russia.[222] Perhaps owing to his midwestern political pragmatism, he hinted that any location was possible, providing that a government existed that was generally recognized.

Felix Cole, back from Archangel and now assigned to south Russia, was clearly frustrated about the lack of American support for Wrangel, but, "now that he is 'up the flue,' . . . the matter is now dead until the next poor devil of a 'white hope' arises."[223] The Russian civil war had become a political charade to many Americans. Cole was certainly not alone in voicing despair over the Russian turmoil. And Herbert Hoover, in a draft memorandum, lamented

> our own lack of decision; there has never been any consistency either in thought or act in this whole stupendous problem. In the face of divided notions, the murderous Bolshevik gets the best of it. It has been the consensus of opinion of many thoughtful Americans, both in Europe and in the United States, that the whole of the policies pursued by the Allies in connection with Russia were the rankest folly. . . . they have been without

220. White to Charles Feron, 24 March 1920, vol. 41, White Papers, MD, LC.
221. White to Dr. Blanche Brown, 29 December 1919, vol. 40, ibid.
222. Francis to Long, 1 November 1919, f. Francis, box 48, Long Papers, MD, LC.
223. Cole to Quantrain, 19 November 1920, DPR 5, Viborg consulate, RG 84, NA.

consistency and without vision, and consisted of taking muddled emergency steps from the beginning, composed of no political or social policy
whatever.[224]

Isolationism was becoming the fashion. In April 1920, Archibald Cary Coolidge,
a founder of Russian studies in the United States, commented, "At this moment the whole international situation looks black enough to suit the most pessimistic. For the time it is the fashion to dislike—to put it mildly—every other
nation."[225] There was much truth to this in assessing blame for why the peace
settlement had not resulted in a really peaceful and stable world.

Americans found much to criticize and to be disillusioned about in the wake
of war in Europe and civil war in Eurasia. There was certainly much soul-
searching, especially among those who had been in charge of Russian policy or
who were long-standing Russophiles. In the wake of so much conflict, confusion, and indecision, they were left to ponder the old Russian dilemma, posed
by Gogol in *Dead Souls:* "Whither Russia?" But to their credit, and despite the
trend toward withdrawal into isolationism, they poured an enormous amount
of relief aid into the region. No doubt some of this was politically motivated—to
strengthen non-Bolshevik elements of the population—but it would also save many
ordinary lives.

The Colby Note

The sense of a lack of direction and indecision in America's Russian policy that
had frustrated so many for so long finally produced a "project" of a resolution
in the State Department. Would the United States recognize the Soviet government as Robins and others urged it to do? Or would it take a more active role in
intervention? Would drift and inaction continue to dominate, or would some
dynamism be found to fuel a more aggressive liberal internationalism? These
were issues that Lansing, Breckinridge Long, and their staffs had struggled with
since the Bolshevik seizure of power. Although Secretary of State Bainbridge
Colby, who replaced Lansing in January 1920, gets credit for proclaiming a firm
refusal to recognize Soviet Russia by the United States in August 1920, the main
catalyst was probably his chief assistant, Norman Davis, who met with the Italian

224. Draft no. 2, Hoover memorandum on Russian policy, 24 January 1920, box 62,
Pre-Commerce, HPL.
225. Coolidge to Dresel, 23 April 1920, Dresel Papers, Harvard-Houghton.

minister several days before Colby addressed his famous note to him, but the actual note was drafted mainly by John Spargo, another erstwhile Wilsonian "socialist."[226]

Events in Poland provoked and shaped the timing of the public statement, informally named "American Note on the Polish Situation."[227] Already at the beginning of the month Colby had sent a cable to the American ambassador in Britain and circulated to other diplomatic missions.

> Desiring the maintenance of Poland's integrity, this Government is in sympathy with arrangements for an armistice between Poland and Soviet Russia, but it does not, at least for the present, see its way clear to participate in plans extending the armistice negotiations in a general European Conference which would involve recognition of the Soviet regime and a settlement of the long-standing Russian problem almost inevitably on the basis of a dismemberment of Russia. . . . Believing as it does that the dismemberment of Russia will complicate and retard a genuine solution of the real problem, it has persisted in denying recognition of the Baltic States as separate nations independent of Russia.[228]

A follow-up memorandum to the president on the Polish situation and a draft statement on nonrecognition were even more emphatic.[229] Landfield, judging from Nicholas Butler's report on an interview with the newly elected president, felt certain that the "radical bunch" in the Republican Party, led by Robins, would have no weight.[230]

The note was not without opposition. Norman Hapgood, for one, thought it was a big mistake and a definite sign that Bakhmeteff and his émigré crowd "had a strangle hold in the department."[231] He thought that it put the Democratic Party in an awkward position and strongly advised its candidate to clarify the matter.[232] Pressure also came from the League of Free Nations Associa-

---

226. David S. Foglesong, *America's Secret War Against Bolshevism: U.S. Intervention in the Russian Civil War, 1917–1920* (Chapel Hill: University of North Carolina Press, 1995), 291.

227. Original drafts, 9 and 10 August 1920, box 3A, Colby Papers, MD, LC.

228. Colby to Amembassy, London, 2 August 1920, ibid.

229. Colby to Wilson, 9 August 1920, ibid. The president returned this note to Colby with the handwritten addition: "Thank you. This seems to me excellent and sufficient."

230. Landfield to Bakhmeteff, 22 December 1920, f. Landfield 1920, box 19, Bakhmeteff Papers, BA, CU.

231. Hapgood to Colby, 4 November 1920, box 3B, Colby Papers, MD, LC.

232. Hapgood to Cox, 25 August 1920, box 11, ibid.

tion, whose motto was "For a Liberal and Constructive American Foreign Policy."[233] The multiplicity of such organizations that had an interest in the Russian situation added more confusion. The Foreign Press Service, managed by Paul Kennady, served as an intermediary between the State Department and the left-wing internationalists and Soviet-sponsored organizations such as "Soviet Russia." Kennady even solicited Elizabeth Hapgood for translation work for him and the department.[234]

The election of Warren Harding in November 1920 did not produce the change toward recognition of Soviet Russia that some, such as Raymond Robins, expected, mainly because of the conservatism of Charles Evans Hughes, the new secretary of state. "In these darkened days I think constantly of Russia, I am wondering whether it is not possible for both Thacher and Wardwell to get a real hearing from Hughes. Also Walter Pettit. Cannot all three of these sound men help in the Russian situation? I have done all that lies in my power."[235] The truth is that the supporters of recognition were politically handicapped by being on the radical fringe or, in the cases of Robins and Hapgood, tainted by the Overman inquisition and nonconfirmation by the Senate, respectively. On the other hand, Harding was under powerful influence from highly respected members of the academic community, such as Columbia University president Nicholas Murray Butler, who opposed recognition of a Bolshevik regime and who, according to Jerome Landfield, spent seven hours cloistered with the president-elect on the subject in November.

The Democratic candidate, James Cox, told Hapgood that he supported recognition:

I have felt from the outset, that the allied policy with reference to Russia is a great mistake. . . . There is too much of a disposition to be sticking to the fetish of international custom rather than considering the flesh and bone of humanity. That's why Root should never have been sent to Russia. When we, with other countries, refused to trade with Russia, we confirmed the contention of the Bolsheviki that the world was trying to starve the Russians. Intended to curb the growth of the Soviet regime, it did quite the reverse, because with threatened starvation, the masses were doubtless driven to an acceptance of the only government in sight.[236]

233. James McDonald, Chairman, to Hapgood, 27 August 1920, ibid.
234. Jacob Hartmann, "Soviet Russia," to Hapgood, 25 August 1920, and Kennady to Norman Hapgood, 29 April 1921, ibid.
235. Robins to Gumberg, 8 March 1921, box 17, Robins Papers, SHSW.
236. Cox to Hapgood, 2 September 1920, box 11, Hapgood-Reynolds Papers, MD, LC.

Despite this vow, it is very doubtful that in 1921 even a Democratic administration would have found such a course of action wise. In fact, it was not an issue in the election campaign.

The Petrograd Children's Colony

Despite a nominal but still quite visible American presence in Vladivostok into 1920, Graves's military command was in a state of withdrawal—or rather of no advance. It could only witness the passage of events, largely controlled by the Japanese from its barracks and manufactured bunkers spread across Siberia along the railroad. For a time this produced an uneasy coalition of Kolchak's forces with the smaller and localized warlords, mainly Semenov and Kalmykov, but also American opposition to the Semenov-Japanese alliance that controlled vital stretches of the Trans-Siberian rising. This situation was engineered mostly by the Japanese to their sole benefit, and they clearly retained the upper hand in the region, thanks in part to the American forces maintaining a low profile.[237] But Kolchak's belated "unity" with the likes of the brutal Semenov forces certainly did not endear him to American authorities, nor certainly to those more concerned with humanitarian relief. Consul General Harris thought this meant disaster for Kolchak. He no longer had an ounce of credibility.[238]

One rare shining light upon the whole Siberian fiasco was the salvation of the Petrograd Children's Colony. This involved the rescue and care of around 800 Russian children of a wide range of ages who were evacuated from Petrograd (and a few from Moscow) by Soviet authorities during the turmoil of early 1918 and taken to the Urals region. They were then caught up in the shifting tides of a brutal civil war. The children were eventually rescued by the Czechs and turned over to the American Red Cross at Chelyabinsk in the fall of 1918.[239] Their perilous situation naturally struck a chord with the relief instincts of both the American Red Cross and the YMCA, and in a cooperative effort the latter naturally took on responsibility for their religious instruction and physical education. They were evacuated east safely out of the zone of military engagement to Vladivostok and housed in an old military barracks in Vladivostok and then on Russian Island in the harbor during the winter of 1919–20. Local American

237. Stevens (Harbin) to Colby, 26 May 1920, box 5, RG 43, NA.
238. Harris to Lansing, 24 January 1920, box 1, Harris Papers, HIA.
239. For an account of this children's crusade, especially in regard to the involvement of her parents, see Jane Swan, *The Lost Children: A Russian Odyssey* (Carlisle, Pa.: South Mountain Press, 1989).

Red Cross personnel jumped to the rescue. Riley Allen became the chief executive officer for this enterprise, and a local Siberian-American recruit to Red Cross work, Hannah "Mother" Campbell, took on the role of mother hen for this unusual brood.

To make a long, much-publicized, and truly wonderfully human story shorter, the Russian children were eventually embarked on a hastily remodeled Japanese freighter, the *Yomei Maru*, in July 1920 and were forced to suffer a long ocean journey in crowded conditions with an often unsympathetic crew, but with the best possible Red Cross care.[240] They saw the sights of San Francisco to much fanfare and—after passage through the Panama Canal—experienced a ticker-tape tribute, as well as pro- and anti-Soviet rallies in New York.[241] Controversy surrounded what some Russians considered to be the children's capture by pro-Soviet elements headed by Ludwig Martens and "the Jewish East Side organizations which, naturally, are in full sympathy with their brethren, at present in control of Soviet Russia."[242] After some give-and-take, and serious consideration of turning them over to White Russian émigrés in France, a resolution by the children and their teachers against that course may have been decisive.[243] In October 1920 they were finally repatriated through Finland back to their families in famine-stricken Soviet Russia—a long and involuntary journey around the world during war, revolution, and civil war. Riley Allen recorded a rare tribute to a measure of enforced Japanese-American cooperation in this venture:

I know that in spite of their eagerness to get home, the Children are saying goodby to the *Yomei Maru* with reluctance and with much sadness. They have come to look upon it as a safe home on the many seas we have traversed. In spite of our shipboard troubles, which have been many, and our daily mishaps inseparable from transporting such a large number of children in close quarters, the children will always remember the *Yomei Maru* as the ship which brought them safely three-quarters of the way around the world. And they will always remember your many kind acts to them.[244]

240. Thanks to excellent record keeping, including a detailed log of the voyage, much information is available in American Red Cross papers on the children's colony, mainly in boxes 869 and 870, RG 200, NA.
241. Keppel to Olds, 9 September 1920, box 869, RG 200, NA.
242. Boris Brasol to F. P. Keppel (ARC), 8 September 1920, ibid. "We deem it our duty, however, to advise you that the sending of these children to Petrograd would be equal to murdering them. The deplorable sanitary conditions in Petrograd, combined with the acute lack of food, make this proposition impossible." Ibid.
243. Petition addressed to American Red Cross, 10 September 1920, ibid.
244. Allen (Kovisto, Finland) to Captain M. Kayahara, 13 October 1920, ibid.

One can still review the debate of the time about whether this was the best out-come—the return of children to their legitimate parents—but perhaps it was one of the better options for all concerned, since it seemed reasonable even to "Red Scare" Americans that Russian children should be reunited with their parents, even if this meant in communist Russia.[245]

This very human episode perhaps signaled a shift in Soviet-American relations from hostility to a major effort at relief, resumption of cultural and economic discourse, and even some diplomatic contact. The beginning of a new administration in Washington coincided with decisions made at the Tenth Party Congress in Moscow in March 1921.[246] Under Lenin's leadership and despite die-hard opposition in the party, the country began a retreat from the extreme, aggressive policies of War Communism that had created so much misery and opposition to the New Economic Policy. This involved restoring a free market in the country, relaxing pressures on the peasantry, and restoring private ownership of small businesses. It also meant a softer approach toward the West and especially toward the United States, the most likely source of much-needed aid and assistance. The opening up of Soviet Russia brought depressing accounts of the conditions there, including reports of mass starvation. It turned out that none of these were exaggerated, as some Western sources believed. And within a few months the largest humanitarian relief campaign yet in history was launched from the United States to help Russians.

245. The literature on one of the happier, human episodes of a this dismal period is considerable and deserving of a dissertation. See, for example, Hannah Campbell, "Petrograd Children's Colony," *Red Cross Courier* 7, no. 1 (2 January 1928); and considerable correspondence and reports in boxes 869 and 870, RG 200, NA. One of the former Red Cross caretakers, Bramhall, arranged a reunion of the surviving "children" in Leningrad in the détente era of 1974.

246. The party of Lenin that now had a complete monopoly of power in Russia was still officially designated as the Russian Social Democratic Labor Party (b), the last letter indicating "Bolshevik." It would soon become the Communist Party of the Soviet Union.

Conclusion

World War I had an enormous effect on both Russia and the United States and the relations between them. Both countries were developing economically before the conflict, the United States obviously at a faster pace. From 1914, Russia would suffer greatly from its main communications routes being cut, while the United States forged ahead as a major supplier to the combatants. As a leading neutral, the United States accepted responsibility for overseeing the large numbers of prisoners of war that resulted from the prolonged and intense fighting on the Eastern Front. This resulted in a much larger American diplomatic and relief agency presence in Russia. Although this produced some strains, relations as a whole remained good.

The beginning of hostilities also coincided with a growth in cultural relations that had begun with American fascination with Russian literature in the nineteenth century and continued into the silver age of the early twentieth century. American exposure to music and art also increased, thanks to their promotion by individuals such as Charles R. Crane. Real centers of Russian studies had emerged, especially at Harvard and the University of Chicago. A number of Americans could now claim to be experts in Russian language, history, and society. They, and many more on journalistic assignments or out of curiosity, ventured into Russia during the war years. These people in the field writing, filming, or working for government or private agencies gained considerable appreciation of Russia's hardships and popular protests about them.

Business and commercial relations were obviously damaged by the war, though at the beginning great hopes were raised for future expansion at the expense of Germany and participants in the war. The Singer and International Harvester factories near Moscow adjusted to the circumstances and filled orders for the Russian military. To meet Russia's increasing needs, purchasing commissions were sent to the United States but were at a disadvantage in competition with allies for similar goods. Nevertheless, large Russian orders were placed in the

United States, especially for rifles, cartridges, and railroad equipment. Few could reach Russia before Russia left the war in early 1918, because of the overtaxing of American industry to produce, shipping delays, and financial problems.

As the United States veered more and more toward support of the Entente in 1916, Russia was feeling the economic strain, especially in regard to transportation, with serious political consequences. Almost all Americans welcomed the February Revolution and the abdication of the tsar, assuming that the basic social structure and diplomatic alignment would continue. The United States was the first major country to recognize the new regime. Both Russians and Americans who believed they had much in common geopolitically and culturally saw Russia becoming even more American in the political and ideological sense.

The changes in Russia also made it much easier for the United States to enter the war a few weeks later and pursue an ideological aim of a stable democratic world. Russia desperately needed American assistance to continue in the war and to cement fragile republican institutions. This was slow in coming, however, because of transport problems, the tendency to want thorough examination and consideration, the pressures from France and Britain to concentrate on the Western Front, and a natural tendency to hesitate about large, specific commitments on the part of government leaders, especially President Woodrow Wilson. Substantial amounts of supplies were finally reaching Russia during the summer of 1917 but became backlogged in Archangel, Murmansk, and Vladivostok because of the ineffectiveness of the rail transport system. As a result of inexperience and mistakes in judgment, the leaders of the Provisional Government were unable to improve this situation, continue an effective military campaign, and meet the challenges of radical revolutionary opponents. In part, this was because they trusted too much in the American miracle to save Russia by direct assistance or by quickly winning the war on the Western Front.

Political and technical missions that were sent to Russia realized these problems but were late to respond to them and then relied heavily on public information campaigns that were poorly funded and would take months to have any effect. With the radical revolutionary movement centered in the soviets growing rapidly on antiwar appeals in the late summer of 1917, disillusionment with the Kerensky-led moderate government set in. The Bolsheviks' seizure of power in November thus came as no surprise. Their ability to stay in power by making a separate peace did.

Americans were perplexed not only by the loss of an important military ally at a crucial time—with Germany launching a major offensive—but also by the failure of "their kind" of democracy. Some, such as Raymond Robins, believed the best course was to work with the government in power and hope either to maintain the Eastern Front or at least to deny Germany a major benefit from the end of the war on that front. Others saw the Bolsheviks as inimical to American interests and as real German agents who should be crushed by any means possible. Pursuing this course, that of direct intervention, was fraught with difficulties: opposition based on political principles, the need to concentrate on the Western Front, public reaction to fighting in distant lands with no clear pupose, and, finally, the inability to find a viable anti-Bolshevik government to support.

After much hesitation, however, Wilson followed the recommendations of diplomats in the field and the State Department and committed the United States to this course, though on a very limited basis in terms of the numbers of men actually sent. This approach had little chance of success, however, due to the limitations, the mistakes, and the lack of unity of anti-Bolshevik forces, and the ability of Bolshevik leaders to forge an effective army under adverse conditions. But they also failed in their inept efforts to divide the interveners, to promote their world revolution, and to satisfy the real wants of the population.

Relief and assistance had always been part of the picture even before the war. Large programs were much discussed because of the obvious desperate condition that prevailed in so much of revolution- and war-torn Russia. Some believed relief could be used as a political tool to tame or overthrow the Bolshevik menace, while many were responding out of sincere humanitarian concern. First of all, the war and especially the civil war that followed created enormous refugee problems. The United States was the only country that could really meet these needs, so it did respond, though perhaps not as soon as possible, because of anti-Bolshevik publicity and a general disillusionment from the failure to make a just peace.

By 1921, Americans were in a quandary about Russia. After so much expectation of it following an American path, the new Soviet Russia was pursuing a hostile direction beyond American control. At least they could take some satisfaction in knowing that Russia as a nation was still intact and not under the influence of another power. The wars and revolutions had done much to shape the future course of both countries in the twentieth century.

Bibliography

Manuscript Sources

Berkeley, California

    University of California-Bancroft Library (UCB)
      David Barrows
      Jerome Davis
      Jerome Landfield

Cambridge, Massachusetts

    Harvard University-Houghton Library (Harvard-Houghton)
      E. L. Dresel
      Joseph Grew
      Curtis Guild (William Thayer)
      Walter Page Diaries and Notebooks
      John Reed-Louise Bryant

    Harvard University Archives
      Archibald Cary Coolidge
      Leo Wiener

Champaign-Urbana, Illinois

    University of Illinois Archives (UIA)
      Paul Anderson
      Donald Lowrie-Helen Ogden
      Russian Student Fund

Chicago, Illinois

    Newberry Library
      William V. Judson

    University of Chicago-Regenstein Library (UC)
      Samuel Harper

Eugene, Oregon

University of Oregon Archives (UOA)
Verne Bright
Jerome Davis
Floyd Ramp

Ithaca, New York

Cornell University Archives
Andrew Dickson White

Kansas City, Missouri

Missouri Historical Society, Kansas City
Charles Colville Jr.

Lawrence, Kansas

University of Kansas Archives
Edward H. Taylor

London

Public Record Office (PRO)
Cabinet (CAB)
Foreign Office (FO)

Madison, Wisconsin

State Historical Society of Wisconsin (SHSW)
Alexander Gumberg
International Harvester
Cyrus McCormick
DeWitt Clinton Poole
Paul Reinsch
Raymond Robins
Edward Ross
Singer Company

Moscow

Archive of the Ministry of Foreign Affairs of Russia (AVPR)
f. 170 Russian Embassy in Washington
f. 133, op. 470 Foreign Ministry

Russian Center for the Preservation and Study of Documents of Contemporary History
Central Committee of the Communist Party of the Soviet Union (TsKKPSS)

State Archive of the Russian Federation (GARF)
 Records of the People's Commissariat of National Economy

New Haven, Connecticut

 Yale University Divinity School Library Archives (DSA)
  John R. Mott

 Yale University, Sterling Library (Yale-Sterling)
  William Bullitt
  Edward House
  William Phillips
  Frank Polk

New York, New York

 Columbia University, Manuscript and Rare Book Department
  Frank Vanderlip

  Oral History Project: Ralph Albertson; Boris Bakhmeteff; Malcolm Davis;
   Stanley Washburn; DeWitt Clinton Poole

  Bakhmeteff Archive Collections (BA, CU)
   Boris Bakhmeteff
   Ekaterina Breshko-Breshkovskaia
   Charles R. Crane
   Ernest Ropes
   Graham Taylor Jr.
   Allen Wardwell
   Dmitri Fedotoff White

  Russian Artillery Commission in the U.S.

 New York Life Insurance Company Archives
  Frederick Corse

 New York Public Library (NYPL)
  Manuscript Division
   Charles R. Flint
   Emma Goldman
   Francis Greene
   Anthony Griffin
   Isabel Hapgood
   George Kennan
   Nikolai Khrabov
   Rand School (Thomas Thacher)
   Lillian Wald

  Billy Rose Theater Collection at Lincoln Center
   Elizabeth Reynolds Hapgood

Princeton, New Jersey

Mudd Library (Princeton-Mudd)
Norman Armour
Ray Stannard Baker
Arthur Bullard
Clinton Decker
Robert Lansing
Woodrow Wilson
Joshua Butler Wright

Rochester, New York

University of Rochester, Rush-Rhees Library Archives
James Wood Colt

St. Louis, Missouri

Missouri Historical Society (MoHS)
John Dearing
David Francis

St. Paul, Minnesota

Minnesota Historical Society (MinnHS)
Peter W. Copeland
Stanley Washburn

San Marino, California

Huntington Library
Charles Janin
Jack London
Theodore Roosevelt
Frederick Jackson Turner

Stanford, California

Hoover Institution Archives (HIA)
American Red Cross
American Relief Administration
Nancy Babb
Fred Bugbee
John Caldwell
Hannah Campbell
Philip M. Carroll
Ethan Colton
William Young Darling
Robert Davis

William Henry Duncan
Edward H. Egbert
George Emerson
Benjamin Fuller
Forrest Funk
Hugh Gibson
Frank Golder
William S. Graves
Ernest Lloyd Harris
William N. Haskell
George Herron
James L. Houghteling
Lincoln Hutchinson
Benjamin Johnson
Frank King
Sylvester Kuhn
Eva Lawrence
Bessie Lyon
Sarah Matthews
Merle Murphy
Stanley Partridge
Carrie (Caroline) Pickett
Chester Purington
Elliott Reynolds
Leighton Rogers
Russkoe Posolstvo (Russian embassy)
John F. Stevens
Norman Stines
YMCA

Washington, D.C.

  Georgetown University Special Collections (GU)
    Richard T. Crane
    Robert F. Kelley
    John F. Stevens

  Library of Congress Manuscript Division (MD, LC)
    Carl Ackerman
    Henry J. Allen
    Alexis Babine
    Newton D. Baker
    Wharton Barker
    Alice Stone Blackwell
    Tasker Bliss
    Mabel Boardman
    Boris Brasol
    Mark Bristol
    Bainbridge Colby
    George Creel

Josephus Daniels
Norman Davis
James Garfield
Herman Hagedorn–William Boyce Thompson
Norman Hapgood–Elizabeth Reynolds
Leland Harrison
Charles Hughes
George Kennan
Robert Lansing
Breckinridge Long
Roland Morris
Francis L. Parker
Riggs Family
Elihu Root
Charles Russell
William Scott
John F. Stevens
Joseph Tumulty
Stanley Washburn
William Allen White

National Archives and Records Service (NA)
RG 24 Logbooks of U.S. Naval Ships
RG 38 Records of the Office of Naval Operations
RG 43 Advisory Commission of Railway Experts to Russia
RG 45 Naval Records Collection
RG 54 (M 840) Bureau of Plant Industry, Expedition Reports
RG 59 (M 316) Decimal Files, 1910–1929, Records Relating to the Internal Affairs of Russia and the Soviet Union
(M 333) Decimal Files, 1910–1929, Records Relating to the Political Relations with Russia and the Soviet Union
RG 80 General Records of the Navy Department
RG 84 State Department, Diplomatic Post Records
RG 120 AEF North Russia
RG 151 Bureau of Foreign and Domestic Commerce
RG 165 Naval Intelligence Reports
RG 200 American Red Cross Papers
RG 395 (M 917) Historical Files of AEF in Siberia

West Branch, Iowa

Hoover Presidential Library (HPL)
Pre-Commerce
Hugh Gibson
James Goodrich

Newspapers and Journals

Chicago Daily News
Chicago Tribune

Christian Science Monitor
Emporia Gazette
Harper's Weekly
Independent
Kansas City Star
Kommersant
Lawrence Journal-World
New Republic
New York Herald
New York Times
Outlook
Philadelphia North American
Pravda
Public
Rossiia

Documentary Collections

The Bolshevik Revolution, 1917–1918: Documents and Materials. Edited by James Bunyan and Harold H. Fisher. Stanford, Calif.: Stanford University Press, 1934.

The Cabinet Diaries of Josephus Daniels. Edited by E. David Cronin. Lincoln: University of Nebraska Press, 1963.

The Diaries of Sir Robert Bruce Lockhart, 1915–1938. Edited by Kenneth Young. London: Macmillan, 1974.

Documents of Russian History, 1914–1917. Edited by Frank A. Golder. Translated by Emanuel Aronsberg. New York: Century, 1927.

Documents of Soviet-American Relations, 3 vols. Edited by Harold J. Goldberg. Gulf Breeze, Fla.: Academic International Press, 1993–99.

Dokumenty vneshnei politiki SSSR. 4 vols. Edited by Andrei Gromyko et al. Moscow: Gosizdat, 1957–61.

Dollars and Diplomacy: Ambassador David Rowland Francis and the Fall of Tsarism, 1916–17. Edited by Jamie H. Cockfield. Durham, N.C.: Duke University Press, 1981.

The History of the American Expedition Fighting the Bolsheviki: Campaigning in North Russia, 1918–1919. Compiled and edited by Capt. Joel R. Moore, Lt. Harry H. Mead, and Lt. Lewis E. Jahns. Detroit: Polar Bear, 1920.

The Intimate Papers of Colonel House. Vol. 3, *Into the World War.* Arranged by Charles Seymour. Boston: Houghton Mifflin, 1928.

John Reed and the Russian Revolution: Uncollected Articles, Letters and Speeches on Russia, 1917–1920. Edited by Eric Homberger, with John Biggart. New York: St. Martin's Press, 1992.

The Letters of Franklin K. Lane: Personal and Political. Edited by Anne Wintermute Lane and Louise Herrick Wall. Boston: Houghton Mifflin, 1922.

The Letters of Lincoln Steffens. Vol. 1, *1889–1919.* New York: Harcourt, Brace, 1938.

Letters of Louis D. Brandeis. Vol. 4. Edited by Melvin I. Urofsky and David W. Levy. Albany: State University of New York Press, 1975.

The Life and Letters of Walter H. Page. 3 vols. Edited by Burton J. Henrick. Garden City, N.Y.: Doubleday, 1925.

Making Things Work: Russian-American Economic Relations, 1900–1930. Stanford, Calif.: Hoover Institution Press, 1992.

Mission to Russia, An American Journal: Letters by Clinton A. Decker. Edited by Clinton J. Decker. New York: n.p., 1994.

Our Man in the Crimea: Commander Hugo Koehler and the Russian Civil War. Edited by P. J. Capelotti. Columbia: University of South Carolina Press, 1991.

The Papers of Woodrow Wilson. Vols. 38–65. Edited by Arthur Link et al. Princeton, N.J.: Princeton University Press, 1976–88.

Papers Relating to the Foreign Relations of the United States, 1914–1921, especially 1918: Russia. 3 vols. Washington, D.C.: GPO, 1931–32.

Papers Relating to the Foreign Relations of the United States: The Lansing Papers, 1914–1920. 2 vols. Washington, D.C.: GPO, 1939–40.

Quartered in Hell: The Story of the American North Russian Expeditionary Force. Edited by Dennis Gordon. Missoula, Mont.: Doughboy Historical Society, 1982.

Rossiia i SshA: torgovo-ekonomicheskie otnosheniia, 1900–1930: sbornik dokumentov. Edited by G. N. Sevost'ianov. Moscow: Nauka, 1996.

Russia in War and Revolution: General William V. Judson's Accounts from Petrograd, 1917–1918. Edited by Neil V. Salzman. Kent, Ohio: Kent State University Press, 1998.

A Russian Civil War Diary: Alexis Babine in Saratov, 1917–1922. Edited by Donald J. Raleigh. Durham, N.C.: Duke University Press, 1988.

The Russian Provisional Government 1917: Documents. 3 vols. Edited by Robert Browder and Alexander Kerensky. Stanford, Calif.: Stanford University Press, 1961.

V. D. Nabokov and the Russian Provisional Government, 1917. Edited by Virgil D. Medlin and Steven L. Parsons. New Haven, Conn.: Yale University Press, 1976.

"A Wisconsin Man in the Russian Railway Service Corps: Letters of Fayette W. Keeler, 1918–1919." Edited by Joe Michael Feist. Wisconsin Magazine of History 62, no. 3 (fall, 1978): 217–44.

Witness to Revolution: Letters from Russia, 1916–1919 by Edward T. Heald. Edited by James B. Gidney. Kent, Ohio: Kent State University Press, 1972.

Witnesses to the Russian Revolution. Edited by Richard Pethybridge. London: Allen and Unwin, 1964.

Memoirs, Autobiographies, and Contemporary Accounts

Ackerman, Carl W. Trailing the Bolsheviki: Twelve Thousand Miles with the Allies in Siberia. New York: Charles Scribner's Sons, 1919.

Albertson, Ralph. Fighting Without a War: An Account of Military Intervention in North Russia. New York: Harcourt, Brace and Howe, 1920.

Anderson, Paul B. No East or West. Edited by Donald E. Davis. Paris: YMCA Press, 1985.

Aten, Captain Marion, and Arthur Orrmont. Last Train over Rostov Bridge. New York: Julian Messner, 1961.

Austin, Walter. A War Zone Gadabout—Being the Authentic Account of Four Trips to the Fighting Nations During 1914, '15, '16. Boston: R. H. Hinkley, 1917.

Beatty, Bessie. The Red Heart of Russia. New York: Century, 1919.

Brown, Arthur Judson. Russia in Transition. New York: Fleming H. Revell, 1917.

Bryant, Louise. Six Red Months in Russia: An Observer's Account of Russia Before and During the Proletarian Dictatorship. New York: George H. Doran, 1918.

Buchanan, George. My Mission to Russia and Other Diplomatic Memories. 2 vols. Boston: Little, Brown, 1923.

Cantacuzene-Speransky [Kantakuzen], Julia née Grant. My Life Here and There. New York: Charles Scribner's Sons, 1921.

——. Revolutionary Days: Recollections of Romanoffs and Bolsheviks, 1914–1917. London: Chapman and Hall, 1920.

——. *Russian People: Revolutionary Recollections.* New York: Charles Scribner's Sons, 1920.

Carey, Donald E. *Fighting the Bolsheviks: The Russian War Memoirs of Private First Class Donald E. Carey, U.S. Army, 1918–19.* Edited by Neil G. Carey. Novato, Calif.: Presidio Press, 1997.

Child, Richard Washburn. *Potential Russia.* New York: Dutton, 1916.

Colby, Bainbridge. *The Close of the Wilson Administration and the Final Years, and Address Before the Missouri Historical Society, St. Louis, April 28, 1930.* New York: Mitchell Kennerlay, 1930.

Creel, George. *Rebel at Large: Recollections of Fifty Crowded Years.* New York: G. P. Putnam's Sons, 1947.

Crosley, Pauline S. *Intimate Letters from Petrograd.* New York: Dutton, 1920.

Cudahy, John. *Archangel: The American War with Russia by a Chronicler.* Chicago: A. C. McClurg, 1924.

Davis, Jerome. *The Russian Immigrant.* New York: Macmillan, 1922.

Davis, Nathaniel P. *Few Dull Moments: A Foreign Service Career.* Philadelphia: Dunlap, 1967.

Denikin, Anton. *The Russian Turmoil. Memoirs: Military, Social, Political.* London: Hutchinson and Co., 1922.

Dillon, E. J. *The Eclipse of Russia.* New York: George H. Doran, 1918.

Dosch-Fleurot, Arno. *Through War to Revolution: Being the Experiences of a Newspaper Correspondent in War and Revolution, 1914–1920.* 2d ed. London: John Lane, the Bodley Head, 1931.

Duncan, Isadora. *My Life.* New York: Boni and Liveright, 1927.

Duranty, Walter. *I Write as I Please.* New York: Simon and Schuster, 1935.

Fedotoff White, Dmitri. *Survival Through War and Revolution in Russia.* Philadelphia: University of Pennsylvania Press, 1939.

Fischer, Louis. *Men and Politics: Europe Between the Two World Wars.* New York: Harper Colophon, 1966.

Francis, David R. *Russia from the American Embassy, April 1916–November 1918.* New York: Charles Scribner's Sons, 1921.

Fraser, John Foster. *Russia of To-Day.* New York: Funk and Wagnalls, 1915.

Gaiduk, M. I. *"Utiug": Materialy i fakty o zagotovitel'noi deiatel'nosti russkikh vooennykh komissii v Amerike.* New York: Russkii Golos, 1918.

Graves, William S. *America's Siberian Adventure, 1918–1920.* New York: Jonathan Cape and Harrison Smith, 1931.

Grow, Malcolm C. *Surgeon Grow, an American in the Russian Fighting.* New York: F. A. Stokes, 1918.

Hammond, John Hays. *The Autobiography of John Hays Hammond.* New York: Farrar and Rinehart, 1935.

Hapgood, Norman. *The Changing Years: Reminiscences of Norman Hapgood.* New York: Farrar and Rinehart, 1930.

Hard, William. *Raymond Robins' Own Story.* New York: Harper and Brothers, 1920.

Hardman, Ric. *Fifteen Flags.* Boston: Little, Brown, 1968. [Fictional version of AEF in Siberia.]

Harper, Florence MacLeod. *Runaway Russia.* New York: Century, 1918.

Harper, Samuel. *The Russia I Believe In: The Memoirs of Samuel N. Harper, 1902–1941.* Edited by Paul V. Harper. Chicago: University of Chicago Press, 1945.

Harriman, Mrs. J. Borden [Florence Jaffray Hurst]. *From Pinafores to Politics.* New York: Henry Holt, 1923.

Harrison, Marguerite. *Marooned in Moscow: The Story of an American Woman Imprisoned in Russia.* New York: Doran, 1921.

Herron, George. *The Defeat in Victory*. London: Cecil Palmer, 1921.

Hoover, Herbert. *The Memoirs of Herbert Hoover: Years of Adventure, 1874–1920*. New York: Macmillan, 1951.

Houghteling, James L. *A Diary of the Russian Revolution*. New York: Dodd, Mead, 1918.

House, Edward M. *Intimate Papers of Colonel House*. Boston: Little, Brown, 1930.

Johnson, Benjamin. "The Trans-Siberian Railway." *Journal of the Worcester Polytechnic Institute* 26, no. 4 (July 1923): 179–85.

Kerensky, Alexander. *Russia and History's Turning Point*. New York: Duell, Sloan and Pearce, 1965.

Knox, Alfred. *With the Russian Army, 1914–1917: Being Chiefly Extracts from the Diary of a Military Attaché*. London: Hutchinson and Co., 1921.

Lansing, Robert. *The Peace Negotiations: A Personal Narrative*. Boston: Houghton Mifflin, 1921.

Levine, Isaac Don. *Eyewitness to History: Memoirs and Reflections of a Foreign Correspondent for Half a Century*. New York: Hawthorne Books, 1973.

Lied, Jonas. *Sidelights on the Economic Situation in Russia*. Moscow: Kushnerev, 1922.

Lockhart, Robert H. Bruce. *Memoirs of a British Agent: Being an Account of the Author's Early Life in Many Lands and of His Official Mission to Moscow in 1918*. London: Putnam, 1932.

Long, Robert Crozier. *Russian Revolution Aspects*. New York: Dutton, 1919.

Magnus, Judah L. *Russia and Germany at Brest-Litovsk: Documentary History of the Peace Negotiations*. New York: Rand School of Social Science, 1919.

Marye, George Thomas. *Nearing the End in Imperial Russia*. London: Selwyn and Blount, 1929.

Masaryk, Thomas G. *The Making of a State: Memories and Observations, 1914–1918*. Philadelphia: Frederick A. Stokes, 1927.

McAdoo, William G. *Crowded Years: The Reminiscences of William G. McAdoo*. Boston: Houghton Mifflin, 1931.

McCormick, Robert. *With the Russian Army*. New York: Macmillan, 1915.

Miliukov, Paul. *Political Memoirs, 1905–1917*. Edited by Arthur P. Mendel. Translated by Carl Goldberg. Ann Arbor: University of Michigan Press, 1967.

Morris, Ira Nelson. *From an American Legation*. New York: Alfred A. Knopf, 1923.

Mott, T. Bentley. *Twenty Years as Military Attaché*. New York: Oxford University Press, 1937.

Nicolson, Harold. *Peacemaking, 1919*. New York: Grosset and Dunlap, 1965.

Noulens, Joseph. *Mon ambassade en Russie soviétique, 1917–1919*. 2 vols. Paris: Librairie Plon, 1932.

Paleologue, Maurice. *An Ambassador's Memoirs*. 3 vols. New York: George H. Doran, 1925.

Pares, Bernard. *Day by Day with the Russian Army*. London: Constable and Company, 1915.

Pettit, Walter W. *The Russian Revolution*. Syllabus for Institute of International Education. New York: The Institute, 1920.

Phillips, William. *Ventures in Diplomacy*. Portland, Maine: Anthoensen Press, 1952.

Pierce, Ruth. *Trapped in "Black Russia," June–November 1915*. Boston: Houghton Mifflin, 1918.

Ponafidine, Emma Cochran. *Russia—My Home: An Intimate Record of Personal Experiences Before, During and After the Bolshevist Revolution*. Indianapolis: Bobbs-Merrill, 1931.

Reed, John. *Ten Days That Shook the World*. New York: Boni and Liveright, 1919. New York: Vintage, 1960.

——. *The War in Eastern Europe*. Illustrated by Boardman Robinson. New York: Charles Scribner's Sons, 1917.

Reeves, Francis B. *Russia Then and Now, 1892–1917: My Mission to Russia During the Famine of 1891–1892 with Data Bearing upon the Russia of To-Day*. New York: G. P. Putnam's Knickerbocker Press, 1917.

Reinsch, Paul S. *An American Diplomat in China*. Garden City, N.Y.: Doubleday, Page, 1922.

Robien, Louis D. *The Diary of a Diplomat in Russia, 1917–1918*. Translated by Camilla Sykes. London: Michael Joseph, 1969.

Root, Elihu. *The United States and the War: The Mission to Russia Political Addresses*. Edited by Robert Bacon and James Brown Scott. Cambridge, Mass.: Harvard University Press, 1918.

Rosen, Baron Roman. *Forty Years of Diplomacy*. 2 vols. London: Allen and Unwin, 1922.

Ross, Edward Alsworth. *Russia in Upheaval*. New York: Century, 1918.

Ruhl, Arthur. *White Nights and Other Russian Impressions*. New York: Charles Scribner's Sons, 1917.

Russell, Charles Edward. *Bare Hands and Stone Walls*. New York: Charles Scribner's Sons, 1933.

———. *Bolshevism and the United States*. Indianapolis: Bobbs-Merrill, 1919.

———. *Unchained Russia*. New York: D. Appleton, 1918.

Sadoul, Jacques. *Notes sur la révolution bolchevique octobre 1917–janvier 1919*. Paris: François Maspero, 1971.

Sazonov, Sergei. *Fateful Years, 1909–1916: The Reminiscences of Sergei Sazonov*. London: Jonathan Cape, 1928.

Scott, Hugh Lenox. *Some Memories of a Soldier*. New York: Century, 1928.

Sisson, Edgar. *One Hundred Red Days: A Personal Chronicle of the Bolshevik Revolution*. New Haven, Conn.: Yale University Press, 1931.

Steffens, Lincoln. *The Autobiography of Lincoln Steffens*. New York: Harcourt, Brace, 1931.

Stillwell, Clyde Scott. "With Harvester Men in Russia." *Harvester World* 8, no. 11 (November 1917): 2–5.

Straus, Oscar. *Under Four Administrations from Cleveland to Taft: Recollections of Oscar S. Straus*. Boston: Houghton Mifflin, 1922.

Thomas, Albert. *Notes sur la révolution bolchevique octobre 1917–janvier 1919*. Paris: François Maspero, 1971.

Thompson, Donald. *Blood Stained Russia*. New York: Leslie-Judge, 1918.

Tyrkova-Williams, Ariadna. *Cheerful Giver: The Life of Harold Williams*. London: P. Davies, 1935.

———. *Why Russia Is Starving*. London: Russian Liberation Committee, 1919.

Ward, Colonel John. *With the "Die-Hards" in Siberia*. New York: George H. Doran, 1920.

Washburn, Stanley. *Field Notes from the Russian Front*. London: Andrew Melrose, 1915.

———. *On the Russian Front in World War I: Memoirs of an American War Correspondent*. New York: Robert Speller, 1982.

———. *The Russian Advance*. Garden City, N.Y.: Doubleday, Page, 1917.

———. *The Russian Campaign: April to August, 1915*. New York: Charles Scribner's Sons, 1916.

———. *Victory in Defeat: The Agony of Warsaw and the Russian Retreat*. Garden City, N.Y.: Doubleday, Page, 1917.

White, William Allen. *The Autobiography of William Allen White*. New York: Macmillan, 1946.

Wightman, Orrin Sage. *The Diary of an American Physician in the Russian Revolution, 1917*. Brooklyn, N.Y.: Brooklyn Daily Eagle, 1928.

Williams, Albert Rhys. *Journey into Revolution: Petrograd, 1917–1918*. Edited by Lucita Williams. Chicago: Quadrangle Books, 1969.

———. *The Russian Land*. New York: New Republic, 1927.

Wilson, Edith Bolling. *My Memoir*. Indianapolis: Bobbs-Merrill, 1938.

Secondary Sources

Abraham, Richard. *Alexander Kerensky: The First Love of the Revolution.* New York: Columbia University Press, 1987.

Allison, William. *American Diplomats in Russia: Case Studies in Orphan Diplomacy, 1916–1919.* Westport, Conn.: Praeger, 1997.

Ambrosius, Lloyd E. *Wilsonian Statecraft: Theory and Practice of Liberal Internationalism During World War I.* Wilmington, Del.: Scholarly Resources, 1991.

Baker, Ray Stannard. *Woodrow Wilson: Life and Letters.* Vol. 7, *War Leader.* New York: Doubleday, Doran, 1939.

Beaver, Daniel R. *Newton D. Baker and the American War Effort, 1917–1919.* Lincoln: University of Nebraska Press, 1966.

Berezkin, Aleksandr. *Oktiabr'skaia revolutsiia i SShA, 1917–1922 gg.* Moscow: Nauka, 1967.

Blum, John Morton. *Joe Tumulty and the Wilson Era.* Boston: Houghton Mifflin, 1951.

Bogdanin, N. A. *Amerikantsy i Amerikanskaia kul'tura.* Petrograd: Obshchestvennaia Pol'ze, 1915.

Borch, Red L., III. "Bolsheviks, Polar Bears, and Military Law: The Experiences of Army Lawyers in North Russia and Siberia in World War I." *Prologue* 30, no. 1 (fall 1998): 180-91.

Bradley, John. *Allied Intervention in Russia.* New York: Basic Books, 1968.

Briggs, Mitchell Pirie. *George D. Herron and the European Settlement.* Stanford, Calif.: Stanford University Press, 1932.

Brinkley, George A. *The Volunteer Army and Allied Intervention in South Russia, 1917–1921: A Study in the Politics and Diplomacy of the Russian Civil War.* South Bend, Ind.: University of Notre Dame Press, 1966.

Buley, R. Carlyle. *The Equitable Life Assurance Society of the United States, 1859–1961.* Vol. 2. New York: Equitable, 1967.

Bykov, Aleksandr, and Leonid Panov. *Diplomaticheskaia stolitsaia Rossii.* Vologda: Ardvisura, 1998.

Byrnes, Robert F. *Awakening American Education to the World: The Role of Archibald Cary Coolidge, 1866–1928.* Notre Dame, Ind.: University of Notre Dame Press, 1982.

Carley, Michael. *Revolution and Intervention: The French Intervention and the Russian Civil War.* Kingston, Ontario: McGill–Queen's University Press, 1983.

Carstensen, Fred V. *American Enterprise in Foreign Markets: Studies of Singer and International Harvester in Imperial Russia.* Chapel Hill: University of North Carolina Press, 1984.

Chubarian, A. O. *V. I. Lenin i formirovanne Sovetskoi vneshnei politiki.* Moscow: Nauka, 1972.

———, ed. *Sovetskaia vneshniaia politika v petrospektive, 1917–1991.* Moscow: Nauka, 1993.

Cockfield, Jamie H. *With Snow on Their Boots: The Tragic Odyssey of the Russian Expeditionary Force in France During World War I.* New York: St. Martin's Press, 1998.

Coletta, Paolo E. *William Jennings Bryan: Progressive Politician and Moral Statesman, 1909–1915.* Lincoln: University of Nebraska Press, 1969.

Costigliola, Frank. *Awkward Dominion: American Political, Economic, and Cultural Relations with Europe, 1919–1933.* Ithaca, N.Y.: Cornell University Press, 1984.

Crissey, Forrest. *Alexander Legge, 1966–1933.* Chicago: Alexander Legge Memorial Committee, 1936.

Daniels, Robert V. *Red October: The Bolshevik Revolution of 1917.* Boston: Beacon, 1984.

Davis, Donald E., and Eugene P. Trani. "An American in Russia: Russell M. Story and the Bolshevik Revolution, 1917–1919." *The Historian* 36, no. 4 (August 1974): 704-21.

———. "The American YMCA and the Russian Revolution." *Slavic Review* 33, no. 3 (September 1974): 469-71.

Debo, Richard K. *Revolution and Survival: The Foreign Policy of Soviet Russia, 1917–1918.* Liverpool: Liverpool University Press, 1979.

——. *Survival and Consolidation: The Foreign Policy of Soviet Russia, 1918–1921.* Montreal: McGill-Queen's University Press, 1992.

Dennis, Charles H. *Victor Lawson: His Time and His Work.* Chicago: University of Chicago Press, 1935.

Desmond, Robert W. *Windows on the World: World News Reporting, 1900–1920.* Iowa City: University of Iowa Press, 1980.

Dubie, Alain. *Frank A. Golder: An Adventure of a Historian in Quest of Russian History.* New York: Columbia University Press, 1989.

Dunlop, Richard. *Donovan: America's Master Spy.* Chicago: Rand McNally, 1982.

Engel', V. V. *"Evreiskii vopros" v russko-amerikanskikh otnosheniiakh: (na primere "pasportnogo voprosa", 1864–1913).* Moscow: Nauka, 1998.

Evgen'ev, G., and B. Shapik. *Revoliutsioner, Diplomat, Uchenyi: L. K. Martens.* Moscow: Nauka, 1960.

Farnsworth, Beatrice. *William C. Bullitt and the Soviet Union.* Bloomington: Indiana University Press, 1967.

Feist, Joe Michael. "Theirs Is Not to Reason Why: The Case of the Russian Railway Service Corps." *Military Affairs* 42, no. 1 (February 1978): 1–6.

Ferrell, Robert H. *Woodrow Wilson and World War I, 1917–1921.* New York: Harper and Row, 1985.

Feuer, Lewis S. "American Travelers to the Soviet Union, 1917–32: The Formation of a Component of New Deal Ideology." *American Quarterly* 14, no. 2 (summer 1962): 119–49.

Fic, Victor M. *The Collapse of American Policy in Russia and Siberia, 1918: Wilson's Decision Not to Intervene (March–October, 1918).* New York: Columbia University Press, 1995.

Figes, Orlando. *A People's Tragedy: The Russian Revolution, 1891–1924.* New York: Penguin, 1998.

Fike, Claude E. "The Influence of the Creel Committee and the American Red Cross on Russian-American Relations, 1917–1919." *Journal of Modern History* 31, no. 2 (June 1959): 93–109.

Filene, Peter G. *Americans and the Soviet Experiment, 1917–1933.* Cambridge, Mass.: Harvard University Press, 1967.

Fischer, Louis. *The Soviets in World Affairs.* 2 vols. London: Jonathan Cape, 1930.

Foglesong, David S. *America's Secret War Against Bolshevism: U.S. Intervention in the Russian Civil War, 1917–1920.* Chapel Hill: University of North Carolina Press, 1995.

——. "Redeeming Russia? American Missionaries and Tsarist Russia, 1886–1917." *Religion, State and Society* 25, no. 4 (1997): 353–68.

——. "Xenophon Kalamatiano: An American Spy in Revolutionary Russia?" *Intelligence and National Security* 6 (January 1991): 154–95.

Fowler, W. B. *British-American Relations, 1917–1918: The Role of Sir William Wiseman.* Princeton, N.J.: Princeton University Press, 1969.

Freud, Sigmund, and William C. Bullitt. *Thomas Woodrow Wilson: A Psychological Study.* Boston: Houghton Mifflin, 1966.

Furaev, Vladimir. *Sovetsko-amerikanskie otnosheniia, 1917–1939 gg.* Moscow: Nauka, 1964.

Gaddis, John Lewis. *Russia, the Soviet Union, and the United States: An Interpretive History.* 2d ed. New York: McGraw-Hill, 1990.

Ganelin, Rafail Sh. "Finansovo-ekonomicheskie otnosheniia Rossii i SShA posle nachala pervoi mirovoi voine." In *Iz istorii imperializma v Rossii,* 270–308. Moscow-Leningrad: Nauka, 1959.

——. *Rossiia i SshA, 1914–1917: ocherki istorii Russko-Amerikanskikh otnoshenii.* Leningrad: Nauka, 1969.

——. *Sovetsko-Amerikanskie otnosheniia v kontse 1917–nachale 1918 g.* Leningrad: Nauka, 1975.

Gardner, Lloyd C. *Safe for Democracy: The Anglo-American Response to Revolution, 1913–1921.* New York: Oxford University Press, 1984.

Gaworek, Norman H. "From Blockade to Trade: Allied Economic Warfare Against Soviet Russia, June 1919 to January 1920." *Jahrbucher für Geschichte Osteuropas* 23 (1975): 39–69.

Gelfand, Lawrence E., ed. *Herbert Hoover: The Great War and Its Aftermath, 1914–23.* Iowa City: University of Iowa Press, 1979.

Goble, Paul. "Samuel N. Harper and the Study of Russia." *Cahiers du Monde Russe et Sovietique* 14, no. 3 (1973): 8–20.

Goldhurst, Richard. *The Midnight War: The American Intervention in Russia, 1918–1920.* New York: McGraw-Hill, 1978.

Good, Jane E., and David R. Jones. *Babushka: The Life of the Russian Revolutionary Ekaterina K. Breshko-Breshkovskaia, (1844–1934).* Newtonville, Mass.: Oriental Research Partners, 1991.

Grabill, Joseph L. *Protestant Diplomacy and the Near East: Missionary Influence on American Policy, 1810–1927.* Minneapolis: University of Minnesota Press, 1971.

Grayson, Benson Lee. *Russian-American Relations in World War I.* New York: Ungar, 1979.

Gvizhiani-Kosygina, Liudmila. *Sovetskaia Rossiia i SShA, 1917–1920.* Moscow: Mezhotnosh., 1970.

Hagedorn, Hermann. *The Magnate: William Boyce Thompson and His Times, 1869–1930.* New York: Reynal and Hitchcock, 1935.

Heenan, Louise Erwin. *Russian Democracy's Fatal Blunder: The Summer Offensive of 1917.* New York: Praeger, 1987.

Hoff Wilson, Joan. *Ideology and Economics: U.S. Relations with the Soviet Union, 1918–1933.* Columbia: University of Missouri Press, 1974.

Hopkins, C. Howard. *John R. Mott, 1865–1955: A Biography.* Grand Rapids, Mich.: William Eerdmans, 1979.

Hughes, Michael. *Diplomacy Before the Russian Revolution: Britain, Russia and the Old Diplomacy, 1894–1917.* London: Macmillan, 2000.

——. *Inside the Enigma: British Officials in Russia, 1900–1939.* London: Hambledon Press, 1997.

Ignat'ev, Anatolyi V. *Vneshniaia politika vremennogo pravitel'stva.* Moscow: Nauka, 1974.

Isenberg, Michael T. *War on Film: The American Cinema and World War I, 1914–1941.* Rutherford, N.J.: Fairleigh Dickinson University Press, 1981.

Istoriia vneshnei politiki Rossii, konets XIX-nachalo XX veka. Edited by V. A. Emets et al. Moscow: Mezhdu-otnosh., 1997.

Jahn, Hubertus F. *Patriotic Culture in Russia During World War I.* Ithaca, N.Y.: Cornell University Press, 1995.

Jeffreys-Jones, Rhodri. "W. Somerset Maugham, Anglo-American Agent in Revolutionary Russia." *American Quarterly* 27, no. 1 (Spring 1976): 90–106.

Kahan, Arcadius. "Governmental Policies and the Industrialization of Russia." *Journal of Economic History* 27, no. 4 (1967): 460–77.

Kalvoda, Josef. "Masaryk in America in 1918." *Jahrbucher für Geschichte Osteuropas* 27 (1979): 85–99.

Katkov, George. *Russia 1917, The Kornilov Affair: Kerensky and the Break-Up of the Russian Army.* London: Longman, 1980.

Kenez, Peter. *Civil War in South Russia, 1918: The First Year of the Volunteer Army.* Berkeley: University of California Press, 1971.

——. *Civil War in South Russia, 1919-1920.* Berkeley: University of California Press, 1977.

Kennan, George F. *The Fateful Alliance: France, Russia, and the Coming of the First World War.* New York: Pantheon, 1984.

——. *Russia and the West Under Lenin and Stalin.* Boston: Little, Brown, 1960.

——. "The Sisson Documents." *Journal of Modern History* 28, no. 2 (June 1956): 130-54.

——. *Soviet-American Relations, 1917-1920.* Vols. 1 and 2, *Russia Leaves the War* and *The Decision to Intervene.* Princeton, N.J.: Princeton University Press, 1958.

Kettle, Michael. *The Road to Intervention, March–November 1918.* London: Routledge, 1988.

Killen, Linda. *The Russian Bureau: A Case Study in Wilsonian Diplomacy.* Lexington: University Press of Kentucky, 1983.

——. "The Search for a Democratic Russia: Bakhmetev and the United States." *Diplomatic History* 2, no. 3 (summer 1978): 237-57.

LaFeber, Walter. *The American Age: U.S. Foreign Policy at Home and Abroad.* 2 vols. 2d ed. New York: Norton, 1994.

Lasch, Christopher. "American Intervention in Siberia: A Reinterpretation." *Political Science Quarterly* 77, no. 2 (June 1962): 205-23.

——. *The American Liberals and the Russian Revolution.* New York: Columbia University Press, 1962.

Laserson, Max M. *The American Impact on Russia, 1784-1917: Diplomatic and Ideological.* New York: Collier Books, 1962.

Lebedev, V. V. *Russko-Amerikanskie ekonomicheskie otnosheniia (1900-1917 gg.).* Moscow: Mezhdu-otnosh., 1964.

Lerner, Warren. *Karl Radek: The Last Internationalist.* Stanford, Calif.: Stanford University Press, 1970.

Libbey, James K. *Alexander Gumberg and Soviet-American Relations, 1917-1933.* Lexington: University Press of Kentucky, 1977.

——. "The American-Russian Chamber of Commerce." *Diplomatic History* 9, no. 3 (summer 1985): 233-48.

Lincoln, W. Bruce. *Passage Through Armageddon: The Russians in War and Revolution, 1914-1918.* New York: Oxford University Press, 1986.

——. *Red Victory: A History of the Russian Civil War.* New York: Oxford University Press, 1994.

Long, John W. "American Intervention in Russia: The North Russian Expedition, 1918-1919," *Diplomatic History* 6, no. 1 (winter 1982): 45-67.

Luskin, John. *Lippmann, Liberty, and the Press.* University, Ala.: University of Alabama Press, 1972.

Lyandres, Semion. *The Bolsheviks' "German Gold" Revisited: An Inquiry into the 1917 Accusations.* Carl Beck Papers in Russian and East European Studies. Pittsburgh: Pittsburgh University Press, 1995.

MacDonald, David M., "A Lever Without a Fulcrum: Domestic Factors and Russian Foreign Policy, 1905-1914." In *Imperial Russian Foreign Policy,* edited by Hugh Ragsdale, 268-311. New York: Woodrow Wilson Center, 1993.

Maddox, Robert J. *The Unknown War with Russia: Wilson's Siberian Adventure.* San Rafael, Calif.: Presidio Press, 1977.

——. *William E. Borah and American Foreign Policy.* Baton Rouge: University of Louisiana Press, 1969.

——. "Woodrow Wilson, the Russian Embassy and Siberian Intervention." *Pacific Historical Review* 36 (November 1967): 435-48.

March, G. Patrick. *Eastern Destiny: Russia in Asia and the North Pacific.* Westport, Conn.: Praeger, 1996.

March, William Barton. *Adventures in Opportunity, Being the Remarkable Story of Herbert L. Carpenter and the Carpenter Container, as Recounted to William Barton March*. New York: William Barton March, 1958.

Mayer, Arno. *Politics and Diplomacy of Peacemaking: Containment and Counterrevolution at Versailles, 1918-1919*. New York: Knopf, 1967.

——. *Wilson vs. Lenin: Political Origins of the New Diplomacy, 1917-1918*. New Haven, Conn.: Yale University Press, 1958.

Mayers, David. *The Ambassadors and America's Soviet Policy*. New York: Oxford University Press, 1995.

McDaniel, Timothy. *Autocracy, Capitalism, and Revolution in Russia*. Berkeley: University of California Press, 1988.

McFadden, David W. "After the Colby Note: The Wilson Administration and the Bolsheviks, 1920-21." *Presidential Studies Quarterly* 24 (fall 1995): 741-50.

——. *Alternative Paths: Soviets and Americans, 1917-1920*. New York: Oxford University Press, 1993.

McKay, John P. *Pioneers for Profit: Foreign Entrepreneurship and Russian Industrialization, 1885-1913*. Chicago: University of Chicago Press, 1977.

McKinzie, Richard D., and Eugene P. Trani. "The Influence of Russian Emigres on American Policy Toward Russia and the USSR, 1900-1933, with Observations on Analogous Developments in Great Britain." *Coexistence: A Review of East-West and Development Issues* 28, no. 2 (June 1991): 215-51.

Melgunov, S. P. *The Bolshevik Seizure of Power*. Santa Barbara, Calif.: ABC-Clio, 1972.

Miller, Floyd. *The Wild Children of the Urals*. New York: Dutton, 1965.

Miller, Martin. *Kropotkin*. Chicago: University of Chicago Press, 1976.

Mock, James R., and Cedric Larson. *Words That Won the War: The Story of the Committee on Public Information, 1917-1919*. Princeton, N.J.: Princeton University Press, 1939.

Morley, James William. *The Japanese Thrust into Siberia, 1918*. New York: Columbia University Press, 1957.

Nash, George H. *The Life of Herbert Hoover: Master of Emergencies, 1917-1918*. New York: Norton, 1996.

Neilson, Keith. *Strategy and Supply: The Anglo-Russian Alliance, 1914-17*. London: Allen and Unwin, 1984.

Noskova, V. V., "Neizvestnye avtografy President SShA Vudro Vil'son." *Russkoe Proshloe* 4 (1993): 350-51.

O'Connor, Timothy Edward. *Diplomacy and Revolution: G. V. Chicherin and Soviet Foreign Affairs, 1918-1930*. Ames: Iowa State University Press, 1988.

O'Grady, Joseph P., ed. *The Immigrants' Influence on Wilson's Peace Policies*. Lexington: University Press of Kentucky, 1967.

Owen, Gail L. "Dollar Diplomacy in Default: The Economics of Russian-American Relations, 1910-1917." *Historical Journal* 13, no. 2 (1970): 253.

Paasiverta, J. *The Victors in World War One and Finland: Finland's Relations with the British, French, and United States Governments in 1918-1919*. Helsinki: Finnish Historical Society, 1965.

Palmer, Frederick. *Newton D. Baker: America at War*. 2 vols. New York: Dodd, Mead, 1931.

Pereira, Norman G. O. "The 'Democratic Counterrevolution' in Siberia." *Nationalities Papers* 16, no. 1 (spring 1918): 71-93.

——. "Regional Consciousness in Siberia Before and After October 1917." *Canadian Slavonic Papers* 30, no. 1 (March 1988).

——. "White Power During the Civil War in Siberia (1918-1920): Dilemmas of Kolchak's War Anti-Communism." *Canadian Slavonic Papers* 29, no. 1 (March 1987): 45-62.

——. *White Siberia: The Politics of Civil War.* Montreal: McGill-Queen's University Press, 1996

Rabinowitch, Alexander. *The Bolsheviks Come to Power: The Revolution of 1917 in Petrograd.* New York: Norton, 1976.

Rhodes, Benjamin D. *The Anglo-American Winter War with Russia, 1918–1919: A Diplomatic and Military Tragicomedy.* New York: Greenwood Press, 1988.

Richard, Carl J. "'The Shadow of a Plan': The Rationale Behind Wilson's 1918 Siberian Intervention." *The Historian* 49, no. 1 (November 1986): 64–84.

Roosa, Ruth AmEnde. *Russian Industrialists in an Era of Revolution: The Association of Industry and Trade, 1906–1917.* Armonk, N.Y.: M. E. Sharpe, 1997.

Rosenberg, Emily. *Financial Missionaries to the World: The Politics and Culture of Dollar Diplomacy.* Cambridge, Mass.: Harvard University Press, 1999.

——. *Spreading the American Dream: American Economic and Cultural Expansion.* New York: Hill and Wang, 1982.

Rosenberg, William G. *Liberals in the Russian Revolution: The Constitutional Democratic Party, 1917–1921.* Princeton, N.J.: Princeton University Press, 1974.

Rosenstone, Robert A. *Romantic Revolutionary: A Biography of John Reed.* New York: Knopf, 1982.

Ross, Stewart Halsey. *Propaganda for War: How the United States Was Conditioned to Fight the Great War of 1914–1918.* Jefferson, N.C.: McFarland, 1996.

Rothwell, V. H. *British War Aims and Peace Diplomacy, 1914–1918.* Oxford: Clarendon Press, 1971.

Salzman, Neil V. *Reform and Revolution: The Life and Times of Raymond Robins.* Kent, Ohio: Kent State University Press, 1991.

Sanborn, Josh. "The Mobilization of 1914 and the Question of the Russian Nation: A Reexamination." *Slavic Review* 59, no. 2 (summer 2000): 267–89.

Saul, Norman E. "British Involvement in the Kornilov Affair." *Rocky Mountain Social Science Journal* 10, no. 1 (January 1973): 43–50.

——. *Concord and Conflict: The United States and Russia, 1867–1914.* Lawrence: University Press of Kansas, 1996.

——. *Distant Friends: The United States and Russia, 1763–1867.* Lawrence: University Press of Kansas, 1991.

——. *Sailors in Revolt: The Russian Baltic Fleet in 1917.* Lawrence: Regents Press of Kansas, 1978.

Schuman, Frederick L. *American Policy Toward Russia Since 1917: A Study of Diplomatic History, International Law, and Public Law and Public Opinion.* New York, 1928.

Sheinis, Zinovy. *Maxim Litvinov.* Moscow: Progress Publishers, 1989.

Siegel, Katherine A. S. *Loans and Legitimacy: The Evolution of Soviet-American Relations, 1919–1933.* Lexington: University Press of Kentucky, 1996.

——. "Technology and Trade: Russia's Pursuit of American Investment, 1917–1929." *Diplomatic History* 17, no. 3 (summer 1993): 375–98.

Smele, Jon. *Civil War in Siberia: The Anti-Bolshevik Government of Admiral Kolchak, 1918–1920.* Cambridge: Cambridge University Press, 1996.

Smith, Daniel Malloy. *Aftermath of War: Bainbridge Colby and Wilsonian Diplomacy, 1920–1921.* Philadelphia: American Philosophical Society, 1970.

Snow, Stacy M. "'Mother' Campbell of the Smile and Great Big Heart." *Red Cross Courier,* 2 January 1928, 6–9, 24.

Somakian, Manouz. *Empires in Conflict: Armenia and the Great Powers, 1895–1920.* New York: Tauris Academic Studies, 1995.

Somin, Ilya. *Stillborn Crusade: The Tragic Failure of Western Intervention in the Russian Civil War, 1918–1920.* New Brunswick, N.J.: Transaction Publishers, 1996.

Sonkin, Moisei Evelevich. *Okno vo vneshnii mir: ekonomicheskie sviazi Sovetskogo gosudarstva v 1917–1921 gg.* Moscow: Mysl', 1964.

Speed, Richard B., III. *Prisoners, Diplomats, and the Great War: A Study in the Diplomacy of Captivity.* New York: Greenwood Press, 1960.

Startt, James D. "American Film Propaganda in Revolutionary Russia." *Prologue* 30, no. 1 (fall 1998): 166–79.

Steel, Ronald. *Walter Lippmann and the American Century.* Boston: Little, Brown, 1980.

Steinberg, Mark D., and Vladimir M. Khrustalev. *The Fall of the Romanovs: Political Dreams and Personal Struggles in a Time of Revolution.* New Haven, Conn.: Yale University Press, 1995.

Stockdale, Melissa Kirschke. *Paul Miliukov and the Quest for a Liberal Russia, 1880–1918.* Ithaca, N.Y.: Cornell University Press, 1996.

Stone, Norman. *The Eastern Front, 1914–1917.* New York: Charles Scribner's Sons, 1975.

Strakhovsky, Leonid. *American Opinion About Russia, 1917–1920.* Toronto: University of Toronto Press, 1961.

——. *Intervention at Archangel: The Story of Allied Intervention and Russian Counter-revolution in North Russia, 1918–1920.* Princeton, N.J.: Princeton University Press, 1944.

——. *The Origins of American Intervention in North Russia (1918).* Princeton, N.J.: Princeton University Press, 1937.

Sutton, Antony. *Western Technology and Soviet Economic Development, 1917 to 1930.* Stanford, Calif.: Hoover Institution Press, 1968.

Swan, Jane. *The Lost Children: A Russian Odyssey.* Carlisle, Pa.: South Mountain Press, 1989.

Taylor, Edmund. *The Fall of the Dynasties: The Collapse of the Old Order, 1905–1922.* Garden City, N.Y.: Doubleday, 1963.

Thompson, John M. *Russia, Bolshevism, and the Versailles Peace.* Princeton, N.J.: Princeton University Press, 1966.

Trani, Eugene P. "Herbert Hoover and the Russian Revolution, 1917–1920." In *Herbert Hoover: the Great War and Its Aftermath, 1914–23,* edited by Lawrence E. Gelfand, 113–42. Iowa City: University of Iowa Press, 1979.

Trask, David F. *General Tasker Howard Bliss and the "Sessions of the World," 1919.* Transactions of the American Philosophical Society, n.s., 56, pt. 8. Philadelphia, 1966.

——. *The United States in the Supreme War Council: American Aims and Inter-Allied Strategy, 1917–1918.* Middletown, Conn.: Wesleyan University Press, 1961.

Travis, Frederick F. *George Kennan and the American-Russian Relationship, 1865–1924.* Athens: Ohio University Press, 1990.

Tuve, Jeanette E. "Changing Directions in Russian-American Economic Relations, 1912–1917." *Slavic Review* 31, no. 1 (March 1972): 57–69.

Ulam, Adam. *Expansion and Coexistence: The History of Soviet Foreign Policy, 1917–67.* New York: Praeger, 1968.

Uldricks, Teddy J. *Diplomacy and Ideology: The Origins of Soviet Foreign Relations, 1917–1930.* London: Sage, 1979.

Ullman, Richard H. *Anglo-Soviet Relations, 1917–1921.* Vol. 1, *Intervention and the War.* Vol. 2, *Britain and the Russian Civil War, November 1918–February 1920.* Vol. 3, *Anglo-Soviet Relations, 1917–1921.* Vol. 3, 4, *The Anglo-Soviet Accord.* Princeton, N.J.: Princeton University Press, 1961–73.

Unterberger, Betty Miller. *America's Siberian Expedition, 1918–1920: A Study of National Policy.* Durham, N.C.: Duke University Press, 1956.

——. *The United States, Revolutionary Russia, and the Rise of Czechoslovakia.* Chapel Hill: University of North Carolina Press, 1989.

Vasiukov, Viacheslav Sergeevich. *Vneshniaia politika Rossii nakanune Fevral'skoi revoliutsii, 1916–fevral' 1917 g.* Moscow: Nauka, 1989.

Wade, Rex A. *The Russian Revolution, 1917.* Cambridge: Cambridge University Press, 2000.

Warth, Robert D. *The Allies and the Russian Revolution from the Fall of the Monarchy to the Peace of Brest-Litovsk.* Durham, N.C.: Duke University Press, 1954.

Weeks, Charles J., Jr., *An American Naval Diplomat in Revolutionary Russia: The Life and Times of Vice Admiral Newton A. McCully.* Annapolis, Md.: Naval Institute Press, 1992.

Weeks, Charles J., Jr., and Joseph O. Baylen. "Admiral Kolchak's Mission to the United States, 10 September–9 November." *Military Affairs* 40, no. 2 (April 1976): 64–65.

Weissman, Benjamin. *Herbert Hoover and Famine Relief to Russia, 1921–1923.* Stanford, Calif.: Stanford University Press, 1974.

Weyant, Jane Gilman. "The Life and Career of General William V. Judson, 1865-1923." Ph.D. diss., Georgia State University, 1981.

Wheeler-Bennett, John W. *Brest-Litovsk: The Forgotten Peace, March 1918.* London: Macmillan, 1963.

White, Christine A. *British and American Commercial Relations with Soviet Russia, 1918–1924.* Chapel Hill: University of North Carolina Press, 1992.

White, John Albert. *The Siberian Intervention.* Princeton, N.J.: Princeton University Press, 1950.

Wildman, Allan K. *The End of the Russian Imperial Army.* 2 vols. Princeton, N.J.: Princeton University Press, 1987.

Williams, Robert C. *Russian Art and American Money, 1900–1940.* Cambridge, Mass.: Harvard University Press, 1980.

Williams, William Appleman. "American Intervention in Russia, 1917-1920." *Studies on the Left* 3, no. 3 (fall 1963): 24–48; 4, no. 1 (fall 1964): 39–57.

Willis, Edward F. *Herbert Hoover and the Russian Prisoners of World War I: A Study in Diplomacy and Relief, 1918–1919.* Stanford, Calif.: Stanford University Press, 1951.

Woodward, David R. *Trial by Friendship: Anglo-American Relations, 1917–1918.* Lexington: University Press of Kentucky, 1993.

Zabriskie, Edward H. *American-Russian Relations in the Far East: A Study in Diplomacy and Power Politics, 1895–1914.* Philadelphia: University of Pennsylvania Press, 1946.

Zashikhin, A N. *Do Dzhona Rida: Amerikanskie zhurnalisty v Rossiia vesnoi-letom 1917 g.: Ocherki.* Archangel: Solti, 1997.

Index